D0999436

The
PINCHOTS
A Family Saga

David S. Patterson

SUNBURY
P R E S S ®
Mechanicsburg, PA USA

Published by Sunbury Press, Inc.
Mechanicsburg, Pennsylvania

SUNBURY
P R E S S
www.sunburypress.com

For information about special discounts for bulk purchases, please contact Sunbury Press Orders Dept. at (855) 338-8359 or orders@sunburypress.com.

To request one of our authors for speaking engagements or book signings, please contact Sunbury Press Publicity Dept. at publicity@sunburypress.com.

FIRST SUNBURY PRESS EDITION: November 2022

Set in Adobe Garamond | Interior design by Crystal Devine | Cover by Noah Regan | Edited by Sarah Peachey.

Publisher's Cataloging-in-Publication Data
Names: Patterson, David S., author.
Title: The Pinchots : a family saga / David S. Patterson.
Description: First trade paperback edition. | Mechanicsburg, PA : Sunbury Press, 2022.
Summary: Beginning in the American Civil War, this book brings to life three generations of the wealthy Pinchot family and their values of serving the public good, including activism in arts, culture, and politics. The saga also features the ambitious Pinchot women and their compelling personal stories of triumphs and tragedies.
Identifiers: ISBN 978-1-62006-950-9 (softcover).
Subjects: HISTORY / Modern / 20th Century / General | BIOGRAPHY & AUTOBIOGRAPHY / Political | HISTORY / United States / State & Local / Middle Atlantic (DC, DE, MD, NJ, NY, PA).

Product of the United States of America
0 1 1 2 3 5 8 13 21 34 55

Continue the Enlightenment!

To the memory of my mother and father,
and to my brother Jim and sister Mimi

Contents

Acknowledgments

The publication of this book was an extended enterprise, involving in-depth research in many manuscript collections in different archives, writing over several years, and negotiating with publishers.

During the research phase, I especially relied on the dedicated staff at the manuscript room of the Library of Congress. In particular, Jeffrey M. Flannery, its head, and Jennifer Brathavde, Bruce Kirby, Patrick Kerwin, and Joseph Jackson went out of their way to obtain the archive boxes I requested from the several Pinchot collections, mostly from an offsite location, and they cheerfully answered my questions and provided cogent advice. Indeed, much of any breadth and depth of research for this project is attributable to their cooperation and support.

I am grateful for the assistance of the research staff at the Yale University Archives, and I profited from my discussions with Judith Ann Schiff, longtime chief archivist at the Yale University Library, who until her recent death was a font of wisdom about the institutional history and many dimensions of the campus experience there.

Also helpful in my research were Tara Willerup and her colleagues at the Simsbury Historical Society. Archivists at the New York Public Library, Franklin D. Roosevelt Presidential Library, and John F. Kennedy Presidential Library and Museum answered my queries, and specialists at the latter two repositories also located and provided photographs for the book. At Grey Towers in Milford, Pennsylvania, ancestral home of several Pinchot family members, Rebecca Philpot, a U.S. Forest Service museum specialist, gave me a hospitable space in one of the towers to conduct some research and a personal tour, during which she shared her knowledge of some Pinchot experiences at the mansion. Katelynn Ulmer, a Forest Service intern at the towers, also helped enormously by locating and sending me many photographs for possible inclusion in the book. Kathleen

Johnson at the Montgomery County (Maryland) Public Libraries successfully retrieved for me several scholarly items on interlibrary loan.

Sandy Crooms, Michael McGandy, Stephen Wesley, and Timothy Mennel offered critical comments on my Pinchot study in its early phases and, perhaps more than they realize, helped me develop a distinctive interpretation out of the massive amounts of material I had assembled and was still digesting. I also benefitted from Marnie Cochran, an experienced book editor, who gave me cogent advice about the academic and trade publishing world.

Academic friends graciously reviewed my manuscript at various phases. John Milton Cooper, Bill Hadden, and James T. Patterson read complete drafts and made numerous suggestions, and early on Cooper also suggested the title. The late Serge Ricard advised on the French dimensions of my project, and Melvin I. Urofsky, Dennis Gilbert, Maurine Beasley, and Fredrik Logevall also commented on selected portions. Their careful perusals certainly helped to improve this book, but any remaining errors of fact or interpretation are, of course, mine alone.

In moving my manuscript toward publication, I particularly thank Lawrence Knorr, publisher of Sunbury Press, who supported my project from the start and helped with many important details leading to publication. I also benefitted considerably from my ongoing consultations with the Sunbury publishing team: Sarah L. Peachey, Taylor Berger-Knorr, and Crystal Devine. Utilizing his impressive artistic talents, Noah Regan prepared the cover art and design for this book. Seth Shibelski, on short notice, skillfully put the Pinchot family tree in presentable form.

Throughout my research for this family history, I received encouragement from Eno-Pinchot descendants and my own relatives. At the start, the late Jackson F. Eno shared with me his incomparable knowledge of the Eno and Pinchot families, and I also benefitted from discussions with Bibi Gaston and her books and articles about her grandmother Rosamond and other Pinchots. Nancy Pittman Pinchot, Amos Pinchot's granddaughter, who has written articles about her Pinchot forebears, and Peter Pinchot, Gifford's grandson, spent several hours with me and answered many questions about the family.

In my immediate family, my wife, Mary Margaret, patiently withstood my tiring ruminations about the Pinchots' adventures, successes, and travails, commented on my drafts, and provided helpful advice and steadfast support over many years. Our son Scott taught his dad how to more efficiently navigate the internet and social media, which are key parts of book publishing today, and his wife, Alix, came to the rescue in the last stages with suggestions for the cover and family tree.

Preface

Vanderbilts, Rockefellers, Carnegies, Morgans, Harrimans, Mellons. They and other super-rich families like them became the closest thing the United States has ever had to a self-made aristocracy. Little is well known, however, about another important family dynasty—the Pinchots of Pennsylvania, New York City, and Washington, D.C.—and I have come to know them as outstandingly different from these families and long overdue for recognition. I argue in this book that they propounded a set of values that went beyond material acquisitiveness and economic dominance and, championing political and social change, made distinctive contributions to the history of their times.

The star in my account is Gifford Pinchot, the first professionally trained American forester and a principal founder of the U.S. conservation movement. He became Theodore Roosevelt's closest confidant and later forged a second successful career as a Republican politician. The ideas and activities of his lesser-known brother, Amos, also attracted me to the Pinchot family, and he gets strong second billing in this account. While writing a previous book, I encountered Amos as a lawyer supporting socialists and radicals in the American peace movement during World War I. Why had this wealthy man, living with his family in a luxurious apartment on Park Avenue in Manhattan, associated with activists from such different backgrounds? I began consulting the Amos Pinchot papers, which started me on a journey of intellectual discovery of this privileged but public-spirited family. I then consulted Gifford's papers, which housed an enormous archive of family letters. These two large collections constitute a fabulous resource, and I realized that the story of their family relationships and involvement in major public issues had to be written and, because of the veritable treasure trove of correspondence, could be told accurately and with authority.

These papers document the Pinchot family members' emigration from France after the Napoleonic Wars, their settlement in Milford, Pennsylvania, and their rise to wealth and social prominence. James W. Pinchot was a self-made business titan in New York City who married Mary Eno, the daughter of a spectacularly successful real estate speculator from an old New England family. James became a patron of Hudson River School artists and supported cultural initiatives promoting Franco-American understanding, including fundraising and designing features for the Statue of Liberty, a gift from the French people. My spotlight is on the ideas, activities, and accomplishments of this nuclear family, the first-generation parents and their children: Gifford, Amos, and Antoinette (Nettie), the middle sibling. The last part of the book covers the more recent third generation, with a special focus on Amos's three beautiful daughters.

The Pinchots belonged to a patrician class in Victorian America, with governesses, live-in servants, private secretaries, and financial advisers. James and Mary were elitists who discriminated between the "ladies" and "gentlemen" with whom they interacted and the rest of society about which they knew little first-hand. They made the most of their money, status, and social connections in their own lives and in the upbringing of their children, who grew up self-confident, fully benefitting from their inherited head start. The parents sent their boys to private boarding schools in preparation for admission to Yale College, and James used his business and social networks to launch Gifford successfully toward his forestry career. He also belonged to prestigious men's clubs and later made sure his sons became club men.

A sense of entitlement is not revered and sometimes even mocked in our more inclusive society today, but what makes the Pinchots stand out is that, beginning with James and Mary, they, despite their elitism, personally and financially supported various cultural and socially beneficent initiatives.

The Pinchots surprised me with their lifelong adventure-seeking and risk-taking. Their activism was evident in the causes they promoted, but they also played hard in their recreational pursuits. The Pinchot parents were inveterate travelers, traipsing around Europe like rich gypsies, and as adults, Amos and Gifford regularly rushed off, occasionally together, on extensive hunting and fishing trips as far away as Florida, Mexico, Montana, and Labrador. In his mid-sixties, Gifford organized a six-month scientific sailing expedition from New York to Tahiti, which combined his love of adventure with his insatiable curiosity about other lands and peoples.

More important and fueling much of the Pinchots' activism were the predominant values of Victorian America, which Mary and James absorbed and taught to their children. This book has an overarching thesis—the various Pinchots' values and their adaptations during their lifetimes to the transformation of American culture from the Victorian to the modern era. The cultural linkage gives the story a coherent structure over the generations. Also featured in this context, particularly in the second half of the book, are the changing roles for women after suffrage but the limitations in their status and what they could achieve in their work life and politics as late as the post-World War II years.

Starting with the first-generation parents, what were their Victorian values? Of course, there are all kinds of values, and sometimes they can be expressed somewhat contradictorily; James and Mary were, first, Christian believers who, as faithful Presbyterians, regularly communicated their religious-moral views and a sense of public service to their children. Gifford especially absorbed these values. Trained as a forester-conservationist in France, he became the man most responsible for the expansion of the nation's system of national forests and the creation of the U.S. Forest Service, working with President Theodore Roosevelt. He believed passionately that America's use of its vast natural resources should be for the greatest good for the greatest number for the longest time. Such a public philosophy has obvious relevance to the troubled social and political life of our own time.

Gifford's emerging views on conservation were part of his gradual transition from a young man with conservative political views to a zealous progressive reformer. Independent-minded, he was no obliging spokesman for upper-class elites, and indeed he was fired from his government forester position for his principled moralism on conservation questions. Why he changed and how his new perspective affected his political positions on many issues are important parts of this story.

I also feature Gifford's commitment to the wider progressive reform movement. He strongly supported labor unions and was committed to ameliorating social problems, such as child labor, income inequality, and poverty. And though the progressive movement mainly addressed urban problems, Gifford sought to improve the economic plight of struggling farmers and the quality of life of rural Americans. Historians have slighted the rural dimensions of progressivism, and this book, giving a broader view of the movement, offers a corrective. Moreover, Gifford was among the vanguard of reformers who prodded Roosevelt to challenge President Taft for the Republican Party presidential nomination in 1912, and when that failed, to found the Progressive Party and choose TR as its candidate.

These pages present new information that revises our understanding of Gifford's evolving views on religion and science as well as eugenics and race relations. Concerning the latter, for instance, at the turn of the century, he, sure of the superiority of American white material culture, was a benign imperialist and assumed the inferiority of African Americans. To his credit, however, as part of his maturation as a modern liberal, he eventually sloughed off his racist views and was outspoken in his attacks against lynching and discrimination. Moreover, most historians are familiar with his controversy with John Muir, leading preservationist spokesman, over utilitarian conservation projects, but I emphasize that Gifford's enthusiasm for the "manly" hunting of wild species, which was an integral part of the elite Victorian cultural ethos, also starkly exemplified his differences with Muir.

Amos, eight years younger than Gifford, also grew up with strong views about what was good and right. His sense of public service prompted him to leave law school to enlist as a volunteer in a New York cavalry unit during the Spanish-American War. He had, however, an unhappy military experience, which shaped his antiwar views thereafter. Amos was a late bloomer, finding his true calling as a gifted political writer during the swelling progressive movement. His polemical writings were consistently critical of business monopolies and conservative political influences, and he joined Gifford and other ardent progressives in the founding of the Progressive Party. The Pinchot brothers' collaboration and sometimes disagreements dominate the heart of the book. To some minds, the two were traitors to their class, but they saw themselves as principled advocates of a more equitable and just society.

Nettie, an outspoken personality, had the same adventuresome spirit as her brothers, and her marriage in the early 1890s to a British diplomat intrigued me. My last book focused on American and European women suffragists who transformed their pre-World War I transatlantic network on feminist issues into advocacy of neutral mediation of the savage European conflict and a set of international reforms for the postwar world. Nettie was part of a quite different social milieu, but, like the suffrage activists, the First World War would transform her life.

Among the Pinchots, Nettie immediately felt the impact of the Great War. Before the hostilities, she and her husband had tried to keep up with the aristocratic conventions of high diplomatic social life. But during the war, Nettie, imbued with the Pinchots' values of *noblesse oblige*, came into her own, and an amazing story, previously untold by historians, emerged. She co-founded, hired staff, and administered a large military hospital in France. Her commitment included the recruitment of her two obliging brothers from across the ocean to help raise large sums of much-needed money to sustain the hospital's successful operations throughout the conflict.

Amos, meanwhile, had moved further to the left politically. He advocated federal government action to regulate and break up monopolies but also believed in the free individual and limited government. Most substantively, before the First World War, he joined avant-garde intellectuals, radicals, and artists in a wide-ranging rebellion against the prevailing stuffy cultural conventions in America. Amos and his wife, Gertrude, supported new social causes like birth control, but his main passion was free speech. He championed press and speech freedoms before the war and strongly defended civil liberties during U.S. belligerency. Afterward, he would be a lifetime supporter of the American Civil Liberties Union.

In some ways, Gifford also moved in new directions. After losing his forestry job, he chose a new career as a politician and, in 1914, ran and lost as a Progressive Party candidate for the U.S. Senate in Pennsylvania. Another change that year was his marriage to Cornelia (Leila) Bryce. Leila, also from a prominent family, was already a staunch advocate of the cause of working women. She loved politics, and Leila and Gifford became a formidable power couple comparable to Franklin and Eleanor Roosevelt, with whom they were well acquainted. Leila assiduously promoted her husband's career as a political reformer and would herself run for Congress three times.

During the business-dominated 1920s, Gifford managed to carve out a successful political career as a reformer in Pennsylvania. Forging a coalition of labor unions, recently enfranchised women, and other reformers, he won election as governor of Pennsylvania in 1922. During his term he fought the private utility industry, won benefits for coal miners in his mediation of a coal strike, and promoted old age pensions and electoral reform.

But if Gifford was politically progressive, unlike his younger brother, he stubbornly held on to the old moral verities of his prewar years and, in the 1920s, emerged as a social conservative. It began as governor with bold policies designed to enforce public acceptance of prohibition in the state. As a young man, he had disliked the taste of alcohol, but he vigorously supported the prohibition experiment as a necessary reform to curtail the unhealthy influence of drinking and the liquor interests on public behavior.

When elected governor a second time in 1930, as the nation descended into the Great Depression, Gifford showed real empathy for the suffering people of his state. He implemented unemployment relief policies and public works projects that presaged some of the New Deal reforms on the national level. Notably, his political career successfully bridged the two reform eras. By that time, he accepted the end of prohibition and worked with both wets and drys to fashion moderate policies for the regulation and sale of alcoholic beverages in the state. Perhaps most significantly, Gifford, who had shown no concern about the suppression of press and speech freedoms during the Great War, spoke out strongly as governor in defense of free speech, whether by Nazi sympathizers or communists, at the state's public universities. And in the conservation field, he no longer shot wild animals and mammals and began to accept much of the preservationist message of wilderness-wildlife advocates. Finally, during World War II, with President Roosevelt's support, he promoted a world conservation conference to move environmentalism into the international sphere. This book explores the reasons for Gifford's emergence as a modern liberal politician and committed internationalist in the 1930s and early 1940s.

The Great Depression was another turning point for Amos, who moved from his left-wing progressivism hard to the Right. His abrupt, extreme change seems incongruous, but I uncovered elements in his political philosophy and personal life that help explain his about-face. He also became a strong anti-interventionist before World War II. In stark contrast to Gifford's and Leila's outspoken opposition to Nazism and anti-Semitism in Germany and support of the Allies, Amos defended anti-Semitic arguments in trying to resist U.S. cooperation with the European democracies against Hitler. After Pearl Harbor, Amos went into an emotional tailspin from which he never recovered.

Woven into the narrative detailing the first- and second-generation Pinchots' public projects and political causes are important changes in their personal lives. The private side receives more attention during the third generation, which takes the family saga into the 1960s. The major theme traces the travails of Amos Pinchot's daughters, Rosamond, Mary, and Antoinette (Tony). All three grew up in an America where the feminist movement after suffrage was fragmented and women's occupational and professional opportunities were still limited. They also lived in fast-paced societies where predominant cultural values, including sexual mores, were changing. Extramarital sex and divorce, for example, were now more tolerated. As a teenager, Rosamond appeared on the New York stage in a starring role but suffered a disastrous marriage and was unsuccessful as a Hollywood movie actress. Her much younger half-sisters, Mary and Tony, were unfulfilled seekers after more emotionally fulfilling lives. The three had connections to the political and social elite at the highest level in America: Eleanor Roosevelt befriended Rosamond, Mary became President Kennedy's favorite lover, and Tony was married for a time to Ben Bradlee, executive editor of the *Washington Post*. All three women lived turbulent lives, and two of them died tragically.

During my research, I immersed myself in the papers of Leila and Rosamond and, along with Gifford's and Amos's, these four manuscript collections, all at the Library of Congress, represent the largest body of family papers in the United States. No historian had delved deeply into more than one of them, and, indeed, except for accounts of the controversial life of Amos's daughter Mary, only one article each about James and Amos, and a memoir-biography about Rosamond, all written by family descendants, have been published. Historians have even slighted Gifford. The only full biography about him was published sixty years ago; another, now twenty-one years old, features his environmental legacy.

The rich tapestry of the Pinchots rivals the history of any great family. Their story includes wealth accumulation, travel adventures, romances, a bank scandal, reform initiatives, responses to cultural shifts, disputes over political and social issues, and foreign affairs, divorces, suicides, and even murder. I have presented a close-up look at the Pinchots' activities, travails, and accomplishments. My challenge in writing this book has been to provide readers with solid historical context and a consistently interpretive storyline. The result, if I have succeeded, will give the Pinchot family members their rightful places in history.

Pinchot Family Tree

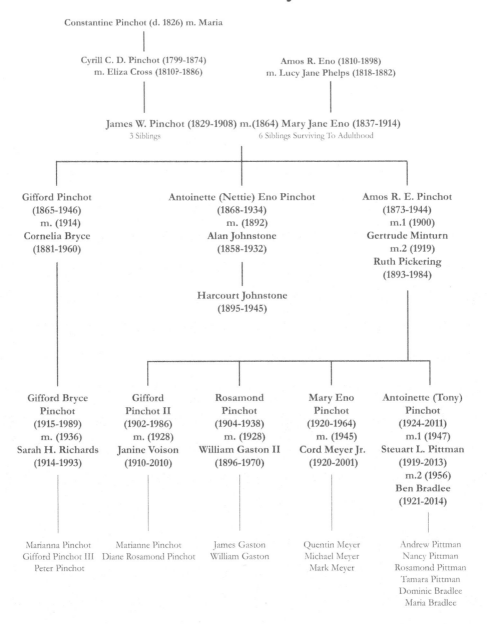

Constantine Pinchot (d. 1826) m. Maria

Cyrill C. D. Pinchot (1799-1874)
m. Eliza Cross (1810?-1886)

Amos R. Eno (1810-1898)
m. Lucy Jane Phelps (1818-1882)

James W. Pinchot (1829-1908) m.(1864) Mary Jane Eno (1837-1914)
3 Siblings   6 Siblings Surviving To Adulthood

Gifford Pinchot
(1865-1946)
m. (1914)
Cornelia Bryce
(1881-1960)

Antoinette (Nettie) Eno Pinchot
(1868-1934)
m. (1892)
Alan Johnstone
(1858-1932)

Amos R. E. Pinchot
(1873-1944)
m.1 (1900)
Gertrude Minturn
m.2 (1919)
Ruth Pickering
(1893-1984)

Harcourt Johnstone
(1895-1945)

Gifford Bryce
Pinchot
(1915-1989)
m. (1936)
Sarah H. Richards
(1914-1993)

Gifford
Pinchot II
(1902-1986)
m. (1928)
Janine Voison
(1910-2010)

Rosamond
Pinchot
(1904-1938)
m. (1928)
William Gaston II
(1896-1970)

Mary Eno
Pinchot
(1920-1964)
m. (1945)
Cord Meyer Jr.
(1920-2001)

Antoinette (Tony)
Pinchot
(1924-2011)
m.1 (1947)
Steuart L. Pittman
(1919-2013)
m.2 (1956)
Ben Bradlee
(1921-2014)

Marianna Pinchot
Gifford Pinchot III
Peter Pinchot

Marianne Pinchot
Diane Rosamond Pinchot

James Gaston
William Gaston

Quentin Meyer
Michael Meyer
Mark Meyer

Andrew Pittman
Nancy Pittman
Rosamond Pittman
Tamara Pittman
Dominic Bradlee
Maria Bradlee

1.

Two Rising Entrepreneurs

The war was over. The thousands of troops in the Union and Confederate armies had disbanded and returned to their homes to resume, as best they could, their former lives, which the hostilities had rudely interrupted. The horrific fighting lasted four years and resulted in more than 700,000 deaths. The nation, though nominally reunited, would never be the same. Tumultuous issues of postwar recovery, racial strife, and sectional reconciliation faced an exhausted populace, and the American Civil War would prove to be a transformative experience.

About the time the fighting ended in early April 1865, Mary Eno Pinchot, who was living in New York City with her husband, James W. Pinchot, a prosperous businessman, returned to her parents' summer home in Simsbury, Connecticut, fifteen miles northwest of Hartford. Married to James a year earlier, Mary was now pregnant, and she chose the house where she was raised to give birth to her first child. She would draw on the support of her parents and other relatives for the coming big event. Attending to his business concerns in New York, James often corresponded with his wife as they anticipated the beginning of their family.

* * *

Although few Americans far away from the battlefields could entirely escape the repercussions of their Civil War, Mary and most of her immediate family relations avoided its direct impact. Mary's paternal ancestors had fled as Huguenot refugees from France (or present-day Belgium) to England in the sixteenth century, then had come to America in the 1640s, establishing deep roots in Simsbury, Connecticut. Since then, her Eno forbears had lived continuously there and made their living principally as farmers.

Amos Richards Eno, Mary's father, was a phenomenally successful businessman, stalwart Republican, and supporter of the Union cause during the

Civil War. Like his Simsbury ancestors, he was a loyal member of the local Congregational church. Attending Simsbury public schools, Amos valued education and would be a voracious reader of books throughout his lifetime.[1] Soon after leaving Simsbury to pursue his business career, he fondly recalled to Lucy Phelps, his future wife and also a Simsbury native, "the old school house where I have spent so many happy hours . . . I cannot but hold it dear in my remembrance . . . [T]here is no place that is home to me except Simsbury."[2]

Amos Eno's love of his hometown was genuine. He nonetheless sought his livelihood elsewhere because opportunities in Simsbury (less than two thousand people) were limited for a would-be entrepreneur and because he believed that the "staid puritanical character of most of its inhabitants" would likely not warm to his capitalistic vision.[3] He was a quintessential nineteenth-century Connecticut Yankee: a Christian believer more concerned about right conduct than doctrine, shrewd but frugal, materially acquisitive but also philanthropic.

At sixteen, he joined John Jay Phelps, a cousin, in Hartford to work as clerks in a dry goods store. Though the same age as Amos Eno, Phelps had already been engaged in business ventures in Connecticut and Pennsylvania. Returning to Simsbury, Amos opened a successful dry goods store, and in 1830, when only twenty, he relocated to New York, where he and Phelps started a wholesale dry goods business. Amos began using his profits from the Eno & Phelps partnership to buy land and develop tracts in the city.[4]

Marrying Lucy in 1835 further linked Amos to the Phelps family, which was already a distinguished name in Connecticut annals. The Phelpses had made their name primarily in politics. Elisha Phelps, Lucy's father, had been a graduate of Yale College and a lawyer in Simsbury. He had played a key role in breaking the Federalist Party's dominance in Connecticut and was instrumental in bringing about the disestablishment of the Congregational Church in the state. Elisha went on to serve multiple terms in both houses of the Connecticut legislature as well as three terms as a congressman in Washington. And as his law practice prospered, he invested in local internal improvement schemes.

Lucy Smith, who married Elisha Phelps in 1810, brought a strong religious faith to their union, reinforcing her determined personality. A daughter later described her as "a woman of great energy and pluck. . . . When some one was fainthearted and easily discouraged[,] she would say[,] 'Oh[,] there is a lion in the way' [Proverbs 26:13] and . . . serves as a stimulant to overcome obstacles."[5]

Amos, successful in real estate, gave up the dry goods trade by the mid-1850s. He was then already a multi-millionaire, but his success story was not that of a poor farm boy coming to the big, impersonal city and striking it rich through pluck and luck. While some luck and especially pluck were involved, his father was a prosperous farmer and a respected town leader, serving a term as Simsbury's representative in the state legislature and also holding several local offices. Amos Eno had financial resources from his thriving business in Simsbury when he first came to New York, and his marriage into the Phelps family broadened his social connections. He shrewdly cultivated contacts among prominent citizens in the Hartford area who had also moved to New York or had business and banking friends there.[6]

Amos Eno's most visible property holding in New York was the Fifth Avenue Hotel, which he built in the late 1850s. Bordering Broadway and Fifth Avenue between Twenty-Third and Twenty-Fourth Streets, the Fifth Avenue Hotel comprised a spacious lobby on the ground floor, which included a bank he founded, boutiques, and, five floors above, accessible by elevators, lavish rooms, appointed with dark red and white marble floors, fine carpeting, rosewood paneling, fireplaces, and private bathrooms. The luxury hotel was sometimes called "Eno's folly" because it was located far uptown from what was then the central business district; however, it quickly became a spectacularly profitable business venture, appealing to well-heeled travelers' preference for comfort and elegance. It would also serve for many years as the city headquarters of the Republican Party.[7]

When Amos R. Eno built the Fifth Avenue Hotel at Twenty-Third Street in Manhattan in the late 1850s, many critics, believing it was located too far uptown, named the hotel "Eno's folly," but it was enormously profitable. (New York Historical Society)

The Enos continued to stay connected to Simsbury, and following his father-in-law's death, Amos bought the large homestead of his wife's parents near the center of town. He was also a family man, spending summers at the Simsbury home, and he supported charities in his hometown and later established a library there. He taught himself Italian and French and read the latter fluently.[8]

Amos Richards Eno's and Lucy Phelps' descendants had a distinctive pedigree, and Mary Eno, the second oldest of their nine children, grew up acutely aware of her lineage and special social status. Mary was twenty-three when the Civil War began.[9] Her older brother, Amos F. Eno (called Amo or Mo), succeeded his father as a partner in the dry goods firm after his father left it, and in 1859, he headed up a new partnership, which dealt mainly in silk and fancy clothes. Most of its business was in the South, however, and when the Civil War erupted, Amo's firm could not collect its debts and went bankrupt. Having lost his business, he perhaps found it easier to join the army, and he would serve in Arkansas and Missouri as an officer on the military staff of his Uncle John Phelps. Amo and his Uncle John's letters sent back home recounting their travails during the conflict provided intimate reminders to Mary and other family members of the personal sacrifices involved in the drawn-out bloody fray. They approved of emancipation but, like most Northerners, believed African Americans were inferior and had strong reservations about racial equality.[10]

In her youth, Mary lived with her parents and siblings in a house near the Battery, but as Amos Eno's business prospered, he moved his family to more upscale neighborhoods uptown. Governesses first taught Mary, and then she went to a boarding school near Union Square. She also studied literature with the writer Caroline Kirkland and music with Kirkland's daughter. Mary's education included intensive religious instruction, and she grew up a Christian believer. Her reading of Harriet Beecher Stowe's *Uncle Tom's Cabin* as a teenager had early impressed on her "that dreadful curse of slavery," and her moralistic outlook would later make her sensitive, at least on an intellectual level, to humanitarian and reform impulses.

For Mary, nonetheless, the problems arising out of the tragic sectional conflict seemed far away. She did not volunteer her services ministering to wounded Union soldiers or participate in sewing circles or other benevolent societies supporting the Northern cause. Instead, as befitted her affluent family status, she was caught up in the local social whirl of chaperoned balls and parties, a major purpose of which was meeting eligible young men from other prominent families for courtship and marriage. When Mary wrote her soldier brother, Amo, in Arkansas about her gay times, he replied that he was "glad" for her but added a sobering note: "People living here seem to think it very strange that the Northern people do not <u>feel</u> the war."[11]

*   *   *

One of Mary's frequent callers, beginning in early 1863, was James Wallace Pinchot. James was then thirty-four years old, or eight years older than Mary.[12] He was born and had grown up in Milford, Pennsylvania, located in the Delaware Water Gap in the northeast corner of the state. James's father, Cyrill C. D. Pinchot, had come to America with his parents, Constantine and Marie Pinchot, from Breteuil, France, a large town sixty miles north of Paris.[13] Their background was petit bourgeois, mainly craftsmen—farriers and locksmiths, for example.[14] They were likely aspiring entrepreneurs, however, and Constantine had enthusiastically backed Napoleon, probably because he seemed the perfect embodiment of the liberating energy and force unleashed by the French Revolution that appealed to small businessmen eager to get ahead materially. In any event, in 1815, Constantine's son, Cyrill, only about sixteen, enlisted in the French Army to support Napoleon's triumphal return to France from his exile in Elba. However, he arrived too late to participate in the ensuing decisive battle against the coalition of anti-Napoleonic nations at Waterloo, which resulted in Napoleon's ultimate downfall.

With the postwar Bourbon restoration, the Pinchot family became persona non grata in France, and Constantine, Marie, and Cyrill fled their homeland to England. Despite their misfortune, Constantine apparently had time to sell his assets before his departure and take goods with him. Two years later, he sailed with his family from England to New York.[15]

The Pinchots continued to value their French heritage, but they saw their adopted country as a land of opportunity and had no thoughts of returning to their native land. Before long, both Constantine and his son became U.S. citizens.[16] Constantine bought four hundred acres of land in Milford, Pennsylvania, which was the seat of Pike County. Other French émigrés and their families, including a few from Breteuil whom they probably knew, already resided there, and there was much land promotion for the newly laid out town lots. Milford was also a crossroads for travelers and commerce between the burgeoning metropolises of New York City and Philadelphia and newer settlements farther west, and the prospect of successful business activity seemed promising to the entrepreneurial Pinchots.

Constantine, in partnership with another Frenchman, opened a local general store, and within a few years, the Pinchots, buying out their partner, became the sole owners. William Bross, a Milford resident, later referred to Constantine's wife, Marie, as "an experienced business woman," and she likely managed the store.[17] After Cyrill's first wife, a Milford native, died shortly after their marriage, he married her cousin, Eliza Cross, also from the Milford area, who bore him four sons and one daughter. James, the second oldest child, attended Farmers Hall Academy (later Goshen Academy), a boarding school about thirty miles away. Much later, a younger pupil there remembered James as "a <u>big</u> boy . . . , its Apollo, its idol."[18]

Aspiring entrepreneurs Constantine and Cyrill indulged in Americans' proclivity for land speculation. They bought up tracts of land as far away as Wisconsin, but mostly they purchased lots in and around Milford. They farmed some of the land, growing a wide variety of vegetables, but many of the Pinchot land purchases were designed to gain access to virgin forests, which they systematically exploited. They were especially involved in the lumber trade, cutting down crops of trees, setting up make-shift sawmills to shape the felled trees into logs, lashing them together into rafts, and then floating them down the Delaware River to processing mills. The Pinchots would then rent or sell the lots, denuded and pockmarked with ugly stumps, to new settlers for farming. Constantine and Cyrill would move on to the next forested tract for similar ruthless abuse. They seemed to have no second thoughts about their complicity in destructive lumbering and the resulting environmental havoc.[19]

Milford was also attractive as a hospitable retreat for urban dwellers seeking an escape from city life. At one point, the town sported eleven hotels, which suggested its tourist appeal. But the lumber trade, with as many as seven sawmills, was the principal economic activity in Milford, and the Pinchots were participating in a widespread, socially acceptable local enterprise. William Bross later provided a jaundiced view of the central place of lumber in the bustling economic scene there. "The stores were all open on the Sabbath, and the streets were full of teams loaded with lumber," he recalled. "In fact, Sunday was the great market and gala day of the week."

After Constantine's death, Cyrill expanded on his father's business exploits, forming a new partnership with another Milford resident, John W. Wallace. He became a stockholder of a regional private toll road and manager of its Milford section and lived in a stately Greek Revival house across from the store. By the 1850s, Cyrill's land holdings were extensive in Pike County, and he was Milford's largest taxpayer. Later, he was also the postmaster of Milford, presumably a patronage job for his loyal support of the ruling Republican Party.[20]

As an adolescent, James participated in the family's involvement in lumbering and land speculation, later admitting that he and his brothers "made occasional voyages to Philadelphia in charge of the great rafts of logs or sawed lumber which descended the Delaware in fleets in those palmy days of the lumber trade."[21] Moreover, in 1849, though only twenty, he used to good advantage his acquaintance with Henry Fitch, one of his former Goshen Academy teachers, who was now general passenger and ticketing agent of the New York and Erie Railroad. At James's request, Fitch gave him a list of Erie purchasing agents who might be interested in buying the Pinchots' lumber for railroad construction and wood for the locomotives, and the business became a predictable purchaser of their wood products.

The advent of railroad lines did not become an economic asset for the Milford community, however. By the late 1840s, as the new Erie Railroad was pushing westward, a Pennsylvania state charter required it to continue the track from Port Jervis, New Jersey, directly across the Delaware River to Matamoros, Pennsylvania, and leading Milford residents wanted a spur built that would connect their town to the anticipated rail bridge at Matamoros, six miles upstream. But the railroad officers argued that the construction costs of blasting through a three-mile rock-encrusted mountain on the Pennsylvania side of the Delaware River near Matamoros were prohibitively expensive. After a multiyear dispute, the Erie agreed to construct the bridge with both a rail track and road across the river to Matamoros and a spur to Milford. But the victory was more apparent than real, as the railroad never used the bridge and the spur was never built. The railroad's bypassing of Milford stunted the town's development, and it would become an economic backwater.[22]

*   *   *

Despite this disappointment, James, as his forebears, became a determined businessman. His entrepreneurial ambition was too large for Milford, a hamlet with a population of only about seven hundred people. Following his brother Edgar, in 1850, he brought his search for business success to New York City, seventy miles to the southeast.[23] Young James clerked for a few years at a mercantile firm and then opened an interior furnishings store near the Battery in lower Manhattan with business partners, first Partridge, Pinchot & Warren, and then Pinchot & Warren. Specializing in window shades, curtains, and especially wallpaper, the firm manufactured some of the items in factories located in New York and Pennsylvania, but it also offered customers a wide selection from other domestic as well as French and English companies. The start-up partnership gradually prospered. Some of its profitability derived from the rapidly expanding population of New York City and rising middle-class people who aspired to decorate their homes and display their affluence.[24]

A counterweight to James's materialistic appetite was his emphasis on the central role of family. When he first went to New York, Cyrill wanted his son to write home frequently. James proved to be a loyal correspondent and once noted that he was writing his father every day.[25] The family operated as an economic unit, and James always wanted to know about commercial dealings in Milford. "How are you doing with the lumber[?]," he would ask his father. "Have you got trams to work at the lumber[?] . . . How do collections progress[?]" For his part, when James sought financial help for his partnership, Cyrill replied, "I will do all I can."[26] James and Edgar also used their connections in New York and elsewhere to purchase and ship home clothing, staples, and other items that might be profitably sold in the Milford store, which their mother and younger brother John managed.[27]

In 1852, James and Fitch pursued a new family business opportunity. Fitch, who knew the agent for German immigrants, and the Pinchots negotiated a business contract whereby the Erie would buy Pinchot land around Milford for $15 an acre and then try to sell it at a profit of $1-3 an acre to newly arrived Germans in New York whom the railroad would transport to the town. It was a tidy arrangement, allowing the Pinchots to sell land without risk or advertisement and with the prospect of future deals.[28]

James's letters home also kept him intimately connected to a loving family. Although business activity was usually "very good" and "first rate," he found the expansion of his new partnerships stressful; exhausted in the fall of 1854, he retreated to the solace of his Milford home to recuperate for a few months. When he returned to New York and again expressed his business frustrations, his father advised him not to "trouble" himself: "you have a home to come to and you are . . . all ways welcome. [W]hat if you should do nothing for one year? . . . you can come home and raise chickens."[29] James persevered in the city but continued to value his family.

Religion was also intertwined with the family's values. The Pinchots were faithful Presbyterians and fairly regular churchgoers. A committed Christian might seem incongruous in the rollicking free-enterprise spirit permeating Milford. And if the Pinchots were righteous, would they denigrate the Sabbath by participating in the town's vibrant business action that day? Operating the general store and being deeply engaged in lumbering surely required the Pinchot family's attention to material matters on Sundays, but the spiritual side still had a place. Protestantism accepted business enterprise as long as it was honestly practiced and the prices were just, and the Pinchots pursued profit while maintaining their religious perspective. The minister of their Milford church later recalled that the prayers of James's father at evening prayer meetings "breathed as pure and childlike earnestness and were as full of faith as any he had ever heard." The pastor's reference to evening meetings suggests that Cyrill worked on the Sabbath but still managed to renew his faith communally afterward.[30]

Father and son sometimes reminded one another that God was in control despite man's best efforts. As Cyrill commented to James, "we are at all time[s] in the hand of him who does all things well and for his own glory. Trust in him and [he] will not leave you nor forsake you." This candid recognition of an all-powerful deity was not Presbyterian predestination, for God was not wrathful or arbitrary but gracious and fundamentally beneficent. Their religion also served as a moral compass in their business dealings. When Cyrill complained about a corrupt judge, for instance, James advised, "Have confidence in a higher power. . . . We must feel superior to the designs of low minded men. . . . If we are united and with the favor of God[,] we are in ourselves a tower of strength and can lau[gh] at their puerile efforts."[31]

In his struggle to maintain an upbeat Christian attitude, James received a spiritual renewal, at least momentarily, in late 1854, when he attended the church of Henry Ward Beecher, the best-known revivalist minister of that era, in Brooklyn, where James then lived. "Went to church with Ed [Pinchot] this morning at Beecher's," he wrote his father, "and heard a very superior sermon," which excoriated Christians for practicing their religion only on Sundays and special occasions. Christian duty required better behavior, Beecher had implored. His admonition of "our carrying our worldliness too far" impressed James, who confessed that "I have lately almost continuously neglected everything else. . . . I am glad I heard him."[32] His religious grounding would later serve him well in the upbringing of his own children.

At the time, however, even with his faith, he continued to find business life demanding. Although his firm survived the serious financial panic of 1857–1858, which, according to James, caused the failure of more than one-half of his business friends, the strain left him physically and emotionally exhausted. Fortunately for James, he understood his predicament. "My fault is that I work irregularly—at times too hard," he confessed, and he left his business affairs behind in 1859–1860 for his health while he went off on an extensive trip on horseback through many Southern states. The break from his business seemed to work, and he returned to New York restored.[33]

Aware of his own physical limitations, James Pinchot took an interest in health matters, and he devoted special attention to his youngest brother, Cyrill, eight years James's junior, when he went off to boarding school in upstate

New York. Taking him under his wing, James exhorted him in letters to study hard, take good care of his health, and write home frequently. He successfully persuaded Cyrill, who was ready to drop out of school, to persevere with his studies until graduation and then enroll in Union College nearby. His prescription for young Cyrill's good health—washing his chest, rubbing his limbs, outdoor exercise, and no smoking—was a constant theme. Indeed, he once wrote him that it was "even more important" that he should be healthy than a good student.

Cyrill's problem was that he was often short of cash, and James admonished him to keep a record of his expenses for their father's perusal. Cyrill received excellent grades but never seemed to measure up to his older brother's perfectionist standards.[34] He considered Cyrill a potentially wayward young man with dissolute habits, including smoking. Despite James's concerns, Cyrill contracted tuberculosis, probably at college while James was on his southern health-restoring trip, and died at home in Milford of consumption in the summer of 1860. He was only in his early twenties.[35]

Cyrill's death shocked the Pinchots, and James's experience with Cyrill seemed to vindicate his emphasis on the critical importance of good hygiene and later would contribute to his near obsession with the health of his own children.

Another counterpoint to the preoccupation with moneymaking was James's growing interest in the American visual arts. He may have been first exposed to the world of New York artists through Launt Thompson, a gregarious Irish-American sculptor and fellow bachelor who shared a house with James in lower Manhattan beginning in about 1858. Soon James became acquainted with a number of landscape painters of the Hudson River school. These artist friends—Albert Bierstadt, Sanford Gifford, Frederic Church, Eastman Johnson, Jervis McEntee, John Ferguson Weir, and Worthington Whittredge—were a considerable presence in the mid-century American art world, and they all lived in or near New York.

As a wealthy businessman and newfound member of the New York leisure class, James joined the Century Association, an exclusive club of the city's cultural elite. Founded by prominent New York writers and artists, by the early 1860s, it began admitting professional people and merchants like Pinchot. He also became a major patron of the Hudson River painters and bought six paintings by Sanford Gifford, arguably James's favorite artist and eventually a special friend.[36] He also tried to find other buyers among his wealthy acquaintances and arrange for showings of their works.

James came to believe that art represented refinement, respectability, gentility. The Hudson River School's depiction of an idealized natural landscape

James W. Pinchot, c. 1860. (USDA Forest Service, Grey Towers NHS)

appealed to James's aesthetic, even romantic, yearnings. He wanted to support American artists and would labor over the years to replace the ordinary, rundown appearance of Milford's downtown with more elegant buildings and surroundings. Over time, he would perceive that destructive lumbering was the antithesis of his ideal of a neat, orderly, refined landscape, but that perspective would emerge gradually.

James valued his painter acquaintances as friends, and his companions enjoyed his company. The artists, sharing a recently constructed cooperative studio on Tenth Street, frequently dined together. Once, when he was away, James sent his friends some partridges for one of their dinner parties. Launt Thompson reported that his gift was "of the nicest quality, plump, tender, and gamey," and the donor was toasted over bottles of sparkling wine, all "toward convincing you that we had a good time and that partridge was popular, also Pinchot." James's and the artists' mutual affection would endure during their lifetimes. McEntee would say, for instance, that "Pinchot is a good fellow and a good friend of mine," and Whittredge would call him "a true friend."[37]

*   *   *

By early 1863, James Pinchot was ready for marriage, and as a rising entrepreneur, he was motivated to seek out a wife from a prominent family. James
had much to offer. Besides his material success, he, though slightly plump, still
cut a good figure, and his light-skinned face sported a handlebar mustache and
bushy mutton chops. Parents in polite society with marriageable daughters were
receptive to wealthy, unmarried men. As Thompson wrote James at the time,
"the mammas regard you with considerable favor, if not more," and "I think the
daughters like you too."[38]

In his search for a possible wife, James attended dances and other social
functions for young adults, and he most likely met Mary Eno at one of the
parties she so enjoyed.[39] Their coming together was fortuitous, and a courtship
began. From a rich and respectable family, Mary, a petite and attractive young
woman, had several suitors. When she was about twenty, she had found true
love, but the relationship had dissolved, and the unhappy experience may have
made her more cautious about future boyfriends.[40]

In any event, Mary was strong-willed, knew her own mind, and easily fend-
ed off those men who did not interest her. She would later recall that, as a young
woman, "society was very much less formal than it afterwards became," and
chaperones were usually not required as long as she was with another acquaintance. Developing a sense of independence, she would go horseback riding with
her friends in Central Park, an expansive public works project that opened in
1859. The park, she later noted, was "at that time in an incomplete state, and
not as well guarded as now, so that we had many wild rides in the unfrequented
parts of the park without any notice from the policemen." And she could be
frank in discouraging male suitors. She refused to dance with one admirer, who
nonetheless later pursued his case during a horseback ride when she said to him
in rejection, "No! No! I could never think of it," and, giving her steed a whip,
"galloped away as fast as I could, leaving that gentleman far behind me."[41]

But the Civil War was then raging, and James, if eligible for marriage, was
also eligible as an able-bodied male to be drafted into the Union Army.[42] The
war thus threatened to complicate his and Mary's relationship. James strongly
supported the Union cause, marveling at the large American flags flying in the
city's streets at the outset of the war. His patriotic feelings might have persuaded
him to join up, and his artist friends Sanford Gifford and John Weir had early
enlisted. But James hesitated. From its outset, he assumed the Union would be
easily restored and viewed the conflict as a hard-headed businessman. Initially,

he optimistically predicted, "We will come out of this unified and will then have another era of prosperity, greater perhaps than we have yet known."[43] One looks in vain in his wartime letters for any mention of President Lincoln, let alone his leadership or his weighty articulation of the war's purposes and meaning or reference to the idealism motivating Union volunteers. Indeed, as the war dragged on, what seemed important to him was the price of gold and the U.S. treasury bonds in which his partnership was invested.

When Robert E. Lee's Army of Northern Virginia invaded Pennsylvania in June 1863 and advanced toward Gettysburg, which was only two hundred miles from Milford, it was feared in Northern circles that a major Confederate military victory there would open the entire eastern part of the state to pillage and destruction. James convinced himself, however, that General Lee's forces were overextended and of no real danger to the Commonwealth. Writing his father from New York on the eve of the Gettysburg encounter, he said that he was so confident in the Union success that his partnership had just bought another $5,000 in treasury bonds (roughly $87,500 today). "Keep cool over it," he wrote, "and wait patiently for the result." And concerning his possible enlistment, James rationalized, "Pike County is of mighty little importance in the number of men she could send, even if all were willing to go."[44]

After the Confederate advance was decisively checked at Gettysburg, James returned to Milford to consult with his father about the draft and perhaps tell his parents about the complicating factor of his budding romance with Mary. Father and son apparently agreed that James should not sign up. Ironically, James's decision came at the same time that violent anti-draft riots, inspired by immigrants' and workingmen's anger at the exemptions of wealthy men, erupted in New York. It would be the worst civic disturbance in the city's history, with more than one hundred citizens killed in the uprising. Launt Thompson gave his absent housemate a sense of the "excitement, fire bells, madness, lunacy, murder and highways midday robbery" pervading the city.[45]

Having decided against enlistment, James intensified his courtship with Mary Eno, bringing her flowers and becoming a regular visitor to her New York home. The romance blossomed, and in September 1863, James was invited for an extended visit at the Eno's Simsbury residence. But when he returned to New York, he learned he had been drafted on October 1, 1863, and ordered to report for service the following month or be declared a deserter.[46]

James presumably doled out the required $300 to pay for a stand-in for his military obligations and seemed to have had no second thoughts on his avoidance of military service. As a successful merchant and an accepted member of the city's cultural elite, he saw himself above the military fray. His calculating decision might seem callous, but James experienced little social pressure to enlist, and hiring substitutes was a common and lawful practice in the North, where the draft was only weakly supported.[47] In any event, having resolved his military status, he continued to see Mary. James had certain advantages—mature in years, well mannered, with solid values, established in business, and committed to American art. Moreover, Mary may have valued their common French background, even if the Pinchots' roots in America were much more recent. Whatever his appeal, Mary encouraged his attention early on, and by early 1864, they were engaged.

Considering the Eno family's wealth and social prominence, the wedding ceremony at the Madison Square Presbyterian Church in New York in May 1864 was a relatively modest affair. Moreover, to James's regret, several of his artist friends did not attend, but McEntee well conveyed to James his appreciation of the event: "Believe me when I wish you all the real happiness you have as good a right to expect."[48]

*　　*　　*

The marriage of Mary and James brought together two prosperous and respectable families, both of which adhered to the Protestant reform tradition. They were not nouveau riche, as both were from and their marriage joined together two economically affluent households already well on their way up. The two's common values and traditions boded well for a compatible marriage, but their union was more than that. It was a love match, pure and simple. James was smitten almost from the beginning, and he came to adore her. About the time of their engagement, he wrote her, "Did my darling miss me and would my own pet have been happier for my presence[?] . . . In a few hours I shall fold you in my arms and kiss the dear face that always claims me."[49]

Right after their marriage, Mary and her new husband set off on their honeymoon for a grand tour of Europe. The transatlantic adventure, of course, further removed the couple physically from the tragic events in America, and James continued to perceive the Union cause mainly in the context of his investments in government bonds.[50]

Mary had previously experienced European life, but the trip was James's inaugural visit to Europe. The couple did not stint on their nearly five months of travels, which took them to England, Scotland, France, Switzerland, and Italy.[51] Besides the romantic aspects, the trip was a cultural experience. James used the occasion to visit leading European art museums to gain a first-hand appreciation of European master painters, and Mary's exposure would also stimulate her interest in the visual arts.

Upon their return to New York, the couple was frequently apart for short stretches because of his business travel and her summer sojourns in Simsbury. During their separations, James plied her with a steady stream of love letters. "My own darling, my pet, my Mary." "I rejoice in your love and thank God for you." "Good night darling. . . . [L]ove me as ever until I see you again." For her part, Mary left no doubt that her marriage was agreeable, and she soon confessed that because of her marriage, "I have a new precious blessing of my husband and his earnest love, and now comes a newer hope, a fresher life to come."[52]

Mary's last reference was to her pregnancy. She had removed to her parents' comfortable home in Simsbury to wait for the arrival of her first child. Her mother and two younger sisters were in attendance, and on August 11, 1865, she gave birth to a ten-pound baby boy. Taking the surname of James's artist friend, the proud parents named him Gifford and made the painter his godfather.

The couple greeted the baby's arrival with delight. Mary early noted that her son showed "decided promise of the beauty which soon caused him to be admired by even those most indifferent to infantile charms," and James, during his occasional absences, was writing his wife, "Kiss the baby for me" and "[t]he dear little fellow has quite won my love anew." His parents gave him the nickname "Gippie" or "Giffie."

Shortly after the baby's arrival, the Pinchots hired Mary McCadden, an Irish immigrant in her early twenties, as a nursemaid. She would subsequently serve as nurse for the Pinchots' other children as they grew up in New York. A devout Catholic, Mamie, her nickname, would gradually gain Mary Pinchot's confidence as an efficient and no-nonsense servant, and her responsibilities would evolve into nanny for the children and housekeeper. Indeed, she would prove to be an invaluable employee in the Pinchot household for fifty-nine years—through James and Mary's lifetimes and then for Gifford's family.

At two years, Mary Pinchot recorded, "Gifford speaks plainly and fluently, is perfectly well, very strong[,] red cheeked, and as rough as a little monkey." He was "a splendid[,] beautiful boy, full of live [life] and joy."[53] By that time Gifford already had a baby sister, Lucy Phelps Pinchot.[54] Born in the spring of 1867, the family called her "Lulie." Gifford "loves her most enthusiastically and admiringly," Mary noted, and referred to her as "me baby," "pendid Lulie," "Lady love," and a "butil girl."

Lulie was delicate, however, and misfortune struck when, nearly two, she became ill and died fairly quickly. As the family grieved, little Gifford, not yet four, mourned the loss of his sister. "[W]hy didn't God take me too!" he exclaimed. "When she was alive I had another guardian angel but now she is my angel, and she watches me always." Lucy, Mary's mother, sympathized with the couple's loss, but she nonetheless took a dim view of letting "Gippie dwell so much upon Lulie. . . . I hope you will all try to divert him from thinking of her too much, or it will surely injure his health."[55]

Lucy need not have worried, as Gifford already had another sister, born on December 30, 1868, who would become his new playmate before long. Antoinette Eno Pinchot, or Nettie as she was known, was apparently named after one of Mary's younger sisters but was also quintessentially French.[56] Gifford was a model child, but he was developing a strong ego. When not yet five, he put on long pants, Mary recorded in her diary, "and stumbled down Broadway with me most triumphantly. . . . Gippie says, . . . 'I am a little wicked, for I can't help being a little proud of my pants and sometimes I feel as proud as a peacock. . . . I am vain too.'"[57]

Nettie showed signs of a much more mischievous temperament. When she was barely two, James reported to Mary, "Yesterday morning she came into my room before I was up and put my shaving brush in the trash. I scolded her and sent her out of the room for that. Then she went into the parlor and put her orange seeds in my tea pot. Then she threw a whole handful of Giffie's marbles in the fire." Her punishment was sitting in a chair in the corner for a long period. A few years later, James confided to his father that "Giffie is first rate and is a real good boy. Nettie is pretty hard to manage but we think will get better as she gets older. She is so overflowing with fun that everything is a joke with her, even a slight punishment." She did improve somewhat, but even at age ten made a short-term resolution: "I promise for on[e] week to try to be agreeable to ever[y]body in the house[;] if during that time if I am cross or bad, there shall be no party."[58]

2.

The French Connection

Returning from their honeymoon, Mary and James lived their first years together in Amos Eno's residences in New York, first on East Twenty-Third Street and, beginning in 1868, a much more spacious, four-story red brick mansion on Fifth Avenue at Twenty-Seventh Street. The mansion became an extended family home for a time, with Amos and Lucy Eno sharing the residence with their three unmarried children, plus the four Pinchots and seven servants.[1] Nobody complained about being crowded, partly because the senior Enos were sometimes away sightseeing in Europe, and James's family was absent during the summers, which they first spent at family houses in Simsbury or Milford or in Newport, Rhode Island.

At the same time, James pursued his vision of a revitalized hometown. He dreamed that Milford would become a pristine example of a charming village that would be aesthetically pleasing and improve its tourist appeal. He first developed plans for transforming Milford into an artist colony. To get his painter friends to visit Milford and paint the local scenery, in 1866, he provided John Weir and his new bride with a bedroom and studio in his Milford house, and the next summer, they lived in a studio in a stone building that James had just built. "Mr. Pinchot is full of enthusiasm for the rare scenic beauties of his native place," Weir commented, "and is never weary of tempting his artist friends to sojourn amidst its hills, cataracts, ravines, and rivers." The studio would become the short-term residence of several painters. James followed with the construction of a smaller building for Jervis McEntee and his new wife, who lived there one summer, as did the Weirs. It was, McEntee recalled, "a suite of rooms which by chance had never been occupied, furnished partly with rare antiques and including a picture-gallery suitable as a studio for large work." The happy outcome was that "I could carry on my work under favorable conditions."[2]

James was involved in other modernization projects. As early as 1863, he had replaced an old building in the town center with a new post office, and later, he envisioned the construction of a chapel that would attract visitors. Weir, warming to James's purposes for Milford, wrote that he hoped the chapel "fulfills the aesthetic demands that associate religion with beauty. Your own life and surroundings says that, so you can[']t get away from it!!"[3]

Most grandiose was James's desire to imbue his hometown with bold French accents. Initially, it involved deference to his father Cyrill's veneration of his hero Napoleon. Cyrill commissioned his son's sculptor friend, Launt Thompson, to create a colossal bronze statue of Napoleon. A life-size work of the real "little" Napoleon of about five-and-one-half feet tall, Thompson's statue was shown at a Paris exposition in 1867, where it received much praise. Cyrill intended to demonstrate his lifelong admiration of Napoleon by displaying the statue in the center of Milford, but many Americans and even some French émigrés, perceiving Napoleon as a tyrant and scoundrel, would not revere such a figure. The transcendental writer Ralph Waldo Emerson had earlier written an essay about the French leader, which had concluded with a scathing critique of him as "intensely selfish," "thoroughly unscrupulous," "a boundless liar," "an imposter and a rogue."[4]

Thompson was personally acquainted with Emerson, and James Pinchot admired him and may have read his essay on the dictator. Perhaps that familiarity and the prospect of a possible adverse public reaction caused him to hold back from a prominent display of the statue until they could see how it would complement other French artifacts he might acquire.

*   *   *

In the summer of 1870, James formed a partnership with Frederick Beck, who had a paper hanging store in midtown Manhattan. The new alliance allowed him to withdraw from all but the financial aspects of the Warren partnership.[5] As Mary later recalled her husband's reasoning, "you did not feel that you could do justice intellectually or in your relations to the world if tied up with [Warren and] that you felt that your ambition for the children's position in the future as well as our own would not be satisfied with the association." James was still interested in profits, but as with Warren, he was primarily an investor in the new firm, not a hands-on manager."[6]

With his business affairs more settled, he and Mary, leaving their two children with her parents, traveled to the Salt Lake area to visit a longtime New York friend, General Régis de Trobriand, a French émigré who had fought with

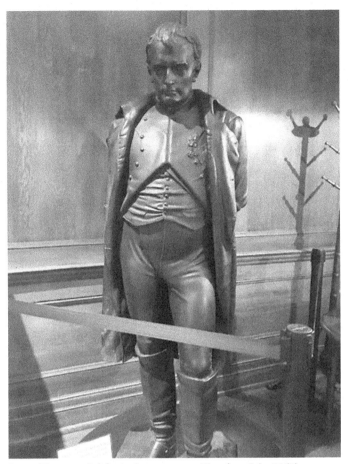

Launt Thompson's life-size bronze statue, Napoleon I (c. 1860), currently installed at Grey Towers; author photo. (Smithsonian American Art Museum)

the Union during the Civil War and was then serving in Indian country in the West. While there, Mary and James first met General William Tecumseh Sherman, commander of the U.S. Army. Sherman was already famously remembered for his scorched earth strategy during the march of his Union troops through the South in the final year of the war. The Pinchots and the general hit it off, and they became instant friends, Sherman even providing the couple with his private railroad car for part of their return journey.[7]

The western trip represented only part of the Pinchots' extended travel schedule. In the previous year, James visited Britain, France, and Italy, for business purposes and to explore Europe's cultural life. In July 1871, the entire family went to live in France for three years to immerse themselves in French life and culture. The Pinchots lived a vagabond existence. After touring Britain, they moved to Paris in the fall. They arrived, finding parts of the city in ruins following the short-lived uprising that spring of the Commune, a socialist movement among Parisian workers after their nation's disastrous defeat in the Franco-Prussian War. The family stayed in Nice for the winter, where General Sherman, who was on an official tour of European military facilities, joined them for an extended stay.

As a war hero, Sherman was at the height of his fame, and a dashing figure still in uniform and only in his early fifties attracted the attention of women, including Mary, who took a fancy to him. He traveled alone, as his marriage was going stale, and he and his wife, who had become a semi-invalid, would eventually have a trial separation. He was already something of a womanizer, but if he had thoughts of a romantic relationship with Mary, a sexual liaison never materialized.[8] In any case, Mary's marriage was rock solid. Despite her admiration of the general, the two seemed to avoid any romantic entanglement, even when they took a long tour together in the spring to a recently unified Italy, visiting Florence, Rome, and Naples. With Gifford and Nettie in tow, James followed afterward and joined them in Rome. James, too, would get along famously with him.

Subsequently, during Sherman's frequent visits to New York, he usually stayed at the Fifth Avenue Hotel and would socialize with the Pinchots in the city. A common bond was their attachment to their respective families. Sherman had six children of his own, and he doted on the Pinchot children in Nice, even playing with them as if they were his own, and his letters to the Pinchots over the years would always ask about their activities and interests. The Pinchots, in turn, would welcome the general's children during their visits to New York.

After Sherman departed, the family spent a month in Florence. Then for the summer of 1872, they rented a house in Dinard—"the prettiest place I have seen in France," James rhapsodized—on the Brittany coast. The family took long walks in the surrounding fields and woods and along the shore, and Mary later recalled, "We all lived much on the beach, and in boats." They also took short trips to nearby Mont St. Michel and the house of Victor Hugo in Guernsey, where the esteemed French author, an ardent democrat who had recently returned to French soil from self-imposed exile. Hugo obliged James by giving him two signed photographs of himself. An agreeable result of their summer experiences, James reported to his parents, was that Mary and the children "are all strong and look brown as arabs." They next visited historic chateaus in the picturesque Loire Valley before settling again in their large Paris apartment near the Arc de Triomphe. They spent the following summer at a spa in Homberg, Germany, and touring Switzerland.[9]

The Pinchots were inveterate travelers, and a defining character trait of the family members, then and later, would be their sense of adventure. In the case of James and Mary, their wanderlust was not wholly without purpose. Of the two, Mary arguably loved travel more, becoming integral to her continuing adult "education." She wanted to see as many sights as possible. James more modestly delved into the European art world, visiting art museums. He relished the experience and exulted in the galleries in Rome: "They are so interesting now that I have had twice to go through them." He did not mingle much with American painters in Paris, but in Florence, James noted, "There are a lot of American artists here and I enjoy visiting the galleries with them."[10]

During their transatlantic adventure, the Pinchot parents were enjoying their children. Far from a burden, "the chicks," as they called them, were mostly "cheerful" and "a great comfort to us," James told his father, and Nettie and Gifford, only three and six, became "capital travelers." The family went sightseeing together, and James ventured alone to Corsica to visit the house where Napoleon was born and probably to Breteuil, his father's and grandfather's native city.[11]

When the Pinchots lived in Paris, they had a chef, and Mamie McCadden provided housekeeping help. Mamie also helped with the children, but the parents viewed childcare as a pleasure. When Mary was away, for instance, he reported to his wife about their children, "How happy you would have been my darling to have seen their bright faces. I took tea with them and then gave them the books I bought," one of which was the children's classic, "Jack the Giant Killer." James claimed that he had already read the story to them twenty times, and "the first thing this morning was their sweet voices asking may I read the Giant Killer again." And when James was away, Mary was engaged with her children. "Every night," she wrote her husband, "I read a little for them after dinner and then we have some other amusement. . . . Tonight the excitement has been soap bubbles."[12]

The children also profited from their time abroad. While in Paris, Gifford had a French lesson each morning, and one of his assignments was to write short letters in cursive French to the parent who was away.[13] Nettie also picked up the language, and she and her brother were soon ordering their meals in French. Gifford also had some special experiences. In Paris, he walked along the top of the Arc de Triomphe; while in Nice, General Sherman arranged for Gifford to get a personal guided tour of the flagship of the U.S. Navy's Mediterranean

Squadron. "He saw everything and came home with most wonderful stories," his father reported.[14]

As James traveled, he offered social commentary on European developments. He had a social conscience. Six months before the Pinchot family left for Europe, he and his Eno in-laws established a charitable fund for New York citizens' relief of the starving and needy Parisians following the German Army's long, punishing siege of the French capital during the Franco-Prussian War.[15]

James understandably sympathized with the French people in that traumatic time, but his observations on the European social order were definitely elitist. During an earlier trip, he had commented, "A more squalid dirty and generally ill looking lot than the lower classes of Rome and Naples it would be hard to find." And upon returning to Europe in 1871, he expressed contempt for "the horrible acts of the dreadful Commune," whose destructive course in many parts of the city made for "a most sad and depressing sight. . . . In fact it is almost too painful to stay here," he told his father. And after a cross-channel boat trip, he disparaged the "disgustingly dirty and sea sick unfortunates crowding the decks."[16] He simply dismissed the lower orders as uncouth and unwashed, and any small, ameliorative efforts would have to come from the charitable efforts of more fortunate and respectable private citizens.

About halfway into their extended European sojourn, James and Mary commissioned Alexandre Cabanel, a well-known traditional French portraitist then living in Florence, to create a painting of his family.[17] Only Mary, Gifford, and Nettie are portrayed in the painting, as James decided not to be included. Cabanel was a demanding artist and required the Pinchot trio to sit multiple times over several weeks in his studio as he worked on the canvas. The completed work depicts the three Pinchots as a proud French noble family dressed in luxurious costumes of a bygone pre-revolutionary era. It says much about Mary's determination to validate her family as rich, specially entitled, and French in background. James paid Cabanel as much as $12,000 ($210,000) in gold. When Jervis McEntee learned of the portrait and the price, he sarcastically commented in his diary, "It is surprising what a respect these European artists inspire in the breast of our travelled Americans."[18]

McEntee expressed a common concern among American artists that art lovers and patrons at home still considered their painters as provincials compared with the masters abroad. European pictures are "imported and seem to find sale, some at enormous prices," Worthington Whittredge lamented to James, "while the Bierstadts, and Churches, Giffords and Johnsons are not sold or even wanted. Some better disposition must be shown by the public for at least our good artists, or art here and our art institutions must die out."[19]

Whittredge and McEntee blamed the American public and not James directly, but they were aware of the Cabanel portrait, and James was guilty by association. The criticism was fair—American art patrons were still enamored with their European counterparts—but not the full story. The romantic naturalism of the Hudson River School had run its course and was in a state of decline, as artistic tastes were changing in a rapidly growing urban-industrial America. By the 1880s, the older American landscape artists would have difficulty getting decent prices for their paintings and would have to adapt to the new realities. Whittredge, for example, began painting in the Barbizon style, which, with its emphasis on light, was a forerunner of American impressionism. In the comparative perspective of French and American civilization, James did not summarily reject one or the other but wanted the best of both. On the American side, he continued his generous support of American artists. He agreed, for example, to lend the Cabanel painting to a New York exhibition, which, according to John Weir, "charmed" the viewers. And perhaps to atone for his indiscretion with the Cabanel, he commissioned Eastman Johnson to paint his maternal grandmother and Launt Thompson to create a marble bust of his mother, Eliza. James, probably with Mary's encouragement, also hired Whittredge to paint *The Mill, Simsbury, Conn.*[20]

At the same time, as a third-generation American, James was comfortable with his French heritage and was motivated to reclaim parts of it. He increasingly tried to blend elements of French history and culture into his continuing vision of revitalizing Milford. Artists sometimes in residence would contribute, but selectively he came to believe that the local population could still learn some things from France and England. He was impressed, for example, with the English countryside, with its neat, white picket fences and tastefully designed gardens. And when he visited a village on the side of a hill facing the sea on the Isle of Wight, he became positively ecstatic. It "is full of shaded walks, shrubbery, beautiful houses most quaintly and unexpectedly placed; rare plants and exquisite blossoms," he wrote his mother. "I wish every one in Milford could see how much could be done in the way of beautifying a village."[21] Though an ocean away, here was a concrete example, he thought, that could inspire the Milford citizenry.

James concocted another cultural scheme. In the fall of 1871, he traveled from Paris to England to visit Louis Napoleon III, the deposed French Emperor living in exile, to ask him to donate his books to the Milford library. Napoleon received him cordially but told James that, unfortunately, nearly all his books had been left behind in France. Encouraged by the American minister in Paris, James followed up and was cautiously optimistic. "I think the result will be that

I shall have something that with the [Napoleon] statue will make Milford quite interesting," he told his father. But Louis Napoleon either thought better of James's proposal or concluded that he had too little to offer, and the initiative died aborning. In the end, James abandoned even the statue as part of his ambitious Napoleonic "plan" for Milford, and after his father's death, he would lend the bronze work for long-term display at the Metropolitan Museum of Art.[22]

*   *   *

The Pinchots planned to return to the United States in 1873, but Mary got pregnant again. The family decided to stay put until the baby arrived. By remaining in France, they avoided the latest financial panic, which suddenly burst on the American scene in the fall of 1873.[23] Then on December 6, 1873, Mary gave birth in Paris to another boy. "Molly was not sick more than an hour and a half and says she can hardly believe it is all over as the baby came so quick," James wrote his father. "Nettie and Gifford are in a great state of excitement." Taking the full name of Mary's father, the parents named the new arrival Amos Richards Eno Pinchot.[24]

The family, now complete, had a scare over the baby's health. At two weeks, Amos fell alarmingly sick with a bad cold, and the family became "very anxious" about him. "We hope God will spare us our dear little boy so that you may see him in Milford," James wrote his mother. Amos's illness came at the same time James received news that his father had died rather suddenly. It was an unhappy time, and James tried to shore up his mother's and siblings' spirits in their time of need until the fate of his own newborn was resolved. He would return home to do his "duty" to the family. James soon reported that Amos was "now much better."[25] An ocean voyage in winter was not advisable, however, and the Pinchots set sail for the United States only after a summer in Boulogne, France, near the English Channel. After three years abroad, the return to American shores was a welcome event. Greeted on arrival by her parents and siblings, Mary noted in her diary: "Oh! The joy of home coming! To find all well and happy! To see so many dear ones and all so rejoiced to see us!"[26]

*   *   *

In many ways, the Pinchots' European experiences had been idyllic, but there were compensations. One involved Mary's desire for more financial independence. Amos Eno, her father, had much earlier given his newly married daughter a generous dowry-like gift of $50,000 (about $700,000 today), which James had invested for her, and then another $50,000 to buy a house.[27] After receiving the second $50,000, she assumed she would also receive that interest income pending the purchase. James invested the money himself, however, and she found in Europe that she wanted that income to meet her own and the children's expenses. Believing her husband was "not entirely right" on the matter, she had confronted him in Nice "to talk upon a subject which I wished never to have discussed between us."[28]

James readily turned over the investment income to Mary, but the question of a permanent home would become an irritant. When they returned to New York, they stayed at the senior Eno's Fifth Avenue mansion, then rented a house nearby. But the family always had summer plans elsewhere—in Milford, Nantucket, and then two straight years in Saybrook (Fenwick), Connecticut.[29] Just before the first of these Saybrook summers, James and Mary left the children with her parents for a three-month sightseeing trip in Europe. Their itinerary was a delightful escapade, taking them to Britain, Scotland, Ireland, Belgium, a boat trip on the Rhine, and Paris. Mary's continual search for more healthful and congenial summer seashore venues continued until, nearly a decade later, the Pinchots settled on Bar Harbor, Maine, which was becoming an elegant summer spot for affluent and urbane Americans. It was full of social entertainment, refreshingly cool, and afforded magnificent views of the sea coast. The setting, Mary rhapsodized, "seems like a dream of the future social life. May we all be there to enjoy it through all Eternity."[30]

Despite the pleasant experiences, their constant movements prolonged their indecision on a permanent home, and Mary, restless at this state of affairs, complained to her husband "that we have no place which we can call our own." "[I]t is not right," she added, "to allow ourselves to be drifted about as we have always done. Both we ourselves and the children have suffered much from our indecision in this way and I dislike to continue in a mistake I so plainly see."[31]

James agreed in principle but somehow managed to persuade Mary that they should still defer a house purchase in the city. Likely gestating in his mind was the prospect of having a home of their own in Milford. James, a deliberate thinker, was not one to promote his plans until they were well developed in his mind, and even Mary may not have known his full thoughts on the subject until he acted on them early in the next decade. He was beginning to envision the building of an elegant mansion, which would complement his commitment to the beautification and modernization of Milford and further identify his family with his native town. During their European sojourn, he had closely observed the historic architecture, admiring, for example, the French chateaus of the Loire, "the most beautiful in France," for their "honest mason work."

And while in Florence, he noted that the hotel where he was staying had once been a palace, with "many spacious and beautiful rooms . . . ; there is nothing I covet so much as one of these massive old houses. They are built to last and do last through centuries. To my mind they are just the thing."[32]

Male pride may have been a factor, too, with James wanting to build and pay for his dream house before using Mary's money for a New York residence. They would still need a place in Gotham, but a home in Milford could serve as a restful retreat, particularly on weekends and in the warmer months. Until his house plans for Milford jelled, buying one in New York could be put off.

Mary understood her husband's attachment to his native town. Milford, even as a retreat, was not an easy sell, however. It lacked the social attractions of a sophisticated New York family. Moreover, her first extended stay at the Pinchot homestead there in the summer of 1875 had been miserable. The "darkey cook," she later groused, "went to balls and got sick, [and I] had to do the cooking for three weeks." The weather was, moreover, "excessively hot," and she caught "a more severe cold than ever before or since," which left her bedridden for a month. Her unhappy experience contributed thereafter to her strong preference for summers at the seashore.[33]

James's continued business career also dissatisfied his wife. Soon after the family had returned from their three years in Europe, James and Beck enlarged their business by taking in three new partners. The new additions brought an infusion of fresh capital to the concern. Although James was not directly involved in the business, he was to receive ten percent of the profits under the arrangement.[34] To Mary, the new deal meant that there would be "no change" in his future business involvement. James had seemed to think that Mary wanted him to make more money, but, mincing few words, she commented sharply that they were affluent and that James's continued pursuit of moneymaking only detracted from his other interests. "I do not think it depends upon the largeness of our income half so much as it does upon our doing what we can with what we have and making the most of what we are," she told him. "I believe you are capable of a higher development than you will get if tied down to paper hangings," she continued, "and I think it is a mistake that a man of such noble aspirations and larger capacity should not fill a larger sphere —all the time."

Mary had an assertive personality and could not help expressing herself even on delicate personal matters. "You know I am subject to fits of sensitivities upon points which at other times do not seem so serious," she admitted to her husband. She also framed her lament in the context of her resolute affection for him, saying, "I love you too well to be happy one moment without your encouragement and sympathy."[35] Her complaint was nonetheless somewhat unfair, as James was becoming a more important player in the American art world. He served on committees for the showing of American art at the Philadelphia Centennial Exposition in 1876 and as secretary of an advisory committee for the selection of American artworks for the Universal Exposition in Paris two years later, both involvements further exhibiting his interest in Franco-American cultural interaction. He also increased his donations to the Metropolitan Museum of Art.[36]

His new partnership, moreover, was limited to five years, which may have been James's way of easing out of the business. Holding him back from an immediate, full break were the growing earnings of the firm, which directly benefitted from the continuing exuberant consumer demand for interior furnishings. Despite James's minimal involvement, the profits, he admitted, were "out of proportion with the amount of capital invested."[37]

Another purpose of Mary's blunt critique was to clear the air of any misunderstanding between them. In this respect, she succeeded, and James got the message. By 1880, he would be out of the wallpaper business—almost. He was still an investor, holding onto a $10,000 mortgage on the company property, and for many years he would continue to receive ten percent of the profits as part of the rent his old partners paid him during the lease.[38] With retirement, he would become more focused on providing a residence, or residences, for his family, assuming a more prominent role as a patron of American and Franco-American cultural activities, and, not incidentally, participating more actively in the rearing of his children. If these actions were designed to please his wife, he would also be well satisfied with the new directions in his life.

Gifford's parents were in the prime years of middle age; of the two, Mary was less ready to slow down. As she wrote her husband, "I must be interested. I would rather die than not do anything nor be anybody. . . . A life of introversion makes me morbid and wicked; it nearly kills me." Her outburst was part of a general criticism of James, who, in her view, was withdrawing socially. "[Y]ou don't seem to care for anything in this world so much as to be alone and to be quiet," she complained to him. "It vexes me to see a man of your possibilities doing so little. . . . [Y]ou have lost courage and are afraid to do and be your best."[39] Because Mary firmly believed they should get intellectual stimulation "more from people than from books," she more easily criticized James's interest in reading and thinking. She also groused that her husband made "the great mistake of keeping things from me," so it was difficult for her to sympathize with him.

As in her earlier criticism of her spouse, Mary claimed that her lament was intended to stimulate James to open up so they could work together toward a mutually supportive, active life.[40] It was nonetheless true and unfortunate for their relationship that the couple was drifting apart somewhat, with Mary now more assertive and active while James was becoming more reflective. Her blockbuster letter may have helped him understand their differences, and he would try to show more interest in her activities. But it did not resolve the extrovert-introvert tension.

Actually, James was still involved in two major activities, but they did not involve Mary directly. His first project at the time was his emerging relationship with the French sculptor Frédéric Auguste Bartholdi, whom the French government had commissioned to design a Statue of Liberty in 1875 as a gift from France to the American people. James would serve on the American committee, which coordinated the complicated logistics of the statue's transport, display, and final erection, and raised money for the design and construction of the pedestal on which the towering Liberty figure would be placed. James gave $5,000 to the endeavor, and in the decade it would take to complete the statue and get it to New York for placement and dedication, he was engaged in many phases of the project. During his 1880–1881 sojourn in Paris, he served as the American committee's representative with the French promoters, including personal contacts with Bartholdi to discuss progress relating to the statue, and the two corresponded afterward on details. The committee hired Richard Morris Hunt, America's best-known architect in the Gilded Age, to design the pedestal, which, rising from a massive base, would be two-thirds the height of the statue, and employed James's sculptor friend Launt Thompson as an assistant.[41] James also had a hand in hiring the army engineer, recommended by General Sherman, who oversaw the pedestal's construction.

The downside to this endeavor was that the American committee promoting the Liberty venture, with James Pinchot as its treasurer, never managed to arouse much popular enthusiasm and support among the American citizenry and fell woefully short in raising the money needed to underwrite the extensive construction and erection costs of the statue. In the end, it would take the efforts of the enterprising publisher Joseph Pulitzer to fill in the large shortfall by publicizing the project in his newspapers and appealing to readers to contribute $1 or more.

James's other priority at that time was the construction of his dream house in Milford that could serve as a family retreat from New York City. He also perceived it as an example of what could be done to upgrade Milford, although

Statue of Liberty, c. 1884, in sculptor August Bartholdi's Paris studio before its dismantlement and shipment to New York City. (French post card)

he seems to have given up his earlier schemes for making the town a tourist mecca. For the site, he bought 102 acres of land on a high hill overlooking the town, with a view of the Delaware River to the east, and he turned to Richard Morris Hunt for the design. Before his involvement in the pedestal of the Statue of Liberty, Hunt had designed palatial residences for the richest Americans in New York as well as numerous public buildings, but he and James were also good friends. Their friendship may have extended back to the late 1850s with one of Hunt's early designs, the Tenth Street studio, which James and his artist friends frequented, and they were both members of the Century Association. Moreover, Hunt's wife and Mary were very close, and Nettie was best friends with the Hunts' daughter, Catharine (Kitty), and would later regularly visit her at another Hunt home in Newport, Rhode Island.

Richard Morris Hunt had an additional appeal. He was the first American architect to be trained at L'École des Beaux-Arts in Paris and had lived in the French capital for many years. He well understood French architectural design, including the long tradition of its country chateaus, and had incorporated French features in his own work in the United States. When James hired Hunt, he had in mind a home modeled after the chateaus that existed during the time of his late father and grandfather in France. Work began in early 1884 and would take two years to complete.

During its building, James, always cautious with his money, scaled back the size of Hunt's plans and was frugal about details. He used competitive bidding to get the lowest price on the many construction parts, and the wood, stones, and other materials for the big house came from the immediate surrounding area, saving money. The massive structure was undoubtedly expensive but, because of James's frugal oversight, was a bargain for an imposing three-story structure of 19,000 square feet. When completed, it would include, among other features, 44 rooms, 23 fireplaces, and three round, turreted towers, 20 feet in diameter and 60 feet in height at the corners of the house.[42]

The Pinchots considered various names for the mansion, and after its completion, James and Mary agreed on Grey Towers. The name avoided direct implications of French pretensions and accurately depicted the towers and gray exterior as prominent features.[43] But Grey Towers was modeled on France's baronial chateaus and was sometimes called a "castle" by visitors. James made sure, moreover, it had distinctive French accents, which included Thompson's imposing statue of Napoleon and a bust of the Marquis de Lafayette by John Quincy Adams Ward, and the Cabanel portrait of family members was prominently displayed downstairs.[44]

Despite its magnificence, James and Mary soon found Grey Towers a mixed blessing. Mary could entertain their visiting friends there, but suffering from uncertain health—rheumatism and digestive problems in particular—she found that even with housekeeping help, the place was burdensome. Even James came to understand that her restful times away from Grey Towers allowed her to escape from "dreading the care it involves."[45] Moreover, Mary still found Milford too quiet for her activist temperament and too hot in the summer. She was drawn to European spas for health reasons, but she also wanted to be around interesting, "attractive looking" people. Otherwise, she could get "tired" of the company and want to move on.[46]

A newly completed Grey Towers, c. 1886. James Pinchot would soon plant many trees to reforest the mostly barren landscape. (USDA Forest Service, Grey Towers NHS)

Almost from the beginning of their occupancy, James was realizing that Grey Towers was more than he and Mary needed; he rationalized, "The children will be pleased with the house and place at Milford when we are gone. This reconciles me to it even if we are inclined to give it up." And increasingly, he found it something of an albatross. It seemed he was always commuting there from New York to attend to the upkeep and various improvements—the construction of a new driveway, farmhouse, outbuildings, and a dam and waterfalls on the Sawkill to create an artificial pond for trout fishing and producing an ice supply in winter for the mansion's yearly refrigeration needs. In short, the Milford estate gave him "little rest and less diversion."[47]

In the Statue of Liberty and similar endeavors, James Pinchot expressed his continuing commitment to the cultural links binding America and France together. However, projects in this area never got far off the ground or were realized mainly with others' more substantial contributions. Even the construction of his Milford mansion, while resulting in a permanent French-inspired icon, would not be an unqualified triumph. James's love of France and its relevance to America persisted, and before long, it would have a tangible influence in pointing his oldest son, Gifford, in the direction of a new profession.

3.

The Education of Christian Patricians

Gifford, Antoinette, and Amos Pinchot grew up under the loving eyes of their parents, who monitored their children's development, and no child was left behind. Yet Gifford, the eldest, received extra attention, and his parents would play a crucial part in molding his character.

That the oldest sibling should receive special parental supervision is not surprising, as the firstborn often has his parents' full attention until the next baby is born. In a male-oriented culture, the fact that his immediate younger sibling was female only confirmed his special place in his parents' eyes. Girls were valued perhaps more in the United States than elsewhere, yet their occupational opportunities were still limited, perhaps more so in wealthy families, where it was assumed that girls would not aspire to success in the business or professional world.

Education was highly valued in the household. James had encouraged his youngest brother, Cyrill, to go beyond high school, and Mary's three younger brothers were college graduates. The parents never enrolled Nettie in a private school, and governesses and tutors taught her basic disciplines.[1] The focus of her education was to provide her with the skills required for a dignified lady in polite society. Nettie also mastered horseback riding to travel short distances by herself, and as a teenager, she took voice and guitar lessons and studied French, German, and Italian. When Nettie was sixteen, her reading consisted mostly of light fiction, and James wanted to encourage her to read more serious literature.[2] But Nettie was largely in the purview of her mother, and Mary's desires would be more important in her social development.

Mary wanted an active life and valued her independence. Paid help relieved her from household drudgery and gave her more time to cultivate her own interests. As late as 1880, the Pinchots had only three servants, Mamie McCadden foremost among them.[3] Appreciating her good work, Mary Pinchot left the details of child care and house management to the Irish woman. Her direction did not always sit well with the children, who occasionally became exasperated with her strict oversight, but she genuinely loved them. McCadden had Mrs. Pinchot's confidence, and that was all that mattered.[4]

Mary Pinchot called on neighbors, went to the theater and opera, attended church, and was involved for a time in the Society of Decorative Art, which offered instruction in New York for women in needlework and the sale of their items in the applied arts.[5] But, society was not her passion, and she limited her commitments so as not to interfere with her frequent absences from the city.

Above all, Mary still loved to travel. As Nettie matured, Mary took her as her companion to Europe at least once a year. It was assumed that Nettie's exposure to the wider world was integral to her education, just as it was for Mary. She had entreated her husband in 1878, "I would not give two straws to go [to Europe] except as a matter of education."[6] She had belated concerns about arranging for her daughter "to go to school or classes with other girls" before "she will be in society," but it never happened.[7]

During Nettie's frequent travels, she learned about the elegant, picturesque places the wealthy people visited. But the semi-rebellious spirit from her childhood remained, and as she became a mature woman would increasingly lead to tensions with her parents. Children invent nicknames to create their own individualistic space in the face of strong-willed parents, and Gifford had already given his mother the affectionate name "Mamee" (Mah-MAY). At age sixteen, Nettie began calling her "Mouse" or "Mousatilla," a creative nickname suggesting her view of the separate parts of her petite mother's loving (Mouse) and forceful (Attila the Hun) personality. She also labeled her father "the Bird" while calling herself "Reed Bird," and in her letters home, she used an imaginary man, "he" or "Mr. R. B.," to replace herself as the writer. On a psychological level, Nettie's masculine nickname could be interpreted as a subconscious desire to be a man, with more opportunities for self-actualization.[8]

*   *   *

Despite the mother-daughter relationship, Mary's favorite child was Gifford, and she never tired of praising him. Mary reminded herself that she loved all her children equally,[9] but her adoring language betrayed her bias. Gifford was "her sunshine and her delight and always has been," she would write him even as a mature adult, and she often called him "my precious boy."[10] However,

Mary did not spoil Gifford, and all her attention encouraged him to develop his own interests. She even accepted his going away to school, although she would tell him that "the sun shines brighter when he is with me."[11]

In his preteen years, James allowed his son to develop his own interests, and Gifford's delight was outdoor activities. During their summer in Dinard, France, he, then seven, had spent hours collecting assorted shells, fish species, and sea plants left exposed on the sand and rocks as the ocean tide receded. Young Gifford also developed a passion for insects. Back in America, he collected potato bugs and other insects, and Mary noted, "Gifford is as enthusiastic as ever about his etymology [entomology]." He captured several large beetles and boasted, "I have caught so many things this summer [and] to describe them all would take a small book."[12] This fascination soon expanded to include amphibians and reptiles.

In the summer of 1879, the family visited Keene Valley in the Adirondack Mountains, a retreat for affluent New Yorkers eager to escape the city's heat, dirt, and noise. Gifford remembered that summer with special fondness. Once while looking for turtles, he spied a trout about eight inches long in a brook. Rushing back to their rustic hotel, he grabbed his fishing tackle and, returning to the brook, captured a grasshopper for bait and soon landed the trout, his first among the hundreds he would catch during his lifetime. He triumphantly took the fish back to the hotel, where it was cooked and eaten. His father gave Gifford his first fly rod a few days later. Then Papa, as the children called him, took him deeper into the Adirondack wilderness to where they camped and fished. One day Gifford was casting his fly rod from a boat, and in another boat nearby, his father remarked to an accompanying friend, "The boy doesn't fish as if he were only thirteen." His father's praise "gave me something to stiffen my backbone then and now and all the years in between," Gifford recalled. "It is a very pleasant memory." His father was letting him know that he was coming of age.[13]

The wilderness also impressed Gifford, and during this adventure, he would hear a bear roar and a panther scream. Concerning the latter, nearly sixty years later, he could still exclaim, "What a thrill!" Later, Gifford remembered, his Adirondack experience "gave me a new and lasting conception of the wilderness, and not improbably it had much to do with making me a forester."[14] Gifford's retrospective comment can be seen as a logical reconstruction of an adolescent's journey toward his chosen profession. His other interests over the next decade would pull him in different directions, but he wrote accurately in his memoirs, "As a boy it was my firm intention to be a naturalist," which was an outgrowth of his love of entomology, and not far removed from forestry.[15]

*   *   *

For Gifford's college education, James and Mary's choice of Yale was a no-brainer. Connections came from Yale graduate Henry Fitch, who had arranged sweetheart lumbering and land deals with James, and several Eno forebears had gone there.[16]

Gifford's preparatory education would prove to be an eclectic mix, however. In New York, he attended two different private grammar schools. Then in 1880, the Pinchots decided to spend another year in Europe. The family would live in familiar Paris but first visited England, where James investigated a number of boarding schools for Gifford.[17] The parents probably chose British preparatory schools, as they were becoming more Anglophilic in their sentiments. Paris was "Paradise" to Mary, but they were developing a natural affinity for their British counterparts' values and social position in a fairly orderly and stratified society. They were also finding the island's seductive scenery irresistible. During their trips there, Mary had waxed ecstatic about the "charmingly beautiful" English countryside and gardens and the "grand" and "pleasing" scenery in the Scottish lakes region.[18]

Finding the British schools oversubscribed, James hired a tutor, the son of an Episcopal rector in Canterbury. Gifford lived with the cleric's family for the fall. Then just before Christmas, he would rejoin his family in Paris. For the rest of the school year, he studied under tutors and visited the Jardin des Plantes to attend lectures on natural history subjects.

The primary responsibility of an upper-class married woman in Victorian America was the home, including the moral instruction of her children, and Mary focused on Gifford's ethical education. She wanted him to become a morally upright and unselfish person, the basis of which was a firm grounding in Christian principles. She made sure he said his prayers at bedtime and had a good understanding of the Bible as guidance for his own behavior. Her letters advised him to accept Christ. "It is the most natural thing in all the world that we should believe in Him who was God's manifestation of himself to us. . . . Our lives are our offering to him."[19] For reading holy scripture, her favorite guide was the apostle Paul. "Every day," she wrote Gifford, "I find in St. Paul's words something which speaks to my soul as if it had been written to me," and she urged him to "read all you can of St. Paul." Gifford received a steady diet of such homilies.[20]

James at first emphasized regular letters home. During Gifford's stay at Canterbury, Papa lectured him, "If you <u>do not wish to write or if you write</u>

irregularly, I shall feel obliged to ask you to leave Canterbury." When he finally received a letter, he bewailed that it had "not answered a single one of your mother[']s questions or of mine." Even Mary insisted on regular correspondence and warned, "Do, my dear boy, pay attention to what I have told you."[21]

Papa also impressed upon Gifford the importance of avoiding extravagance. He required a report on his son's monthly expenses and details of his lessons to see if he was getting his money's worth out of the tutor. "I cannot afford too much expenditure," James stressed, so frugality was required, and he complained about the money Gifford spent on candy and other pleasures.[22] Finally, James tried to refocus his son's attention on his studies and personal health. The health advice was a monologue of common sense: lots of exercise and avoiding exposure to the cold. Regarding his lessons, he urged Gifford to spend five hours of study daily, soon expanding to seven. "Education like civilization is growth, not a plunge," he advised.[23]

All the commands from an unreasonably demanding father did not seem to hurt Gifford. Children need parental love but also boundaries. Gifford was on a short leash, but it was also elastic, and James's bark was worse than his bite. When Gifford apologized for shortcomings in his correspondence, for example, his parents quickly backed off and insisted on letters only two or three times a week. Gifford more than met that standard, and his letters, usually several pages long, were full of his opinions and news of his adventures. Whether his parents knew it or not, they were giving Gifford good training in expository writing.[24]

James's letters to his son were also full of affection, and he sent him baskets of fruit and visited him at Canterbury. Papa and Gifford consulted on his studies, and the constant health reminders were harmless as long as Gifford stayed physically sound. Knowing that his father, for all his hounding, was deeply interested in his welfare, Gifford was appreciative and wrote his mother from Canterbury, "He is the very best father that ever was."[25]

Returning home, the parents enrolled Gifford at Phillips Exeter Academy, a private boys' boarding school in New Hampshire. Gifford maintained a religious outlook there, profiting, he said, from his reading of a biography of St. Paul that his mother had sent him.[26] She also pestered him about joining the church. It was, she wrote him, a real commitment, "only to be assumed when our hearts are so in accord with His will that we feel impelled to assume them by our own uninfluenced wills."[27] Gifford was ready and decided to become a Presbyterian. His parents had sometimes attended an Anglican church in Milford, he had lived with an Episcopal minister's family in Canterbury, and Episcopalians predominated at Exeter. But the family's Presbyterian roots stuck with Gifford, who concluded that the Anglican religion was "very high church" and had "too much ritual" for him.[28]

As his father required, Gifford sent home accountings of his expenses and claimed to study nine hours daily (including three hours of recitation).[29] Despite such discipline, young Gifford was enjoying himself. He twice went on chaperoned sleigh rides with classmates and some town girls and, during a snow storm on the second, was designated after drawing lots to go back with a driver on a cutter to inform the girls' families that all were safe. After delivering the news to the girls' homes, he got up early to study and bragged to his parents, "I was the only fellow who did not miss a recitation." Gifford's exploits made his mother "very happy and proud of my boy;" but, giving them religious meaning, added, "still more is my heart gladdened by the knowledge that your life is 'hid with Christ in God,' and that the priceless treasure of this love brightens your every day and hour."[30]

Gifford exuberantly described his extracurricular experiences at Exeter, but Papa wrote him, "Don't think all the time of sleighing trips and your pleasure. Study is the thing now and your health." After relating more of his good times, he was reproached again: "If you are never to have any backbone or resolution . . . , your education is thrown away, and the money and time spent useless."[31]

His father's constant tugging on Gifford had no untoward effect. His parents knew he was a well-behaved, extroverted boy and would strive to be the best he could be, and eventually, his father would tell him, "I take it for granted you will act judiciously."[32] James had spared the rod on young Gifford, and Mary had not spoiled him. They had imposed a disciplined structure within which the value system they imparted in him could flourish. The result was a self-confident personality that would serve him well in getting respectful attention, but that could also lead him to insurgent action in pursuit of goals that seemed good and desirable to him but were unreachable at the time.[33]

The steady parental hammering had some effects, however, as Gifford early internalized certain values—particularly, a compulsive work ethic. His energy and intensity prompted his brother, Amos, to comment later, "You make hard work out of everything you do—even loafing and doing things for fun!"[34] His father's emphasis on discipline and purposeful activity got through to his oldest son, so any backsliding made him feel guilty. Thirty years later, for instance, Gifford would write his mother, "I'm afraid I have . . . let a day or two slip by without a letter—but I didn't mean to." He was particularly hard on himself when he relaxed. As a young forester, for example, he would complain, "Have been perfectly useless all this week and am disgusted with myself;" or, more succinctly, "Am a footless ass."[35]

*   *   *

Gifford had entered Phillips Exeter as a junior (tenth or lowest grade), but because of his uncertain education, the school put him in a preparatory class that was not formally a part of the academy. Gifford impressed his teachers with his effort, his Latin teacher telling him, "I worked better than any other boy he had ever had who had spent much of his time abroad." He was nonetheless behind in algebra and Latin and was told that spring that he did not yet qualify as a junior.[36]

Gifford soon made up the deficiency and continued to thrive. He was elected president of a religious society, and his first autumn, he took up lacrosse and, the following fall, was elected captain of the team.[37] During the long winter months, he indulged in ice fishing and bought an ax to cut down dead trees and search for grubs and insects. Once, after he and a classmate felled a rotten tree, they found five baby owls in its top, two of which survived the fall.[38]

But then he began to have trouble with his eyes and had real difficulty doing his assignments. Gifford probably suffered from astigmatism, which his long evening study hours and poor lighting aggravated. His father urged him to see a doctor and offered health advice, while a "troubled" Mamee advised, "Give up all evening pleasures and duties of any sort," get plenty of sleep, and finish his homework "by full daylight." Over the next year, Gifford saw his Uncle Henry Eno, a physician, and doctors and oculists, but their advice was sometimes contradictory. Anyway, the prescribed treatments of eye wash, glasses, and cod liver oil did not seem to help.[39]

When he could not read his lessons the following fall, his father hired a tutor as a reader, and Gifford quickly impressed him with his "combination of frankness, generosity and purity of spirit," but the problem persisted. It was more frustrating because Gifford otherwise was growing toward his full size of six feet and 160 pounds and was in excellent health.[40]

By the fall of his third year at Exeter, however, Gifford, still struggling with his eyes, lamented, "I cannot but feel blue at times over my inability to do my work," and it might make it "almost impossible for me to enter Yale next fall." His parents were taken aback, and an annoyed Mamee replied that instead of study, "you do everything [else] first, tire yourself with games, being up late nights, eating all kinds of trash, thereby damaging your digestive organs which react upon your eyes. . . . If I am too severe I am sorry [but] my standard for you is very high."[41]

Gifford got the message and wrote home, "I ask your forgiveness for the pain I have caused you, and I will try not to get blue again and [will] go on with my work in a manly way."[42] Somewhat mollified, Mary nonetheless reminded her son that he came from a privileged background with "everything before you. . . . You can study, thank God, without being hampered at every step with the necessity of gaining your own bread. You have only to have patience, prudence and determination to get on and be useful to your day and generation." The notion of *noblesse oblige* was rarely expressed more explicitly to an adolescent.[43] And Gifford's use of the word "manly" probably satisfied his papa. In James's value system, it was a favorite word, which, besides acting grown up, meant an internalized, stoic resolve to persevere amid setbacks. One of James's complaints about his younger brother, Cyrill, had been his "want of manly courage shown in his neglect of his studies," while he considered a tutor's evaluation of Gifford's "manly" approach to his lessons the highest praise.[44]

In preaching "manly" behavior, James was espousing a form of Christian manliness—a value system that was fairly widespread among upper-class Protestants in Victorian England and America. Christian manliness emphasized physical health, morality, civic virtue, and personal responsibility. Except for Emerson, James never really explained the sources of his cultural and intellectual beliefs in his correspondence, so the precise influences are somewhat speculative. But James likely absorbed this ethos from his frequent visits to England and, as an avid reader, from books, perhaps even of English novelists who were popularizing the concept of Christian manliness.[45]

But for Gifford's eye problem, manliness was insufficient. He suffered from a medical condition that no amount of willpower could remedy. Finally, his parents, hoping to relieve the strain on his eyes, withdrew him from Exeter at the end of the fall.

Meanwhile, Nettie had been suffering from serious sore throats and sickness that fall, and the family doctor, believing the city environment endangered her delicate health, prescribed an extended time of study in the Adirondacks. Now a precocious fourteen-year-old, Nettie disliked the plan.[46] But her parents sent her to stay with a family in a comfortable cabin at Saranac Lake for the entire winter, and with Gifford removed from Exeter, they sent him there too. Among other benefits, it would relieve James of chaperone duty and put her under the watchful eyes of her older brother.

Gifford's stay at Saranac was meant to improve his overall health. James, encouraged by the family doctor, was acting out his theory that cold, fresh air (with precautions) and exercise were conducive to good health. He also thought his son would profit from a mixture of study and outdoor activity.

Still, Saranac was a curious choice. It was positively frigid there (Nettie reported one reading of -32°), and on clear days, Gifford complained, the glare of the bright sun on the snow "brings on dimness and pain" to his already "troublesome" eyes. Armed with a lesson plan, he studied on his own with occasional help from a tutor in mathematics and would send home slips of paper showing completion of assignments. He spent more time doing woodcraft and shooting. With a native guide, Gifford regularly donned snowshoes and went hunting. He failed to shoot a fox but bagged many rabbits. "I killed them all without a miss, and the last one made the eleventh I have shot without a miss," he boasted.[47] He also claimed he could break bottles with a rifle at seventy-five yards. How Gifford, with his failing eyes, could be a crack shot is puzzling. Anyway, his parents were unimpressed with his shooting escapade, his mother commenting, "The more moderate effort necessary for reading and studying would be less harmful."[48]

When the two teenagers returned to Manhattan, Gifford continued his studies with tutors. When he returned to Exeter in June, he passed tests allowing him to graduate with the class of 1884. Yale was prepared to accept him with conditions in as many as five subjects, which, he and his parents agreed, was a daunting prospect.[49] Still not yet ready for Yale, he would spend the next year at home in New York preparing for examinations to remove the conditions.

* * *

During this upsetting time, the construction of Grey Towers in Milford started. Mary and James also began house hunting in Manhattan, but a wrenching financial scandal would deflect the couple's search.

In 1881, Amos Eno installed son John Chester Eno, only thirty-three, as president of the Second National Bank, located in the Fifth Avenue Hotel. John was a likable young man who had been elected the most popular man in his class at Yale, but neither Amos nor the bank's directors provided careful oversight of its operations. Unfortunately, John speculated in the stock market at a time when it began to drop dramatically during a recession in 1883–1884. Faced with staggering losses eventually amounting to perhaps $4 million, John began using depositors' money to pay for his losses, which he then concealed by making false entries in the bank's books. Rumors spread about John's misdeeds, and by mid-May 1884, depositors began lining up at the bank to withdraw their funds.[50]

Confronted with a run on the bank, Amos moved swiftly. Though reportedly worth $20 million, most of his assets were tied up in real estate. Nonetheless, he managed fairly quickly to raise about $2.6 million in cash from his own resources by mortgaging his properties, including the Fifth Avenue Hotel. The bank directors believed that Amos was morally obliged to cover all the losses since he had installed his son as president under his responsibility.[51]

The Second National Bank survived a run on its deposits without ever closing its doors. When John feared arrest, he fled to Quebec, Canada. Flight across the nation's northern border by embezzlers, popularly known as "boodlers," was a fairly common practice in the 1880s; during that decade, for example, an estimated two thousand fugitives, most of whom were bank employees, would abscond with funds from their U.S. institutions and find safe haven on Canadian soil. In John's case, he was brought before a Quebec court, and the question was whether he could be extradited to the United States.

The prospect was not promising. One reason for these "boodler" flights was the deficient extradition treaty between the United States and Canada, which covered many crimes but not embezzlement or bribery. Would-be swindlers working in U.S. banks thus may have been more tempted to embezzle funds, believing they could evade the arm of the law by fleeing to Canada.[52] Once in Quebec, the question became whether the Canadian authorities would determine that his crimes included "forgery" under the terms of the extradition treaty and send him back to New York for trial.

Mary Pinchot's assets were mainly in bonds, which John had managed at the bank. Before the scandal broke, he had sent her regular statements of her investments so that "you may know how rich you are."[53] To cover his losses, John had used those bonds (along with their sister Antoinette Wood's large investment and his father's securities) as collateral to finance his speculation in stocks and perhaps more of her holdings without her knowledge. Mary, who had relied on the interest income from the bonds, soon found herself short of cash. She would shortly ask James for Amos's first $50,000 dowry gift to her, which he had invested. James readily complied, although he had to sell some land for whatever money he could get and with a mortgage in her name for the rest.[54]

John's indiscretions violated Mary's moral code, but he, ten years younger, was her favorite brother. There was also the honor and reputation of the Eno family. As the crisis unfolded, Mary spent several "sad," "anxious," and "dreadful" days and "sleepless" nights worrying about John's possible prosecution and his painful split with his father, who had lost his trust.[55]

But Mary was not one to let justice take its course. Her first thought was to find a way to get John to Europe, where he might be beyond the reach of U.S. authorities and, for this purpose, seemed willing to evade the nation's laws and diplomatic procedures. In developing her scheme, she turned to General Sherman, sending him a frantic letter to forward to President Chester Arthur.[56]

Willing to help Mary, Sherman forwarded her letter to the president along with his own supporting arguments. He admitted John's "terrible fraud" but blamed the bank's directors for their poor oversight. Hoping the administration would temper justice with mercy, he suggested that if the secretary of state could "shut his eyes for half an hour," presumably to allow John's U.S. passport to be validated so he could travel to Britain, then, he "honestly" believed, the secretary "will sleep the sounder in years to come."[57]

Sherman hoped the U.S. government would not try to extradite John, but he did not mention that prospect to the administration and made no other appeals on her behalf.[58] Nevertheless, to some legal minds, Sherman's and Mary's pleas might seem perilously close to attempted tampering with the wheels of justice. The White House replied that the decision regarding John Eno's extradition rested entirely with the Canadian government.[59] That was technically true, but the state department, prompted by the New York district attorney, did formally request Eno's return on the charge of "forgery" under the terms of the extradition agreement, and his case came before a Quebec court. The charge was a stretch because although John had made untrue entries in the books, he had likely not forged documents, and the judge determined that there was no clear evidence of forgery to send him back to New York. John Eno had found asylum.[60]

Throughout the continuing imbroglio, General Sherman tried to calm a still agitated Mary, "[Y]ou will always know that I will stand by you and yours though the heavens fall." The problem was that in New York, "money is your God. It is idolised, worshiped, and men fall down before it." John, a victim of this pernicious culture, "has taxed his good father dear, and will all his life bear the penalty; yet I hope his young life will not be poisoned by one mistake." He also assured her, "your father is a clear-headed businessman and has seen New York in the [financial] collapse of 1837, 57, 73, etc., so that this squall of 1884 must seem to him a tempest in a teapot."[61]

Providing soothing words is what any good friend would do in a traumatic time, but coughing up millions in short order was more than a "squall" for Amos, who also suffered real emotional strain from his son's indiscretions and his own difficult dealings with the bank's directors and stockholders. It was a messy family affair, and the healing process would be slow and imperfect.[62]

Earlier, the James Pinchot family and John Eno had both lived at Amos Eno's Fifth Avenue mansion, but James's pleasant memories of the lively household turned painful after John's transgressions. He now referred to the "unfortunate" and "depressing" influence of the house and vowed never to live there again.[63] The family misfortune would intensify the Pinchots' search for their own home. Moreover, John's misbehavior grossly violated James's code of personal responsibility—indeed, his cowardly behavior displayed unmanly behavior at its worst.

James nonetheless went to Canada to try to smooth over the family rift. He learned that John was yet unwilling to communicate with his father. His wife, Harriet (Hattie), and their children had joined John in Quebec, and James found her understandably sulking and having a hard time. And back home, he, like Sherman trying to lift his wife out of her funk, advised that her father "is quite willing to do what is entirely reasonable as to your money. You must write him affectionately." Mary likely followed through. Amos helped mend relations with his daughters by providing restitution for Antoinette's losses, and for Mary's, he offered to put up the money to buy her a house for which his much earlier gift, now lost, had been intended.[64]

As a fugitive, John could return to the United States at great risk of being arrested. Mary and other relatives would labor for many years to get the U.S. government formally to drop the charges. That effort failed with President Grover Cleveland, even though Mary and James managed to secure a social engagement at the White House with Frances Cleveland, the young first lady, at which they likely pleaded John's case. And with the succeeding Republican administration, Sherman counseled, "[President] Harrison will be influenced by the effect (on votes) of granting a nolle prosequi [no prosecution order] to John without doing the same for all the parties who have gone to Canada to avoid arrest and extradition." He urged her to get the attention of Harrison's attorney general, who had authority in the matter, with the aid of a sympathetic U.S. senator as an advocate. The attorney general's views were critical, and he opposed a pardon, arguing that he objected to clemency when the accused had refused to abide by the decrees of American courts. Harrison agreed and denied the pardon, despite Sherman's and other friends' endorsements of John Eno's application. John's father, Amos, "had his heart set" upon clemency, Gifford noted, and news of the president's decision "hit him hard."[65]

Meanwhile, John was getting well settled in Quebec. Many Canadians were appalled at their country becoming a refuge for American white-collar criminals, but some prominent citizens in smaller cities like Quebec believed that the stolen money and business acumen that these American exiles brought with them boosted the economy.[66] John was a beneficiary of this conflicted environment, and the American and Canadian press published stories of John's supposed luxurious lifestyle, which included owning the best horses and sleigh in the city and taking his wife to a society ball "glittering in diamonds." He did prosper, buying a large house in the city, becoming treasurer of a Canadian railroad, and investing in several commercial enterprises in the country.[67] It seemed John had found a foreign refuge and would no longer intrude on the Pinchots' lives.

Nine years later, however, John Chester Eno would again shock the Pinchot family when he, accompanied by his family, suddenly arrived unannounced in New York. The fugitive brother turned himself in, was arrested, and released on $20,000 bail. John never really explained why he returned. He may have calculated that President Harrison, while earlier denying his application for a pardon, might reconsider if he had given himself up on U.S. soil in the final days of a lame duck administration when presidents traditionally announce pardons. In any event, none for John was forthcoming.

John may also have returned for reasons of his children's education or family peace. He probably wanted somehow to reconcile with his father, Amos, in hopes that he, or at least his children, would be included in his will. Amos was, in fact, setting up trust accounts of $100,000 each for his descendants but excluding John. (John's children were probably not included, but they, along with Amos's other grandchildren, would be beneficiaries in his will.) Amid these events, John's reappearance was to Amos, who was beginning to suffer from dementia, a "new blow at the age of 82," Gifford commented. "It seems pretty hard."[68]

Mary found her brother's attitude "most painful." John was, she noted, "just as gentle[,] as kind, as calm as possible, and just as obtuse as ever," thinking the charges against him were some kind of conspiracy. Only "punishment will open his eyes," she thought.[69] Mary was preparing for the worst while working toward a less disturbing denouement. General Sherman had died in early 1891, and Mary carried on her quiet lobbying alone. Nearly a year after John's homecoming, she contacted Frances Cleveland, requesting an appointment, and the first lady, remembering Mary's visit during her husband's first term, replied that she would meet with her privately in the Executive Mansion to "talk to me."[70] Their conversation probably had no direct result, but it did not hurt that Mary could explain John's situation and its impact on the family to Mrs. Cleveland, who was closest to the president's ear.

In this confusing situation, John's relatives had tried to get John pardoned to clear the Eno family name and have him remain ostracized in Canada, but they failed. John at least managed to salvage something. Upon his return to New York, he hired high-powered lawyers to quash any charges brought against him, and in the end, no jurisdiction prosecuted him.

*   *   *

When the banking crisis had first broken, Gifford was studying with tutors and taking classes at the private Berkeley School. Then in March 1885, his parents, leaving behind thoughts of the bank scandal, went on a month-long jaunt to Southern states, and Gifford and Amos (Nettie was staying with the Hunts in Newport) were under the care of Mary McCadden and a relative. During their absence, Gifford reported to his parents that it was "very quiet and lonely in the house."[71] That was only partly accurate, as he was beginning a courtship with his sister's best friend, Kitty Hunt, then sixteen. Kitty and Gifford's romance was entirely platonic and nurtured through their letters since Gifford was in New York while Kitty was in Newport. Gifford's and Kitty's friendship blossomed into expressions of mutual love; he proposed marriage and she accepted. He sent three letters to his parents with news of their betrothal, which they received during their return trip.

Mary's first reaction was "Greatly pleased." She liked Kitty and could envision their marriage binding the two friendly families more closely together. The couple was young, but girls often married early. Moreover, Gifford's letters presumably assured his parents that marriage could be delayed until he was well settled into his studies at Yale. Their relationship may have been what later would be called "going steady." Exactly what Gifford said in his letters to his parents is unknown, because none of them has been found.[72]

Gifford's father would have none of his son's love interest, and he still controlled his future. After receiving his son's letters, James hightailed for New York to confront Gifford, and James surely lectured his son on what he considered inappropriate behavior. Mary, meanwhile, no doubt prompted by her husband's strong feelings in the matter, wrote Kitty's mother about the impending broken engagement. The break was complete. The couple was never again linked romantically, although the two would occasionally correspond about family matters, Kitty calling him her "ex-fiancé."[73] James tried to soften Kitty's hurt feelings by sending her an Easter gift. Gifford recovered from the disappointing experience, and Nettie soon observed, "I am glad that Gifford is all right, or nearly so."[74]

With Gifford's first love experience behind him, James sent him to New Haven that summer so he could study with tutors in preparation for removing his conditions. In September, Gifford took the examinations and passed everything. The college secretary told him that all conditions could have been removed in June.[75] Perhaps the extra effort had been unnecessary, but Gifford was better situated to begin college with no academic concerns. His eye problem would gradually subside, and by his junior year, he would excel in his studies and extracurricular activities.

4.

A New Profession

Before heading off to Yale College in September 1885, Gifford was relaxing with his parents and a few friends on a piazza at Far Rockaway, a beach community close to Manhattan, when James suddenly asked Gifford, "How would you like to be a forester?" Sixty years later, Gifford began his memoirs with his father's query. It was an "amazing question," Gifford commented, because no American had heretofore made forestry his profession, no timberlands in the United States were under forestry management, nor were there any schools in the nation for study of the subject.[1] Still, his father's question intrigued Gifford, who would turn to forestry as his life's work after college, and he naturally credited his father with pointing him in this direction. James had raised the subject after carefully reflecting on the possibilities of a new profession in the United States with his son at the forefront. His query served as another crucial step in nurturing Gifford's genuine boyhood interest in the natural world.

*   *   *

How did James Pinchot get interested in forestry, and when did he begin considering it a possible career choice for his oldest son? Clearly, a real purpose of the family's Adirondack summer adventure in 1879 was to foster Gifford's interest in natural history by allowing the fledgling teenager to develop some skills as an outdoorsman.[2] The connection to forestry is more circumstantial, but clues suggest that the widespread destruction of lumbering and the search for remedies were gestating in James's mind by the late 1870s. James had read books, learning about wilderness from Thoreau and nature from Emerson, and he likely was aware of *Man and Nature* (1864) by George Perkins Marsh, a Vermont native. Marsh's book was a detailed indictment of man's destruction of forests in both the Old and New Worlds and the consequent deleterious effects on the drainage of soils, the flow of rivers, and the climate. "We have now felled forest enough everywhere, in many districts far too much," Marsh wrote.

Marsh also warned that the destruction of the Adirondack woods would be "as injurious as those which have resulted from laying bare the southern and western declivities of the French Alps," which he also described in his book.[3] Marsh's treatise was a powerful early indication of more general stirrings among concerned citizens about the deforestation of the American landscape. The themes in Marsh's book struck a responsive chord among literati and the educated elite at the Century Association, where James was a member. Another sign of this interest was the founding of the American Forestry Association in 1876, although it remained pathetically weak for decades.

Closer to James's inner world, the Hudson River painters were capturing the beauty of the natural landscape on canvas, sometimes in contrast with its despoliation. One painting, in particular, *Hunter Mountain, Twilight* (1866), by Sanford Gifford, James's good friend, depicts the forested mountain in the southern Catskills silhouetted against a brilliant red-orange sky at sunset. Stretched across the foreground of the painting is a clear-cut area inundated with many tree stumps, a grim reminder of man's rude and irresponsible invasion of nature. The tree stumps were the remains of hemlocks that had been cut down to extract tannin for industrial uses. One can also interpret the solitary man, cattle, dwindling steam, and homestead in the center of the scarred foreground of Gifford's painting as part of the necessary deforestation to support agricultural life. Growing up in the Catskills area, Sanford was an astute observer of the subtle environmental changes over time to the Hudson River and surrounding landscape, and he almost certainly was familiar with Marsh's recent book, in which the author criticized the harmful impact of cattle in requiring the clearing of forested lands. James was the first owner of Sanford's painting, one of the artist's best, and James would later display it prominently in his various homes. He saw the symbolic contrast between the beautiful mountains and scarred lands in the same painting, and his discussions with his other painter friends who had similar concerns reinforced the contrast.

Moreover, during his extensive travels abroad and from reading about the history of European deforestation and conservation practices, James was familiar with several continental nations' first efforts at reforestation and management of timber in their national forests. He became an admirer, not surprisingly given his Francophilia, of Jean-Baptiste Colbert, a perceptive minister of Louis XIV two centuries earlier, and Bernard Palissy, a French naturalist, potter, and philosopher more than a century before that, who had warned of the dangers

of forest destruction and urged state forestry management. Neglect of the forest, Palissy had asserted, was "not a fault, but a curse and misfortune to all of
France," and Marsh's book extolled Palissy's contributions to forestry.[4] Perhaps,
James mused, Americans could learn from the French visionaries and come up
with solutions for their own country.

With the disappearance of the forests from lumbering in the Milford area,
James believed that "something ought to be done," as he would put it twenty-
five years later, but admitted that he had no remedies then.[5] The systematic
exploitation of the natural world in pursuit of profit and the preservation of the
wilderness were indeed polar opposites; yet both co-existed in James, the former
because of his forebears' and his own early involvement in the lumber trade and
his business values, and the latter from his growing identification with artists
and other publicly spirited New Yorkers who were showing concerns about
the environment. Indeed, deeper down, some guilt over his and his forebears'
participation in forest destruction may have been involved, though never clearly
articulated. Although not an intellectual, James was thoughtful and willing to
wrestle with the materialistic/idealistic dichotomy. The resolution would take
time because he was not one to summarily reject the occupation that had fos-
tered his father's prosperity. Only when distanced from the practice and exposed
to new ideas would he gradually work out his own perspective on the problem.[6]

In the end, though, much of the timing of James's interest in forest conservation is speculative. Gifford later claimed that his father should be acknowledged as the "Father of Forestry in America," but the claim would have been
moot if Gifford had not responded enthusiastically to the prospect and made it
a success. Moreover, James never mentioned Marsh's book to his son, who first
discovered it on his own during his college freshman year.[7]

James's main contribution to the creation of forestry as a profession was
first mentioning and sustaining his son's exploration of its prospects in the
United States. This would be no mean achievement, as there would be landscape gardeners, botanists, and European-trained foresters who, doubting the
possibilities of forest preservation, would try to persuade Gifford to abandon it
or subsume it to other aspects of natural history.

*   *   *

Yale had little to offer a young man interested in forestry. In those days, the
Sheffield Scientific School (Sheff) and what was known as the academic (liberal
arts) curriculum at Yale were separate schools located on different parts of the
campus. Gifford, not having any science courses at Exeter, would concentrate on

the academic curriculum and venture to take only a few Sheff courses. Majoring in a discipline did not begin until fifteen years later. Gifford seemed to have plenty of choices in electives and took courses in meteorology, botany, geology, and chemistry, all of which would be invaluable to anyone trying to understand flora and fauna and the scientific reasons for their growth and decay.[8]

His main discovery during his freshman year was a professor of agriculture, William H. Brewer, who was intrigued by Gifford's interest in forestry. The professor commented to him that it was "a science to found," and Gifford reacted, "This is certainly as good an opening as a man could have."[9] He learned much more about the non-existent field from Brewer, who, like many intellectuals in that era—Marsh was an outstanding example—was more of a generalist than a specialist. Brewer would consistently support Gifford's forestry efforts after graduation. Years later, Gifford reflected that "Brewer knew far more about forests at home and Forestry abroad than any other man at Yale," and "His service to Forestry in America should never be forgotten." For Christmas during his sophomore year, Gifford asked his parents only for a microscope to assist him in his forestry studies.[10]

Despite lingering problems with his eyes, Gifford studied hard and earned the equivalent of dean's list in his freshman year. Thereafter he fairly regularly made the middle ranks of honor roll, and he would later credit mainly Brewer with inspiring him academically.[11] He found early that there was much more to college life than the curriculum. He enjoyed the many diverse aspects of college, which was also a social experience for him. He was beginning to show that, more than reflection, he preferred action, and for pleasure, he later admitted that he preferred watching a movie over reading.[12]

Gifford fell in with a good crowd of classmates. He was pleased with his choice of eating club consisting of a "company of fellows who are congenial, gentlemen and whom I know something about."[13] The remark could suggest some snobbery, but it was intended to persuade his socially conscious but penny-pinching father that spending a few more dollars a week on his elite club was justified. He certainly valued wealth and status but also appreciated his student friends' character and values; he would later financially assist some of his less affluent classmates in their post-graduate pursuits.

During his first semester, Gifford found a compatible roommate, Edward (Ned) Parsons, who had a strong religious focus, and he soon wrote Mamee, "He is one of the best and most Christian fellows I know." Founded at the beginning of the previous century as a bulwark of Calvinist teaching, Yale still had a strong religious focus. The two were elected deacons in their freshman year and would remain roommates until graduation.[14]

Because of his delayed college entrance, Gifford was now twenty, or two years older than most of his classmates, but that presumed maturity was not immediately on display. He was a joiner, and he participated enthusiastically in undergraduate rituals. Just before the start of classes was the traditional freshman-sophomore rush in which each class formed a solid column and, advancing, tried to push the other back. During the event, he "was lifted off my feet and carried quite a distance" and lost "a few buttons and the integrity of my trousers." Gifford was involved in three other encounters with sophomores, and at one, he told his parents, he was stripped of his clothes and "went home in a borrowed overcoat though richer by two Soph hats." Papa, of course, was not amused and urged him to avoid hazing.[15]

Gifford was independent and maturing into a young man. When James visited his son during his freshman year, he found the walls of his room adorned with photographs of General Sherman and Sanford Gifford, as well as an etching by Eastman Johnson. And when James called the students "boys," they quickly corrected him by asserting that they were now "men."[16] James would find it hard to accept full adulthood in all three of his children, even into their thirties, but at least for Gifford's first few years of college, he was not far wrong in assuming his son was still a "boy." His good grades notwithstanding, Gifford himself later reflected that his eager participation in Yale student rituals displayed more energy than study.[17]

Gifford initially indulged in sports. At Exeter, his mother had warned him away from the "most violent" and "dangerous game" of football, and early at Yale, his father implored him "to avoid" the sport. The parents' concern was justified, as football was then played with light or no padding and no headgear, and Harvard, as James reminded his son, had banned the sport as too violent. But Gifford was already practicing with the freshman football squad and was soon elected captain unanimously. Because of his lingering eye problems, however, the Pinchots' family doctor urged Gifford to abandon football, and together with his father's objections, Gifford resigned as captain and then reluctantly gave up the sport.[18]

Tall and thin but physically strong and well-coordinated, Gifford relished the competition. He had shown flashes of athletic ability at Exeter and the Berkeley School. He tried other sports at Yale his first spring, finishing second in his class in the shot put, competed in a freshman tennis tournament, and was elected vice-president of the lacrosse team.[19]

Gifford also became a cheerleader. After a freshman baseball game at Harvard, Gifford wrote home, "I had the pleasure of leading the cheering and as a direct result I can hardly speak, and I am so lame through the shoulders that I can scarcely raise my hand about my head, from waving my arms to mark the time." Papa had had enough. What Gifford was doing, he bellowed, "is more than foolish[;] it is outrageous. I must command you to stop and <u>now</u>," and he emphasized twice more that Gifford had to stop "the leadership of shouting."[20]

Gifford complied for the Princeton game, but after the team's victory, "we all went right off and bought tin horns and when the crowd began to blow[,] the noise was so great that I would not hear my own horn!" That evening he and other students "patriotically proceeded to steal some empty boxes . . . to help along the bon fire." His behavior might seem "very wicked," he wrote home, but he rationalized that "in college ethics that's all right and proper."[21]

*   *   *

At the end of Gifford's freshman year, the Pinchot mansion in Milford was completed, and the family moved in on August 11, 1886, Gifford's twenty-first birthday. Fittingly, Amos's present to his older brother on that occasion was a copy of Marsh's forestry volume, and the Pinchots raised glasses of champagne in appreciation of both events.[22]

That same winter, Mary and James used her father's money to buy another residence in Manhattan. Located at 2 Gramercy Park, a private, gated enclave at Twenty-First Street, it was a large red brick house with brownstone trimmings. It needed considerable work, but the parents were pleased with the purchase. And so, James and Mary, who had spent more than the first twenty years of their married life without their own home, found in short order that they now had two.

At Yale, Gifford grew a mustache, which would become a readily identifiable part of his visage. He also became more actively engaged in non-athletic activities. His service as deacon soon expanded to include participating in daily religious services and Bethany, which sponsored Sunday school and Bible study, joining the YMCA, and frequenting as a student representative to their off-campus convocations. In addition, he loved to write. He published articles in the *Yale Literary Magazine* and, in his junior year, aspired to be an editor. The subject of his short writing submission for the position was the last will of Isaak Walton, the author of the classic *The Compleat Angler* (1653), which displayed Gifford's interest in fishing and an appreciation of Walton's sympathy for the poor.[23]

His classmates voted on the editors, but Gifford was not one of the five elected. The outgoing editors wanted Gifford, however, and told him, "Your work has been of too high a character to pass over, . . . and the Lit deserved you quite as much as you deserve the Lit." When Gifford failed in subsequent ballots, the editors simply named him an editor in place of one of the five. Flouting the will of the class was too much for Gifford, so he declined the position.[24]

Gifford's parents tried to soften his disappointment, saying he had behaved "beautifully." Gifford continued to write occasional pieces for the Lit and made his presence felt on campus. His brother heard that "you were the most popular man in your class." Gifford's failed election to the Lit suggested that was an exaggeration, but he was becoming a big man on campus. In the spring of his junior year, he was elected to Skull and Bones, Yale's oldest and arguably most prestigious secret society. It likely helped that two of his Eno uncles had been members, but Gifford was an obvious choice. Indeed, he was made the president of the fifteen rising-senior members. Not hearing from her son in a while, Mary inquired "whether you have even emerged from that mysterious bourse whence no messenger returns. I have been expecting to learn whether your mustache had fallen a victim of its solemn rites."[25] Many of Gifford's close friendships would be with his fellow bonesmen, and he would write of one of their first reunions after graduation that "It was just grand. . . . That was the best night I spent since leaving" Yale.[26] He was also awarded the prize in French at the end of his junior year.

Gifford's main preoccupation in the fall of his senior year was football. His eyes had not bothered him for a year, and he was anxious to participate. He had to persuade his parents to let him play, but how? He argued that he now had "perfect use" of his eyes and would quit immediately if the problem returned. There were, moreover, only six weeks left in the schedule. But he also framed his request in the context of his loyalty to Yale and how he could contribute to the team whose promise was "not bright," even "very glum." "I could perhaps help Yale is reason enough in the college world why I should make some sacrifice for that purpose."[27]

His pleading, seemingly heartfelt letters persuaded James and Mary reluctantly to acquiesce to their son's request. But the suspicion exists that Gifford was putting on his parents. When he wrote about Yale's poor prospects, he did not mention that the team had already won its first three games by the lopsided margin of 175–0. And despite his strong interest, the players did not welcome him with open arms but added him to the roster as a substitute. Trying to reassure his worried parents, Gifford continued to argue that the Yale eleven would still be hard-pressed to finish in second place.[28]

Yale would, in fact, go undefeated in thirteen games, and its point totals that season would be 698–0. Indeed, that 1888 Yale team, led by two future All-Americans and legendary coach Walter Camp, was the most dominant football presence in the early history of the sport. The most that can be said in defense of Gifford and his sob story was that when he entreated his parents for permission, the success of the football eleven was not an absolute certainty, and the team did have a struggle in the final game against Princeton, which was then also undefeated and unscored upon before falling to Yale, 10–0. As a reserve, Gifford scored two touchdowns (out of Yale's season total of 126), and eating at the football training table added seven pounds to his wiry physique. But mostly, he had the satisfaction of playing a competitive sport he enjoyed, and on a championship eleven, earning a letter Y. He would make sure that he attended a team reunion twenty-five years later to relive those bygone glory days.[29]

* * *

Gifford's last semester was his busiest. Part of his time was spent overseeing and enjoying the company of his brother, Amos, who had developed into an extroverted boy. Growing up, Amos had several playmates and was especially close to several Phelps and Dodge distant cousins. At age ten, his mother had commented on how "very funny" he looked strutting around in new gloves and overcoat, with a red carnation pinned on the collar.[30] He would, in fact, always be well dressed and projected a classic, refined appearance. Amos was also fun-loving, adventuresome, and witty, often telling jokes at the dinner table, and the family had given him the nickname Toots. He had the same thin physique as his older brother but a more angular face and naturally curly hair, which William Walter Phelps called "beautiful."[31] He, like Gifford, developed a keen interest in canoeing, fishing, and shooting and received instruction in the violin.[32]

James and Mary left some of Amos's tutelage to Mary McCadden, and as with Gifford, her exacting direction did not always sit well with young Amos, who later hinted at her arbitrary ways by referring to her jokingly as "Barbarian Miss McCadden." Amos's personality was pleasing, and after one of his visits to Grey Towers, the artist Jervis McEntee wrote James that Toots, then twelve, impressed him as "a dear little fellow. You ought to be proud of him and I dare say you are."[33]

There was genuine brotherly love between Amos and Gifford. When Gifford was attending Exeter and Yale, they wrote to each other about their experiences. Gifford tried to expose Amos to the natural world by encouraging him to capture frogs and insects and having him describe them to him, and Amos would sometimes send him chestnuts or other goodies. Once, he frankly confessed that he missed Gifford, for without him, "there is no more canoeing . . . fishing and little shooting."

The brothers were thrown together again after Christmas during Gifford's last college year, when the Pinchot parents rented their Gramercy Park home and began a six-month journey by train that took them and Nettie south to Mexico City, then to the Pacific coast states, and finally across the continent back home. To prepare for boarding school, Amos, now fifteen and in eighth grade at the Berkeley School, the parents sent him to New Haven to study under a tutor during their travels.

Gifford found an off-campus rooming house for Amos and hired one of his bones classmates, Herbert S. Smith, as a tutor. Smith liked Amos, telling Gifford, "it is a pleasure to teach him. Toots is a great favorite."[34] Amos took to college life, attended some lectures with his brother, and gloried in extracurricular life as a shadow participant. The result of this interest, Gifford soon informed Papa, was that Toots "keeps dropping in here continually, indeed almost too much."[35] And in a moment of juvenile high spirits, he gave one of his tutors a shower bath. The arrangement was not working well, and Gifford soon enrolled his younger brother at Hopkins Grammar School, a private day school in the city, which provided a more pedagogical structure. The two nonetheless managed to go ice skating and take long walks together during Toots's New Haven sojourn.

Otherwise, during the semester, Gifford was focused on academics and career choices. During spring break, Amos went off to stay with his Uncle Henry Eno and family and his grandpa, while Gifford remained in New Haven to write a paper in competition for the Townsend Prize, given for the best senior essay in history. He put his vacation time to good use, winning the prize for his study of Quakers in the seventeenth century.

His subject was a curious choice since he was neither a Quaker nor an aspiring historian and had shown no special interest in social reform, a defining trait of the religion. But there were many Quakers in Pennsylvania, if not in Milford, and the essay, an offshoot of a course he took on the subject that spring, reflected his continuing religious perspective. The Society of Friends, he reasoned in his essay, was too extreme to succeed as a major religious movement, but in raising their voices against slavery and for toleration, peace, and justice, the Quakers set forth "the progress of civilization in charity, humanity and beneficence for two hundred years."[36] Not incidentally, Gifford's topic, like his earlier interest in Isaak Walton, suggested a distinctly empathetic personality, which would develop into a passion for social justice later in his life, especially in politics.

Continuing her fetish for nonsensical family nicknames, Nettie had recently begun calling her older brother "Spick" or "Speck," and she applauded him for the awards. "Three cheers for little Spicky!" she wrote him, and, of course, his "proud" and "puffed up" parents, as well as several relatives and friends (including Kitty Hunt), sent him effusive congratulations.[37]

*　　*　　*

With graduation looming, Gifford, like other seniors, began to fret about his career. In the fall, he had consulted with a professor of botany, Daniel Eaton, who "advised me to stick by my original purpose of studying forestry. . . . I do not see that I can be more useful in any other way, or so successful or happy." He developed an inventory of trees in New Haven with Eaton, which became an "extraordinarily interesting" project, and forestry was clearly uppermost in his mind as a career choice throughout his final year.[38]

Still, committing to a new field and deciding how to pursue it were rather daunting prospects, and Gifford sought the advice of knowledgeable men with hands-on experience with the subject. In his freshman year, he discovered on his own investigation that there was a division of forestry in the department of agriculture in Washington, D.C., and he obtained literature about it. Then on a visit to the nation's capital over Christmas vacation his senior year, he called on George B. Loring, a former department commissioner, and Dr. Bernard E. Fernow, the chief of the forestry division, to get their opinions.

Both were advocates of forest preservation, but Gifford found that these men would not confirm his inclination toward the profession. Of the two, Loring was the more discouraging, telling Gifford that the nation had "no centralized monarchical power" to develop a disciplined forestry policy, and in any case, the second growth of the forests was so rapid. When Gifford met with Fernow, he volunteered to serve as an unpaid intern under the chief for the next year. "He accepted gladly," Gifford reported, so he at least had a start in the field if he wished to pursue it after graduation. But otherwise, Fernow, a Prussian who had become a U.S. citizen, advised Gifford that forestry should be a secondary interest to more established fields like botany and landscape gardening. Thus began what would, over time, become an awkward relationship between the two men, both committed to forestry but with seemingly different perspectives on its future. Gifford also interviewed Charles S. Sargent, head of the Arnold Arboretum at Harvard, who gave the same opinion.[39] The three men's negative pronouncements gave Gifford pause. "If I knew more definitely about Forestry[,] I should feel better about it," he admitted.[40] Indicative of his indecision, Gifford recorded no career choice in his class yearbook.

He considered several other possible short-term choices until he could decide about a program for forestry education. The easiest alternative career to dispense with was the entreaties of his grandfather Amos Eno, who wanted to set Gifford up with a well-paying position in his real estate empire, with the good possibility of inheriting it. The offer would have tempted many young men, but Gifford was never interested. For family peace, he had to decline Eno's proposals politely, which only brought forth renewed overtures over the next several years. Fortunately for Gifford, his parents supported his disinterest in Amos's business, his father telling him after he had diplomatically turned aside one of his grandfather's offers, "You did exactly right."[41]

Gifford's most tempting calling was religion. As his spiritual focus intensified, he developed firm friendships with some Yale colleagues who would make the ministry their calling. One was his roommate, Ned Parsons, who would become an Episcopal priest; another was James B. Reynolds, Yale '84, who, while at Yale Divinity School, mentored the undergraduate deacons and ran Bethany and the local YMCA. In the spring of Gifford's senior year, Reynolds asked Gifford to serve as the YMCA secretary in New Haven for the coming year. Gifford was interested, partly because he admired Reynolds as "one of the finest men I know" (the two would remain close lifelong friends), but also because the job would only be half-time and allow him to explore forestry further by taking additional science courses at Yale. Reynolds, who would soon travel to France as a missionary, also suggested to Gifford that following his YMCA stint, he should join him in his proselytizing endeavors abroad.[42]

Gifford also found that a career in religion might not be an ideal choice. He seemed to share the thoughts of one of his closest classmates, Ted Donnelley, who had complained after attending a religious convention that the ministry seemed "an unnatural strained sort of life" and lacked the qualities of "divine help and motive power" that were central to their faith. Moreover, Gifford's involvement with Bethany took up a lot of time, and midway through his senior year, he gave it up, telling Mamee that his decision was "a great relief and satisfaction." The ministry was a worthy profession, he seemed to be saying, and he could still take up the cross later but was not ready to take the plunge.[43]

Gifford's considerations of scientific-oriented forestry and the ministry, seeming opposites, as possible professions are not easily explained. To be sure, both science and religion involved "an ideal of selflessness, or truth, of the possibility of spiritual devotion . . . in a context seemingly far removed from the sordid compromise implied by most other careers," and that perspective also helps account for his interest in becoming a physician, another calling, as it required both a firm grounding in the sciences but also a moral commitment to serving humanity.[44] Gifford then perceived the religion-science dichotomy mostly as a metaphysical one between mind and matter, awkwardly blending the two. Attracted to the "laws and disorders of the mind," he seemed to disdain pseudo-scientific explanations.[45] At the same time, however, psychic or supernatural phenomena, especially hypnotism and spiritualism, fascinated him, and this focus would gradually lead him to the emerging discipline of psychology, telling a college classmate a decade later that "psychological questions, as you know, have interested me deeply for years."[46]

As a religious person, Gifford also could not avoid the growing controversy over Darwinian evolution. The emphasis in Charles Darwin's writings on "natural selection" and "survival of the fittest" seemed to contradict Christianity's teachings of a God-centered world and troubled serious religious people. But social Darwinism—the application of biological evolutionary "laws" to society—could work differently. It could imply ceaseless conflict and the ultimate triumph of might over right, but it could also be perceived more optimistically as a theoretical framework for man's steady, inevitable improvement from a brute, physical world of constant struggle toward a more moral, even enlightened existence. Some clergymen of that era even came to believe that Darwinism was divinely inspired and interpreted it teleologically. Gifford did not go that far but was exposed to the religious perspective at Yale. He took a required course of eight lectures for seniors on evolution by the renowned geologist James Dwight Dana. The course syllabus, containing statements like "Faith has nothing to fear from evolution," "an upward tendency in the [evolutionary] development," and "A Divine purpose throughout the history," indicates that Dana believed evolution was no threat to Christianity. Gifford found the lectures "very interesting" but, after graduation, would continue to wrestle with this intellectual and spiritual problem and try to reconcile the contradictory aspects to his satisfaction.[47]

A writing career was also appealing. After winning the French prize, a publisher asked him to edit and translate into English the works of the French feminist writer George Sand, which would be published in some fifteen volumes. The offer tempted Gifford. "I should get my name before the public as a writer," he thought, and he liked the proposed remuneration. Significantly, however, he wanted that financial independence to support himself abroad, presumably while studying forestry.[48]

Gifford's parents would be his chief counselors concerning his professional concerns. Ambitious for her son, Mamee warmed to forestry, which appealed to her sense of adventure. During her European travels, she reported on the progress of forestry on the continent and sent him literature about forestry degree programs. In his sophomore year, she told him, "I think you have made a wise choice" in forestry as a career. As Gifford seemed to waver in his senior year, she said she would support his career decision—but could not resist downgrading the editing project.[49] And despite her Christian bias, she applauded his break with Bethany and disparaged the YMCA job. Not to appear too overbearing, she joshed in conclusion, "I've succeeded perfectly in writing a completely impartial statement of the case." She also offered to finance a European trip after graduation so that he could explore forestry and other options. And regarding missionary work in France, she gave practical advice: "I have not very much faith in the success of Protestants in Catholic countries."[50]

His father's role was crucial. Besides correspondence with his son about forestry and other choices, he also visited him in New Haven twice during his senior year to discuss Gifford's future. He did not seem overtly insistent about forestry but always reassured Gifford of his financial and emotional support if he moved in that direction.

In the end, Gifford gave up the other options and committed himself to forestry. "In spite of the unfavorable opinion of those who know," he wrote his father, "it appears to me there must a future for Forestry in this country. At any rate I should like to study it for a year or so, and even if I am forced to give it up at the end of that time my work will not have been wasted." The stimulus for his decision, he later wrote, was that he "craved" adventure. "The fact that Forestry was new and strange and promised action probably had as much to do with my final choice of it as my love for the woods."[51] He was surely adventuresome and more than willing to accept a challenge. Perhaps he could prove the naysayers wrong; in any event, he wanted to give it a try.

Dramatizing his decision, he spoke as a class representative at a college dinner at the end of the academic year. Gifford, "on the spur of the moment," he later recalled, dropped his prepared subject and proceeded to talk about the importance of forestry in the nation and his decision to choose it as his life work. His remarks, the first public announcement of an intended career, must have baffled the uninterested audience. The real significance of the event was that Gifford's father was with him and witnessed his public commitment to this new field.[52]

                                    *   *   *

Gifford spent that summer of 1889 at Grey Towers, where he entertained his college friends and conducted an inventory of trees on the estate. He loved the place. Forestry work would take him to distant places for extended periods, but he could comment early in his career, "The satisfaction in getting back to Grey Towers each time is something wonderful."[53] Indeed, he would escape there whenever his demanding work schedule allowed it; much later, he would make it his residence. Gifford's enjoyment of Grey Towers made up for his parents' perception of it as a mixed blessing.

At the end of the summer, the Milford leaders invited Gifford to give the featured address for the town's celebration of the centennial of the U.S. Constitution. The invitation was a tribute to Gifford's success at Yale but also suggested the local citizenry's esteem of the Pinchot family. The theme of his speech was civic responsibility. "We are trustees of a coming world," Gifford proclaimed, but "We are first of all . . . citizens of Pike County, Pennsylvania, and it is here we are to realize, if at all, the blessings of our great birthright which has descended to us from the courage, perseverance, and energy of our forefathers." A reciprocal obligation was involved: "not only that we have a share in the commonwealth, but that the commonwealth has a share in us," even "a right to our service, our thought, and action."[54] Here Gifford intertwined notions of republican virtue and *noblesse oblige* (or stewardship), all deeply ingrained family values shared by elements of the upright patrician elite nationally. He would do his best to live up to these high-minded standards in his public life.

5.

Practical Forestry

When Gifford sailed for Europe in early October 1889, he planned to consult with leading European forestry practitioners, explore forestry school programs, and return home by Christmas. He and his parents would then contemplate his next steps. As he later wrote, "It was my simple intention to buy a few books and come home—proof enough that I was still lost in the fog."[1]

Without a set timetable, he did some sightseeing in England. While in London, he called unannounced at the forest department of the India Office, where the head, hearing of Gifford's interest in forestry, loaned him books on the subject and provided letters of introduction to others. Gifford marveled at his "disinterested kindness to a total stranger."[2]

He would then visit Sir William Schlich and Sir Dietrich Brandis, well-trained German foresters working for the British government. Brandis had introduced forest management in India and Burma in the 1850s and was, Gifford later wrote, "the first of living foresters."[3] Schlich had succeeded Brandis as inspector-general of forests to the Government of India. Brandis was then in Bonn, so Gifford first saw Schlich, who explained the system of instruction in Britain and gave Gifford an autographed copy of the first volume of his *Manual of Forestry*. He urged the neophyte to focus on creating national forests in America but warned him of the hard road ahead. After the interview, Gifford reflected, "As I learn more of forestry, I see more and more the need of it in the United States, and the great difficulty of carrying it into effect."[4]

Gifford moved on to Paris, where he enjoyed various events at a centennial exposition celebrating the French Revolution. Despite these pleasures, forestry increasingly absorbed his time. He took copious notes at a forestry exhibit at the exposition. Gifford also met a young French forestry student there, who told him he could not learn forestry just by visiting its schools and recommended that he should enroll in L'École Nationale Forestière at Nancy in Lorraine. It was serendipity. It was as if Gifford needed someone to point him forcefully in the direction of formal study, and he decided to enroll in the Nancy program unless Brandis objected during his Bonn visit.[5]

Dr. Brandis, in his mid-sixties, was a big man, austere and formal—indeed "a perfect Prussian in appearance," Gifford remembered—but he probed the seriousness of interest in a forestry career. Gifford passed the test, and Brandis wrote a letter of recommendation for him for the Nancy forestry school. Afterward, a relieved Gifford wrote in his journal, "Dr. Brandis is splendid. Energy, power, thought, determination—all these and much more. He was more than kind. He was inspiring."[6]

Gifford and his parents would debate over the next year how long he should study forestry. Professor Sargent, Brandis, Schlich, and other European experts in the field would urge him to spend at least two or three more years of European study, ideally combined with fieldwork. The range and depth of knowledge were vital, but just as important, Brandis warned him, was that his training had to be "on a par with the young German foresters that are sure to be imported" to the United States, and their training could last seven years.[7] From this awareness, Gifford began his forestry studies.

Gifford's courses at Nancy encompassed three areas: silviculture, which deals with trees and forests, their growth, care, harvesting, and reproduction; the economic aspects (forest capital, rent, interest, and sustained yield); and forest law. He learned a lot in class, except for the boring law lectures, but valued the student trips into the nearby forests, and he benefitted more from his own exertions than from his professors. Used to informal discussion with his Yale professors, he was turned off by the Nancy instructors' show and tell and their discouragement of discussion.

Gifford was also unimpressed with the French students. He formed some friendships, but his classmates were mostly interested in carousing with their girlfriends and drinking. Gifford found little pleasure in alcohol. His parents imbibed moderately, but he preferred abstinence. He also was not interested in the social scene and dubbed the forestry dances "Very rotten."[8]

He also developed negative views of Catholicism, whose teachings in France, imposed from above and full of superstition, were really "awful." Recalling his mother's earlier warning about taking up missionary work in France, he confessed to her, "the longer I am here the truer your remark about the impossibility of foreigners helping Christian work among Frenchmen seems." He also despaired of French immorality in stark contrast to American society, "where the man who does take part in [vice] is regarded as simply an ass." Only French gastronomical skills won his respect; "they certainly do know how to cook," he admitted.[9]

Gifford's deflationary views of the French people were, in part, a reflection of the social prejudices of an upper-class, well-educated young man toward the rough, rural elements he encountered, but he was also trying to understand the contradictions in the French national character. Despite his father's love of France, he encouraged his son's dissection of French traits, even when the conclusions were negative. Thus, when Gifford unfavorably contrasted "the average French student [who] has no more moral sense than a bull frog" to his own religious beliefs, Papa praised his display of "Christian feeling and a manly attitude toward the students" and, paraphrasing Emerson, added, "Character in the long run goes for more than anything else. It does my heart good to think of you as always striving for the right."[10]

The deficiencies of French pedagogy and his father's entreaties for him to return home in the fall were enough for Gifford to end his studies after a year, but he kept getting contrary advice from the "experts." In consequence, he admitted at one point, "Personally I don't know what to do."[11] He decided to participate that summer in extensive excursions, led by Dr. Brandis, into German and Swiss alpine forests. During this experience, Gifford found the German, Swiss, and British forestry students just as deficient as the French. The Germans, for instance, had a "sad" preference for hunting game over protecting and caring for the forests, and they indulged in heavy drinking. "All drink and no forestry [are] not my meat," was his succinct appraisal.[12]

Gifford's European stay was making him more patriotic. Many things, not just French, compared unfavorably with America. About his physical surroundings, he wrote, "I have seen nothing yet that approaches the Saw Kill, not a country house that I liked in any respect[,] as I do ours," and even the trout in Europe were "ugly and not so good as ours." At a deeper level, the American democratic tradition and its culture were superior. Toward the end of his work in the Black Forest, he reflected, "I am getting more enthusiastically American the longer I live in it. [The Germans] are hugely self-satisfied and ridiculously jealous, and with it all the great German people is subject to the beck and nod of a young man [Kaiser Wilhelm II] in Berlin[,] who would have had the same power he has now if he had been the stupidest instead of one of the brightest of Germans and as malicious as he seems to be full of good intentions." A further criticism was that "they are taxed as they are in England for the support of a church to which they do not subscribe."[13]

During that summer, Gifford spent most evening hours composing articles for the monthly magazine *Garden and Forest*, which Professor Sargent, the editor, accepted. As a forestry neophyte, Gifford confined himself to descriptive articles about the forestry school and the Swiss and German forests. The factual pieces, he wrote his father, would avoid "any important or even slight mistake bearing on my career at home, while I shall get a good deal of free advertising" with publication.[14]

During the summer excursions, Gifford's admiration for Dr. Brandis's knowledge of forestry and his "perfect kindness and courtesy" grew. "He's one of the finest men I ever knew," Gifford commented.[15] The learned German forester's strong advice to study for two more years in Europe clarified Gifford's thoughts on forestry education. He now conceded that "a year is altogether insufficient time to make a forester," and he planned to enroll in a forestry school in Munich for the following year.[16] Otherwise, he came to doubt European forest practitioners' call for still more education. He perceived that training beyond two years brought diminishing returns and had "not counted with Yankee push and Yankee woodcraft." With chances for advancement few and slow in European countries, foresters there never developed an esprit de corps and were steeped in pessimistic attitudes. Gifford understood why they preferred hunting and drinking as diversions.

Book learning had its place, but Gifford preferred field work and direct observation. In that regard, he realized he had never been west of the Alleghenies in his own country and had not seen the extensive southern pine forests, magnificent California redwoods, or the towering Pacific Northwest sequoias. Early in his European forestry studies, he confessed, "how foolish I have been not to get more fully acquainted with America."[17] If he were a pioneer in the American forestry movement, he would have to visit the forest lands there as soon as possible. These thoughts heightened his desire to return home. At the end of the excursions, Gifford returned to Nancy, where he passed examinations in silviculture and forest organization, received his certificate, and said pleasant farewells to his professors.

Meanwhile, James had been following developments in the nascent conservation movement in the United States and was trying to guide his son. Although politically conservative, James had mildly reformist views and believed government action would be required to stop the destructive lumbering. Having experience in the lumber trade and observing the relentless tree cutting nationally, he was skeptical of Brandis's view of philanthropic businessmen buying and harvesting forested lands for a modest return. Instead, the goal of an

American lumber company, James argued, "is to destroy as quickly as possible, in fact to do anything for immediate profit. Future results would not be cared for," and lumber companies were inventing ways to cut down the forests "with greater and increasing activity."[18]

State action in Europe eventually established protected forests, and James predicted that "in ten or fifteen years the subject will be forced upon the attention of Congress and the [state] Legislatures in a way that will demand action of some kind." He was, in fact, "sure that the subject will soon have to be seriously considered."[19]

Although Gifford lauded the American democratic experience, his political views were fundamentally conservative. As a college student, he opposed government regulation of business and had written that railroads "own the tracks and the cars. . . . Then why shouldn't they charge what they please."[20] Similarly, his approach to public opinion was distinctly elitist. When his parents wrote him that a Milford resident had gone missing, Gifford responded, "If a considerable percentage of the population of Milford were to do the same thing, it would be good for the village."[21] Pretty strong words for a young man who, in his earlier address to its townspeople, had exhorted them to become good, responsible citizens. But in his mind, there was no contradiction, as a message of his address had been moral uplift, with the enlightened social elite—that is, people like himself—leading the rest of the citizenry on the path of republican virtue.

A top-down approach to public opinion would be a hallmark of many progressive reformers a decade later, but these reformers would also enlist popular support—from rising middle-class professional people, for instance. In 1890, however, James, and to a lesser degree Gifford, assumed that well-meaning, upper-class citizens concerned about deforestation could draw on their exalted social position and political connections to bring about conservation legislation. The participation of middle-class elements, let alone a popular-based movement, was not really considered.

Mary Pinchot, too, was status conscious about the family's social position and had recently criticized Gifford for his inclusive use of the word "gentleman," which "sounds rather too much like the stage driver and Western cowboys," when the terms "gentlemen and ladies" should be reserved "for discriminate use." At the same time, however, she perceived that a broader movement, with constant pressure, might be required to agitate for forestry programs. "You have to help make a public opinion which will force the government to do what ought to be done," she advised her son.[22]

Gifford was considering how non-governmental organizations might make a difference in mobilizing public opinion in favor of government action. Concerned citizens were organizing forestry groups, and he wrote his father that he had joined a more active Pennsylvania Forestry Association, but civic lobbying was barely considered.[23]

Gifford, like his father, also disagreed with Brandis's opinion that it would be enlightened lumber companies that would bring about forest management but was more optimistic about government action. Partly it was his youthful faith in the nation's capacity for change, and he was more enthusiastic about signs of public stirrings for conservation of America's forests and its possibilities. As James plied him with newspaper clippings and reports issued by state commissions recommending government action to preserve the Adirondack woodlands, Gifford, greatly encouraged, wrote his papa "that the repeated attempts to get legislation on the subject will at length produce something;" and he believed the Adirondacks might become a model for national forest policy.[24]

Brandis and Schlich, he was realizing, saw forestry in terms of their autocratic traditions, and even German-trained Fernow, Gifford would eventually conclude, viewed forestry in America through European eyes. The exception to this negative appraisal was his visit to more democratic Switzerland, and Swiss forestry leaders, particularly Forestmeister Ulrich R. Meister, impressed Gifford with their flexible approach to forest management. Meister also told Gifford what he wanted to hear—that he could promote forestry in America without more formal study.[25]

*   *   *

As Gifford resigned himself to a year of study in Munich, he received a letter from Fernow indicating that a doubling of appropriations for the agriculture's forestry division in Washington included a new position as assistant chief. Fernow was well aware of Gifford's forestry studies, but he nonetheless offered him the assistantship in case Gifford thought he was far enough along to curtail his training and take on the job. Fernow also mentioned as a sweetener that the "position means of course heirship to the chief place" if he should leave.[26] Though only thirty-nine, Fernow had previously hinted that he might resign and return to Germany.

Gifford was ecstatic. He consulted Brandis, who surprisingly told Gifford to take the job, but only after another year of study. Mamee also thought he should accept. To Gifford, the advantages of the position were "many and obvious," including finally earning his own living and his possible early elevation to head forester. The forestry division was then tiny, but Gifford, believing that the future success of forestry and conservation depended on bold federal government initiatives, wanted to be at the center of the action. Harboring such thoughts, he cabled his acceptance, asking Fernow only to allow him to defer his start until the beginning of the next year (1891).[27]

The offer proved too good to be true. Professor Sargent argued that his acceptance would be "a serious mistake," as the agriculture department was "simply a political machine and has ruined anyone who has had anything to with it," and the forestry division "is of no account whatever. It has no control over forests, or sufficient money or popular support to amount to anything even if the personnel were different." That assessment reflected Sargent's negative assessment of the future of forestry and his conservative bias against government generally, but Sargent's letter "rather upset" Gifford.[28] More important, Papa wrote Gifford that Fernow was "always posing and insincere," and you should be "completely on your guard."[29] James likely had made his own inquiries and came away with a low opinion of Fernow.

Ultimately, before Gifford had to weasel out of his acceptance of the position, he received two more letters from Fernow, saying he would hold the position for Gifford until he had completed his studies. It was confusing, Gifford mused, but ultimately, he was somewhat satisfied because his father offered to suspend judgment on the Fernow offer until father and son could further discuss it.[30]

Knowing he had a job offer in America, Gifford found it easier to come home and consult with his parents about his possibilities. Even then, he thought he would return to Europe, but he would, in fact, never resume his forestry studies. He sometimes conceded, "I begin to feel the scantiness of my preparation."[31] But he found it somewhat comforting that he was better prepared for forestry than any other American and that pioneers in the field elsewhere, including Brandis, had largely educated themselves through their own study. And years later, he reflected, "I covered all the ground I could in the time I had for preparation" and "I am still convinced that my decision was right."[32]

*   *   *

Upon returning home in late 1890, Gifford presented a paper on government forestry abroad at a scholarly conference. His essay, a ponderous survey of forestry practices in many foreign countries, summarized his early impressions of forestry issues. One idea was the importance of state-owned forests, a trust held for all the people. In his view, the state had the right and duty to control the amount of cutting on private forest lands to assure their continued productivity and issue regulations to prevent erosion and insure water courses, all while respecting private property rights. Further, the principles of rational forest management, Gifford asserted, were the same everywhere: the protection of forests. This did not mean a "hands off" attitude or the "sentimentalism" of wilderness advocates but long-range, "scientific" planning based on more utilitarian approaches. Specifically, trees were a crop but required many years to reach a merchantable size, and a fresh crop could not be harvested every year from the same land. In practice, this meant no cutting more trees than were replaced each year; prohibiting large immediate profits and acceptance of smaller returns, say 2.5 percent, that would be sustained and hopefully increase indefinitely; and balancing public-private needs over privately owned forests.

Gifford explained that because of often widely dissimilar local conditions, the methods by which these principles were applied could vary considerably. Touching only briefly on his conclusion on the implications of forestry policy in the United States, he cautiously asserted that "We are surrounded by the calamitous results of the course that we are now pursuing," which was then an odd mixture of laissez-faire biases and a hodgepodge of poorly thought out state and federal legislation. What was now required was wide-ranging, flexible, pragmatic government action, similar to Swiss practices but adaptable to the American experience. Believing that American lumbermen were already far advanced in exploiting the nation's timberlands, he surmised that European conservation methods might not work well in the United States. A much more vigorous government involvement was needed, but he argued only vaguely for the federal government's "intelligent application of the general principles of forestry through the medium of forest organization."[33]

Gifford next sought a job in the field. He was still considering Bernhard Fernow's offer, but checking with European foresters before returning home, he had found that Fernow had never been involved "with the practical management of forests." That limitation, Gifford thought, explained why Fernow was not "at all anxious to have his division spread into the great center of national forest management that he says it ought to be." Forestry in America, Gifford concluded, could not advance if it was led by Fernow, a bureaucrat who lacked "force" and was "not master of the situation."[34]

Gifford wanted to work independently at first and find his own way. Before long, a large resource extraction firm owning timberlands and mines in several states hired him as a consulting forester to make recommendations for its timber holdings in Pennsylvania. James, trying to help Gifford get established in forestry, likely made the arrangements to bring his son and the company together. Sometimes James left a paper trail revealing his promotion of his son's interests. At other times, he acted more as a hidden hand, maneuvering discreetly behind the scenes. One of James's early efforts was arranging for Gifford's election to the Century Association, and Gifford may have been the youngest man elected to the prestigious private men's club.[35]

Soon after the Pennsylvania survey, the company asked Gifford to evaluate the firm's timber lands in Arizona. Gifford used the assignment as an opportunity to see many places in his vast native land for the first time. Taking a circuitous route at his own expense, he visited Niagara Falls, the Grand Canyon, Yosemite, Oregon, and Washington, before returning home via Canada. The entire western trip was an eye-opener. "Whereas I had been blind, now I began to see," he later wrote. Seeing the various climates and magnificent tree specimens first-hand, he more clearly perceived that the unique conditions would require different forest management plans.[36]

Then Gifford, trying to keep on good terms with Fernow, accompanied him on an inspection trip of forested areas in several southern states. Their experiences on the trip confirmed their different philosophies of forest conservation. On the surface, it appeared as a personality conflict between the German-bred, imperious, highly opinionated chief forester and the more phlegmatic, optimistic younger American, who was becoming increasingly cocksure himself. Gifford thought Fernow, though well-intentioned, rejected any criticism while attacking others "with tiresome uniformity" and wanted "credit for everything." He was, in short, a "very queer man."[37]

*   *   *

At the end of his southern trip, Gifford detoured to Asheville in western North Carolina to visit the estate of George W. Vanderbilt, who was planning a gigantic house surrounded by landscaped gardens and forest. James had suggested that Gifford make the stopover. "Then you could look over the land of Geo. Vanderbilt a little," he wrote Gifford, and at some point, "talk it over with him intelligently." Papa saw it as a possible opportunity for his son. Gifford did not meet Vanderbilt during his Asheville visit but pronounced the climate and land at his place "just right for forest management . . . Hilly, but regeneration of conifer and deciduous both excellent."[38]

George W. Vanderbilt was the twenty-nine-year-old grandson of Cornelius Vanderbilt, one of America's first self-made millionaires, and the youngest son of William Henry Vanderbilt, who had doubled his father's fortune. When

William died in 1885, he was arguably the richest man in the world and had left George $10,000,000 in his will. George was not interested in making more money but was a sensitive man who loved books and wanted to become a patron of the arts and culture in America. He also became fixated on spending a good portion of his wealth on developing his Asheville property, a favorite spot of his mother. He had bought more than eleven square miles of land situated on a plateau between the Blue Ridge and Allegheny Mountains for his estate, which he soon named The Biltmore. He asked Richard Morris Hunt, then at the height of his fame as an architect, to design the house on land near the French Broad River and the town, with gorgeous views of the lush surrounding landscape and forested mountains beyond. The chateau, when completed in late 1895, was a virtual palace consisting of 250 rooms, including 34 bedrooms, 44 bathrooms, an indoor swimming pool, a gymnasium, and a bowling alley. It was (and still is) the largest private residence in the United States.[39]

Vanderbilt's grandiose pretensions were an extreme manifestation of the exorbitant spending on mansions and purchases of rich tapestries, famous paintings, antique furniture, and other priceless cultural artifacts by newfound millionaires who wanted to validate their status as the new American aristocracy. Such showy displays were easy to criticize, especially in an era when public suspicion of the power and influence of big business was rising rapidly.[40]

Vanderbilt also employed Frederick Law Olmsted. Widely acclaimed for his numerous city parks, including Central Park in New York, the almost seventy-year-old Olmsted was famed as the pre-eminent landscape architect of that era. The young Vanderbilt intended to make the land into a giant park, but Olmsted argued that a park would be expensive to build and maintain. Vanderbilt would do better to make the vast area a forest preserve, in which careful management would permit trees to be harvested and sold.

Though receiving no formal forestry training, Olmsted was an American pioneer conservationist, and his aesthetic sensibilities had early caused him to reject the growing destructive lumbering practices. His work as a landscape architect disturbed nature, but he always tried to blend natural elements with his designs. He was also a preservationist and, after exploring the Yosemite in California, had written that it "should be held, guarded and managed for the free use of the whole body of the people forever."[41] Olmsted also often discussed forestry matters with Charles Sargent, his neighbor in Brookline, Massachusetts.

Olmsted argued for "a thoroughly well organized and systematically conducted attempt at forestry made on a large scale" at Biltmore.[42] Gifford could not have made a better case for practical forestry. Many municipalities sought the famed landscape artist for new parks and some commissions, however, and Olmsted thus told Vanderbilt that he would need to employ a professional forester full-time to develop a management plan for his woodlands. He recommended Gifford Pinchot for the job. The prospect of deriving income from his lands appealed to George Vanderbilt, who accepted Olmsted's proposal.

That Olmsted suggested Gifford indicated the young forester's name recognition, but there was also a social connection. Gifford later wrote that his father and Olmsted were "good friends." The two surely knew each, but there is little evidence of a close relationship.[43] Still, Olmsted's approach to filling the forestry position was professional. He recommended Gifford to Vanderbilt only after meeting with him twice and asking him for his thoughts on forestry work at Biltmore. Finally, Vanderbilt invited the young forester to his Asheville estate. Olmsted took a grandfatherly interest in the young forester, who, in turn, was careful to discuss his proposals with him before gaining Vanderbilt's approval. Olmsted "always raises me very much in my own opinion, by the way he asks my views, and attaches importance to my work," he wrote his father. "After talking with him the ultimate great objects of my work always stand out."[44]

Getting along famously with Olmsted facilitated Gifford's tasks at Biltmore. He found too that Vanderbilt, "a simple minded[,] pleasant fellow, full of his place," was easy to work for. As fellow bachelors, the two spent evenings playing pool or whist together, and Gifford attended some of his employer's house parties. Soon they were calling each other "Brother Pinch" and "George." Gifford was not disposed to criticize him, even privately. Whatever his eccentricities, Vanderbilt, unlike many other plutocrats of his generation, was not rapaciously plundering the natural resources on his lands; he was committed to conserving them. As part of the world of social privilege, Gifford then easily accepted Vanderbilt's affectations as the natural order of things, relishing, for instance, that his traveling on Vanderbilt's private railway car "is something almost too good to be true."[45] Early into the job, Gifford employed two assistants to survey the forest and hired local lumbermen to do the cutting and hauling.

Of course, Gifford's acceptance of the Biltmore job further soured his relationship with Fernow, who still expected him to become his assistant. "There having been no obligation on either side," Gifford explained to him, "I felt myself entirely free to accept Mr. Vanderbilt's offer." Fernow shot back that although there was no legal contract, Pinchot had nonetheless reneged on their understanding. He also ridiculed Vanderbilt's experiment and, after visiting Biltmore, challenged Gifford: "If you can 'make forestry profitable' . . . within the next two years, I shall consider you the wisest forester and financier of the age."[46] Though Fernow thought the future of their profession belonged in private forestry, he could not resist denigrating the large foray before it had begun.

As an early American experiment in scientific management, the Biltmore forest, if it could be made economically viable, might inspire similar ventures elsewhere. But upon investigating Vanderbilt's forested lands, Gifford discovered that he had been too optimistic during his first visit to Asheville. He now realized that "the condition of a large part of the forest was deplorable in the extreme." He nonetheless developed a plan for thinning the forest and planting or nourishing new tree growth. "It will be a good fight," he wrote his father, "I must make it pay. And I shall."[47]

Profitable forestry at Biltmore was also improbable, because lumber then was generally inexpensive. Moreover, transportation outlays would be a large part of the expense of forest management, and finding cost-effective methods to get the cut trees out of the rugged hills and mountains to free-flowing streams and rivers and passable roads for transit to market would be a major logistical problem.

Gifford also gave much attention to related projects. One was the development of an exhibit on Biltmore forest for the Columbian exposition in Chicago. Olmsted suggested the exhibit to Gifford, who enthused that it would be good publicity for him and provide exposure to forestry education for the thousands attending the fair.[48] Gifford visited the windy city twice to oversee the Biltmore display, and he wrote an explanatory pamphlet, which was given to exhibit visitors and sent to newspapers.

Gifford followed with a short book about his first-year experiences in Biltmore forest management. Gifford claimed in the book that the forest made a twelve-percent profit. His reasoning was badly flawed, however, as more than one-half of the income was his "value" of the cut inventory not yet sold, and he did not include his own salary as an expense. The income stream was also abnormally high that first year, because the ease of extensive cutting of various big trees nearer to the mansion yielded more lumber and much less transportation expense. Such advantages could not be sustained, and new sources of income would have to be found. But Vanderbilt appeared satisfied that his forest was under competent management and was bringing in some revenue.[49]

His accounting gimmickry did not fool his mentor, Dietrich Brandis, or Fernow, the latter writing the Biltmore forester, "I . . . agree with Mr. Brandis when he called the experiment 'verfehlt' [failure]—from that point of view (profitableness) only." Despite these negative analyses, Gifford would maintain fifty years later that the first year was profitable. (He would also assert subsequently that the national forests he administered likewise made money, though more dispassionate economic assessments have strongly suggested that none did.)[50]

*   *   *

Gifford soon explored new opportunities. It was his "growing impatience for fresh fields and pastures new," he later remarked, but it was also his awareness that Biltmore would prove a long, rough slog. During a brief trip to Europe, he consulted Brandis, who stressed that Biltmore was a small operation and advised his protégé to move on to larger challenges. Gifford concluded, "I must get at bigger work as soon as possible."[51] Vanderbilt allowed him to open an office as forestry consultant in New York City at a drastic cutback in his salary and duties at Biltmore.

He was reducing his role at Biltmore just when forestry there promised to become a much bigger undertaking. In entertaining thoughts of making forestry an enormous commercial enterprise, Vanderbilt asked Gifford in August 1892 to venture much deeper into the nearby woodlands, later named the Pisgah Forest, and make judgments on promising timber.[52] These lands were mostly virgin forests, and Gifford rhapsodized over the beauty of this untamed wilderness. "The forest is exceedingly fine," he gushed to his parents, "the streams are as beautiful as any I have ever seen, except for our Sawkill." And he wrote a sometimes girlfriend, "I have had no use for money recently, having been out in the wild, wild woods, sleeping on the ground, conversing with moonshiners, and feeding on warmed-up dough." After Gifford reported enthusiastically to his employer about the woodlands, Vanderbilt pursued the land purchases and now owned more than 80,000 acres around Asheville.[53]

Although George Vanderbilt's purchases in the Pisgah Forest suggested a bigger forestry enterprise ahead, Gifford wanted to reduce his role even further at Biltmore. Vanderbilt at first decided not to do anything with the new tracts, and Gifford believed that, despite the purchases, his employer "seems to be rather losing his interest in forestry." So prompted, he concluded, "I shall be glad to find some more active work in the near future, while retaining my present position in some ways unchanged."[54] Supported by Olmsted, he persuaded his boss to hire a new resident forester. With no other trained American foresters available, Vanderbilt turned to Brandis and accepted his recommendation of Carl Schenck, a German with five years of forestry education and a newly earned Ph.D. in the field.

Schenck's introduction to America was inauspicious. When Gifford greeted him in New York in the spring of 1895 and took him to his parents' home for lunch, his father did not even shake hands with him and peremptorily announced that they would have to go elsewhere for their meal. Gifford at first told Schenck very little about Biltmore, and when he sent him off to Asheville, he remarked, "You will be forester and I shall be chief forester during your term of employment."[55] In their cool welcome, father and son let Schenck know he would be watched in his new position.

As a newcomer, Schenck tried to be accommodating and only belatedly asserted himself. He much later wrote his own account about his Biltmore experiences, which differed fundamentally from Gifford's. Vanderbilt told Schenck, for example, that "Pinchot's connection with Biltmore Estate had ended and that I was in no way subject to his orders or to his supervision," but there was, in fact, a division of responsibility. At the start, it had been agreed with Vanderbilt that Gifford's sphere would lie on the technical side and not at all on the monetary side, of which Gifford was "very glad," while Schenck dealt with the day-to-day operations in the forests.[56]

These were general categories of responsibility, however, with some overlap. Gifford continued to act even in his diminished capacity as if he was still chief forester. Partly he wanted to ensure his already developed scheme for the Pisgah Forest would be carried out. In this regard, Vanderbilt affirmed to Gifford, "In case of any difference as to methods between you [two,] your advice and instructions I expect to have carried out." Gifford also had strong doubts about German foresters' willingness to adapt to American conditions, and he only partly succeeded in training him.

Carl Schenck later wrote that soon after he arrived at Biltmore, he realized that German forestry was "impossible of success. . . . A brand-new sort of forestry was needed." Some Old-World biases persisted, however.[57] Regarding forestry policy, for instance, Schenck's approach was more conservative than Gifford's. Where the German saw problems, his American counterpart saw opportunities. The German was a product of a mature European forest system, but he had had no experience with a primeval forest like the Pisgah, and he had deep reservations about harvesting the tall, majestic tulip poplars. He preferred a smaller operation. However, Gifford was determined to make the Pisgah a big, paying operation and calculated that up to four million board feet of poplar could be cut in an area called Big Creek. His plan involved harvesting large numbers of these magnificent specimens and cutting them into logs up to seventeen feet long to be processed into lumber and sold on the open market at an attractive price. The remoteness and complicated logistics of the Pisgah operation would incur high costs, and Gifford knew that the economies of scale of a large operation were required to bring in sufficient revenues to make a profit.[58]

It was acceptable to cut the enormous trees, Gifford believed, because he had discovered many poplar seedlings in open areas of Big Creek receiving more light, and he calculated that the plethora of seeds falling onto the soil from the felled poplars would be exposed to more light and produce bounteous progeny. The big poplars would be cut down with care to avoid hurting the seedlings, and the logs would then be lugged to Big Creek, where a splash dam would be built with big lumber booms holding the logs. When the water from the dam was released, the lumber would hurtle down the mountainside toward the Mills River, a tributary of the French Broad River, and finally downstream to an Asheville sawmill Vanderbilt had bought for processing and marketing.

The bold scheme troubled Schenck. Besides feeling "guilty" about the destruction of the primeval forest, there was also the transportation issue. Constructing a dam was a tricky process with potentially disastrous results. He would have preferred building a series of roads connected to the nearest public roads. As a newcomer, he did not push the idea but later bemoaned that although the expense might have been ten times greater, roads would have been "twenty times cheaper in the end!"[59]

Then there were the seedlings. Contrary to Gifford's observations, Schenck later claimed he found no poplar seedlings in Big Creek Valley. On this basis, Schenck likely complained to Vanderbilt, who nonetheless reaffirmed, Gifford noted, that he "was entirely in accord with me as to my directing the forest policy at Biltmore, and not Schenck."[60]

The operation encountered major difficulties. The poplars were cut down, but a drought did not provide sufficient water in the dam to push the logs when released into the river. Thus, a second dam was built and the process repeated. Eventually, the logs reached the Mills River, but it did not have enough water to float the logs downstream to the French Broad; when heavy rains came, the logs became wild in the turbulent waters, and many were lost downstream or stranded on flats. The hurtling lumber often damaged farmers' lands and bridges, resulting in lawsuits Vanderbilt had to settle.

A few years after the commencement of the Big Creek operation, Schenck and Gifford walked through it. Gifford was highly pleased with the regeneration of the forest. "There is a magnificent growth of young yellow poplar on Big Creek," he exuded. "This is a complete justification of my plan of cutting and fulfills my prediction." Even Schenck compromised his first concerns about the absence of poplar seedlings by admitting later that he saw a profusion of new poplars growing there. Still, he remained skeptical. He noted, for instance, that eighty percent of hardwood seedlings that had been planted with care on the estate had died, and the vicissitudes of nature could bring about the same failure to the Big Creek seedlings.[61]

Schenck also claimed that the Big Creek operation was a financial "debacle." In his memoirs, Gifford would write that the venture had been profitable the first year, though not subsequently. He did not provide details, and one wonders whether he included Schenck's and his own salaries or other expenses (including the lawsuits). He would further admit that Big Creek had been a learning experience and encountered problems—working with new men, the enormous size of the trees and felling them unbroken, and the damaged terrain despite the precautions—but he touched only lightly on the difficulties. And he remained unapologetic about the grandiose scope. "The trouble," he wrote Brandis a decade later, "was not that we cut too much, but that we did not get logs enough to the [Vanderbilt saw] mill." And he told Schenck "how foolish" the German forester had been in executing the Big Creek plan.[62]

When Gifford returned to Big Creek in 1937, it was now a national forest thanks to his own efforts in persuading the Vanderbilt heirs to sell it to the federal government. The flourishing tulip poplars there, which were being harvested commercially, reaffirmed his vision. Overall, he concluded, "Big Creek was the first successful attempt in America to secure the natural reproduction of a particular tree by commercial lumbering under forest management." Other analyses have confirmed that, profits aside, the operation provided worthwhile lessons in the planting and regeneration of American forests.[63]

6.

Affairs of the Heart and Mind

Of the Pinchot children, Nettie would be the first to experience a serious romantic attachment. By 1886, Nettie, now seventeen, was maturing into a beautiful young woman, and her mother took notice. "[D]o you realize," she wrote her husband, "that she may be married in two or three years more?"[1] She had the figure of a fashion model, tall at five feet, seven inches, with an attractive face featuring a firm chin, high sculpted cheekbones, and a regal nose.   •

Three years later, she tried to pull away from her parents' oversight. When James and Mary planned to take her with them on their multi-month trip to Mexico and the West Coast, she was "Terribly blue about going . . . Awfully homesick."[2] A redeeming feature of the journey was a two-week stay in Washington, D.C., where she attended some social functions and attracted the attention of some young British diplomats at the Legation. George Barclay, an attaché, particularly interested her. "He is awfully nice, the nicest man here," she emphasized, and having to continue on the family trip made her "melancholy."[3]

When she returned home, Barclay had left the Legation, but another young British diplomat there began courting her. The maids accompanying Nettie to Virginia Beach the following spring told Mamie McCadden about "one young gentleman at the Beach [who] stayed several days longer than he expected to get a[c]quainted with her." And upon her return, Mamie reported that Nettie had "Two admirers to dinner last night, one English man, the other American." The English guest was likely Alan Johnstone, a young diplomat at the British Legation, and he had probably been the beach suitor too. Nettie began to see a lot of him. A romance ensued, and by early 1891, Alan wrote to Nettie's parents that he had proposed to Nettie and added, "I may say that she perhaps returns my feeling."[4]

A serious complication, however, was Nettie's poor health. She had a weak heart aggravated by a nervous condition and was often laid up with a sore throat or fever. Still, Alan continued to see her in New York and Washington. In the summer of 1891, an illness prompted her parents to send her to stay with friends in western New York to recuperate and separate the couple for a time. Nettie was much in love and wrote her mother that her romance was "no passing fancy, Mama dear, but a thing which must last as long as I live." Soon Mary, seeing that her daughter would not change her mind, let her go out with him daily.[5]

Gifford described Alan Johnstone, eleven years older than Nettie, as "a very nice straightforward honest fellow, without much apparent ability, pleasant, a true gentleman" and "fairly interesting." But though not a scintillating personality, Alan had an even temper that was a salubrious influence on high-strung Nettie. For Alan, the art of diplomacy involved not just international relations but family relationships. His perseverance aggravated the Pinchots; they wanted him to move on. Gifford surmised that he was "making no end of trouble" for everyone and was "Not half big enough" for his sister.[6]

Despite the family obstacles, Alan and Nettie stuck it out. Besides her health, there was his social position. Alan was the fourth son (among nine siblings) of an earl, who was a former member of Parliament and a large landowner with an estate in Yorkshire. But under the British custom of primogeniture, the first son inherited all land and more, and the younger siblings had to make their own way in the world. Alan graduated from Eton, but instead of university, he studied with tutors and took and passed the examinations for entrance to the diplomatic corps. Being in the foreign service conferred social prestige, but diplomats were paid modestly and required independent means and social connections to advance professionally. And he was only a third secretary in Washington (soon to be promoted to second). He admitted that he could not bring many financial resources to their union, telling Mary, "The only real claim I can put forward is that I love your daughter with all my heart, honestly and thoroughly."[7] The consent of Nettie's parents to their marriage would mean a Pinchot obligation to provide long-term financial help. It was a delicate situation.[8]

Reacting negatively to Alan as a future son-in-law, James demurred their betrothal. Nettie understood that the family's worry was, as she indelicately put it, about his "poverty."[9] A hefty dowry and some subsidization of their married life was a burden, but James also disliked that, despite his financial support, Nettie would be living far away in London or other foreign capitals. Instead of dwelling on these sensitive matters, he stressed that Nettie's poor health made her unready for marriage. Both he and Mary were also musing that her emotional disposition suggested an infatuation, although Gifford thought "it may be much more than that."[10]

The parents' concern for their daughter's well-being was not misplaced. She was an invalid much of the time and also easily excitable. At a large family Christmas dinner, for example, she had a nervous attack and "Went all to pieces," Gifford noted, which made the dinner "very gloomy." James said that she would have to wait two years to announce her engagement, but then he and Mary relented somewhat, telling Alan that, while "there is no engagement at present, the decision when her health permits rests only with you and her, the announcement and marriage to take place as soon as you both choose and circumstances permit."[11]

The Pinchots' longtime family doctor pronounced that, because of Nettie's weakened state, she and Alan should not write to or see one another until he gave permission. Indeed, she was sent off again, this time to family friends upstate so she could focus on her health. After her departure, Nettie related to Gifford, "I did not dare to speak to Papa, as I was so nastily nervous. . . . Mama never said one word to me, but she told Alan in Washington that [the engagement] should be announced" later. The prospect arose that the couple would be incommunicado for six months, and Nettie, believing that nothing would happen while she was sick, resolved, "I must get well."[12]

Alan pressed his case. He produced an engagement ring and asked if the doctor had any objection to her receiving it. Echoing the doctor, Mary told him that "anything which reminds her of you sends her pulse up."[13] Nettie's health improved somewhat, and she went to Europe for rest and bath treatments during the summer of 1892. Alan informed them that he, too, would be in England to be near her. His father, Lord Derwent, had meanwhile written James that he supported Alan's attachment to Nettie and was prepared to contribute £10,000 ($1.42 million now) to him and Nettie jointly in safe securities as a "settlement" for their marriage.[14]

Nettie dug in her heels, too. While reluctantly acquiescing in her separation from Alan, she continued expressing her undying love for him and complained that she still had no voice in the matter of their communication, even though she was twenty-three. She was particularly perturbed that they could not announce their engagement, and she began a campaign for a fall wedding.[15]

Accompanied by her mother, Nettie spent the summer at Aix-les-Bains in France, alternating daily baths and electrical shock treatments. The regimen helped considerably, with Mary reporting that Nettie was "jolly and just like her old self again." Mary's resistance was weakening. She found Nettie "more serene when he was far away" but also understood "she thinks of no one else and perhaps she would be more tranquil if he were here. . . . I don[']t know." Without having any good excuse, she wrote her husband, "We may as well acknowledge the engagement, and possibly she may see reason to change her mind."[16]

Giving in to Mary, James ended the suspense by inviting Alan to dinner at Delmonico's in Manhattan, where he consented to their engagement. A month later, he, Mary, Nettie, and young Amos visited Alan and his parents at Lord Derwent's Hackness estate. James provided the couple an allowance, and Mary also contributed. Mary's supplement, Alan gratefully wrote her, made the engaged couple feel like "millionaires. . . . [and] anywhere but in Washington we would live in a palace and entertain royalty."[17]

Antoinette Pinchot and Alan Johnstone were married in December 1892, although when Nettie became ill again, the Pinchots gave up a church wedding and held the ceremony in their home in Gramercy Park. It was all Nettie could do to get up for the nuptials and then return to bed upstairs afterward. The Pinchot parents adjusted to their new son-in-law, and it was not long before Mamee could remark to Gifford, "Your Papa likes Alan very much and so do we all more and more."[18]

* * *

During Nettie's romantic travail, Gifford Pinchot also showed interest in the opposite sex. At Yale, he had enjoyed meeting girls and hosting informal parties with classmates in their rooms for visiting females on dance weekends. His good looks, his family's wealth, and his outgoing personality gained the attention of unattached young females. He had been voted the most handsome member of his college and earned the nickname "Greek god," although Sam Fisher, a close Yale classmate, regaled in calling him "you darn old woolly headed Greek god." His early accomplishments suggested an interesting man with real potential. For one, Ted Donnelley's sister-in-law gushed, "Mr. Pinchot—well[,] he is just <u>glorious</u>."[19]

Gifford's views on sex were conventional, and he unquestioningly accepted the strict Victorian standards that intimate sexual relations were reserved for marriage. Part of his disdain for his fellow forestry students had been his disapproval of their loose sexual behavior. However, he was curious about such matters and, before beginning his forestry studies, had ventured out in Paris with Jim Reynolds for some risqué entertainment. At the Folies Bergères, they watched a ballet, which Gifford called "the most carefully arranged bit of indecency that I ever saw." Following the performance, one of the cabaret's "tough looking maidens . . . put her arm around me and invited me to a game of 'billiard[s] Anglais,'" but "I kept my face closed" and firmly turned down this "bagatelle." Later, a dealer on the riverbank enticed the straight-arrow Gifford to come inside his shop where he showed him "the filthiest lot of photos imaginable," and the shocked Gifford was "awfully sorry" he had gone in.[20]

Gifford's first real female interest was Maria Furman, one of Nettie's friends, but their relationship did not develop smoothly. Just before Gifford began his forestry studies, the two had met in Paris, ridden together in a hot air balloon, and ascended to the top of the newly completed Eiffel Tower. Maria and Gifford were "chums" who could have fun and intellectual discussions together. She wrote him gossipy letters at Nancy, and they had met again briefly in Paris during his Christmas vacation. She especially valued Gifford's seriousness and steady influence, but she also asked him for "more sprees, built on the plan of the old ones." But Gifford did not dote on her—indeed, she seemed a low priority. When he delayed his return home from France, Maria joked that the only way his family could get him back was to bribe her to go back to Europe, "and then you will come contentedly home and stay until I return which as usual will be the signal for your departure." He was also a poor correspondent. When he wrote her a letter but posted it belatedly, she replied with a cutting question: "did you think it would improve with age?"[21]

Gifford was also distracted by a new female friend, Beatrix (Trix) Jones. Their parents were neighbors both in New York and Bar Harbor. It was at their Maine retreat in the summer of 1891 that Gifford and Trix, nineteen, became constant companions. She was an outdoors person and liked to go canoeing and shoot skeet, and she quickly impressed him with her knowledge of botany, having discovered, for instance, a new kind of orchid. She also knew a lot about trees and was interested in learning more. Gifford loaned her Schlich's manual of forestry, outlined a course for her, and tested her on the topic, giving her top marks.

Soon he was having long talks with Trix and noted in his diary, "Saw a great deal of Trix, in fact saw nobody else." Rumors soon surfaced that they were engaged, and Gifford reacted, "Cuss!" The problem was that while he enjoyed her intellectually, "somehow," he reflected, she "is not attractive."[22]

That evaluation put a damper on romantic involvement. Trix had had plenty of warning of Gifford's romantic disinterest. He had broken dates with her, and when she had asked him to do something, he would find that he had "to go away just then to examine something at Kalamazoo or Tahiti." He was also an indifferent correspondent, and an exasperated Trix warned him, if "you don't answer my carefully concocted epistle, you shan't get any more, as I am mad with you." His inattentive behavior was reminiscent of his earlier treatment of Maria, only with much less romantic interest on his part.[23]

Gifford then tried to reconnect with Maria Furman. When she and her parents visited the Pinchot family at Grey Towers for four days, the experience, he enthused, was "beautiful, beautiful," "wonderful," "True chumsship."[24] His feelings for her, he soon related, "grew stronger and stronger very rapidly," and he called on her again at her parents' summer place in Roslyn, Long Island. The two had a long, serious talk in the garden. He professed his wish to see more of her, but Maria, somewhat taken aback, rather firmly rebuffed him. As Gifford tactfully described their meeting to his fellow bonesmen, "we decided that we did not care enough for each other, although we did care a great deal. Then I kissed her good night, which was perhaps the most solemn thing I ever did, and in some ways the most sacred, and that was the end" of their quasi-romance.[25]

Not quite. Right after their tête-à-tête, Maria wrote him sympathetically that she was "very glad and relieved to find that you are very human after all, . . . and I do love to be loved, and it is very great that a man can think well of me." She was trying to let him down easily and cheer him up, but the affectionate tone of her letter prompted Gifford to write again, asking to talk about their relationship. This time she minced no words, telling him that at their meeting, "what I said was that I liked you very much and that we would call 'it' off forever. . . . this is the end." Gifford seemed to get the message. In later recounting his continuing mooning over Maria to his Bones friends, Gifford ruefully admitted that he had "managed to make an imperial ass of myself."[26]

Maria had earlier discouraged Gifford because she was already seriously involved with Bond Emerson, a New York stockbroker, and Gifford soon received word that she and Bond were engaged. The news "hit me very hard, much harder than I had the least idea of before," Gifford penned in his diary. "Feeling decidedly broken up." The next day, Gifford had a "splendid talk" with Maria, noting, "We are true friends anyway, so the best part is left. . . . [A]nd so it ended," he sighed. "I am very sorry and very glad."[27]

Later that year, when Gifford returned from Biltmore to New York for his sister's marriage, his mother was sick while Nettie was indisposed, and no one had given any oversight to the wedding preparations. Natalie Bayard Dresser, Nettie's longtime Newport friend, was there as maid of honor, and she came to the rescue by cheerfully organizing every detail.

At Yale, Gifford had shown some interest in Natalie, inviting her in his senior year to a college event, and afterward retained an odd attraction for her, commenting that she was a "Smooth maiden. Has always great charm for me." But also finding her "somewhat impassive and uniform," he was not smitten.[28] However, her performance at Nettie's wedding was so outstanding that Gifford became an admirer. With mistletoe around the house during the Christmas season, she consented to his request for a goodnight kiss after the wedding. "It all seemed quite natural and right, and it was," he thought. They exchanged presents the next day and promised to write to each other.[29] Gifford then twice wrote to Sam Fisher about Natalie. Disturbed at Gifford's sudden ardor, Sam lectured him, "You do not want for a wife . . . 'a kissable girl'—as you express it. You want a <u>woman</u> and above all one that you can respect on that side." The latter represented "<u>true</u> love," while Gifford's fascination with Natalie's physical attributes "does not draw the best out of you."[30]

The potential romance went nowhere. Natalie embarked on a long trip to South America with her three sisters and then moved to Paris, and their correspondence never developed.[31]

*   *   *

Gifford next had a diverting experience with Florence Adele Sloane, whose mother was the daughter of William Henry Vanderbilt. Despite her fabulous wealth and luxurious lifestyle, Adele wanted to experience "real things" beyond the exclusive world of the super-rich, and she imagined taking an assumed name to "travel, go everywhere, see what poverty, sickness, and sorrow really were, what misery and crime meant." Gifford had gotten to know her the previous spring when George Vanderbilt, her youngest and favorite uncle, hosted an extended house party at the Biltmore. Only eighteen, she stayed for three weeks, and Gifford had found time away from his work to have "many very shining talks and rides" with her. He wrote admiringly to his mother that Adele "is not afraid of anything and is a hearty, natural sort of maiden."[32] They also saw each other that summer at Bar Harbor, and by then she had fallen for him completely. Perceiving his commitment to forestry, she read up on the subject to nurture his interest in her. Soon, she was writing him long letters, peppered with her "dry facts" and other "scientific" observations about the natural world.

Gifford was unimpressed, however, and now "kicked" himself for giving her attention. The following February, he visited Vermont to talk to Dr. William Seward Webb, who had married George Vanderbilt's sister. Webb was buying hundreds of thousands of acres in the Adirondacks, and Gifford had prepared a report on the forest and hoped to manage it. He arrived when Webb was hosting a large house party, and Miss Sloane was there as part of the Vanderbilt

George Vanderbilt with relatives and friends, including Gifford Pinchot (sitting, center), at a Biltmore outing, c. 1892. Adele Sloane, Vanderbilt's niece, who had a romantic crush on the young forester, is standing directly behind him. Vanderbilt valued the "snap" that Gifford brought to the local social scene. (Biltmore)

entourage. Gifford found himself forced to amuse her. "I do not give the weakest cuss for her," he wrote his Bones classmates, but "People come and squeeze my hand and look deep into my eyes and evidently want to say[,] Go it, old boy, and I just curse and curse"—to himself. He tried to show her "that I am not pining, but she is just blank thick headed."[33]

Adele continued her pursuit. She already had a suitor who was ideal in many ways. But that was "not enough," she wrote in her diary; "I want so much more." She visited the Chicago exposition later that spring, partly hoping to see Gifford again, and she ran into him twice. At the second, Gifford, accompanied by his mother, greeted her with a deep bow, which was his unsubtle way of telling her that she was not a familiar friend. Adele, of course, was upset; from her private railroad car on the return trip to New York, she sent him what she confessed was a "foolish . . . mad" letter. She wanted him to know, however, that "I hate formality, and I hated [your] bowing . . . as if I had never spoken to you in my life." She said "goodbye" but could not forget him and continued to write him notes. She stayed in New York because she knew Gifford would establish an office there as a consulting forester. "I am sure it will be a horrible winter for me," she lamented. "And how often he will hurt me through and through! I believe the more he hurts me, the more I will love him."[34]

*   *   *

When Gifford returned to Biltmore in the late winter of 1893, he had not yet experienced any serious love commitment. The easy explanation is that he was just unlucky in love. Beginning with Kitty Hunt and extending eight years later with Adele, it seemed that one thing or another got in the way of his girlfriends. Still, there was a pattern to Gifford's elusive behavior toward the fair sex. He might well have won over Maria but dithered and let her slip away. And it was easier to profess a momentary, strong attraction to Natalie, knowing that she would soon be continents away for an indefinite future. One explanation was his parents. He was their pride and joy, and their concerns for his welfare would mean they would never be far away from him emotionally. James was an ideal parent in some ways, and Maria reported to Gifford, for example, that he "is so pleased about you that he smiles all the time he is talking of you."[35] The father and son's regular consultations on forestry matters brought them closer together.

However, Papa was a control freak when it came to romantic attachments. Nettie's long, frustrating experience before her marriage was proof of his domineering behavior. Gifford knew he was expected to become well-established in his profession before considering marriage. When he returned from his trip to see Maria on Long Island, his father and mother confronted him, saying they were "disturbed" that a romance might develop between them. And several months later, James commented almost gleefully about Kitty Hunt's engagement. "Gifford's neck is out of joint now surely," he wrote Mary, and he asked her to tell Gifford "not to mourn as he is not yet quite ready to undertake the uncertain experiment. . . . I will hunt up a good wife for him some of these days if he is too busy to do it himself."[36]

Gifford had long since gotten over Kitty, but James's reference to picking a wife for him served as a reminder that Papa still did not think Gifford, now twenty-six, was ready for marriage and that his approval would be required for any future mate. He left little to chance and, worrying that there might be something between Gifford and Trix, cautioned him, "She is just too much interested in what you do."[37]

The role of Gifford's mother was more complicated. She closed ranks with her husband on Kitty and Nettie's situation and was reluctant to lose Gifford, who was still mama's "precious boy." She had warned him at Nancy, "You won[']t let some pretty girl gobble you up[,] will you[,] so that I can[']t have you too?" She assumed Gifford would marry eventually, but she wanted to enjoy their emotional bond as long as possible. "One of these days," she once wrote him, "you must have a nice little house next door to us somewhere, and a dear little wife who will not hate her mother in law and then we will all have a good time together."[38] Moreover, during his frequent travels, she nonetheless managed to arrange her itinerary so that she could visit him. There was nothing oedipal in their relationship, but Mary felt a steady pull to be with him and could write him, for instance, "I so long to see you that sometimes I fear that I can not wait."[39]

For his part, Gifford harbored no thoughts of disobedience and fully accepted the closeness of his parents, especially his mother. When Mary was with Nettie at Aix-les-Bains and asked Gifford if he could come and help out with his sister's health care, Gifford left Biltmore for two months to join them.[40] Under such constraints, for Gifford to fall seriously in love and contemplate marriage would likely be a trying experience for him, just as it had been for Nettie.

* * *

And fall seriously in love is precisely what happened once he returned to Biltmore in the winter of 1893. His love commitment would be Laura Houghteling. The same age as Gifford, Laura lived with her mother in a comfortable mansion on fourteen acres of manicured lawns and gardens at Strawberry Hill in Asheville. Situated just above the French Broad River, the mansion afforded gorgeous views of the surrounding mountains. Gifford had briefly met her when he was first exploring the Biltmore position. A few months into his new job, he spotted her riding horseback in the nursery, and he took off on his own horse to intercept her. Calling her by her first name, he felt a blush come across his face. As they separated after their brief encounter, she misspoke, saying goodbye to "Peter." Despite the embarrassment, the ice had been broken.

Adele Sloane, during her visit that spring, was instantly jealous of Laura; afterward, she had written Gifford from New York that in reminiscing on Biltmore, she and George Vanderbilt had "both imagined you in a blissful frame of mind dining at Miss Houghteling's—the very name sends shivers down my back—but no, honestly, I think she is perfectly lovely and so pretty." Laura was indeed a beautiful woman, and Gifford had taken notice.[41]

There would be, however, a serious obstacle to any romantic relationship—her poor health. A photograph of Laura Houghteling at the time shows a tall, curvaceous woman with blond hair piled high on her head but also reveals the pallid complexion and gaunt face of what might be an ailing person. She had grown up in Chicago, where her father was a businessman, but a few years before meeting Gifford, she had begun long visits to Asheville with her mother. Because of its temperate climate and clean mountain air, Asheville was a popular retreat for wealthy people for rest cures at sanitariums and a semblance of high society in a country setting.

Laura suffered from tuberculosis, or consumption as it was usually called, although the historian looks in vain for specific references to the disease in the extant documents. Tuberculosis was associated with the poor and slums of industrial cities, and the social stigma attached to the disease may have prompted the Houghteling and Pinchot families never to mention it in their correspondence. It is also true, however, that laboratory tests were just beginning to detect the disease, so one could hold out some hope, if the symptoms were not too virulent, that perhaps the patient might have some other kind of chest infection. In any event, the uncertainties of diagnosis made it possible to avoid mentioning the unmentionable disease.[42]

Before the advent of antibiotics fifty years later, there were no magical drugs or promising treatments for tuberculosis, which was a leading cause of death. Among diseases in the late nineteenth century, it was a scourge, equivalent to what polio, cancer, and AIDS would become in the following century. Gifford was well aware of its deleterious consequences. It was prevalent in France, for example, when he lived there. Moreover, two of his Skull and Bones classmates contracted the disease within two years of graduation and soon died.[43]

Gifford, in love, minimized the possible downside, however, and gradually began seeing more of Laura. His optimistic outlook allowed him to believe that his fervent love for her, combined with her own inner fortitude and the best medical care, might "will" his sweetheart back to good health. In addition, she seemed to be holding her own and was receiving close attention from her doctor, S. Westray Battle, famous as an expert on consumption and Asheville's favorite society doctor specializing in treating wealthy patients like Laura. In any event, Gifford visited her during his free time. Laura could venture outside for short periods when she was feeling better. But she was still semi-invalid and would always be available for him. By that summer, they were a committed couple.

Their attraction was physical. Early in their relationship, Laura sent Julia Sullivan, her nurse and confidant, out of the parlor to bring some tea to Gifford and her. Upon her return, she found the couple locked in a passionate embrace on the sofa by the fireplace. It was their first embrace, Julia soon learned. "I was so frightened I came near dropping the tray," she wrote Gifford much later. "She told me all about it that night."[44]

The couple's intellectual interests greatly reinforced their love. Laura had an active, curious mind, and they began sharing their interests in literature and poetry. She, too, was a good Christian, and they indulged in Bible study, particularly the Gospel of John and Revelation, texts appropriate for someone contemplating the possibility of approaching death.

Laura was also receptive to Gifford's fascination with spiritualism. His interest in psychic phenomena at Yale had grown while studying in France. He had attended lectures in Paris on hypnotism, mesmerism, and spiritualism and had gained a long interview with the physiology professor Charles Richet, who was researching but doubtful of the phenomenon of extrasensory perception.[45] Gifford had soon read a new book, which tried to reconcile the conflict between evolution (or science) and religion, and was impressed by the scientific language undergirding the author's spiritual message. Psychologically, it bolstered his Christian faith when the world of science seemed to be eroding it. "Needed such a book," Gifford penned in his diary then, and after reading it again a year later, he commented, "Always an impressive book."[46] Gifford may not have exposed Laura to this treatise, but together they read Emerson and the mystic Emanuel Swedenborg, who claimed to have visited the afterlife with a touring guide. And they shared many novels depicting spiritualist themes.[47]

Spiritualism spread across the nineteenth-century American landscape as a social movement and grew considerably after the Civil War as people, still mourning the deaths of their loved ones during the hostilities, searched for meaning in the enormous death toll. Spiritualism provided a vision of a friendly, material heaven in which familiar, recognizable people built a perfect society and tried to communicate with the living. There was hokum, even fraud, in the movement, and it appealed more to women and to uneducated and less religious people. Gifford, a well-educated Christian man, thus does not fit the stereotypical spiritualist. Some Christians even attacked spiritualism as blasphemy. However, like Gifford, many people, still more believers than skeptics, were prepared to perceive spiritualism as neither unscriptural nor sacrilegious. They found comfort in the spiritualists' emphasis on making contact between departed spirits and mortals. The spiritual world would have a more powerful pull in times of great bereavement when family members and lovers wanted to reunite with their lost ones, now living in an afterworld without sin, death, and misfortune—a world that they, too, would eventually enter.[48]

Gifford would early confide about Laura with his fellow bonesmen, who gradually dragged out from him Dr. Battle's pessimistic prognosis.[49] Gifford's Yale friends who visited Gifford and saw Laura were circumspect and emphasized her great beauty. Donnelley remarked, "she is certainly a <u>queen</u> [double underlined]," while another Bones classmate thought she was "a <u>very</u> attractive girl" and alluded only in passing to her poor health.[50]

Gifford put off telling his parents about his newfound love. In his letters, she was first "Miss Houghteling" and, by the spring, could mention their common intellectual interests and "very jolly times together." He soon hinted, "She and I have always been very good friends, and especially so of late," and also let on that she was an invalid and not expected to live but provided no details beyond praying for her recovery.[51]

He was clearly vexed to reveal everything to his parents when he was unsure whether he and Laura would have a future together. Why, they would want to know, had he fallen in love with a sick woman who would likely complicate his promising career? And why get them worked up about his love if she never recovered? Dr. Battle seemed to have no cure for her except rest, various medicines to numb the pain, and occasional trips to more congenial climates, but it is doubtful whether her condition really improved, because she rarely complained and put on a brave face even when suffering. As a woman friend noted, "Laura's buoyant spirit and great courage make her impatient of her weakness and prompt her to conceal it as much as possible."[52]

That fall, Gifford finally wrote his parents about their love for each other and noted only that she was not "strong and well." But his parents, especially James, were upset because Gifford had told them in a letter rather than personally. James demanded more details about Laura and her family's social position and questioned his son's judgment and commitment to his career. While apologizing for causing his father "so much pain," Gifford affirmed that the Houghtelings were "the best and most refined people in Chicago" and emphasized Laura's "high character and refinement." "I have not known another woman so able and gentle," he added, "or with so fine a nature . . . or so universally beloved, or whose reputation for kindliness and helpfulness, and patient courage, was so high." He complained that his papa was treating him like "a sick child" or "a criminal fool."[53]

Nettie also spoke her mind. Delighted with her brother's love, she became the couple's fervent advocate. "It is rather hard luck that Miss Houghteling has health problems," she wrote her mother, "but there is nothing like happiness to cure—look at R.B. [Reed Bird, i.e., Nettie] himself!!" In other words, her union with Alan had greatly improved her health, so it could work for Laura too. "It's a blessing to see him so entirely recovered from the melancholy young person of last summer and I must say I feel as if Laura Houghteling had led us back to the old cheery Gifford . . . he deserves to be happy, doesn't he?" And she urged her mother, "Please, dear Mouse, don't let the Bird [Papa] get worried about Gifford. I know you will be angelic to him."[54]

As James's questions persisted, Gifford and Nettie commiserated on their father's negative reactions to their intendeds. "You poor little Spick," Nettie wrote him, "undergoing your first taste of the family displeasure! They always disapproved of me so the roaring didn't seem so unnatural! I am sure Laura is worth a thousand times the trouble, isn't she? . . . Alan sends his love, and says that he pities you, having been in the same hole so far as the Bird is concerned! . . . Hold the fort," she concluded. In reply, Gifford apparently made some "very funny" remarks to Nettie about their papa's intrusive behavior.[55]

When James learned more about the Houghteling family's social prominence and Gifford's assurance of delaying their engagement until her health improved, he backed off. Meanwhile, Gifford continued to send more realistic appraisals of her poor prospects to his friends but was much more optimistic with his parents. As winter approached, he would tell Ted Donnelley, for instance, that Laura "has not improved materially" but would report to his mother almost in the same breath that she "is better than I have seen her in a year."[56]

In December, she declined noticeably, and her parents moved her to Washington, D.C., where they hoped new doctors might bring some improvement to her condition. Gifford made regular trips from his New York forestry consulting office to see her in Washington, staying at Alan and Nettie's small rental house on Dupont Circle. On New Year's Eve, Mary visited Laura for the first time, and with great effort, Laura came downstairs to greet her. In a few days, however, she was completely bedridden, and soon after that, her doctors gave up hope. When Laura was told her fate, she was, her nurse Julia later told Gifford, "so calm and collected. And she told me she expected it. And then she said[,] 'Oh, Julia, how can I tell Gifford.' She knew you would not believe it, but it had to be. She had felt it for a long time."

Gifford intimated that if she did not make it, they would continue to commune together after she was gone. Whatever her fate, he now wrote his father, "It seems as though it must come out as we hope, and are not afraid because we know it can be nothing more than a temporary separation, short for her, however long it may be for me. She is so splendidly brave about it, so strong and unselfish, and we feel so strongly what I have just said, that it is all much less terrible than it must seem to you and indeed to anyone but ourselves." Laura Houghteling died a few days later, on February 8, 1894. Her body was immediately taken to Chicago for burial.[57]

Right after Laura's death, Nettie wrote their mother, "He is wonderfully calm and brave and takes his sorrow in the most beautiful way. . . . He seems to feel that the separation is only for a time which comforts him greatly and that they are to go on caring and longing for each other until the time comes to be reunited. . . . His faith and trust are beautiful, you can well feel he would be. Poor Mamie [McCadden] is wild with grief for him."[58]

*   *   *

James and Mary had sent Mamie to Washington to attend to Nettie, who was pregnant with her first child, but she also ended up looking after Gifford during his frequent stays at the Johnstone household. McCadden's sorrow soon extended to Nettie, whose baby girl, born seven weeks after Laura's death, died within ten hours after birth. Compounding the extended family's woes, fourteen months after John Eno's return to New York, his youngest daughter, Antoinette, died at age twelve from an abscess on her ear that spread to her brain. "It was a sad time made more so by the circumstances surrounding John," James commented.[59] It had been quite a year, and the first months of 1894 had been tragic. Grandfather Eno's advancing dementia made for further unhappiness.

The saving grace was that the immediate Pinchot family members were mostly in good health and would move on with their lives. Shortly after the Johnstones returned to London for his next assignment at the Foreign Office, Nettie got pregnant again; barely two months along, she fell down some stairs and began hemorrhaging internally. Certain she had suffered a miscarriage, Nettie was naturally "depressed" and braced for the painful aftereffects, but her doctor offered a steady, hopeful message—"we must give [the baby] a fair chance" to survive and grow. Nettie's condition soon improved, and in mid-May 1895, Nettie gave birth to a healthy boy whom the proud parents named Harcourt, a distinguished name among several of Alan's forebears.[60] Nettie, however, came up with another of her creative nicknames, "Crinks," after the many wrinkles on the newborn's face, and the name would stick with him in adult life. The Johnstones would have no more children.

Meanwhile, Gifford went into mourning over Laura and wore mostly black clothes for more than a year. He deeply felt, however, that he had not lost his love and that Laura's spirit lived on in him. He would soon write in his diary,

"My darling is with me, and I know it clearly." Several days later, he added, "She spoke to me again and filled and warmed me. She and God." Eight months after her death, he asserted that "we have been growing closer." "[H]ow thankful I am for her, and how splendid it is that what is between us is stronger than death or anything else." He continued to commune with "my Lady," and even after more than fifteen years, still felt her presence, writing, for example, "A good day. I dreamed of my Dearest last night."[61] Having his own spiritual love, Gifford Pinchot, it seemed, would be a confirmed bachelor and, with one exception, would not look at another woman for twenty years.

The exception would be Maria. Following her marriage to Bond Emerson, she continued corresponding with Gifford, even writing him on her honeymoon. She early found that marriage brought "a lot of new (and unpleasant) experiences," and after Laura's death, she arranged for him to come to lunch at her house in the suburbs when Bond was at work in the city so she could talk to him, among other things, about her husband's "peculiarities." Gifford apparently better met some of her emotional needs. He confided in Maria about his love affair with Laura, which brought them closer. "I think of her so much and of you and of all the good you are doing in the world," Maria wrote him.[62] The two remained special friends, and for the next half dozen years, Gifford continued to visit her alone on occasion when Bond was away. In later, more prurient times, it would be easy to believe they were having an affair, but that was improbable. For Gifford, the heart was allowed to love romantically and spiritually, but the mind, prescribing a Victorian ethos of sexual abstinence outside marriage, was still in control. Bond knew about Maria's and Gifford's continuing friendship, and the two's correspondence suggests no physical intimacy.

7.

Forestry Stirrings

During the mid-1890s, Gifford reduced his presence at Biltmore, but his forestry commitments rapidly expanded. One of his first endeavors was surveying the white pine in the Dodge woodlands in Pennsylvania. Because that species was the most commercially harvested timber, Gifford believed better knowledge of the tree would help the forester and lumberman develop sound policies for its widespread cutting. His assistant in this effort was Henry (Harry) Solon Graves. While a freshman during Gifford's senior year at Yale, the students had met as fellow deacons. Gifford had given Graves reading suggestions to nourish his interest in forestry, and Graves later wrote that his mentor's description of the expanding needs of forestry had "appealed to my imagination." After deciding on forestry, Graves soon became Gifford's assistant in his consulting business. The forester then arranged for him to study under Sir Dietrich Brandis in Germany for more than a year, and upon his return, the two completed a book together, *The White Pine* (1896). Graves was the second American forester, and Gifford liked to tell people that his younger colleague was better trained in the field than he was. Though unassuming, Graves was enthusiastic about his new profession, dependable, and intelligent, and he would become Gifford's closest associate on forestry matters for many years.[1]

Well organized, Gifford could be at Grey Towers, his New York consulting office, visiting Biltmore, or off in the Adirondacks at any time. All this rushing around worried James. Earlier, he had complained to his son about his "feverish haste" and "going at too rapid a pace." Seeing the same hyper-activity, young Amos chimed in, "it is harder for you than for most people to be lazy but I wish you would be sometimes."[2] All the familial advice had no effect, as Gifford took on more consulting jobs. He was making a decent living as consulting forester, earning perhaps $3,500 a year (about $70,000 today).

Gifford's growing forestry commitments made his foray into New York City's social problems and politics increasingly problematic, and soon he was too enmeshed in a new national forestry campaign to continue his involvement in them. The forestry issues also required extensive travel. Seeing his friend's enforced absences, Reynolds would write him a few years later, "I hope you will not let the bond of friendship and of experience, through which we have passed together, weaken even though we do not see much of one another during these days."[3]

Except for a job in New Jersey, Gifford's work had been entirely with private foresters, but the future of public forested lands nationally, a vastly bigger undertaking, was inexorably moving into the political limelight. All the nation's territories acquired since the founding of the American republic were initially public lands, and Congress had enacted a series of laws over time to allow for the sale and settlement of its billions of acres. The theory was basically democratic—to encourage farmers and other settlers to buy land at an affordable price and settle and live off their purchases—but unscrupulous speculators and mercenary interests had developed ingenious and sometimes blatantly fraudulent methods of evading the letter and force of the land laws. The result was extensive land grabs by private interests, and the few in the national government with authority on the issue who resisted the violators had little success. In 1889, Carl Schurz, a former interior secretary, had deplored "this wanton, barbarous, disgraceful vandalism," but the people seemed unmoved. "Deaf was Congress, and deaf the people seemed to be," he commented.[4]

But the small public opinion that Gifford Pinchot and other concerned citizens had aroused was not deaf, and a somewhat different civic mood was developing simultaneously. Since the 1870s, bills had been introduced into Congress, providing some kind of forest protection or a commission to develop a plan. In 1888, Bernhard Fernow, the government's chief forester, had drafted a bill, which the American Forestry Association arranged to have introduced in Congress, giving the president the power to create national forest reserves. In 1891, Congress rescinded some timber legislation and added an amendment authorizing the president to create forest reserves. This seemingly innocuous new provision was nonetheless, Gifford accurately commented later, "the most important piece of legislation in the history of Forestry in America. . . . This was the beginning and basis of our whole National Forest system." President Benjamin Harrison used his authority under the act to announce the first forest reservation, the Yellowstone Park Timberland Reserve of more than a million and a quarter acres. His action became "the seed from which the National Forests grew."[5]

While giving the federal government title to new reserves, the law prohibited lumbering, mining, or grazing and outlawed building roads on forestry land. It might please preservationists, but it was not an enviable model for many westerners, who saw the bountiful forests as their section's precious resource and were eager to exploit the reserves, even if regulated in some ways. Not surprisingly, they resented the precedent of withholding all legal access to national forests. The law also provided no provisions for forest administration or enforcement and penalties, so violations inevitably occurred. Over the next five years, attempts to close loopholes in the 1891 act failed to pass Congress.

When exploitation of public forest lands aroused popular opinion, it seemed to prefer outright prohibitions (as in the 1891 federal law) against harvesting trees or mining minerals. In New York, for example, a constitutional convention in 1894 passed an amendment to the state constitution prohibiting the state from selling any of the lands it owned in the Adirondacks or the cutting and selling of trees in them, and the people overwhelmingly approved the amendment in a referendum. Gifford's ideas on applying carefully developed plans for harvesting and reforestation of forested lands seemed to have little support.

It was into this fluid situation that Gifford Pinchot and others interested in the uses of the nation's prime forests intruded. The first mover in this early phase was Charles S. Sargent, head of the Arnold Arboretum at Harvard University, who, beginning in 1889, promoted three proposals in his *Garden and Forest* magazine: the temporary withdrawal of forest-bearing public lands from sale or production, the temporary assignment of the military to protect them, and the appointment of a commission to develop an administrative plan for forestry reserves. Gifford would come to believe the first two were too controversial or unworkable, but he and other advocates of forest management seized on the commission idea as a possible opening for developing a rational plan for the nation's forests.[6] The American Forestry Association endorsed it, as did Gifford, some newspapers, and Robert Underwood Johnson of *Century Magazine*.

In the summer of 1895, Gifford met with Sargent and Dr. Wolcott Gibbs, head of the National Academy of Sciences, the most distinguished group of American scientists, who pointed out that Congress had authorized the academy, when called upon by any department of the government, to investigate and report on any scientific subject. Sargent and Gifford agreed that an academy of scientists, including individuals with some forestry expertise, could develop an action program for the national forests, free from political interference.

Supported by Johnson and others, the plan was presented to Hoke Smith, Cleveland's secretary of the interior, who, in February 1896, asked the academy to establish the commission.

Accepting the call, Gibbs made appointments to the academy's national forest commission. None of the members was a politician, and the scientists who served on the working commission included: Sargent as chairman; General Henry L. Abbott, an army engineer; Gifford's old Yale professor, William Brewer; and another Yale graduate, geologist Arnold Hague. Only thirty, Gifford was half the average age of the other members, the only non-academy member, and the only forester on the commission, which elected him secretary. The commissioners served without pay, but Congress appropriated $25,000 for their expenses.[7]

Smith and President Cleveland emphasized early completion of the commission's work so Congress could act on its recommendations during the current session. Cleveland's presidential term would end in March 1897, but he still hoped for congressional approval of an action plan for national forests during his lame-duck months. Anticipating resistance in Congress, he counseled that the commission should first consider the more modest, less costly question of a forest service and then tackle the question of more forest reserves.[8]

As the commission began, Gifford wrote Dr. Brandis that he planned to "keep rather quiet" and "not attempt to direct the course to be pursued," but he was not quiet. To get started, Sargent asked Gifford and Hague to draw up an action plan for the commission. Gifford seized the opportunity, and the Hague-Pinchot plan called for the commissioners, accompanied by many assistants, to visit selected forested regions, assemble a wide range of data about the forests, and advance proposals for their management. In short, the commission should get ready for practical forestry. They argued that "such data were needed for the discussion of even the broadest lines of policy and . . . would be indispensable when the Commission is called up to justify its recommendations, and to answer the question of what a forest service will do when it is constituted, and how the reserves are to be used."[9]

Sargent was a cautious man, however, and he frittered away the opportunity. He was also autocratic and reluctant to take advice. He had his own ideas and opposed Cleveland's plan. He and his main ally on the commission, General Abbott, whom Gifford privately described as "pitiably ignorant of the whole subject," likewise objected to the Pinchot-Hague proposal for gathering data as too detailed. As the author of several illuminating books on American trees, Sargent was the preeminent American arborist of his generation. Nothing would move forward without his approval, and with such an august reputation, most commission members were reluctant to oppose him.[10]

Gifford, too, had great respect for Sargent—at first. However, respect did not necessarily mean agreement on forestry matters, and Gifford had reservations about the man. Earlier, Sargent's pessimistic views of government action in the forestry field had upset Gifford, and he was thus initially inclined to work with other forestry advocates such as Johnson of *Century Magazine* on a plan "to get Congress to do something." To stimulate readers' interest, Johnson asked several knowledgeable individuals to give their reactions to Sargent's outline for military administration of the nation's forest reserves. Gifford opposed the outline but, out of deference to Sargent, probably softened his criticism at the time.[11]

Gifford's involvement with Sargent on the commission soon greatly increased the young forester's displeasure. Sargent's deliberative approach bothered the young forester, but what particularly disturbed him was Sargent's lack of interest in forestry. The commission chairman wanted to preserve the forests but not put them to constructive use. As Gifford sarcastically put it later, "he couldn't see the forest for the trees—the individual, botanical trees." And after a commission session, the forester wrote, "Sargent opposed to all real forest work, and utterly without a plan, or capacity to decide on plans submitted. Meeting a distinct fizzle."[12]

When Sargent denied Gifford's request for another forester to accompany him on the fieldwork, Gifford, at his own expense, took Harry Graves with him. The two went out six weeks ahead of the other commissioners, spending half their time together in northern Montana, exploring the reserve there, then tramping into northeastern Idaho. They also found time for hunting and fishing. Gifford shot the only bear he ever killed and a Bighorn ram. (He cleaned the ram's head himself and had it shipped home for mounting.) The other commissioners joined them in July, and they spent almost four months visiting vast forested areas in six far western states and the Arizona and New Mexico territories.

The one distinctly pleasurable part of the trip for Gifford was his experiences with John Muir, a founder of the Sierra Club and the preeminent naturalist of that era. Muir was not a commissioner but, invited by Sargent to join their party, tagged along part of the way as an enthusiastic woodsman and preservationist. Always eager to ingratiate their son with luminaries in his field, James and Mary Pinchot had hosted Muir a few times at dinners at their Gramercy Park home. Appreciative of the gracious hospitality, Muir fondly recalled those "delightful evenings I shall never forget." Coming to the United States from his native Scotland as the young son of a poor family, Muir's background was very different from Gifford's, and his religious reverence for nature contrasted with Gifford's more scientific perspective. And Gifford, a joiner, saw the forestry commission as an opportunity to forge a progressive national forest policy, while Muir preferred his role as an independent outsider. But the two men had gotten off to a good start at the Pinchots' New York dinners, Muir telling Gifford, "you are choosing the right way into the woods. Happy man. Never will you regret a single day spent thus."

During their western adventure, Gifford, to his "delight," found Muir with the party, and the two men went fishing and traipsed off into what Muir called "God[']s woods." Their highlight together was sleeping in freezing weather on beds of cedar boughs next to a campfire they had prepared above the rim of the Grand Canyon, where the naturalist, a wonderful storyteller, entertained Gifford; they talked until midnight, all the while gazing up at the heavens above them. Muir soon regaled his new friend about "our own big day of sunshine and starshine along the verge of the tremendous and divine Colorado Can[y]on with heads level and hearts level and eyes upside down," and even many years later, Gifford could recall, "It was such an evening as I have never had before or since."[13]

Otherwise, Gifford continued grumbling about Sargent. The least of Gifford's worries was James, who implored his son to avoid independent explorations and, as secretary, stay with the party and exchange ideas with the other commissioners. They were "trained and able men," he wrote Gifford, "and will have much to say that will be of value to hear and consider." He complained again when Gifford ignored this advice. James had been a team player in business, the Statue of Liberty design and fundraising, and other public committees. Why, he was saying, could not his own son behave in a similar, responsible way?[14]

The boundaries had shifted, however. James had served on committees involved in limited artistic and cultural endeavors, but Gifford, much more of an activist, perceived the stakes—the entire future of national forest policy—as critically important. In any event, the outdoor experience confirmed what he already believed about Sargent. The Harvard professor was no woodsman, Gifford observed, and did not fish or hunt or know "anything about the mountains." The whole time, Sargent was collecting specimens that made the expedition's baggage more cumbersome, and he was once headed off trying to take thirty-six cans of condensed milk for a side trip. At the same time, Gifford claimed his own small group needed only six or seven. Later, Gifford found Sargent "still without any plan of work," and following a long talk with him about forest policy, he concluded, "Sargent utterly wrong on all points, as usual."[15]

Sargent was not optimistic about getting congressional action, but, prompted by Gifford and other members, he agreed to submit a preliminary report to the lame-duck president, which recommended that he proclaim, under the 1891 law, thirteen new forest reserves totaling twenty-one million acres in seven western states. Cleveland genuinely supported the desirability of the new reserves, but perhaps also surmising he had nothing to lose as a retiring president, he proclaimed ten days before the end of his term all thirteen reserves, which more than doubled the acreage of the national forests. In effect, his announcement violated his earlier advice of focusing on creating a forest service ahead of new reserves.

In recommending the reserves without any management plan, the commission had put the cart (reserves) before the horse (forest service). The commission had been at loggerheads on administering the new reserves. Some members objected to Sargent and Abbott's plan for appointing forest superintendents and temporarily using the military to protect the reserves, but the commission could not agree on Gifford's outline proposal for a forest service organization.

Problems with military supervision included the army's control over an obviously civilian matter and necessary additional education on forestry for military officers. Gifford also believed that the "temporary" policy, once started, would take on a life of its own and be difficult to reverse later. Moreover, successful forestry policy required local cooperation, but the frontiersmen entering the reserves would resist being subjected to military principles. Failing a civilian forest service, Gifford put forward a fallback position, calling for the commission to make a strong public statement that the newly announced reserves were not being taken out of circulation permanently and would permit some settlement and timber cutting under a regulated plan. That proposal likewise failed.

Without an administrative plan, Cleveland's grandiose announcement unleashed a firestorm in Congress. Many western members, in particular, attacked the new reserves as a sudden and complete withdrawal from entry or disposal, announced hastily without adequate examination and promulgated without any consultation of Congress. The result, a representative from Wyoming whined, was that "we of the West are to suffer as we have suffered from the actions of men who sit in their studies and formulate pretty theories based on the action of European nations in densely populated regions."[16] Only six days after Cleveland's proclamation, the Senate passed an amendment to an appropriations bill that rescinded Cleveland's order and returned all thirteen reserves to the public domain.

Gifford conceded that the complaints were valid. He noted, for example, that to his knowledge, the commissioners had made no effort to talk to local newspapers during their field trip. The result was that the announcement of the reserves surprised the affected regions, and the commissioners had not set foot in a few of the reserves included in Cleveland's proclamation. The congressional outburst forced the commission into damage control. Cleveland's secretary of the interior, together with the commissioners, lobbied hard though unsuccessfully with friends of conservation in Congress, and Cleveland then pocket vetoed the legislation.[17]

Two months into the incoming McKinley administration, the national forest commission issued its final report. In belatedly recognizing that the natural resources in the reserves should be open for public use under government regulation, the commission came a long way in trying to harmonize western interests with national forest conservation. The report also resurrected the provisions for temporary military control of the reserves and drafted five bills for military oversight until a forestry bureau could be created in the interior department.[18] Having to decide whether to endorse it or make a minority report, Gifford agreed to sign after some soul searching. If he refused, he reasoned, he would be alone in dissenting and would underscore disunity when, in the face of western attacks on it, an undivided commission was needed. He may also have perceived that a minority report would have no immediate effect since Congress had already decided to move forward after further wrangling on a forestry bill without military control.

The forest legislation, finally approved on June 4, 1897, authorized the U.S. Geological Survey to survey the new forest reserves; suspended all but two of them for nine months, at which time the lands not taken up would again become national forests; defined and limited the conditions for new forest reserves; and put the secretary of the interior in charge of the reserves and gave him authority to make rules and regulations for their administration. The secretary also received discretion to allow bona fide settlers, farmers, miners, and prospectors the free use of forest reserve grazing lands, timber, and minerals. The measure proved to be another key milestone in developing national forest policy.

From his experience with the national forest commission, Gifford learned a lot about the variegated topography, different water courses, various kinds of trees and their condition, and the destructive effects of forest fires; more importantly, it confirmed the widespread public ignorance and misunderstanding about the principles of scientific forest management as he understood them. The main benefit of the commission, Gifford believed, was that it had aroused opinion on government forestry policy. No longer would the nation's forests be neglected, and forestry matters could sometimes be on the front burner as a domestic issue.

At the same time, however, he concluded that the commission's report had virtually no impact on Congress. What stuck with him about the entire experience was his intense introduction to the political process. It was like taking a crash course in American civics—observing how the government actually worked and got things done and how political it was. The presidents were not a problem, but Congress was a challenge. He learned about the relevant congressional committees involved in drafting and approving forestry bills; the importance of transparency, including hearings on important forestry matters; the desirability of cultivating party power brokers, key committee chairmen, and congressmen from the affected areas; the difficulties in neutralizing the "sweetheart" relationships with mining, lumber, and other commercial companies; and the willingness to compromise when it became apparent that larger goals were politically impractical.[19]

Above all, the experience strengthened his belief in the importance of nourishing a wider public opinion to bring sustained and informed pressure on politicians to support constructive forestry. Even as the national forest commission was formed, Gifford had mostly, through his own efforts, won the endorsements of the New York business groups for Sargent's initial proposals; one of his main objections to Sargent on the commission was the professor's opposition to involvement in the legislative process. At the height of the congressional debate in the last days of the Cleveland administration, for example, Sargent wrote Gifford, "It is more dangerous to talk than to keep silence," and he decried Gifford's statement before the conference committee on the bill as "the worst thing that has happened yet."[20] Gifford thought speaking out might be counterproductive, but fighting for the correct principles was worth the risks. Henceforth, he understood that conservation advocates, their associations, and friendly commercial interests would have to step up their agitation for forestry legislation and try to win over other individuals and groups with concerns about the long-term fate of the nation's forests.

8.

Brotherly Love in Peace and War

Young Amos Pinchot was growing up fast. James and Mary enrolled their youngest as a ninth grader at the recently founded Westminster School, a small boys' boarding school on the banks of the Hudson River in Dobbs Ferry, New York, thirty miles from Manhattan. The headmaster was William Lee Cushing, a Yale graduate. Amos was never far away, and Mary liked having him home on some weekends, particularly because Gifford was rarely around, and Nettie, in her early twenties, was spreading her wings and going out on her own. When Amos was at their Gramercy Park home, she often took him to the theater or opera. He was growing to his full size, six feet tall and 160 pounds, the same as Gifford.[1]

Amos enjoyed Westminster. In letters home, he told his parents that he was having "a very jolly" and "bully time" and "have made friends with a good many fellows."[2] He had a corner room in his dormitory that afforded scenic views of the Hudson. One time, when Amos got sick, his concerned papa, acting out his health theories, complained that Amos's overheated room was the cause of his malady, but Cushing rejoined that Amos was not "fault-finding" and "gave no hint that he was uncomfortable."[3]

Amos knew he was subject to certain standards, such as receiving religious instruction and writing home regularly. Cushing believed, and Mary soon concurred, that "Tootsie's mental and moral status are very satisfactory." She believed that Amos "will get at Yale quite enough of Yale manners and work," and before that exposure, she hoped to get him some instruction in music, art, and languages. What she wanted was a well-rounded, refined, accomplished son. She was not really successful on the aesthetic side, however. Amos joined the glee club at Westminster and took violin lessons, but Mary regretted that "you had not been willing to learn to dance and I fear that one of these days you will wish you had paid more attention to your music." Amos vowed to take up the violin again, but nothing came of it. If he avoided dancing lessons, he nonetheless succeeded thereafter in enjoying himself on the dance floor.[4]

During Amos's four years at Westminster School, he excelled academically, regularly getting grades in the nineties (and once a perfect score in algebra), and he was ranked first in his class at one point. Mary, of course, was "delighted," but Amos took it in stride. "He is quite pleased that he finds himself at the head of the school," she wrote Gifford, but "he seems to think he does not quite see why he should be." Amos was well prepared for the Westminster curriculum, which included a heavy dose of foreign languages—Greek, Latin, French, and German—and may not have been overly demanding. Recalling Gifford's earlier arrangement of his younger brother's schooling in New Haven, Mary gave him some credit for Amos's scholastic success. "You will find your account in it I feel quite certain," she wrote Gifford.[5]

There is no doubt that Amos was a conscientious student, and the small classes were an added benefit, with Amos reporting that they made "our recitations very pleasant." Personal attention from Cushing and the other teachers also provided an intensive yet informal learning experience.[6]

Amos especially enjoyed athletic competition. Like Gifford, he was well coordinated and developed a keen interest in sports. In his free time, he often went sailing on the river, but by his senior year, he was enamored with playing on the winning school baseball team. The agreeable result was, "I am enjoying this term more than any other of this school year." As graduation approached, Amos reflected, "I have had such a good time here and I like the Cushings so much. Mr. C is the most ideal school teacher I ever saw."[7]

In the fall of 1893, Amos began his freshman year at Yale. He had an excellent academic record and passed the examinations without conditions, but the loyalty of other Yale relatives, especially Gifford, and a Yale alumnus like Cushing touting his candidacy, undoubtedly made his acceptance there a certainty. Gifford accompanied Amos to Yale, took him around to meet his former professors and President Dwight, and helped get him settled in his sunny room, which Amos labeled "delightful." Amos told his parents that Gifford's attention "was of the greatest advantage to me."[8]

Gifford remained interested in his younger brother's development, advising his parents on Amos's curriculum and urging them to send Amos to Europe during summers for direct immersion in foreign languages and cultures. When

Laura Houghteling died midway through Amos's freshman year, Amos wrote a sympathy note to his grieving brother. He had never met Laura and had been immune from family tragedy, but he wrote from the heart, saying, "I hope God will be with you and comfort you and I am deeply thankful that you are both good Christians."[9]

When Amos entered Yale, he was fairly devout. As a youngster, he said his prayers at bedtime, and until he went to Westminster, he regularly attended Bible classes—"as usual," Mama wrote in her diary. Gifford's minister friend, Jim Reynolds, still connected to Yale, told Gifford that he had heard that "your brother came out and made a strong Christian stand at the first prayer meeting of his [freshman] class."[10] But his religious faith was not deeply ingrained, and he would grow more nonobservant through college.

Amos's four years at Yale were unremarkable. At the outset, he assured his concerned papa that he had escaped the "harmless" hazing during freshman rush, and he and twelve other classmates formed an eating club. Academically, his seeming lack of interest in his studies may have been partly due to his choice of friends at Yale who were more interested in having a good time. He would early exude, for example, "I have gotten to know my crowd well, and it certainly is a smooth crowd with a few exceptions." No members of his eating club, for example, made high honors during college. One of them, Sumner Gerard, became Amos's roommate for their last three years of college and was Amos's best friend. A standout athlete, Gerard excelled on the Yale crew and track teams but was also a gay blade.

Amos may have improved somewhat academically in his last two years, making the lowest of the honors categories.[11] One professor who had some impact on him was William Graham Sumner, a conservative social Darwinist. He had published perhaps his most influential essay, "The Absurd Effort to Make the World Over," which ridiculed reform ideas that challenged the well-established ideology of classical laissez-faire economics. Controversial in his views, Professor Sumner was a commanding presence on campus. He was a popular, stimulating teacher, and students flocked to sign up for his classes. Amos may not have enrolled in one, but he absorbed the Sumnerian ethos of individual liberty, equal opportunity, and hostility to government-sponsored change. In his later conservative years, Amos sometimes mentioned Sumner as an enduring influence in his political thought.

James and Mary occasionally ventured to Yale for football games, which Amos reveled in, and they showed up for the sophomore dance weekend. Moreover, his Uncle Will (William P. Eno) and Aunt Alice, who lived in

Saugatuck, Connecticut, and Uncle Henry (Henry C. Eno) and Aunt Antoinette (Eno Wood) from Simsbury sometimes came to New Haven and took Amos out to dinner and attended a play or college event, and Amos also visited his relatives.

In his first college years, Amos served as treasurer of his class crew club and played as a lower-ranking member of the tennis team. Amos had taken up tennis before college, and at Yale, he concentrated on the sport, competing in local tournaments and becoming an accomplished player, usually beating, among others, his older brother.

Amos wrote home regularly that everything at college was "first rate," "very jolly," "very pleasant," "gay," and "no end of fun." He also attended many dances, and his class elected him to the senior prom committee. Indeed, in a poll of classmates, he was a runner-up among those shining "most brilliantly in the social realm." He also joined a fraternity and, like his brother, was tapped by Skull and Bones at the end of his junior year. Impressed by the secret society's initiation festivities—"except for my song which was rotten"—he looked forward to bonding with his bones classmates, who included Gerard. After pleasant visits from two of them in Bar Harbor that summer, he exclaimed to Gifford, "What a year we ought to have!"[12]

During his senior year, Amos and his friends lived in a suite of spacious rooms just off campus. Otherwise, his senior year seemed not much different from his earlier ones. The one area in college where he showed some talent was as a writer. Gifford encouraged him to write for the *Yale Literary Magazine*, but Amos had only one piece accepted there. It was an impressionistic essay depicting a man on horseback amid the lush scenery taking in a beautiful sunrise near Pisgah Mountain.[13] He also competed for the Townsend Prize in his senior year. Gifford read two drafts of Amos's Townsend essay, and on a visit to New Haven, the brothers stayed up until 2 a.m. going over the final version. "Very good, I think," he concluded of Amos's submission, but it did not win the prize.[14]

For the class yearbook, Amos wrote a humorous essay on the more frivolous adventures of his class during their junior year. Amos's piece included witty vignettes about the class members' involvement in many extracurricular activities, such as the senior prom, which, Amos claimed, "knocked the whole progression of Prom. improvements 'galley west,' as regards girls, other improvements and general excellence." He also referred to some dissipation—drinking a Toby (cocktail) at Moriarty's (later Mory's) bar near campus and pipe smoking.[15] Amos did not smoke but was exposed to drinking and, unlike his abstemious brother, would enjoy imbibing alcoholic beverages.

As long as Amos behaved, wrote home regularly about his adventures, and persevered in college, his parents seemed to tolerate his innocent pleasures. He even managed to wheedle money out of his papa to pay for his college ventures. The contrast with Mary's and James's rigorous oversight of Gifford is striking. They had been so heavily invested in Gifford's upbringing and career that they would have had to have been extraordinarily disciplined to impose the same demands on Amos. They did not require much of their younger son, however, and they were also considerably older. And Gifford was a surrogate mentor.

Mary also viewed her youngest child as a social companion. An unwritten rule among families in high culture in Victorian America was that parents and their children had obligations of "duty" and "responsibility" to each other. If parents provide their children with a good life and exposure to highbrow culture, it was assumed that their youngsters would later look after their parents' welfare in their older years. Almost by default, Amos became his mother's escort during her travels. She continued yearning to travel and meet new, interesting people but could not venture out alone. After the Johnstones' 1895 move to Alan's new post as first secretary at the legation in Copenhagen, Nettie was no longer around as a sometime companion. And Mary's reclusive husband was increasingly averse to extensive travel and could not keep up with her wanderlust. He had found The Players, a men's social club only a few doors away from the Pinchots' Gramercy Park house, which became a comfortable refuge where he could retreat and spend long hours reading and writing letters in peace. Mary continued cajoling James to accompany her on her trips to Bar Harbor and abroad. Sometimes her pleas were good-natured, but she could also be blunt, writing him, "I am not going to live so isolated a life any more. I want companionship and I am going to stay more where I can get it."[16]

Amos was a welcome substitute. He enjoyed traipsing around Europe during summers with his mother, telling Gifford while still at Westminster he would have liked to have spent another month there. In the summer of 1895, he joined Mamee at the Johnstones' London residence and the estate of Alan's parents in Yorkshire. Mother and son then visited France and enjoyed Paris, Versailles, and even Dinard, where the Pinchot family had spent a happy summer before Amos was born. "Toots loves the gayety of it," Mary enthused about their journey, "and so do I."[17]

*   *   *

The events of 1897–1898 would again unite the two brothers. The first stimulus was new forestry development. Because the June 1897 law suspended the eleven newly created forest reserves for nine months, Cornelius N. Bliss, McKinley's interior secretary, anticipating further congressional action, decided to gather more information about the reserves—their needs and relationships to lumbering, agriculture, mining, grazing, and settlement—and he asked Gifford to serve as a special agent of the interior's land office. Gifford objected since many special agents had been political hacks who ended up serving special commercial entities. However, agreeing to the job as "confidential forest agent," he spelled out the terms of his employment, which allowed him to make recommendations concerning a forest service to manage the new reserves.[18]

When Gifford started west in July, Amos accompanied him, much to Gifford's pleasure. Freshly graduated from Yale, Amos wanted to test his outdoor skills. An advantage to Gifford's per diem service was that he was paid only for the time he worked, so he could spend other days hunting and fishing with Amos. Joining them were a guide and a cook, and, for parts of the trip, Henry L. Stimson and his wife. When Gifford got to know Stimson, he was already a lawyer in Elihu Root's law firm in Manhattan. Both lawyers would be rising stars in the Republican Party, but, at this time, Stimson was providing legal advice to the forest commission and shared Gifford's enthusiasm for hunting. The Pinchots and Stimsons started their trip at the St. Mary's lakes in Montana, then moved on to Priest National Forest Preserve in Idaho and the rugged peaks of the Cascade Range in Washington State. Sometimes Gifford would go off with a small party to explore the forest reserves and then rejoin the others.

Amos's trip was his first to the great American West, and he marveled at the "wonderfully beautiful country," with "magnificent mountains rising on every side, some of them, in fact most of them, snow capped." Indeed, he commented, "everything is very new and different from the East and I have enjoyed it all exceedingly." Heading out from Spokane, they were ready for hunting. "If I have fairly good luck," Amos believed, "I should get a Rocky Mt. sheep and, also a goat, if I learn to shoot decently with my 30-40 Winchester which I have not become used to yet."[19]

Each brother killed billy goats—Amos wrote that Gifford's was "as big as a good large Shetland [pony], to our delighted eyes"—and, along the way, a deer, rattlesnakes, and grouse. Gifford then went off to forests in Washington State while his younger brother, hunting with Stimson in the Rockies, bagged a young bull elk and two rams. In early September, Gifford arrived in Seattle and was "[m]uch delighted" to see John Muir again.[20] Then Amos and Gifford returned to the St. Mary's area, where they again indulged in profitable hunting and fishing. In October, Amos returned to New York, while Gifford visited more forest reserves in Montana and South Dakota. At the end of his western foray with Amos, Gifford proudly commented that it had been a "really long adventure trip."[21]

*   *   *

Meanwhile, Gifford's decision to serve as a consulting forest agent had set off Sargent. He considered Pinchot a traitor for accepting the position, which, he assumed, the young forester would use to advance his own forestry ideas at the expense of the commission's unanimous report. It was not an unreasonable assumption since Gifford could include in his survey an endorsement of his own management plan by professionally trained foresters instead of the commission's endorsement of military administration. Sargent was particularly upset that Gifford had not consulted his fellow commissioners and "has gone over to the politicians." Sargent expressed his views to Dietrich Brandis in Germany, and the professor wrote Gifford that if Sargent's letter were true, Gifford's behavior would retard American forestry by twenty years and, he concluded, "The appearances . . . are against you."[22]

Gifford, at first, showed some restraint. When the commission disagreed over forestry policy, for example, he wrote Brandis for his advice on creating a forest service, and his mentor sent him a twenty-page reply. Gifford thought he was promoting his German mentor's emphasis on the gradual development of a civilian service based on a practical and theoretical education in forestry that would instill a healthy esprit de corps among its members. Gifford held back until he discussed the situation with his father and his supporters on the commission. Already nervous about Gifford's criticisms of Sargent, a deeply pained papa had a long talk with his son. Apparently, Gifford persuaded him that he was promoting the best forestry principles and that the problem was Sargent's ignorance and inflexibility. At any rate, James soon wrote him apologetically, "I may have said and done things that seemed querulous and petty. . . . If I should ever hurt you, you know that I am at the same time more hurt myself. You know you have my love and approbation. Always, even if sometimes shown in a queer way."[23] It was a difficult admission for James, a proud man, but it was the kind of manly act he had often preached to his oldest son.

William Brewer and Arnold Hague wanted Gifford to move deliberately, with Hague bluntly advising him, "Cool down." But Gifford, already warmed up, went ahead anyway and explained his position to Sargent. His service as a government consultant, he wrote, had the full approval in writing from a majority of commission's members, "and in their view it has been in direct accord with the main features of policy recommended in the Commission's report." He hoped, therefore, that "the present misunderstanding may not continue." But Sargent, having had enough of the young forester, replied sharply, "Different persons have different standards which govern their conduct and yours and mine are evidently so unlike that it is useless to discuss the subject" further.[24] The split was regrettable, but the entire episode provided a foretaste of Gifford's forthright approach to important policy questions. Thereafter, although he might be open to discussion, what he said and wrote is what he meant, and there would be little, if any, trimming.

Gifford's report as a consultant boldly reaffirmed his beliefs in the necessity of a flexible national forest policy. He emphasized the immediate need for a professionally trained forest service, which would manage the forest resources and protect them against fires, with the flexibility to exclude lands more valuable for agriculture and regulate areas suitable for grazing. Throughout the expedition, Gifford, expressing his maturing thoughts on public opinion, prioritized talking to local ranchers, lumbermen, and miners to mollify resentments at the nascent national forest policy. He also gave interviews to newspapers in cities and towns to try to win support for the government's new national forests. From these discussions, he wrote in his report that an informed public opinion would support the creation of the national forests. He thought his public relations efforts had softened the opposition, but he urged greater publicity to inform interested but mostly ignorant constituent users of the national forests.

The June 1897 law granted broad powers over the national forests to the interior secretary, but there were still no trained foresters to administer the reserves. Gifford's report did not recommend any federal department to manage the forest service and the forests. The interior department already had authority over them, but Gifford, already disillusioned with the department, was likely unwilling to give it his further endorsement. Gifford found that Secretary Bliss, longtime chairman of the Republican National Committee, perceived his department as a jobs reservoir for party loyalists and, to Gifford's mind, was giving the interior's land office commissioner a free hand in increasing the number of special agents to manage the new forest service. To Gifford, some of the commissioner's appointments had been "abominable," and he feared "a wholly political service and the complete failure . . . at decent management." Gifford surmised that his only recourse was an appeal to President William McKinley.[25] When the national forest commission had met with him eight months earlier, Gifford then recorded that the new president was "strong for the reserves. He impressed me very favorably."[26]

Believing the danger of "going wrong" on forest matters was "real and immediate," Gifford hatched a scheme in personal politics. It turned out that Gifford's initiative to get McKinley's attention was too complicated, and nothing further happened. Hague and others soon persuaded Gifford to "let matters simmer a while."[27] For one thing, Gifford learned that western members in Congress would strenuously fight against a forest service filled with Republican appointees. For another, by early 1898, the administration was too deeply absorbed in the contentious issues with Spain over a surging rebellion in Cuba, its colony, to give attention to forestry issues. Gifford turned in his agent's report to Bliss on January 26, 1898, just as the diplomatic tensions with Spain hurtled out of control.[28]

* * *

In these first months of 1898, transforming decisions by each brother would before long put them in direct contact again. The first was Gifford's decision to accept a government position in Washington, D.C. He had his eyes on leading the agriculture's forestry division, telling his friend Jim Reynolds in 1894 that he viewed his private forestry jobs as "training for Head Forester of the United States."[29] The obstacle there was his old nemesis, Bernhard Fernow, who vacated the position in early 1898 to accept an appointment as head of a new forestry school at Cornell University.

Fernow's departure prompted James Wilson, secretary of agriculture, to ask Gifford to assume the position of chief of the forestry division. Gifford refused the offer, which seemed to contradict his earlier coveting of the position. He may have perceived the division of only eleven employees as too small and devoted to churning out research studies as a position without much future promise. Still working for Dr. Webb in the Adirondacks and with another job in the South, he felt no pressure to accept the offer.[30]

Secretary Wilson was persistent, however, and promised Gifford carte blanche regarding appointments and the direction he wished to take the division. He even promised to hold the position for him for three years. "Couldn't have said more," Gifford admitted, but he hesitated. He consulted his professorial allies, Arnold Hague and William Brewer, and others he respected on forestry matters, and they all urged him to accept Wilson's offer. Harry Graves told Gifford that if he took the job, he would serve as his assistant.[31]

Finally, Gifford accepted the position. It was a path-breaking opportunity, and he would make the most of it. He would serve in that position for eleven years, and his main accomplishments as a forester would be during this tenure.

Because it was a civil service position, an examination was required to test his professional competence for the job. But when nobody could be found to devise the test questions, Secretary Wilson asked Gifford to write out his own. Ultimately, the secretary appealed successfully to President McKinley to exempt Gifford from the examination and avoid an obvious absurdity. By late May 1898, Gifford began his new job, ensconced in a small attic office of an old red brick building housing the agriculture department, and Wilson changed his title from division chief to chief forester. His salary for several years was a modest $3,500. Harry Graves soon joined him as an assistant.[32]

Simultaneously, Amos made a fateful decision that would result in a new direction in his life. The transforming event was the explosion and destruction of the U.S. battleship *Maine* in Havana harbor on February 15, 1898, causing the death of some 266 American sailors. A rebellion in Cuba against Spanish control over the island was raging at the time, and Spain's cruel and repressive policies had inflamed the American public, which increasingly demanded U.S. military intervention to end Spanish injustices on the island and bring about Cuban independence. The cause of the *Maine*'s destruction was almost certainly an internal explosion rather than an external Spanish mine. Still, American opinion, fanned by a jingoist press, would countenance no further delay in intervening militarily against Spain on the island. A naval investigation's conclusion without explanation that the explosion was external confirmed Americans' widespread belief that the horrific event was a dastardly Spanish deed. Thereafter the United States moved rapidly toward war with Spain.

Given Americans' long-term interest in Cuba, close to American shores, and the intensification of Spain's savage military repression on the island, the prospect of war with Spain was already rising, and that tragic incident made it inevitable. But a surging bellicose nationalism was also at work. Earlier in the decade, the United States fomented or aggravated a series of incidents with foreign nations, and the one with Spain finally brought on military conflict.[33] To some extent, it was a case of the United States, a rising economic powerhouse, flexing its muscles and incautiously asserting its will in its foreign relations even at the risk of possible war. Perhaps, too, a deeper emotional crisis in American society, resulting from the deepening depression of the mid-1890s, rising labor-business confrontations during the nation's rapid industrialization, and the challenge of the Populist revolt made an already uneasy public more accepting of vitriolic rhetoric expressed by combative politicians and the yellow press.[34]

The Pinchot and Johnstone families had already experienced the effects of Americans' surging bellicosity over a boundary dispute between Venezuela and

British Guinea, and war between the United States and Britain in 1896 had become a distinct possibility, with Alan, a British diplomat, and Nettie, his American wife, caught in between. Fortunately for Anglo-American relations, cooler heads prevailed, and the boundary dispute was arbitrated without hostilities.[35]

As the United States hurtled toward war with Spain in early 1898, Amos, now twenty-four, could have stayed comfortably at home, but within two weeks of the *Maine* disaster, he signed up as a private in Troop "A," a New York cavalry squadron in the U.S. Army. The cavalry appealed to him because he loved horseback riding. As an adolescent at Grey Towers, he had sometimes spent an entire morning or afternoon riding, and Nettie had even remarked that Amos, learning polo, "hits the ball every time." And when Amos had visited Gifford at the Biltmore, the latter had noted, "We are in the saddle a good deal, and he enjoys that immensely."[36]

After graduating from Yale in June 1897, Amos was accepted as a law student at Columbia University. However, he was bored with his law studies, telling Gifford, "It is uninteresting as the deuce but it seemed to be the only thing there was."[37] Given that attitude, it was not difficult to conclude that an army stint might be a diverting experience. He was also likely caught up in the surge of patriotic fervor in the early months of 1898, with the *Maine* tragedy as the catalyst for abruptly dropping his studies and enlisting.

Still, Amos was no super-patriot and was probably as much influenced by peer pressure. As examples, a good family friend, Munro Ferguson, and Sumner Gerard both enlisted in the Rough Riders, another cavalry unit from New York City led by Lieutenant Colonel Theodore Roosevelt. Many graduates from the oldest eastern colleges and several others of Amos's classmates, as well as the sons of many other recognizable family names in the city, volunteered for military service at about the same time. Early in his training, Private Pinchot noted that, of the eighty (including himself) from his squadron to be sent to Camp Black in Hempstead, Long Island, fifteen to twenty were Yale men, and "the rest were a first rate crowd."[38] A sense of adventure and patriotism combined with feelings of humanitarian duty as leading scions in society—*noblesse oblige*—to help liberate the Cubans from their Spanish oppressors prompted many of them to enlist. When Nettie learned that Amos had volunteered, she interpreted it as part of a broader patriotic surge involving members of their social class. "It's very fine to see how every one longs to fight," she wrote her mother. "No one can again say that the New York club men are useless."[39]

Amos seemingly never consulted with any family members about his enlistment. As James had already demonstrated during the American Civil War, his code of personal and social responsibility did not extend to military service obligations in wartime. Amos made his decision, however, and the family had to make the best of it. Volunteers in the cavalry were then allowed to provide their own horses. Although his papa (and Gifford, too, when he was in New York) went with him to nearby stables looking for one, Amos never found a suitable steed and took his chances with the army issue. From Camp Black, Private Pinchot sent postcards and letters home, assuring his worried parents that the camp was "comfortable" and the food "good." Indeed, he concluded that "The whole thing is lots of fun so far and I think it will be pleasanter still as we get used to the regular hours and discipline."[40]

Meanwhile, if Gifford had any thoughts of enlisting, his mother's "depressed, nervous state" over the prospect of Amos going into battle made him worry about her welfare first. As Laura Houghteling's mother wrote Gifford, "Of course I agree with you that the first duty is to her, letting Amos do the patriotic part." Mary's distress was more acute because she felt powerless to help her youngest. "I don[']t seem to have any 'pull' any where now a days," she lamented.[41]

In early June, Amos's troop was transferred to Camp Alger in Falls Church, Virginia, just outside Washington, D.C. He found that the mount he was assigned there was the "most obstinate horse I ever saw." He had distemper, Amos complained, and had "already fallen with me twice—once down a six foot bank into a dug road and once into a muddy ditch of about the same depth. . . . I lost my glasses and it took me three quarters of an hour to find my dispatches and get myself ready to start on. . . . The men have named him the 'Mole' as he keep[s] his eyes shut in the day time in a grouchy manner." Gifford looked again unsuccessfully for another horse for Amos. There was indeed a shortage of good ones, which the officers needed.

Gifford visited Amos several times at Camp Alger, bringing him bottled water and other provisions, for which his grateful brother thanked him: "I don't know what we should have done in our tent but for your help."[42] Gifford found that his interest in helping Amos outweighed initial concerns about his mother's welfare and his new job. Amos's experience would eventually propel Gifford willy-nilly into much deeper involvement with his brother's activities.

In late July, Amos's troop received orders to deploy to Puerto Rico. The U.S. Navy had already won a smashing victory over the Spanish fleet in Manila Bay, Philippines, and Americans had triumphed on land and sea at Santiago, Cuba. Hearing the news of the Santiago victories, Mary exulted, "I feel like singing a te Deum[,] indeed I am 'singing in my heart with joy unto the Lord.' Isn't it wonderful and blessed?" The conflict was almost over, but it was alarming to the family that Amos might be involved in subduing the Spanish forces in Puerto Rico. Gifford traveled to Newport News, Virginia, to see his brother off. And as her son disembarked at Ponce, Puerto Rico, Mary exclaimed, "Heaven protect them! And bring them all home in safety."[43]

The main role of Troop "A" in Puerto Rico was occupation. On August 10, Amos left Ponce with a detail of sixteen men as an escort to a supply cavalcade on a march northward through mountainous terrain to Utuado, where they would join another army unit. Bogus stories of recent ambushes by Spanish troops and inflated worries of impending attacks unnerved the cavalrymen. Amos became a victim of this jittery environment. Assigned nighttime guard duty upon reaching Utuado, he heard a rumble about midnight that shook the nearby building and sounded like distant artillery. Rushing to his commanding officer, he reported that the Spaniards were firing in the hills. The officer awakened his forces and summoned them to arms, but they soon learned that the rumble was an earthquake.

Two days later, Amos participated in a three-day march to the town of Ciales under a flag of truce to inform the Spaniards of a recently negotiated armistice between the U.S. and Spanish authorities ending the fighting. Entering the town, they met Spanish soldiers who had not yet received official notice of the armistice. With guns cocked on both sides, a standoff ensued until, fortunately for the men's safety, the Spanish officer in charge received the armistice protocol from his superiors. As the Americans withdrew, they discovered that they had been surrounded by Spanish forces concealed on both sides of the road and would have been massacred if shooting had started. This episode was the closest Amos came to military action, and Troop "A" saw no real combat and suffered no military casualties in Puerto Rico.[44]

In his first days in Puerto Rico, Papa sent him a telegram to come home, but Amos would wait until the entire troop was sent back. His father persisted, however, and somehow managed to persuade the war department in Washington to have Amos discharged. In James's view, his son had served honorably, and his services were no longer needed once an armistice was signed. The discharge order reached Amos in Utuado on August 18, six days after the armistice. It was an unusual action and must have embarrassed Amos, as later that day, the troop, leaving the mustered-out Amos alone to look after a fellow sick cavalryman, began a long march to the West Coast. But if Amos was resentful at his father's interference, there is no evidence of it.

*   *   *

Besides the perils of combat, James wanted his boy home, safely removed from possible sickness and disease. There were indeed real health concerns. The main danger was the "fever"—yellow, typhoid, or malaria—and, sure enough, the Pinchots would soon learn that, right after his discharge, Amos fell terribly sick in Utuado. At Camp Alger, Gifford had confirmed Amos's good health, and Nettie had commented that "the danger from fever is very small if one had always led a very temperate life, as our boy has."[45] But Amos was not a perfect physical specimen, as he suffered from neuralgia, or severe nerve pain, and on their western trip a year earlier, Gifford had noted that his brother was "much troubled" by it. Perhaps Amos's neuralgia was congenital and similar to Nettie's more serious nervous condition.[46]

Amos's neuralgia had probably weakened his immune system, the hard army training further wore him down, and finally, the tiring work and exposure to the torrid summer heat and tropical rains in Puerto Rico brought on Amos's fever. On the Ciales expedition, Amos and his companions were in the saddle for nearly twelve hours with only occasional dismounts. He may also have been a victim of horrid, unsanitary conditions. Upon first reaching Utuado, his troop and another army unit, because of rumors of a Spanish night attack, had been crammed together for a few nights in an old guard house, which one of his Troop "A" cohorts described as a "filthy, venomous" place. In fact, the entire guard house floor, where they tried to sleep, was "alive with big, shiny, brown cockroaches fully three inches long," while the stable yard behind "was a foot deep in a vile smelling compound of mud, manure and stagnant water, the odor of which pervaded the whole region, and must have reeked with germs of all the diseases that flesh is heir to."[47]

Dr. Criel, a physician, attended to the ailing Amos at Utuado and sent him to Ponce for treatment. Gifford, meanwhile, was in Boston when he learned of Amos's fever. He soon found that the U.S.S. *Relief*, an army hospital ship, was leaving New York for the island, and he told his parents that the ship would bring Amos home. It was good luck for the Pinchots, but even more fortunately, Gifford secured passage aboard. Taking leave from his job and agreeing to travel to Puerto Rico, Gifford told his parents, "I will do whatever is best when I get to Ponce," and a grateful Papa replied, "God bless you my dear boy for your kindness and courage." Gifford then met a doctor on board, a Yale graduate and fellow bonesman, who would help, as needed.[48]

The parents' anxiety level further receded when they received a cable from an agent of James's bank in Ponce, saying that Amos had a temperature of 100° and was receiving the best care in Margaret Chanler's private hospital there. Soon another one, from Chanler herself, explained that she had been with Amos, who was resting comfortably with the same temperature. The Pinchots were acquainted with Margaret Livingston Chanler, three years older than Amos and from a prominent and public-spirited New York family. Two of her brothers had enlisted to fight against Spain, and though not a trained nurse, she went to the island to set up a private hospital for the sick and wounded in the war. Her discovery of Amos was another piece of good fortune, and Mary could only "thank God!" for this hopeful news.[49] James cabled money to his banking agent in Ponce and Miss Chanler's hospital for Amos's care.[50]

Gifford located Amos convalescing in her hospital. His brother, he noted, was "out of danger" and "doing splendidly after a very close shave," but "Could speak only very slowly." Gifford brought him back safely on the *Relief* to Philadelphia, where the Pinchots arranged for him to be picked up and brought to a hospital in the city. Amos was still weak, and his improvement would be slow. After two weeks in the hospital, James and Mary moved him to Grey Towers, and later that fall, he could ride a horse and go shooting with his brother. Mamie McCadden thought, "he look[s] splendid and seems as Happy as can be," but he was still unwell, and his recovery would never be complete.[51]

Amos suffered from malaria. The first cable from his banking agent, James wrote Gifford, "almost assured us that he had a single malarial fever," and his malaria was soon confirmed.[52] Malaria was no stranger to New York. Mosquitoborne, it is generally perceived as a tropical disease, but it also afflicted areas of the northern United States during the Civil War and years afterward.[53] It was a serious illness and without a ready treatment. Anyone contracting the disease would have the parasite in the bloodstream for life and, even after seeming to recover, could be susceptible periodically to low-grade fevers and headaches. It could be completely debilitating, even life-threatening. There was no magic cure for malaria (even today, there is none).

For treatment, Amos consulted at least four doctors at various times, and they likely prescribed some antimalarial drugs, especially quinine, which interferes with the parasite's ingestion of hemoglobin and can mitigate the illness. To be effective, the patient needs to consume large quantities of quinine, which has downsides—its bitter taste and unpleasant side effects, including headaches and nightmares, both of which Amos experienced. One wonders whether his intake of quinine was sufficient to make a real difference or whether he might have sloughed off on his medicines when he encountered discouraging side effects. His neuralgia likely persisted, too, and in combination with malaria, it would make treatment more challenging.

Ward scene on the Army hospital ship
USS *Relief*, on which Gifford Pinchot
traveled to Puerto Rico during the
Spanish War and brought safely home
his sick brother, Amos, a private in an
army cavalry unit. A Swedish surgeon
commented that this new ship was "a real
hospital . . . a model for all the world."
(Naval History and Heritage Command)

Amos knew his prognosis was unfavorable and uncertain. He was not well enough to return to law school and suffered the deleterious effects of persisting malaria more acutely by the end of 1898. He soon wrote Gifford, "I'm certainly not improving now and I'm not likely to." His doctor told him, "I've still got some of the malaria or relics of the fever. . . . Every afternoon my grouch comes on at about three or four and everything seems absolutely out of tune and a good deal like a bad dream . . . ; it makes me, as you know, a rather rotten person to have around at such times." In the longer term, he realized, he should be choosing a profession and getting on with his life. And for that to occur, he concluded, "it seems pretty plain that I ought to get into condition just as quick as I can." What to do? He consulted with Henry Stimson, his doctors, the minister of the Episcopal church the Pinchots sometimes attended, and others, and he decided that the one attractive remedy was the West. Perhaps going there for a while would significantly improve his condition.[54]

Amos headed south by train to the Biltmore, where he camped for a few days, and then southwestern New Mexico. The wildness and remoteness of the American West attracted him, but the actual location was less important than the prospect of good hunting. He lived in a tent in the desert but also in hotels in nearby towns. Amos, then joined by a New York friend and an experienced guide, felt well enough to set off on a three-week hunting trip in the mountains and into the canyons of the Sierra Madre in Mexico, where he hoped to find that "the bear or the mountain lion are 'rising'." On one stretch, they tramped "very hard" for three full days and covered about 250 miles. Physically, at least, he was coping. Amos's choice of season and place was unfortunate, however, as the bears were still in hibernation mode and the one mountain lion he saw eluded him. Moreover, there was closed season on antelope, deer, wild turkey, and quail.

Despite the unsuccessful hunting, Amos believed "the trip did me good." He satisfied himself with duck shooting and another two-week hunting venture, netting no wild game. His main acquisition on his western foray was "the dirtiest[,] ugliest, most weather beaten, war scarred, mongrel bull dog I ever saw." Some Mexicans had so terribly treated the animal at a ranch that he almost died, so Amos, also finding him "the mildest[,] sweetest[,] most affectionate" dog, rescued him and brought him back as a gift to Gifford. His name was Patch, Gifford explained amiably, "because he came from the Apache country, because of his mixed ancestry, and because he has one over his eye." Gifford nonetheless seemed relieved to give him up to the wife of Grant La Farge, the architect the Pinchots had recently hired to design a new house for Gifford in the capital city.[55]

9.

Family Matters

The death of Amos R. Eno, Mary's father, was a transformative event in 1898. Struggling with dementia, Amos spent most of his last years at his homestead in Simsbury. In January, he went into a steep decline and died at his New York home a month later. At the end, Mary wrote, "He went to his repose as sweetly[,] gently as a baby falls to sleep." He was eighty-seven.[1]

The settlement of Amos's estate was a challenge, as his many illiquid land and building assets would require appraisal and procedures for their distribution. He left five children, including Mary, as immediate surviving heirs, and only John, because he had precipitated the Second National Bank scandal, would inherit little, if anything. Amo, the oldest, had resigned from the U.S. Army after the Civil War and amassed a fortune as a real estate investor. He was the executor of his father's estate and, with the family lawyers, oversaw the writing of Amos's will during the mid-1890s.[2]

Wayward John remained a problem. After his return from Canada, he had no regular job and was, young Amos Pinchot thought, "exceedingly hard up." John had asked more than once for an allowance and presumably some inheritance but was rebuffed. Shortly before their father's death, the siblings (except Amo) agreed to contribute to the establishment of generous trust funds of $500,000 each (about $17 million today) out of their estate shares for John's two children, Florence and Mary, with payments deferred until they reached the age of twenty-five. A grateful John was "as agreeable and conciliatory as possible," James told Gifford. "He has evidently changed front completely."[3]

Amo's curious personality further complicated the relationships. He was an honorable man, and an initiative shortly before his father's death exemplified his moral probity. His action involved the creditors of his bankrupt partnership at the onset of the Civil War. Even though the firm's liquidation legally released the partners from any further financial obligations, Amo decided, thirty-six years later, to hunt up the creditors and pay his share of those debts plus four percent annual interest. A newspaper story of his altruism related that all the creditors were astonished at Amo's determination to find them or their heirs. Amos F. Eno's generosity—the interest was more than the principal owed—likely cost him more than $500,000. His beneficence was in stark contrast to his thieving younger brother.[4]

But Amo was also highly opinionated and could be overbearing. His refusal to contribute to the trust agreement for John's children and his penchant for suggesting changes in the will, most of which served to benefit Amos's childless heirs at the expense of the Pinchots', increased family friction.[5] James was all for family, but most of all for his immediate family, and he and Mary had resisted the changes mostly unsuccessfully. Caught up in this internecine undercurrent, a frustrated Amo gave up his role as executor a month before his father's demise. A committee of family members, including James, served in that capacity.

Following probate, each of Amos R. Eno's five children received one million dollars ($34 million). Payments of $350,000 to the four grandchildren (three of whom were the Pinchot siblings) would follow in due course.[6] After all smaller amounts had been paid out to other relatives and numerous charities, the residual shares were divided among his children and grandchildren. The Simsbury homestead was left to the children as a family home. As Amo put it, it was to be maintained "in the family and for the family." Antoinette Wood lived in it (except in winters when she resided in Washington, D.C.), but it was available for other family visits.[7]

When carrying out the terms of Amos Eno's will, the youngest sibling, William Eno, complained that James was procrastinating. James, a conservative investor, wanted to move forward deliberately, but Will, involved in real estate speculation, wanted more cash quickly so that he could buy more properties. As an experienced businessman, he challenged James on the delays.[8] Despite the tensions, the family eventually liquidated Amos's properties at three public auctions and shared in cash rewards totaling more than $11 million ($376 million). Will bought the Flatiron Building and, with brothers Amo and Henry, the Fifth Avenue Hotel at the auctions, and the three established a land company to manage the property.[9]

*   *   *

Meanwhile, after his extended western hunting jaunt, Amos returned home to pick up his law studies, transferring from Columbia to New York Law

School. Living with his parents in Gramercy Park, he commuted downtown to his classes. He still struggled with his health, and Mamee commented, "I don[']t find A any better." He improved somewhat that summer, indulging in less cerebral pursuits in Newport and Bar Harbor. When Nettie learned about his active social life, she joshed, "Toots is a very frivolous young person, to be running about all day as well as night!"[10] On his doctor's advice, Amos went to Bermuda that winter for a few weeks to try to shake off the periodic headaches he was still experiencing. He was then courting his newfound girlfriend and would have preferred to be enjoying her company at home.[11]

His lady love was Gertrude Minturn, who lived with her mother and other siblings in Gramercy Park. Beginning with her grandfather, the Minturn family had amassed a fortune in international shipping, with Gertrude's father, Robert B. Minturn, Jr., adding to the family's prosperity before his death in 1889. One year older than Amos, Gertrude was one of six children and the second youngest of the four daughters. The Pinchot and Minturn families were New York neighbors. Involved in philanthropic and social activities, Mary and Susanna Shaw Minturn, Gertrude's mother, were particularly close, and Gertrude was a favorite young person. Mary and Gertrude had earlier worked together in the Society of Decorative Art, and the two went to church and on local shopping excursions together. Amos, seeing a lot of her from family contacts, began dating her. They went to the horse races together and corresponded during his Bermuda interlude. Two months later, they were engaged.

Gertrude, Amos explained to Gifford, "has been such a good friend of mine for so long that it seems absolutely natural that we should be engaged except that it is almost too good to be true." Mary was "Very happy" with their betrothal, and Nettie exulted to her mother, "I know how fond you are of Gertrude and what a thoroughly nice girl she is." Even James could not object to his son's union with the daughter of a locally prominent family. His parents' positive reaction mildly surprised Amos, who commented, "I did not expect it would give them so much pleasure."[12]

Amos passed his law school exams that summer, and his pleased mother was "very proud" of his "perseverance and ability." He could put off the state bar exams until after his marriage and honeymoon. As a last bachelor outing, he went on a hunting expedition to New Brunswick, Canada, with Gifford and Henry Stimson, who had hunted together there a year earlier. On that occasion, each man had killed a moose and had them mounted. "It is the best head I have in the house," Stimson bragged, and of his, Gifford pronounced, "I had no idea what a big beast he was until I saw him stuffed." The two men decided to try again, with young Amos joining them. On this trip, Amos tracked but failed to come out of the wilds with a moose, and Stimson commiserated, telling Gifford that Amos was nonetheless "most wonderfully amiable" about his "bad luck."[13]

Amos and Gertrude's large wedding ceremony at St. George's Episcopal Church was a highlight of the New York social season that fall. "What a bully wedding we had," Amos soon wrote his brother, the best man, "and how good you were and have always been to us both!"[14] After honeymooning at a hideaway in Connecticut, the newlyweds embarked on an eight-month trip to Europe. Gertrude had not gone to college but was an experienced international traveler fluent in French and Italian. (Her affectionate name for her mother-in-law was "Madama.") They met up with Nettie and family, who were vacationing in Cannes, France, well south of Darmstadt, Germany, where Alan had assumed his new position as chargé d'affaires. Amos and Gertrude then spent nearly three months in St. Moritz, Switzerland, and moved on to Paris and Rome. Amos wanted a slow travel pace, and ideally, he said, "I would like to be on the water," as his doctor had advised.[15]

After Italy, Amos and Gertrude retreated to a German spa. During the nuptial celebrations, the Pinchots had never really considered Gertrude's health, but she was thin and frail and seemed sicklier than her husband in Europe. She took the cure, consisting of several weeks of mineral and mud baths, and in mid-June, she suffered from appendicitis, requiring an appendectomy. Performed in Heidelberg, the surgery was successful. After a slow recovery, the couple soon returned to New York.

More disturbing was that Amos was still debilitated. Indeed, Gertrude had earlier sent Gifford a much more alarming evaluation. "You can have no <u>faint conception</u>," she emphasized, "of what an effort to Amos the slightest responsibility is or any arrangements for daily life—any decision—any work. I am convinced that for the past 2 years he has lived on his nerves and is now feeling the effects. Yesterday, . . . he said[,] 'this letter writing makes me feel like hell.' . . . It shows you what his condition is if such a little thing affects him so," and she wanted to induce her husband to take the "mental rest cure" a New York doctor had urged. Two other doctors, she continued, had said that it was imperative that Amos take a few years off from any work. Gertrude was convinced that only this combination of outdoor interests and complete mental rest could make him "fit for any work the rest of his life."[16]

Gertrude proposed that he should go alone to live on a horse ranch for a year, to which Amos concurred in principle. He again showed the effects of his festering illness when Gifford briefly visited him, and Amos later wrote his brother, apologizing for his "rotten temper. . . . I seemed all upset and nervous and tonight I can[']t sit still and am horribly irritable."[17]

*   *   *

Shortly before Gifford left, Amos, James, Mary, and Nettie arrived in Cannes for the family rendezvous. Nettie's interaction with the assembled immediate family proved an irritant to family peace. Plainly and simply, she was difficult. Her problem, as always, was her precarious health. Nettie suffered from Graves' disease, a thyroid malady affecting mostly females, resulting in an aggravated heartbeat, sleep disturbances, and irritability. While her condition was mostly under control, her doctor said that any overexertion could threaten a recurrence. And despite her weak heart, Nettie had taken up smoking which, she finally realized, worsened her condition, so she cut back on the habit.

Her shaky physical condition was not the whole problem, however. Alan and Nettie moved in different social circles in Europe, and their behavior increasingly disturbed Mary and James. Nettie accepted without much questioning the artificial conventions and values of the European diplomatic world. It was not the politics of that world but the culture. Politically, almost all the diplomats the Johnstones associated with were conservatives, but Alan resisted the reactionary elements. He was a Liberal and supported his party's reform agenda. When Parliament drastically increased the estate tax, his parents fumed that their eldest son would have to give up the Hackness estate. Alan believed, however, that the tax was a necessary corrective to redress inequality in British society. Nettie, agreeing with her husband's political views, had argued that the "one good thing" about Denmark was that "it is farther advanced in state socialism than any other country, there are old age pensions, and all sorts of excellent things. I wish we had some of it in America."[18]

Culturally, however, Nettie had bought into the diplomats' high society with its formal protocol and entertainments. Despite Alan's salary supplemented by James's allowance, the Johnstones still could not afford a sumptuous lifestyle, but they thought it was important to keep up appearances. They had a few servants, a full-time nanny, and, as often needed because of Crinks's various illnesses, a nurse, and Nettie always seemed to need a new dress or gown, jewelry, or other accessories for the parade of dinner parties and receptions. She went into debt and wrote to her mother, "[D]o you think that anyone would advance me a few pennies, as I haven't any at all and I owe a good deal; and I <u>hate</u> owing."[19]

Among the prerequisites for upper-class living was renting a summer house during the hot weather. While still in Denmark, Nettie was outbid for one, and in her "great disappointment," she wrote her mother, "I confess that I cried like a fool, as I'd quite set my heart on it."[20] The Danish villa they rented for a few summers was equally big and glamorous, furnished with a study, terrace, large dining room, and blue room. It even had a stable with horses and a bathhouse on a beach. And it was costly. The result was that Nettie pleaded with her parents for substantial financial help. Her excuse was that Alan had no security to get a loan, so she had to do it. She had already borrowed $5,000 (about $170,000 today) from her mother to pay debts and cover household expenses but quickly found herself strapped for cash again. "[T]he great expense of the house in the country, the rent and the extra expense of living there," including entertaining "a good deal, . . . have taken everything," so she asked for another $2,000.[21]

Because of her poor health, Nettie bought a new Stanley Steamer motor car, abandoning her bicycle even for short rides. In all these matters, Nettie's view was that she would soon inherit a sizable chunk of money—generating an income of perhaps $25,000 a year, she estimated—from her grandfather Eno's estate. That prospect led her to exclaim, "It's nice to be rich!" While expressed with good humor, she was looking forward to her new wealth.[22] In the meantime, she continued borrowing against her family's future.

Nettie's husband embraced the affected pleasures of his profession. Intelligence and performance were valued in the diplomatic service, but advancement usually required social networking within and outside the service. As an ambitious diplomat, Alan willingly played that part of the career game. Nettie admitted that while she liked to "get a certain amount" of social recognition from hobnobbing with the nobility, "it[']s really Alan, who loves it."[23] He had recently bought and raced six horses in England, three of which sometimes finished in the money, and he had traveled back to his home country to take in the horse racing season, including the annual Ascot races, a high point of the aristocracy's social life.[24] He also went off regularly on hunting outings to Hackness or the estates of wealthy gentlemen.

One episode highlighted his understanding of the social expectations of the diplomatic corps. In the summer of 1901, King Edward VII visited Homberg, and Alan, as the senior officer at the Darmstadt Legation, attended to the desires and needs of the new monarch. Over several days, he and Nettie socialized with the king and escorted him to a local exhibition, and Edward came to the Johnstone house for dinner. It was a big event for Alan and Nettie, and Alan played bridge with Edward and others afterward. The Johnstones were soon known as social favorites of the king and queen.[25]

James and Mary, who had their own set of firm beliefs, had great difficulty accepting their daughter's lifestyle, and a tense relationship would erupt into family acrimony during their German rendezvous.[26] Questions about Nettie's extravagances were involved, and Nettie behaved poorly. Amos wrote Gifford that their sister was "absolutely pugnacious[,] unreasonable and incapable of seeing two sides to anything. . . . Nettie is in bad shape in my opinion and that is why she is so sensitive to opposition and so silly in her tenets on various subjects." Much of her argument was with her strong-willed father who, Amos continued, "insists on fighting with Nettie whenever the occasion offers."[27]

Mary, too, became "very anxious" about her daughter's conduct, "quite as much as to her mental and moral condition as to her physical. . . . She seems to be under an almost hypnotic condition, just as she was long ago before she had met Alan." Most disturbing to Mary was Nettie's absorption of the outward trappings of European diplomatic culture. The result was that Nettie and Alan's "world is no longer our world," and "our standard is not in the least theirs," and the pernicious "influences" were "unfortunate for her present life and still worse for her future unless they are checked." Among the consequences was that while America provided "a healthier moral tone," Nettie "does not seem to care for her own country." What she really needed, Mary believed, was a good dose of religion—"God's holy spirit"—but she had little confidence that it would happen.[28]

Nettie was indeed fixated on money and ostentatious living, and Mary's negative feelings may have partly been her nostalgic remembrance of a bygone time when "N's life and mine were bound up together." To be sure, marrying into the British diplomatic corps meant becoming a citizen of the United Kingdom, and Crinks would be thoroughly English. The Pinchots could hardly have expected less. But Nettie tried hard to stay close to her mother, writing regularly and visiting with her parents in America every year that they did not travel to visit her. Moreover, in focusing on Nettie's psychological faults, Mary downplayed her real physical problems. At any rate, her mother's belief that her doctors exaggerated her ailments angered Nettie. Later that year, a leading heart specialist told her that she was "seriously ill." She was mostly forthcoming to her parents about her various maladies, although she concluded there was "[n]othing very serious but enough to bother me." To her friend Kitty, however, she admitted, "I am . . . thoroughly frightened about my health."[29]

The Pinchots were not one big, happy family, and on top of those strains, Amos had to endure his papa's stern lectures expounding his theories about medical matters. "He has almost driven me crazy worrying about my health and telling me the danger of various things," Amos wrote Gifford.[30]

Nettie at least began looking after her health, following the regimen laid out by her doctor, visiting spas for rest, massages, and hydropathic treatments in Homberg, Nice, and Cannes, often for many months over several years. She also received serum shots every other day, which, she grumbled, made "my poor hind legs look like pin cushions." Nettie's doctor "strongly" warned her not to risk visiting her mother in America. But then her health gradually improved, and she soon reported, "I am better," with a much lower heart rate.

Of course, extended health care came with a high price. "Being ill is so d--- expensive," Nettie complained, and she was soon "very hard up." Instead of using the interest on her inheritance (about $8,000), which she had not yet received, to pay off her other loans from her mother, she asked her parents to send her the money for her current living expenses.[31]

James was more interested in the monetary side. When Nettie received her first bequest of about $1 million ($34 million) from her grandfather Eno's estate, she and Alan tried to assure him that they and their financial advisers would manage their portfolio conservatively. Papa lacked confidence in their money management plans, however, and he was in no hurry to complete the sale of the last of the Eno properties, which would bring Nettie more than $900,000 in residual inheritance money.

Fundamentally, Mary wanted to remain close to her only daughter and would not let the Johnstones' extravagances damage the family relationship. She tolerated the excesses of British high society, and her complaints about Nettie and Alan's lifestyle carried little authority because she had never refused to lend Nettie the money she requested. She also spoiled her with gifts. One particularly expensive present her mother sent was eighty-five chinchilla furs. The gift, Nettie wrote, thanking Mary, "simply takes away my breath! Also," she added with only a trace of guilt, "I feel like a murderer, and can hardly wait to rejoice over the remains of my victims."[32]

Mary, trying to soften James's attitude, said they needed to acquiesce to the Johnstones' lifestyle. "I know they spend too much," she wrote him, but "I think they are for the most part very careful." She admitted that "N is extravagant in clothes and their house is kept up in more style than seems necessary to me, but we must remember that we are not accustomed to the sort of society they are in . . . . At all events," she concluded, "it is their own affair not ours." She soon exerted her influence among the family executors and lawyers to settle the final details of the Eno estate and release the residual money, with Will's pushing.[33] Their determination may have had some effect; Nettie (and the others) received the rest of her inheritance five years after Amos Eno's death.

*   *   *

Meanwhile, James and Mary asked their newly appointed forester son to search for a house in the nation's capital for him and themselves. Gifford found a lot at 1615 Rhode Island Avenue in northwest Washington. Set back from Scott Circle and close to downtown, the location passed the critical eye of business- and race-conscious Papa, who concluded that the house they built there would be close to the stately mansions and embassies on Sixteenth Street and removed from the large African American population. "The darkies once away[,] the property in that St[reet] will soon be very valuable," he concluded.

The Pinchots purchased the lot. They were friends with the prominent New York architect Grant La Farge, who designed the new Pinchot house, and James often consulted with him on the many details. Built in about nine months, Gifford moved in by late 1901. Soon the parents moved their furniture from Gramercy Park to the Rhode Island Avenue house and offered their New York residence for sale.[34]

The Pinchots' new house was built in a grand style. Really a mansion, it had four floors, with the main floor raised a half story. Below were the laundry, garage, and large storage rooms, parts of which Gifford later made into an exercise gym and shooting gallery. Gifford also set up an area for tetherball on the roof. The main floor consisted of a large entrance hall, parlor, man's (service) room, dining area, and library, and the bedrooms and servants' quarters were on the top floors.[35] After visiting the Pinchots in their new abode, Ellen Maury Slayden, wife of a veteran Texas congressman, commented: "I like the house better than any I have seen in Washington. It doesn't glitter, or jingle with money, and the furniture belongs to no period but that of good taste and comfort. There is nothing artistic in the strained modern sense but everything pretty and restful." She saved her most glowing remarks for the spacious sixty-foot library, "with bookshelves practically all around it and from floor to ceiling. The books look as if they had been read and might be read again at any time. There was an open fire, and over the mantel a picture built into the wall."[36]

Now in her sixties, Mary had advanced the money to pay for the lot and house. Having often visited her sister Antoinette Wood, her daughter, and Alan in the first years of their marriage, Mary knew the capital city and enjoyed good entertainment. When she had told Nettie about Bar Harbor's congenial social life, her daughter replied, "You really do seem to be the most dissipated person I have ever known. . . . The tea parties with music must be delightful."[37]

Mary wasted no time getting known in Washington society. Compared with New York City, the nation's capital was only a large town, and Nettie, who had lived in both places, even declared that "Washington after New York is like country." However, many interesting people lived there, including a large nucleus of well-established families and all the foreign diplomats and politicians and their wives. Mary was in her element; she liked entertaining and was good at it. She hosted teas and dinner parties in her new home, partly to get Gifford better known but also on her own. At one of Mary's entertainments, Ellen

Pinchot Mansion, 1615 Rhode Island Avenue, N.W., Washington, D.C. (Historical Society of Washington, D.C.)

Slayden found her dressed "in dark-purple silk, Irish lace, and long amethyst chain, but so easy and humorous that I was not surprised to find myself sitting on a sofa beside her laughing over the queer thick underclothes we used to wear and wondering what had become of our flannel petticoats."[38]

Mary's parties were usually small and never ostentatious affairs; her refinement and good taste further ingratiated her to the Washington elite. To those she liked, she confided that she did not go out calling much at her age but encouraged them to visit her. People came and, enjoying the company and conversation, often returned. Her hosting had no overt intellectual pretensions, but as informal and seemingly spontaneous gatherings, her house increasingly became a salon. Before long, some Washingtonians were calling her a "grande dame." Nettie appreciated her mother's social success, but the apparent incongruity between the nickname she had given her and her honorific title amused her. It was "pretty fine," she chortled, "for a Mouse to be called 'grande anything.'"[39]

The house bustled with social activity. Besides Mary's parties, Gifford used the library for meetings with his work colleagues and associates in the Society of American Foresters. Founded by Gifford and other foresters in 1901, the society grew as a professional body interested in exchanging ideas with others in related scientific fields, and it held weekly evening meetings in the Pinchot library. In addition, two government commissions on which Gifford served regularly met there. James prized the library as a place for his reading and reflection, but finding it almost never quiet, he built an addition on the back of the house, which became his new private retreat.[40]

*   *   *

To Gifford, being a forester was more than a job; it was an opportunity, and he was determined to make the most of forestry as a growth industry. He started at a disadvantage, because the national forests were still under the control of the interior department—he was truly "a federal forester without federal forests."[41] Undaunted, he got his employees out into the field to develop working plans for conserving the forests.[42] Moreover, because of the interior land office's limited knowledge of silviculture and the actual conditions of the American West, it relied on the technical expertise and on-the-ground experience of the forestry division's personnel in surveying, planting, and dealing with homesteaders, lumbermen, and sheep herders. And Secretary Wilson always supported him, which prompted Gifford to comment, "The more I see of him the more I like him."[43] From these beginnings, forestry became much more visible, and Gifford's division expanded exponentially.[44] Gifford early perceived the need to mollify or persuade this congressman or that committee about the importance of forest conservation. As he told a key sympathetic senator, forestry "is just beginning to get on its feet. If the impression were to go abroad that the growth had stopped, public interest would be checked, young men would be discouraged from going into the work, and there would be real loss."[45]

Gifford recognized that if forestry was to be successful in the United States over the long term, professional education in forestry was vital. Aside from Harry Graves, Gifford, and a knowledgeable staff he inherited, there was no cadre of professional foresters in the United States. Gifford would hire a few energetic, young recruits like Overton Price, who had received forestry training in Europe and under Carl Schenck at Biltmore. He thought, however, that it would be impractical for Americans interested in the emerging discipline to go to Europe in any numbers; in any case, he had enough of Prussian-trained foresters like his frenemies Fernow and Schenck. "What we wanted," Gifford summarized much later, "was American foresters trained by Americans in American ways for the work ahead in American forests."[46]

That perspective required developing forestry education programs in the United States. James Pinchot had early proposed the founding of a national forest school, with Milford, Biltmore, and Washington, D.C., as possible locations, but Gifford had argued that the "first thing is create a [popular] demand for trained foresters." Until then, he commented, "I shall not commit at all."[47] Papa then outlined a plan for a forestry school in Pennsylvania, but Gifford remained skeptical.[48]

Fernow and Schenck also saw the need for forestry education in America, and both acted before the Pinchots. In 1898, Schenck, with George Vanderbilt's approval, opened Biltmore Forestry School, which offered a one-year curriculum. And Fernow was now head of a New York State College of Forestry affiliated with Cornell University. Some students in the two programs would join Gifford's forestry bureau, but both ultimately failed. Schenck's program was a shoestring operation and would close in 1907 after he had a falling out with Vanderbilt. At Cornell, Fernow developed a four-year forestry program. Gifford presciently predicted "a very serious failure," and Fernow soon got in trouble with the Cornell trustees, state legislature, and the governor, leading to the school's closing by 1903.[49]

Despite these inauspicious beginnings, professional forestry education was always in Gifford's thoughts, and now with added new dimensions—his grandfather's bequests, his government forestry job, and perhaps with other Eno and Pinchot benefactors—he could underwrite the founding of a forest school.

Gifford's location of choice was his alma mater. Yale had tradition and prestige behind it, and with underwriting by the Pinchot family, the university might be persuaded to support a forestry school. Yale was also what he knew, and he had contacts like Professor Brewer, who was still on the faculty. Through his active alumni involvement, he came to know Arthur Hadley, Yale's new and first lay president, who was interested in public service initiatives, and the president's closest associate, Anson Phelps Stokes, Jr., the university's secretary, who was a distant relative on the Eno side of the family. As an insider, Gifford had no difficulty getting a respectful hearing for a proposed forest school.[50]

Gifford's main sounding board for ideas on a forest school at Yale was Harry Graves, his assistant chief in the forestry division. The two had drawn close. While earlier living together in Gifford's rental house in Washington, they had spent evenings developing an outline plan and curriculum for a two-year graduate degree program. They also told President Hadley that they had discussed their proposal with George Dudley Seymour, a respected alumnus actively involved in university affairs. The timing was right, as Yale had recently received a bequest of a large faculty house and land adjacent to the campus, but the site could also provide a convenient location for the classrooms and school offices. Hadley stressed that the estate was encumbered in debt and provided no endowment, and as much as $200,000 would be needed just to maintain the botanical part. He did not venture an estimated cost of a forestry school but asked Gifford for the names of possible benefactors.[51]

Hadley soon dropped his inflated estimates when Gifford let it be known that the Pinchot family was seriously interested in underwriting the cost of a new forestry school. Amos also endorsed Gifford's vision: "I think it would be a good thing to contribute to on a large scale," and the parents believed "strongly" that a gift was "as a fine thing for the family to do."[52] Mary, Gifford, and Amos contributed $150,000 ($5 million) to endow the forest school, which would have adequate funding at the start.[53] The details fell neatly into place. The president and trustees approved the founding of the Yale Forest School, which opened in the fall of 1900 with an enrollment of seven graduate students, and the numbers soon swelled.

Graves, anointed by Gifford, became the first director of the new school and would prove to be a capable administrator. As he set off to New Haven for his new assignment, he told Gifford, "Everything that I have received has been directly or indirectly from you," and he thanked him for giving him this "great opportunity" and for making "a very happy home for me" for two years in

Washington. Gifford's involvement with the school included presenting annual lectures to the students, as his busy schedule allowed.[54]

James Pinchot was not a direct financial benefactor of the new Yale Forest School, but he reveled in its founding. As part of the gift, Yale also accepted his free lease of land (ultimately more than 1,700 acres) surrounding Grey Towers for twenty-one years as a summer·school for practical fieldwork. James began buying tents, constructing wooden and stone buildings on the Milford site and a meeting hall in the village, locating a field station, hosting welcoming entertainments for the students, and arranging other details for the eight-week summer programs. For these efforts, Yale would award James an honorary degree in 1905.[55]

*   *   *

Amos, meanwhile, seemed in mostly decent health but had relapses, and his mother-in-law described him as "weak" and "almost on the verge of nervous exhaustion." His doctors and Gertrude continued urging him to go off to a ranch for a year. That could be problematic, however, as he had already spent weeks away on several occasions but always without more than incremental improvement. Would Amos explore the prospect of other types of treatment? In any event, the couple faced some big choices—finding their own place to live, deciding on a career path, and starting their own family. All would be more difficult to fulfill if Amos's malarial and nervous afflictions continued.

Because Gertrude became pregnant shortly after their return from Europe, Amos deferred a western trip. Instead, the couple bought a cottage in Bar Harbor, and in June 1902, Gertrude gave birth to a baby boy there, whom the parents named Gifford 2nd, with Gifford as godparent. Amos was a proud father, but with a nursemaid to help care for their newborn, he managed to escape for local fishing trips and another fall hunting trip to New Brunswick, during which he killed a small moose and brought home the head with eight-point antlers.[56]

Still, Amos wanted to find a serious job and complained, "The idea of pottering around any more is terrible." But Amos was not ready for the grind of steady work. He continued to suffer "headache and other irregularities" and sleepless nights. Soon, Gertrude bewailed, he was "miserable," with the red corpuscles in his blood only a little over fifty percent of normal levels. The cause of his extreme anemia, his doctor thought, was injured nerve centers. "He is morbid now, negative, and unhappy," Gertrude informed Gifford, "but everything worries and disgusts him. He is so sensitive." She and the doctor agreed that he could not work unless he changed "absolutely and radically." Again, the desired prescription was to go out West and live on a ranch for an extended period. Though averse to family separation, Amos left for a retreat on Catalina Island off the Southern California coast, which Gifford had recommended.[57]

Amos had a relaxing stay, but he grew restless. Claiming to feel "infinitely better" after three months, he went again to the St. Mary's area of Montana to go camping and hunting with a friend. He shot a brown bear, which, he noted, "will make a very fine robe for the baby," and returned home refreshed. Gertrude wanted him to stay away much longer, as she was "sure" that his removal from "all family, and worry, and all the thousand ills of civilization, for 8 good months, are needed to give him the strength to take up his winter's work." She, too, was under a physician's care for her own nervous trouble, but by the time Amos was reunited with the family, her condition had improved, and they spent a restful summer at Bar Harbor.[58] Most promising, Amos found a new doctor who prescribed electric shock treatments. The new therapy would not help his malaria, but he responded well and seemed less nervous.

Gifford sought Amos a job as a government lawyer, perhaps on conservation matters, and he bought the house for sale next door and enticed his brother to rent it. Amos's family was "very glad" to accept Gifford's "delightful" offer of living in Washington so close to each other, and they moved in that winter. Gifford was more confident in opportunities for Amos, as he now had a close working relationship with Theodore Roosevelt, who had become president after McKinley's assassination in September 1901. After mentioning the prospect of Amos's employment to him, Gifford claimed that he and Roosevelt "talked about it frequently" while at the president's Oyster Bay home.[59]

Amos had first met Roosevelt during his senior year in college when TR, then New York City's police commissioner, gave a talk at Yale. Afterward, Amos and his roommate Sumner Gerard hosted a reception for him in their room. After Amos moved to Washington, TR arranged with W. W. Rockhill, the famed Sinologist heading the Bureau of American Republics between ministerial appointments, to offer Amos a job. During one of his legendary walks, the president talked to Amos about it and intimated that if he liked the work, he could succeed Rockhill to the directorship. Despite Amos's admitted ignorance of Latin America, Rockhill offered him a writing position. Preparing for the job, Amos began studying Spanish. But perhaps realizing that the bureau job was far from his interests, he also looked elsewhere. Shortly after, he won appointment as a deputy assistant district attorney in New York City, and in 1904, Amos and Gertrude moved back to Manhattan.[60]

Though regretting his brother's departure, Gifford believed that because of Amos's and Nettie's improving conditions and their parents' general good health, there was reason to expect that "the Pinchot family will be once more fairly on its feet." Nettie had quit smoking, though not entirely—she would flout social conventions by smoking at formal events where it was presumed women would not indulge in the habit—and her husband gave her a clean bill of health.[61] However, Alan's career suffered a setback when he was passed over for high positions in St. Petersburg and Vienna. Instead, he was appointed the British Minister to Denmark, and the Johnstones would return to Copenhagen, living there from 1905–1910. Alan also had a knighthood conferred upon him. Trying to make light of the award, he called the ceremony "foolish," but he admitted he had hoped for a higher honor. Alan and Nettie would now be formally addressed as "Sir" and "Lady."[62]

Meanwhile, Amos's continued progress prompted Gertrude to enthuse that her husband was "better than I've ever known him to be." In October 1904, she gave birth to a girl, Rosamond, and she would soon write, "I hope everything will turn to happiness and good for all of us, and that our new treasure will be as great a joy as little Gifford is."[63]

10.

Political Awakenings

The Pinchots' improved health and new career advancements occurred while hopeful signs of political and social changes permeated America. The previous decade of the 1890s had been a time of growing unrest but only little progress toward meaningful reforms. Western and southern farmers, aggrieved at low prices for their farm goods and convinced they were victims of powerful railroads and industrial monopolies, formed a third party, the Populists, before the election of 1892, but the rising big businesses seemed indifferent to the plight of labor and consumers. The ruthless suppression of strikes at the Homestead steel mills outside Pittsburgh and the Pullman Company in Chicago two years later dramatized the labor-capital strife and stimulated public discussions of the sectional and class inequities in American life.

Close to home, James Pinchot supported civil service reform and Republicans' resistance to the patronage politics practiced by the Tammany Hall political machine in New York, which controlled the local Democratic Party. Although Republicans were a distinctly minority party in the city, by the 1890s, increasing numbers of citizens had grown disenchanted with Tammany's widespread corruption. Charles H. Parkhurst, the Pinchots' minister at the Madison Square Presbyterian Church, spearheaded the rising anti-Tammany campaign. The senior Pinchots, though conservative politically, admired their minister's moralistic fervor. Mary praised one of Parkhurst's "red hot" sermons in which he arraigned "everyone, himself included on the love of money. It was masterly and I felt as if I would like him to stand on the steps of the Treasury building in Wall St. and preach it again."[1] Parkhurst lambasted the police department for its collusion with Tammany in protecting gambling halls and houses of prostitution, and by 1894, a coalition of church activists and several civic groups championing political change put forward a slate of reform-minded candidates endorsed by the Republican Party to try to repudiate graft-ridden Tammany in the upcoming municipal election. On its eve, Mary commented, "Everybody is waked up and all seem to be doing what they can against Tammany and we do hope for success this time. It is wonderful how Dr. Parkhurst has made himself felt. . . . and all the Good Government Clubs are alive and working. If this had only come years ago[,] what sin and suffering might have been spared."[2]

When the reformers won the election, the Pinchots rejoiced. "Dr. Parkhurst is the hero of the day," James wrote Gifford. "Tammany is gone root and branch. . . . everyone seems sure that we will have, for three years at least a decent city, government by respectable people."[3] Tammany was far from finished, but some reforms occurred. Most conspicuously, Theodore Roosevelt, appointed police commissioner after the election, vigorously enforced the laws impartially and instituted a merit system of hiring and promoting policemen.

Of the Pinchot parents, Mary was much more responsive to political reform. As early as the early 1880s, while vacationing on the Virginia shore, she had visited "a full-blooded darkey church at Hampton [Institute] and heard a very good sermon;" and after touring the campus, she commented, "I cannot but feel it is doing a great work." Her seeming support of African Americans was only rhetoric, but she showed a willingness to experience a vastly different culture and respond positively to it. And though not enamored of books, she later read Harriet Beecher Stowe's *Uncle Tom's Cabin*, which gave her a new understanding of the humanitarian impulse behind the Union's "great righteous war" for freedom.[4] Similarly, during mounting labor unrest, she would prove sensitive to the plight of the working masses. "Labour in a good cause is a blessed thing," she believed, "even if it does not win each time[,] for it will 'rise again' and keep on till the eternal years have brought the glorious battle to a close."[5]

She also approved of the growing women's movement that challenged societal stereotypes of her sex as weak and restricted to the home. The fairly rigid gender divide bothered her more than the denial of suffrage. When James went to a men's dinner, for example, she complained, "the pigs! Why [not] let women in too!"[6]

There were distinct limits to the senior Pinchots' reform interests, however. They were loyal Republicans and could tolerate conservative Democratic leaders like Grover Cleveland. But they were aghast when the upstart westerners, led by William Jennings Bryan with his mellifluous oratory and free silver ideas, won the Democratic presidential nomination in 1896. During the campaign, Mary predicted "anarchy" if the Democrats won the election, and James rejected

Bryan's "unsound opinions." Fortunately for the Pinchots, the nation was not yet ready for his advanced reform program, and the Republican nominee, William McKinley, swept to a decisive victory in the presidential election.[7]

By the mid-1890s, Gifford was gradually drawn into the wider reform orbit. The process began with Jim Reynolds, who was reinventing himself. As an ordained clergyman, he was concerned with the growing problems in the inner cities. He became the head worker at a social settlement house on the lower east side of New York, trying to alleviate poverty and bring about the acculturation of the new immigrants.

Reynolds had many friends in the city and counted Gifford "at the head." In fact, he drew considerable support from the Pinchots. Upon moving to New York, for instance, he stayed at their Gramercy Park home until he was settled in his own quarters. One of his experiments in the settlement home involved taking young immigrants who had abandoned factory work to try their hand at alternative occupations, and Reynolds persuaded the Pinchots to try out beginning chambermaids for a year. At one point, he advised Gifford that he could send his parents an Italian if they did not like the Irish incumbent and added, "I can also give you a Jew if you wish one."[8] James and Mary became generous contributors to the settlement house, helping erase its debt and funding a new building.

Settlement work interested Gifford, and soon he was a member of the governing council. Reynolds also used Gifford for fundraising, telling him, "If you meet Uncle Amos[,] please touch him for a few thousand or any[one] else who might yield to your appeal." Gifford later wrote of his maturing liberal views after his time with the settlement home: "I came into operating contact with the other half and learned something of how it lived and thought and why, whereby my original conservative opinions were greatly changed, to my very marked advantage."[9]

Reynolds's other passion was municipal reform. After the victorious 1894 election, he and other "goo goos" (as the Good Government Club's members were called) braced for a long-term fight against Tammany. Gifford attended the club's convention to endorse candidates for local and state offices in the next election, and he was soon serving on its finance committee. The Good Government Club morphed into a broader reform coalition headed by Reynolds, the Citizens Union, to continue the fight. Gifford was enlisted to speak at one of its open-air rallies in the city. It was the first of his many political speeches over the next fifty years, but his inaugural "talk" was never delivered, as the reformers were harangued by an unfriendly crowd of hecklers who "would not let us speak."[10]

*   *   *

Theodore Roosevelt would nourish Gifford's political awakening. The Pinchot and Roosevelt families were well acquainted with each other—both were New Yorkers and solid Republicans from the same privileged milieu. Mary and James made social calls to Theodore and his wife Edith in New York. When Roosevelt was a civil service commissioner in Washington, D.C., Nettie and Alan invited the couple for dinner at their Dupont Circle home. Roosevelt provided his young hosts with "delightful" nonstop conversation on many subjects.[11]

Gifford Pinchot and Theodore Roosevelt had likely first met at another of Alan and Nettie's dinner parties in May 1894, at which the two apparently discussed forestry. The next day, Roosevelt sent Gifford an appreciative note: "I did not begin to ask you all the questions I wanted to."[12] And with Gifford's introduction to urban reform in New York, he had further contact with Roosevelt, an aspiring political activist in the city. They also had mutual acquaintances. In particular, Grant La Farge, the architect of the Pinchots' Washington house, had encouraged his close friend Roosevelt to consult Gifford on forestry issues, and Gifford's enduring friendship with Theodore Roosevelt really began during the latter's tenure as governor of the Empire State. A hero returning from his daring exploits in the Spanish-American War, TR, popularly dubbed the Rough Rider, had found immediate political reward with his election to the governorship.[13]

Roosevelt was an outdoorsman and a hunter and, having lived in and written extensively about the American West, had developed a deep interest in conservation issues, which lay at the core of Roosevelt's being. What most interested Governor Roosevelt was the forester's views on scientific forestry questions and managing the state's forests, parks, and fish and game. He was also a sympathetic listener. At this first meeting with the new governor in February 1899, for instance, Gifford presented an argument for changes in the state forestry commission, and Roosevelt acknowledged to the forester, "You have given me just the information I wanted."[14]

They both practiced the strenuous life, though Roosevelt's incentive was more Darwinian. Gifford soon proved he was a survivor among the fittest—just barely. After his February meeting with the new governor, he and La Farge set off to climb the snow-covered Mount Marcy, New York's highest peak, unaware that the great blizzard of 1899 was moving in. Bucking ferocious winds and blinding snow in sub-zero temperatures, two badly frostbitten guides early gave up, and La Farge, finding his freezing legs failing him, stopped below the summit.[15] But Gifford "crawled on over glare ice holding [on] by rocks that stuck through, to the top," La Farge later wrote. Gifford took photographs of the signal there, and then rejoining his companion, the two retreated. As they found a more sheltered spot, "we looked at each other," La Farge recounted, "and burst into laughter—truly we presented a peculiar appearance. . . . Icicles hung even upon our eyelashes, and Pinchot's beard was coated so solidly with ice that he looked like . . . perhaps, a walrus." Gifford's ears were frostbitten despite wearing a thick sealskin cap pulled down over them, as were his neck and upper lip through his mustache, but they made it down the mountain. Normally careful about his outdoor exploits, Gifford admitted that his determined climb was "Foolish."[16]

At an Albany meeting that November, the forestry issue TR raised with Gifford was settled in short order, but the sequel was spontaneous. Before dinner, Gifford's aggressive host challenged the forester to a boxing match. After squaring off, Gifford threw a solid punch, which sent Roosevelt to the floor. The stunned governor got up, embraced Gifford in a clinch, and, falling to the floor with him, gained the advantage. The boxing-wrestling encounter, which ended almost as quickly as it began, was a draw.[17] Gifford's boxing success against Roosevelt, an experienced pugilist, was not entirely luck. As an adolescent, he had received some instruction and practice in the ring and thus understood some fundamentals of the sport.[18] Also in his favor, he was a full three inches taller than Roosevelt and with a longer reach, giving him a physical advantage.

The Roosevelt-Pinchot relationship gradually became more intimate. Roosevelt already respected Gifford for his honesty and forestry expertise, and their boxing-wrestling fray served as a bonding exercise between the two men, confirming for Roosevelt that Gifford was no patrician dilettante but a real man ready to accept a challenge, even a fight.

Their emerging friendship paid off unexpectedly when TR was nominated as McKinley's running mate in the presidential election of 1900, then in September 1901, when TR assumed the presidency after the assassination of McKinley. Gifford was now the new president's closest adviser on forestry questions.

To Gifford, the foremost conservation issue was administrative—transferring the national forest management from the interior to the agriculture department and developing a genuine professional forest service. The former was a prerequisite for the latter. Gifford had been working with Interior Secretary Ethan Hitchcock, who was committed to forest conservation, on a plan that would make him a special agent and forester in the interior without giving up his place as forester in the agriculture department. He wanted a free hand to get results until Congress passed legislation making the transfer permanent.

Inheriting this situation, the new president endorsed the proposed transitional arrangement and received promises from Hitchcock that his department would fully cooperate. However, bureaucrats in the interior were unwilling to give up control over the millions of acres of public lands without a struggle. Raising technicalities, Hitchcock did not follow through and soon created the interior department's own forestry division to enforce the land laws. Through the president's intervention, Gifford had competent foresters run it, but the interior's general land office, still steeped in old routines, effectively prevented changes in forest management.

TR was a hands-on administrator who sought experts in their respective fields. He asked Gifford and Frederick H. Newell, an experienced engineer on water issues, to prepare the section on forest and irrigation matters for the president's first message to Congress. Using their draft language, Roosevelt affirmed his commitment to the "practical usefulness of the national forest reserves to the mining, grazing, irrigation, and other interests of the regions in which the reserves lie." He also asserted, "The forest and water problems are perhaps the most vital internal questions of the United States," and recommended that the various functions of the general land office (protection), United States Geological Survey (mapping), and the agriculture's forestry bureau should be consolidated in the forestry bureau, "to which they properly belong."[19]

However, he did not make transferring the interior's forest responsibilities to the agriculture department a priority issue. To Roosevelt, getting the 1904 presidential nomination and winning the election in his own right were paramount. Until then, he would be an activist president but did not directly challenge the prerogatives of powerful and mostly conservative Republican leaders, who would wield considerable influence at the party's nominating convention to choose their presidential candidate. Most of the president's achievements in his first three years in office were undertaken without congressional action. With Gifford's input, TR also proclaimed fifteen more national forests in his first year but none thereafter in his first presidential term. His main legislative achievement in conservation was the passage of a 1901 law that established a reclamation service in the interior department to investigate water courses and develop irrigation systems to reclaim arid western lands in sixteen states.

* * *

Gifford was soon on his way to the Philippines. As a fruit of its war with Spain, the United States annexed the Spanish colony as American territory. Forest management would be among the challenges in governing the thousands of distant islands from the continental United States. Under Spanish rule, the islands had a forestry bureau, laws, and regulations but lax enforcement. Moreover, an ongoing Filipino rebellion for independence would make forestry administration problematic. At the same time, however, the publicly owned and richly forested lands there provided the United States with a major opportunity in forest conservation.

Gifford had no experience with tropical forests but realized he would be involved in their administration.[20] Captain George Patrick Ahern, the new U.S. head of the forestry bureau in the islands, would focus Gifford's attention on the archipelago. A graduate of West Point and a career military officer, Ahern early developed a passionate interest in forestry and taught himself the subject while stationed in the American West. Subsequently stationed in the east, he studied forestry while earning a law degree at Yale before returning to his post in Montana. He began peppering Gifford with questions about forestry. In 1896, he submitted suggestions to the national academy's forest commission, and Gifford met him during his trek west with the commissioners that summer. Gifford then pronounced Ahern's views on forestry "very sensible." They met again between Ahern's courageous military service in Cuba during the Spanish War and his forestry assignment in the Philippines.[21]

In the Philippines, Captain Ahern wrote Gifford that he would "reverence any suggestions" that he, the "greatest practical forester on God's Green Earth," might make regarding the Philippine forests. Gifford wanted to support him. Ahern experienced local resistance to his initiatives from natives and lumbermen while trying to enforce forest regulations. He may have exacerbated the problems with his opinionated and outspoken personality. Because of the difficulties, rumors surfaced of Ahern's removal, which prompted Gifford to write William Howard Taft, the U.S. governor-general in the islands, of his "very high regard" for Ahern, who was "well fitted" for the work of the Philippine Forestry Bureau. When Ahern continued complaining that he was "hampered" and "threatened," Gifford persuaded Secretary of War Elihu Root that he should go to the Philippines and make recommendations. A pleased Ahern wrote the chief forester that he would "show you more kinds of timber than you ever dreamed of seeing. I will talk your head off and never let up on questions."[22]

Gifford's trip became a four-month round-the-world adventure. He embarked from New York to England, then across Europe to Russia. Along the way, he met with George Seymour, his New Haven friend, who provided lively company on the trip. They crossed Russia on the newly completed Trans-Siberian railroad to Vladivostok.[23] Gifford's party then traveled through Manchuria and China to Hong Kong and eventually to the Philippines.

Upon Gifford's arrival in October 1902, Governor General Taft provided him with an armored gunboat for his investigation of the forests. "Nothing could be more delightful than cruising among these wonderful islands," he soon reported, "where there are new things to be seen at every landing, and where the variety of forest and topography is so great that interest never flags." In his six weeks in the Philippines, Gifford, Ahern, and Seymour logged about 3,000 miles, visiting all the larger islands and several hundred smaller ones. The rebellion for independence among Filipinos required caution, so Gifford's landings were controlled, and he admitted that he was only able "to see a good deal of the islands from the ocean." What he saw was nonetheless impressive and humbling, and he wrote his father, "it was full of the keenest interest, although somewhat bewildering to be dropped into the midst of a forest[,] not one tree of which I knew."[24]

Despite the new challenges, Gifford and Ahern agreed on a forestry policy for the islands, and Ahern wrote large sections of Gifford's report. Gifford discussed his preliminary recommendations with Taft, who "Agreed full[y] with forest program. Said of law, 'Let me know what you want and we'll pass it.' Said of measures, 'Tell me whatever you want and I'll see that Ahern carries it out.' Situation most helpful," Gifford concluded of their meeting.[25] Soon his party was on its way home across the Pacific.

McKinley's decision to annex the islands had sparked a domestic anti-imperialist movement, nearly defeating the peace treaty with Spain in the U.S. Senate, and the Democratic Party had made it an issue in the election of 1900. Like many Americans, Gifford showed little interest in foreign affairs before the war, but he never criticized administration policy during the debate over American imperialism.[26]

The numerous skirmishes between the occupying American military force and resisting Filipinos resulted in gruesome reports of U.S. atrocities. Gifford never questioned the soldiers' past actions and assumed that because they were well disciplined during his visit, they could not have engaged in torture, random killing, or the wanton destruction of property.[27] Indeed, knowing of Roosevelt's keen interest in the fighting there, Gifford provided TR with a glowing justification for the American military's behavior. The enlisted men acted with restraint even without officers present, he wrote the president from Manila. "These are the men whom the Anti-Imperialists are trying to exhibit as bloodthirsty brutes. . . . Nothing has impressed me," he went on, "more than the quality and bearing of both officers and men. . . . [T]he officers" under Captain John J. Pershing "are manly, upright, clear-eyed, honest gentlemen, and the men of so high a grade that it makes me proud to be an American every time I see them."

TR, an enthusiastic imperialist, was delighted with Gifford's message and had it published in the *Washington Star*.[28] The motivations of American expansionists were both material and spiritual, but Gifford emphasized the latter. He believed U.S. rule brought civilized values, education, scientific expertise, and medical help to the natives. Given his sturdy Christian perspective and his assumption of the superiority of Western culture, Gifford had early supported Yale-sponsored Christian mission activity there—what would become Yale-in-China, which was nondenominational and emphasized education and social service activity rather than proselytism. During his Asian trip, he visited Christian missions in China and the Philippines. He never wavered from this belief that missionaries were a strong, positive force in the world, though less for saving souls than for their good works. Indeed, many years later, he would write unapologetically, "I have always been a champion of foreign missions, and the more so the more I learned about them."[29]

During his trip, Gifford did not mingle extensively with ordinary Filipinos, but he had definite views about them and people of color generally. Still early in his forestry career, he had used the "n" word, and at Biltmore, he had easily accepted the status of African Americans exclusively as a source of menial labor and servants. He also did not complain about the imposition of black disenfranchisement and legal segregation in the South and, at its worst, the widespread heinous lynchings of African Americans there.[30] When it came to the Filipinos and other colonial peoples at the turn of the century, Gifford, unlike Roosevelt and many other imperialists (and some anti-imperialists too), was no social Darwinist and did not use racially loaded words such as "Anglo-Saxonism" or "inferior." His strong Christian background probably precluded such stereotypes, but he clearly believed Caucasians were superior.

Blended with his Christian outlook was his strong nationalism. He viewed the American people as a force for good in the world, and he did not then consider cultural relativism and diversity. Gifford believed the Filipino people, though underdeveloped, had great potential, but as he revealed to Yale forestry students upon his return home, "The Filipinos are not as good as the best kind of white men, of course." He considered the islanders mainly as laborers, who, if wisely handled, were faithful and reliable. He was a modest contributor to Booker T. Washington's Tuskegee Institute, which promoted manual labor training for uplifting black Americans. Gifford's benign imperialism was far removed from race equality, but it was a mildly progressive view for a white American in that repressive era.[31]

Gifford and Ahern's approach to Philippine forestry was a pragmatic blend of Spanish, American, and Philippine practices. Most Spanish rules were acceptable, and the Philippine forestry bureau, in cooperation with the war department, would develop new ones. The Philippines opened new possibilities for American lumber companies to exploit the tropical forests and the natives for rich profits. But Gifford wanted such capitalistic penetration to be government regulated and managed for the broader public good. He and Ahern assessed that more than one-half of the islands were deforested, and he urged the prohibition of the sale of timber in the public domain except for lands that the Philippine Bureau of Forestry could verify were more valuable for agricultural purposes. He also called for bans on lumbering where the cutting of trees had been rampant but, in less harvested forests, recommended more lenient license terms to encourage lumber companies to consider operations in the islands. Many of the recommendations were incorporated in forestry legislation that Congress soon passed.

For the future, Gifford emphasized that more rigorous inspection and management would be required, which meant training more foresters. Education was crucial, and he urged a decisive role for the new Yale Forest School. Before he visited the islands, he asked President Hadley to consider admitting and giving tuition help to some Filipino students to attend the school. He also wanted to train American foresters to venture there. It was, he told Graves, a "great chance" for professional foresters, "and your men ought to have it, . . . for there is certain to be a large demand out there." The preparation, he advised, would include some language training in Spanish. He continued lobbying Hadley and Taft, a Yale graduate, in the same way. For the longer term, Gifford recommended establishing a forestry school in the Philippines to train Filipino foresters in their native country. Graves would also visit the islands a few years later and actively consulted with Gifford, who remained a government adviser on the Philippine forests.[32]

The motto of Gifford Pinchot's university was, "For God, for country, and for Yale," which formed the final, climactic line of the alma mater. "God" and "country" were reason enough for Gifford to support American expansion, but "Yale," with graduates Pinchot, Ahern, Taft, and Graves, the quadripartite designers of U.S. forestry policy in the Philippines, provided a neat complement to the justification of active American involvement in that distant land.[33]

*   *   *

Gifford Pinchot made himself available to his chief to take on extra assignments,[34] and Roosevelt soon appointed him to government commissions on public lands and government efficiency. Gifford eagerly served as secretary of the former commission. Here was a chance to expose the defective land laws and mismanagement of the nation's still-enormous public domain, totaling about twenty times the size of the state of Pennsylvania.

Gifford later admitted that he also had an ulterior motive—both commissions were opportunities to promote his ideas on transferring the forest service to the agriculture department. The efficiency committee actually recommended the transfer. The report of the lands commission exposed the corrupt oversight of the land laws that large landholders frequently crowded out honest homesteaders using fraudulent methods. Neither commission had much immediate impact except for Roosevelt's orders to withdraw coal lands and national forests on the public domain from purchase.[35]

Meanwhile, Roosevelt relied more on Gifford for advice and support. He obliged his forester by visiting the Pinchot home to give a pep talk—which Gifford had written—to a gathering of the Society of American Foresters. He was also turning to Gifford for grist for his speeches and soon told him that "he favored my material for his speeches more exactly than that of anyone else."[36]

11.

Empire Builder and Anti-Preservationist

After President Roosevelt's impressive electoral triumph in November 1904, congressional opposition to the transfer of forest management responsibilities eroded. The transfer bill, in which the forestry bureau was renamed the U.S. Forest Service, moved forward. When Roosevelt signed the new act, Gifford received a directive from Agriculture Secretary Wilson, specifying that "all land is to be devoted to its most productive use for the permanent good of the whole people, and not for the temporary benefit of individuals or companies." And when "conflicting interests" arise, "the question will always be decided from the standpoint of the greatest good to the greatest number in the long run."[1] Here was the utilitarian notion of what forest conservationists have subsequently called "wise use:" the forests could be cut as long as there were restrictions and reforestation to assure their permanence.

Public opinion may have made a difference in the outcome. Thanks mainly to Gifford's prodding, the American Forestry Association, called a forestry congress in Washington in early January 1905 to promote transfer to a new forest service. Roosevelt spoke to the congress, which passed a resolution endorsing it, and Congress authorized the transfer a few weeks later. The AFA had grown steadily in the previous fifteen years, with membership increasing from some 300 to 2,200 members in early 1904.[2] There was a slowdown in membership after that, but government forestry continued expanding, and Gifford was busy hiring well-trained people. Many of the newcomers to the original forestry bureau and the new forest service were Yale Forest School graduates, and he recruited Yale classmates to fill management positions.[3]

One was George Woodruff, who had played football at Yale, been captain of the crew, and was a fellow Skull and Bones member. Now a lawyer, he handled the forestry's legal work and shared Gifford's belief in active government. He would become perhaps Gifford's best friend, serving him later in other positions, including as his personal lawyer. Other recruited classmates were Philip Wells, Woodruff's assistant, and Herbert A. (Dol) Smith, also a bonesman, who directed the forestry's public affairs arm, including the increasingly important task of publicity.[4]

Gifford, well aware of the incestuous drift of government forestry, confessed to Smith, "The Bureau of Forestry will be the worst case of Nepotism since Grant, but if all the Nepots are of your type I shan't mind." Indicative of his trust, Roosevelt sometimes turned to Gifford for suggestions on presidential appointments. Gifford put forward names, many of whom had graduated from his own university, and he commented to TR, "You will notice that this is again a Yale man, but that is almost the only kind I know." For his part, the amused president commented that because he was a Harvard man himself, "he had been forced for that very reason to take more Yale men into his administration than men from any other University."[5]

Gifford's support of Jim Reynolds, his Yale friend, well exemplified the reach of the old boy network. Reynolds had undergone another career change. From missionary cleric to settlement house worker and urban reformer in New York, he then studied law and soon worked in the office of the city's new reform mayor, Seth B. Low. Reynolds took a sabbatical to study municipal government in 1903 and let Gifford know he was interested in using his skills in law and public policy in the federal government. Because of their earlier common interests in political reform, TR was well acquainted with Reynolds and later remarked that it was through him that "I first became interested in settlement work on the East Side." He also admired Reynolds's reforming zeal and commitment to honest government. It was Gifford, however, who kept his name before the president, and after his election, Roosevelt appointed Reynolds as an assistant secretary of the treasury.[6]

Because Gifford recruited many college friends, he could be seen as an ingrown elitist. To be sure, the civil service system gives an advantage to educated, professionally trained prospective government employees, but Gifford was willing to go outside the system, if necessary, in his hiring decisions and recommendations. "[I] will not let the civil service examinations stand in the way of our getting good men," he told Roosevelt.[7] In other words, in place of the old patronage politics, he developed a personal network of like-minded individuals who would be loyal to him and Roosevelt. Of course, Gifford evaded civil service requirements, mostly for senior managers in the home office, and his main requirement for supervisors in the field was men who possessed technical training in forestry and "a good knowledge of western conditions, combined with integrity, intelligence, and practical sense."[8]

Moreover, Gifford insisted upon on-site inspections before approving promotions, which were based on officers' performances. Hobnobbing with the many forestry graduates from public universities, he appreciated foresters' outdoor skills, including shooting and horseback riding, rather than their pedigree. He urged the Yale Forest School to give students practical knowledge of horses since they heavily relied on them as foresters. His colleagues warmed to his involvement in their work and affectionately referred to him as G.P. He himself made clear, "I am getting too much office work for the good of my soul," and "I must get out into the field." He mingled freely with homesteaders, ranchers, and sheep men, and he was as much at home eating his bag lunch in a cramped government office with other employees as dining at the refined Cosmos Club. As one associate later remarked, "One of G.P.'s finest qualities was his capacity to understand and work with men whose background was totally different from his own."[9] Gifford had definite ideas on the service's management, and his approach was professional yet informal. One of his requirements, undoubtedly influenced by his parents' earlier insistence on timely letter writing, was ensuring that all correspondence is answered promptly.[10]

The service's foresters and rangers were far from the home office, and each location had unique challenges. Decision-making, except for crucially important questions, was fundamentally decentralized. To guide the newly authorized forest service, he and his staff compiled a pocket-sized *Use Book* manual of 120-pages, which provided officers in the field with extracts of relevant laws and decisions and the basic rules, instructions, and guidelines for operations. The *Use Book* was invaluable to Gifford, marking "the beginning of sound, clean, and effective Government forest administration in America."[11] Even so, he expected officers in the field to be flexible and exert their authority with restraint. In admonishing one officer who had been overzealous in enforcing forest regulations, for instance, he, borrowing a Roosevelt phrase, advised, "'Step softly and carry a big stick.' But don't use the stick. It is especially important that irregular methods . . . and quarrels with local residents should be avoided."[12]

Gifford and Reynolds prevailed upon the president to appoint another committee on government efficiency to investigate the operations of several executive departments. The two were both enamored, as were many progressive reformers, with the utilization of "experts" to investigate deficiencies and recommend changes in many areas of American life. Among the president's appointees to the efficiency committee were Gifford and Garfield, who headed the bureau of corporations before becoming interior secretary. Like the previous one, this commission did not garner headlines, although a Washington newspaper provided a front-page article covering Roosevelt's appearance at the Pinchot house to talk to the assembled seventy committee and subcommittee members. Mary received the guests with charm and grace, and Gifford pronounced the meeting "a great success."[13] This time, the committee's reports on waste and mismanagement in individual departments over two years resulted in better procurement practices, management controls, and the elimination of some duplication.

Gifford early discovered that his relationship with the president was not only work but play. Even as vice president, Roosevelt had singled out Gifford as a sporting companion. "I am looking forward to seeing you at Washington," he wrote him, "and playing with you there."[14] Gifford became a regular player in the "tennis cabinet" on the White House court with the president, often as many as four or five sets.[15] The first lady, Edith, sometimes served tea to the sweaty athletes after their matches.

Another of TR's preferred exercises was leaving the White House on late afternoon walks to Rock Creek Park or the Potomac River.[16] One of these outings included Gifford. On short notice late one afternoon in October 1905, the White House summoned Gifford and Assistant Secretary of State Robert Bacon, both of whom were in good work clothes, to join the president on a walk. The three men came to a swampy area on the bank of the Potomac. It was raining, but both Gifford and Bacon had umbrellas. They sloshed around in the mud for a while, getting wet to the knees, then came to an inlet a few hundred feet wide, just west of the Washington Monument. No boat was available, so Roosevelt put his valuables in his hat, placed it back on his head, and swam across the water. Bacon and Gifford did the same, swimming with their umbrellas in their hands. Raising his halfway across, Bacon sang, "A lot of good this is doing me now." The three men walked back to the White House "in great merriment," Gifford recorded. When he returned home, Mamie McCadden, his Irish housekeeper, seeing his sodden condition and knowing of TR's outdoor escapades, exclaimed, "Drenched! You've been out with the President."[17]

*   *   *

Gifford's enthusiastic reaction to his wild romp with Roosevelt was symptomatic of his upbeat attitude. Reflecting on his own good fortune that Thanksgiving, Gifford, now forty, gave his father an effusively sanguine assessment: "I think we all have more and more, year by year, to be thankful for, . . . as I see how every year more clearly how God's good purposes in us are being worked out . . . in nearly all matters that I can think of. . . . [I]t is a great thing to be beyond the need for money. . . . Indeed that is almost an unfair advantage in a man's work, as I see it now. It is very little to my credit to have succeeded even so far as I have, in view of all the help I have received from you and from many others."[18] Deeply grateful for his success, steeped in religious faith and notions of *noblesse oblige*, and assuming inevitable progress, he was ready, even eager, to play a more active part in improving the world about him.

Gifford's optimism was also a reflection of the improving times in the nation. As prosperity returned after about 1900, many Americans who had gradually awakened to the many abuses of industrial America began pressing for political and social reform. The reformers came from many walks of life, but a new, confident middle class, eager to tame the abuses of industrial America, became a major engine for change, and Roosevelt would be their willing champion. From well-born backgrounds, TR and Gifford did not fit the profile of rising middle-class insurgents but represented the well-educated part of these stereotypical progressive reformers.

In Gifford's case, religion played a role in steering him toward reform. Before moving to Washington, the Pinchot family, without rejecting Presbyterianism, began attending the church in Manhattan of W. S. Rainsford, an Episcopalian minister, and he and Gifford sometimes played golf together. Rainsford was deeply involved in the rapidly expanding social gospel movement among the Protestant churches, reacting to rising social inequality and the challenges facing immigrants flooding American cities. In Rainsford's words, "if the Churches do not attempt to draw the well-to-do to meet the poor, and to make the general community feel that it is in the House of God they must understand each other—for if we cannot accomplish something in this direction, there is going to be monstrous trouble in this land sooner or later." Gifford pledged $200 a year to support this work.[19]

In the nation's capital, Gifford found an energetic young Episcopalian clergyman who established a mission in northeast Washington to help the poor and unfortunate. "My chance to do work is small, on account of my erratic habits," Gifford admitted, "but that is the sort I should like to be connected with."[20]

Gifford's new reform interest was young people, especially the problem of child labor. Businesses' exploitation of children in the workforce was a major problem in America. Children as young as five were often employed at menial wages and required to work twelve hours or longer in squalid factories.

In reaction, voluntary organizations like the National Child Labor Committee (NCLC) campaigned to curb the widespread abuses. Gifford's close friend Albert Beveridge, a progressive Republican senator from Indiana, was committed to child labor reform and nourished the forester's interest in the issue.[21] He strongly supported Gifford's forestry work, and Gifford became an NCLC board member.

As the Indiana senator introduced legislation in Congress to abolish child labor, Gifford optimistically believed that Beveridge's bill would succeed. From 1905–1906, Congress had recently passed, in addition to the transfer law, major legislation providing for meat inspection and the regulation of foods, drugs, and the nation's railroads. Political reform was on the march as muckraking writers revealed the unsanitary conditions in Chicago's meat-packing plants, which led to swift passage of the meat inspection law, so Gifford believed the NCLC's and journalists' exposés of the inhumane treatment of children in the workforce would also achieve quick success. "The beef inspection bill," he wrote Beveridge, "gives an absolutely satisfactory precedent, and . . . has all the simplicity of big ideas."[22]

But reform legislation did not always come easily, even with President Roosevelt's prodding. Federal legislation abolishing child labor in certain businesses engaged in interstate commerce would not become law until 1916, and the Supreme Court would later deem the law unconstitutional. The NCLC also pursued anti-child labor laws in the states. Gifford's assignment was the District of Columbia. Roosevelt soon pushed successfully for the passage of a law prohibiting child labor in the city, but conservatives in his own party stymied further measures. A related commitment of Gifford would be his lifelong support of the Boy Scouts of America, with its strong emphasis on moral values, character building, and manly endeavor, from the founding of the organization in 1910.[23]

*   *   *

The last two years of the Roosevelt presidency would be Gifford Pinchot's busiest, most productive, and most contentious. Strong cross-currents were at work, and a confusing picture emerged. On the one hand, the reach of the newly created forest policy expanded to include water power, navigable rivers, and mineral lands. On the other hand, the opposition was more determined. Gifford's new ally on the government side was Secretary of the Interior James Garfield. Committed to conservation, he worked closely with Gifford in designing and implementing the new Roosevelt policies. Gifford and Garfield became hunting and fishing companions, and Gifford would soon comment about his new friend, "The more I see of him the better I like him, and the better time we have together." They also shared a religious perspective, sometimes attending church and performing mission work together. "We talk over everything, including our committee work, and have lots of fun over it," Gifford told his mother.[24]

Despite his emphasis on scientific forestry, an evangelistic tone permeated Gifford's presentation. He brought the good news about forestry and was confident that the truths he preached would disarm its opponents. At first, he was mostly respectfully received when he explained government forestry policy in speeches to gatherings of lumbermen, ranchers, sheep men, miners, and settlers. These meetings passed resolutions, sometimes drafted by Gifford, endorsing national forest policy. He would always view lumbermen with some suspicion, but through most of the Roosevelt administration, he believed he was winning them over. He was, after all, not a preservationist but engaged in utilitarian forestry. His message was that, through competitive bidding, lumber companies could obtain access to large areas of timberland in fair condition in the national forests and cut timber equal to what they leave but of much better size and more valuable.[25]

In turn, increasing numbers of lumbermen viewed Pinchot, the government's point man, as practical and pro-business. The forest service could help enormously, for instance, in preventing and fighting forest fires, a rapidly growing problem. And even on their company-owned forest lands, government policy might support their interest in curbing rising taxes on the growing amount of cutover land that would not produce revenue until the maturation of a new crop of trees. The government would also maintain tariff barriers against lumber imports from Canada and elsewhere. As late as 1910, when he was losing faith in business cooperation, Gifford asserted, "The first great fact about conservation is that it stands for development."[26]

Gifford's message of government-business cooperation impressed Frederick E. Weyerhaeuser, whose lumber company was the nation's biggest and had made a fortune cutting trees mainly in the Northwestern forests. He was "curious to know more about the plans" of the forestry division.[27] Gifford and Weyerhaeuser gradually developed a personal relationship. Gifford arranged for him to meet with TR, and Weyerhaeuser soon became a vice president of the American Forestry Association. When Senator Weldon B. Heyburn (R-ID), a vigorous critic of national forest policy, attacked him as "the largest land grabber," Weyerhaeuser thought his affiliation with the association might hinder its work and offered to resign, but a pleading Gifford wrote him, "it is so clear that forestry can not succeed unless it has the support of great timber owners that I think it would be a very real misfortune for you to draw out."[28]

Gifford exaggerated westerners' favorable reception of his message. He came close to believing he made converts of several western politicians who had previously been sharp critics of the forest reserves. He contended that the few continuing complaints on details mostly came from those whose "toes are being trod on for the public good." He even reported to TR in the fall of 1905 that "organized opposition to your forest policy in the West is completely at an end."[29]

To be sure, thanks to Gifford's extensive public relations efforts—especially his regular meetings with cattlemen, lumbermen, and other western insurgents, at which he confidently and smoothly (but politely) explained the necessity of grazing fees on federal lands and other restrictions—more westerners became accepting of national forestry policy. Simultaneously, however, a strong prejudice against federal government control and regulation continued permeating large sections of the American West. Large numbers of westerners believed that the incredibly abundant virgin lands in their states comprised an inexhaustible, God-given "garden," which they had the "freedom" and "rights" to develop without interference from the federal government. Sectional feelings existed, and forest service pressures under the Roosevelt administration for more sweeping government regulation of the national forests exacerbated them.[30] To these complainers, forest service employees were effete eastern bureaucrats out of touch with the daily needs of enterprising, hard-working westerners. Despite Gifford's efforts to get his foresters to mingle with the local people, the service seemed far away and became a ready target of national forestry critics. Senator Charles William Fulton (R-OR) charged, for example, that foresters in the nation's capital "sit within their marble walls and theorize and dream of waters conserved, forests and streams protected and preserved throughout the ages," while "the lowly pioneer is climbing the mountain side where he will erect his humble cabin, and . . . engage in the laborious work of carving out for himself and his loved ones a home and dwelling place."

Forest policy was becoming a hard sell to westerners and a hot political issue in the forested states. In 1905, for example, the Republican governor of Idaho told Gifford he fully supported national forest policy, but a year later, he began criticizing it.[31]

A manifestation of the resistance to forest service authority was an amendment attached to an agriculture appropriation bill in early 1907 that effectively rescinded the president's power to create new national forests in six Northwestern states. Roosevelt was reluctant to veto a measure containing many other necessary provisions but adopted Gifford's strategy. His forest service associates had already planned prospective national forests in the six states and drafted presidential proclamations for new reserves incorporating the main features. As Congress approved the bill, TR signed the proclamations, creating twenty-one national forests totaling sixteen million acres in these states, and signed the appropriations measure into law.[32]

Roosevelt's action further galvanized the western opposition to the administration's conservation policies. That summer of 1907, for example, the governor of Colorado and other opponents called a public lands convention to air their grievances publicly. Pinchot, Garfield, and Newell spoke and corrected some misconceptions of federal government policies, but the decidedly unfriendly audience gave them short shrift. In the end, though, the resolutions were only mildly critical. The convention "was intended to be packed and was packed," Gifford reported to Roosevelt, but "that fact," instead of a cause for concern, "became so evident as to destroy its capacity to do harm." Indeed, "the forest policy is now a dead issue."[33]

A newly emerging issue was electric power. As electricity spread to run American factories and light American homes, power dams on American streams and rivers were becoming critically important. Congress had constitutional authority over the nation's interstate waterways but had traditionally given away the rights and privileges for water power development to private power companies, which then had a monopoly over the generation, distribution, and rate charges of electricity. Perhaps one-half of public lands containing waterways suitable for future power dams lay in the national forests now under the administration of the forest service. Gifford wanted the government to lease water power sites in the national forests to power companies for up to fifty years at a reasonable charge. Nonetheless, private power companies continued opposing government control and fought any legislation that imposed a charge or time limits. In his last year in office, Roosevelt vetoed two bills that omitted those provisions.[34]

In the final months of the Roosevelt administration, Gifford identified other public lands containing potentially valuable dam sites, which TR withdrew from sale until Congress could act, hopefully, to protect them. Congress earlier authorized the removal of water power sites from public lands for future government reclamation projects. With Roosevelt's approval, Garfield and Pinchot also withdrew additional sites as places for ranger stations. In their haste, however, some were surveyed quickly and made larger than necessary, and some were deliberately located on water power sites to assure government control until regular site withdrawals could take place. The power companies and conservatives generally were displeased with these actions.

*　*　*

Gifford Pinchot's involvement in protecting timber in national forests engaged him in public lands policy, homesteader rights, and grazing, ranching, and mining interests but expanded to include concerns about sufficient water supply, electrical power, navigation, and irrigation and soil preservation for continued fertile farming. All the nation's natural resources were connected, and the "conservation of natural resources" became the catch-all phrase to describe the interrelated components and the necessity of coordinating them through coherent government policies. Gifford later claimed that this holistic conception came to him "all of a sudden" while horseback riding in February 1907. In an instant, he realized it was not several overlapping relationships among competing government agencies separately overseeing parts of the nation's natural resources. Now he saw the big picture: "the one great central problem of the use of the earth for the good of man."[35] Whether he had such a eureka moment that winter morning is questionable, but he discussed his broader conception with senior government colleagues. Later, Gifford acknowledged that W. J. McGee, former head of the Bureau of American Ethnology, refined the new, comprehensive policy into a philosophical vision—"the use of the natural resources for the greatest good of the greatest number for the longest time."[36] Gifford directed his staff to include the slogan in letters drafted for his signature.

Conservation had come front and center as the priority issue in America. One indication was a rising interest in the nation's inland waterways. Conservationists now better understood that the nation's many navigable rivers and canals, the Great Lakes, and the Intracoastal Waterway could be harnessed more fruitfully for flood control purposes and as railroad competition in transporting nonperishable goods. Embracing this wellspring of interest in March 1908, TR persuaded Congress to authorize a temporary Inland Waterways Commission to investigate the transportation and conservation dimensions of the nation's waters. To conservationists, the creation of the commission signaled the triumph of science in a now-modernized nation-state, and they looked forward to the commission experts advancing several coordinated water projects that would produce a more efficient and productive economy. The commission's report soon recommended that plans for inland waterways "shall take full account of all resources connected with running waters, and shall look to the protection of these resources from monopoly and to their administration in the interests of the people." Sectional divisions in Congress prevented agreement on the commission's extention, but meanwhile, Roosevelt joined Gifford and the commission members on a steamboat traversing the Mississippi River. TR publicized the commission's promise in speeches during stops at towns and cities along the way.

Twenty state governors from nearby states joined the river excursion, and interest soon swelled for a meeting of state leaders to discuss common conservation issues. Delighted with this interest, Roosevelt invited all the state governors to a White House conference in April 1908. Thirty-four came and the other twelve sent representatives.[37] It was the first time in American history that the governors had convened together, and significantly, the issue of the conservation of the nation's natural resources was the stimulus for their meeting. Moreover, representatives from about seventy private associations concerned with conservation issues were also invited. In a fitting complement to Gifford's hard work, his mother hosted a huge reception for the delegates at the Pinchot home and received some 1,000 guests.[38]

The main achievement of the high-profile conference was publicity. The extensive press coverage raised national consciousness about forestry and conservation, and Gifford was "as pleased about it as a hen that has laid an egg," he wrote La Farge.[39] Capitalizing on this interest, TR created a National Conservation Commission of about fifty representatives from government, industry, and science to work with similar groups in the states and prepare an inventory of the nation's national resources. It was Gifford's suggestion, and TR appointed him as its head.

The administration's rapidly expanding conservation agenda created a swift, unrelenting adverse reaction. One sign was Congress's rejection of the president's request for $50,000 to fund the National Conservation Commission, which took six months to prepare a three-volume report providing careful estimates of the amount and adequacy of the nation's natural resources. President Roosevelt praised the report to Congress as "one of the most fundamentally important documents ever laid before the American people," but Congress refused payment of expenses of any board or commission that Congress had not authorized.[40]

Critics of conservation also began attacking the forest service's public affairs activities. A first reaction came in early 1908 when a wary Senate passed a resolution requiring the secretary of agriculture to submit a summary statement listing the names of forest service personnel attending meetings and conventions during the previous year. Gifford and Smith sent the service's publications to greatly expanded mailing lists, and they flooded print media with press releases giving current news on forestry matters. This revved-up publicity mill later prompted one historian to assert that Gifford Pinchot "may have been the best press agent of his time." These actions brought Gifford closer to crossing the line into propaganda for activities that Congress had not specifically sanctioned. Beveridge warned his friend about the criticism, but Gifford claimed he simply reminded the public that the forest service was busy.[41]

President Theodore Roosevelt and Gifford Pinchot on a trip down the Mississippi River with the Inland Waterways Commission, October 1907. (Bain Collection, Library of Congress)

The chief forester's attempts to avoid the appearance of lobbying were not convincing. For instance, Gifford persuaded Senator Jonathan Dolliver (R-IA) to pay for the printing of 100,000 copies of his Senate speech favorable to forestry, which the forest service then sent to names on its mailing lists. Gifford conceded that press publicity had to be "scrupulously confined to its legitimate field of education" but asserted that he was not glorifying himself or the forest service because neither name appeared on the publications. Congress nonetheless prohibited the use of government funds for the preparation of magazine or newspaper articles.[42] However, the measure did little to stifle the service's publicity endeavors.

In the wake of negative reactions, Gifford's benign view of a voluntary business-government partnership began to fray. Businessmen would go their own way if they believed the government regulations seemed too onerous and worked to their competitive disadvantage. The forester now saw the opposition in terms of "special interests," such as the water power "trust" or profit-mad lumbermen and selfish sheepherders, working for private gain against the common good. To Gifford, the conservation agenda was obviously just and right, so nefarious intriguers had to be deliberately distorting the conservation message and congressional opponents willingly did their bidding. He was surely right in defining the fundamental issue as one of the ideas between the public good and private gain. There were indeed concerted efforts among land speculators, lumbermen, and developers in the West to undercut the Roosevelt conservation policies and tarnish his chief forester's image. Gifford had experienced hard-nosed corporate lawyers representing power companies interested only in their clients' aggrandizement. A real battle was in the offing.

But Gifford did not allow for additional motivations.[43] He minimized the potentially negative impacts of strong sectional feelings, political partisanship, and congressmen's concerns over their prerogatives in reaction to an assertive president willing to stretch or evade the law through executive orders and commissions. Gifford's allies had warned him about the possible downside of these other factors. Regarding the plan for presidential proclamations creating additional forest reserves in the Northwest, for example, a worried Secretary Wilson inquired, "Have you thought this over carefully? Have you resolved that it is not coming up to make you a good deal of trouble when Congressmen learn what has been done?"[44] Gifford, however, minimized these concerns and framed the issue in terms of "the inevitable opposition of the men whose private interests have been made to yield to the general good," and he did not foresee "any serious difficulty" in achieving the latter.[45]

His enthusiasm and evangelism, each reinforcing the other, made him instinctively assertive for progress toward achieving his policy goals, and the same qualities could make him resistant to compromise with those who had different ideas and policies. Gifford also exuded a belief in democracy and faith in experts—that the people were willing to be led by professionals like him toward more democratic rule—although the tension between expert elites and democracy would prove to be an unstable mix for the long-term success of progressive governance.

*   *   *

Besides attacks from special interests, Gifford faced severe criticism from preservationists. Gifford was an avid hunter and had no qualms about shooting animals and game. How could he reconcile the conservation of the forests with the seemingly wanton destruction of wildlife? To the forester, there were no second thoughts; other conservationists like Roosevelt were also avid hunters, even bloodthirsty in their passion for shooting large animals. To them, hunting was an assumed male trait in American culture.

The exclusive Boone and Crockett Club was a manifestation of seemingly contradictory elements. Founded in 1887 by Theodore Roosevelt and other patrician New Yorkers interested in hunting, the limited-membership club promoted "manly sport with the rifle," and a prerequisite for membership required killing three different species of large American game. The club's mission was killing, though preservation also had a place. The club's sportsmen resisted market hunters making their living shooting large numbers of wild animals. They were also at the forefront of public efforts to save the American bison, which had been hunted to near extinction in the 1880s, and they supported regulations to preserve large game in the nation. Stimson was an early member; Gifford had joined in 1897.[46]

However, Gifford did not really absorb the club's preservationist part. In 1903, he proposed to his brother that they take a "whack" at California grizzlies, which were "almost extinct," he admitted, "so it would be a great feather in our caps if we could bring away a hide." Though not an excuse for his predatory behavior as a hunter, the best that can be said about Gifford was that he was a sportsman, not a greedy market hunter, and sometimes took time to cut up and eat much of his take.[47] He also practiced catch-and-release for most fish that were not to be eaten.

In the first years of Roosevelt's presidency, Gifford turned to saltwater fishing. It was a "fun" experience, he first admitted, and shortly said, "I had rather go to Florida in the fishing season than into the mountains after bear, and that is saying a good deal for me." In subsequent years, Gifford would pursue jewfish, sharks, manta, tuna, marlin, porpoises, barracuda, and even whales.[48]

The mounting criticism of wild animal killing from preservationists, led by Muir, made Gifford back away from hunting trips in favor of deep-sea

Gifford Pinchot, an avid fisherman, with one of two big marlin, each more than eight feet in length, he caught off the California coast, 1906. This one was apparently already stuffed, and soon both were displayed on the walls of Grey Towers. (Gifford Pinchot, *Fishing Talk*, facing p. 205)

fishing—Gifford simply transferred big game shooting to the pursuit of water species. Off the Southern California coast in 1909, for instance, he took position on the stern of a 25-foot launch and proceeded to shoot with a revolver at orcas swimming nearby. To Gifford, the water "hunting" and the wounding (or worse) of the mammals was simply another good sport.[49]

John Muir may not have known about Gifford as a sea plunderer, but he became Gifford's severest critic. During their first encounters much earlier, Muir and Gifford's viewpoints on conservation issues had seemed compatible on the surface. Muir had accepted that the nation's development needs meant that lumbermen's regulated cutting in national forests was "inevitable." The land office was blatantly corrupt, but with Gifford's help, Muir would "hope for the best and do what we can to head off blundering plundering moneymaking officials." Gifford also supported some preservationist initiatives, such as saving the wondrous Crater Lake as a national park, and he was a member of Muir's Sierra Club.[50]

Gifford Pinchot, shooting a revolver at fairly close range at three orcas off the California coast, 1909. In his mature years, Gifford increasingly emphasized salt-water fishing over the hunting of big game but here combined the two. (Charles Frederick Holder, *Recreations of a Sportsman on the Pacific Coast*, facing p. 324)

Gifford, like the preservationists, negatively viewed sheep grazing on America's public lands. It was no small matter; in some reserves, the number of grazing sheep reached hundreds of thousands. Gifford had early observed that sheep trampled tree seedlings under their sharp hoofs and chewed up grasses before moving on to other pastures for more abuse. Despite this despoliation, Gifford approached the problem pragmatically.[51] In 1906, Gifford and Roosevelt supported a measure that restricted sheep's access to national forest lands and charged herdsmen for grazing rights there, but sheep men fiercely protested the government's regulations and charges. Gifford spent much time on a western trip trying to smooth over the disagreement. "It is always a good thing to talk these matters over frankly," he said and believed too optimistically that the sheep men were "very much quieted down and most of them are quite satisfied with the results."[52]

Muir and the preservationists wanted near total exclusion of animals, but Gifford kept them on the margins. Neither Muir nor other preservationists were invited to the governors' conference on conserving the nation's natural resources. When preservationists complained, Gifford disingenuously replied that the White House gathering was not a forestry meeting but had grown out of the Inland Waterways Commission.[53]

The utilitarian-preservationist tensions escalated into a major controversy involving the proposed construction of a dam in the scenic Hetch Hetchy Valley on the Tuolumne River in Yosemite National Park. Its supporters argued that a dam was needed at the valley's lower end to create a reservoir that would provide a sustained water supply and hydroelectric power for San Francisco and the surrounding Bay area 150 miles away. In April 1906, the damage from the catastrophic San Francisco earthquake, and the even more destructive fires immediately afterward, dramatized the city's fragile infrastructure. During the ensuing rebuilding effort, public attention focused on the desirability of the Hetch Hetchy site for San Francisco's long-term, stable water requirements.[54]

Garfield and Gifford were both persuaded that the city's water needs were genuine and that the Hetch Hetchy dam would provide the desired supply, and they so advised the president, who approved the project. Gifford believed it was a case of the greater good for hundreds of thousands of Bay area citizens, and he then perceived almost no preservationists' opposition.[55]

The Hetch Hetchy controversy exposed that John Muir and Gifford Pinchot, already on different trajectories, represented two sides of the conservation cause. The tension between them, sometimes complementary and sometimes conflicting, thereafter defined the citizens' conservation movement. For one thing, Gifford, like TR, loved sport hunting, while Muir, an uncompromising advocate of the "rights of animals," forcefully criticized "the murder of business of hunting."

It was a fundamental, philosophical difference involving, for example, the education of young Americans. To Muir, boys needed to learn how to move away from "natural hunting blood-savagery into natural sympathy with all our fellow mortals—plants and animals as well as men." Gifford later related an anecdote, revealing their different viewpoints. During his and Muir's excursion to the Grand Canyon in 1897, Muir had not allowed Gifford to kill a tarantula. To Gifford, the poisonous spider was of no value, but Muir believed the spider had as much right to live as humans.[56] Always outspoken and uncompromising in his religious enthusiasm for the natural world, Muir had impressed Roosevelt during a carefree camping venture in Yosemite in 1903, sharing his passionate antipathy to hunting; however, TR remained enamored with big game shooting for sport.

Led by Muir, the Sierra Club was somewhat divided because many of its central California members, who would benefit from the new water source, were sympathetic to the dam project. It was a complex issue, as many opponents were reformers who did not want to reward what they perceived as "corrupt" San Francisco city fathers with a municipal water supply. In contrast, other progressives, opposed to a private company water monopoly, wanted the dam and a publicly controlled water supply. The preservationists belatedly mobilized in protest, but Congress would finally authorize construction of the Hetch Hetchy dam in 1913.[57]

*   *   *

Historians have rightly viewed the progressive reform movement as a widespread national response to the problems and challenges confronting a rising urban-industrial America. Even conservation questions directly affecting rural areas usually had an urban connection. San Francisco's water needs affected the rural Yosemite area. Moreover, the growth of lumber and power monopolies impacted rural areas, and the requirements for their regulation were part of the nation's industrial maturation. People were fascinated by new scientific and technological breakthroughs such as the telephone, electricity, the airplane, and the automobile, rapidly becoming Americans' preferred mode of transportation. Material "progress" was indeed intertwined with the progressive reformers' faith in a better future. Even the farm economy was being transformed with the introduction of large gasoline-powered combines and reapers to produce wheat and other crops on a much more extensive scale; agribusiness was expanding.

But the United States was still predominantly a nation of small towns and rural communities. In this ongoing urban-industrial transformation, what would become of the millions of ordinary farmers eking out a living on their family farms? Were they to be left behind, even forgotten? Was the Jeffersonian ideal of the yeoman farmer now an obsolete shibboleth? Roosevelt was sensitive to small farmers' needs, and the reclamation act and his advocacy of electric power regulation would benefit many of them. In his annual message in 1904, he wrote, "Nearly half of the people in this country devote their energies to growing things from the soil. Until a recent date little has been done to prepare these millions for their life work." But his administration did not really focus closely on the question of farm life until Sir Horace Plunkett, an Irishman who had promoted agricultural cooperatives in his home country, called on Roosevelt in early 1908.[58] An intrigued president referred Plunkett to Pinchot, who immediately warmed to the Irishman's enthusiastic message and engaging personality.

Gifford shortly developed the notion of a commission to investigate country life in America, which TR endorsed. The result was his appointment of an unpaid commission of experts knowledgeable about rural America. Economically, it would explore ways to help American farms become more profitable but would also focus on educational opportunities and cultural outlets. As Roosevelt charged the commissioners, "Agriculture is not the whole of country life. The great rural interests are human interests, and good crops are of little value to the farmer unless they open the door to a good kind of life on the farm."[59] Roosevelt included Gifford as the administration's lone representative on the committee, which conducted extensive visits to rural areas throughout the nation, held public hearings, and distributed a questionnaire to hundreds of thousands of farmers asking for more information about them and their families.

Gifford was too busy to participate in the commissioners' deliberations. Moreover, city-bred himself, his knowledge of the American farmer at the time was impressionistic. At the same time, he never really liked big cities or their corrupt political machines. His forestry career had given him considerable exposure to rural America and some sensitivity to its problems. Gifford later wrote of American farm life that, as a forester, "I had seen no little of its hardships, and especially of the hardships of farm women, and I was more than glad to help" the commission.[60] He thus followed the commission's hearings with interest and, given his reform perspective, was privately critical of its comparatively mild recommendations. It called for improving rural roads, for instance, but squandered the opportunity to make bold recommendations. Gifford even complained that the commission's "accepted plans have been thrown overboard without ceremony" in the final report, but as an administration loyalist, he nonetheless offered no public protest and signed it.[61]

The commission experience convinced Gifford of the plight of American farmers and their importance as the backbone of solid American values. It also brought him into close contact with leading spokesmen of the movement for scientific farming and improvements in agronomy, like Plunkett and three generations of the Wallace family in Iowa.[62] And the report's recommendation of improved rural roads would be a subject Gifford would promote aggressively during his later political career. More immediately, it moved him closer to Charlie Gill, a former Yale classmate, star tackle on the football team, and a Skull and Bones colleague, who served as the pastor of small Congregationalist churches in rural northern New England after divinity school. Gifford contributed monetarily to help Gill's churches survive and meet their communities' social service needs.[63]

As part of the social gospel's soul-searching into Protestantism's shortcomings, Gill gathered materials on the problems of the rural and small-town churches. Pairing up with Gifford, the two published a book together. Gill did the research and writing, but Gifford genuinely endorsed the effort and supported it financially. Their book, focusing on country churches (including Catholic) in several counties in New Hampshire and Vermont, was a self-conscious effort to understand the problems caused by a more urban and secular America, suggesting some antidotes to restore their influence in their communities. Gill and Gifford would later publish a follow-on study of rural churches in Ohio.[64]

The Roosevelt administration was not quite finished with its conservation agenda, and TR and Gifford were also determined to leave markers indicating the future international direction of the movement. Again, mostly at Gifford's prompting, in the summer of 1908, Roosevelt sent the forester as his personal emissary to Ottawa and Mexico City to invite their nations to attend a North American conference in Washington for the discussion of common natural resource issues affecting the continent. The two governments sent delegates, and the U.S. representatives were members of TR's "tennis cabinet:" Garfield, Bacon, and Pinchot. A significant conclusion of the exchange of information and views at that gathering, which held daily sessions only two weeks before the end of the Roosevelt administration, was that the natural resource questions were worldwide in scope and required concerted international action. It formally asked Roosevelt to call a world conservation conference.[65] Again, TR and Pinchot were already working on that possibility, and the state department prevailed upon The Netherlands government to invite fifty-eight foreign governments to an international conference later that year at The Hague to discuss the world's natural resources and their proper utilization.

*   *   *

Theodore Roosevelt and Gifford Pinchot had come a long way together, and the president jocularly commented to Archie Butt, his military aide, that "Gifford truly has an affection for me. . . . It is almost fetish worship, and . . . Pinchot truly believes that in case of certain conditions I am perfectly capable of killing either himself or me. If conditions were such that only one could live[,] he knows that I should possibly kill him as the weaker of the two, and he, therefore, worships this in me." Perhaps TR's weird Darwinist analogy did not include rethinking their boxing-wrestling encounter a decade earlier, but Roosevelt's assessment of Gifford as a willing acolyte was accurate.

It was also true, however, that TR found Gifford Pinchot an indispensable adviser on many issues and was clearly fond of him, as Butt also observed.[66] Toward the end of his presidency, Roosevelt stroked the forester's ego with high praise. He identified Gifford, for example, along with Root, Taft, and Garfield, as his most valued advisers and told him directly, "I have never known a more disinterested public servant than you are, or a more efficient one—there couldn't be." More effusively, he soon added, "As long as I live I shall feel for you a mixture of respect and admiration and of affectionate regard. I am a better man for having known you. . . . For seven and a half years we have worked together, and now and then played together—and have been altogether better able to work because we have played; and I owe to you a particular debt of obligation for a very large part of the achievement of this administration."[67] The solid friendship of the two men would endure, and before long, they would embark on a remarkable collaboration in a new chapter of American politics.

12.

Family Turmoil

At Thanksgiving 1905, when Gifford offered a paean of praise for the good fortune of the Pinchot clan, he singled out the improved health of the family members. His father was "so much better than a year ago, and Mamee also, and Amos too," he had noted. Nettie was also in the best physical shape she had been in a decade, and Alan reported to the family that at dinner parties, "she looks quite magnificent in her tiara and smart dresses, quite the gem of the corps diplomatique."[1]

Gifford's rosy assessment of the Pinchot family's robust health would prove ephemeral and, in short order, several misfortunes befell family members' well-being. Amos first told Gifford, "I like the law work very well" at the district attorney's office "but cannot do much work and without Saturdays and Sundays coming along I don't think I could keep it up." He also confided to Gifford, "I am economizing my energy and going to bed early" and that his future plans were "rather undecided."[2] Moreover, Gertrude had a miscarriage in 1906, which made her almost helpless, and Amos, suffering burn-out from his lawyer's work, complained in April 1907, "I've been so stale that almost any change would be welcome." It was, in fact, "an awful grind if continued long enough and next month I shall try to get transferred" to another division.[3] Amos was then diagnosed with appendicitis. He had a successful appendectomy and, during his slow convalescence, resigned from his position.

James's problems were next to interrupt the activities of the Pinchots. It began with family worries. Papa's attachment to the Yale summer school at Grey Towers was a labor of love, but he was suffering bouts of depression, which the deaths of his two brothers and his reclusive nature probably accentuated. His penchant for fault-finding extended even to criticism of Gifford's friendship with Harry Graves. Papa believed that the head of the Yale Forest School was taking credit for Gifford's accomplishments and trying to undercut him, and James, always the formalist, deplored the two friends' greeting of one another with an affectionate hug as "both childish and foolish . . . I am beginning to hate to have him around."[4]

James's greatest concern was Gifford's awe of Roosevelt. He had rejoiced over TR's election in 1904, and Theodore and Edith had entertained the senior Pinchots several times at the White House. But James never warmed to Roosevelt and thought the president was using Gifford for selfish purposes. Gifford was, James told his eldest son, "sacrificing" himself for the president and would "soon be a used up man. . . . If you are to have [a career] of any kind you must begin to prepare for it," which he could not do while adoringly serving that "vampire" Roosevelt.[5]

While there was a little wisdom in Papa's advice to maintain some distance from Roosevelt, his comment can be dismissed as that of an old fuddy-duddy. TR was no vampire, and James was out of touch with his son's important role in helping his chief guide the growing progressive reform impulse in constructive

Mary, Gifford, and James Pinchot at Grey Towers, early 1900s. (USDA Forest Service, Grey Towers NHS)

directions. Gifford was also making a name for himself as TR's alter ego and as the acknowledged leader of a more robust conservation movement. Moreover, Mary could become exasperated with her husband for his finicky behavior. James complained, for example, that when he went to Grey Towers without a full complement of servants, he had to hire additional temporary help to attend to his needs. Mary rejoined that "with three servants you could stand it for a few days without telegraphing to N.Y. for strangers. . . . Now do settle down and keep quiet," she implored.[6]

Despite his crotchety attitude, James seemed physically sound during the summer of 1907 when he, now seventy-eight, and Mary visited Europe. Mary exuded about him, "It is really most pleasant to see him so well and so amused," and upon his return, Gifford reported, "Father is flourishing."[7] But within days, James fell sick. His condition did not improve, and doctors warned the family members that James, suffering from kidney failure, might not recover.

Family was first to all the Pinchots, and Nettie thought she should be near her failing father. Her dilemma was that King Edward VII was considering a visit to Denmark, and she would be expected to serve as hostess during his sojourn there. "Of course if anyone is ill," she wrote her mother, "Ed- may go hang, but it would be a bore for Alan if all were well and to have to entertain alone." When her father's condition deteriorated, Nettie and Alan booked passage to America. James died on February 6, 1908, with Mary and the three children at his bedside. He did not suffer much in his last days, and, Mary reflected, "He had a very happy life and went to his repose as he would have liked."[8]

After leaving the district attorney's office, Amos opened his own law practice in lower Manhattan but did not seek new clients. Family estate matters initially kept him well-occupied. Mary inherited everything from her husband, except for Grey Towers, which went to Gifford and Amos jointly at Mary's request, and his other Milford properties were distributed equitably to his three children. Amos took over responsibility for the maintenance of Grey Towers and advised his mother on her investments. Although Mary's brokers gave her advice on investments, Amos nonetheless made his own suggestions for buying and selling bonds and stocks. His recommendations, he counseled, were "safe and such as father would have approved of and I believe thoroughly that they are."[9]

Though a generally accurate statement, Amos was willing to take on more risk. His main financial interest was real estate in Manhattan, which offered potentially huge profits but was a volatile market. Earlier, Amos had gone through an embarrassing learning experience. On his own, he had bought property lots and then found he was cash poor, with insufficient money on hand to pay for the costs of a big, new apartment building for his family on Park Avenue at Eighty-Fifth Street and the mortgages on his other properties. He needed $30,000, which Gifford came up with as a short-term loan. His brother's generosity, a grateful Amos wrote him, "helps me out of a hole and I will pay you back as soon as I possibly can."[10]

Amos was more a speculator than investor in residential real estate. After James's death, for example, he advised his mother to sell three of his father's houses and realize "a quick profit of a large amount," and he urged her to buy a lot close to his new Park Avenue apartment house, which, he explained, was appreciating rapidly in value. If she purchased the property, he claimed, she could divide it into several lots and then sell them. "There would be good profit in it," he counseled. Mary ignored his recommendations and seemed little interested in the complications and worries that might arise from changes in her late husband's conservative investments. Undeterred, Amos bought properties on his own, and soon Gifford would note that "[h]is investments are turning out very well indeed."[11] That was likely true, although the prosperous times helped.

Amos also turned his attention to Republican politics. In the spring of 1908, he declared himself a Republican candidate for the New York State Assembly but, as a novice among the party, did not get the nomination. He also served as party captain of a district and, according to his wife, was "very successfully turning out a lot of voters who usually don't go to the polls, by actually pulling them out of bed, or saloons."[12] Then his plans to participate in the 1908 presidential campaign were interrupted when Gertrude had a second miscarriage and was "in dangerous condition" for a time. Still trying to recover her strength the following winter, she went alone to Europe for several months. She loved her children dearly but was too debilitated to oversee them, and Mary and Mamie McCadden in Washington also looked after them sometimes. Gertrude's departure was part of a recurring pattern of long separations that could not help but strain her marriage.[13]

During Gertrude's absence, Amos was not alone. The family had as many as eight servants and a governess living with them who tended to his basic needs and their spacious apartment.[14] With no regular job, he spent more time with his college roommate, Sumner Gerard, a lawyer with an office near Amos's. Gerard was still a bachelor living a gay life in the city. Amos sometimes joined him in his merrymaking, and Gerard even moved into Amos's home, which, Amos thought, "makes the house more cheerful." Opinionated and carefree, Gerard was clearly not a salubrious influence on Amos, who admitted that his friend was a difficult personality at times. Once when he was ill, for instance, he refused to stay in bed, insisted on reading the newspapers, considered his nurses useless, and despite a fever of 105°, "kept right on twitting the doctors on their inability to cure disease." Still, the two men remained close social companions.[15]

After Gertrude had been in Europe for five months, Amos planned to join her. She indicated, however, that she probably was not yet well enough to bring the children along, so Amos, willing to do his part, managed to leave their two children with Mrs. Minturn in New York and soon went abroad to join his wife, accompanied by his mother.[16] While Mary went off to visit Nettie, Gertrude and Amos rented an apartment in Venice for a few weeks.

The couple's reunion was a disaster. Amos reported that Gertrude was in a "queer nervous condition," which Mamee believed was partly the result of "her solitary life with no diversion." Amos also disclosed that she was "in poor spirits," and on his way home, he arranged to take her to Lausanne, Switzerland, to put her under the care of a leading nerve specialist.[17] Following her contretemps with Amos, Gertrude wrote Gifford, whom she worshipped for his empathetic personality, describing in blunt terms their unhappy Venetian encounter and frankly appealing to him for support. What particularly annoyed her was Amos and Sumner Gerard cavorting together in New York during her European convalescence. Gertrude emphasized that she clearly disliked the "very bad effect" of Gerard, and "I wish Amos could never see him again." She believed their companionship harmed her husband's sensitive personality. Completing the psychological portrait of him, she added, "Just now Amos is profoundly discouraged and skeptical about himself, and absorbed in his own feelings, and looking for entertainment to forget it all," she lamented, "and nothing could have been worse for him than to have me away all the winter and Sumner."

In her view, Amos had come to a "most critical" time in his life, "which will make or mar our whole future," but "I shall be a wretched woman and he an unhappy man if he tries to fill the void by a life of effort after fun." Despite his health problems, she believed he made a serious mistake giving up his deputy district attorney job, and she wanted him to find another one. Amos often felt ill in his previous position, Gertrude acknowledged, but "I don't think Amos will be either well or happy till he makes up his mind to do some regular work for which he has to make sacrifices and be bound down if need be," and he "would improve gradually when he settled down." "Making investments will never absorb him so as to give him contentment," she argued, and he needed "to be tied soon by work in order to grow into the kind of man he could be."[18]

Gifford must have found Gertrude's dire warning about his younger brother's condition unsettling, but he gave Amos and his behavior the benefit of the doubt. During Amos's care for Gertrude after her second miscarriage, for example, he told his mother, "Amos is a far larger man than any but a few of us know, and he will make it appear, too." He was also in touch with his brother's needs and aspirations, and the two took a trip with Henry and Mabel Stimson to Montana, which Gifford wrote enthusiastically to Mamee, was "a great success. I have had no such time with Amos for years, and I enjoyed it to the full. Also, I think it did him much good."[19]

If Gertrude was worried about her husband's health, his mother was beginning to wonder about Gertrude's. To Mary, having Amos with her on the trip to Europe was like their old travel times, and she commented, "He is such a comfort and joy to me." Already partial to her son, she commented that Gertrude "has been rather rash" in her judgments. In fact, Gertrude's retiring nature made her seem somewhat dull, and Mary had earlier criticized her daughter-in-law, who, even in good health, "does not go to dinners, luncheons, or teas—or give any."[20]

Gertrude could also be tactless. She thought Alan Johnstone was "a little snob" and preferred to socialize with Nettie only when her husband was not around. Alan was no snob, although his aristocratic pretensions and sucking up to royalty could make him appear something of a fop to democratic Americans. In any case, it did Gertrude no good to express her prejudice so insensitively, and Nettie, aware of her disdain, was standoffish. "I wonder if Gertrude hated a note I wrote her," she told Amos. "I meant it to be nice but had misgivings after."[21]

Poor Gertrude. The Pinchot family seemed put off by her behavior, and even Gifford, who was usually upbeat about family matters, was ambivalent about his sister-in-law. After her return from Europe, he noted she was "very evidently in an excessively nervous state." Still, he added, "she is such a fine girl," and he predicted she would be "coming back to normal soon." At the same time, not surprisingly, he defended his brother from Gertrude's plaint, arguing that Amos despised men who shunned work and denied Gerard's bad influence on him. This prompted another letter from Gertrude, who elaborated on her deep fears concerning Sumner's presence in the house, but Amos had pronounced that "S. is to live with us always." The result of this impasse, she lamented, was that "Amos is estranged from me." "All these things were opened to me in Venice, and after I went to pieces," she admitted. Gertrude prepared herself to save their marriage. It would be "a long and hard fought fight," she acknowledged, "all the harder because I can do so little."[22]

The two were growing apart, and their problem was both physical and psychological. The physical explanation is that they were sexually incompatible. Women of her social milieu in Victorian America were not expected to

Gertrude Minturn Pinchot, c. 1910. (Bain Collection,
Library of Congress)

have much interest in sex or enjoy it, and Gertrude found sexual relations with
her husband unpleasant. (Her poor health likely exacerbated their sexual tension.) Her repeated desire for Amos to extend his absences indicated her lack of
interest in their physical intimacy. When Amos was trying to recover from his
malaria and nervous condition, her suggestion of up to a two-year separation
was extreme; she subsequently went away or asked him to stay away, even when
his health improved and they had family responsibilities together. Their son
later confirmed, "She and my father never got along sexually because of the
inhibitions of that Victorian family of hers."[23]

In any case, during this turmoil, Gertrude fell under the spell of spiritualism, which further removed her from the real world. Curiously, her and
Gifford's common interest in the supernatural world gave them an emotional
connection. She told him she had communicated with "The Light," and the
clarity of this "most extraordinary experience," which involved receiving messages from his deceased father, grandfather Amos, and his beloved Laura, made
it "unquestionable that spirits from beyond are with us." A sympathetic Gifford

told Mamee that he was "delighted" to hear about his sister-in-law's "remarkable séance."[24]

Gertrude knew her brother-in-law could help Amos get a job in the conservation field. Helen Garfield, James Garfield's spouse, took it upon herself as a friend to remind Gifford of the possibly tragic costs for Amos and Gertrude as well as their children if their marriage failed (she spoke from experience, as her brother's marriage had dissolved in divorce). Helen's "warning note" urged Gifford to get Amos involved in the conservation movement and "keep up his interest and not let it flag." [25]

Helen and Gertrude may not have been aware of the extent of Gifford's involvement with Amos's job problem. The forester had already invited Amos to "take up this conservation campaign" and give talks on "the economic, political, or sociological sides, the human sides, and I would keep more in touch with the natural resources end. . . . Think it over," Gifford urged. "It looks good to me."[26] Amos did not accept the offer, but Gifford did not see him as a pleasure-seeker. He knew of Amos's interest in political issues, for instance.[27] Gifford (and his mother, thinking similarly) could well assume that Gertrude's illnesses and absences, together with her sensitive personality and quirky spiritualism, were as much to blame for the couple's problems.

What was really going on? Amos probably suffered from what psychiatrists today call high functioning bipolar disorder, or manic depression, a condition afflicting someone who can appear perfectly normal and performs adequately for a time, only to experience severely depressed periods. A person can have seemingly ordinary work days, for example, only to be down and out in the evenings or weekends. Amos exhibited this type of erratic behavior while employed in the district attorney's office, claiming to like the work but complaining of the grind and exhaustion until he gave it up. Gertrude would see him in every mood, but such a condition would allow him to show only normal behavior to those acquaintances, such as his brother and mother, who saw him only occasionally and in more relaxed circumstances. As she told Gifford, "You can hardly understand as he only shows you his best side."[28]

If Amos was bipolar, it was undiagnosed, comparatively mild, and not far removed on the same psychiatric continuum from what psychiatrists would later call hypomania, which is less gloomy or negative. Indeed, hyperactive behavior, while still restless, can be exuberant, enthusiastic, and creative; it would not be long before Amos would get over his funk as an unemployed lawyer and, finding a new calling and meaningful activity, would exhibit a much more upbeat personality.

Sumner Gerard was another problem. Gertrude was probably right in see-ing him as using Amos's unhappiness to pull the two men toward hedonistic pursuits. But even before Gerard, he had sometimes been miserable from his malaria and nervous condition, either of which (or in combination) was more likely directly linked to his poor psychological condition, and Gerard may have accentuated his malaise. But if Amos was a victim of high functioning bipolar disorder, Gertrude's insistence on regular work was wrong. Many people with a personality abnormality do not perform well in a bureaucratic job environ-ment, and Amos, who had briefly tried it unsuccessfully, seemed to be one of those. Gertrude knew that her husband "hates being <u>held</u> [to a job] worse than anything" but could not suggest any possible cure beyond another job.[29] Amos would later show bursts of great productivity as an independent writer, but his success would come from writing articles, broadsides, and essays, and without long-term discipline, he would never finish the two book projects he would undertake.

13.

Political Rebellion

In early 1909, Gifford was busily fighting entrenched interests and congressional opposition to conservation and other Roosevelt reform initiatives in Washington, D.C. Having won all but two presidential elections dating back to the Civil War, the Republican Party was becoming a victim of its own success and was more receptive to business influences. Although President Roosevelt had revived the reform orientation of the party, the momentum of progressivism had stalled. A year earlier, Gifford noted that Roosevelt "thinks with me that no crisis except the Civil War since the Revolution is as serious as the present in determining great policies."[1] Still, Gifford was cautiously optimistic. Roosevelt anointed William Howard Taft as his successor, and he and the Republican platform were committed to his predecessor's policies. Gifford recognized Taft's evident abilities and approved of his victory over Bryan in the election.[2]

He worried, however, about Taft's cabinet appointments. Although some speculated that Garfield would continue as interior secretary and Gifford's name was rumored to head the agriculture department, that scenario was soon demolished when Taft kept Secretary James Wilson but replaced Garfield with Richard A. Ballinger, a corporate lawyer and former mayor of Seattle. Heretofore Roosevelt, Gifford, and Garfield had devised conservation policy, but under Taft, the triumvirate was reduced to Pinchot alone. Miffed at the slighting of his friend Garfield, Gifford assumed that Taft's commitment to conservation was shallow. The new president's appointment of four other corporate lawyers to his cabinet also suggested the new administration's conservative direction.

Taft also abandoned an international conference on natural resource issues, a Roosevelt-Pinchot proposal. The diplomatic reasoning was that there was insufficient foreign interest, but the initiative's main purpose had been to stimulate nations' engagements with conservation subjects.[3] It would take another generation before there would be a further attempt to give conservation an international dimension.

Pinchot was already acquainted with the new interior secretary, as he had served as the interior's land commissioner under Garfield, and Gifford had run-ins with him over the disposal of public coal lands. Under Taft, he feared "Ballinger and I might clash."[4]

Garfield, aware of the incoming secretary's opposition to the policy of removing waterpower sites from public lands, accelerated the removal process before Ballinger took over. The new secretary showed his disapproval when he ordered a gradual restoration to the public domain of most of them and denied the agriculture department's requests for ranger stations, arguing that Congress had not approved them.[5]

Ballinger was no conservationist, but neither was he an extreme anti-conservationist. Early on, he withdrew certain oil fields in California and Wyoming from entry. He also firmly believed that executive branch officials were duty-bound to limit their actions to what Congress sanctioned and he was merely undoing the previous excesses. His views as a constitutional conservative were far removed from Gifford's nationalist notions of the implied powers of the federal government in general and the president in particular.

More hopeful of Taft, Gifford managed to gain three interviews with him at which he pressed his case. In the short term, he was successful, as Taft directed Ballinger to reverse the policy and withdraw the power sites again. Gifford was elated and soon told Garfield, "Taft is getting more and more committed to conservation. He will simply have to stick now."[6]

Rather than "stick," Taft vacillated; Gifford would wonder if "the influence of the last man consulted" would be a factor in Taft's policies. In any event, Ballinger, temporarily frustrated on the power sites, went after his subordinate in charge of the power withdrawals, F. H. Newell, head of the reclamation service. Ballinger's prime interests throughout the controversy were his department's control over public lands and the loyalty of his employees. His continued badgering deeply upset Newell, who began asking for the forester's help finding a new job.[7]

*   *   *

Gifford recognized that his continuing disagreement with Ballinger might force the president to choose between the two. Four months into the administration, however, he persuaded himself that Ballinger was "a nuisance, but not for long. In the language of the small boy," he told his mother, "he is on the toboggan."[8]

Gifford and Ballinger refrained from personal attacks, but the press played up their differing viewpoints.[9] Still, Gifford remained cautiously sanguine. He believed that the people supported TR's conservation programs, and the best evidence was the enthusiastic response to Gifford's short speech to an irrigation congress in Spokane, Washington, prompting him to marvel, "Never in my life have I had such a reception." Meanwhile, Ballinger "was not warmly received," Gifford surmised, and "It is remarkable he should have so little support in his own State."[10]

A new crisis over public lands in Alaska sharpened the conflict. It began with Louis R. Glavis, a young chief inspector in the interior's land office, who, from his own investigations, believed that investors' claims to coal lands in Alaska were likely fraudulent. Glavis typified the young, zealous reformer, sensitive to corruption and methodical in gathering evidence. The investors were known as the Cunningham group, named after one of thirty-three claimants, which a J. P. Morgan-Guggenheim syndicate had an option to finance. Ballinger was deeply involved since he had supported the claimants during his tenure as land commissioner, only to have Secretary Garfield deny them. Then before becoming interior secretary, Ballinger had provided legal advice to the investors. Glavis thought the new secretary was uncooperative with his investigation and pushing to authorize the claims. Because the disputed land lay in a national forest, a frustrated Glavis turned to the forest service for assistance. He briefed Gifford, the latter's deputy, Overton Price, and A. C. Shaw, a forest service lawyer, saying he had "damaging and conclusive evidence" of Secretary Ballinger's misconduct.[11] Gifford was "mighty glad" to hear the inspector's story. Glavis's worst suspicions, if confirmed, would provide proof of the interior's dishonesty, and Ballinger, who had approved the licenses, would be discredited and forced to resign. At the forester's urging, Glavis and Shaw took the concerns directly to Taft and gave him a fifty-page report detailing their allegations.[12]

*   *   *

President Taft's handling of the situation was crucial. He studied Glavis's charges and asked Attorney General George Wickersham and Ballinger for their comments on the report. Taft soon sent a letter to Ballinger saying he and the attorney general found only "suspicions . . . without any substantial evidence" in Glavis's charges and authorized the secretary to dismiss Glavis "for filing a disingenuous statement, unjustly impeaching the official integrity of his superior officers."[13] Although a law allowed the dismissal of disobedient employees, Taft's approval of Glavis's firing without first allowing him to defend himself was a mistake. Glavis's supporters and journalists pointed out the cavalier treatment he had received at the hands of a president, himself a serious student of jurisprudence. Taft also brushed aside Ballinger's previous role as lawyer for the Cunningham group. He still believed the Pinchot-Ballinger conflict was a bureaucratic tussle over control of natural resource policy, and he would soon "clean up the whole matter."[14]

But the controversy only sharpened. Gifford and the president had several personal talks that clarified their widely different perspectives. Taft showed his penchant for order and formality, which were part of his legalistic view of politics. The president also complained that the forester's idea of the law was "wrong" and that Pinchot had wanted him to "set aside [the] will of Congress and make law."[15] In his Spokane speech, Gifford had, in fact, overreached. Obedience to the law works in the vast majority of cases, he then acknowledged, "But the law is not absolute. . . . [A] law is a means . . . to be used for the public good, to be modified by the public good, and to be interpreted for the public good. . . . The people, not the law, should have the benefit of every doubt."[16] His viewpoint suggested that an administrative officer could willfully ignore or reinterpret a law if he disagreed with it.

Gifford correctly perceived that Taft deferred to the "good intent" of Congress and was merely "carrying out what Congress ordered." On the question of water power sites, for example, Taft wanted Congress to settle it "one way or the other," but Gifford asserted, "I wanted it settled one way only."[17] He also bluntly told Taft that he might be forced to make his objections public and that the president might have to fire him, but he still commented, "I do not believe there is any danger of my being fired."[18]

Taft wanted Gifford to remain in his position. As the popular forester, if he were dismissed, he would go public on a hot-button topic and weaken the administration. But Gifford's belief that he would not be fired was misplaced. Taft regarded the forester as rather "radical" and a "crank," and he thought Pinchot's "fanaticism" had a religious basis. Gifford "has a good deal of the guile attributed to the Jesuits in his nature," he wrote his wife, and "seizes shreds of evidence as conviction stronger than the Holy Writ." The president also complained that Gifford and Roosevelt "both have more of a Socialist tendency." He wanted a more regular bureaucratic chain of command and would instinctively support a cabinet secretary (Ballinger) instead of a mere bureau chief (Pinchot) unless hard evidence showed malfeasance in office.[19]

The reform impulse encouraged Gifford's sense of moral indignation. Insurgent progressives in Congress were making themselves heard, successfully curtailing (with Democrats' support) Joseph Cannon's powers as House Speaker and vigorously protesting the passage of a higher tariff law. The reformers often framed the issues in moralistic terms, and Gifford confidently announced to his mother, "Our safety now lies in making the people see that the control of the special interests is a moral question." Heretofore he had criticized his opponents as biased and uninformed, and implicit in his attacks on the "interests" was an ethical component. Now, however, morality was explicit, and the opposition was seen as immoral, even villainous. He even told a religious friend, "I do believe I am on the side of the Lord and the electorate." A sense of self-righteous indignation would lead him to criticize even moderate and more patient reformers.[20]

Glavis expressed his views of the Alaska coal lands in *Collier's Weekly*, a popular magazine. Norman Hapgood, a crusading editor, had already written editorials attacking Taft and Ballinger for their harmful conservation policies. Glavis's piece did not argue that Ballinger was dishonest, but the subtitle of the article, "The Whitewashing of Ballinger," and the text contained intimations of the secretary's probably illegal dealings with the Cunningham group.[21]

*   *   *

When Congress appointed a joint committee to investigate the allegations, the majority-Republican members would likely support the administration's case unless presented with compelling evidence to the contrary. Gifford hired his old friend Henry L. Stimson and then George Wharton Pepper, a prominent Philadelphia attorney, as his legal counsel. In preparing his case, Gifford often instructed his staff to avoid publicity about the controversy in his absence, and he would report in October that "Price has been handling things beautifully in my absence."[22]

But during their boss's absence, Price and Shaw gave information about the Cunningham claims to print publications, wanting to make public the details of the Alaska coal episode. The two men provided Glavis with documents from the forest bureau files for his report to the president. They even shared copies with three journalists before Taft saw it and commented on drafts of Glavis's *Collier's* article. It is hard to believe that Gifford did not generally know what his two subordinates were doing. When he asked Price and Shaw for their reactions to Ballinger's demand that the congressional committee investigate "the pernicious activity" of forest service officers, they admitted their "irregular" conduct in many areas.[23] Price, trying to save Gifford from further embarrassment, went to Secretary Wilson, offering to resign. When Wilson asked Gifford for an explanation, Gifford turned to Stimson, who counseled him to discount any advice of Price, who was "a perfectly helpless baby so far as mature judgment is concerned," and even Amos, whom Stimson knew well.[24]

But ignoring the advice, Gifford revised the letter, with Amos's considerable help, and sent it to Senator Jonathan P. Dolliver, a progressive Republican, who had asked for a statement and read it on the Senate floor. Gifford thought he had the secretary's approval to forward the letter, but Wilson later remembered their discussion differently, claiming he may have approved the letter but could not recall its contents.[25]

Gifford's letter to Dolliver was a ringing defense of his subordinates. Again citing his expansive view of the law, he claimed he was "bound, at any personal risk, to do everything the law will let him do for the public good." Shaw and Price "broke no law" when they publicized the Cunningham claims, he argued, "and at worst were guilty only of the violation of official propriety." And because of "the purity of their motives" and "the results which were accomplished, their breach of propriety sinks well-night to insignificance." He conceded only that their behavior "deserved a reprimand, and has received one" in writing.[26]

Here were direct challenges to the chief executive's actions and authority, and Taft fired Gifford for his disrespect. "By your own conduct," Taft wrote him, "you have destroyed your usefulness as a helpful subordinate to the Government, and it therefore now becomes my duty to direct the Secretary of Agriculture to remove you from your office as the Forester." A messenger delivered the letter to the Pinchots' house during a dinner party. Gifford, waving the letter, announced, "fired." Mary Pinchot was not in the least surprised. "Great rejoicing. Lots of reporters," she recorded of the event.[27]

*   *   *

To retain his government position, Gifford needed less confrontation and more friends telling him to "cool down."[28] If he did not want to be fired, he was clearly determined to force the issue, but Stimson was virtually alone in trying to restrain him, and then only briefly.[29] Gifford had surrounded himself in the forest service with like-minded subordinates who were, if anything, more zealous than their chief. Gifford's hiring practices for the forest service, while assuring personal loyalty and passionate commitment, resulted in groupthink and a failure to consider alternative approaches.

Gifford's family members also tried not to hold him back. Mary agreed with Gifford's principled stand and worried only about the strain on him. Moreover, during the controversy, Amos was "tremendously thrilled by all that is happening." Ballinger was "a stinker" and "sh[oul]d be shown up." He believed that public opinion was behind his brother and had also supported Glavis's search for good evidence "where Ballinger has lied."[30]

Gifford's firing was a defeat, but he landed on his feet. In early 1909, he had created the National Conservation Association as a citizens' action group and, during the controversy, had the association as a fallback, writing that "Even if Taft should bounce me, . . . I should go straight on with the Conservation work."[31] After his dismissal, he became the association's president.

The congressional investigation lasted four months, and the published record would fill more than 7,500 pages. The difficult challenge to Gifford's lawyers was that the laws and regulations relevant to the Cunningham claimants' proposed clear listing and patenting of public lands far away in Alaska were a complicated tangle, sometimes overlapping and conflicting, and open to various interpretations. Louis Glavis was nonetheless an impressive witness.[32] Gifford appeared before the committee, but his testimony proved unsurprising. He reviewed his differences with Ballinger but stopped short of charging him with malfeasance.[33] Gifford lost in the sense that the investigation failed to show clearly illegal conduct, and none of Ballinger's critics managed to prove that he was clearly dishonest or incompetent. Doubtless, there was some fraud in the Cunningham claims but no smoking gun. It was thus a foregone conclusion that the committee would exonerate him.

In other respects, however, the Glavis-Pinchot forces could legitimately claim victory. Their success resulted from their understanding of the political ramifications of the dispute. To Gifford, the hearings were a venue for courting public opinion—"to win before the country."[34] Amos Pinchot's most distinctive contribution during the controversy was understanding the important role of print journalism. He was a newspaper junkie, buying several papers each morning to sample editorial and public reactions.

The lawyers on Gifford's side allowed Louis D. Brandeis, a well-known Boston lawyer and supporter of labor rights who represented *Collier's* at the hearings, to direct their case. It proved to be an inspired choice. His strong views on public morality and the public good mirrored Gifford's progressive outlook. Brandeis recognized the difficulty of proving the Glavis charges and adopted a broader strategy accordingly. "We're not trying to prove a fraud," he explained; "we're just trying to protect the public interest."[35]

An indefatigable researcher, Brandeis assembled a large tranche of interior department documents, and from this collection, he exposed several inconsistencies in the administration's case against Glavis.[36] In withering cross-examination of Ballinger, he exposed the secretary as a flawed public servant and produced evidence, contrary to Ballinger's testimony, that the secretary had earlier served as a lawyer for the Cunningham claimants.[37]

Brandeis also learned from a conscious-stricken stenographer in Ballinger's office that President Taft had based his exoneration of Ballinger and the firing of Glavis not on a collection of documents prepared by Attorney General Wickersham, as the president had said, but from a summary memorandum hastily prepared much later by an assistant attorney general.[38] He got Ballinger to admit this mistake and release the memorandum; to make matters worse, the president, unaware of Ballinger's action, falsely insisted on the administration's earlier argument. When this discrepancy was exposed, Brandeis and Amos were "both in great glee." Brandeis later commented, "It was the [administration's] lying that did it. If they had brazenly admitted everything and justified it on the ground[s] that Ballinger was at least doing what he thought best, we should not have had a chance."[39]

Brandeis believed that government officials should be held to a high standard and that Taft, violating the public trust, had, in essence, lied to the American people. Gifford and other progressive reformers shared his strong moralistic outlook and vivid sense of public service.[40] In fairness to Taft, however, when he received the summary memorandum, he had also already received many documents from his attorney general, but he erred by denying that the memorandum was predated and insisting that his decisions were based upon his own careful review of the full documentary record.

Moreover, Ballinger's lawyers bungled their presentation. They presented details on points of law and procedure at the hearings but were insensitive to their political significance. They ridiculed conservation as a "fad" and conservationists as "men who have gone to seed on the subject" and often criticized the press,[41] which sympathized more with Gifford as fighting for the "people" against the "interests." In the end, Gifford savored his side's "victory" and congratulated Brandeis: "The way you brought the investigation to an end seemed to me simply beyond all praise."[42]

Taft's appointment of Harry Graves as Gifford's successor to the forester position was further vindication of his side.[43] It turned out that the disputed coal lands in Alaska were not really lucrative, as Glavis had claimed, and the majority report, though critical of Gifford and making no judgment on the Cunningham claims, recommended retention of coal lands under public ownership, legislation for their leasing, and continued withdrawal of lands from entry pending congressional action. These were all proposals Gifford and Louis Glavis had championed.[44]

In a larger sense, though, the coordinated national planning on conservation issues that Pinchot assiduously forged and promoted with Roosevelt had fragmented. Congress had already resisted conservation initiatives toward the end of the Roosevelt administration, and the Taft presidency further undermined them so that the broad conservation and development purposes of the Inland Waterways Commission, for instance, gave way to the initiatives of individual components, special interests, and individual states. The dream of a federal regulatory state supported by a popular democratic base survived, but its future realization remained problematic.[45]

* * *

After his congressional testimony, Gifford Pinchot went to Europe, traveling under a fake name to consult with Colonel Roosevelt, as he was called in his post-presidential years. After hunting in Africa, the former president traveled to Europe for several honorific events. Once in Europe, Gifford met with TR in April 1910 on the Italian Riviera, and the two talked all day about the unraveling of the conservation legacy. "One of the best and most satisfactory talks with T.R. I ever had," he recorded.[46]

The Ballinger episode, meanwhile, had energized Amos, who turned his attention to political activism and writing. Previously unpublished, it was something of a surprise when *McClure's* accepted his first article submission, which compared the crisis of the American political parties in the 1850s with the current situation. His article argued that, like the antebellum slavery issue, which had led to the collapse of an ossified Whig Party and the rise of a new Republican Party, so was the situation in 1910 showing the disintegration of the Republican "oligarchy" from rising insurgent reformers.

Gertrude, believing her husband had found his calling as a political writer, rejoiced, "You deserve great credit for it, . . . This is the beginning of y[ou]r work—and very encouraging to you." Helen Garfield also marveled, "Why has [Amos] been shutting himself up so long and not letting us know on the outside what he can do?" After several such fulsome compliments, Gifford enthused that Amos's piece gave him "an important position at one stroke."[47]

His article moved him closer to Republican progressives, whose eyes looked toward Theodore Roosevelt, who soon embarked on a western trip. His speechmaking became his opportunity to discuss current issues and promote a reform agenda for the Republican Party.

The defining moment of his tour was his speech at Osawatomie, Kansas, where the fiery abolitionist John Brown had fought against raiders from Missouri in 1856. At the former battle site, Roosevelt looked directly at the Civil

War veterans amidst an assembled crowd of 30,000 people. "There have been two great crises in the country's history," he shouted; "first, when it was formed, and then, again when it was perpetuated." Roosevelt then launched into an exposition of a rising third crisis. Corporate boardrooms allied with backroom political bosses were corrupting American political life, he charged, and he called for full publicity of corporate activities and a law prohibiting the use of corporate funds for political purposes. Further, he called for more federal regulation of all industrial combinations, with board members liable for antitrust violations, a judiciary that favored individual over property rights, a graduated federal income and inheritance tax, workmen's compensation laws, and child and women's labor legislation. His talk articulated what he called "New Nationalism," and his speech would be a benchmark against which progressives would compare subsequent reform programs. He made clear that he wanted new, "genuinely progressive" leadership.[48]

The writing of Roosevelt's Osawatomie speech showed the hands of several progressives, especially Gifford, who wrote the final draft. Their chief, he exulted to Garfield, had endorsed almost their entire platform. "He is ready to fight if necessary, and the situation could not be better."[49] Gifford was doubly pleased with the reception at Osawatomie. "I have never seen a crowd that affected me as much as that one did," he wrote Mamee. "They listened to T.R. for nearly an hour in perfect silence."[50]

Gifford identified himself with the most ardent progressives. After Democrats and insurgent Republicans made impressive victories in the 1910 midterm elections, he claimed, "My feeling is very strong that the people generally are far more progressive than nearly all the progressive leaders themselves, and that unless the Republican [P]arty is able to put itself squarely in line with genuinely advanced political principles, the condition in which it finds itself today is likely to be lasting, for the principal reason that the party will have deserved it." Overall, the election revealed a pervasive restlessness in many parts of the country, and the progressive case seemed to be surging. Moreover, the progressives' already notable achievements on the municipal and state levels, especially in the middle and far west, seemed to be harbingers of a new era.[51]

*　*　*

Roosevelt's New Nationalism speech barely mentioned the conservation of natural resources; the Taft administration's moves on environmental issues would make it more difficult to emphasize them as presidential failings. The administration asserted, for instance, federal control over water power, Ballinger resigned, and his statement that he would have patented the Cunningham claims seemed to validate the protest against them. As Gifford wrote Brandeis, "If anything further was needed to justify our fight[,] that [statement] was certainly it."[52] Moreover, the Taft administration resolved the status of the Cunningham land claims favorably to the conservationists' cause. Finally, the land office recommended canceling the Cunningham claims, which the new Interior Secretary Walter L. Fisher approved. "So that job is done," Gifford rejoiced in his diary, and Theodore Roosevelt wrote him triumphantly, "What a superb vindication it is!"[53]

After recovering from the Ballinger affair, Taft would indeed end up withdrawing more lands from public sale in his four years as chief executive than his predecessor, Roosevelt, in nearly eight. Gifford privately conceded that Taft's conservation initiatives and other moves toward the political center had resulted in "the successful confusing" of the issues.[54]

Suspicions of the Taft administration's collusion with powerful corporate interests nonetheless continued, and its principals spent a lot of time defending their policies.[55] Gifford traveled to the Alaska territory for six weeks to see the lands he and other conservationists had made such a fuss about. Initially, his Alaskan reception was decidedly unfriendly. Even before he reached the territory, citizen groups from two towns had burned him in effigy; one, in imitation of the Boston Tea Party, had also dumped Canadian coal into the harbor.[56]

Despite Gifford's professed support for free enterprise, many Alaskans perceived him as a preservationist opposed to private development.[57] Gifford nonetheless received a respectful hearing at public meetings. His message was simple: It was fraudulent land deals, not conservation policies, that inhibited the development of the territory's resources, and he opposed those "who were trying to plunder and monopolize Alaska from carrying out their plan."[58]

A sequel to these Alaskan episodes would again demonstrate Gifford's belief that he was championing the people's interests against greedy capitalists. In 1917, Daniel Guggenheim met with Gifford to persuade him that he had been "unjust" in condemning the Morgan-Guggenheim syndicate for seeking monopolistic control in Alaska. Guggenheim admitted that his syndicate had been interested in commercial development and financial rewards there but argued that it had never violated U.S. laws and regulations. In a long letter, he detailed the syndicate's scrupulous behavior and concluded that the syndicate "never attempted to obtain a monopoly" in Alaska. Gifford did not dispute Guggenheim's facts but, in his reply, refused to accept any blame and argued that the "inevitable result of what was actually done in your name . . . was to produce the impression that an effort was under way to monopolize the resources of Alaska." Indeed, Gifford asserted that any charge of injustice should be directed at the Guggenheim syndicate. Here was an example of Gifford's moralistic "impression" trumping a more deliberative weighing of solid evidence.[59]

*   *   *

Meanwhile, rebellious reformers tried to organize a challenge to Taft's renomination the following year. Refusing to believe that Taft's mid-course correction on conservation issues amounted to a conversion experience, Gifford rationalized that the president, a candidate for reelection, had approved measures to try to defuse the conservation question as a campaign issue. He also argued that Taft had shown his true colors at the outset of his presidency by choosing corporation lawyers for his cabinet and allying with conservatives in Congress.[60]

Insurgent Republicans wanted Roosevelt as Taft's challenger, but they were long stymied by his insistence that he would not run. For the 1910 congressional elections, TR, a savvy politician, had also endorsed Republican conservative candidates, and he told Stimson that Gifford's course would "relegate himself to the company of single taxers, prohibitionists and the like."[61] To Gifford, however, principle and an advanced program trumped party allegiance. He wanted progressives to unite behind a candidate to defeat Taft's nomination and, if that failed, to start a third party.

Mamee, the matriarch of this close-knit Pinchot family, initially urged Gifford to go slowly for tactical reasons. But still smarting from his firing, she was also strident in her rhetoric. "Hurrah for the progressives!" she cheered, and if the Taft forces could be defeated, she joked, "I am very moderate in my desires and would not ask more . . . than the scalps of a dozen or so."[62] Ellen Slayden, an astute chronicler of the Washington scene, received a dose of Mary Pinchot's prejudices at one of the latter's tea parties. Slayden admired her as "my ideal of what an oldish lady of the best society should be," wearing clothes "as if she put them on just because she enjoyed wearing pretty things, and not at all to be dressed up" and holding forth as "stately and gracious, but absolutely direct and unpretentious." But Slayden cringed at her hostess's political enthusiasms. "Mrs. Pinchot's hatred of the Administration is an obsession," she wrote in her journal. "She talked about 'Progressives,' 'Insurgents,' and such political shades and plans until I pictured her and Gifford as a pair of deep conspirators with Jimmy Garfield stepping softly in front carrying a dark lantern."[63] And seeing Amos's involvement in the mounting insurgency, Mary beamed, "I am proud and happy and the more so that my <u>two</u> boys are in it for the right together and both getting recognition."[64]

Throughout 1911, Gifford and Amos tried persuading Roosevelt to come out openly and challenge Taft for the nomination.[65] Prominent among their arguments was that Taft was "dishonest." Amos drafted a magazine article highlighting Taft's deceptive practices. Though convinced of Taft's improbity, he admitted that his article was "the hardest thing I have ever struck," and even a well-argued piece might not persuade a magazine to publish it.[66] Soon Gifford was also telling Roosevelt "for the nth time" that "Taft is dishonest," but his former chief protested "as usual." When Congressman William Kent, a friend of the Pinchots, wrote the colonel that Taft was "a contemptible individual and a disgrace to the office," TR replied in exasperation, "Come, come! You and Gifford are altogether crazy about Taft . . . you use language about him that is not justified." And to his son, he wrote, "Gifford Pinchot is a dear, but he is a fanatic, with an element of hardness and narrowness in his temperament, and an extremist."[67]

With Roosevelt seemingly unmoved and indeed still a veritable sphinx over the next six months, most Republican reformers supported Robert M. La Follette, who had compiled an impressive reform record as progressive governor of Wisconsin and then as a U.S. senator and was currently assailing Taft's support of high tariffs and resistance to reform. "Fighting Bob," as he was known, fearlessly championed his reform agenda and showed considerable strength in the Midwest.

The Pinchot brothers perceived La Follette as "the one man available at the moment to carry on the fight against reaction" and Taft.[68] Each contributed $10,000 to jumpstart the senator's candidacy and encouraged La Follette's presidential run. Temperamentally and ideologically, the brothers were closer to La Follette (the radical insurgent) than to Roosevelt (the progressive reformer); however, they held back from formally endorsing him.[69]

The brothers were not a stalking horse for Roosevelt but were prepared to change horses if he declared his candidacy.[70] Also holding Gifford and Amos back from La Follette was the disquieting belief among many Republican reformers that he had little stature in the eastern states and could not wrest the nomination from Taft. Amos said he was "entirely unsuccessful" in recruiting volunteers in New York for the senator's campaign, and his several requests for La Follette campaign literature had gone unanswered.[71] After talking to western governors, Garfield reported that "many people" there, including farmers and laborers, were "against him."[72] Given this pessimistic undercurrent, Gifford's strategy was to try to withhold endorsements of La Follette while keeping the reform forces unified.[73]

With La Follette's candidacy eroding and a Roosevelt challenge more certain, Gifford mused, "Must find a way to let Bob down easy." The senator's deteriorating mental and physical health, accelerated by a recent operation and his grueling schedule in Congress and presidential run, "bids fair," Gifford had worried, "to break him down altogether."[74] And that happened on the evening of February 2, 1912, when an exhausted La Follette gave an important speech in Philadelphia. It was an unqualified disaster, as he spoke emotionally during a two-hour rambling rant.[75]

Right after La Follette's blunder, Roosevelt told Gifford that he would enter the race. Gifford then wrote the Wisconsin candidate, bluntly criticizing his campaign and asserting that he should support Roosevelt. He also insensitively struck at the senator's health and concluded self-righteously that he had to "stick to his principles and let [La Follette] go." Far from letting down Bob "easy," Gifford's criticism displayed some "hardness" and "narrowness" that had perturbed Roosevelt, and the Pinchot-La Follette frosty relationship endured for the rest of their respective political careers.[76]

*   *   *

When TR declared his candidacy, Mary Pinchot immediately gave $5,000 to his campaign. Her brother Will and sister Antoinette would also each contribute $5,000, and the latter's fervor for Roosevelt prompted Mamee to comment, "She's the fiercest Rooseveltian I know."[77]

Amos, the uncompromising reformer, maintained a surface cordiality with Roosevelt, who straddled or fine-tuned issues to curry favor among Republicans and independents disillusioned with Taft, but their tense relationship would gradually unravel. When Amos saw a draft of Roosevelt's speech declaring his candidacy, he complained about its "qualifying clauses" and "conditional and hypothetical premises" on the major issues. "I differ with you, Colonel, radically as to the need of your showing just how progressive you are; just what your attitude toward the tariff, child labor, the trusts, etc, is." Gifford wholly agreed with Amos's criticism but would always be more deferential than his brother to the former president. Trying to accommodate advanced progressives, TR revised portions of his speech "to give an exact and clear view of my meaning." On a deeper level, he allowed, he might be wrong on the issues. "But that I have the right attitude I am absolutely certain." TR would also gently reproach

Gifford for his radicalism, prompting Mamee to complain to her eldest, "I wish Roosevelt wouldn't call you anarchistic even in fun."[78]

Amos admitted that TR's reply was "mighty nice" compared to "my rather mean" letter to him, but he remained unconvinced. The two got along well as long as they agreed on reform principles. Thus, when the new candidate called for the selection of delegates directly in preferential primaries instead of "by the spoils politicians and the patronage mongers," Amos praised him for his "powerful" statement and concluded, "It is bully!"[79]

Roosevelt thought well enough of Amos to encourage him to write a broadside featuring Taft's abandonment of the Roosevelt legacy. The resulting pamphlet, "Theodore Roosevelt and William Howard Taft," was put out by the Roosevelt League without authorship but was Amos's handiwork. The league promptly circulated 100,000 copies of it nationwide.[80] TR would also prove receptive to Amos's completed magazine article on Taft's supposed character flaws. Several magazines rejected the manuscript as too contentious, but *Pearson's Magazine* finally agreed to publish it.[81] The thrust of Amos's article was that Taft's mistakes and flawed personality had resulted in a failed presidency. His depiction of Taft avoided words like "liar" or "dishonest" and was mostly a detailed rehash of the president's blunders during the Ballinger controversy and an indictment of the reactionaries in his administration who opposed clean government. He charged that Taft, having "given sanction of his great office to those outworn and devious methods which we are trying to banish from our national life," did not deserve to be the Republican presidential nominee.[82]

Amos sent his published piece to Roosevelt along with an annotated copy with the documents cited in it. A grateful TR replied, "This is just what I wanted. . . . I do not want to make this a personal fight if I can help it, but if I do want to hit him, I want to hit him hard." His earlier protestations against the Pinchots' and others' maligning of Taft as "dishonest" largely dissolved now that he was a candidate and wanted further validation for his sharpening criticisms of the president. The Taft-Roosevelt contest for the nomination descended into mudslinging, and Roosevelt, abandoning the course he professed to eschew, launched personal attacks on Taft (who called him "neurotic," a "dangerous egotist," and a "demagogue"), labeling him a "reactionary," "puzzlewit," and "fathead," among other epithets.[83]

Controlling the party machinery, the Taft forces would receive support from most delegates selected in state caucuses and conventions. At the same time, Roosevelt's hopes for the nomination required decisive victories in the thirteen presidential primaries, and Roosevelt would win ten of them (La Follette, who had stayed in the race, prevailed in two) by commanding margins. By the end of the primaries, Roosevelt won 294 delegates to Taft's 126.[84]

Gifford and many other progressives now predicted TR's nomination, but when the Republicans descended on the Coliseum in Chicago for their convention, Roosevelt still had far fewer delegates than those already pledged to the president. The Taft forces also dominated the Republican National Committee, which orchestrated the election of conservative Senator Elihu Root, once TR's good friend but now supporting Taft, as chairman of the convention, and controlled the credentials committee, which would consistently decide on the seating of Taft slates among the contested delegations.

Believing conservative forces and entrenched bosses in the Republican Party were depriving him of the nomination, the embattled Roosevelt framed his challenge as an evangelist crusader. "We fight in honorable fashion for the good of mankind," he proclaimed to his supporters at the convention, "fearless of the future, unheeding of our individual fates, with unflinching hearts and undimmed eyes, we stand at Armageddon, and we battle for the Lord."[85]

Convinced of thievery, three-fourths of the Roosevelt delegates withdrew to Orchestra Hall nearby and bolted to form a Progressive Party. TR soon helped his followers channel their rage at the "stolen" Republican nomination into momentum for a new political campaign; journalists, picking up his exhortation that "I'm feeling like a bull moose," dubbed the new Progressive Party with a more popular name, Bull Moose Party.[86]

*   *   *

Amos and Gifford Pinchot attended the Progressive Party's convention in Chicago in early August, where the faithful formally nominated Roosevelt and his running mate, Governor Hiram Johnson of California, pressed for an advanced progressive platform. TR and his intimate advisers essentially recast the New Nationalism reform proposals into specific planks. Gifford, in particular, worked long hours in the resolutions committee. He and Amos believed an advanced program for change was needed for its own sake but also as necessary to show progressive-minded voters its clear contrast to the Democratic Party's milder reform platform, which eschewed positions on women's suffrage and child labor.[87]

The Progressive platform stopped short of advocating, as the American Socialist Party propounded, government ownership of public transportation and utilities,[88] but the Progressive platform was breathtaking in the broad sweep of its demands. The one major omission was any mention of race relations. Despite Gifford's and Amos's (and other Progressives') rhetoric touting "human rights," "democracy," "justice," and their avowed concerns for the downtrodden, their progressivism was generally for whites only. Racial toleration in the northern states was at its nadir, and Gifford was now telling Booker T. Washington that he was too committed to other causes to continue his modest contributions to his Tuskegee Institute. In any event, African Americans had historic ties to the Republicans, the party of Lincoln and emancipation. As an alternative to the Taft Republicans' inclusion of blacks, the Progressive Party leadership decided to court southern whites. Since African Americans were now legally disenfranchised (and also segregated) throughout the South, the party's silent contempt for their plight could be viewed as acceptance of a practical reality. Still, it surely limited the party's appeal to African Americans in northern states where they could vote. Gifford agreed with this strategy, arguing that "the negro in the South will not take a front seat" in the new lily-white Progressive Party. Amos later summarized the ineffectiveness of this strategy nationwide while exhibiting the same insensitivity toward blacks: "They loved Massa Roosevelt, but they loved Massa Taft, too."[89] Racial issues aside, the Progressive Party's domestic program was the most progressive of any major political party in American history at that time, and its reform planks would not be matched in number and scope for another fifty years.[90]

Meanwhile, Gertrude, Amos's wife, showed concern over the plight of working women. In March 1912, she traveled to Lawrence, Massachusetts, to show solidarity with the striking textile workers, who were protesting against the inhumane conditions in the local mills. Gertrude provided no compelling reasons for her visit, but she had a social conscience and was surrounded by political activism. She already knew about Gifford's concerns about child labor abuses and her husband's expanding range of political interests. Moreover, New York City had become a hotbed of activity among women progressives, including many from similar privileged backgrounds.[91]

But probably mixed in with these benevolent motives was a personal element. Gertrude, worried about her strained relationship with Amos, likely hoped that her involvement in work related to her husband's might save their shaky marriage and probably bolstered her decision to visit Lawrence alone for eight days and get directly involved. Gifford encouraged her to observe the conditions of the Lawrence workers engaged in a bitter strike against their employers.[92]

The Lawrence experience was eye-opening. She had gone there, she related afterward, as a "sociological investigator" of the living conditions and the charges of police brutality, but it became much more. At first, the strikers were suspicious of this well-heeled woman, thinking she might be a detective. When she told them she was Gifford's sister-in-law, "they readily let me in." She observed the miserable conditions of the workers and the excessive police methods, but what caught her attention was the self-respect and self-discipline of the working men, women, and children living there. She went to a meeting of six hundred strikers representing multiple nationalities and, because of its orderliness and the thoughtful argument, called it "the most impressive I have ever attended." She used her fluency in French and Italian several times to communicate with foreign workers, and the strikers accepted her as one of their own. Their warmth and affection, in turn, deeply touched Gertrude, who commented, "Nowhere else have I felt the glow of the brotherhood of humanity as at Lawrence."[93]

Encouraged by this positive experience, Gertrude headed a women's committee for Roosevelt. Antoinette Wood gave $500 to her group, and Mary said, "I am going to do the same if she needs it," and Gifford soon donated $1,500.[94]

Amos's main contribution to the election campaign was the publication of a thirty-eight-page pamphlet extolling the promise of the nascent reform movement. Entitled "What's the Matter with America," his treatise developed a concise macro-historical interpretation of the past four hundred years of the Western world. History, in his progressive view, was the story of political change. He saw progressive insurgency as the most recent of a long line of reform movements, starting with the "revolution" in religious thinking and scientific inquiry in Europe in the sixteenth century and continuing with the emergence of democratic ideas.[95]

The emphasis in Amos's pamphlet was decidedly economical.[96] His interpretation likened the current progressive revolt to America's earlier War for Independence and the Civil War. "It is the same old story," he claimed, of a powerful, privileged class preying upon the public, just as Britain's special interests had exploited the American colonists and the slave and cotton interests had promoted false, vicious commercialism. Now, in the modern industrial era, it was the "predatory" and "powerful" trusts, together with "the money power" (Wall Street), that were enslaving America, and he cited the enormous profits that monopolies like American Sugar Refining, General Electric, and Standard Oil were making. He also documented the pitifully low wages big businesses paid their workers and emphasized the widespread "exploitation of women and children" in the workforce, which further underscored the maldistribution of the nation's wealth.

Severe income inequality was indeed a fundamental problem. Amos argued that the current progressive movement was radical but also "a practical movement, because it deals chiefly with a more just distribution of wealth, which is at the very bottom of the bread question in every land and age." The progressives saw "the immediate necessity of taking the control of our nation out of the hands of the privileged class and placing it once more in the hands of the people." Amos avoided specific policy remedies, but the pamphlet highlighted the seriousness of the economic problems and the need for urgent change. And despite the powerful resistance of the "old order," its outlook was decidedly upbeat. In such a great awakening, Amos felt no need to mention Roosevelt or other reformers, and the movement "will go on irrespective of men and party lines, because it has the living power of the whole nation behind it and a constructive program of usefulness before it."[97]

*   *   *

The Progressive Party organizers wanted to run a campaign that demonstrated a semblance of a national organization with roots in local communities, but its late formation meant scrambling to recruit reformers to run as party candidates in the upcoming elections across the country. In this hasty process, New York's progressive leaders asked Amos Pinchot to become their candidate in a congressional district in midtown Manhattan.[98]

Amos accepted the challenge. Caught up in the exuberance of reform politics, he perceived that his candidacy would help Roosevelt and publicize the progressive cause. Now thirty-nine and in better health, he worked with Lindon Bates, Jr., who was running as a progressive for Congress in an adjoining district.[99] They walked the streets together, stood on chairs rounded up from nearby saloons, and preached their message. A crowd would gather, and Amos was impressed at their reception. "It is extraordinary how the people seem to listen," he wrote Hiram Johnson. He also enthused to his mother, "I have a lot of good stuff to say and it is only a question of getting it to the people."[100]

From the start, Amos recognized that his candidacy would fail. Never having run for public office, he was a neophyte in electoral politics. Moreover, he faced a Democratic incumbent, Thomas G. Patten, in a Democratic district. The vote-getting appeal he mustered would likely draw away as many Republican as Democratic votes in the election.[101]

He privately conceded that Patten was "a very good man" but gathered information revealing that the congressman had been absent in sixty-three percent of roll call votes during his current term. Although Patten had been paired with a Republican member on many votes, a procedure Amos thought "ought to be against the law," he still had no recorded position on twenty-one percent of the roll calls and no enunciated position on progressive issues, such as a proposed children's bureau or bills affecting labor.[102]

The election, he argued to his constituents, was a clear choice "between the people and special privilege." A "small but powerful group called the privileged class" controlled the two traditional political parties, he contended, and the new Progressive Party had been formed "to break the grip of the old corrupt parties" and respond to "the people's need for justice."[103]

With some financial support from his wealthy mother, Amos mostly bankrolled his own campaign. To voters in his district, he mailed postcards and 40,000 copies of his campaign leaflet, which included effusive endorsements by Roosevelt, Oscar Straus (the Progressive Party candidate for governor of New York), and several senators, congressmen, and governors across the nation.[104]

Gifford was delighted with Amos's congressional run. He corresponded with him regarding campaign strategy and endorsed his brother at a New York rally as "faithful, honest and with his heart in the right place."[105] Amos, in his turn, helped Gifford with his speeches in support of Roosevelt and fired off letters to him suggesting ideas for his talks on conservation issues.[106]

Amos and Gifford then seemed to be virtually one in their political views. Besides identifying with Roosevelt, the two criticized backroom politics in favor of more open, democratic governance. The brothers particularly assailed the "trusts," whose extraordinary powers had to be curtailed. They developed misgivings about Frank A. Munsey and George W. Perkins, the main financial angels of the new party. Munsey, the wealthy owner of *Munsey's Magazine*, generously paid for the Roosevelt publicity but, to the Pinchots, distorted the reformers' message. At the same time, Perkins, previously associated with the House of Morgan and a board member of the Harvester and Steel "trusts," was the party's executive secretary, playing a key role in emasculating the anti-monopoly plank of the platform. As Amos explained, "Munsey is painting us, as he has no right to do, as the party of protection, while Perkins is giving people an opportunity to assume that we help the defenders of the trusts," and "I think this is hurting us." Gifford agreed that Amos was "exactly right" to limit Perkins's and Munsey's prominence.[107]

Both brothers also believed in authoritative government and advocated vigorous federal regulation of monopolies. Amos was more inclined to use government power to break up monopolies, but the slight differences were obscured at the time, partly because Amos also endorsed the creation of a new government commission to regulate businesses until antitrust proceedings had been successfully launched, but more because of their shared anti-monopoly bias and concerns about the unhealthy influence of Perkins and Munsey.[108]

Gifford had never run for office, but it was easy to believe that he, too, having a prominent public profile, would become a candidate for some important position. But Gifford would have been an awkward candidate in 1912, as he was a man without a state. He had been a registered voter in the District of Columbia but did not register in Pennsylvania until 1911. In 1912, there was no race in the state for the U.S. Senate or governor, positions he would later covet.[109]

As Amos predicted, his Democratic opponent for the congressional seat won handily with fifty percent of the vote. Amos finished a respectable second, however, and as Norman Hapgood, his journalist friend, put it, fairly "drubbed" the Republican candidate.[110] Nationally, the split in the Republican ranks allowed Woodrow Wilson, the Democratic Party's presidential nominee, to prevail easily over Roosevelt and Taft, winning 435 electoral votes, although garnering only forty-two percent of the total popular vote. Roosevelt could take small satisfaction in crushing Taft, who won only two small states.

14.

New Directions

Five days after the 1912 election, Mary Pinchot motored out to Sagamore Hill to visit the defeated candidate. "I never saw either the Col or Mrs. R look so well, or so happy, or he so young," she informed Gifford. "There was not a line on his face but an expression of serenity, as well as sincerity, that I have never seen before. We talked of you of course in the most appreciative way, and [he] told me what position Gifford would have had in his cabinet—you can guess if you don't know." Before Mary gave him the answer, the colonel sent Gifford a letter with the salutary opening: "O Mr. Secretary of State that was-to-have-been!" Though the vanquished could afford to be generous to his loyalists, Roosevelt meant what he said. Well-traveled, fluent in French, and sharing his chief's robust foreign policy views and enjoying his confidence, Gifford would have been Roosevelt's first choice for the position.[1]

Needing a break after the frenetic politicking, the Pinchot brothers planned a fishing venture. When they invited Nettie, who was arriving from Europe, to accompany them on their ten-day trip to south Texas, she joyfully replied, "I'd like it better than anything I can imagine." During their sojourn, however, Nettie and her accompanying maidservant were sick much of the time, and the fishing in the Gulf of Mexico was poor. The two men then went duck hunting, where Gifford bagged twenty-three, and Amos killed a huge rattlesnake nearly five feet long, two inches across the head, and seven inches around.[2]

Following their vacation, the brothers contemplated the future of the Progressive Party. Fielding candidates in every state except for some southern ones, the new party had shown promise, electing a few congressmen and some local officials. Its supporters could claim it was the most successful political third party in U.S. history. Whether it would flourish as a reform party would depend mostly on Roosevelt, only fifty-four, who could still be a powerful force

Antoinette Pinchot Johnstone (Lady Johnstone) during one of her many trips from Europe, with her younger brother Amos Pinchot, New York, c. 1912. (Bain Collection, Library of Congress)

in national politics. Its fate was also tied to the incoming Wilson administration, which, if successful in co-opting key features of the Bull Moose reform program, would diminish its relevance as a party alternative.

Determined to make the Progressive Party grow, Amos and Gifford spent many frustrating months in mostly fruitless arguments with Roosevelt and his advisers about the party's future. The main disagreement came over the Pinchot brothers' determination to remove George Perkins as chairman of the party's executive committee. In their view, Perkins symbolized Wall Street. Although he previously resigned from his lucrative executive position in the International Harvester company, he remained a director of the monopolistic U.S. Steel Corporation and was no faceless manager. He was always impeccably dressed in expensive, tailored suits as befitted a Wall Street operative. He had supported TR in 1912 mainly because the candidate, reacting negatively to President Taft's prosecution of some monopolies, had emphasized government regulation of trusts instead of dissolving them.

Gifford's and Amos's arguments had some merit. In post-mortems on the election, some commenters argued that many voters perceived the Bull Moose party as allied with the trusts, which the progressives were supposedly fighting, and failed to win over the laboring classes. Gifford noted that "both the Harvester Trust and the Steel Trust exclude union men from their works. This, I think, has had a good deal of bearing on the attitude of the unions during the past campaign." And fundamentally, he asserted, "Unless we as a party are radical enough to be clearly separate from both the old parties we can hold few people indeed."[3] The stridently moralistic brothers wanted stronger antitrust legislation, and they judged Perkins as representative of the rule of Mammon that they were trying to topple. And besides anti-monopoly, they wanted the party to confront the problems of income inequality and poverty in America. As Gifford succinctly commented, "we are fighting for those who have not been able to help themselves, and against those who have helped themselves too freely."[4]

Roosevelt firmly resisted Perkins's removal, stressing that in 1912 "we could not have carried the fight at all without him." TR had needed Perkins's money to finance his campaign, but he also enjoyed his company socially and appreciated his "sane radicalism." Above all, the party needed first-rate organization, and he insisted that Perkins was a skillful organizer.[5]

Most party leaders deferred to Roosevelt, their leader. One of them, Albert Beveridge, argued privately with the brothers. "Talk got very sharp at times," Gifford noted. "Amos joshed B." The first showdown came at a national convention of the Progressive Party in December 1912, and the executive committee lined up solidly behind Roosevelt. "Evident feeling among a lot of men that Amos and I are troublemakers," Gifford conceded after the meeting.[6]

The Pinchots subsequently won a few partial victories, including, at Amos's insistence, the party's endorsement of the missing plank in the platform on antitrust law. Roosevelt remained unmoved, however, and he asserted that in 1912 the progressives had lost a million voters or more who found their party "overradical," was "jeopardizing property and business," and that the assault on Perkins "would wreck the Progressive cause."[7]

Because of his long association with Roosevelt, Gifford had no desire to break with him, and he concluded one of his early letters to his chief with, "Whatever differences in judgment I may have with you, they will not dim my affection for you." But the blunt language in his letters to Roosevelt continued, and the two brothers, sharing their correspondence with Roosevelt, reinforced each other. Gifford wrote Amos, "The trouble with [Roosevelt] is that he is surrounded by people who tell him what they think he wants to hear, irrespective of his own good and the good of the cause."[8] Soon his Irish friend Plunkett warned Gifford, "I had better keep away from T.R., who was still 'sore.'"[9]

The Pinchot brothers had misjudged Roosevelt. Because they had moved him to challenge Taft for the presidential nomination and then bolt and form a third party, they assumed he would come around to agree with the advanced progressives. But TR had a strong, pugnacious streak and would become angry with his prodders. As Elihu Root had earlier commented of his former ally, "He is essentially a fighter and when he gets into a fight he is completely dominated by the desire to destroy his adversary."[10] Perkins's opponents would have done better to line up behind an alternative candidate and convince Roosevelt that their choice was best for the party's long-term health. But no alternative candidate surfaced who could provide the required commitment, energy, and leadership.[11]

*   *   *

Meanwhile, Roosevelt decided he would write his autobiography, then explore the Amazon River region. For his book project, he asked Gifford to prepare a chapter on his administration's conservation policies, and Gifford dutifully provided a full account, with TR assuring him several times that "he would give me much credit" for his services.[12] But the colonel's draft chapter only referred a few times to Gifford, who was somewhat miffed about the slight. He reasoned, however, that the autobiography was, after all, his chief's.

But when Gifford read the draft to his mother, she became "very indignant." Mary dashed off a letter to Roosevelt complaining about the "little importance" given to her son, "the soul and fount of Forestry," and how he could be "only incidentally connected" with his many successful policies. This "is history you are writing," she reminded him, and "there is little record of him except the shameful treatment of the last administration and the vituperation of those who, being envious of righteousness and truth, hate him." Because Taft had fired Gifford, it was the duty of Roosevelt, his friend, to restore his reputation. "It is for future generations that I wish his name to be vindicated and his services honored," and she concluded, "I think you will not be surprised if I am disappointed."[13]

Roosevelt mollified Gifford with kind words and defensively replied to Mary, "I have mentioned [Gifford] twice as often as I have mentioned anyone else in connection with my administration." But making amends, he added a passage that extolled Gifford Pinchot as "the man to whom the nation owes most for what has been accomplished as regards the preservation of the natural resources of our country" and praised "his tireless energy and activity, his fearlessness, his complete disinterestedness, his single-minded devotion to the interests of the plain people." Immensely pleased with these laudatory words, she thanked Roosevelt "for your admirable tribute to Gifford."[14]

*   *   *

Meanwhile, Mary Pinchot's health was faltering. Her writing hand was "stiff with rheumatism," but more seriously, she suffered from poor digestion and had exploratory surgery on her stomach in June 1910. Mary's illness was diagnosed as stomach cancer. She had operations in 1911 and 1912, but the cancer persisted.[15] When she was gone, who would be Gifford's companion? Might not a suitable wife be found who would become his valuable helpmate in advancing his future ambitions? In her twilight years, such thoughts surely crossed her mind, but her correspondence or diary never hinted at such a concern. He was a mama's boy, to be sure, but Gifford had many interests to keep him occupied.

But then, in June 1913, Gifford invited Cornelia Bryce to Grey Towers. Leila (her nickname, pronounced LEE-la) was thirty-one years old—sixteen years younger than Gifford. From a wealthy New York family, Leila's father, Lloyd Stephens Bryce, a banker in Manhattan, had earlier served a term as congressman. He was also an avid sportsman and had been publisher and editor of the prestigious *North American Review* in the 1890s. Leila, the second of three children, could also claim, on her mother Edith Cooper Bryce's side, a distinguished lineage, as her great-grandfather, Peter Cooper, and grandfather, Edward Cooper, were both New York industrialists and inventors as well as political reformers fighting Tammany Hall. Leila's mother and father had a home on upper Fifth Avenue and a country house in Roslyn, Long Island. They were well-acquainted with the Roosevelts, who lived just down the road in Oyster Bay. President Taft had appointed Lloyd Bryce minister to the Netherlands in 1911.[16]

Leila's childhood, she later reflected, had been "commonplace and uneventful," but her education was entirely with governesses and she never attended a school or college. As she matured, she later admitted, "I had not the faintest idea what I did want. I only knew that I was 'agin' everything the family wanted—all its traditions, all its theories, all its works." Her sense of revolt could be explained as a normal rebellion of a young person against parental authority and social conventions of the rich, but it became part of Leila's personality. She refused to come out as a debutante and, in her twenties, took off with a friend on a trip to the West Coast and back.[17]

Still, her rebellion mostly gave her some independent space. She seemed content to participate in charitable balls and other benevolent causes that were reserved for the social elite in the New York metropolitan area. She became an accomplished horsewoman, winning prizes at horse shows, participating in fox hunts, and even joining other society women in competing successfully in polo matches "against hard-boiled masculine competition." This competitive drive helps explain Leila's subsequent energetic involvement in many forms of political activity. She also became a suffragist and took up the cause of working women.[18] Growing up in a family environment steeped in politics, she easily warmed to the issues and drama permeating the swelling progressive movement.

Leila had suitors in the past but apparently no serious romantic interest until Gifford came along. Initially, Gifford took no special notice. His one comment about her before their first date was to the head of the Progressive Party's public affairs arm: "I had a talk with Miss Cornelia Bryce [who] has a great deal of money, is greatly interested in the Progressive movement, as well as in modern advance of all kinds, and I think could be gotten to take a vivid and productive interest in the work of the Progressive Service."[19]

Not surprisingly, given Gifford's love of angling, he and Leila went trout fishing together along Sawkill Creek on their first date.[20] Leila was the only woman he had more than looked at since the death of Laura Houghteling, his true love. What had happened? Had his mother, aware of her approaching mortality, nudged him toward finding a marriage partner? She, too, knew the Bryces, and Leila had visited her at Grey Towers for a few days in October 1911, and over the next twenty months (up to Gifford's first date with her), Mary had stayed in touch with her at social events.[21] Mamee, of course, had many friends, but it was unusual for someone of Mary's advanced years to befriend a woman half her age. It could be assumed that Mary was carefully promoting Leila as her son's possible mate.[22]

There is, however, a more innocent explanation. When Mary first invited Leila to Grey Towers, her father was just starting his service as the U.S. Minister to the Netherlands. Mary, who had earlier stayed with Nettie at The Hague, likely invited Leila to tell her about her daughter and husband, Alan, at the British Legation and the diplomatic social landscape in the Dutch capital in case Leila visited her parents there. Leila traveled to Europe at least three times during her father's two-year tenure at The Hague, and she had some contact with Nettie.[23]

For Gifford, the number of "not a clear day" references to Laura Houghteling in his diary supplanted the "happy" ones. As memory of her faded, he more easily contemplated a new love interest. With many productive years ahead of him, would not a real, live mate, if compatible, be preferable to a withering, spiritual one? Was it not important for a politician to be a married man? Might the prospect of possible progeny also have a place in such thoughts? Because Gifford never commented about his willingness to give up bachelorhood, his reasons are speculative.

But Gifford left a few clues. He must have found her attractive, and if he were considering a possible new sweetheart, he should show some interest. On their fishing date, he recorded that she wore "a kind of Blouse and rubber boots," an unusual observation since he seldom commented on a woman's attire. Besides her good looks, Leila possessed stellar pedigree, wealth, and shared political perspectives—everything a man in his position might want. In any event, three months after their first date, Leila invited Gifford to visit her and stay overnight at the Bryces' Roslyn house, and he accepted. Later, in March 1914, Leila spent a few days at the Pinchots' Washington residence. [24]

Leila seemed fixated on Gifford, later claiming, "I marked down, pursued, and captured" him. Inviting Gifford to visit her was part of her pursuit, but her capture did not come fast and easy.[25] After their first dates at Grey Towers and Roslyn, little is known about the process leading to Gifford's and Leila's slowly blooming romance, although the two stayed in touch.[26]

Of course, Gifford was busy after he decided to run as a Progressive Party candidate for the U.S. Senate in Pennsylvania in early 1914. William Draper Lewis, dean of the University of Pennsylvania Law School, was the Progressive candidate for governor, and the two campaigned throughout the Keystone State.[27] But in Gifford's free time, he gave Leila no special attention. Despite the many "not a clear day" entries in his diary, he still had an occasional "clear and happy day" remembering Laura; in early April, he noted it had been "twenty years and two months today" since her passing.[28]

Then he again turned his attention back to Leila when his mother's condition worsened. Mamee, despite her "superb" and "unbroken" spirit, was obviously failing. She was wracked by cancer, which had spread to her lungs, and her left hand and foot were useless. She likely told Gifford that if Leila were his intended, she wanted him to marry her while she was still around, and Gifford, who loved his mother, wanted to please her in her last days. Gertrude rooted for the couple's romance, telling Amos, "Perhaps . . . if yr. Mother's illness hadn't come, this also might not have come."[29]

In May, Lady Johnstone arrived from Europe to visit her ailing mother, who gratefully noted, "My Girlie came."[30] Nettie was prepared to stay on to comfort her mother in her last days, even after the outbreak of war engulfed the European continent in the first days of August. Right after the assassination of the Austrian archduke and his wife on June 28, Mary Pinchot "thought it meant war and [was] very distressed about it."[31] She might not have predicted how widespread the European maelstrom would become, but that soon ensued with Britain's early involvement. The Great War, as it would be called, had begun. [32]

Gifford finally proposed to Leila in late July, but the thought of marriage gave her pause. She wondered if she were really ready to tie the knot. She wrote to Gifford, expressing her reservations. "I know in my soul, I am not giving you enough to ensure that this [marriage] should never happen between you and me. . . . I am not good enough for you on any count, not the same class of animal," and "I know I ought not to marry you so." Although admitting in her confused state that it might "all be bloodlessness or lack of courage and deci-sion," Leila concluded, "you had better forget me completely and marry one of the other ladies I have picked out for you."[33] Despite her hesitation, the couple reconciled and planned to marry sometime that autumn.

But with Mary declining precipitously, Gifford asked his fiancée to move up the wedding day. Unprepared for the change, a startled Leila rushed off to Seal Harbor, Maine, and wrote Gifford, "I have thought it over and am begin-ning to see clear. . . . it seems to me brutal to do it immediately—any time after the 3d or 4th of September will suit me." But in the end, Leila, tired of the haggling and uncertainty, acceded to Gifford's wishes and consented to August 15 as the marriage date.[34]

The modest matrimonial ceremony took place in the Bryces' Roslyn home, with Amos serving as best man and Gertrude, Aunt Antoinette Wood, Uncle Will Eno, and a few other friends, including Theodore and Edith Roosevelt and Jim and Helen Garfield, in attendance. The couple soon visited Mary, who had removed to Will's home in Saugatuck, Connecticut. Mary was surely delighted with the marriage but too weakened to participate in the nuptials.[35] She died ten days later, a month short of her seventy-seventh birthday. The newlyweds attended her funeral in Saugatuck, and she was transported for burial at Grey Towers next to James.

*   *   *

Marriage and a new career as a politician were turning points in Gifford's life. His campaigning for the U.S. Senate with Leila was a fitting introduction to the kind of political activity that would become part of the couple's future. His wife, too, would later run for elective positions in her own right.

For his Senate campaign, Gifford had a few advantages. In 1912, Roosevelt carried Pennsylvania, which suggested popular support for political reform statewide, and his endorsement of Gifford was crucial. "One of the strongest arguments of going in," he wrote TR, was the former president's backing. Moreover, Gifford was unopposed for the progressive nomination and could concentrate his political attacks on the other party nominees. On the Democratic side, his opponent was A. Mitchell Palmer, a three-term congressman, but Gifford paid little attention to him, mainly because the Democratic Party was weak in Pennsylvania, a state no Democratic presidential nominee had won since the 1850s.[36]

Instead, Gifford directed his criticisms at the Republican incumbent, Boies Penrose. Running for reelection to his fourth term as U.S. senator, Penrose was the acknowledged boss of the state's Republican Party. He had supported Taft in 1912, and Gifford, then campaigning for TR in Pennsylvania, had spoken out against the senator and predicted he would be defeated for reelection two years later. In 1914, Gifford relished the challenge of opposing a representative of boss rule and the entrenched interests he thoroughly disliked. Penrose had a reputation as a hard-drinking politician; during the campaign, Gifford emphasized that the Republican incumbent was tied to the liquor interests and accepted contributions from Standard Oil. The Pennsylvania senator replied in kind, arguing that Gifford was a carpetbagger with no roots in the state and sneered at his virtuous character and do-good program. And whenever mentioning Gifford's name, he would mispronounce it as "Pin-shot."[37]

Gifford stressed the trust question, but he soon conceded to Garfield, "Wilson seems to have completed in fine style his job of taking our platform." He was referring to the president's recent speech calling for new antitrust legislation and an interstate trade commission. Congress would not pass these reform measures for another eight months, so Gifford believed he could differentiate his party's position on monopolies from Wilson's during his campaign. Gifford emphasized "efficiency" as a standard for accepting big business units, which the government would regulate, but he was willing to prosecute the most bloated behemoths among them.[38] His position on trusts, in fact, did not deviate much from Wilson's proposed legislation and, in any event, did not seem to take hold with the electorate. The zeal for reform was in decline, partly because of the progressives' successes on all governmental levels but also because the public was becoming skittish about accepting the reformers' long-term struggle for social and political change.

Gifford also had to deal with his querulous brother as their positions on the issues diverged. Despite his radical instincts, Gifford continued to be more careful in his assertions. Both were anti-monopoly, but the problem had become Amos's obsession. Amos was prepared to accept large corporations if real competition still existed but never monopolistic ones, which represented concentrated wealth and overwhelming economic power. He argued that a regulatory commission was hobbled by lawsuits, and besides, "the ordinary result of commission regulation has been control by corporations of the body that is supposed to control them." Above all, he wanted to strengthen and enforce the Sherman antitrust law. The most powerful monopolies would be dissolved, and a freer economy would emerge, giving the man on the make a fairer chance to compete and get ahead. He also wanted the government to take over, own, and operate the railways because "the railroads and the great industrial producers are controlled by the same group of people." He allowed that government control might be less efficient, but the rates and fares would be fairer for the users. Ethics trumped economics in such matters. He likewise advocated government control of other "natural" monopolies, such as the telegraph, telephone, and electricity, and he provided examples of lower rates charged by municipal power companies compared with privately owned ones. Otherwise, he opposed socialism as contrary to natural economic laws and stifling initiative.[39]

Amos's emphasis on breaking private monopolies was quite different from the Roosevelt-Perkins view.[40] Like his brother, Gifford believed that the U.S. government might take over some of the monopolistic anthracite coal lands and supply coal to consumers at a reasonable price. The government could take over the railroads, too, if they did not cooperate. But Gifford's political handlers persuaded him to drop the initiatives as too radical.[41] Similarly, he agreed with his brother's position on government ownership of "natural" monopolies, except for railroads, since the people, while accepting rate regulation, were not ready for government ownership.[42] Moreover, Amos wanted to break up large landholdings, but despite his prodding, Gifford avoided the issue of land reform. Pennsylvania had traditionally favored protectionism, so he endorsed a high tariff, which Amos opposed.[43]

During Gifford's Senate campaign, Amos became a hindrance. He wrote letters to prominent reformers nationwide seeking their endorsements of Gifford. But then rumors surfaced that Amos, believing Perkins would promote a pro-trust candidate for the U.S. Senate in neighboring New York, was seriously considering a run for that seat. Worried that Amos's more radical politics as a candidate might tarnish the mainstream reform program of his older brother, Gifford's political advisers strongly opposed his brother's candidacy.[44] And in one of her last letters, their mother bluntly told her youngest that his running without "a ghost of a chance" of winning would hurt Gifford's candidacy. Amos agreed to stay out if "it might be a bad thing for the Penna race," but his reply, a sustained attack on "the Progressive Machine" in his home state, confirmed he had considered a Senate bid.[45]

The disappointing vote in the May primary was a warning to Gifford's political hopes. Gifford was the top vote-getter among his party's candidates but polled only 47,000 votes compared to Penrose's 220,000 against light opposition. He had much work ahead to have a chance in November.

Then, right after the primary, an Amos broadside sent to the party's national committee demanding the removal of Perkins from the executive committee was leaked to the press.[46] Heretofore, the intraparty bickering had been private, but now Gifford publicly defended Amos's letter as "right. . . . Perkins has had and will have nothing whatever to do with my fight against Penrose in Pennsylvania." Gifford's allies nonetheless called Amos's contretemps "folly" and predicted it would hurt their candidate in the coming election. Republicans also pointed out the anomaly of Gifford denouncing Perkins as a party leader while welcoming the support of another business magnate and political boss, Bill Flinn of Pittsburgh, a bitter enemy of Penrose.[47]

Gifford campaigned at a grueling pace. His main political adviser in his campaign was P. Stephen Stahlnecker, whom Gifford hired as his personal secretary in 1909. German-American in background, Stahlnecker gradually won Gifford's confidence as a loyal aide and shrewd party worker. By 1914, he was also planning his boss's campaign stops and speeches. With good political instincts, "Steve," as Gifford called him, complemented Gifford's more idealistic outlook, and he would be the real director of Gifford's political operations for the next twenty years.

Determined to visit every corner of the state, Gifford mainly relied on the automobile, a relatively new mode of transportation in American politics and necessary in Pennsylvania as the nation's second most populous state and the second largest geographically east of the Mississippi. His mother's final illness prevented comprehensive coverage, but he still shook hands with hundreds of workers at a time entering or leaving factory gates and coal mines and countless citizens at rallies. His barnstorming likely prompted Penrose to campaign actively for the first time in his long political career.[48]

Gifford's positive message was that he represented the needed fresh air for political reform, spoke out for women's suffrage, and courted labor and farmers. Gifford also tried to make a campaign issue of prohibition, which was surging in importance in the state. Allying with the Anti-Saloon League, churches, and civic organizations, he emphasized local option, allowing counties to vote to ban the sale of alcoholic beverages. Because he never really liked alcohol since his student days, he had no problem advocating temperance reform.[49]

He even sought to make inroads in the African American community. Despite the Progressive Party's disinterest in black support in 1912, Gifford, looking for votes, saw no such constraints in a northern state. Booker T. Washington believed Penrose had "deceived" the "restless" colored people and introduced Gifford to a black pastor from Philadelphia who would rouse African Americans behind his candidacy. Moreover, a black employee in the U.S. Forest Service, calling Gifford "a true friend" of African Americans, put him in touch with relatives and other black ministers in Philadelphia, Pittsburgh, and Harrisburg. Gifford funded a black preacher from Washington, D.C., who had friends in the Keystone State to lead the quest for African American votes. Black Americans then comprised less than three percent of the Pennsylvania population, so making inroads among this relatively small racial group would be an uphill quest. Penrose also organized rallies of African Americans, most of whom were traditional Republicans, and, if Stahlnecker is to be believed, was actively buying their votes.[50]

Gifford's willingness to court black votes was a practical political decision but also displayed his evolving perspective on race. Previously assuming that blacks were inferior in mental development, he may have been somewhat seduced by a burgeoning eugenics movement that tried to categorize racial stereotypes and prevent the mixing of the races that would, so eugenic enthusiasts believed, result in degenerate offspring and the undermining of white civilization. Politicians and prominent professionals flocked to the eugenics movement and boosted its legitimacy. Among them were Theodore Roosevelt; Irving Fisher, an economics professor at Yale; and Dr. John Harvey Kellogg, who ran a health sanitarium in Battle Creek, Michigan.[51] Gifford had visited Kellogg's sanitarium to try the doctor's famed low-carb diet and health regimen. Savvy in public relations, the Michigan doctor welcomed prominent people to his sanitarium and used Gifford's and Fisher's names, among many others, as endorsements for his health regimen.

In January 1914, Dr. Kellogg hosted the first National Conference on Race Betterment at his Battle Creek sanitarium. Because of his scientific interests, Gifford was attracted to the search among eugenics practitioners for verifiable conclusions about race, and he, his friend Sir Horace Plunkett, also a previous beneficiary of the health regimen of the sanitarium, and Fisher agreed to serve on the five-man planning committee for the conference.[52] But that was the extent of Gifford's commitment, and he did not attend the conference or show any subsequent interest in the eugenics movement. Indeed, in the absence of good data on racial hierarchies, he would move steadily in the opposite direction, avoiding racial stereotypes and seeing the fundamental humanity in all people. Later, he would early denounce the Nazis' anti-Semitism, and during World War II, he would express his "grave doubts" about the incarceration of Japanese-Americans in domestic concentration camps.[53]

During his campaign, Gifford featured his positions and endorsements in a pocket-size booklet entitled "What Gifford Pinchot Stands For."[54] TR's involvement in his contest, however, meant the most to him, and he visited Roosevelt at his Oyster Bay home. The colonel was happy to oblige his old friend, but he also relished the opportunity to attack Penrose, an old enemy, and pungently criticize the Wilson administration. "TR was just like his old self," Gifford noted of their meeting.[55] Roosevelt spoke with Gifford at rallies in Pittsburgh and Philadelphia and, in the final week of the contest, was signed up for a railway trip across the state involving many whistle stops and major addresses. But the former president had nearly died from a fever during his Amazon adventure, and his other travels and campaigning for progressives elsewhere had worn him down. Roosevelt asked to be relieved of some speechmaking. But now the shoe was on the other foot, and Gifford implored, "I have never asked you for anything personal before. I ask you now to keep this schedule." TR could not comply because of already conflicting commitments, but his Pennsylvania appearances gave more visibility to Gifford's candidacy.[56]

Gifford genuinely believed he had a good chance of winning, but he fell woefully short. On election day, Penrose amassed 520,000 votes, almost double Gifford's total of 269,000. Gifford had outpolled Palmer but by only 3,000 votes.

Gifford fairly accurately explained some of the reasons for his defeat. Trying to make an issue of Penrose as a sleazy character failed, he acknowledged to his sister, as "Church people threw us down and voted for Penrose and 'prosperity' where they voted at all, which most of them did not do."[57] That could have been an admission that voters' interest in reform issues was waning, but Gifford would continue to believe that his party's message of honest government and curbing abuses in industrial America remained relevant. He also did not admit the difficulty of third-party candidates in capturing the imagination of voters in a fairly stable two-party system. Roosevelt and the Bull Moosers had temporarily rocked the Republican Party in 1912, but it recovered sufficiently to endure as the conservative alternative to Wilson and the Democrats. Indeed, except for Gifford and two races in California, no other Progressive Party candidate for major statewide offices finished better than third.[58] Gifford had waged a strong fight, and his defeat served as a useful learning experience, gaining knowledge about Pennsylvania and its problems that would be indispensable for future campaigns. At the time, however, the result was discouraging, and he would not actively seek public office for another eight years.

*   *   *

Marveling at her mother's adaptability, Nettie earlier wrote, "The Mouse is the only person of that generation who has an elastic mind and isn[']t shocked by progress."[59] Mary Pinchot had indeed adjusted to the growing demands for political change in her last years, but her elasticity had limits. Culturally, she remained a traditional Victorian and hinted at her unease about societal changes while spending the summer of 1913 in Newport with Amos and his family. The Rhode Island retreat for wealthy Americans offered cool breezes and many activities, and she observed that "A and G are dancing madly day and night." "Newport really is a wonderful place," Mary concluded, but at the same time, she felt uncomfortable among "the gay foolish set who are doing all they can to spoil it."[60] Mary likely witnessed Amos and Gertrude trying out new dances like the turkey trot, bunny hug, and tango, which had become a rage in New York and spread to outlying places like Newport. They attracted the young and also middle-aged people like Amos and Gertrude. If not an active part of the "gay, foolish set," they adjusted easily to the new social conventions. A cultural revolution was underway. In the slow transition to modern America, morals and manners were changing, and a newly emerging intellectual climate influenced large parts of American thought.

The changes had come gradually to about 1908 and, by 1913, penetrated widely over many areas of American life. In science, it involved developments in atomic physics and the theory of relativity. New psychology and psychiatry fields arose, emphasizing the irrational and the interpretation of dreams and instinctual behavior. There were entirely novel developments in literature, architecture, music, and art. The latter, departing from representational forms striving for refinement and beauty, became more realistic with the emergence of the Ash Can school of painters and graphic artists, who depicted grim scenes of everyday life in American ghettos and brawny boxing matches, or nonrepresentational, with cubist paintings and abstract sculpture. Greenwich Village was the center of this new literary and art world, located fairly close to the Tenth Street Studio where James Pinchot had visited his much more conventional Hudson River School painter friends a half-century earlier.

Gertrude and Amos were becoming immersed in what has been called an innocent pre-war rebellion of artists and intellectuals.[61] The couple embraced the new currents of thought. For Amos, one part of his rebellion was his disillusionment with the progressive movement and his political radicalization, but another aspect was his outspoken support for free speech.

From 1913–1914, he became involved in three disputes. The first was a strike by silk mill workers in Paterson, New Jersey. During the protests, some leaders of the Industrial Workers of the World (IWW), a revolutionary labor group that came to the strikers' support, were arrested and convicted for making incendiary remarks during demonstrations. Amos did not sympathize with IWW theories, but believing that "a very vital principal of American life is at stake—the right of free speech—of public discussion and protest," he sent $500 to one of its leaders for an appeal.[62]

A second involved the fallout from a violent labor strike in Colorado. The operators of a Rockefeller family mining company in Ludlow had used company police and the Colorado National Guard to attack union strikers. The ensuing gun battle, which resulted in the deaths of many miners, miners' wives, and their children, became known as the Ludlow Massacre. Concerned about the violence, a radical preacher in New York gave advance notice that he would point out the inconsistency between real Christianity and the Rockefeller actions in Colorado at a Baptist church in Manhattan where John D. Rockefeller worshipped. When the preacher stood during a service to ask a question, he was seized by ushers and policemen, taken to the streets where he and some friends were beaten with clubs, and arrested, and he and some of his supporters were given six months in jail. In response, Amos, though not religious himself, wrote a public letter of protest to the mayor in which he contrasted the city's violent behavior in this affair with the treatment nearly two thousand years earlier of Jesus, who had criticized the Pharisees' commercialism and corruption. Jesus, Amos mocked, was not arrested in Jerusalem, "a semi-barbarous oriental city [where] a spirit of official and religious tolerance and freedom of discussion existed which is absent in Christian New York today."[63]

Amos's third and more enduring involvement was his support of the radical monthly magazine, *The Masses*. Max Eastman, the new socialist editor, had turned what had been a nondescript socialistic publication into the most avant-garde periodical of its day. Its masthead defiantly proclaimed that it was "a revolutionary and not a reform magazine . . . with a sense of humor and no respect for the respectable: frank, arrogant, impertinent, . . . printing what is too naked or true for a money-making press, and . . . conciliat[ing] nobody, not even its readers."[64]

Amos loved *The Masses*. Eastman later told the story of Amos telephoning him one day and saying, "I called up to tell you fellows you're getting out a swell paper." With *The Masses*' subsidy from rich benefactors running out, Eastman and the managing editor, John Reed, were in Amos's office the same afternoon, and "we came away charmed by his sagacious humor, and richer by two thousand dollars."[65] Subsequently, to sustain its operations, Amos gave a regular subvention, solicited other patrons, and paid for subscribers' renewals in advance to produce enough cash to print the next issues.

Amos was drawn to public questions, especially free speech, that *The Masses* discussed in its pages. The magazine had accused the Associated Press of slanting its coverage of a coal strike in West Virginia in favor of the employers. Accompanying the article was a cartoon by Ash Can artist Art Young, showing the AP poisoning the waters of public opinion. In response, the AP sued Eastman and Young for criminal libel. Rallying with other leftwing radicals, Amos managed a defense fund and argued that the AP did "color and distort the news [and] . . . is a monopolistic corporation not only in constraint of news, but in constraint of truth."[66] *The Masses*' criticism of fellow journalists, who also championed freedom of the press, resulted in a hostile response from elite metropolitan newspapers but was indicative of the magazine's readiness to attack any vaunted American institution, including its own. The results in the free speech cases involving Amos's efforts were mixed.[67] But Amos's point, win or lose, was to support strikers, both financially and in the press, who were fighting for better wages and working conditions, and backing the accused adversaries would improve the chances for fair trials and appeals.

What linked Amos's interests in both large economic problems like monopoly and individual rights and free speech was their common commitment to ordinary, powerless citizens against concentrated power. His political philosophy was basically Jeffersonian but mixed with a few Hamiltonian ingredients of activist governance. The cornerstone of democracy for him was the Jeffersonian free individual, and he believed that his and like-minded protests would defend citizens' rights and prompt the "people" to elect reformers to an aroused Congress, which would pass legislation utilizing the government's countervailing power to break up corporate and land monopolies. But on the positive side, he also advocated enacting federal legislation to fight poverty and economic insecurity in the modern industrial era. In favoring the state ownership of natural monopolies, he even wanted to go beyond Hamiltonian means.[68]

The federal government's enactment of the Federal Reserve banking system, the Clayton Antitrust Act, and the Federal Trade Commission provided clear evidence that progressive reformers were succeeding, but public discussion of Amos's advocacy of land reform, social security, and unemployment insurance was then barely discernible in the United States, which, compared with European countries, was larger and more ethnically diverse, decentralized, and individualistic. He recognized that his vision of comprehensive reform was ahead of its time. As he told a fellow reformer, "Nothing that we can put over in a year or two years is worth doing." And he perceived that "the fight against privilege is going to be harder and harder," because "the Rockefellers, the Steel Corporation, and other large groups of power," through their funding of private pension plans and other philanthropic activities, were "painting themselves up as benevolent God the Father. . . . Why don't people see it? It is unbelievable that intelligent people should stand for this false charity. And yet they always have stood for it, and perhaps will during our time."[69]

Amos was expressing the perplexity of politicians and political analysts over the millennia. He wanted to believe that people were rational actors who, perceiving their economic interests, would vote for politicians who best expressed them. The fact that cultural biases, obfuscating rhetoric, and other factors muddied the political landscape and undermined reform was discomfiting. Amos was more persuasive in presenting the big picture—the struggle between "privilege" and "the people," capital and labor, monopolies and consumers—than in providing a strategy for bringing about the desired changes.

Most progressive reformers were practical idealists. They had an idealistic vision of the good society but also promoted a pragmatic reform program that they would strive to achieve incrementally over time. Amos had plenty of idealism, but his vision was more grandiose than practical in a time of general prosperity. He perceived that Americans were restive and that an economic revolution was at hand, and Amos's writings provided anecdotal examples of the deep social malaise he perceived. But he still saw himself as a political writer, not an organizer, and his problem-solving strategy was mainly a long-term education campaign, which his writings promoted. He was an elitist who assumed that ordinary, aggrieved citizens would somehow discern the wisdom of his and other reformers' ideas and demand changes from their elected officials. It is doubtful, however, whether his ideas had much popular impact beyond progressive and socialist leaders who already shared much of his perspective.[70] And unluckily for advanced reformers like Amos, worries over foreign policy would increasingly deflect the American public's attention from their domestic reform goals.

* * *

As a polemicist, Amos greatly valued *The Masses'* incisive coverage of political issues (even when he disagreed with its socialist message).[71] But besides his transition further to the political left, he also identified with *The Masses'* irreverent attacks on Victorian culture in America. He rejoiced in the magazine's satires of the staid, stuffy social elite. "We are not popular among the best people," Amos confided to George Bernard Shaw, and the exclusive men's clubs to which he belonged had "banished" *The Masses*. "This is a pity," he joshed, "for heretofore a number of old gentlemen at the University Club got their exercise by walking up and down the library, tearing the Masses up and throwing it on the floor."[72]

Dedicated to political and social change, the magazine promoted women's rights. It went beyond suffrage, however, to include the liberation of the female from what the young literary writers believed to be the female's liberation from the vestigial feudalism of the home and the artificial narrowing of her personality and activities, while more women entering the workforce was a positive development, making the "new" woman more like men, more interested in ideas, more honest, and less finicky. The Victorians would have said that these women had become like men, coarsened, but these new intellectuals liked her.[73]

Among feminist issues, *The Masses* championed birth control, whose pioneer leaders in the United States were Margaret Sanger and her husband, William. Sanger and her sister, Ethel Byrne, set up a birth control clinic in Brooklyn to provide the female sex with informed knowledge of contraception and planned parenthood, and women, often poorly acquainted with the subject, flocked to the site for advice. Mrs. Sanger was adept at attracting public attention to her cause. Deliberately violating a state law prohibiting the dissemination of birth control advice and devices, she and her sister were arrested, as they were determined to test the constitutionality of the law. Out on bail, Sanger and her co-workers kept the clinic open while Mrs. Byrne, still in jail, went on a hunger strike and refused to bathe. When prison officials continually force-fed her, public concerns against the cruel treatment of this dedicated woman mounted.

Amos Pinchot provided legal advice to William Sanger after his arrest earlier for disseminating birth control information, and Gertrude stepped forward to champion Margaret Sanger's cause.[74] Perhaps Gertrude's own sexual ignorance as a young woman caught her attention, but already sensitized to the plight of working females who often had much larger families than they could afford, birth control was in line with her new reform interests. Knowledge about birth control would benefit all women, Gertrude believed, but Americans were still mostly uninformed. "The taboo on the subject is hideous," she complained to a newspaper reporter. The United States was practically the only country opposed to birth control, and "People do not look the facts in the face."[75] At first, she contributed financially to help the Sangers get out of debt and keep their children enrolled in a private school. She then organized fundraising luncheons and dinners to help with Mrs. Sanger's and her sister's legal defense, sat through Sanger's trial as a show of solidarity for her movement, devised schedules for volunteers to administer the clinic, and paid Sanger's small fine when she was found guilty of violating the state's obscenity law. Staffing the clinic involved the risk of police raids, but Gertrude and other Sanger backers provided volunteers to replace those arrested.

The birth control movement attracted the interest of upper- and middle-class women who did not really need the information, but the poor and working females for whom it was mainly intended were too absorbed in their daily toils to get much involved. Gertrude's and other society women's efforts in these first struggles might suggest a radical chic aura to the birth control cause, but Gertrude was more than just a wealthy patron. Encouraged by Amos, she headed a delegation to Albany, for example, to ask the Republican governor to release the weakened Mrs. Byrne and appoint a commission to study the question of birth control.[76] The commission was never appointed, the governor released Byrne only after her distressed sister accepted the terms of pardon on her behalf, and the appeals of the Byrne and Sanger convictions failed, but the movement persevered. Despite the obstacles, the Sangers managed to advance citizens' interest in birth control, and Gertrude remained committed to the movement.

15.

A Military Hospital

The Great War in Europe would directly and profoundly affect Alan and Nettie. Before the hostilities, the centers of the couple's daily routines were in the Netherlands and England. The Hague had advantages for the Johnstones. It was close to England where their son, Harcourt (Crinks), began attending Eton in 1910, and Mary Pinchot had purchased a house for them in London that year where they could stay closer to their son and the British social scene.[1]

When the Great War began, Crinks, now nineteen, was a student at Oxford, and the conflict would pull him, and his mother, away from college and society. Britain had no military draft until 1916, so Crinks could have escaped military service for the first part of the war, but while still in America, Nettie received a cable from her son saying he had volunteered for the armed forces. The patriotic upsurge in support of Britain's military involvement was strikingly visible among the privileged Oxford and Cambridge students who left college in droves and signed on for military service. Crinks was not an able-bodied student-soldier. He had always been plagued by poor health, and Gertrude described him in 1912 as "such a tall fellow, with sweet and rather sad eyes, not strong looking." Indeed, it is somewhat surprising the army accepted his enlistment.[2]

Nettie was anxious about her only child. She reported that "Crinks seems to like soldiering so far, tho' the hours of drill and work, fr[om] 6 am to 6 [pm] don't sound very pleasant to me. If all goes well with him and he gets thro' this war it will be the making of him." Some of his training occurred in the biting cold while living in tents on the Salisbury plain in the shadow of the great cathedral, with nearby Stonehenge his only recreation. Nettie's concerns escalated when, in mid-1915, he was sent for service in France. "He seemed so terribly young to be allowing him to go," she wrote Gifford, "but it was all very sweet and matter of fact and he said it was more like going to a private school than going to war." Crinks's assignment was as an aide to General Walter Norris Congreve, which relieved Nettie, and he would never have to fight in the trenches or experience poison gas attacks. Later in the war, Nettie admitted, "Of course if these were normal times, I'd be distressed about his health but now I rejoice as he isn't well enough for the trenches. I'm not really a Spartan mother at all!"[3]

Until the end of 1914, Nettie stayed mostly at The Hague, "as it seems to be my job" as a chief of mission's wife. "I can see that Alan is looked after, that he goes out. I can grin and grin and make feeble jokes, wh- seems to be my permanent business." While there, she also helped with the relief effort for the hundreds of thousands of Belgian refugees fleeing Germany's invasion of their country. Her witnessing of the Belgians' dislocation, poverty, and misery paled in comparison with the enormous casualties on the battlefields but was nonetheless unsettling. "What a world we live in!" she exclaimed. "It all seems too bad to be true, but we are going to win." She soon surmised, however, that her relief work was not really appreciated, "as I find the Dutch ladies a little touchy about the help of foreigners, and the most I can do seems to be to write cheques."[4]

The war would transform Lady Johnstone from a social dilettante to a woman with a purpose. In 1911, on one of Nettie's visits to America, Mary Pinchot hosted a tea party for her. Ellen Slayden, the acerbic diarist of Washington society, had commented that Nettie at the "charming" affair was "the only one who seemed quite indifferent to the company, going through it as if just to humor her mother's little fancy. . . . Lady Johnstone is tall, athletic and handsome in an unfinished sort of way," Slayden had continued. "She belongs, I think, to the every-hoydenish Roosevelt school, taking enough up to twenty-five years, or so very little longer, but confusing socially when it extends into the thirties."[5] Unaware of Nettie's many health problems, Slayden was unfair in her assessment, but she was correct in her comment about Nettie's awkward transition from a high-spirited, young American personality to a life as Alan's wife of European diplomatic formality.

There were two sides to Nettie. On the one side, she loved high society and enjoyed making a fashion statement at formal social functions. (By such standards, Mary's tea party might have seemed ordinary to her.) While visiting Mamee in Washington in November 1913, for example, she appeared regularly at embassy receptions and dinners, and the Washington newspapers, intrigued by the visit of a foreign Lady and daughter of a prominent local resident, delighted in descriptions of her stylish evening gowns, usually with a long and full train.[6] The other side was that she was public-spirited, well-informed, and possessed an impulsive temperament to speak her mind on public issues she felt strongly about.[7] Before the war, both sides of Nettie had shown themselves at a White House tea hosted by President Wilson and First Lady Ellen to greet foreign diplomats and their spouses, which Nettie, as the wife of one (though abroad), had also attended. A society writer for a local newspaper had described her appearance in a dress of "tête de nègre' satin" and wearing a "broad-brimmed, low-crowned hat" in detail.[8] More substantively, during the reception, she had engaged Wilson in conversation about the British and U.S.'s markedly different responses to the unfolding Mexican revolution. She bluntly told him she disapproved of the U.S. policy. Several years later, in fact, she would still refer to her "awful row about Mexico" with the president.[9]

The transformation of Antoinette Johnstone went beyond spirited conversation to concrete action. She had internalized some of the Pinchot family's sense of *noblesse oblige*, and she acknowledged early in the conflict, "All the values have changed, have become more real." Searching for a way to make her values work for something positive during the war, she developed ambitious plans for service in wartime. She thought she might become a nurse but soon surmised that what was needed, and where she might make a real difference, was establishing a hospital for wounded soldiers in France. Such an institution would be her contribution to her adopted nation in wartime and serve as a memorial to her mother, although she did not publicize the latter.[10]

A hospital was a tall order, but Lady Johnstone was undaunted in pursuing her goal. She shared her plans with American Red Cross officials traversing Holland, who gave her helpful suggestions, and she solicited donations from relatives and wealthy friends in Britain and America. Her Uncle Will and Aunt Antoinette contributed, the latter giving $1,000 (soon increased to $5,000), and to her surprise, even quirky Uncle Amo Eno, after rejecting her and his nephew Amos's appeals, changed his mind and donated $5,000. The younger Amos also acted as a valuable liaison with Mabel Boardman, head of the American Red Cross in Washington, D.C., and a longtime acquaintance of the Pinchot family.

From his contacts with Boardman, Amos passed on information about how Nettie could purchase American ambulances and additional medical equipment at a discounted, government-sponsored rate. He was also handling the details of their mother's estate, which left everything equally to her three children, and assured his sister early on that she could borrow against her inheritance money, which would not come for another year. "Don't take any more than you need now, please," Amos advised. "But, of course, whenever you do need it, I will see that you get it."[11] Receiving assurances from British authorities, Mrs. Boardman soon recruited several nurses and sent Nettie additional equipment totaling over $4,000, which Amos paid for until his sister could reimburse him.

Gifford also became involved with Nettie's project. At first, though, right after his Senate election defeat, he and Leila went to Florida on a delayed honeymoon. They spent much time fishing, and Leila, already an accomplished sportswoman, experienced the excitement of the saltwater kind. As Gifford reported to a favorite fishing buddy, "You would have been pleased to watch her fight a seven foot shark in a sixteen foot canoe, lifting his head out of the water with the rod in her left hand, and shooting him with a .45 caliber Colt with her right. It was well done I can assure you."[12]

The couple returned to their Washington house, where Boardman told Gifford that the Red Cross was eager to help Nettie and her proposed hospital. It wanted only assurances that the French authorities would use the American doctors and nurses in meaningful work. It agreed to pay for some supplies and a unit, including the salaries of three surgeons and up to twelve nurses for at least six months, and the French government would be expected to pay for their room and board.[13] With this support, Nettie was assured that more of her funds would be freed up to purchase additional equipment. Even so, her initial goals were modest. "I'll begin quite small if money doesn[']t come in," she had thought, and she contemplated a staffed and equipped hospital tent unit of thirty-six beds.[14]

In January 1915, Gifford and Leila sailed to Europe, in part, to support Nettie with her hospital initiative. They arrived at a time when his sister was in the midst of attending to wifely duties at The Hague Legation, helping the Belgian refugees, and trying to launch her hospital project.[15] Another reason for his trip, however, was to offer his services to the relief efforts of displaced people on the Continent. He received an appointment as a special agent of the U.S. State Department to distribute food to a few thousand hungry French civilians inside the German battle lines. Here was a chance to do some meaningful humanitarian work, he thought. But Germany reneged at the last minute on his entry onto its occupied territory on the ground that "my sister had married an Englishman." He also sought a job with the American Commission for Belgian Relief, providing food and other needed supplies in their occupied country. He often met with Herbert Hoover, who was in charge of the program. A phenomenally successful American mining engineer, Hoover, living in London at the start of the war, helped stranded Americans obtain financing for the return passage home before organizing the relief effort. He offered Gifford a position feeding some 200,000 Belgians in the southwest part of the country. But the German authorities imposed one obstacle after another to delay his work, and the position dissolved. "The Governments decided to transfer the population elsewhere," he complained, "so now I am out of a job, and coming home to find one."[16]

Gifford's European journey had been a frustrating experience, but the one positive result was that Leila became pregnant. They had wanted children from the start of their marriage, but nothing had happened, so Leila consulted with a specialist in Britain and had a surgical procedure. Gifford commented that the operation was "very successful and very necessary." And it worked, for within two months, Leila had conceived. She was under doctor's orders to avoid travel, so the two did not return to the United States until May 1915.[17] Three days before Christmas that year, she would give birth to a baby boy, to whom they gave the name Gifford Bryce. Five weeks later, the proud papa joked, "It looks as if this youngster of mine was going to weigh 27 pounds by the time he is 27 weeks old, if this chart curve keeps up." Realistically, he judged, however, "that won't happen."[18]

* * *

Nettie, meanwhile, first offered her hospital project to the British Red Cross, which was in charge of an American ambulance corps servicing the French Army. In conversations with the head of the French medical corps, she had worked out the terms for the placement of her hospital in northern France, but she soon found her negotiations with the British Red Cross "tiresome," and the French war ministry dragged its heels. Wanting to be sure that the Americans coming to France had no German relatives or sympathies, the French government was scrupulously checking their references. Meanwhile, the American equipment had arrived, as had the willing doctors and nurses who had to be paid for doing nothing. The delay was bad enough, but the French official she had negotiated with was promoted to another position, and his successor reneged on the arrangement. Nettie was outraged. "The d--- old hospital is bust," she exploded to Amos. "The French with their usual red tape . . . have done us in, d--- them."[19] Nevertheless, Nettie turned to the British Royal Army Medical Corps, and Gifford, trying to help before his return to America, received assurances that they would accept her offer. When he went to complete the deal, however, he was told that the British did not need more privately managed hospitals, and her proposed one would be too small. Gifford was indignant and "blamed the British medical leader severely for creating the impression that he had accepted, and then refusing." The Belgians also declined, saying that their government (in exile) could not accept any foreign doctors or nurses. A real bureaucratic disaster was in the making.[20]

Reacting to the British authorities' complaint (the French were thinking similarly) that economies of scale required a much larger hospital, with a minimum of about one hundred beds and more equipment, surgeons, and nurses, Nettie found a partner. Harold J. Reckitt, an affluent British Quaker, also wanted to found a hospital but, like Nettie, was constantly frustrated by the balking Allied military and medical bureaucracies. Their coming together was serendipity. The two could make a more practical offer to the allies by pooling their resources. She could offer the beds, medical staff, and supplies, and Reckitt would provide the ambulances and other motorized transport. Together, they could afford to support a hospital of one hundred beds.

A breakthrough came during one of Nettie's visits to Paris in the spring of 1915 when she discovered a fitting building. Located in the village of Ris-Orangis (near Fontainebleau) on the Seine River, fifteen miles southeast of the French capital, it had once housed a Catholic monastery that had been unoccupied for more than a decade. The building was large, and Nettie would have preferred a location closer to the British lines, but it was only about forty years old and structurally sound. Reckitt later remarked that it was "perfectly wonderful for a hospital." Having decided on the building, Nettie negotiated the terms with the French government, which owned it and was more amenable since the hospital project was now well developed. The two founders then set to work to transform the building into a fully equipped hospital along with ambulance services from rail stations and other places closer to the front.

The enterprise was multi-national. It was a French military hospital servicing mainly wounded Frenchmen, while the lay staff and orderlies were British, and the physicians and trained nurses were mostly American. It specialized in serious surgical cases among the wounded, but because of the fierce fighting on the Western Front that summer and fall, the French government paid to double the number of beds to 210. In the fifteen months from its opening in September 1915, surgeons at the hospital operated on more than 1,000 wounded soldiers, and the beds were almost always full.[21]

Nettie's focus on the hospital was stressful. Among other things, travel logistics to Ris-Orangis were nerve-wracking, requiring her to cross the perilous North Sea from Holland to Britain by ship, then to the French coast, and eventually to Paris. Nettie would follow that complicated route and back several times. She and Reckitt agreed that they would take turns in its direction. He would be in charge when she was away, and she would take over during his absences (traveling to Britain or North America to raise funds). Of course, they had other capable administrative officers. One, in particular, was Celia (later Lady) Congreve, a British friend of Nettie's and the spouse of General Congreve on whose staff Crinks was serving. She had already worked for the British Red Cross in Belgium and northern France; when Nettie returned to The Hague, Celia acted as her representative at the hospital. Finding the travel and other demands on her health too wearing by the end of 1915, Nettie decided she had to give up her administrative role. However, she still visited the facility on occasion.

Another of her accomplishments was hiring Dr. Joseph A. Blake of New York as head of surgery at the hospital. Dr. Blake was one of the surgeons to perform the major operation on Mary Pinchot in 1911 and then continued as a medical adviser. At the outbreak of the Great War, he had gone to France to volunteer his services as a surgeon in an American ambulance unit. The French quickly came to admire him and his team for their mastery of war surgery. Soon after the Johnstone-Reckitt Hospital opened its doors, the head surgeon, an American, resigned and returned to the United States. Nettie then persuaded Dr. Blake to become his successor. Reckitt was not acquainted with him or his professional accomplishments, but Nettie argued, "I feel it is our duty to give these French soldiers the very best that we can get for them and if I had anyone who was near and dear to me who required the aid of a surgeon, it would be Joe Blake that I would send for." Acquiescing to her choice, Reckitt later commented that Blake's appointment "was in my judgment one of the most fortunate events in the history of our hospital."[22] A year into his job, Nettie commented that Dr. Blake was "a wonder," and by all accounts, he was an outstanding head of surgery for the eighteen months he stayed with the hospital.

Nettie also took a personal interest in the human side. When she visited the hospital ward, she informed Amos, "I hold the men's hands when the dressings are very bad and sit with the ones who are in pain. And I make no end of surgical dressings. . . . And the rest of the time I try to present news and heal disputes."[23] A French physician offered a fuller report:

> To-day Lady Johnstone has come back to us; the news spreads quickly through the hospital and the old *blessés* who know her make haste to tell the new arrivals. In each ward the *poilus* wait. . . .
>
> She enters, dressed in the simple costume of an English nurse with a long white veil which lengthens her silhouette without detracting from its

distinction. In this ward, filled with wounded, she is at home; she goes from one to the other, talking a very pure French, offering cigarettes, asking like a friend about the circumstances in which each was wounded, mingling in their talk and their games. Then, bending over a poor devil, hit mortally, unable to silence his moans by her soothing words of hope, she suddenly draws herself up and goes toward the ward-surgeon, a question in her eye, her glance almost hostile as though, saddened and vexed at not being able to lull the soldier's pain, she blamed the doctor for his powerlessness to cure.

This simple scene shows better than a long narrative how Lady Johnstone loved our wounded and how the staff, following her example, petted and cared for them.[24]

* * *

Throughout her involvement with the Ris-Orangis hospital, Nettie always felt the pressure for more funding. As the hospital began operations, for example, the Red Cross promised her $10,000 (nearly $300,000 today) in supplies, but when little arrived, she had to spend the money she had raised privately. During a hospital visit in the late winter of 1916, she discovered that Reckitt had spent £14,000 (about $70,000) in the first five months, which should have funded the hospital for a year. Nettie was flabbergasted, telling Gifford that Reckitt "never gave me a full idea of what was going on as he always said he was 'well within the estimate', wh- I like a fool, believed. I begin to think that he's not very honest beside[s] being a fool." Reckitt may have overspent, but more likely, the hospital's operating costs were much higher than they had estimated. By the end of 1916, Nettie let on that, despite much better financial discipline, the hospital's operations were costing $10,000 a month.

Nettie wrote Reckitt that the hospital was now "bankrupt," and without the French government's contribution, they would have to shut down soon. But she also indicated she was not yet giving up. She informed him that she had persuaded her brothers to promise $5,000 each and she would try to raise another $5,000, but he would have to do the rest.[25] Nettie was herself "frightfully in debt," she explained to Leila, "not thru my own fault but besides the expense of my journeys[,] etc., I have to give money away all the time." She even disposed of some jewelry, selling one expensive piece for £400 and pawning another for £500. It was a personal struggle to give up the affluent trinkets of her old lifestyle. "Of course I'm silly not to let the jewels go and have the anxiety off my mind," she confessed to Leila, "but I want the jewels. It seems fearfully silly when real things only are important. . . . [but] I enjoy them very much every day."[26]

Another source of money would come from her mother's bequest, from which she had already borrowed, but by the spring of 1916, the finances of her estate had still not been completed. For five months, she complained, she had been writing Amos, "asking if there is or ever will be any regular recourse for Mama's money and he won't answer. Surely I have a right to know. Either there is or there isn't."[27] Part of the problem with the settlement was trying to ascertain whether the large chunks of money her mother had given her over the years were gifts or loans. If the latter—and it was eventually determined some of them were—they would have to be deducted from Nettie's inheritance.

Also promising, though in the longer term, was the prospect of a bequest from her Uncle Amo F. Eno, who died in New York in October 1915 at eighty-one. Though the oldest of eight brothers and sisters, he outlived all except Antoinette Wood and Will, the youngest. Amo had prospered in real estate and, at his death, owned about ninety properties in New York City and a country home in Saratoga. His estate's value at the time of his death was as much as $15 million ($440 million), sixty percent of which was in real estate holdings.

Nettie could well believe that her uncle, a lifelong bachelor, would leave her and her brothers generous bequests, but the Pinchot siblings were shocked when they learned the terms of Amo's last will. He had written a will in January 1914, which left about $2 million to his brothers and sisters, except John, whom Amo had never forgiven for his embezzlement of funds from their father's New York bank. But after John, Henry, and Mary all died later that year, Amo, in 1915, a few months before his own death, drafted another will, which provided only $250,000 to Will but nothing to Antoinette, his other sibling, and the same amounts to nephews and nieces except Henry's son, who was to receive almost nothing. After many other bequests to public and charitable organizations, Amo's last will left the residuary part of his estate amounting to about $4-7 million to Columbia University. His will baffled and angered the Pinchot and Eno beneficiaries. Why had he left so much money to Columbia, when he had left nothing to the institution in his previous wills? He had lived near the university but had shown no interest in it during his lifetime, and he had rather disparaged the value of a college education. Had he not been of sound mind? Or, sane or not, had he much underestimated the value of his estate and the millions that would go to Columbia after the bequests?

Late in life, Amo Eno had become more irascible, and seven months before his death Amos Pinchot reported to Gifford, "Uncle Mo has been terribly down in the mouth. He takes it out in condemning everything in the world. He says the trouble is that the poor are not working enough and expect too large wages. He is in a continual rage with me but I can[']t make believe I agree with him and he <u>wants</u> me to disagree I think."[28] Probably still smarting from his brother John's flight to Canada after his bank embezzlement, Amo also stipulated in his last will that the trust funds set up for the children of his deceased siblings would lose the interest if they ceased to be U.S. residents; however, he made an exception for Harcourt Johnstone, whom he barely knew, by leaving him $1.5 million since he was already living abroad. (Presumably, Amo had a soft spot for military veterans, as he had been a Union soldier fifty years earlier.)

Nettie, who said she did not expect that her Uncle Amo would leave her much, was of course "very glad" for the "unexpected" bequest to Crinks but to "give to a beastly rich old college this year when every penny might save some-one[']s life," she complained to Amos, "makes me boil."[29] The Pinchot brothers agreed that Amo's will did not make sense and, along with Will, decided to contest it. The plaintiffs' strategy involved the presentation of a united family front, which meant including the neglected Aunt Antoinette and cousin Henry in their suit. If they won, the generous bequests to six family members—three Pinchots (including Nettie), Will, and John's two children—would be divided among eight of them. Amos managed to get the other beneficiaries to agree, if successful, to accept lesser bequests than they would receive from either of Amo's last two wills.[30]

The plaintiffs had a good case, and nobody accused the family members of selfish grasping after Amo's money. Nettie gave her power of attorney to her brothers for the ensuing legal proceedings and supported her relatives' action, as they (though not her son) would be the main beneficiaries if their suit was successful. During the ensuing jury trial, more than two hundred interested parties testified. Although the Pinchot plaintiffs won a verdict in July 1916, Columbia successfully appealed, setting in motion a long, drawn-out legal struggle. It was obvious that the Pinchot siblings could not rely on Amo's inheritance to help Nettie with her hospital's finances. A second trial would take place in 1922, and the Pinchots would finally accept a compromise settlement with Columbia.[31]

*   *   *

Nettie, meanwhile, continued to administer the Ris-Orangis hospital. When the United States entered the war on the side of the allies, fundraising at first became easier. Now there was a patriotic reason for Americans to contribute. But at the same time, the U.S. military's demands for medical supplies, nurses, and doctors severely stretched the hospital's resources. Dr. Blake left in the spring of 1917 to head a new military hospital in Paris, and after that, it would be harder to get and keep good surgeons who were much in demand.

The Ris-Orangis hospital survived. Harold Reckitt first came to the rescue, guaranteeing funding for the hospital for six months. He traveled to the United States, where he organized a New York committee from his contacts and a list of names Nettie gave him. Herbert L. Satterlee, a New York lawyer and friend of Nettie, agreed to serve as the committee chairman, and his wife, Louisa, was the daughter of J. Pierpont Morgan. The couple each contributed $2,000 and proceeded to tap their wealthy friends for donations. Gifford and Gertrude also became committee members, aiming to raise $60,000 for the hospital. And when these donations flagged, the New York committee persuaded Mae Plant, married to one of the city's wealthiest businessmen, to provide a monthly subvention of $2,000, which, along with additional contributions from Reckitt and the French government, allowed the hospital to continue its operations well into 1918.[32]

Nettie also "begged" Gertrude to approach Henry Ford since he had supported the women's peace movement, in which she was involved. She believed that Ford had "half promised $25,000" to the hospital. "I suppose I'm pushing," she whined to Gifford, "but I always see people when I want to!"[33] Nettie was expressing her poor opinion of her sister-in-law, but Gertrude made appointments to see the automobile magnate only to have his secretary cancel them, and Ford, surrounded by protective aides, was indeed elusive. Gertrude raised $3,500 from her affluent contacts, but feeling guilty about failing to see Ford, she promised to do more. "It's hard to do it but I must," she wrote Gifford. From her efforts and funds collected at entertainments, the committee was soon sending the hospital $5,000 a month.[34]

Nettie became increasingly frustrated with her enterprise. She wrote in the spring of 1917, "I ought to be at the hospital," but physically exhausted, "the doctor won't let me move much." Then one day, she tripped and fell on a rug at her London home, suffering a concussion, injuring her back, and breaking her right arm and shoulder blade, and her travels were put on hold indefinitely. Because of staffing (though not financial) difficulties, the Ris-Orangis hospital finally closed down two months before the end of the war. Shortly after the armistice, Nettie got to Paris, where she told Reckitt, "I have not always agreed with you in what you did at the hospital, but I always remembered that you were on the spot and I wasn't. . . . I think our hospital is unique in the history of the war. We finish our three years' work together with a balance in hand and are still on speaking terms."[35] It was an accurate summation of a long, successful collaboration under trying circumstances.

16.

War and Dissent

Despite the Pinchot brothers' steadfast support of their sister's humanitarian venture, the contentious issues of the First World War opened a chasm between Amos and his siblings. Nettie and Gifford identified closely with the Allied war effort and sharply disagreed with Amos, who championed an anti-interventionist position for his nation. Amos saw himself as an internationalist but firmly opposed U.S. military intervention into the maelstrom. Contrariwise, his siblings championed democratic France and Britain as fighting for liberty and democracy, which a militaristic and autocratic Germany was determined to destroy. As Gifford expressed it, "The whole future of civilization is at stake in this war." Prominent among Germany's many wrongs was its army's wanton destruction of Belgium, which "is one of the great crimes of civilization. . . . If Germany wins," he warned, "the doctrine of might makes right will be established as the rule of the world." When Germany engaged in submarine warfare resulting in the loss of American lives, he was ready to support U.S. belligerency.[1]

Among anti-interventionists, Gertrude was most active. Many women involved in suffrage and social justice movements were eager for action and, finding the male-dominated peace societies overly timid, formed a new national peace group, the Woman's Peace Party, in December 1914, with Jane Addams as its president. The WPP opposed U.S. belligerency and promoted conflict mediation by the United States and European neutrals. The organization also articulated a broad program of international reform for the postwar world, much of which would appear in Woodrow Wilson's liberal peace program of fourteen points three years later. In the WPP forefront, New York women formed a branch, and Gertrude Pinchot became a vice-chairman.

Amos's experience during the earlier Spanish adventure had shaped his anti-interventionist perspective. Unlike his brother, he favored early independence for the Filipinos and, in 1907, had questioned the high cost of a naval fleet and "the risk of a big war. . . . I think what Antis [anti-imperialists] everywhere need is cod liver oil and iron, or a chance to run things and try their methods." And concerning the Wilson administration's military incursion into Vera Cruz, Mexico, in April 1914, he commented, "I have seen a little of one war and I pray that we may be spared another."[2]

Early in the Great War, Amos charged in an article that compulsory military service in Europe had transformed "free men to [military] slaves." He at first believed the United States could stay out of the war, but the sinking of the British passenger liner *Lusitania* by a German submarine off the southern Irish coast in early May 1915, with the loss of some 1,200 lives, including 128 Americans, starkly dramatized the possibility of U.S. belligerency. Amos conceded, "we see the possibility of being drawn into the war."[3]

President Wilson used firm diplomacy to resolve the *Lusitania* crisis without war, but that sinking and other incidents contesting America's neutral rights fueled citizens' agitation for increased military preparedness. Theodore Roosevelt and others, mainly from the Northeast, led the movement, setting up private military training camps in response to America's perceived military vulnerability. There was a certain logic to the preparedness argument. Roosevelt had always championed a big navy, and the European conflagration was an urgent reminder of the need for enhanced security measures to protect the nation's long continental coastlines and holdings abroad. Some also believed that a healthy dose of military training would provide discipline to what they perceived as a society of slouchy, undisciplined young men and challenge their materialism. As a newspaper friend wrote Amos, preparedness would be worthwhile "if it only served for a time to lift this nation out of the sordid pot-bellied, fat-joweled state into which it is getting as a result of its orgy of money-making." Furthermore, a flabby, multi-ethnic society might promote social unity and a sense of national purpose.

Amos Pinchot rejected such arguments and, along with many pacifistic liberals and socialists, emphasized the dangers of militarism. They charged that the escalating European arms race had brought on the war, spreading to America's shores and eroding civilian control of foreign policy, and might bring the United States into the maelstrom. As Jane Addams commented, "If we get ready for war, it will surely come."[4]

In December 1915, antimilitarist activists founded the American Union Against Militarism (AUAM), which became the most visible among voluntary associations opposing major increases in U.S. military spending. The respected social worker Lillian D. Wald and other New York reformers were AUAM leaders. Despite its pacifistic orientation, the organization tried to project a non-pacifist stance. Their members were not against "sane" and "reasonable" preparedness but opposed the creation of a large standing army, major armament increases, military training in schools, and compulsory military service. In direct language, they claimed that "preparedness is militarism," and the central issue was "democracy versus militarism."[5]

Amos supported the AUAM financially and was one of its articulate spokesmen. To his mind, the boosters of American military preparations were less patriotic than self-interested, and he sought to expose the links between the major preparedness groups and prominent Northeastern industrialists and bankers who were financing the campaign for a military buildup. As he wrote President Wilson, "the shouters of exorbitant armament are using preparedness as an argument with which to [e]ntrench more firmly the doctrine of the sacredness of monopoly and extortion." Amos was revealing, in protean form, the lineaments of what would become the military-industrial complex. He remarked in a talk, "I am not a peace-at-any-price pacifist. I believe in an efficient army and navy, and I am a pacifist because I believe that pacifism leads to democracy."[6] From his AUAM involvement, he drew closer to many like-minded antimilitarists and pacifists like Eastman's sister, Crystal Eastman Benedict.

In late 1915, President Wilson announced a multi-year program for enhanced military preparations and, in a tour of several Midwestern states, argued that his program was "necessary," "practical," and "reasonable." At his last stop, he referred to the preparedness opposition as "hopelessly and contentedly provincial" and challenged them to "hire large halls" and present their contrary views. The AUAM took up the challenge, and eight anti-preparedness advocates, including Amos Pinchot, made forceful presentations of their position to overflow crowds in eleven cities. The anti-preparedness message resonated better west of the Alleghenies, where opinion was more isolationist.[7]

The anti-preparedness advocates directed most of their criticism at the military program rather than President Wilson, whom most of these reformers liked. Rabbi Stephen S. Wise, one of the foremost anti-preparedness spokesmen, for example, denounced "militarism" but voiced disapproval of those who criticized the president. Indeed, Amos viewed the preparedness issue as the only real question mark in an otherwise promising Wilson administration. He had approved the new administration's lower tariff law, the Clayton Antitrust Act, and the creation of the Federal Trade Commission as important steps in breaking monopolies. He particularly reveled in the nomination of Louis Brandeis

Antiwar activists Amos Pinchot and Crystal Eastman Benedict, c. 1916.
(Bain Collection, Library of Congress)

to the U.S. Supreme Court. Amos had written Wilson, "We need his kind, especially now when there is such a powerfully driving impulse away from the democratic idea," and he informed Norman Hapgood, "It took courage . . . to make this appointment and I take off my chapeau to the President."[8]

Wilson's nomination of Brandeis was designed, in part, to appeal to Roosevelt Republicans and independent progressive reformers like Amos Pinchot. Indeed, if Wilson were to be reelected in November, he would need to win over large numbers of them. Amos predicted that the appointment of Brandeis "will pull a strong oar for Wilson" in several "Roosevelt strongholds." Some opposition to Brandeis was murmured sotto voce since he was Jewish, and the prejudice against his religion, along with his pronounced liberal views, was well entrenched in places.[9] And when the Senate confirmed him, the news to Amos was bittersweet. Though appreciative of his elevation, Amos wrote Brandeis, it also "makes me feel pretty sad" because those like himself fighting privilege would "sorely miss" his presence.[10]

Closer to home, Amos and Gertrude opposed military bills in the New York State legislature that called for military training in schools, compulsory military service for boys over sixteen in summer camps, and mandatory registration in case of a draft in wartime. Amos objected, however, that such legislation would promote a Prussian-style "unthinking obedience to authority," which threatened "liberty" in America. When the New York State legislature nonetheless passed these measures, backed by the state National Guard and other preparedness boosters, the WPP and AUAM appealed to Governor Charles Whitman to veto the pending legislation. Reacting to the "wave of hysteria" that led to "the conscription of children," he wrote a statement Gertrude took to Albany and used in her presentation.[11] "No country in this world, not even those in the throes of war," it warned, "has gone so far along the path of autocratic militarism as this legislature has gone in presenting you these bills." Gertrude and other speakers opposing the bills were received respectfully, but the governor signed all the military training measures into law.[12]

As Congress considered preparedness, an AUAM delegation, which included Amos Pinchot, Lillian Wald, and Max Eastman among its six members, gained an interview with President Wilson at which they presented their report on their western speaking tour.[13] During their meeting, Wilson patiently argued that some basic army training was no threat to democratic values, came out against universal military training, and noted that the proposed increase in the army seemed large only because it had previously been at a minuscule level. He concluded with a standard deterrence argument: "if you say we shall not have any war, you have got to have force to make that 'shall' bite."[14] Wilson's presentation impressed his erstwhile critics, Eastman enthusing that "The whole interview in [Wilson's] hands became a friendly harmonious discussion of how 'we' could meet the difficulties of national defense without the risks of militarism." The president, Amos allowed, seemed to be winning over him and other AUAM stalwarts.[15]

Congress passed most of the administration's preparedness agenda, expanding the nation's military establishment but not as far as the crusading preparedness leaders desired. Wilson and congressional Democrats had, in fact, framed a security policy that would satisfy all but the ultranationalists on the one hand and fervent isolationists and pacifists on the other. To be sure, the president had sometimes gotten carried away in boosting his preparedness program, but throughout the debate, his sentiments were closer to the radical and pacifist groups than the capitalist or militarist elements.[16]

*   *   *

The antimilitarists soon found themselves deeply involved in an international crisis involving Mexico, where a political revolution erupted in 1910. After Wilson's ill-advised military intervention in Vera Cruz, he withdrew U.S. troops. In October 1915, his administration recognized the newly established but still shaky government of Venustiano Carranza. Complicating the U.S.-Mexico relationship was Pancho Villa, a Mexican revolutionary whose forces challenged the Carranza regime and its surrogate ally. In January 1916, Villa's forces attacked a train in northern Mexico and murdered seventeen American citizens. Two months later, his marauders, invading Columbus, New Mexico, killed several U.S. citizens and soldiers. In response, President Wilson sent U.S. troops commanded by General John J. Pershing into northern Mexico in pursuit of the Villa bandits. Wilson's cabinet and Congress were united in wanting to defend U.S. honor in the face of these desperadoes' actions. But the threatened Carranza army commander's resistance to Pershing's troops carousing on Mexican soil presented Wilson with a real dilemma. He explored possibilities for the peaceful resolution of the international crisis, and in any event, he wanted to keep the nation's powder dry in case the United States was drawn into the European catastrophe.

Then, on June 21, 1916, a U.S. Army patrol confronted some Carranza forces at the Mexican town of Carrizal, and the U.S. Army captain rashly advanced with his men. The Mexicans opened fire, and in the ensuing gun battle, many on both sides were killed, and seventeen U.S. soldiers were taken prisoner.

While the president awaited Pershing's report on the Carrizal incident, the AUAM established an unofficial commission of private American and Mexican citizens to mediate the dispute. Their purpose was to provide a model for the kind of mediation the two governments might adopt. Amos Pinchot served as publicist for the joint commission, which assembled at the Willard Hotel in Washington, D.C. Speaking for the commissioners, he asserted that such a group "can get at the facts, present them with fairness to both sides, and give the President and the people of both countries a chance to avoid a wicked and senseless war." He followed with a telegram to Wilson arguing, "Peace sentiment is increasing," and with forbearance, "the country will stand for almost anything you do toward peace."[17]

Gertrude Pinchot, along with two college professors, then presented an antiwar resolution to the president. Drawn up by the AUAM, WPP, and other concerned New York civic groups, the petition urged arbitration. Wilson received the delegation on June 28, just when he was contemplating whether to ask Congress to declare war against Mexico. He told his visitors that, to avoid war, "acts must follow words," and he insisted "that the lives and liberty of our own people shall be safe from the depredations of Mexican bandits."[18] Wilson wanted to avoid war, and the flood of antiwar messages against hostilities from peace, religious, and reform groups persuaded him to pursue a peaceful solution if still possible.

Wilson soon received Pershing's report, which showed that the U.S. Army captain had exceeded instructions and forced the issue leading to the bloodshed. Moreover, Carranza announced that he would return the American Army captives. As the president used this information to defuse the crisis, Amos wrote a detailed account of the Carrizal incident in an open letter to the *New York Times*, which published it as a full-page spread. His account included the dispatches from military witnesses on both sides that the unofficial commission had gathered to demonstrate that the fault was not the Mexicans and that American citizens should resist the unscrupulous newspapers that distorted "facts" and promoted war between the two nations. Finally, he urged citizens to write their congressmen to forestall a war resolution.[19] As tensions receded, Gertrude and Amos sent Wilson another telegram praising his resolve for a mediated solution, and the president thanked them for it "with all my heart."[20]

The United States and Mexico soon established an official commission, just as the AUAM had proposed, to resolve the issues; the situation did not stabilize until the first months of 1917, when a peace accord was finalized and Pershing's troops left Mexico.[21]

*　　*　　*

Meanwhile, in the summer of 1916, the presidential election campaign was heating up. Gifford still believed TR would run for president in 1916 as a progressive and perhaps also receive the Republican nomination. When the Republican and Progressive Party nominating conventions met at the same time in Chicago in early June, Gifford, a delegate on the progressive side, wanted the party to nominate Colonel Roosevelt. However Old Guard Republicans, still unforgiving of TR's apostasy in 1912, would make his nomination on a fusion ticket a distinct longshot.[22]

Gifford represented a faction among progressives who wanted to nominate Roosevelt early in the proceedings and pressure the Republicans to accept him as their choice. George Perkins and others, hoping to work out a fusion deal with the Republican leadership, preferred to wait until the Republicans had nominated their candidate and Perkins had his way. When the Republicans shunned TR and nominated Charles Evans Hughes, a former moderate reform governor of New York and currently a justice of the U.S. Supreme Court, the progressive forces immediately voted for Roosevelt by acclamation. Roosevelt abruptly dashed his loyal progressive supporters with a curt message to the convention, saying he could not accept their nomination. Shocked at his mentor for leading on the delegates and then brusquely rejecting their endorsement, Gifford wrote Nettie that he had never seen anything "more cruel and unnecessary. . . . you never saw a madder lot of men in your life than the Progressives when his message reached them."[23]

Though "heartbroken" at this turn of events, Gifford grudgingly accepted the reality of Hughes as the alternative to Wilson. "It is tough though, and no mistake."[24] He accurately predicted that Hughes would be a lackluster campaigner constrained by the conservative Republican stalwarts who engineered his nomination, but, rationalizing that the nominee was honest and could stand firm against the party's more reactionary elements, he eventually endorsed him.

Because Wilson was a progressive and had seemed sympathetic to conservation, it could be believed that Gifford might be attracted to him.[25] But Wilson's apparent propensity to change his mind on domestic issues annoyed Gifford. He believed the Democrats were the party of state rights, and Wilson, as their standard bearer, could never fashion a genuine national reform program. He worried that the president might support proposed legislation favorable to water power interests—"the grabbers," Gifford often called them.[26] Wilson was on top of the issues, however, and had confided to his secretary of the interior that "It might be better to do nothing about the use of water power than to do the wrong thing." Congressman Kent would write Amos that Wilson "will put a crimp into any water power grabs." Indeed, he added, "I cannot for the life of me see why any Progressive should accept the bunk and husks that are being handed out by the Hughes's aggregation, unless, like Jim Garfield and Gifford, they blindly follow the Mahdi, or unless they have greasy motives."[27]

Gifford was even more critical of Wilson's handling of international affairs. He believed, for instance, that the president's diplomacy after the *Lusitania* incident had not resolved the submarine issue and might result in future submarine attacks with "the bitterest possible insult" to the United States. "I have gradually acquired a contempt for Wilson greater than I have ever felt for any other public man of our day," he wrote Nettie. The president's preparedness and Mexican policies only intensified Gifford's criticisms. He has "kept us so weak" for so long, he groused. "If it were not so deadly serious, so dangerous, and tragic, it would be nothing but broad farce."[28] Gifford's loyalty to Roosevelt, who was sharply attacking the administration's foreign policy, bolstered his criticisms. TR stumped for Hughes and forcefully accused the president of cowardice on foreign policy issues.

Amos was moving in the opposite direction, although there was still the question of whether he would endorse the Democratic incumbent and work for his reelection. He was so independent that "I don't think that I will ever again acknowledge any affiliation to any party."[29] But Wilson skillfully exploited independent reformers' sympathies, and perhaps one-half of the progressives who had crafted TR's reform program in 1912, Amos among them, would end up supporting Wilson's reelection. In March 1916, he was still "rather at sea" politically; but his journalist friend Norman Hapgood headed a group of independent "volunteers" for Wilson, and Amos soon joined it.[30]

In September, Gifford wrote Amos, "I greatly hope you are not going to support Wilson." Amos publicly endorsed Wilson two weeks later and, making light of their differences, replied to his brother, "I wish we could have been on the same side, but the next best thing is to be on opposite sides and have it make no difference."[31]

Three weeks before the election, Amos, a spokesman for a group of Wilson volunteers, affirmed to the president at his summer residence, "In all the great issues that came up you have taken the democratic point of view and given everybody a square deal." Amos next led a group of these volunteers on an automobile caravan across New York State to showcase the president's support among independents and former progressives. Wilson failed to carry New York on election day, but the president squeaked out a victory nationally, winning by twenty-three electoral votes.[32]

Amos displayed his emotions in the campaign when, in its last days, he released an open letter to Roosevelt to the newspapers, which revived the charges that he and Perkins had "secretly" conspired to cut out a strong antitrust pledge from the Progressive Party platform in 1912. His letter also claimed that the colonel endorsed the party's national defense plank that had denounced war as "barbaric," called for the pacific settlement of international disputes and a smaller naval building program, and made no mention of the army or coastal defense. In short, Amos continued, he had supported "a clear and unequivocal pacifism worthy of Tolstoi" in 1912. The clear thrust of his charges was that TR's current criticisms of Wilson were politically motivated. Amos's plaint ludicrously ignored other progressives' less conspiratorial explanations of the omitted antitrust plank four years earlier and ignored the entirely different prewar era when "peace" was in the ascendancy domestically and a complete contrast to the current perils facing the United States internationally.

Roosevelt had had enough and wrote Amos, "When I spoke of the Progressive Party as having a lunatic fringe, I specifically had you in mind. On the supposition that you are of entire sound mind, I should be obliged to say that you are absolutely dishonorable and untruthful."[33] Amos was of "sound mind," but his hypomanic penchant had taken him over the edge. It was not a promising sign, and his emotional exuberance, if unchecked, might take him into the political wilderness.

* * *

Shortly after the presidential election, Leila told Amos that "it hurt Gifford horribly to have you blind to what he considers the fundamentals." It was not just Amos's support of the hated Wilson, she noted, but Amos's pacifism in opposition to his older brother's boosting of military preparedness. But trying to be a good sister-in-law, she professed, "I don[']t feel that way at all. You both see life from different angles. But the main will and purpose is the same"—making America "a better place."[34] The brothers' views on their nation's place in world affairs were diametrically opposed. Gifford, a traditionalist, perceived the world as a moral universe, and the misbehavior of bad actors like Germany should be firmly resisted. To be sure, he did not want to appear as a warmonger and believed political decision-makers should exercise self-control, but he was ready to support war against an immoral Germany. By contrast, Amos's secular pacifism was derived from his own miserable experiences in the Spanish conflict. He opposed war not because it was sinful but as stupid and horrific in the modern industrial era and could be avoided in most cases.

The final war years and the peace settlement would further test familial relationships. At first, Amos optimistically wrote that Wilson's election victory showed "a shift of power from Wall Street toward the people" and that the peace vote in the western states had determined the result. When Wilson offered the belligerents his mediation of the protracted military stalemate, Amos asserted that the president, serving the cause of peace and reconciliation, "has now raised a new flag . . . of internationalism. He argued that Wilson's subsequent call for a "peace without victory" in Europe "has, in some degree at least shifted the balance of power away from physical force toward the realm of the mental and spiritual."[35]

Amos's pacifist bias made him an apologist for Germany's military excesses. The Johnstones believed that German soldiers committed atrocities against innocent Belgian citizens, as reported in the American press, but Amos could acknowledge only that "the enslavement of the Belgians and the Zeppelin raids [on London] are atrocities, although, in fact, mere fringes of the huge fabric of cruelty woven by the super-atrocity of war."[36]

There was also a realistic element in Amos's thinking, however. From his knowledge of European history, he argued in a speech that Germany's autocratic government and militarism were "only surface expressions of something that is going on deep in the European soul." For a thousand years, Germans suffered humiliations and were largely immune to democratic ideas. And following unification, Germany found itself surrounded by distrustful neighboring states. Compensating for a sense of inferiority in its long history, the German state cultivated an ultranationalism in its subservient people "until it has become a religion and finally a fanaticism." Given this history and its psychological implications, even if defeated on the battlefields, Germany could not be entirely crushed. Its industries would be revived, and Amos predicted, "fifteen years from now Germany, left with a grudge, will have practically as many men of fighting age as she would have had if the war had never happened." He believed a negotiated peace might incorporate new concepts that would allow for a reintegrated and more democratic Germany in the postwar world order.[37] If that was a tall order, it was no more than President Wilson envisioned.

Gifford believed, however, that a negotiated peace was unrealistic in a still anarchic world and, at a deeper level, that compromise with Germany was immoral. He thus denounced the president's mediation offer as "a slap in the face of the [allied] men who are fighting for the principles of human liberty on which our nation was founded." He complained to Nettie that "Wilson seems to be going from bad to worse."[38]

*   *   *

On January 31, 1917, Germany announced it was introducing submarine warfare on the seas against all enemy and neutral ships. Unrestricted U-boat warfare was a calculated German policy to try to cut off supplies to the Allies and force them to accede to its war demands before the likely military intervention by the United States could rescue them from their downfall. The world had suddenly turned upside down for Wilson.

The new crisis came at an inopportune time for Amos, as he was bothered by the inflammation of an old hip injury. He also suffered from serious abscesses in his gums and rotting teeth, resulting in several sessions in the dentist's chair, and he was generally worn out from his barnstorming for Wilson's reelection. Amos, "pretty well banged up," complied with his doctor's orders to take two months off from work and speech-making.[39]

But he did not stop lobbying. Responding to the German U-boat announcement and Wilson's break in U.S. relations with Germany, AUAM leaders sent appeals for restraint to the president. They and other concerned New Yorkers placed advertisements with the same message in several newspapers nationwide. The antimilitarist group called for a league of armed neutrals to defend those nations' rights on the seas as an alternative to full belligerency, and Amos wrote letters to print media touting its present possibilities. On February 26, Wilson asked Congress for authority to arm U.S. merchant ships, and two days later, he received an AUAM delegation, which included Amos Pinchot, to discuss its proposal.[40]

The timing could not have been worse. Wilson had learned only a few days earlier of a telegram sent by Arthur Zimmermann, the German foreign secretary, to its embassy in Mexico City with instructions to propose a military alliance with Mexico and the promise of assistance in recovering the lost territories of Texas, New Mexico, and Arizona. Though not yet revealing its contents, Wilson told the delegates that he had received information about Germany's perfidious intentions.[41] The Zimmermann telegram, combined with the sinking of several U.S. ships and the loss of American lives, would push the nation toward war. After a few senators engaged in a filibuster, the president, as commander-in-chief, ordered the ships to be armed on his own authority.

Amos wrestled with the implications of the recent events for U.S. policy. He looked at the crisis "from every angle" and was "puzzled and doubtful at all times of my own intellectual process." But he could not bring himself to accept war without a struggle. He complained that the administration's armed neutrality, "not circumscribed or defined, will lead to war." He added, "I think it is unquestionably wrong for us to go to war for the purpose of forcing contraband through the war zone, or on account of American passengers lost or munition-carrying ships of any nationality whatever. I do not believe the people would stand for this."[42]

Cooperating with pacifists in resisting American military intervention, he embraced an initiative put forward by a new group, the Emergency Peace Federation, for a nationwide referendum on the decision for war. Derived from progressive reformers' faith in popular referendums on the state level to refer issues directly to a vote of its citizens, the war referendum initiative generated interest, especially among citizens in more inland areas. It had well-known supporters like William Jennings Bryan, who had publicized such a measure since the start of the Great War.[43]

However, U-boat attacks on American shipping continued. President Wilson finally asked Congress to declare that a state of war existed between the two nations and added, "The world must be safe for democracy" as the central purpose of U.S. intervention. Congress shortly voted for war against Germany, with only six negative votes in the Senate and fifty in the House. On April 6, Wilson signed the war resolution.[44]

*   *   *

Antoinette Johnstone, welcoming the U.S. decision for war, wondered to Gifford, "How does Amos like being a belligerent?" Their younger brother did not like it at all. Amos wrote to Hapgood that war "takes out of human nature the one most beautiful and adorable quality—that of being happy, and of being moved by the play spirit. It seems to me too horrible the way a curtain of gloom has descended over the world. Most people even in normal times are unable to be as good, as kind or as happy as they naturally want to be. Now we have got to be everything that we hate."[45] But accepting the unpleasant reality, he wanted to define the purposes for which Americans would fight. He founded another group, the American Committee on War Finance (ACWF), which promoted a progressive income tax to pay for the war.[46] He stressed that the ACWF had no connection to the pacifist movement and was solely focused on war financing. The group released the names of its supporters; initially, it had only six paid staff members, and Amos paid the lion's share of its expenses.[47]

In his view, people with annual net incomes less than $2,000 ($3,000 for married couples) would be exempt from the tax, but more privileged elements would pay an additional war tax, which would rise steeply on incomes over $100,000 and would continue until all bonds and other war obligations were paid for. The desired result would be "a pay-as-you-go war, financed by the [higher income] people who can do so without great sacrifice."[48] He advanced his proposals in congressional testimony and communications to reform congressmen and key committee chairmen. "The time is short," he entreated progressive and radical allies across the nation. "May we count on you to help us?"[49]

Amos's financing scheme had merit. Learning to use the new income tax, congressional reformers had already passed legislation that greatly increased the tax rate on higher incomes to pay for the recently enacted preparedness program. With full belligerency, the ACWF quickly received endorsements from like-minded progressives and several labor unions. More conservative elements would prefer Liberty bonds, as they would be called. However, they were voluntary investments and even desirable because the government, desperate for revenue, would offer fairly generous terms to the purchasers.

For Gifford, his brother's changing focus from peace action to war finance was an improvement. Just before America's war declaration, Gifford had written his minister friend Rainsford, "I am not reading Amos' stuff anymore." But impressed with press reports touting Amos's new group, he told Nettie that their brother "has had a real influence, . . . and in this matter at least I am heartily with him."[50]

Because of Amos's previous antiwar activities, some hesitated to support the ACWF.[51] Moreover, two key members of Congress promoting progressive taxation as the principal vehicle for financing the war—La Follette, chairman of the Senate Finance Committee, and Claude Kitchin, chairman of the House Ways and Means Committee and house majority leader—had both voted against the war resolution. The two were often perceived as promoting increased taxation to make belligerency unpopular in America.

Amos had initially hoped that the ACWF would lead the fight to stop loans altogether. Toward the end of the war, however, he came to accept loans when it became apparent that taxation alone was insufficient to finance the escalating costs of the extended war effort. He even bought $20,000 in liberty bonds, giving two reasons: "first because the country needs the money, secondly because it is a good investment."[52]

Still, Amos remained interested in tax policy. In mid-1918, when large additional revenue was needed for the war, he supported doubling an excess profits tax to eighty percent, arguing that the pocketbooks of American businesses, already fattened by profitable trade during U.S. neutrality, could well afford that rate.[53] Amos correctly asserted that his committee "actually did get the thinking started" about tax policy for financing the war and that several congressmen told him that the ACFW's work had influenced the current legislative proposal to raise forty to fifty percent of revenues through taxation. The excess profits bill languished in committee until the war ended, however, and then was passed in much-diluted form.[54]

*   *   *

Amos got caught up in two other questions: the draft and free speech. He continued to oppose compulsory or universal military training, the results of which would debauch the American ideals of voluntarism, freedom, and individualism and push the nation inexorably toward the hated "old European system" of coercion and regimentation.[55] The Wilson administration, realizing that voluntary enlistments would be insufficient to assure adequate fighting forces, called for a selective draft but stopped far short of universal military training. Amos objected to any compulsion, but by the time Congress passed the Selective Service Act in July 1917, he was absorbed in questions of free speech that the rising war hysteria at home threatened. In his war message to Congress, Wilson promised "the firm hand of stern repression" against disloyalty. Only a week after the U.S. war declaration, Colonel House told Amos and several of his compatriots that the only effective way for democracies to fight autocracies was to give their governments dictatorial powers in wartime.[56]

Congress soon passed the Espionage Act, which gave the government the power of press censorship and control of the U.S. mail to prevent the dissemination of materials through the mail in violation of the law. Postmaster General Albert S. Burleson immediately targeted the Socialist Party, whose rank and file had passed a manifesto opposing U.S. military involvement and urging "vigorous resistance" to military conscription, censorship, and the curtailment of labor's right to strike.[57]

Concerned over the suppression of the mail and the threat to individual freedoms, dissenting liberals and radicals in New York set up the Civil Liberties Bureau (CLB), which split off from the American Union Against Militarism. Amos was a CLB member, but while maintaining ties with the Wilson administration, he avoided more militantly radical groups. Civil libertarians had a reason for concern, as the administration showed little sympathy. Wilson gave an address in which he labeled "pacifists" (a convenient euphemism for all war opponents) as "the agents and dupes of the German Imperial Government." Amos believed that Wilson's rhetoric "flourishes the knout over the objectors and all who would oppose the temporary little fatherhood which he is assuming to order to discourage autocracies in other climes."[58]

Burleson ordered local postmasters to withhold dissenting socialist and radical print publications from the mail. One of the first was the August 1917 issue of *The Masses*, which contained cartoons satirizing compulsory military service—one showed the Liberty Bell smashed to pieces—and an editorial and a poem supporting draft resisters. Amos joined *The Masses'* editors in writing President Wilson a letter complaining about the censorship and asking him to receive a small delegation to discuss the situation. Wilson declined and rejected their request to make a public statement on the free speech question but said he had read their letter "with a good deal of interest and sympathy" and would take up the matter with Burleson. Despite the refusal, Amos was satisfied initially, believing "the matter has been called very sharply to his attention."[59]

Wilson did seem to care. He asked Burleson for a report on *The Masses* complaint and added, "These are very sincere men and I should like to please them." But the postmaster general replied to his chief executive that the ban on publications was limited to those that would generally obstruct the prosecution of the war. Wilson forwarded Burleson's letter to Amos, asking for his "most friendly consideration," but did not countermand his department head.[60] Amos was also encouraged when, at a hearing of the *Masses* case, Learned Hand, a federal judge, granted a temporary injunction against the post office, ruling that the government could not just say that a publication was subversive or seditious but had to "point with exactness to just that conduct which violated the law." Indeed, Amos believed that the post office would soon pull back from its suppressive actions.[61]

The larger truth sank in when Amos and four others gained a long interview with Burleson. The perspectives of the two sides could not have been more different, with Amos and his colleagues, culturally sophisticated and politically radical New York professionals, confronting Burleson, a coarse Bryan Democrat from Texas. The delegates promoted Hand's objection and argued that suppression was unwise in an unpopular war. Afterward, Amos wrote a journalist friend, "I do not think I made the slightest impression on Mr. Burleson." The administration seemed to operate "in an atmosphere rather remote from the things that are being thought and felt by the majority of the public."[62]

Amos's comments neatly captured Burleson's insouciant self-assurance about civil liberties during U.S. belligerency. At the same time, however, Amos's belief that a "majority" were opposed to a war that Congress had authorized by a lopsided vote was wishful thinking. The war was weakly supported in many areas, but the opposition was not "widespread." He nonetheless expressed his opinion in a long letter to President Wilson and stressed that suppression was counterproductive. It might have been enough to warn the president that his administration's repressive policies would undermine his political support among liberals and the left. But Amos showed little tact and made excessive claims. Even the left was divided over the war, as the Socialist Party, hopelessly split, would disintegrate during American belligerency. Moreover, Samuel Gompers, head of the American Federation of Labor (AFL), was a practical man and saw more benefits to his union of skilled workers in supporting the war than resisting it. Amos saw the war revealing divisions between its supporters and opponents, but not within the latter.

Congress went further in the fall by passing a trading with the enemy bill, which required foreign language publications to submit English translations of all proposed articles and editorials about any belligerent government or the conduct of war to the post office department. Amos and five other CLB stalwarts protested to Wilson, arguing that the bill practically subverted constitutional rights and a free press, but Wilson would sign the bill into law.[63] He asked Burleson to apply censorship with caution, but the postmaster general expanded the range of publications for suppression. Moreover, Attorney General Thomas W. Gregory cared very little about civil liberties and, pressured by fearful local and state officials at the social unrest in their communities, vigorously prosecuted the editors of the dissident publications that Burleson identified.

Wilson's speeches that fall, castigating all doubting voices in the country, did not help matters. "Woe be to the man or group of men that seeks to stand in our way in this day of high resolution," he warned. "What I am opposed to is not the feeling of the pacifists, but their stupidity. My heart is with them, but my mind has a contempt for them. . . . They may be left to strut their uneasy hour and be forgotten."[64]

A few months later, Wilson, again showing concern, asked his postmaster general for leniency in the *Masses* case, which had gone to trial. When Burleson threatened to resign, the president backed down. He gave his department heads considerable slack in running their agencies and never fired him despite his misgivings about Burleson. Colonel House noted that Burleson "is in a belligerent mood against the Germans, against labor, against the pacifists" and used the free hand the president gave him by hounding all measures of publications for the duration of the war.[65]

In any event, Woodrow Wilson focused on winning the war and preparing for the peace settlement. Though even prowar liberals like Herbert Croly warned the president that the repression was excessive and counterproductive for his future success, Wilson failed to moderate the actions of his lieutenants.

Amos Pinchot next found himself actively engaged in supporting the candidacy of Morris Hillquit for mayor of New York City. Hillquit was a socialist, staunch antimilitarist, opponent of U.S. belligerency, and strong advocate of municipal ownership of utilities, which, for Amos, was the paramount local issue. Hillquit lost the election but gained more than 100,000 votes, or five times the usual socialist vote in the city.[66]

The exhausting Hillquit campaign, Amos believed, was worthwhile but had distracted him from his war finance committee, and his involvement in multifarious radical activities was compromising his influence. In consequence, he declined an invitation to serve as a director of the Civil Liberties Bureau, which would reconstitute itself as the American Civil Liberties Union (ACLU) after the war.[67] Amos was not a founder of the new group, but as a staunch defender of individual rights dating back before the Great War, he was a spiritual father of the new organization and would remain a loyal ACLU supporter for the rest of his life.

* * *

Gifford, meanwhile, had his own difficulties with the Wilson administration. While pleased with U.S. belligerency, he hoped to organize foresters into a fighting force in Europe. Alternatively, he wanted to join with Theodore Roosevelt, who, though fifty-eight, eagerly sought the chance of leading a voluntary division into battle and promised to make Gifford a lieutenant colonel if the administration approved his request to head a military unit. The last thing the Wilson administration wanted was Roosevelt gallivanting off on a romantic military escapade in Europe, capturing the limelight and detracting from allied military coordination.

Gifford did not pursue the forestry division possibility, in part because Leila had become pregnant again. He would stay nearer her and their son. Leila then had a miscarriage in August 1917 and had a slow recovery. He sought nonmilitary ways to support the U.S. war effort and focused on farm production. He believed that an urgent priority was encouraging farmers to plant more crops and raise more livestock posthaste to meet the surging Allied demand for food in Europe. He sent a letter to 5,000 editors, suggesting that the government should guarantee fair prices to farmers, and went on a speaking trip to several southern states to promote agricultural output. He also offered his services to Herbert Hoover, who headed the U.S. Food Administration. When its operations began, Hoover appointed Gifford as a member of the livestock committee in his agency, whose mandate was to increase livestock production. "I am tickled to death to be at work again," he wrote Amos.[68]

Hoover told Gifford that he wanted him to take charge of the entire livestock area gradually, but the relationship quickly went awry. They agreed that farmers needed to be encouraged to increase pork production but disagreed on the desired policy. For Gifford, the meat packers had to guarantee sufficiently high prices to swine farmers. He was in the farmers' camp, and his old friend Henry C. Wallace was chairman of a food administration's subcommittee on hogs. But when the meat packers balked, Gifford asked Hoover to support his price-fixing scheme. Pressure from the food administration would bring about the packers' acquiescence, Gifford thought, and he argued that the food administrator had "the power under the law, in addition to the moral weight of the War situation," to take over the packing houses, if necessary.[69] Hoover believed, however, that he lacked that authority and, in any event, objected to government coercion.

Gifford twice aired his complaints to Colonel House and followed with a detailed written list of his many grievances. After these experiences, Wilson's intimate adviser predicted an "imminent" break between the two men. Hoover soon offered to move Gifford to a new job distributing tractors in France but gave him only a day to accept. Not unreasonably seeing the offer as a ploy to get rid of him, Gifford wrote Hoover a terse letter of resignation. He had lasted only ten weeks in his position.[70]

To Gifford, a nationalist, Hoover's behavior reminded him of the Taft administration, with Hoover the new embodiment of timid, limited government. Hoover was certainly cautious, but Gifford may not have known that undergirding Hoover's skepticism about centralized state power was his sturdy faith in individualism, voluntarism, and cooperation among the various economic components in society. He preferred public appeals to farmers' "patriotism" and "duty" to meet the U.S. and allied needs in the war emergency. To agree to the hog farmers' demands for a still higher guaranteed price seemed excessive and smacked of extortion to him, although Wallace and Gifford argued that high prices were needed to convince all swine producers of the necessity to raise more hogs. It was easy for Hoover to believe that Gifford and Wallace and their allies might be in bed with greedy, unpatriotic farm interests and for his opponents to assume that the food administrator sympathized more with the meat packers and business interests generally. Philosophically, Pinchot and Hoover could not have been much farther apart.[71]

The episode further displayed Gifford's egotism and intense moralism, which made him sharply judgmental and compromised his ability to work with those with different perspectives. First, it had been Ballinger and Taft, then Wilson, and now Hoover. He might succeed as a chief executive officer, it seemed, but not as a subordinate unless his boss, like Roosevelt earlier, shared his basic views.

Gifford's frustrations would continue. Toward the end of the war, he prevailed upon the National Board of Farm Organizations to include him in a commission to be sent to Europe to develop proposals for postwar farm reconstruction. But the department of state, in rejecting their applications, said the agriculture secretary whose department had already sent over a competent commission, was the only one mandated by President Wilson to deal with the issue. Gifford, angered, appealed personally to Secretary Lansing, arguing that this denial of the right to farmers "would be in line not with American democratic ideals, but rather with the policy and practice of autocratic governments," but the state department was unmoved.[72] Gifford also had turned to Theodore Roosevelt, who wrote an army general detailing Gifford's eagerness to get near the front lines and recommended him for an intelligence position. The director of military intelligence in the war department showed immediate interest, and Gifford seemed slated for an assignment as a civilian, ostensibly as a forestry investigator in Switzerland or Scandinavia. But then nothing happened until two weeks before the armistice when the war department informed him that its efforts to get a passport for him had failed.[73]

Gifford, believing the Wilson administration was engaged in a political vendetta against him, grew more bitter. To his Republican friends, he resented Wilson's interest in lenient peace terms for the defeated Central Powers and his dream of a league of nations. And right after the armistice, he wrote Roosevelt, "What a pitiful spectacle at Washington. Unready for war, unready for peace, without a plan or a policy."[74] Gifford was well off the mark, as the American representatives to the Paris Peace Conference, headed by President Wilson, were well prepared and would advance a coherent liberal peace program. Despite the enormous obstacles, conflicting pressures, and complex issues, he would courageously fight for and gain acceptance of a good part of his agenda and managed to embed the covenant of the League of Nations in the Treaty of Versailles. The truth was not that Wilson had no program but that Gifford strongly disagreed with it.

*   *   *

During this interim, Amos was caught up in the ideological upsurge in radical thinking emanating out of the Bolshevik violent takeover in Russia. He was convinced that the revolution, with its anti-imperialist, antiwar program, was a counterweight to western imperialism, which had brought on the war. "As long as there is imperialism," he soon wrote, "there will be militarism. . . . That has been the story of the last twenty years of armed peace" in Europe. The United

States, a later player, was also culpable. Amos wanted radicals to embrace a peace program modeled after the Bolsheviks and the British Labour party.[75]

Amos still had faint hopes for Woodrow Wilson and his liberal peace program of fourteen points, which the president issued in January 1918, partly as an alternative manifesto to the much more radical Russian agenda. He allowed that the Wilsonian program "can make it as clear as sunlight that our objects in this war have nothing to do with imperialism, territorial acquisitions and trade privileges," but the peace settlement could "give just and equal commercial opportunity to all nations, and self-government wherever possible."[76] It was a fair statement of much of what Wilson also wanted.

Nevertheless, the president's handling of the problem of civil liberties thoroughly disillusioned Amos, and he felt loyalty to his antiwar friends at *The Masses*. The editors' trial ended with a hung jury, but the government decided to prosecute them again. Dismayed over the prospect of another trial, Amos wrote Wilson, protesting the administration's zeal, and reminded him of the larger issue—that "if rights like that of common counsel are taken from the public in an emergency, they can never be restored as <u>rights</u>. They have become revocable permissions."[77]

Again, Wilson seemed concerned and commented to Attorney General Gregory, "Mr. Amos Pinchot is not always very wise, but he is always very sincere, I believe, and his letter, I must admit, has made some impression upon me." But Gregory proceeded with the second prosecution of *The Masses'* editors, and Wilson did not acknowledge Amos's letter. "It's the first letter of mine he never answered," Amos complained.[78] Wilson, it appears, was conflicted between his fear of mob passions undermining personal freedoms and his perception that public passions were required to prosecute the war to a victorious conclusion. The result of his standoffish behavior, however, was a serious undermining of civil liberties. The only satisfaction Amos would receive was another hung jury at the second *Masses* trial, but the harassed magazine had folded.

Despite the Wilson administration's failure on civil liberties, Amos was conflicted, believing the president's liberal internationalist principles offered the best hope for the upcoming peace talks. He urged American and Allied liberals to see to it that the old order's "plan of selfish aggression . . . is not countenanced in the peace treaties. We cannot afford to lose the war by returning to armed peace. . . . The world," he added, "had seen enough sorrow. There is a great deal of work to be done; let us all join hands and help."[79]

His hopeful words notwithstanding, Amos's rejection of the American president would soon be complete. He worried first about Wilson's apparent penchant for secrecy. In late October 1918, when the state department withheld the text of a German note relating to armistice negotiations, the refusal, to Amos, constituted a backward step toward secret diplomacy in which the American people were treated "as if they were children."[80] Moreover, Amos interpreted "open covenants openly arrived at," the first of the president's fourteen points, to mean that treaty negotiations would be conducted in public. Wilson, however, believed that the negotiations might be confidential. Still, their process would be publicly reported during the talks, and the full treaty, when completed, would be available for citizens' comment and criticism. Thus, when the Big Four leaders at Paris—Wilson, Georges Clemenceau, David Lloyd George, and Vittorio Orlando—held some closed sessions to thrash out sensitive matters, Amos viewed Wilson's acquiescence in this procedure as a betrayal of his own principles. He believed the Big Four were "a little bunch of old school profiteer diplomats, closeted behind the closed door of a palace."[81]

He also deplored the continuing repression at home. A powerful reminder was the arrest of Socialist leader Eugene Debs for speaking out against the war in violation of the Espionage Act. When the U.S. Supreme Court decision upheld his conviction in March 1919, Amos circulated a dissenting pamphlet, claiming that the highest court, ignoring the First Amendment to the Constitution, sustained Debs's conviction, not because of his opposition to the war, obstruction of recruiting, or his socialism, but because he "is a dangerous agitator, who demands from the ruling classes in society a social order embodying a degree of justice which the ruling classes are unwilling to concede." He continued that the court's decision, along with other recent ones "against organized labor and in favor of child labor, has simply been over eager to protect the old order."[82]

During the peace negotiations in Paris, Amos claimed that the Big Four "seem to be preparing new wars for us, driving the world into anarchy and . . . shouting for liberty and grabbing for loot. Meanwhile Bolshevism . . . is gathering strength and gaining immensely." The victorious powers were now "hastening to prevent the catastrophe of a Kulturless world by endeavoring to clamp on our own. It all seems to[o] mad[,] this craze for forcing everybody but ourselves to be law abiding Christians."[83]

Like many liberals, Amos objected mostly to a punitive peace and the continuing economic blockade on Germany during the peace conference. He also condemned the dispatch of U.S. troops to Russia during its revolution and, concerning the economic blockade of that nation, charged that one could "search history in vain for any more brutal crime." Early turned off to the conference proceedings, he mostly touted the socialist-communist line of the victorious capitalist-imperialist nations imposing their will on defeated peoples.[84]

Amos's disillusionment with the Paris talks brought him superficially closer to his brother in their political thinking. Indeed, Amos commented to Gifford, "I congratulate you for your early appraisal of the Great Father [Wilson]. He is what you thought him[—]a man without a policy. . . . He has thrown his fourteen points to the sharks and abandoned his league of nations in favor of an international gang of bullies." Appreciating Amos's indictment of the president, Gifford replied, "I am very much interested and pleased that you have come around to my view of Wilson."[85]

When the American president returned home after the conference, he would make several major missteps contributing to the Senate's rejection of the peace treaty signed at Versailles. For Amos, the secret treaties became the coup de grace for his complete disaffection. Wilson had been informed about the secret provisions in treaties of alliance among the European allies but denied knowledge of them when critical senators asked him about them at a White House meeting. Amos concluded that Wilson had lied, and he fired off letters to Senators Hiram Johnson and William E. Borah, two severe critics of the peace treaty, telling them so.[86]

* * *

Nettie witnessed the unfolding peace process in Paris. She wanted the peace negotiators to succeed, but she knew about her older brother's difficulties with the Wilson administration and had no enthusiasm for the president.[87] During the conference, she spoke with Wilson at a diplomatic reception. According to Nettie's account, he remembered her from their testy exchange about Mexico nearly six years earlier. She mentioned that there was an ill feeling in Europe because he had not visited the devastated areas. Wilson explained that he had avoided them because he believed peace had to be free from hate. Nettie re-joined that "a peace founded upon truth was not helped by ignoring facts."[88] Wilson then asserted that "the German people were in complete ignorance of the war, and how it was waged. I said they were the best-informed people in the world—their newspapers had gloried in their crimes. He said he must (always he) make a peace as if it were fifty years after the War. I said the Bible never spoke of pardoning unrepentant sinners."

The two then commented on Theodore Roosevelt, who had died eleven days earlier. His legacy was widely discussed in the press, and he was especially in the minds of Nettie and Gifford, who had known Roosevelt so well and revered him. Wilson, according to Nettie, "spoke of Theodore rather flippantly," and she defended him. Persevering, Nettie then brought up the denial of Gifford's passport, and the president said there could not have been anything personal in the refusal. When Nettie disagreed, Wilson added, "I know nothing about it."[89]

In recounting this episode to her older brother, Nettie admitted that it sounded as if she and the president had quarreled, but she added, "We didn't. Quite the contrary. It was a sort of match, both using personal charm like mad." Although she concluded proudly, "As you can gather it was one of my good evenings, and he won't forget" that she was distressed at Wilson's egotism. "[A]ll this I," she reflected. "No wonder people are afraid of him."[90]

The three Pinchot siblings' disillusionments with Woodrow Wilson were unanimous. Only Nettie, sophisticated in the world of diplomacy and its ameliorative purposes, had the slightest hope for the Paris negotiations, but she worried that Wilson's forceful personality would subvert intelligent discussion of the complicated issues. "Today, and a nasty cold, windy day it is," she wrote Leila as the peace commissioners assembled at Versailles, "they are going to sign what they call peace! And Poland is being attacked and there are 22 other wars going on. But the job was too great for human beings to tackle. If I were the Bon Dieu I'd finish up this planet tonight and let us begin again—w[ith] a nice clean one." And she had already feared, correctly, that partisan politics would contribute to the defeat of the Versailles Treaty in the United States.[91]

Nettie may have exaggerated the amount of violence, but during the Paris conference, there had been continual labor strikes, ethnic turmoil, clashes over contested national borders, and the toppling of governments, and widespread social discontent permeated even the victorious nations. Her bleak picture captured a pervasive sense of malaise and disillusionment with the entire irenic process. The world seemed broken, and the postwar era began without much solid evidence of real peace and reconciliation.

17.

From the Depths

While contesting his nation's foreign policies, Amos Pinchot was also absorbed in personal travails. First, there was his son Gifford 2nd, who, in 1915, enrolled at Westminster School, Amos's alma mater.[1] Unfortunately for the boy, he soon received many demerits for infractions like marking up his desk. Unwilling to see his son as deficient, Amos argued with William Lee Cushing, who was still the headmaster. Cushing also involved students in military-style exercises, but Amos, rankled by compulsion, directed his son not to participate and told Cushing that his son had a spinal malformation. Amos's excuse was likely untrue yet his way of defusing the petty disagreement. Soon Amos resigned as a director at the school, claiming he was too busy to attend the meetings.

Gifford 2nd stayed at Westminster until early 1918, when he became severely ill with the grippe, and his "anxious" parents withdrew him from the school. Amos had no intention of having his son return to Westminster, telling Cushing, "I do not agree with the [school's] general fundamental ideas of education." Amos also discontinued his funding of the Pinchot Cup, awarded annually to the school's best athlete.[2] That fall, Amos sent Gifford 2nd off to another private boarding institution, Lake Placid School. As a further irony, the nation was still at war, and Giff signed up for the military training exercises. This time his father paid for the extra charge while hoping his son would drop the training "if an opportunity offers."[3]

Gifford 2nd's educational change occurred just as his parents' marriage was falling apart. Outwardly, Amos and Gertrude seemed compatible; the couple had worked together in birth control and peace activities, and in 1917, both took a lively interest in constructing a large "cottage" close to the Grey Towers mansion. Gertrude assumed primary oversight of their children, but Amos did not neglect his family.[4] The couple's correspondence was affectionate but lacked intimacy.

And then, Amos became involved with another woman. Her name was Ruth Pickering, twenty years younger than Amos. Ruth had grown up in Elmira, New York, in a family dominated by women: two assertive Quaker grandmothers and two sisters. The family was lower-middle class, thanks to the nearly bankrupt business her father had inherited, and she hated the menial housework required of her. Her progressive parents supported women's suffrage, and Ruth rebelled against her economic handicaps, determined to attend college and become independent. She believed her feminism came easily because, as she later wrote, she and the other females in her family "had to earn our own living; no feminist faith was necessary."[5]

Max Eastman, ten years older, had admired Ruth's natural beauty during his own youth in Elmira. At seventeen, "Ruth was," Eastman recalled later, "a lithe, strong, beautifully proportioned girl, ash blonde, with a petulant mouth, mostly lovingly tender and far-seeing blue eyes, . . . and she was a poet—a girl who concealed under a great deal of silence a rare and individual gift of speech."[6] She had then enrolled at Vassar College, where she majored in English literature and wrote verse for student publications. After graduation in 1914, she came to New York City to pursue a career in journalism, and Max, his wife, and his sister Crystal helped her settle in Greenwich Village. Ruth worked at *The Masses* before getting a paying job as an assistant editor at the socialist-leaning *Pearson's Magazine*, in which she also published a few articles.[7]

Amos undoubtedly got to know her from his association with the Eastmans and his involvement with *Pearson's*. The U.S. government did not prosecute the magazine for its heretical views during the war, but like other radical publications, it went into receivership. Amos identified with *Pearson's*, which had published two of his long pieces, and he appealed to wealthy friends for donations to keep the magazine afloat. *Pearson's* survived, but in the discussions over the magazine and his possible roles, Amos began seeing a lot of Ruth Pickering, who served as the editor's assistant.[8]

Ruth was attractive, well-educated, progressive, and already showing some accomplishment as a writer, all qualities that might attract a man in Amos Pinchot's position. Amos accepted the stimulating lifestyle of Greenwich Village in which Ruth participated. For her part, Ruth saw Amos as a mate in upward social movement. As she wrote her mother at the time, "On the strength of the future I have drawn all the money I had in the savings bank out to buy me a new coat and a new dress. . . . I am beginning to get a fatal desire to dress like a princess. . . . I ought to give [my face] the decoration which is its due."[9]

Soon Amos and Ruth were linked romantically. In February 1918, she joked to him, "It seems a pity my valentine to you must be a business letter,"[10] and their sexual liaison probably became intense that summer when Gertrude, as was her annual wont, was away on vacation with her mother and the children in Canada. At one point, Amos gave Ruth a present of andirons. It was a practical gift, but Ruth, taken with her new lover, waxed poetic in thanking him. To Amos, the experience of physical intimacy after years of sexual denial with Gertrude was likely exhilarating.[11]

Upon Gertrude's return home, Amos told her about his new relationship and said he wanted a divorce. Gertrude was shocked and took it hard. In retrospect, Gertrude could have seen the warning signs. Amos, only forty-four, was a good-looking man with an interesting personality, engaging and articulate. Moreover, in the liberated, bohemian society in which Amos thrived, extramarital affairs and divorce, compared with the rest of America, were more tolerated.

At one point, Amos reconsidered divorce. He wondered, for instance, how it might adversely affect their teenage children. But a pained Gertrude opposed reconciliation and wanted to begin divorce proceedings immediately. "It is impossible for me to break my heart and cripple my life again," she told her husband. "The things that are sacred to me and what I feel most deeply, are negligible to you. . . . I have to 'step easy' every instant for fear of irritating and displeasing you, and with the greatest desire to give you everything you wanted I have succeeded less and less during eighteen years."[12]

Amos still thought his spouse's uncompromising position might soften, and his lawyer and confidant, Sumner Gerard, told Amos that he and Gertrude should try to "stick it out." The fate of their marriage was indeed off and on again that fall, and Ruth wondered how it would play out, closing a letter to her lover with, "And please come soon to dinner? Aren't you ever coming?"[13]

When Amos moved out in November, Gertrude made no effort to win him back. To her, Ruth was simply Amos's "mistress," and she scorned those of Amos's friends who socialized with her. As Gerard's wife, Helen, commented, "G is absolutely unwilling and because of her uncompromising nature incapable of being sensible and getting the best she could out of things as they were." Nettie, who understood the couple's sexual incompatibility, told Amos, "I couldn[']t live without male society any more than you can without female, and that's a point which Gertrude will never understand."[14]

During the couple's deteriorating relationship, Gifford remained silent, but holding strict views on marital fidelity, he was doubtless appalled at his brother's taking up with another woman. By contrast, Leila became a sounding board for their grievances and, in the process, became Gertrude's most trusted confidant. Like many in the extended Pinchot family, Leila initially did not take Gertrude seriously, but they had apologized to each other for misunderstandings on small matters. Leila, desperate to have another child, gave birth to a stillborn baby and suffered another miscarriage not long afterward. It was Gertrude who provided loving concern to her sister-in-law through these painful and emotional months, and she also empathized with Leila, who was trying unsuccessfully to bear more children.[15]

The acrimony between Amos and Gertrude continued for some time. Amos wrote Leila that friends were telling him that Gertrude "is talking violently and not truthfully about me saying I was a frequenter of houses of prostitution and brought disease back into the home. . . . I do think Gertrude says things which people who want to damn me can use as the foundation of malicious exag[g] erations." The only saving grace was that "it's better for her to spill the bitterness than to repress it, for I don't want it to poison" Rosamond against him. Gertrude indeed had unshakable views about adultery. As one of her friends confirmed, "She is almost fanatical on the subject of her particular code of sex morality . . . and anyone who doesn't and always hasn't lived up to that code is beyond her ken."[16]

Gertrude obtained a divorce decree, which became final in March 1919. She received custody of Rosamond, and Amos was given responsibility for Gifford 2nd, but each child would also visit the other parent for two months each year. The estranged couple managed to get on speaking terms and, with their lawyers, arranged for alimony and the distribution of their personal effects.[17] But Gertrude remained bitter and jealous toward her former husband, and news of Amos and Ruth's engagement set her off. "A. is marrying this girl," she bewailed to Leila. "It is terrible to have him throw away his place in the world. How could the children be with him if he does [marry], for what kind of a home atmosphere does it mean, and I should doubt if it lasted a year or two, knowing both their characters and views of life."[18]

To make matters more tense, Leila sided with Gertrude on the child visitation arrangement, which prompted Amos to dash off a five-page rebuttal, explaining that Gertrude had freely consented to the divorce terms and that Rosamond's two months with her father was a salient corrective to the "Minturn dry-rot atmosphere, in which there is tremendous repression and mighty little humanity or generosity of judgement."[19] Amos's and Leila's contretemps would become an evolving love-hate relationship. Ruth and Amos were married in a small civil ceremony five months later at his Uncle Will Eno's home in Saugatuck.[20]

*   *   *

In politics, Amos, looking forward to the election of 1920, concluded that both major parties were "chained to out-of-date fictions. . . . They are in the hands of reaction." In his alienation, he professed to see "indications that a new party, not socialist, will come into being before very long and play an important part." He had plenty of company among radicals, advanced progressives, and disillusioned Wilsonians. Herbert Croly of the *New Republic*, Oswald Garrison Villard of the *Nation*, historian Will Durant, and publicists Gilson Gardner, Allen McCurdy, and Frederic C. Howe were among the disgruntled reformers and intellectuals whom Amos considered his friends. He wanted to build a political movement like the British Labour Party, which was emerging as that country's second-largest party.[21] A third-party alternative drew support from discontented farmers and workers, especially in the Midwest, and many of the same middle-class progressive reformers that had earlier championed Senator Robert La Follette's insurgency.

Amos soon allied himself with a Committee of 48, which former Progressive Party faithful and independent reformers hatched in mid-1919. Unlike the earlier Progressive Party, the Committee of 48 had no leading standard bearer, and its main claim was that it offered a reform alternative to the stand-pat parties. As its name connoted, it was initially interested in spreading its program and developing networks with reformers and disenchanted voters in every state. Amos perceived that he and his independent-minded friend George Record were prominent among the new party's intellectual heavyweights, and together they would fashion an economic program for the new party. His political thought, a refined version of his prewar philosophy, began with two premises: "All big political fights in this country have been waged upon economic issues," so his program would have a fundamental economic component; and "Man is a libertarian animal. . . . He wants to work for whom he pleases, when and where it pleases." The private sector, Amos urged, "should be encouraged to the utmost," and as he had expounded earlier, the government should own or operate only in two areas—transportation and natural resources. He argued that both economic sectors, when left in private hands, tend to create monopolies, whereby production is restricted, prices are raised, and employment is decreased. The combinations in transportation, fuel, or raw materials use their unfair advantages "for their own good and to the detriment of the rest of the community."[22]

During U.S. belligerency, the government had taken over the railroads in the interest of efficiency, and the question was what to do with them afterward. The railroad owners and conservatives argued that everything would be returned to the private owners at the end of the war, but the railroad brotherhoods, other unions, and many reformers supported what became known as the Plumb plan, which would continue public ownership, provide compensation to the rail companies for their loss, and create a centralized administration with representatives from labor, management, and the public.[23]

Amos approved of the Plumb plan but objected to reformers' fixation on it.[24] A second part of his economic remedy was overthrowing large corporations monopolizing the nation's natural resources—generally its water courses and raw materials. The required prescription for smashing "privilege," he insisted, was government takeover of the country's basic natural resources and public control and operation of transportation. These measures might result in "limiting individualism" but were "a necessity of protecting society from those [monopolists] who themselves would limit opportunity."[25]

Well connected to J. A. H. Hopkins, the Committee of 48's executive head, Amos served on the executive committee and the platform committee. In December 1919, the party adopted a program calling for "Equal economic, political and legal rights for all citizens," increasing taxes on idle land, and the "immediate and absolute restoration" of First Amendment freedoms. Amos claimed that the new party's platform was "so simple, so definite, and so centered on our great economic crisis" that it would soon spawn "a party big enough to outbray the Democratic jackass or swing the Republican elephant by the tail."[26]

Amos optimistically believed that laborers, farmers, and "the great middle class . . . if they would only realize it" were "in a sense, members of one class in that they are equally the victims of the monopolistic group." The postwar spike in inflation and the high cost of living, he continued, "may have the one redeeming feature of forcing these elements to recognize their solidarity in the social struggle."[27] There was much social dislocation right after the war—high unemployment, strikes, racial and ethnic strife, and farmers' discontent were all reasons to believe a new party might unite disaffected citizens.

Unfortunately for the incipient political movement, however, many urban race riots and a mounting feeling of insecurity, even paranoia, were making Americans more amenable to citizen demands for law and order, even repression.[28] Immediately, the committee had to deal with the public reaction to anarchist and Bolshevik revolutionary ideas spreading to the United States. When the delegates arrived in St. Louis for their convention, they found that the American Legion had picketed the meeting, and local businesses had threatened to boycott the convention hotel. Also, agents from the Department of Justice attended and compiled a stenographic record of the proceedings. The DoJ presence was a milder version of the "Palmer raids," which Wilson's attorney general launched against left-liberal and radical groups suspected of concocting subversive plots against the U.S. government. Of course, these threats to free speech rankled Amos and convinced him that the only way to protect this precious right and stop the government's abuse of power was to win the election and "take the power clean away from them."[29]

Like Amos, most of the 48ers were dedicated and idealistic progressives. Still, they had little experience in political organization—the tiresome process of raising money, knocking on doors, and drumming up support at the ward and precinct levels. Moreover, many of its spokesmen were patrician reformers who had not directly experienced the lower classes' deep-seated grievances, assuming they would obligingly defer to the 48ers' program. In addition, Northeasterners like Hopkins, Record, McCurdy, and Amos dominated the executive committee, so the party was not well connected to the complaints of ordinary, working-class citizens out on the hustings.

To coalesce with other discontented elements, the Committee of 48 turned to the American Labor Party.[30] Like the Committee of 48, the new party was expanding its appeal to other insurgent workers, agrarians, and reformers. Informal talks with Labor Party leaders raised hopes for a labor-liberal coalition in an amalgamated party, and the two groups agreed on some fundamentals: the restoration of civil liberties, nationalization of transportation facilities, and public ownership of utilities. What Amos and most 48ers wanted from labor was assurances that it would reduce the class emphasis in the new party, and he was initially optimistic. "They are pretty reasonable," Amos surmised after talks with Labor Party representatives. "They see that a purely class movement has no future." Soon he expressed the predominate thinking of the committee leadership: "it looks as if there would be a union of the American Labor Party, the Committee of Forty-eight and other independent groups; and the formation of a new party. If this happens, as I believe it will, a national ticket could easily be put in the field in all states, except in some southern states."[31]

In this seemingly cooperative mood, both parties decided to hold their nominating conventions in Chicago at the same time in mid-July 1920. Over nine hundred earnest delegates from forty-three states represented the Committee of 48 at its convention. In its negotiations with the Labor Party, the committee had three challenges: to find a party name, a platform, and a presidential candidate.

The fusion effort failed miserably. During the war, large elements of organized labor became more militant, and many Labor Party leaders, perceiving the Committee of 48 liberal leaders as "coupon-clipping intellectuals," "plutocratic philanthropists," and "slick lawyers," refused to compromise their class-conscious perspective and sought the committee's support solely on its own terms.[32] It adamantly maintained that "Labor" or "Farmer-Labor" should be part of the new party's name, and it rejected the inclusion of "liberal" or other bourgeois reform labels. The Labor Party leaders went well beyond what Amos and most 48ers wanted by insisting on a nearly fully socialist program, which advocated the nationalization of utilities and all large industries, and they wanted to give labor unions a large measure of the management and operations of these industries.

Most liberal 48ers shared Amos's view "that nationalization of industry is bad economics, and that government should only invade the field of industry . . . to destroy private monopoly or remove the privileges that sustain private monopoly." And they shared his conviction that government employees, representing the public generally, rather than unions, should run the nationalized companies. Amos even allowed that the government-owned natural resources (though not the railroads) could be leased to private companies for their operations.[33] But there was also resentment among elements of the Committee of 48's rank-and-file at the party's elite. As one middle-class member at the Chicago conventions put it, "How deep and wide the breach in our social fabric must already be when such sons of privilege as Amos Pinchot . . . who go into a movement . . . draw back . . . towards the side of privilege when they come cheek-by-jowl with the dead in earnest multitude awakening to a sense of its wrongs."[34]

Amos was not pleased with the criticism. From his perspective, he had avidly supported the rights of labor, going back to his financial and legal support of the Paterson and Ludlow strikers and continuing through the war. He now conceded that his belief in industrial democracy was not as advanced as the labor leaders' but argued that labor had to recognize the necessity of "playing a bigger game . . . and of frankly joining . . . with the rest of the public . . . in freeing all the exploited classes together."[35]

The two parties also failed to agree on a suitable candidate to convey their message to the wider public. Amos and others from both sides wanted to entice

Robert La Follette to head the amalgamated ticket, as he could resolve the "complicated" differences between the two parties' platforms.[36] Toward the end of the conventions, a delegation from the two groups, Amos among them, appealed personally to La Follette. The senator was interested but insisted on his own "Wisconsin platform." The labor people resisted, however, and when La Follette finally turned down the invitation, the unification effort collapsed. The labor faction came up with its own new name, the Farmer-Labor party, and would select an obscure presidential candidate, but the party dismally failed both locally and nationally in the fall election.[37]

Afterward, Amos admitted that he and the other committee leaders "did not realize, until too late, the type of [uncompromising] men who controlled the Labor party." And to the socialist Lincoln Steffens, he added, "We made silly mistakes quite naturally—and we were busted." A friend offered a harsher judgment, charging that the 48er leaders "were amateurs. . . . We permitted ourselves to be jockied in the conference negotiations and to have our time wasted until it was too late to act as a separate convention as we might have done."[38]

Amos soon resigned from the party. He grudgingly realized that despite his, Record's, and others' efforts, "there has been no intellectual conversion to our ideas on the part of a great many of the members." That was an accurate assessment, but Amos could not seriously contemplate that his program, despite its apparent simplicity, was too sophisticated to generate much enthusiasm at the Chicago gatherings.[39] And Amos saw only the shortcomings of the committee in failing to boost his vision. "The intellectual leadership is furnished by people who are not grounded in economics," he complained, and "the majority" of the 48ers in Chicago "knew nothing about the propositions which they voted upon and made no effort to discuss them."[40]

Amos signaled his disenchantment in a satirical article in which he said he would vote for Warren G. Harding, the conservative Republican nominee, in the 1920 election. Harding's handlers, he joshed, had made him over during the campaign so that "he has become humble and open-minded too and swallows with fortitude every bolus of social justice and feminism that his trainers bring." He even favored a landslide victory for Harding that would result in the "annihilation" of the Democratic Party, which disgusted him.[41]

*   *   *

Gifford was meanwhile assessing his future course in public life. The demise of the Progressive Party and his frustrations with Hoover and the Wilson administration during the war had been low points in his career, but he would nonetheless try to claim a prominent place in American politics. On the positive side, Leila proved to be an invaluable ally. Their union might have seemed a matter of convenience, with the two combining their wealth and pedigree to augment their political influence.[42]

Leila's marriage did not detract her from her commitment to women's issues—the plight of working women, suffrage, and birth control. From helping unemployed women in New York, she gravitated to the Women's Trade Union League, the predominant national lobbying organization for the protective legislation of women workers. By 1919, she was a member of the WTUL's executive committee. A WTUL priority issue at the time was suffrage, and Leila also served as secretary of the Pennsylvania Woman Suffrage Association.

Moreover, Leila possessed the zest of Gifford's mother for an active social life, and she enjoyed hosting entertainment. Events at their house in Washington, D.C., involved a guest speaking on general interest topics. In Milford, veterans and residents visited Grey Towers for an afternoon of refreshments and speakers. Despite the physical and social distance between the Pinchots at their hilltop chateau and the ordinary townspeople below, the couple genuinely tried to mingle with them as common citizens.

These supposed nonpolitical entertainments might benefit Gifford and Leila as aspiring politicians, and Leila arguably loved the political game more. She reveled in considering the tactical and strategic moves that might be required for her own or her husband's political success. As Republican progressives, they understood the difficulty in achieving their objectives in a conservative party but did not abandon reform. Shortly before Roosevelt's death, Leila, concerned about Gifford's difficulties in the web of Pennsylvania politics, asked the former president for advice on Gifford's political career, and TR frankly declared that Gifford was too radical to be successful, although he hoped that conditions might change.

Gifford and Leila were, moreover, a loving couple. Older than most newlyweds, they knew their own minds, and in their maturity, they gave each other space to develop their own priorities. Their various causes and commitments meant they were frequently away from each other. During their absences, their letters habitually reaffirmed their mutual love. "You have no idea how much I have missed you this time," she wrote during one of his trips. "All the while there has been a numb[,] incoherent but persistent kind of pain next to my heart which is just wanting you. . . . All my love to you[,] beloved." Gifford was no less effusive: "What should I have been without [you]—a wanderer and a homeless man, with nothing vital to live for and no real life at all." He usually referred to her affectionately by her first two initials, C.B.[43]

Already somewhat known in the state from his 1914 campaign for the U.S. Senate, Gifford planned his reentry into Pennsylvania politics. Because the state constitution limited the governor to a four-year term, the incumbent Republican could not run again in 1918, and Gifford would have a chance to run in the primary. Gifford believed there were "ten chances to one" against an announced Republican reform gubernatorial candidate, adding, "I had no idea I had so much strength in the State." But he discovered that the other progressive aspirant had already received promises of endorsements from many party officials, unions, and associations. A disappointed Gifford backed away and admitted to Nettie that "the controlling reason against me [is] that I have been too much absent from the State during the past two of three years . . . . It is a lesson which I shall not forget."[44]

Gifford earnestly courted farmers and labor unions in the state. He joined the Grange, for example. He also hired George Woodruff to work for him half-time in Philadelphia as his attorney and adviser, and the two collaborated with the AFL and Grange in Pennsylvania, especially on issues involving the conservation of the state's natural resources.[45] Developing ties to farmers and labor would be the backbone of his future political support, and his support of prohibition was welcomed in rural areas of the state. After the Penrose gubernatorial candidate William C. Sproul, a respected businessman and long-term state senator, won the primary and was comfortably elected in November, Gifford wished him success: "I for one shall be delighted to do anything I can to make it so."[46] The Pinchots moved to populous Philadelphia for a time, and he gave frequent speeches at rotary clubs, churches, Grange picnics, and labor groups. In these various ways, Gifford was mending his political fences and keeping his name before the public.

In 1920, both Pinchots considered possible candidacies. Gifford thought he might want to oppose Boies Penrose again, but his criticisms of the senator as "the most perfect living representative of the worst type of politics in America" had little effect. Penrose retorted pungently, "Mr. Pinchot seems to me about as important as a cheap side show outside the fence of a county fair, like the tattooed man or the cigarette fiend." The easy victories of Penrose candidates in local primary elections in September 1919 convinced Gifford that the time was not ripe for a second challenge for his Senate seat.[47]

Meanwhile, Leila fleetingly pondered a run for Congress in 1920. By the spring of that year, thirty-five states, or one short of the required three-fourths, had ratified what would become the Nineteenth Amendment to the U.S. Constitution, enfranchising women, and she thought Delaware might be the thirty-sixth. Hearing of her sister-in-law's possible candidacy, Nettie volunteered that it "would be glorious. . . . a brilliant idea."[48] But when the vote in the Delaware legislature was delayed, Leila abandoned such hopes. As she explained to a friend, "my own political ambitions came to an ignominious end, partly because it was possible that even if the Suffrage went through in Delaware, the mechanics of making out [voter] lists and assessing the women would not be put through in time to have them vote in the primaries here." The amendment, approved by Tennessee, was finally ratified in August, and Leila "joyfully" wrote Carrie Chapman Catt, a national suffrage leader, giving her credit for "the success of the whole fight. . . . It's magnificent, isn't it[?]"[49]

*　*　*

Leila's political liberation extended to the social sphere. If she was not a typical Flapper, flaunting conventional norms, she dressed smartly in tailored clothes according to the latest fashion, and she colored her naturally auburn hair with reddish accents. She was also representative of the emerging New Woman, who was willing to defy some of the traditional roles of her sex. One was drinking. When the Eighteenth Amendment prohibiting the manufacture and sale of alcoholic beverages took effect in January 1920, Leila, who liked to imbibe occasionally, did not serve them at her social entertainments, which might have been embarrassing to Gifford's strong support for the so-called noble experiment. But at the same time, she thought it was "extremely pusillanimous" to decline a drink in someone else's home, "so I always take all cocktails that are offered to me, in order to assert my independence."[50]

As the presidential election approached, Gifford had wanted Roosevelt to be the Republican nominee. TR had moved to the right politically and made a semblance of peace with the regular party leaders, and he, with enthusiastic backing from Gifford and other Republican progressives, would have been a virtual shoo-in for the GOP nomination in 1920. With his unexpected death in January 1920, however, Gifford, making clear his preference for another reform-minded candidate, announced, "I shall oppose the nomination of a reactionary like Senator Harding . . . or any other supporter of special privilege."[51]

Because he was a relative outsider to regular Republicans, Gifford tried to ingratiate himself with at least some of the more moderate Republican leaders. One of whom he had friendly contacts with was Will Hays, the Republican Party's national chairman, who put Gifford on an advisory committee for the party platform. Gifford was pleased that the party adopted his planks on the farmer and conservation. He privately lamented, however, that none of the GOP candidates "stands for just what I believe." He settled on General Leonard Wood, a Roosevelt confidant, as "the best chance to beat the reactionaries."[52]

General Wood's candidacy did not catch fire with Republicans, however. At the convention in Chicago, the party bosses picked Harding as the most acceptable compromise candidate. Gifford viewed the selection with dismay. Among other things, Harding had severely attacked TR's candidacy in 1912, and his nomination rekindled old political wounds. "Yes the old Guard did the thing in style," he commented acidly to Jim Reynolds. "Harding was not only the worst candidate they could have chosen from the point of view of the Republicans, but of every Progressive and every friend of Roosevelt's."[53]

Gifford decided to support Harding, "bitter" though it was, and after meeting with the nominee a month later, publicly endorsed him, even claiming that his position on conservation questions was "admirable." He also stumped for him in the campaign, now believing that Harding was "by no means the reactionary I thought him" and that former Progressives were still getting their positions "far more widely accepted in the platform. . . . I still have the feeling that our day is not over."[54]

But reformers' days would be in eclipse under Harding, who was resoundingly elected president that November. To Gifford, the main bright spot was the president-elect's selection of Henry C. Wallace as secretary of agriculture.[55] Gifford himself was not considered for a cabinet post, and Harding's other appointments favored his crony friends and Old Guard conservatives. Gifford dubbed the choice of Albert B. Fall as secretary of the interior as particularly unfortunate. Indeed, it was "not altogether easy," he reflected, to believe that there might possibly have been a worse selection.[56]

A priority of the Harding administration was government reorganization, including the transfer of the forest service to the interior department. Although the president argued that it was more efficient and economical to combine oversight of all the nation's natural resources in one department, Gifford objected.[57] It was not just his suspicions of Interior Secretary Fall's well-known hostility to forestry that prompted the opposition. Gifford's old prejudices against the interior department, especially his battles with Richard Ballinger, remained deeply ingrained in his psyche, and he adamantly wanted to preserve the greater independence of the forest service and the national forests in the agriculture department. Working with his political adviser Harry Slattery of the National Conservation Association in Washington, Gifford lobbied Congress hard to block the move. At a White House meeting, the president acknowledged to Gifford that he did not have the votes in Congress for the transfer, adding, "I pay you that compliment." The transfer was soon dropped from the reorganization.[58]

Gifford's move toward the political center involved abandoning his earlier, more extreme views and a tactical accommodation to political realities. As the transfer issue suggested, however, he did not bend on conservation issues. The other conservation question receiving Gifford's continuing close attention was waterpower and its uses. Following Roosevelt, Gifford and the National Conservation Association successfully lobbied for congressional passage of the Federal Water Power Act of 1920, which had brought some government oversight to interstate electric power development.[59]

A year later, he was the first public figure to criticize Henry Ford's proposal to buy the U.S.-owned plants at Muscle Shoals, Alabama, in the Tennessee River Valley. Slattery provided his employer with details of the automaker's initiative. The plants had been used to manufacture nitrates for explosives during the First World War. Ford proposed to take them over, produce fertilizer for American farmers, and generate electric power for the surrounding area. Gifford professed his willingness to see Ford profit from Muscle Shoals, but he argued that the automobile executive's offer was demonstrably one-sided and unfair to the public and would produce exorbitant returns for the investors. It was, above all, "in every important point directly contrary to the Roosevelt water policy," whose principles of public control the waterpower act had just affirmed. Gifford's exposé of the Ford initiative resulted in considerable press coverage. He received support from progressive members in Congress, especially Senator George W. Norris from Nebraska, who would almost single-handedly block private developers' plans for Muscle Shoals in Congress until a decade later, when it would create the Tennessee Valley Authority for the federal government's development of the area.[60]

On these issues, Gifford appeared as a moderate progressive, willing to support the Harding administration without compromising his core beliefs. He spent most of his time in Pennsylvania, trying to become a prominent player among the Republican state leadership. He had a few things going for him. From his progressive Senate candidacy in 1914, he had enunciated a clear reform message and developed a network of loyal reform-minded allies across Pennsylvania. In addition, he had endorsed women's suffrage in his earlier Senate campaign, and from former suffragists and other activist women, now energized with the franchise, he could expect strong support.

Leila Pinchot was a proven asset among women voters and would get her husband's message to them. She was actively involved in the League of Women Voters, the successor of the main national suffrage organization, and near the outset of the Harding administration was a member of a delegation of league women, who gained a meeting with the president at which they urged passage of a bill providing federal funding through the states for maternity and child-care. Harding, in fact, soon endorsed the bill. Enacted later that year, the law was a sign that progressive reform still had some life in the early 1920s.[61]

Organized labor, especially the United Mine Workers (UMW), also viewed Gifford favorably, and he had connected with farmers and voters in rural areas. Pennsylvania was more urban than rural, but thirty-five percent of its residents still lived in hamlets and small towns, and his main base of support would always be those parts of the state.[62] He had past connections to rural residents from his brief service with the wartime food administration, so his identification with farmers' concerns came across as genuine. And particularly important, teetotaling Gifford had a ready link with "dry" voters, who mostly lived in the rural sections of the state and supported prohibition. To be successful, the "great experiment" would require strict compliance at both the state and federal levels, but in the first years of the amendment, there was an outward public willingness to see if it would work in practice. From the start, though, as Leila commented, the topic "excludes all others in interest—and the ferocity of the emotions that are developed over it is leading everyone into an early and I should think distracted grave."[63]

The onset of prohibition posed a tricky issue for politicians. They might pay lip service to it, but many wanted alcoholic drinks served at social engagements. In her acceptance of drinking, however, Leila did not at first see its possible negative impact on politicians, and she sent Amos a check for some whiskey she would serve at Grey Towers. Her brother-in-law, super-cautious on this issue at least, refused to cash it, fearing it might leave a paper trail that could be used against Gifford if he were later accused of violating prohibition. He explained to Leila the possible ruinous political fallout if it got into the newspapers that "there was a secret stock of booze on the premises. [Gifford] would have to do a lot of explaining that the liquor was yours and not his, and the more he explained the more people would laugh." Amos soon bought their supply, which he stored in his own cottage nearby. In this way, Amos joked, they could "go right on ministering to the thirsty" at Grey Towers by sending their guests to his place for refreshments, and anyone who asked would be told that the alcohol belonged to Gifford's "wet and wicked brother."[64]

Gifford also developed direct ties with the state government. In 1918, the Pennsylvania Grange appointed him chairman of its conservation committee. Under his leadership, the committee issued a report critical of the state's forestry department and urged new forestry initiatives.[65] Impressed by this work, Governor Sproul soon appointed Gifford a member of the five-person state forestry commission. Gifford was an activist commissioner from the start. The chairman, Robert S. Conklin, had political allies but was not a trained forester, which, Gifford thought, should be a prerequisite for the job. Gifford soon complained that the chairman was a lackadaisical administrator whose "main trouble was that the path ahead is always full of lions."[66] Gifford developed a rapport with the other commissioners, especially venerable Dr. Joseph Rothrock, recognized as the founder of forestry in Pennsylvania. Gifford and his commissioner allies sent a stinging indictment of the chairman to the governor, which Sproul used to reassign Conklin to another post, and then appointed Gifford the chairman.[67]

Pennsylvania forestry was a small universe compared to the U.S. Forest Service, but Gifford found it "real fun to be on an executive job once more."[68] He promptly reinvigorated publicity to make the commission a visible force in the state. He published an article, which decried man's destruction over time of five million acres, resulting in "Pennsylvania's Desert," and emphasized the prevention of forest fires, a serious problem nationally. These barren and desolated lands, he argued, needed to be taken over by the state forests and made productive again. His department received sufficient funds to buy up burned and exhausted lands, planted countless trees, and erected many fire observation towers.[69]

Gifford's agenda had only begun. When the legislature balked at his request to hire more foresters, Gifford paid for consultant foresters with personal funds. Moreover, he objected to the low salary of the commissioners, but there was a prohibition against increasing the salaries of incumbent members. Gifford's ploy, arranged with Governor Sproul, was to have all the commissioners resign from their positions, get the legislature to increase the commissioners' salaries, and have the governor reappoint them. Gifford did not need the extra money, of course, but was nonetheless accused of a "salary grab." He would spend some time during his subsequent gubernatorial campaign trying to explain the increase.[70]

18.

The Limits of Power

Despite Gifford's growing visibility in Pennsylvania, it would be an uphill battle in a quest for statewide office. Boies Penrose's iron hold on the Republican organization involved his alliance with entrenched party bosses. Most prominent were the Mellon family from the Pittsburgh area—Andrew W. Mellon was then Harding's secretary of the treasury—and W. W. Atterbury, a Pennsylvania Railroad executive. Other powerbrokers included the Vare brothers, Edwin and William, who were in the construction business and served respectively as state senator and U.S. Congressman from South Philadelphia. A final player was Joseph R. Grundy, who used the district offices of his Pennsylvania Manufacturer's Association Casualty Insurance Company to put up and finance his own candidates. These political barons supported the Penrose machine in return for control of public-sector jobs and patronage. They were wealthy and powerful men, and Gifford, as a Republican office aspirant, would have to forge alliances or maneuver around them.

When Penrose unexpectedly died on New Year's Eve, 1921, his death raised the prospect of a changing landscape for the party. Would other GOP state leaders cooperate in sharing political power without him, or would one of them gain control of the old machine? With agreement from the Republican organization, Governor Sproul appointed George W. Pepper, one of Gifford's lawyers during the Ballinger controversy, to fill Penrose's seat until a special election. But otherwise, an internecine struggle for control of the party machinery prevailed.

Because of the confusion, Gifford, independent of the Republican machine now, had a better chance of success vying for the governorship. He lined up key supporters, declared his candidacy in mid-March 1922, and campaigned across Pennsylvania.[1] He took out a mortgage of $75,000 on three Washington, D.C., properties to finance his campaign and, with help from Leila, would underwrite almost its entire cost.[2]

For the gubernatorial election in 1922, Grundy and the Vare brothers had their own candidates, but Vares, worried about the competitiveness of their own office-seeker, along with other Republican machine leaders, put forward the name of George E. Alter, the state's attorney general, as their "harmony" candidate. Having also served as house speaker, Alter was well known in the state but a reluctant political aspirant. The party organization nonetheless touted him as a "real" Republican, not the synthetic type represented by Pinchot. But Alter's selection also angered Grundy, who, realizing that his candidate, and Pinchot, the other leading contender, could not prevail against the Republican organization in the approaching primary, withdrew his choice and endorsed Gifford. Grundy was less enamored with Gifford than he was determined to defeat the regular party group. Reducing the major candidacies to two was a big help for Gifford, but he was endorsed by a distinct minority of Pennsylvania's newspapers and was the underdog.[3]

Gifford used Alter's selection to his advantage. When he heard rumors of the party machine's move to put forward their own candidate, he decried "deals and set-ups" and warned that "no candidate who has the slightest taint of a deal can win this year." Instead of backroom shenanigans, he asserted, what was required was a truly open primary.[4]

Gifford's strategy was to take his message around the state, and he would visit all but one of the sixty-seven counties during his campaign. The aspirant added some unorthodox features that further set him apart from Alter. One was to resign from his state job as forestry commissioner. He wrote the forestry staff, "you must not use your official position to advance my candidacy," and as individuals, they could "support any candidate." Gifford then challenged Alter to do the same for his attorney general's office and criticized his rival when Alter continued in his government position and used his office workers as campaign supporters.[5]

Another was Gifford's emphasis on administrative reform. The state government was hamstrung and woefully inefficient, and in 1921, Governor Sproul appointed Gifford one of the commissioners to prepare a reorganization plan for the state government. From this work, he learned that the governor had little control over the executive agencies of government that were responsible only to the legislature and often exceeded their budgets.[6] During his campaign, Gifford touted his experience serving on federal commissions dedicated to government efficiency in the Roosevelt presidency and, more recently, what he had learned close-up about the "mess in Harrisburg." However, his remedy for Pennsylvania's problems was not more government regulation, which might alienate conservative voters. Instead, he supported extensive government reorganization and the imposition of an executive budget that would modernize the state agencies and get them to work more efficiently.

Gifford also appealed to particular constituencies. He and Alter had both announced as "dry" candidates, but the Vares, who endorsed Alter, were anti-prohibitionists and compromised their candidate's position. Moreover, as attorney general, Alter supported a law allowing saloons to keep their licenses and sell beverages containing one-half percent of alcohol as permitted under the Volstead Act. The law, Alter claimed, allowed the state to control liquor sales, even though the licensed saloonkeeper would regularly dispense drinks well above the legally permitted alcoholic content. Objecting to the law and practice, Gifford received strong endorsements from the Women's Christian Temperance Union and the Anti-Saloon League. Gifford also courted organized labor, particularly the coal miners who were periodically on strike against the coal operators; the miners, despite their "wet" preferences, flocked to his banner.[7]

His most important innovation was the mobilization of women behind his candidacy. Leila's role here was critical. In 1921, she joined with other like-minded Republican women in Pennsylvania, demanding that their sex share power equally with men on the party's state executive committee. They did not get full parity but agreement on more gender power sharing.[8]

The leader of these Republican women was Mary (Minnie) Warburton, the daughter of John Wanamaker, the Philadelphia department store magnate. Miffed over the machine leaders' failure to consult women when they had privately picked Alter as their harmony candidate, Mrs. Warburton soon came out with a "wonderful statement" endorsing Gifford. Leila noted that "the women everywhere are rallying for him."[9] Another ally was Leila's New York activist friend Esther Lape, who assembled a cadre of women volunteers and traveled around the state to recruit more women to spread Gifford's message to female voters.[10] One of their techniques was using a relatively new instrument—the telephone—while Gifford used the radio, another new electioneering device, for addresses in the Philadelphia area.

In the flush of the victory for women's suffrage, many women were motivated to become more active citizens, and Gifford likely benefitted from this enthusiasm. He believed that, for the 1922 election cycle, as many women as men were registered voters. The press regularly noted the many zealous women promoting his candidacy and attending his rallies.[11]

Gifford also championed a federal anti-lynching bill, and when Alter said that southern states and local governments should deal with the problem, African American leaders severely criticized him. Moreover, Gifford issued a statement strongly supporting black political and civil rights and equal opportunity, while Alter failed to respond. African American newspapers across the state featured their markedly different attitudes and endorsed Gifford.[12]

Throughout his campaign, Gifford, eschewing personal attacks on Alter, put forward a positive message of his qualifications and exploited the party voters' disenchantment with boss rule and the possibility of a new, more transparent political regime.[13] He also benefitted from the state's financial mismanagement, which had resulted in unpopular increased taxes on gasoline, coal, and inheritances, and he presented himself as an agent of conservative reform. Perhaps most significant, the public release of a special auditor's report of the state treasury's books only ten days before the primary seemed to validate Gifford's claims of financial abuses. As one of his supporters noted, "The daily disclosures of crookedness in the State Treasurer's department [are] most helpful to the campaign for Pinchot and Reform." One of his campaign broadsides promoted Pinchot as the candidate with the widest experience in government work and "[b]eyond all question the best man in the State to straighten out the muddle in Harrisburg."[14] He also looked the part. Upon seeing a newspaper photo of her uncle, Rosamond Pinchot, Amos's daughter, commented, "He looked at least 80!"[15] Hers was the reaction of an impressionable teenager, but Gifford, now in his late fifties, did appear older: a considerably receded hairline, thinning hair turning silver-white, and a bushy mustache with a salt-and-pepper hue. His more mature visage complemented his campaign literature, which depicted him as an accomplished, sagacious statesman.

Near the primary date, Gifford believed he was ahead but worried that "the use of money and cheating in the count" might defeat him."[16] Voting fraud was a serious problem in Pennsylvania, with the Republican organization in some areas keeping deceased residents on the registered voter lists and having their loyal supporters vote multiple times for their candidates. That happened in this election when Gifford's statewide majority of about 50,000 was reduced by a late influx of last-minute votes from the Philadelphia area to a winning margin of only 9,000 out of more than a million cast. Fortunately for him, his cushion in the more rural areas of the state sufficed to preserve his victory.[17]

Esther Lape rejoiced to Leila on election night, "I'm sublimely happy. It's just one of those <u>right</u> things that it takes a miracle to bring about. . . . [M]any people said to me today[,] 'it means a new day in Pennsylvania.'" Gifford's analysis was that his nomination was a "most remarkable combination of circumstances—one that could not be repeated . . . in a thousand years," and "it could not possibly have been won without the women, and especially not without Leila, who organized the women on that side."[18]

Although now the Republican gubernatorial candidate, Gifford still faced resistance from the regular leaders, who soon installed their choice for state party chairman by more than a two-to-one margin. Among the bosses, Gifford consulted only the experienced Grundy, asking him how he could best balance his independence and his deference to the party organization during his campaign. But on some matters, Gifford was uncompromising. He threatened to run as an independent unless the party agreed to abandon the practice of requiring state employees to give up three percent of their annual salary as political contributions. He argued that the practice was unethical, and the machine leaders reluctantly acquiesced to his demand. He also refused to disband his campaign organizations in the counties.[19]

Because Republicans had three times as many registered voters as Democrats, the campaign for the November general election was not onerous. His Democratic opponent was a friend, John McSparran, the respected head of the Pennsylvania Grange. They were both drys, and their common message in the campaign would be state government reform.[20] Gifford began crisscrossing the state again two months before the general election. He succeeded in his election strategy to hold onto Republican predominance in several cities and stay competitive with McSparran in rural areas. Gifford did surprisingly well in all sections of the state and easily prevailed, garnering fifty-seven percent of the popular vote. It was an impressive victory, and he led the statewide Republican ticket in votes.[21]

*　　*　　*

Following Gifford's primary victory, Antoinette Johnstone exuded, "Isn't it glorious about Spickey[']s triumph! Of course he, and only he could have done it."[22] Her older brother's electoral ambitions nourished Nettie's interest in politics, which the involvement of her son, Harcourt (Crinks) Johnstone, swelled. After the First World War, Crinks returned to Oxford, received his college degree, and then held different jobs in the business sector. "I hope he'll stick to it," Nettie had commented, "but he will loathe it." He stuck to it and viewed these positions as providing hands-on knowledge of commercial matters, which, he argued to his mother, "is going to be[,] from now on, necessary in all political affairs."[23]

He was preparing himself for a life in politics. In 1922, though only in his late twenties, he ran for a seat in the House of Commons from Willesden East in London, just when his Uncle Gifford, 3,000 miles away, was running for governor. Following Alan and Nettie, Crinks was a free trade Liberal, but his party was squeezed between the Conservatives and the rising Labour Party. Nettie got caught up in her son's political aspirations. "I made my first speech fr[om] any platform on Monday night and Crinks was pleased," she wrote Leila immodestly. Her son, she believed, "has the making of a _real_ speaker in him. . . . I see something of Gifford[,] though not Gifford[']s quality of being an apostle. Anyhow, I'm very proud of the child and so happy he has found his job." Nettie continued to tout his candidacy in remarks at his rallies and would help with his campaign financing. Crinks lost his first race, but when the sitting Tory soon resigned, he ran again and won the by-election. He was reelected at the end of 1923 by the tiniest of margins—114 votes.[24]

Then another family matter threatened to complicate personal relationships. Unsatisfied with Gifford's electoral triumph, Cornelia Pinchot convinced herself that Amos could be a liability to her husband's governorship. She worried that her brother-in-law's radical ideas were sometimes confused with her husband's.[25] She remembered how, in 1914, Amos publicly broke with the Progressive Party and threatened to derail Gifford's campaign. Now, she was determined to separate the two brothers' views in the public mind. Leila asked Harry Slattery if he could arrange for the publication of such an article. Slattery, Gifford's long-time paid lobbyist, was working as much for Leila and her causes.[26] Among other things, she suggested that the piece would show how Amos was an "agitator" in contrast to Gifford's "record of achievement," "how Amos always disliked T.R. and never lost an opportunity of attacking him, and how T.R. referred to him as 'one of the lunatic fringe'; how Amos was a pacifist during the war; voted for Wilson while Gifford was campaigning for Hughes, etc. etc." More than that, she wanted the article to demean Amos's personal life. "I suppose it would be a rather dirty trick to talk about his admitted 'free love' theories because they might hurt Ruth," she insinuated, "but it might be possible to refer to the divorce which is constantly saddled on Gifford." "Of course," she emphasized to Slattery, any such article "should not come from us."[27]

Leila's letter was scurrilous and conveniently pushed aside some inconvenient truths. For one thing, Leila disagreed with her husband about U.S. entry into the war, remarking, "Two minds don't think as one, it would be dreary if true." She had then tolerated Amos's antiwar ideas and had even asked her brother-in-law for advice concerning her older sister Clare, a radical pacifist, that might steer her away from illegal war resistance activity and possible arrest.[28] Although Amos may have talked to Leila about free love, no evidence has been found. Moreover, believing that his brother's divorce "constantly saddled" Gifford's reputation was far-fetched. Amos valued family peace and knew where to draw the line in his disagreements with Leila so that a measure of co-existence continued, and he had avoided publicizing his political differences with his brother.[29]

Leila's letter to Slattery showed her passionate identification with her husband's political career, even if it might mean disparaging her brother-in-law. Slattery was on fairly good terms with Amos but gave Leila his own "slant" in handling her brother-in-law. He probably fed Leila's prejudices against Amos to journalistic friends, and two years later, a Philadelphia newspaper editorial appeared, praising Governor Pinchot while severely ridiculing Amos. Ruth Pinchot correctly labeled the piece "pro-Gifford and anti- anti-Amos." Whether Leila or Slattery was behind this specific attack is unknown, but the issues and language in the editorial resembled those in her earlier letter to Slattery.[30] Gifford himself was not involved.[31]

*   *   *

In January 1923, Gifford, Leila, and son, Giff, now seven, moved into the executive mansion in Harrisburg.[32] From the start, Gifford was determined to exploit the popular mandate he had received in the election. Responding to prominent female support, he appointed seventy-nine women to supervisory positions in his government and a woman cabinet member. His old Yale classmates and forestry loyalists George Woodruff and Philip Wells became attorney general and deputy attorney general, respectively, and Steve Stahlnecker served as his secretary.

In his inaugural address to the general assembly, the new governor proposed legislation to help farmers, equalize taxation, and protect working men, women, and children. Perceiving that only a few issues laid out plainly could arouse the electorate, he commented, "If you succumb to espousing every good cause, you keep building up the number of your enemies. Soon they reach such proportions that you cannot possibly be reelected."[33] Avoiding a scattershot approach, Gifford stressed three major goals for the legislature: a balanced budget, the reorganization and modernization of the state government, and the enforcement of prohibition.

Governor Pinchot affirmed in his address that he equated his purposes with TR's Progressive Party in 1912. "Both were based squarely on the proposition that the public good comes first," and that proposition, he argued, would be his "foundation stone, and upon it [his administration] hopes and intends to erect a structure of honest and effective service to all the people, without distinction of race, creed, sex, or political complexion." His concluding remarks took on an evangelical tone, decrying the "breakdown in law enforcement" and the people's toleration for "indefensible" conduct in their public servants and proclaiming "that Pennsylvania needs a new birth of political righteousness."[34]

He got off to a good start with the legislature. The house accepted his choice as speaker, and the legislature, which commanded a decisive Republican majority, discussed reorganizing the state's finances.[35] As he promised in the primary campaign, he created a citizens committee to study the state's finances and appointed Clyde L. King, a professor at the Wharton School of the University of Pennsylvania, as its chairman. Gifford would rely heavily on King's advice during his four-year term; and King, relishing the chance to help the governor, informed Amos, "This is my first and no doubt it will be my last opportunity to give everything to one in whom I believe implicitly all the time."[36]

The legislature overwhelmingly approved a new administrative code, which brought 107 agencies under eighteen departments and three commissions, and introduced an executive budget overseen by a newly established budget office.[37] The legislature also enacted a retirement system for state employees and a modest old-age pension plan (which the courts soon declared unconstitutional) and provided for direct state control over mental health and children's hospitals. Highways, welfare, security, education, and health all increased in importance, and Pennsylvania, among the large, industrialized states, needed to adjust to the rising public needs.

Gifford used his gubernatorial position as a bully pulpit for Pennsylvania, just as TR had done earlier nationwide. At the same time, though, he wanted change without increasing the cost of government. Among other considerations, many of his rural supporters, while wanting honest government, remained conservative in their objection to tax increases. Gifford inherited a state budget deficit of about twenty-five percent, and his reaction was to tell department heads that extensive cuts would be forthcoming unless the legislature raised more taxes, which was its business, not the governor's. At the end of Gifford's term, King told him that, compared with the previous Sproul administration, his had saved the state $100 million.[38]

The new governor also confronted the drinking issue head-on. To Gifford, prohibition was part of the U.S. Constitution, the supreme law of the land, and it was a moral duty to respect and enforce it. In his inaugural address, he promised to appoint only drys in his administration and urged public officials down to the district levels to pledge to support the U.S. Constitution and the Eighteenth Amendment. As the governor wrote at the outset, "I have started my drive to clean up the bootlegging. . . . It won't be a short job, but I think we have more than a chance to put it over."[39]

Leila also got involved. Supporting her husband's anti-liquor crusade, she argued that failure to enforce the nation's laws "means destruction to any civilized society." She even proposed that women should serve as prohibition agents. Such women officers might convince the public that "law enforcement is a moral question." She claimed that churches and women's clubs could put forward the names of "outstanding women" around the country who would be willing to "undertake the work of prohibition enforcement as a moral duty . . . and that a group of women so chosen would be literally unbribable." She conceded that women would not inspect saloons but believed that the government generally would not have "to give special protection to women officers, nor plan to save them from potential danger." As an analogy, she mentioned that once women were employed as election officials, their presence eliminated most of the "'rough stuff' and the dangerous places became as peaceful as Sunday Schools."[40]

Indeed, she confided to Slattery, "It would be a magnificent publicity stunt" if she could get an interview with Harding on the subject. Perhaps with his help, she managed to finagle another meeting with the president to ask him to consider her dry proposal as an experiment. Harding, who was not overeager to enforce prohibition, told Leila that he would talk to the treasury official overseeing prohibition but promised nothing. Afterward, Leila admitted, "I am not very hopeful."[41]

Prohibition was a daunting problem, requiring effective enforcement on both state and federal levels. The only federal enforcement legislation was the Volstead Act, and Gifford pushed a bill in the legislature that ended all licenses for saloons and gave law officers extensive powers of search and seizure of suspected possession of intoxicating beverages, with the burden of proof of innocence placed on the accused. After furious lobbying on both sides, the measure squeaked through the state senate by four votes and the state house by two.[42]

Gifford's vendetta against anti-prohibitionists extended to censoring movie pictures containing drinking, even if innocuous and set in a pre-prohibition era. Such restrictions were part of Gifford's general mindset, which involved the broader enforcement of public morality. During his governorship, Gifford was willing to curtail free expression involving such questions. He closely monitored the state's motion picture censors and often complained when the plot line was too racy or the characters were not respectfully clothed. He similarly opposed gambling and vetoed a legislative action subsidizing county fairs since it provided no ban on gambling or immoral shows. He also supported the state's "blue laws," restricting recreational and commercial activity on the Sabbath.[43] Despite his political progressivism, Gifford remained a social conservative. To more modern minds, he came across as an old-fashioned Victorian, a sanctimonious prude, but many Pennsylvanians, particularly in rural districts, agreed with him.

Gifford expressed no interest in civil liberties during the First World War and seemed different from his brother, who had strongly defended them. But in principle, they were not in fundamental disagreement. During U.S. belligerency from 1917–1918, Gifford faced a dilemma, not unlike President Wilson and other prowar liberals in valuing free speech but accepting the suppression of dissent during wartime. For Gifford, there was a distinction between the state's responsibility to set standards for and enforce public decency, which he promoted, and the right of free speech in the political and academic realms, which he would later champion.[44]

On the prohibition question, Gifford faced an uphill struggle with the legislature. The house rejected supplemental bills, which would have provided the necessary funding for more effective enforcement law, especially hiring special agents who would search for violators of the new act. Pennsylvania would have to rely on existing resources to enforce compliance.[45]

Despite the disappointment, Gifford overall had a successful first legislative session and was pleased with the results, telling Nettie, "It is beginning to look as if I was coming out of this Legislature with nearly everything I wanted—very much more, I will admit, than I expected."[46] He had, in fact, accomplished a lot.

The Pennsylvania general assembly met only in odd-numbered years, and with the legislative session's conclusion, Gifford focused more attention on prohibition enforcement. He would receive indifferent support at the federal level. Andrew Mellon's treasury department was in charge of the agents authorized to arrest and prosecute individuals violating prohibition.[47] Early in his governorship, Gifford had charged that Mellon, who had been a major investor in a distillery before he became treasury secretary, failed to act aggressively against the brewers and distillers in his home state. After Gifford's continued public complaints, Mellon finally responded that he had given up his whiskey investment when he became treasury secretary and was enforcing prohibition within the limits of the funds Congress granted him.

Gifford derived satisfaction from drawing out Mellon's public comment. "I don't know whether Andy has enjoyed it or not," he wrote a forester friend, "but I am having a grand time out of it myself." Staying on the offensive, he publicly criticized "the disgraceful failure of the Federal Enforcement Service" and concluded that it was "wrong" for a man who has been in the whiskey business for forty years to be at the head of the law enforcement.[48] It was, of course, easier to criticize Mellon, who was part of the Pennsylvania "gang" he was fighting and implementing an ultra-conservative fiscal policy at treasury that was highly favorable to the wealthy. Still, Gifford would have objected to Mellon's lackluster enforcement of prohibition in any case.[49]

The main argument of prohibition opponents was that it encouraged criminal elements to develop extra-legal methods to supply consumers' demand for alcohol. The opposition claimed it undermined public morality and encouraged corruption. At its worst, it led to violent shootings between competing gangs. From their vantage point, it was preferable to legalize and better regulate the trafficking and sale of alcoholic beverages. The sale of beer and wine, for instance, might be tolerated.

Governor Pinchot rejected any such legislation (and likely, so would have the courts), but his efforts in Pennsylvania were mixed. He continued receiving strong support from church and other dry groups. The Pennsylvania WCTU was particularly active in promoting the governor's anti-liquor crusade, and its energetic president, Ella M. George, became one of Gifford's loyal confidantes on prohibition strategy.

Moreover, after the legislature failed to grant the governor the enforcement funding he requested, the state WCTU raised money for a fund of $250,000, and Attorney General Woodruff ruled that such private funds could be used to assist the state enforcement departments. During Gifford's governorship, the WCTU raised over one-half of the fund goal, and all of that amount was expended on state prohibition enforcement—particularly, the hiring of several special agents, often working undercover. Gifford also relied on the state police, which conducted vigilant campaigns against the production and distribution of alcohol. By 1926, the police reported that they had destroyed more than 10,000 stills and over 58,000 gallons of alcohol, 15,000 gallons of moonshine, and almost 50,000 barrels of beer across the state.[50]

The crackdown required effective cooperation at the local levels with mayors, sheriffs, police, district attorneys, and grand juries, and prosecuting lawbreakers in the cities remained an even greater challenge. Many saloons still operated openly in Philadelphia, the state's biggest metropolis. In one saloon there, Gifford claimed he witnessed "the law-breaking drinkers surrounded the illegal bar four deep . . . there was as little secrecy about it as there is about the Washington monument. . . . A policeman stood at the very door."[51] The enforcement was so lax there that the mayor hired General Smedley Butler of the U.S. Marine Corps on a temporary assignment as director of public safety to reorganize the police force and reduce crime. Butler, a forceful and flamboyant personality, waged war on the saloons. In his first five days in office, he closed 973 of them. Gifford was gleeful. "Every good citizen in Pennsylvania," he wrote in an open letter to Butler, "will be delighted with the vigor and earnestness with which you are going at the difficult problem of cleaning up Philadelphia. May you have every success." Butler continued his enforcement operation for two years.[52]

If prohibition in Pennsylvania was a work in progress, the governor's other successes prompted speculation about Gifford Pinchot as a GOP aspirant for the presidency, the more so because rumors were spreading about possible criminal behavior in the Harding administration. Gifford's political star was rising while Harding's was in steep decline. One scenario was that the president might decide not to run, even if he survived the allegations of corruption among crony friends. In any case, his tainted administration might allow other Republican aspirants to contest his renomination. Nettie warmed to the thought of her brother seeking the presidency. "[O]f course H[arding] will want the nomination," she wrote him, "tho' I know he'll die or something before [the nominating convention] next June. I do feel that all is going yr way fr- now on." Sixteen days after she wrote this letter, Harding died of a heart attack, and Calvin Coolidge became president. Gifford mused that he was "a melancholy substitution," and Nettie chimed in, "I hope Coolidge will do no end of stupid things and clear the way to the throne."[53]

Gifford quickly pressed for Coolidge's cooperation with the states on prohibition, but the new president demanded little from Congress or Mellon and his department. At a conference of governors, which Gifford attended, the president told them that enforcement was a joint responsibility of the federal and state governments but left little doubt that he believed the main action had to come from the states.[54] When General Butler's assignment in Philadelphia ended, Gifford visited Coolidge at the White House to appeal personally to allow Butler to continue in his city post. He was unsuccessful, however, and would complain, "Lord, how I wish [Butler] was back here in the war! It would change the whole complexion of everything."[55]

Gifford's national profile became better known because of his involvement in a serious labor strike in the anthracite coal regions of the state. Anthracite coal was still the preferred fuel for heating Americans' homes, and most of it was mined in northeastern Pennsylvania. The UMW, challenging the coal companies for better wages, hours, and working conditions, had gone on strike for several months in 1922. After a short-term settlement, the UMW prepared to strike again in the fall of 1923. A coal stoppage with the cold winter months approaching could foment a serious national crisis. Gifford would cite figures that 6,000 Pennsylvanians had died in the freezing weather during the previous strike.

Gifford saw Coolidge in Washington and assured him of his cooperation if the new president decided to mediate between the two sides.[56] But Coolidge, fundamentally cautious, did not act. Then, with the strike deadline only a week away, the governor directly appealed over the telephone for his intervention. The president finally invited him to the White House to discuss the matter, but from their meeting, Gifford surmised that the federal authorities' thoughts did not run beyond hiring substitute coal miners—strikebreakers—and that Coolidge did not want to get involved.

The governor then invited the parties to meet with him in Harrisburg. Through his good offices, the UMW and the coal operators reached a two-year agreement that gave miners a ten percent wage increase and an eight-hour day. The settlement gave Gifford greater luster to the pleased miners and highlighted his name nationally. Coolidge praised the governor for his role but included a curious sentence: "It was a very difficult situation in which I invited your cooperation." It was Gifford, of course, who had taken the initiative, while Coolidge, unwilling to take on the risks, nonetheless wanted to share in the credit.[57]

In the labor-owner negotiations, Gifford had been less an impartial mediator than a true friend of organized labor. Believing the miners had genuine grievances, he saw it as a question of simple justice. He had suggested both the wage hike and hour limitation, arguing, as he said afterward, that they "on their merits were completely justified. The anthracite workers deserved and should have had both of them, wholly without reference to the threatened strike."[58] But the coal operators accepted the settlement partly because the governor also had figures showing that the coal companies' recent profits had increased and they could afford concessions.

Gifford had earlier entertained more radical notions about coal mining. During his Senate race in 1914, he had toyed with the idea of state ownership of the coal mines in Pennsylvania but had stopped short of proposing it. However, a year later, he had urged that the U.S. government take over the Colorado mines owned by John D. Rockefeller as an indispensable step toward ending the labor strife there. "It seemed to me the right time to say something about Government Ownership, and I have gone straight at it," he had written Amos, who expressed his delight at his brother's "first rate" speech on the subject.[59]

For Amos, the serious coal problem in Pennsylvania was fodder for advancing his anti-monopolistic ideas, and he wanted his brother to put them into practice. He wrote a series of articles for *The Nation*, advocating for a government takeover of the railroads. Since railroads owned most of the anthracite coal mines, the situation in Pennsylvania was a textbook case of nefarious collusion between producers of the nation's natural resources and their distribution to market at artificially high prices.[60] Unions retaliated with strikes. Seeking to end the monopoly and the cycle of labor-capital strife, Amos urged Gifford to condemn and have the state buy and then lease out the coal mines to businesses, "in the same way that the government so successfully owns and leases to private developers water power, grazing and lumber lands on federal reserves," and also take ownership and operation of one or more of the anthracite hauling railroads.[61]

The proposal was fraught with difficulties.[62] In any event, Gifford was already committed to collective bargaining in this instance. After successfully negotiating a labor agreement with the owners, he told Amos, "I wasn't able to follow the line of your suggestions at this time." He also indicated that, contrary to his brother's assumptions, the independent operators, without exception, sold coal at a higher price than the railroad companies.[63]

*   *   *

After a successful first year as governor, Gifford encountered stiff opposition that would persist for the rest of his term. Following the strike settlement, the coal owners raised the price of anthracite to consumers to pay for the increased labor wages, then went on the offensive, blaming Pinchot for the increase. Citizens were upset, and the governor, championing consumers, tried but failed to get Congress to pass a bill empowering the Interstate Commerce Commission to hold down retail coal prices.[64]

More significantly, the Republican Party machine had tolerated his leadership in tackling some of Pennsylvania's serious problems, but it was now pushback time. They were determined to teach Gifford some lessons. Incumbent governors had traditionally been a delegate to the GOP national convention and sometimes were put forward as "favorite son" presidential candidates. In early 1924, Gifford decided not to ask for instructed delegates, as it would set off a bitter intraparty fight that might result in only a few delegates pledged to him. He believed he had an understanding with the state party bosses that, in the interest of unity, they would support his election as a statewide delegate in the upcoming primary. But the bosses conspired to deny him that honor at the upcoming nominating convention in Cleveland.[65] Only days before the primary election, the bosses spread the word to their loyalists that the maverick Gifford Pinchot, in his attacks on Mellon, had been disloyal to the Coolidge administration. Instead of the governor, they should get out the vote in support of a wealthy newspaper publisher, who strongly backed Coolidge.[66] Gifford learned of the move too late to counteract it with any effect, and he was soundly defeated by 220,000 votes.

Gifford lashed out in defeat, claiming that the result was "merely proof of the old alliance between liquor and gang politics in the State." He again appealed for "the help of every friend of law, order and clean politics."[67] Prohibition was only part of the organization's determination to regain a decisive upper hand in the control of the party in the state.[68]

Gifford publicly denied any interest in the nation's highest office, but he was realistically considering the prospect. As he had told Nettie in early 1924, "whether I have or have not a chance for the Presidency does not depend in any sense on Pennsylvania, but altogether with the West, which will be the deciding factor beyond all question." But the only revolt among western progressive Republicans that year was in support of the third-party candidacy of La Follette, whom Gifford loathed. (La Follette would garner nearly five million votes in the election.) There was still the possibility that GOP leaders might conclude that a conservative like Coolidge could not defeat a strong Democrat, especially after the Harding scandals and Teapot Dome oil affair. Even so, Gifford privately admitted that his presidential chances were "exceedingly small," and he soon accepted the inevitable and endorsed Coolidge.[69]

When Coolidge won the election easily, a discouraged Gifford told Horace Plunkett that "this country is at the moment falling back under a more complete domination by the plutocracy than for many years past, and eventually something has got to be done about it."[70] But change was not in the offing, and it would be Gifford's political misfortune that the Old Guard leadership retained firm control of the GOP machinery in the mostly prosperous 1920s.

The "gang" continued to undermine the Pinchot administration. In the 1924 election, they worked hard to elect loyalists to the state legislature, and the house decisively rejected the returning speaker, Gifford's ally, in favor of a wet. Gifford noted that the "people in control in the House especially are certainly a bad bunch." They started out having "a hot time" in manipulating the budget and causing general mischief, and Gifford accurately predicted that they would cause "plenty of trouble yet before they adjourn."[71]

Gifford focused on preventing his opponents from undermining the accomplishments of his first year as governor, and he presented only two major items for the 1925 legislature. One was prohibition enforcement. Anticipating a new legislative struggle, Gifford convened representatives of dry organizations and sympathetic women and media in the state to prepare for the coming session. He made two appearances before joint meetings of the legislature to tout his law enforcement program. But his authority was waning. Partly, it was the erosion of support for his hardline position against alcohol. William Vare, for example, cited statistics showing that, despite the administration's efforts, alcohol-related crime was rapidly increasing, and he adroitly played to citizens' concerns over its overreaching enforcement measures and invasions of their privacy. Gifford had already expended his patronage powers and lost political leverage as a lame duck. As he commented earlier, "The second session of a Governor who can't be reelected is not exactly huckleberry pie."[72] The opposing factions narrowly defeated the enforcement bill in the house, and the legislature rejected his request for $500,000 for enforcement measures.[73] The anti-Pinchot coalition was clearly in control.

The other issue was electrical power. Gifford had perceived the enormous potential of electricity in the transition to modernity, and he would try to do for Pennsylvania what he and his conservation allies were promoting on federal level. Governor Pinchot turned to Morris Llewellyn Cooke in the state utilities bureau. The two had similar backgrounds as patrician progressives and admirers of Theodore Roosevelt, and they became close allies on the power question. Moreover, Cooke, an engineer from Philadelphia, was concerned about the quality of country life. Electric power had made city dwellers' lives more comfortable, but inhabitants of rural Pennsylvania were being left behind. Agriculture was a "sick" industry during that decade, and farmers began demanding government help. Agrarian reformers raised their voices and began shouting, among other complaints, that the monopolistic power utilities were ignoring the less populated areas or bringing electricity to them only at prohibitively expensive rates. For example, a frustrated John McSparran charged, "we have tried regulation, and these giant corporations laugh in our faces."[74]

Governor Pinchot at President Coolidge's inauguration, Washington, D.C., March 4, 1925.
Gifford borrowed the horse from his Uncle Will who owned a house in the city. (USDA Forest
Service, Grey Towers NHS)

On the positive side, Cooke and other progressives believed that the state
government should regulate utilities in the public interest and disseminate
cheap power to all its citizens, including rural inhabitants. However, the rapidly
expanding power industry was well ahead of the states in sensing the enormous
potential of electricity. In 1921, Northeastern utilities had written a super-
power report, which propounded the development of giant generating stations
and interconnected transmission lines. It did not mention rural electrification,
but Cooke and other progressives thought the report seemed to be the product of profit-minded businessmen. And when Secretary of Commerce Herbert
Hoover set up a northeast super-power committee, reformers concluded that
they could not expect help from the federal government.

As public interest in electric power swelled, Governor Pinchot prevailed
upon the legislature in 1923 to provide funding for a giant power survey board
to investigate Pennsylvania's water and fuel resources and the most practical
methods for generating abundant and cheap electricity. Gifford was chairman,

and his loyal lieutenants Woodruff and Wells were also members. The new board named Cooke as its director. By the end of 1924, Cooke and his entourage had completed their comprehensive study, entitled Giant Power.

The survey recommendations were fairly moderate, containing no mention of government-owned plants. But the survey called for state agencies to actively plan, license, and regulate the private companies producing the electricity and transmission lines. Because no large rivers ran through the state, it emphasized using its plenteous natural resource, bituminous (soft) coal, as the energy source. Instead of railroads transporting the coal to generating sites around the state, it pressed for building generation stations next to the coal mines. These plants would produce "giant power" via transmission lines that would also reach country residents, who would be encouraged to form rural power districts and farmers' cooperatives so that farms would now have access to reasonably priced electricity for their homes and water pumping operations.[75]

The governor was enthusiastic about the report, telling Cooke that it was "of larger significance and importance to the people of the United States and indeed of the whole world." He presented it to the legislature in February 1925 with the challenge that if electric power could be regulated in the public interest, "It can be made incomparably the greatest material blessing in human history. . . . Of a truth, we are in the valley of decision. . . . Either we must control public power, or its masters and owners will control us."[76]

The legislators soon realized that active state involvement in the industry challenged the political status quo. Business and engineering groups and the utilities attacked giant power for its advocacy of a new rate structure and "communistic ideas." Despite pockets of strong support, rural elements proved insufficiently united in opposition, with more conservative farm organizations unwilling to stand tall against utility pressure. The administration's bills to implement the survey board's recommendations never got out of the house committee. Moreover, the state's public service commission also failed to represent consumer concerns consistently. Governor Pinchot fired two of its members, holdovers from previous administrations, and appointed Cooke as one of the replacements, but the commission still fell short of full-scale regulation of the utilities in the public interest.[77] The conservative political climate in the 1920s would frustrate substantive progress on giant power. The Pennsylvania experience was typical of private companies holding the upper hand in the utilities field, and their predominance would become more evident in the last years of the decade.

In the fall of 1925, Gifford revisited another energy crisis. The earlier two-year anthracite coal agreement expired in September, and the coal miners went on strike again. When early efforts for a settlement failed, Gifford once more deferred to Coolidge's intervention. Again, the president chose not to get involved.[78] Governor Pinchot then invited labor and owner representatives to Grey Towers to confer on the issues. From the information he gathered there, he drew up the outlines of a proposed settlement. He also mobilized public opinion behind his efforts to end the work stoppage. He called the legislature into extra sessions to learn about the conditions and pass laws regulating the anthracite coal industry. He proposed, for example, that the legislature declare that the industry was a public utility, subject to control by the state's public service commission. The fallout from the earlier strike convinced him that the owners' freedom to raise coal prices needed to be controlled. If a public utility was not to be government-owned, as his brother Amos preferred, it was a clear message that private industry had to serve the public good. Another initiative was his invitation to all the mayors and town leaders in the anthracite region to meet with him in Harrisburg to discuss the situation and share information about living conditions in their communities. He used the strike to publicize the squalid, miserable plight of the mine workers and their families, their indebtedness, and their need for food and other welfare assistance. He intended to build public sympathy for the miners, which would pressure the owners to agree.

The legislature rejected his utility plan, and when the strike was finally settled, Gifford, embroiled in other issues during the extra legislative session, did not participate in the final bargaining. A small reward for his determined efforts during the shutdown was that his picture was featured on the cover of *Time Magazine*. Perhaps his most substantive achievement during the strike was the imposition of a careful investigation of coal and iron policemen, a good number of whom were thugs and gunmen used as strikebreakers, and he revoked the commissions of hundreds of those who were demonstrably unfit to serve as police officers.

Despite Gifford's best intentions, anthracite coal was another "sick" industry, operating at less than half capacity, and the recurrent strikes resulting in uncertainty and increased fuel costs to consumers hastened its decline. During the work stoppages, Americans imported more foreign coal, and they turned to alternative energy sources, such as modified bituminous coal or coke, and more affluent households converted to oil heat. Gifford understood these powerful economic trends but lacked the authority to counteract them.[79]

*   *   *

Gifford's decision to reconvene the legislature in extra sessions was a gamble, given the opposition he had already faced. But besides the coal strike, he had an unfinished agenda and hoped to achieve at least some of it. He proposed eight items, including prohibition enforcement, clean elections, banking reform, and cheaper electric service. An undercurrent in the political discussions over Gifford's legislative program during this session was his political future. Everyone presumed that he was preparing to run for the U.S. Senate seat held by George Pepper in the 1926 election. The signs were unmistakable. He had already begun criticizing Pepper. In the late summer of 1925, Stahlnecker, his secretary, arranged an extensive automobile cavalcade for the governor across Pennsylvania to inspect the state-run hospitals, asylums, and homes. Gifford was genuinely interested in the status of public institutions (prisons were a special concern), but he had also used the trip to make speeches at local events where he had touted his accomplishments as governor and castigated his opponents.

Besides prohibition, a major theme of his addresses was electoral reform, especially for the citizens of the state's smaller communities. Pennsylvania had a long history of widespread voting fraud, and last-minute ballot stuffing in Philadelphia had almost cost him his election as governor. "The gang controlled majorities in the great cities," he thundered in his talks, are "the most dangerous factor in American public life today." He organized a Committee of 76, composed of Democrats and independent Republicans, which reported on the "gross . . . scandals" and "brazen" theft of votes in Pittsburgh, Philadelphia, Scranton, and elsewhere, and the committee recommended the passage of several laws to reform the election system.[80]

But Gifford's enemies were united in their determination to deny him fresh legislative achievements, and ultimately almost all of his initiatives went down to defeat.[81] He admitted to an old ally "that pretty nearly everything has been massacred, but we shall get something out of the wreck and what we get will amply justify the extra session." That "something" was passage of a law authorizing state regulation of distilleries, but he lost the battle for control of the breweries. After the rejection of his agenda, he charged that "the gang" had broken its promise to consider his administration's proposals and had "killed" its bills regulating giant power and insuring bank deposits, and had "put itself clearly on record against clean elections."[82]

After the special session, Gifford declared his candidacy for the U.S. Senate. He was, he emphasized, "a supporter of President Coolidge, and an enemy of the gang," and he was the candidate of the "plain people," who had no one in the Senate to represent them.[83] George Pepper, the incumbent, was a moderate

Republican, but Gifford thought he was vulnerable. The senator was a dry but more as a defender of the law than from conviction, and Gifford called him a "damp." Many drys nonetheless found Pepper's position acceptable and were prepared to vote for him. He also had the backing of the Mellon organization. As a wet, Congressman Vare, realizing that Pinchot and Pepper would likely divide the dry vote, saw his chance to move to the Senate. He also entered the race, emphasizing his opposition to prohibition. A three-man contest ensued. Gifford ran against "the gang" controlling the state GOP organization and for law enforcement and electoral reform. He had support in rural areas and the unwavering backing of the United Mine Workers. A not uncommon sight during the campaign was Gifford appearing at outdoor rallies before thousands in mining areas where he was flanked on either side by John L. Lewis and Philip Murray, the UMW's president and vice-president.[84]

Believing he could not make inroads on Vare's supporters, Gifford directed his criticism against Senator Pepper, who "stands for nothing," was a "colorless" and "milk and water" candidate, and, during the race, was "fading" and "mostly water over the dam."[85] Leila campaigned strenuously for her husband, sometimes giving as many as nine speeches a day. She also believed that Gifford was gaining support, telling Amos, "Things are beginning to look better and better—the swing to us I verily believe is on." Moreover, she continued, Pepper and his campaign team "have made every kind of mistake" in double-crossing the gubernatorial candidate attached to the senator's candidacy if likely to win him more votes and blindly approving "the wise leadership of Mellon," which she found "senseless." She labeled the entire chaotic primary as "the damn[d]est campaign you've ever seen—all mixed up in the most unbelievable confusion."

Adding to the confusion, Leila noted, was that some of Gifford's old political friends were now "agin['] us in many cases." Minnie Warburton, for instance, endorsed Pepper, who came from the same Philadelphia aristocracy, and took away some female support, though Leila asserted that "middle class plain women are with us strong—and working like the very devil."[86]

By election day, Gifford exuded confidence. However, he was running against two well-known, liberally financed, experienced politicians, and the primary results went decisively against him. The governor did well in "wet" coal and "dry" rural areas, but Vare, effectively mobilizing his Philadelphia base, won the election handily with 597,000 votes (over one-half from his home city), with Pepper trailing with 516,000 and Gifford with only 339,000, including a paltry 28,000 from Philadelphia. The growing anti-prohibition sentiment was a powerful factor in Gifford's defeat, and reform no longer seemed to excite the general electorate.[87]

Vare would go on to win at the polls in November, but allegations of excessive campaign expenditure in the primary undermined his election. Even before the general election, the U.S. Senate began investigating primary winner Vare for his lavish campaign spending. Governor Pinchot weighed in, calling Vare's expenditures "disreputable beyond exaggeration" and charging him with involvement in electoral fraud.[88] As governor, Gifford's responsibility was the certification of the results of the Senate election, but he refused to do so, telling the U.S. Senate that "I am convinced, and have repeatedly declared, that [Vare's] nomination was partly bought and partly stolen, and that frauds committed in his interest have tainted both the primary and the general election." When the Senate completed its investigation, it cited Vare's excessive primary expenditures to deny him a place in its august institution.[89]

Besides the conservative political drift, voters also seemed tired of Gifford's constant assertions that his opponents were wrong and selfishly tied to corrupt political elites, while his self-promoting publicity and political ambition, first as a possible presidential candidate and then as Senate candidate, made him far from angelic. To some minds, he seemed willing to use machine methods he supposedly abhorred to advance his political career.[90]

But for Gifford, even after several defeats, the bombast continued. He was determined, he told Nettie, "to go out of office here with head up and tail over the dashboard, instead of oozing out of office as so many Governors have done." Among others, he directed his wrath at Philadelphians. Speaking in Independence Hall, he contrasted the Americans who, in their revolution 150 years earlier, had overthrown British tyranny to the current city citizens' toleration of vote stealing by a "gang tyranny." "Does the blood of Philadelphians today run less warm than that of their ancestors?" he asked pointedly. "Why don't the people speak?"[91]

The coup de grace of these excoriations was his farewell address to the general assembly. At the end of his speech, he ripped into his opponents, saying he was leaving office "with the hearty contempt not only for the morals and the intentions, but also for the minds of the gang politicians of Pennsylvania." Besides Vare's corruption, he attacked the Mellon and Mitten machines (which controlled the Philadelphia transit system), castigated the "respectable element" for joining "organized crime" in supporting the city regimes, and railed against "great monied interests" controlling state politics, while the "people got little more than crumbs which fell from the rich men's table."[92] Needless to say, he received strong applause only from his supporters.

As he explained to his sister about his address, "I really had a great time writing it, and even more fun delivering it. You ought to have seen the opposition squirm." There are a few memorable presidential farewell addresses, but fewer by governors are remembered by anyone except true devotees of state political history. But Governor Pinchot's final speech to the legislature was one. It was a veritable jeremiad combined with a ringing call for reform, and its fighting, defiant tone suggested he would compete for political office again. As if to counter any doubts, he commented as he prepared to leave the governor's mansion, "There is no good-bye to it. I'll be back."[93]

19.

Women's Aspirations

As Governor Pinchot's battles with entrenched business and political elites starkly revealed, the 1920s were inhospitable to reformers. Amos Pinchot, except for unsuccessfully promoting his transportation-resources proposal and supporting Robert La Follette as the Progressive Party's presidential candidate in 1924, mostly stayed closer to home, writing opinion pieces for magazines and newspapers, to which he had added a book project, a history of the Progressive Party from 1912–1916.[1]

Ruth and Amos were enjoying their new daughter, Mary, born in 1920, and he remained involved with the education of Gifford 2nd and Rosamond. For his last two years of preparatory school, Gifford 2nd had enrolled at Philips Exeter Academy. In 1922, he was accepted at Yale. Amos also made sure that Rosamond spent her allotted two months each year with him, usually during the summer at his and Ruth's house at Grey Towers.

Even before her parents split, Rosamond had an unstable childhood. Because of Amos's and Gertrude's travels and participation in their activist causes while she was young, she had often been looked after by a governess or Mary, Amos's mother. Mary had warned Amos of her interest in the Yale students at the forestry summer school during a visit to Grey Towers when Rosamond was only about seven. "You are going to have your hands full with that bewitching little coquette of yours," she warned. "I am afraid she is going to be too fond of attention, especially from men, to whom she is irresistible and probably will be. Her flirtations with foresters are amusing now, but she will soon be getting too conscious of their admiration."[2] It was an accurate premonition, as Rosamond craved affection and was an attractive girl. Except for her older brother, she had had no special playmates while staying at Grey Towers, and her identification with the quiet atmosphere likely reinforced the introspective side of her personality.

A fledgling teenager when her parents divorced, Rosamond adored her father and called him Dole, or Doly. Rosamond lived with her mother in Manhattan and attended the exclusive Miss Chapin's School on the upper east side, so Amos likely saw her on occasion. She enjoyed swimming and loved horses.

For her last two school years, she entered the Ethel Walker School in Simsbury, Connecticut, in 1921. For a private boarding school, Walker's was a logical choice. It was not far away, so Amos and Gertrude could occasionally visit her. He also knew the town well, most recently from Gifford 2nd as a student at Westminster nearby. Moreover, Amos's own Aunt Nettie, now eighty, would occasionally invite Rosamond to a meal at the old Eno house in Simsbury, where she lived part-time each year. After one of these visits, Rosamond confided to her dad, "Aunt Nettie has been very sweet to me. She may use horrible perfume and have horrible taste but she has a very kind and pleasant hospitable atmosphere in her house. She really is remarkable for a woman of her age."[3] Amos would visit Rosamond sometimes and send her fruit, sweets, and newspaper articles for her current events class.

The Ethel Walker school was a poor match for Rosamond, who was perpetually homesick. She would write in her second year, "I just dream of New York all the time." She disliked the "dreary" school routine and the strict rules, which kept her "on bounds" because of poor grades or a messy room. "Oh how I hate the place!" she complained. Even the food was "so awful and dull." In a rebellious moment, she sprayed some girls with water and was grounded again, which only depressed her.[4] Rosamond participated in sports but had little appreciation for Walker's emphasis on study and learning. She knew she was no student. "I really can't go to college." she wrote her father, "but I will work."[5]

After graduation, Rosamond and Gertrude went on an extensive sightseeing trip to Europe. She had blossomed into a beautiful woman. Five feet, ten inches tall, long-legged, lithe, and svelte, with blonde hair cut close and gracefully sculpted facial features, she turned heads everywhere. Not all the looks were adoring, however. Among those who ogled her, the Italians were the worst. "I can't imagine more unpleasant people than ordinary Italian men," she commented; "they follow us, talk to us and make the most absurd eyes at us. . . . Of course I can't go out alone at all."[6]

The voyage back on the *Aquitania* in late October would be a life-changing experience for Rosamond. On board was Max Reinhardt, an innovative Jewish theatrical director from Austria, who was on his way to New York to oversee a religious pantomime play called *The Miracle*. After a European tour, Reinhardt decided that he would bring the play to the United States in 1923.[7] Americans,

Prominent among young Rosamond's athletic interests was her love of horseback riding. Undated photo. (Rosamond Pinchot Papers, Library of Congress)

he pondered, might be tired of vaudeville and the follies and would be ready for more serious fare.

Despite many auditions, Reinhardt had found nobody suitable to fill the role of the nun, a central character. But when he espied Rosamond on the *Aquitania*, he, not an English speaker himself, had his assistant ask Rosamond to meet with "Professor Reinhardt" about a part in the play he was preparing for the New York theater. Rosamond replied candidly that she was only nineteen and had no acting experience, but the next morning, she and her mother showed up to hear Reinhardt's and the assistant's presentation about the plans for the December opening of *The Miracle* at the Century Theatre in Manhattan.[8]

The Miracle was about a bored young nun lured into leaving her convent by an evil piper. During her wanderings through haunting landscapes over seven years, she has many exhilarating and depressing adventures before she returns to her cloister and is forgiven by the Madonna despite her sinful ways. The script was wordless except for the nun reciting the Lord's Prayer at the end, thus realizing the redemptive message of the play.

Reflecting on Reinhardt's offer, Rosamond made a decision. It was, she later wrote, "a great chance. . . . The one thing that stood out clearly in my mind was that I wanted the part of the Nun more than I ever wanted anything else before." She soon told Reinhardt that she wanted the part, even begging until she cried. Reinhardt, understanding her interest, replied simply, "sehr gut."[9]

Rosamond's parents were prepared to defer to Rosamond's determination, under proper safeguards, to give the acting trade a try. Amos, serving as her agent, would negotiate the terms of her employment. A contract was deferred until Reinhardt received the approval of his producer and publicity director, Morris Gest, in New York. When Gest discovered that Rosamond was from a prestigious New York family and the glamorous daughter and niece of two wealthy and well-known namesakes, including a sitting governor, he needed no prodding to hire her. Gest was a publicity hound, and he soon leaked Rosamond's name and her upcoming role to the press, and interest in the play swelled.[10]

Amos drove a hard bargain with Gest. He learned that Rosamond, as the liberated nun, would be required to do a lot of tiresome prancing on the set. He thus arranged for an understudy as a substitute for two to four performances a week. He also exploited Gest's craving for her publicity value. During the negotiations, he noted that "With the exception of Reinhardt, [the managers] are a very rotten lot, cold blooded exploiters, who care nothing for art, nothing for beauty and lack every quality of mercy. The only way to deal with those people is to kick them as soon as you get in the room, and very hard. Then they develop a very high regard for you."[11]

Rosamond began rehearsals, and the theater interior had been radically transformed into a gothic-style cathedral. The set was a tour de force, and the play became an elaborate, three-hour-long pageant. Throughout the performance, there was incidental music by the opera composer Engelbert Humperdinck played on an organ sometimes accompanied by invisible choirs, an enormous cast, which kept reappearing in exotic costumes, and elaborate choreography. "The result," Reinhardt affirmed, "was such a spectacle as this country had never seen before."[12]

Opening night was January 15, 1924. Amos and Gertrude were there, but Ruth was in a nearby hospital, having given birth that same morning to her second child, Antoinette (Tony). Both mother and baby were doing well, and

Amos soon wrote Nettie, "This has been a terrific week, between the events at the Sloane Hospital and the Century Theatre." The reviews, if sometimes dismissive of the play and its fantastical storyline and obscure symbolism, approved of the scenery and the acting. Amos was especially pleased that two major New York newspapers, the *World* and the *Times*, were "enthusiastic" about Rosamond, the latter complimenting her "naif animal grace and physical vitality," while her "passionate utterance" of the Lord's Prayer at the end was "both richly emotional and intelligently phrased."[13] Leila Pinchot was also in the audience. She had befriended Rosamond during her many visits to Grey Towers and regularly corresponded with her. Sharing their common interests in horseback riding, they had a good relationship. Leila was ecstatic about Rosamond's "wonderful performance" and a few days later was still "seeing lovely pictures of her [acting] in my mind."[14]

The Miracle, with Rosamond in a starring role, had a successful New York run for nearly a year. The play then went on the road to Cleveland. Her parents consented to the travel, but Rosamond disliked the city and found the daily acting boring. Was she going to become a stage actress by profession at a young age, especially when her livelihood did not depend on it, and she might do better exploring other interests? Rosamond and Gest failed to agree on a new contract, and her father supported her decision to leave the production. Rosamond thought she was done with *The Miracle,* but Reinhardt soon prevailed upon her to perform her role again during the Salzburg festival that summer. He owned a castle there where he sometimes put on plays, and he was a co-founder of the festival in the town. Upon her return home, she acted in another play in Rochester and New York City, with Morris Gest again the producer, but she was not sure she wanted to be a professional actress.

*　*　*

Despite her fast-paced social life, Rosamond was not enamored with New York City, nor did she enjoy living with Gertrude, whom she found too conventional and fussy. The country atmosphere of Grey Towers attracted her more. Part of it was being with her father, but she also enjoyed horseback riding and walking alone. In June 1926, after the final performance of a New York play, Rosamond drove out to Grey Towers and took a long walk deep into an isolated meadow.

"All ugliness, all hurry, all heat seemed so far away. I feel happier than at any time in months. . . . It was hot so I took off all my clothes. What a marvelous feeling! I ran around the meadow like a horse, jumping over azaleas and watching my shadow. . . . I started off to the woods. The wind and sun were warm and I ran along. There was a chance of meeting someone but that didn't make any difference."[15]

Rosamond was a sensitive, lonely romantic, finding inner peace in her natural surroundings.

She soon took a train to San Francisco. Her trip was an act of independence, and she admitted, "I have no idea how long I will be gone or what I am going to do." However, she was now twenty-one, a seasoned traveler, and had some general thoughts. One was to experience other parts of the work world on her own. And running away from her life as a Broadway star, she arrived in the Bay city with an assumed name, Rosamond Peters. She purposely brought only a few hundred dollars with her, forcing her to seek employment. Living first at the YWCA, she scanned help-wanted newspaper ads, and she confided to her diary, "I fixed my hair in points the way all the girls do here, and I put on my hideous little straw hat over my eye." When she was dressed, "I looked awful, particularly when I slumped over in the approved fashion."[16] Suitably frumpy, Rosamond found a job peeling peaches in a cannery staffed mostly with Armenian women workers. She shared an apartment with two other women, took courses in shorthand and typing, and bought an old Buick so she could explore other parts of California.

The Armenian women got suspicious of her urbane habits, such as wearing rolled silk stockings, and newspapers soon publicized that she was in San Francisco and perhaps had given up acting. Her car trips eventually took her to Los Angeles, where she found a job as a photographer's assistant. She wrote Amos enthusiastically about earning her own living, and he informed Nettie that Rosamond was having "a great experience which will teach her many things about life which she could get in no other way, certainly not by hanging around New York and going to parties."[17]

Morris Gest, the producer, told Rosamond that she was still under contract, and he asked her to play the role of the nun again in *The Miracle*, which was on a cross-country tour. He finally caught up with her in Los Angeles and sent her a shawl as a kind of peace offering. Her resistance softened, and she reluctantly consented to perform as the nun in the play during its local run. She also took the part of Hippolyta, queen of the Amazons, in Max Reinhardt's production of Shakespeare's *A Midsummer Night's Dream*. She returned to New York in the winter of 1927.

Reinhardt persevered and recruited Rosamond one more time to play in *The Miracle* in Dortmund, Germany, and Salzburg that summer. Once again, her performances drew acclaim. At Dortmund, she badly sprained her ankle during marathon dress rehearsals just hours before the performance, but after getting a shot of medicine, she ignored the doctor's orders and acted her part, exhausting dances and all, and fainted afterward. Her fortitude impressed the cast, and the *New York Times*, learning of her injury, headlined "RP Saves 'Miracle'." She was the "heroine" of the hour and had performed, the story went on, "with a dramatic verve that lifted the German audience," who did not know about her accident, "right out of their seats." In Salzburg, she received reviewers' praise for her acting in *A Midsummer Night's Dream*. Speaking her lines in German, the reporter marveled, "served to emphasize the amazing scope of the young girl's talent." Her "talent," in this case, was a tribute to her determination to become fluent in the language. She had taken German classes at Ethel Walker and had supplemented her recent contacts in Germany and Austria with German-speaking lessons.[18]

Upon her return to New York, Rosamond began seeing William Gaston, a Harvard-trained lawyer who, hoping to become a successful playwright, was abandoning a law career. She had met Bill at a Beaux Arts ball in New York City two years earlier, and they had stayed in touch. They had certain common interests. They both knew the theater scene, and, seven years older, Bill seemed worldly to Rosamond, and he was tall and strikingly handsome. With her own father a writer, she could perhaps more easily identify with an aspiring wordsmith like Bill Gaston. On a personal level, he was a good conversationalist with a magnetic quality that could make the introspective Rosamond feel comfortable with him. He also came from an old, wealthy Massachusetts family with deep roots in the Democratic Party. His grandfather had been mayor of Boston twice and had been elected governor. His father, William A. Gaston, called "the Colonel," had been a Harvard law graduate and had held public positions until he narrowly lost the U.S. Senate race to Henry Cabot Lodge in 1922.

Rosamond, awestruck by Bill's good looks and seeming self-assurance, did not consider that he was also self-centered, irreparably alienating his father. The Colonel mostly objected to Bill's stubborn pursuit of playwriting that was, he believed, distracting him from public service and tarnishing the family name. If Bill Gaston had some talent as a playwright, it did not show in his first effort. When his play, *Damn the Tears*, opened in New York in January 1927, critics dismissed it as a "grasping effort," a "conglomerate and heterogeneous mess," and another asserted that "it drove about one-third of its friendly first night audience, by twos and fours and half dozens, out into the ugly sanities of thirty-fifth street."[19] Colonel Gaston also had not approved of his son's flings with various women—earlier, Bill had secretly married and divorced another actress. The last straw occurred shortly before the Colonel's death that July when he discovered that his son had become part owner of a speakeasy in central Manhattan. In his will, he left nearly everything to his other son and two daughters, and Bill would have to make his own way in the world.

Rosamond was in love and remained committed to Bill, and on January 26, 1928, they were married in a small civil ceremony near Philadelphia. Amos and Bill's mother attended. Hearing details about the ceremony over the phone from Leila, Gertrude commented that she was "as happy" as Amos and wanted to meet Bill and "see Rosamond actually in love and happy."[20] After a honeymoon in Canada, the couple settled in a penthouse flat in midtown Manhattan.

One of Bill's few assets was Crotch Island off the coast of Maine, which he had bought in 1926 after the falling out with his father. The Gaston family had summered on the nearby island of North Haven, so he was familiar with the surroundings. His own small island symbolized his independence from the Gaston heritage. Crotch Island was rather remote and mostly deserted, but Bill felt a part of the island and the natural surroundings. Rosamond commented that he was "terribly fond of it. I believe he knows and loves every stone." Enjoying country living, she also appreciated Crotch Island, calling it "a lovely place" and liking "such a quiet healthy life." Their time together on the island was idyllic, Rosamond wrote her father. "Bill has been awfully sweet and really made everything very nice."[21]

*   *   *

Meanwhile, Ruth Pinchot was trying her hand at journalism again. Her contribution was an essay in *The Nation*, which ran a series of articles on the "modern woman." Ruth wrote about her rebellious childhood and emerging feminist views, but now comfortable as a wife and mother of two small girls, she perceived her feminism as "part of my age and perhaps nothing more. . . . I have traded my sense of exhilarating defiance (shall we call it feminism?) for an assurance of free and unimpeded self-expression (or shall we call that feminism?)."[22]

Ruth's article was anonymous, but she shared it with Leila "because," as she told her, "I love you and want you to know what I've been and what I do." Leila liked the article, and the two women began exchanging views on women's current status. The suffrage movement had provided the intellectual and emotional glue that united women in a common cause, but once achieved, feminism seemed to splinter in different directions. Leila and Ruth's views suggested the diverse, unfocused feminism of the era. Ruth affirmed that women were asserting their independence, but there was no social movement, and Leila argued that it was not so much male opposition as women's timidity that hindered feminism. "[W]hy in heaven's name," she complained, "don't women get out and make the world the way they want it instead of sitting and bemoaning about conditions and biological facts[?]"[23]

Encouraged by Ruth, Leila wrote her own essay, which was soon published anonymously in the series. After recalling her early assertion of her independence and her marriage, she constructed a grand vision of what the feminist movement could achieve. She was the modern super-woman who did it all, and so could others. She allowed that childbearing and childrearing could delay female aspirations for a time, and she vaguely recognized the need for "constructive action" to realize women's economic independence. Her optimistic perspective was very idealistic, however, and offered no program for advancing women's status in the working world and public life generally. Indeed, she simply affirmed boldly in conclusion, "My feminism tells me that women can bear children, charm her lovers, boss a business, swim the Channel, stand at Armageddon and battle for the Lord—all in a day's work!"[24]

Ruth and Leila were drawing closer, but almost immediately, the issue of prohibition threatened to push them apart. Right after Gifford's governorship, the brothers planned a fishing jaunt with their sons to Florida, but a potential problem was that Amos would bring liquor with him. Again, Slattery was involved.[25] When he heard about the upcoming Florida trip, he sent Amos a letter firmly asking him to give up alcohol for the fishing event. He told Amos that "the Prohibition crowd, largely a low grade outfit in the South at least," was engaged in indiscriminate searches looking for alcohol, and the downside from getting caught was too great a risk to take any with them. Slattery argued that Amos would not want to give political enemies a chance to damage the Pinchots' public reputation, but he was trying to protect Gifford, who might still have a promising political future.[26]

After Slattery's warning, Amos became, Ruth noted, "too uncomfortable" and gave up the trip. However, Amos told Slattery only that because of his absence, "the 'buzzard [prohibition] agents' are still sharpening their beaks in vain." The incident nonetheless disturbed Ruth. Unknowing of Leila's earlier attempts to enlist Slattery's assistance in besmirching Amos's reputation, she argued in a letter to her sister-in-law that Gifford had pursued a "round-about method" of approaching his brother about the problem, and Amos too had been "cowardly" in not telling Gifford personally. The result, she intoned, was pent-up, repressed animosity rather than direct and honest "give and take" between them, and "it is profoundly important to the happiness of both of them that they have a deep—and expressed—understanding." Ruth had a point. Normal sibling rivalry could become destructive unless the brothers could find a way to express their divergent views. It is unclear whether Amos and Gifford had a heart-to-heart talk, but at least Ruth's clear-eyed intercession may have eased the fraternal tension.[27]

As an anti-imperialist, Amos continued expressing his views opposing U.S. military and economic interference in Latin America, from which he pressed for the early withdrawal of U.S. occupying marines.[28] And he also gathered materials on the rise of big business and monopoly in America. It is unclear whether he was starting another book project or, for his Progressive Party history, expanding its scope to try to document an intimate nexus between predatory banking and business interests and the Theodore Roosevelt and George Perkins party leadership. Either way, the new research likely deflected him from completing the first history and was not sustainable if Amos had undiagnosed high-functioning bipolar disorder. That may have been the case then, as Amos, finding himself rundown, went off to Santa Fe, New Mexico, for five weeks with Ruth and their two daughters.

It was a pleasant respite, and only one issue distracted Amos—the trial and execution of Nicola Sacco and Bartolomeo Vanzetti. The two Italian-born anarchists had been arrested, convicted, and sentenced to death for killing two men during a robbery in a Boston suburb in 1920, and time was running out for the condemned men.[29] Amos fired off a statement from his Santa Fe retreat, which was read at protest demonstrations in New York and Boston. Like many supporters of Sacco and Vanzetti, who had continued to profess their innocence, he criticized the inquiry and the Massachusetts governor for trying to justify the conviction instead of looking carefully at the facts of the case. In consequence, despite the "doubt and disgust" with the verdict, "we are about to see executed two men innocent of the crime charged and denied the retrial which would long ago have been granted them had their social beliefs not been repugnant to the judicial and political authorities of the Commonwealth."[30] All such arguments and appeals were in vain, and Sacco and Vanzetti were executed on August 23, 1927.

A year later, Amos learned that his and Gertrude's son, Gifford 2nd, was engaged to a French girl, Janine Voisin. Married two months later, the newlyweds and her parents booked passage to New York to introduce the bride to his parents and other relatives.[31] Gifford 2nd (sometimes called Long Giff to distinguish him from his namesake and his shorter and stouter cousin, Giff) had dropped out of Yale after his sophomore year and taken courses in the science and engineering curriculum at Columbia before enrolling at L'École Polytechnique in Paris. He met Janine Voisin in the French capital. Voisin was a household name in France. Janine's father was Gabriel Voisin, a famous aviator who, a quarter century earlier, had been right behind the Wright brothers in successfully flying man-powered gliders. Before the Great War, he had founded airplane and automobile companies. The French Air Force, during that conflict, owed a good measure of its aerial successes to Voisin's skills as an inventor and engineer. In the 1920s, with demand for airplanes down, his firm produced luxury cars.[32]

The marriage of Giff and Janine, both from wealthy families with French names, was perhaps not so remarkable. Janine was only eighteen—eight years younger than Gifford 2nd—and had ambitions to become a musician or an actress. Another aspiring woman had joined the extended Pinchot family, and the newlyweds would have to sort out whether they would live in France or America and handle the ensuing personal and social adjustments.

*   *   *

Following his Florida fishing trip, Gifford wrote a history of his four years as governor. It was a personal account of his fight against bossism and corruption in Pennsylvania, and "the gang" was in the title of all but a few of the thirty-three draft chapters. The writing was often angry, and the purple prose probably served as a cathartic release for Gifford. But publishers, concluding that the manuscript displayed more heat than light, quickly rejected it. A few years later, Gifford asked noted historian Charles A. Beard to look at it, and Beard bluntly told him that his language was unnecessarily vindictive. Gifford accepted the criticism. "My story," he wrote back, "was written when my temper was still hot from the four-year fight, and I am sure I can greatly improve it by reducing the billingsgate."[33] But Gifford, involved with other matters, would never return to it.

The next presidential year was 1928, and politics would absorb the attention of nearly all the Pinchots. It would first preoccupy Leila, who wanted to run for office. Her choice was the congressional seat comprising five counties in northeast Pennsylvania, including Pike County, where Grey Towers was located. Her opponent was Louis T. McFadden, a small-town banker. He had already served seven terms and seemed too entrenched to dislodge in the Republican primary.

Moreover, women had only modest success running for Congress so far: eight had been elected to the house, and only one was from an eastern state (New Jersey). If anything, by the late 1920s, female success in politics was

Gifford and Leila at Grey Towers, sometime in the 1920s. (USDA Forest Service, Grey Towers NHS)

declining.[34] But Cornelia Bryce Pinchot's electoral chances were arguably as good as any woman's. She had money, was a proven energetic campaigner from her husband's previous races, and had some name recognition as a former first lady of the state. She also had a competitive spark and loved the game of politics. "It is a merry life, this political one," she had earlier written Ruth, "and I really enjoy every bit of it—the downs as well as the ups."[35]

Leila well knew McFadden's political strength, telling Nettie that he "has all the money he needs . . . and still has the Gang with him. However," she added, "it is fun to try, and I might get in."[36] Gifford helped as she launched a vigorous campaign. Her platform continued Gifford's, emphasizing prohibition enforcement, "clean" government, aid to farmers, and keeping the Sabbath. With memories of the suppression of civil liberties in the First World War, Leila advocated free speech and consulted Amos for ideas and examples.[37] She urged women's more active participation in public affairs and touted her involvement in education, winning election to the local school board and displaying a real interest in pedagogical concerns ranging from classroom discipline to improving teacher pay.

Leila received endorsements from the Pike County party chairman, the Anti-Saloon League, the presidents of the WCTU and the AFL, and county prohibition enforcement groups. She also featured Theodore Roosevelt in her campaign literature, claiming he had said that Cornelia "knew more about politics than any other women among his friends" and that he had "consulted her frequently on public affairs."[38] Leila argued that McFadden was unsympathetic to farmers' problems and criticized him for voting three times in Congress against veterans' benefits. Still, she exposed nothing serious against McFadden that might capture the public imagination. The incumbent's organization pushed back by disparaging Leila as a woman upstart out of her league in politics.[39]

The prosperous times surely worked in favor of the incumbent, and McFadden prevailed in the primary. An anti-feminist bias among the electorate may not have hurt Leila's chances, and she won Pike County by a large majority, took a neighboring county, and even carried McFadden's hometown of Canton, but she lost almost everywhere else. Overall, she garnered forty-six percent of the vote and more votes than McFadden had received in the previous primary. She more than held her own against her opponent, and Gifford claimed she was beaten "by the Pennsylvania Railroad, the Lehigh Valley Railroad, the big bankers, and the Pennsylvania state machine."[40]

Bill Gaston also got involved in the political game. At the end of his and Rosamond's Maine honeymoon, Bill returned to Gotham, where he found a job with the campaign of New York Governor Al Smith, the Democratic Party's presidential nominee, who was running against Herbert Hoover. Bill's position was the head of the Negro division, and his assignment was to get out the black vote for Smith nationwide. Rosamond was unsure whether her husband's position was "rather thankless" or "very important," but he had his own office and "spends most of his time," she commented insensitively, "with coons." Rosamond also got involved peripherally. Serving the campaign as an "instructress" of women speakers, she taught them how they could most persuasively convey the Smith message to voters.[41]

A month before the election, her father composed a seven-page letter vigorously endorsing Smith. Amos liked that the nominee was a wet, and he lauded his stands on hydroelectric power and domestic reform. In his letter, he confessed his growing distaste for politics, but Smith, "frank" on all the important questions, had revived his interest in political reform.[42]

Almost immediately, however, Amos worried that the Democratic nominee had not clarified his position on the utility question. Specifically, he wanted to know if Smith was for public or private operation of the power plants, and he sent Smith and John Jacob Raskob, Smith's campaign manager, some literature on the subject. Amos may have sensed that conservative influences were steering the nominee away from a clear commitment to the utility question.[43] Raskob, in particular, was the wealthy chief financial officer of General Motors and a Republican conservative who had signed on as Smith's campaign manager, mainly because both men were confirmed wets.

Amos and the Gastons had committed themselves to the Democratic side, but Gifford had to decide whether to support Herbert Hoover, the GOP nominee. He applauded Smith's positions on electric power and farm relief, and a few Republican progressives, like Senator George Norris of Nebraska, believed that power was the "great fundamental issue," supported the New York governor. But Hoover favored prohibition, and Gifford, still a Republican, reluctantly concluded that he would "let the wet and dry issue decide my stand."[44] Gifford had even hoped to do some limited campaigning for Hoover, but newspapers reprinted Gifford's 1917 resignation letter criticizing Hoover's management of the food administration and his statement during a Hoover boomlet for the presidential nomination in 1920 that the engineer-humanitarian was "wholly unfitted to be President." Not surprisingly, Republican regulars had little use for Gifford's help in the 1928 campaign. Toward its end, he told Nettie, "I am doing what I can for little Herbie," but it was "a queer world and no mistake."[45] Hoover needed no such help and easily won the election.

20.

The Widening Horizons of Conservation

Besides politics in the 1920s, Gifford Pinchot was actively involved in two other projects. The first was his re-engagement with forestry questions. From the First World War era, he worried about the direction of professional forestry. He believed the forest service had lost its spirited leadership, and what he had considered the gold standard among federal agencies was in decline. U.S. forestry policy was in a state of transition. The national forests were essentially demonstration areas that showed how forest management under federal protection could work. But what about the vast acreage of private woodlands that lumber companies extensively exploited throughout the nation? Did the federal government have the resources and constitutional authority to oversee these timber areas, or should some regulations be devolved to the states? Implicit in these questions was the problem of industrial forestry, which now had the technology to cut vast swaths of timber in a short timeframe. How should the lumber companies be persuaded or required to prevent forest devastation and motivated to practice reforestation on these lands?

Gifford had become more pessimistic about the sustainability of American forests. Early in his governorship, he published an article in which he charged that Americans were "the most wasteful people in the world—wasteful in living, wasteful in manufacturing, and wasteful in handling their natural resources." As evidence from his own statewide travels, he cited the examples of several Pennsylvania towns that had boomed as lumbermen moved in to reap the plentiful supply of tree species, but they brought with them no forest renewal plan and cut everything in their path. With all the trees gone, these bustling communities, some of which housed a thousand people or more, became ghost towns almost overnight. In economic terms, the forest devastation had cost Pennsylvania dearly, which now had to import its lumber and other wood products. The same problem of forest depletion was occurring nationally. He emphasized that forest devastation was, more than an economic concern, a human problem that had to be dealt with as part of a broader social vision of serving the public good.[1]

As governor, Gifford continued his efforts to reverse the course of deforestation in the state. Besides initiating reforestation and fire control policies, in 1923, he helped draft an administrative code whose purpose was "[t]o provide a continuous supply of timber, lumber, wood and other forest products, to protect the watersheds, conserve the waters and regulate the flow of rivers and streams of the state, and to furnish healthful recreation to the public."[2] He also created a sanitation water board to enforce laws prohibiting pollution of the state's thousands of rivers and streams. Public health moved front and center as a priority in conservation. The lawyers in his administration upheld the board's regulatory authority to stop industrial waste from befouling water supplies and brought suit to stop a mining company from dumping mine-acid waste into a watershed and polluting a local reservoir. Moreover, encouraging cooperation with neighboring states, Gifford negotiated an interstate conservation agreement for the Ohio River, in which the signatories agreed to protect water supplies from tarry acid wastes.

These interests continued after his governorship ended, when he campaigned successfully for approval of his successor's initiative for a state bond issue to raise $25 million for state forestry projects, which would provide free hunting, fishing, and recreation for Pennsylvanians, rejuvenate wildlife, and have long-term public health benefits. In all these environmental endeavors, of course, his love of the outdoors and fishing informed his acute awareness of the supreme importance of clean streams and rivers.[3]

Given the complicated present-day web of local, state, and federal environmental regulations—and the continuing difficulty in assuring clean drinking water—these measures might seem overly cautious. Gifford and his legal team were careful not to demand too much from industry polluters, which might leave the state if pressed. And notions of effective federal action were still in the distant future. But seen as the first state initiatives, they were path-breaking in asserting the expanded responsibility of government oversight of environmental questions affecting public health.[4]

Still, Gifford focused on the big picture of national forest policy and was disturbed by its new directions. Chief Forester Harry Graves had initiated cooperative policies with state forest departments until he resigned in 1920. His successor, William B. Greeley, continued these practices but adopted a policy of greater cooperation and accommodation with the lumber industry. He and his supporters in the service viewed the lumber industry as depressed and believed it was impractical to force more restrictive forest policies on them.

Greeley, a skilled bureaucrat, shrewdly advanced his agenda for American forestry. But he had detractors, Gifford foremost among them, who disparagingly labeled the federal-state-private cooperative policy "Greeleyism." Gifford conceded that a small number of lumbermen supported forest conservation, but the great majority were focused on short-term profits. He had long argued that lumber interests were strong "states righters," since it was easier for them to dominate forest policy at that level. He warned that if the lumber interests gained control of four large western timber-producing states, they would, in effect, be in control of national forest policy. Greeley's cooperative policies with lumber associations and in support of enhanced state involvement made him a pawn of commercial interests. He asserted that the forest service leadership was, in short, supine, and being coopted by the lumber industry. Gifford understood that the strongest support for forest conservation still came from the eastern and industrial states, which served as a check on lumber's greater political strength in the major timber-producing areas. Urging federal authority over the forests, he supported a bill that Senator Arthur Capper (R-KS) first introduced in 1920, which imposed a tax on timber cut on private lands but rebated a large amount if it was cut in compliance with federal regulations.

Gifford's warnings about the influence of industrial forestry at the expense of a weakened forest service were astute, but criticism of statewide cooperation arguably went too far. Surely not just easterners but large numbers of westerners liked their parks and forests and believed in conservation. However, they had suspicions of Washington politicians, reasonable or not, and a determined insistence on some local control. Partly because of this ambivalence, the forest service leadership and many other conservationists supported educational and other conservation initiatives at the state level. The conservation of natural resources was a struggle for people's hearts and minds everywhere, and framing the issues as an "us" versus "them" dichotomy might only further alienate western opinion. As forester under President Roosevelt, Gifford had believed westerners generally understood the importance of conservation, but in the reactionary 1920s, he was losing faith in anything but a reinvigorated national forest policy without western support.

Forest policy in Congress was in a stalemate. Neither Capper's bill nor an alternative supported by Greeley got far in Congress, which passed a compromised

version of the Clarke-McNary Act in 1924. Greeley embraced the law, which
provided for federal-state-private cooperation in the protection of forests and
included incentives and tax benefits to private owners who protected forested
lands. It did not include provisions on the regulation of timber cutting.

Following his busy governorship, national forest policy again became
Gifford's major interest. In late 1928, Greeley resigned to accept a position
as executive secretary of a lumber company association, which was Gifford's
confirmation that Greeley was a willing lackey of that industry. His replacement as forester was Robert Y. Stuart, who had been Gifford's deputy in the
Pennsylvania forestry department and then its head when Gifford moved to the
governorship. Gifford emphasized to Stuart that the forest service, thanks to
Greeley's "poison" of putting the interest of lumbermen ahead of conservation,
had been declining for some years, and, further, Hoover's lack of interest in the
service and his ties to business interests meant that "the Service will be more
open to attack and weaker . . . than any time in its history." Vigorous action
was needed, he claimed, to reclaim popular support for forest conservation.
But Stuart's perspective was quite different. Concerning Greeley, he bluntly
stated, "I think he did a splendid piece of work as Forester." He also defended
"the strength and standing of the Forest Service" and used examples to claim
that forestry was definitely "progressing" in the states.[5] Gifford accepted state
actions and forest regulation on all levels of government but argued that they
were insufficient. He asserted, "We need a great expansion of public forests" to
prevent the destruction of private timber areas.[6] His forthright views may have
impacted Forester Stuart, who increasingly seemed to want to appease all sides
on forestry questions.

Gifford's emerging internationalist perspective on forestry during the Roosevelt presidency reinforced his negative views of industrial forestry. During the
1920s, he watched with increasing alarm as lumber interests despoiled large areas of forests abroad. He had concluded an article on Pennsylvania's ghost towns
by mentioning the experience of "decadent" China as "an excellent example of
what deforestation means." A year later, he spoke to the Pan American Union,
warning against the growing and uninhibited destruction of large swaths of
Latin American forests.[7]

Reinforcing Gifford's pessimistic outlook was his reconnection with George
P. Ahern, his former protégé, who had administered the Philippine forests for
fifteen years. After he retired from the U.S. Army, Ahern conducted his own investigation of the status of American forests and was appalled at the destructive
lumbering practices he found. The lumber industry, he admitted, was heavily

in debt, but its search for additional revenue prompted widespread ruthless cutting of more timber on private lands without much, if any, follow-up reforestation. The wanton forest devastation and loose regulation also contributed to the epidemic of major forest fires that wrought further forest depletion. A dangerous trajectory of the destruction of America's timber resources was at hand, he warned.

Working with his old friend, Gifford wrote the foreword to an Ahern pamphlet entitled *Deforested America*. Ahern's study presented many examples of the worsening deforestation and was severely critical of industrial forestry and forest service leadership. Ahern argued, for instance, that "The foresters at [Washington] headquarters should be held responsible" but "have fallen down on the job in failing to get the real facts [of deforestation] before the people." He charged, "Foresters and lumbermen offer nothing worthwhile to stem the tide of forest devastation."[8] Senator Capper, Gifford's ally, also helped, circulating 10,000 copies of Ahern's pamphlet as a Senate document.[9]

Gifford was initially pleased with its reception. Coolidge's lame-duck secretary of agriculture thanked him for publicizing Ahern's statement. Gifford reported to an old forest compatriot, Raphael Zon, that he and Ahern were "almost completely dazed" at the friendly reception to the pamphlet. "[N]ot a word was said in criticism but a lot in praise," he noted. Gifford believed that Greeley's "malign influence having been removed, the foresters were returning to what they had known all along was the right point of view."[10]

Despite that optimistic appraisal, Gifford knew that lumbermen, many advocates of Greeleyism, and perhaps Forester Stuart would push back vigorously at Ahern's savage indictment of U.S. forest policy. At first, it was the lumbermen. The National Lumber Manufacturers Association replied with a mimeographed paper entitled "Reforested America," which labeled the Ahern report misleading and asserted in an advertisement in the American Forestry Association's journal that the lumbermen were practicing good forestry. They offered free copies of "Reforested America" to readers. To Gifford, the advertisement was evidence that timber interests were now in control of the association and protested that the journal ought not to "hold its columns open for the dissemination of propaganda intended to facilitate the continued destruction of American forests."[11]

*   *   *

Toward the end of 1928, Gifford put agitation on forest policy on hold as he thought about a new adventure—a family trip around the world, part of which they would navigate themselves in a big sailboat. Whoever was elected president would not consider him for a cabinet position, so he, Leila, and Giff, now thirteen, were free to travel. Giff had enrolled at a private school, Avon Old Farms, near Simsbury, and his roommate was his boyhood chum, Steve (Stiff) Stahlnecker, the son of Gifford's aide and two years older than Giff. The Pinchots' son would graduate, however, when he was sixteen, which was too young for starting college, his father thought. Because of Gifford's consuming conservation work and governorship, Leila provided most of Giff's daily oversight, so her husband thought Giff was "terribly dependent on his mother." A year of travel with his father would be a good growing-up experience for him. At the time, Leila believed her husband's talk about a South Seas adventure was "just moonshine and conversation" and would never happen.[12]

Gifford's interest in an extended sailing voyage was a long-standing dream. He claimed that he and George Woodruff, while still in college, had vowed to undertake a sailing trip to the South Seas. Since then, he had sometimes investigated the purchase of a large sailboat for water journeys without results.[13] This time, however, he was determined in his search. He soon found a "wonderful" steel-hulled, 148-foot, three-masted, top-sail schooner for sale in New York and bought it.[14]

Why such a big ship? Gifford's priority was safety, so for a long voyage through open waters, he needed a large, seaworthy vessel with sufficient ballast in heavy seas. His purpose, however, was more than a yachting cruise. He wanted it to be a scientific expedition, with sufficient room on board for some scientists who would accompany them to study the flora and fauna of the many remote islands they would visit. The scientific-naturalist part would help justify the trip's high cost and make the voyage "ten times as interesting with a definite object in view." To his delight, the National Museum of Natural History in Washington, D.C., provided collection equipment, labels, and a long list of specimens it wanted from the islands the group visited. As Gifford had eagerly collected insects as a small boy, so would he now have a chance to relive that passion in the South Pacific. He also recruited a biologist, conchologist, ornithologist, and physician.

He refurbished and refitted the schooner with a new engine, sails, and seven smaller boats for exploring trips during their island wanderings. The ship's original name was the *Cutty Sark*, surely not one a teetotaler would accept, so he renamed it *Mary Pinchot* after his mother. In honoring her memory, he wrote, "The best thing we could hope from any vessel was that she would turn out to be the kind of ship that Mary Pinchot was a woman." Leila continued expressing doubts about the trip and decided to join them in the end, though she would be the only woman and did not come on board until the ship reached Key West.[15]

On board with the parents were Giff and Stiff Stahlnecker; the Pinchots' private secretary, Morris Gregg; and the perennial Harry Slattery for the first part. An inexperienced sailor, Gifford hired a captain along with a first and second mate, cook, engineer, and additional crew members for the journey. Altogether, more than twenty people were on board.

Mary Pinchot, the three-masted schooner that Gifford Pinchot purchased and outfitted for his scientific voyage to the western Pacific islands. (USDA Forest Service, Grey Towers NHS)

Leaving New York harbor on March 31, 1929, the ship sailed down the East Coast to Key West, then across the Caribbean Sea to the Panama Canal, and once in the Pacific Ocean, headed to the South Seas. The *Mary Pinchot* expedition lasted more than six months and included visits to several Caribbean islands, the Canal Zone, the Galapagos, French Polynesia, and Tahiti.

The entire venture was an enormous success. It was an intense educational experience for Giff, who learned first-hand about sailing, shells, assorted wildlife, and the native inhabitants of these largely unspoiled, remote places. The youngster also received close-up knowledge from informal lessons and conversations with the scientists on board. Fishing included encounters with sharks, porpoises, whales, tuna, giant rays, swordfish, marlin, and squid, and they also investigated snails, lizards, iguanas, and angleworms. Moreover, they identified and collected many new species of insects, reptiles, crustaceans, and birds and shipped a huge tortoise from the Galapagos to the National Zoo in Washington, D.C.

On the human side, Gifford remained a benign imperialist in lauding U.S. control of the Panama Canal. "Every American can be proud of what Uncle Sam has done at the Canal," he asserted. "What we have done there in honesty, efficiency, intelligence, and humanity of administration we can do anywhere else—on the same condition." Given his hero worship of Theodore Roosevelt, who orchestrated the U.S. takeover of Panama and boasted grandiloquently that "I took the Isthmus," perhaps Gifford could not comment otherwise.[16] But he was also becoming a cultural relativist to the extent that he was learning that modernity was not an unmixed blessing. He gained a deeper appreciation of the native peoples he encountered—from their dress, ceremonies, unique cuisine, and other customs, and especially their natural friendliness to him and his party everywhere.

Gifford's published account of the trip, entitled *To the South Seas*, faithfully told the story of the group's many adventures.[17] It was not quite complete, however, as it glossed over the serious difficulty that his party experienced with Captain Beale. The skipper was an experienced but careless navigator, failing to take soundings or post a crewman on the rigging as a lookout as they entered shallower waters, so the ship went aground three times before they reached the canal. The groundings damaged the rudder and jostled the engine loose from its moorings, and the resulting vibrations caused a cracked crankshaft, which delayed the trip for a month on the Caribbean side of the canal while the voyagers waited for new parts and repairs. In addition, the skipper seemed to have "a phobia," Leila believed, about giving orders and had no rapport with the crew. He was, in short, "largely impossible . . . a dead loss."

To Leila, the captain was only part of the problem, as the cook "was a silent[,] sullen, mysterious Dane" and "served food that would have been excellent in a Maine lumber camp in the dead of winter." When Leila learned he had contracted a venereal disease in Key West, she said he had to go. The first and second mates were, moreover, wholly lacking in leadership, uncooperative, and undisciplined. The entire situation was, in sum, "a Hell of a mess."[18]

Leila detailed these difficulties in long letters to Amos, and she worried the expedition might have to be abandoned. She even emphasized that her husband was at loose ends. "Gifford seems to be completely nervously exhausted—I've never seen him like this before." In fact, she claimed that the trip has "'blown up' as far as he is concerned—he hates it, hates everything about it and would only be too glad to have the ship sunk tomorrow, so that we could go home." In the absence of a sinking, they were looking for a good excuse "so as not to seem a quitter."[19]

A purpose of Leila's plaint was to ask her brother-in-law to recruit a replacement for the faulty captain if Gifford determined to continue onward. Amos, trying to be helpful, soon identified a qualified and willing sailing friend, whom Gifford accepted. After firing Captain Beale, new Captain Fred Brown undertook the long journey to Panama to join the expedition.[20] Leila soon noted approvingly that the replacement seemed "competent . . . and generally in command of the situation," and Amos also came up with a new chef and another doctor. Leila and Gifford both thanked Amos profusely for his successful actions. Leila later wrote him appreciatively that he had "pull[ed] us out of our hole . . . like a rabbit out of a hat."[21]

Gifford wrote Amos about the difficulties, describing the first captain as a "queer duck" and "evidently the victim of fits of depression" and criticizing him for his "slackness." He never expressed thoughts about cutting the expedition short, however, and none of Leila's sense of crisis appears in Gifford's writings about it. Of course, Leila exaggerated the problems because she was not enamored of the voyage and was prepared to abandon it. She adapted well to the island visits, exploring caves, taking hikes to learn about the vegetation, and interacting with the local inhabitants, but she was a landlubber, not a sailor. For instance, during the crossing of open waters in the Caribbean, her lone diary entry reads, "More damned sea." Even Gifford, who usually boasted about his wife, commented to Amos that "Leila is inclined to groan because of the shipwreck not's [sic] coming off." And Gregg, her secretary, reflected that Leila "is considerable as an actress you know," and she could overdramatize negative experiences to Amos as a way to get his help for their plight.[22]

Another purpose of the expedition was publicity. Gifford was never shy about promoting his views and achievements, and a popular story of the voyage, especially if the downsides were minimized, was in the same vein. The Pinchots took lots of photographs and brought five movie cameras and seven miles of film to document their adventures. The visuals and his book would help keep his name (and Leila's too) before the public and, given a positive spin as a scientist-adventurer, add another interesting dimension to his public persona.

Media outlets were indeed interested. During the voyage, Gifford sent home several descriptive accounts, some of which found their way into newspapers. The *New York Times* printed a full page of photographs showing the Pinchot family members investigating native wildlife. Following their return, a New York theater presented an edited edition of their film footage, which Gifford, Leila, and Giff narrated in person during the showings. The *Times* called it "a splendid film . . . beautifully photographed" and praised their "nicely worded talk." Leila soon arranged for a "talking" version of the film, which was distributed nationally.[23]

Gifford also hurried with the completion of his book. Already an accomplished writer of many magazine articles on the natural world, he told his story about the expedition in a popular writing style. It was published six months after his return home and had a respectable sale of almost 8,000 copies by the end of 1930. In addition, Giff would publish his own book about the trip, aimed at young readers, which would outsell his dad's. It was not altogether a coincidence that Giff's later professional career would be as a research scientist and that he would become an avid yachtsman, both interests fundamentally nourished by this sailing experience to the South Seas.[24]

* * *

Soon after they arrived in Tahiti, Gifford and family took a steamer to San Francisco and then a train to Washington, D.C. "Conservation work," he wrote in his book, required that he get to his Rhode Island Avenue home by early November 1929, and the *Mary Pinchot*, having to fight prevailing trade winds, would never make it in time.[25]

The conservation work involved his participation in the still-evolving controversy surrounding Ahern's *Deforested America*. The lumber industry continued attacking its premises, but many professional foresters also balked at its dire conclusions. Most forest service personnel closed ranks behind Forester Stuart and the current leadership. Gifford agreed that the forester was well-meaning but viewed lumbermen too optimistically as partners in industrial forestry. To

Gifford, despite some exceptions, lumbermen should be treated as adversaries. However, many of Gifford's longtime friends in the conservation movement, including Yale classmate Herbert (Dol) Smith, who was still public affairs chief in the service, also took a more moderate position. After arguing with Smith and getting nowhere, Gifford came away convinced that "he has the Greeley point of view in the worst way," which made "me angry enough to chew carpet tacks." Harry Graves also backed Stuart, and a report of the Society of American Foresters that December endorsed the forester's perspective. Afterward, a dejected Pinchot concluded that the Greeleyites "have lost confidence in the usefulness of the forest, and apparently have reached the definite conclusion that forest devastation is not worth worrying about." The Pinchot-Ahern faction nonetheless filed a minority report, which argued that the rate of deforestation over new growth had grown from four to six times in the previous ten years.[26]

Voluntary associations are often in tension between more moderate members interested in long-term educational goals and more activist supporters who see the need for urgent change. The tension can be constructive, even creative, if held within the bounds of civil discourse. Despite their disagreements, the foresters were professionals, civility prevailed, and Gifford and Graves remained friends.[27] The debate among foresters kept before them the fragility of American forests and the continuing question of how best to sustain them over the long term. The forest service soon would have a new chief forester who was in accord with Gifford's views, and with the nationalist perspective of Roosevelt's New Deal, Gifford would feel that forest policy was again in good hands.[28]

Another compelling reason for Gifford's return home from Tahiti was electric power, another form of "conservation work" but now of widespread public interest. When he earlier geared up for his struggle with the Pennsylvania General Assembly on the issue, he predicted, "there is many a years['] work in this thing." After the legislature killed all his power bills, he added, "it looks to me like war to the knife, and I am more than ready for it."[29] After his governorship, he gathered information from an investigation by the federal trade commission into the extensive propaganda efforts of the electric company trust across the nation in trying to stifle public criticism of its monopolistic power and high utility rates. "Nothing and no one is neglected," Gifford charged of their public relations efforts.[30] He followed with a pamphlet indicting the greed of the utility companies. In deference to Hoover, he delayed its release until after the presidential election but was prepared to battle with the incoming administration on the issue. As he told a friend, "watch my smoke on the electric question. . . . Hoover is just as wrong on that as the devil itself."[31]

As his comment suggested, Gifford wanted to be back home to participate in the political debates and perhaps run again for political office. During his absence, for example, Stahlnecker urged Gifford to run for governor in 1930 on the need for a strong utilities commission. Needing little prodding, Gifford replied, "My interest in what you have written is so great that I have temporarily lost interest in the trip because of it."

The political landscape was changing. Gifford arrived home right after the stock market crash in October 1929, and it gradually became apparent that the plunge in stock prices was a surface manifestation of fundamental structural weaknesses in the American economy. Businesses began to contract and lay off workers and went bankrupt in increasing numbers. Despite the growing economic hardships, Gifford saw the opportunity for political change. The collapse in share prices, he surmised, "had taken a good deal of the paint off" Andrew Mellon and regular Republicans. Further, he predicted, "the haughtiness of the old Gang was going to be quite considerably mitigated in the next few years," and he wanted to be "present when the mitigating takes place." Indeed, he said he could "smell the beginnings of a new Progressive movement."[32]

21.

Toward a New Deal

Launching his gubernatorial bid in early 1930, Gifford campaigned across the state and gave some radio talks, and Leila also gave speeches. His advanced reform program included old age pensions, unemployment insurance, and major improvement of country roads. His main issue was replacing the utility-dominated public service commission with a "fair rate board" elected by the people. He mostly avoided the prohibition issue, which was losing popular support.

Gifford benefitted from the continuing factionalism in the Republican Party establishment. William Vare's well-heeled organization put up its own candidate for governor, Francis Shunk Brown, a former state attorney general, who was also endorsed by the Mellon organization and W. W. Atterbury, now president of the Pennsylvania Railroad and a Republican Party national committeeman. Grundy, realizing his gubernatorial candidate could not prevail against the Vare choice as in 1922, had his man withdraw and threw his support behind Pinchot. Gifford charged that Atterbury, the head of a major business in the state, should stay out of politics, and as a national committeeman, he "violated the rules of decency" in taking sides in a party primary.[1]

Pouring a lot of money into the Philadelphia area, Grundy helped Gifford make headway against the Vare political machine. Gifford had a good organization in the rural districts and the Pittsburgh area to counter the Mellon forces, and he thought the up-state machine would prefer him to Brown. The coal miners backed Gifford's candidacy, and he made inroads among African American voters, who were more convinced that the Republican organization had not helped their race. With only a few weeks to go, Gifford mused, "I keep watching myself not to become overconfident."[2]

The entrance of a third Republican candidate into the gubernatorial contest nourished Gifford's confidence. Thomas W. Phillips, a former congressman and a wet, decided to run because Brown had straddled the prohibition controversy by favoring a referendum on the issue. Phillips likely drew many more voters away from Brown than from Pinchot. On primary day, Gifford was badly out-polled in the Philadelphia area but overall won sixty of the sixty-seven counties to win election by only 20,000 votes.[3] Gifford then assumed that because of the Republican Party's statewide dominance, he would easily win in the general election.[4]

But Vare's powerful Philadelphia organization, backed by Atterbury and other business executives and wet proponents, coalesced in a determined effort to defeat what they called "Pinchotism." Their strategy involved rallying behind Democratic nominee John Hemphill, a young Philadelphia leader of the movement for prohibition repeal, and painting Gifford as anti-business. Traditional Republican control of the Philadelphia area, by far the most populous in the state, was now in jeopardy.[5]

Now in for a real fight, Gifford campaigned furiously over the state. He stepped up his attacks on William Vare as the leader of gang politics and, taking his campaign into Vare territory, promised to support development projects in the Quaker city. "Is it not time for a new deal?" he asked presciently. "Is it not time to have the affairs of the Republican party in this city administered by public servants who are not willing to serve solely their own selfish interests?"[6]

He also forged new political alliances. A benefit of Hemphill's candidacy was that some dry Democrats rebelled and moved over to support Pinchot, including John McSparran, Gifford's gubernatorial opponent eight years earlier.[7] That Grundy, anti-labor and opposed to social programs, and Pinchot, the reformer, cooperated was a case of strange bedfellows finding a way to coexist for mutual political benefit. In a delicate tightrope, Gifford explained that he would accept the help of anyone who endorsed him and that not many people "think that I am in any way under the influence of Grundy or anybody else."[8] Gifford also had to deal with the Republican Party chairman, Edward Martin, an army general in the National Guard, who had an iron grip on the Republican organization in the state. Gifford had failed to oust him from the chairmanship. Fortunately, for Gifford's candidacy, Martin strongly believed in party loyalty, supported Gifford as the GOP primary winner, and argued to voters that Gifford's election would not harm utilities.

Pinchot prevailed over Hemphill in the 1930 election with a margin of 59,000 votes. His narrow victory was a remarkable triumph, and he would be the only candidate in Pennsylvania in the twentieth century to return successfully to the governor's chair for a nonconsecutive second term.[9] A *Collier's*

editorial touted the election of the "ascetic . . . Gifford the Spotless . . . as
something good for [Pennsylvania's] soul after too much of the Vares, Mellons,
Grundys, and pious Peppers." More effusively, *Christian Century*, a premier
liberal magazine, rejoiced that Gifford Pinchot "stands out today as one of the
political leaders with whom America must reckon. He has shown the heart and
arm of a warrior."[10]

The old party loyalties were fraying, and the championing by the GOP's
Vare forces of a Democratic gubernatorial candidate served as a precedent for
possible future party realignments.[11] Acknowledging the blurring divisions,
Gifford appointed McSparran as his secretary of agriculture. He made George
Woodruff the governor's adviser on public utility matters, again selected a
woman as secretary of welfare, and appointed capable Jews and Catholics to
judgeships and other high positions despite criticism. He also placed an African
American on the state athletic commission, the highest state appointment thus
far for that race.

*   *   *

Gifford's short inaugural address affirmed that his governorship would
represent "the plain people" instead of "the hidden forces" working undercover
for "a few." At the top of his legislative agenda was utility regulation, and he
asserted, "We have no more compelling duty than to destroy the corruption
upon which the power of the utilities depends."[12]

The GOP solidly controlled both legislative houses, the senate overwhelmingly, but conservative Republicans dominated the upper body. The president
pro tempore of the senate had the power to appoint members to that chamber's
committees, but he was loyal to the Philadelphia machine and had supported
Hemphill, and Gifford lobbied hard for his own choice. His loss of that contest
by two votes presaged the difficulties he would face in getting legislative approval of his reform program.

Utility reform went nowhere, as the uncooperative senate rejected the new
governor's proposal for a joint investigation of the utilities and stymied in committee the house bills framed by Pinchot loyalists, which would have abolished
the public service commission and allowed the governor to appoint members of
a new fair rate board.[13] Gifford denounced the senate for its "most contemptu-
ous defiance of public opinion" and charged that the Republican organization
was now "owned and operated by the public utilities."[14]

Ultimately, Governor Pinchot found a way around the recalcitrant legislature to bring about utility reform. Benefitting from several resignations and

term expirations, he appointed new members more sympathetic to his goals and exploited a scandal involving the commission's chairman, who soon resigned his position.[15] Among those Gifford appointed to fill the vacancies were close allies George Woodruff, Clyde L. King, and Steve Stahlnecker. By the fall of 1932, the governor had a clear majority on the commission.

His success was more apparent than real, however, and Gifford and King, both strong-willed and temperamental, soon quarreled. Gifford wanted quick decisions upholding the public interest. King preferred a more deliberative commission and grew resentful of Gifford's attempted interference in the commission's work. Their disagreements escalated into name-calling.[16] A second problem was that the senate failed to confirm any of Gifford's five nominees until four months before the end of his term. It would be a pyrrhic victory, however, as the incoming Democratic administration would abolish the public service commission and create its own.[17]

*   *   *

By the summer of 1931, unemployment rushed to the fore to supersede utility reform. Even before his inauguration Gifford perceived the growing jobless numbers as a government concern. He appointed a committee composed of a spectrum of citizen and economic interests to develop relief plans. The failing national economy increasingly disturbed the governor, and he commented to Nettie, "People are angry in this country . . . and I think we will have trouble before the winter is out."[18]

Unemployment in the state had risen sharply to nearly twenty-five percent by July 1931, and many employees were now working fewer hours. Miners, particularly in the depressed western coal fields of the state, were upset at their low wages and went on strike. Their families endured a miserable existence, subsisting on a diet of dried beans and no milk. Even a coal industry president admitted that "the children are starving in our coal district." Communists took control of the strikes in some areas, and a miner's wife commented, "Sure I'm a Bolshevist, and so's my old man and my four kids. . . . You'd be a Bolshevist, too, if you didn't have enough to eat."[19]

Concerned about the rising rebelliousness and frustrated at the Hoover administration's inadequate response to the unemployment crisis, the governor became impatient. Private charitable groups proved unable to keep up with the massive levels of assistance required, and much of the funding of poor boards by the state was spent ineffectively. The county and local governments had pitiful financial reserves, and the state constitution forbade appropriations for direct relief (food, clothing, shelter) and limited the state's indebtedness to $1 million.[20]

How to get around these limitations bothered Gifford, who wanted to spend much more and go into debt to alleviate the problems of hunger and homelessness. He always believed that government should provide a human face and meet the people's basic needs in desperate times. As it was, he strove to maximize funding for unemployment relief, which within the constraints of a balanced budget meant severely limiting other government expenses. Calling an extra session of the legislature, he stressed the urgent need for state action. "The Declaration of Independence tells us that the right to life, liberty, and the pursuit of happiness is inalienable," he intoned. "But in an emergency like this that right means nothing to millions of men and women unless it carries with it not only the right to live but also the right to work. For the right to work is included in the right to live."[21]

During the special session, Governor Pinchot proposed the creation of a state commission on unemployment relief, which individuals would fund for relief purposes by purchasing "prosperity bonds" at four percent interest. He also urged legislative enactment of a two-percent emergency tax on gasoline and taxes on cigarettes and billboards. Altogether, he wanted to raise $35 million for relief.[22]

The legislature eventually appropriated $10 million for the poor boards to be spent on direct relief. Its proponents in the house argued that, despite the state constitution's ban on direct relief, the bill was a justified use of the state's police power. The senate went along. The legislation provided no taxes, however, to fund the measure. As one critic of the lawmakers noted at the time, "They want to give the money and at the same time create no present burden," and Gifford labeled the session party chairman "Martin's folly" and a "fraud on the people."[23] The state supreme court upheld the direct relief law but ordered the government to take $10 million from other government programs to keep within the state's constitutional debt limit.

Another relief measure involved hiring the unemployed in a road construction public works program. Gifford had campaigned on the issue of "taking the farmers out of the mud," and at the outset of his governorship, he persuaded the legislature to transfer control of 20,000 miles of the 73,000 miles of rural roads to the state highway department, which had more resources for their upkeep and improvement. More substantively, he initiated an extensive road-building program to improve transportation for farms and small towns in the state. The new roads were paved, though of rudimentary construction, and some were only one lane wide. Still, they accomplished the governor's stated purpose of "more miles of good road rather than fewer miles of faultless boulevards."[24]

Anticipating the later Civilian Conservation Corps in the federal New Deal, Gifford established work camps for road construction. His priority was creating jobs for the neediest, most able-bodied persons, and he ordered the placement of several camps in the eastern and western rural coal counties where unemployment and homeless rates were highest. He firmly overturned instances of political favoritism involved in hiring decisions. The laborers worked out of these camps, which had canvas tents where the workers slept and ate their meals. The number of applications escalated, but the $1 million debt ceiling greatly limited the scope. The road camps were, at best, a makeshift program allowing many unemployed people to get temporary work and nourishment for their bodies.[25]

Gifford increasingly turned to the federal government for assistance. As a TR progressive, he thought in national terms and urged the U.S. government to provide financial relief to the unemployed, because the crisis was nationwide and well beyond the capacity of private charity and state and local governments. During the summer of 1931, he went on a nationwide speaking tour, and his main message was the need for more aggressive federal action on unemployment. In a major address in Detroit, he argued that unemployment was a nationwide human problem. "[T]he only power strong enough, and able to act in time, to meet the new problem of the coming Winter," he emphasized, "is the Government of the United States. This is a national emergency. It is a national calamity as well. The nation must help to meet it."[26]

By mid-1932, unemployment in Pennsylvania from the deepening depression had reached 1.11 million (plus 800,000 working only part-time), and about a third of the state's population lived in households with no income. In the face of this widespread reality, it was more difficult to believe that prosperity might soon return.[27] But well-rooted American values of self-reliance, individualism, and voluntarism worked against the quick development and expansion of government relief programs. The state's revenues derived mainly from real estate taxes, and many property owners resisted assuming a heavier financial burden. The predominant mood in the legislature was for economy, even retrenchment.[28] Still, Gifford continued exhorting the legislature to provide adequate unemployment relief funding and strategizing with its leaders and federal officials in cobbling together workable reform packages.

At a subsequent special legislative session, he announced that $60 million for unemployment relief was needed for the next year, even though that amount would only provide qualified earners about $5 a day, which was below the minimum level for food for a family of three. Again, the overriding priority was assistance to destitute families. "Let it never be said of this great Common-wealth that it turned a deaf ear to the cry of the hungry. . . . The honor of the Commonwealth demands a different reply." He also warned that the growing restlessness might lead to rioting and bloodshed.[29]

Pennsylvania had no state income tax, and instituting one would require a time-consuming amendment to the state constitution, and Gifford did not press the matter.[30] The lawmakers soon passed a one percent emergency sales tax for six months, estimated to bring in $12 to $15 million, and doubled the $10 million for relief that the legislature had earlier passed. The governor objected to the regressive tax, but needing state revenue, he allowed the measure to become law.

He also requested $45 million from the Reconstruction Finance Corpora-tion, which Congress had recently established to provide unemployment relief and financial aid to the states. The RFC would give Pennsylvania about two-thirds of that amount, and Gifford insisted on the "honest" dispersal of basic necessities to the needy without regard to color, sex, creed, or "politics."[31]

Gifford did not like special legislative sessions, which cost the taxpayers more money and resulted in stalemates on issues. However, he gave credit for the legislators' accomplishments, and at the end of the special session, he announced, "The General Assembly did its work promptly and well. It made $20,000,000 available for relief without additional tax and guaranteed that no one will go hungry in Pennsylvania. . . . I congratulate them."[32]

*   *   *

As the 1932 election approached, Gifford, who had presidential aspira-tions, convinced himself that regular Republicans, among others, believed that Hoover could not be the nominee and would lose the election if nominated. He said, of course, that he was not a candidate, though claiming support in every state. Senator Norris announced that Gifford was "an excellent man and I am for him five hundred times more than I am for President Hoover." No one among other possible progressive Republican candidates from western states openly opposed Hoover's renomination, so theoretically the field was open for a challenge from Gifford.[33]

Because of speculation about his supposed presidential ambitions, Gifford went out of his way to say that the "nation has come to a pretty pass if a man cannot say what needs to be said in the public interest without being charged with a political intention."[34] He nonetheless created files of speeches he might deliver as a presidential contender, the dates of the primaries, and the names of the delegates to the previous GOP national convention and the Republican state chairmen. More audaciously, he drafted a letter, which he persuaded his old Midwest progressive ally, Harold L. Ickes, to send out under his own name to Republican leaders nationwide, arguing that Gifford Pinchot "would carry the next Presidential election just as surely as Hoover would lose it."[35]

The replies were profoundly discouraging, however, and Ickes commented to Gifford, "Republicans are going to take their licking lying down." Gifford agreed, and in June 1932, Hoover would be nominated on the first ballot at the GOP convention.[36] In Pennsylvania, the Republican organization recently affirmed its dominance of the party machinery when the senate incumbent had drubbed Pinchot's choice in the primary—General Smedley Butler, his old ally in enforcing prohibition. A discouraged Gifford commented afterward that the "church people" had not supported Butler and prohibition. "Some cynic once said," he wrote Ickes, "'The preacher and the pimp finally vote the same ticket.' . . . I am not so sure he isn't right. The hold the over-rich have on the pious is something to make angels weep."[37] Doubly disillusioning, Leila again challenged Congressman McFadden in the primary but lost, this time more decisively.

But then, the Democratic Party's presidential nomination of Franklin D. Roosevelt buoyed Gifford's spirits again. Franklin and Gifford were friends. In early 1912, young Franklin, as chairman of the senate forest, fish, and game committee in New York State, had invited Gifford to give a lantern slide lecture on conservation in the assembly chamber. Two slides particularly impressed Roosevelt. One was the reproduction of a painting created about 1500, which depicted a city in northern China nestled in a valley surrounded by mountains teeming with luxuriant forests, with a stream running down the hillside through the city. The other was a photograph taken of the same spot some four hundred years later showing a desert, with only rocks on the mountains and no grass or trees, the city below in ruins. Over time, the Chinese had decimated the trees for their use and profit without practicing reforestation and soil conservation. Roosevelt took the message to heart and would recall Gifford's two slides again as president to emphasize the importance of the conservation measures he was then championing.[38]

The two also revered FDR's distant cousin Theodore and his example of activist government. And in the early 1930s, as governors of adjacent states, they cooperated in initiating and hosting conferences on the surging unemployment problem with officials from other states, and the two met again at a governor's conference in Indiana.[39] As a Republican, Gifford did not openly endorse Roosevelt for president and commented only that he "voted for the majority of the Republican ticket" in the election, but he sent FDR a congratulatory letter on his election victory. He did not want a "job or anything else," Gifford claimed, but offered "to come a runnin'" to Washington if he could help. FDR soon reciprocated by inviting the Pinchots to his inauguration. And when the president-elect narrowly escaped an assassin's bullet, Gifford cabled him, "Thank God you are safe. The Nation needs you right now."[40]

The link between their spouses was arguably closer, as Leila and Eleanor had gone to dancing school together as children and shared a commitment to the Women's Trade Union League as the core organization for improving women's

Neighboring Governors, Franklin D. Roosevelt (New York) and Gifford Pinchot (Pennsylvania), at a governor's conference, Fort Lick, Indiana, June 2, 1931. (Franklin D. Roosevelt Library)

working lives. When Eleanor visited Harrisburg shortly before the presidential inauguration to give a speech on malnutrition, Leila hosted a highly publicized "relief" dinner for her and about fifty guests that she purchased at a nearby "model" community market at a total cost of only $2.72. Mrs. Roosevelt was reportedly "pleased" with the meal.[41]

*   *   *

Leila's dinner for the future first lady was part of an experimental program in which the state provided funds to local relief agencies that distributed staple necessities to citizens without money. The program served a real need, but the publicity of the Roosevelt dinner backfired. Critics noted that the announced cost figures did not include the beverages, butter, dessert, and condiments served to the guests, and the hamburger, which Leila had ordered, had been cooked by a French chef. More criticism of the program followed, and Gifford allowed it to expire.[42] In any event, Pennsylvania's relief needs still went far beyond such experiments. For 1933, Gifford estimated that the state would require $125 million for relief. The legislature managed to cover more than half that sum, and Governor Pinchot asked the RFC for another $45 million. In late 1933, with the imminent end of prohibition, the state had the prospect of more tax revenue from liquor sales. Accepting the inevitable, Gifford called another special session of the general assembly to work with "sincere wets" in establishing control policies that would minimize the evils of alcoholic beverages. Among other measures, the legislative response was the establishment of state liquor stores, but liquor sales were disappointing.

In the last months of his tenure, Governor Pinchot sparred with officials of the Federal Emergency Relief Administration over relief payments to Pennsylvania until a new legislature convened in January 1935. FERA was an early New Deal agency providing major financial aid to states. It covered relief costs in Pennsylvania through March 1934 but required the state to meet its obligations beyond that. President Roosevelt personally appealed to Governor Pinchot to get his state to provide its share. Gifford pushed back and cited statistics showing that Pennsylvania, with some federal help, had so far met its relief costs, contributed a larger percentage share of the costs than thirty-eight other states, and, in absolute terms, spent more on relief than any other state except New York, which could more easily borrow money. His figures were correct, but after March, the state contribution to relief had dropped precipitously. Harry Hopkins, FDR's aid administrator, would not budge from FERA's position, and Gifford had to call another special legislative session to approve more relief dollars. The general assembly appropriated the necessary funds and adjourned without discussing repayment, which was left to the next legislature.

Despite the continuous struggle for funding, Gifford could be fairly satisfied that the Pennsylvania legislature had met its relief obligations. And he could be proud that there was no hint of scandal or mismanagement in spending the immense sums of money for relief. He had hired competent, dedicated administrators, and federal officials were unstinting in their praise of the management of the relief programs in the Keystone State.

*   *   *

Besides accepting the end of prohibition, Gifford agreed to the legislature's weakening of the state's blue laws during his governorship, and he no longer censored movies as during his first gubernatorial term, which might undermine conventional morality. It could be said that the demanding social and economic issues of the depression precluded his attention to the old cultural norms. But in acquiescing to these social changes, Gifford accepted a modern reality. Indeed, he went further, championing free speech for teachers and academic freedom in higher education, whether on the left or right. Amos's and Leila's emphasis on free speech had likely nudged Gifford toward his more liberal position, and the social upheaval and rising anti-Semitism convinced him that repression bred intolerance, hatred, and disloyalty and that free expression was necessary for a democratic society.[43]

In Gifford's first year as governor, the legislature passed a modest reduction in maximum working hours for children. In 1932, the Democrat representation in the house in Harrisburg nearly tripled, which was promising for reform. Although still a minority party, many Democrats backed the governor's social programs, and at the end of the legislative session, Gifford wrote President Roosevelt of the Democrats' welcome support. The president let Gifford's Democratic allies know about the governor's "awfully nice letter" and approved their cooperation with him.[44]

Another promising development was that the Republican machines in Philadelphia and Pittsburgh, stung in the election, became more amenable to social legislation. With the Pinchot Republicans and Democratic support, the prospects for major social and economic changes in the legislature seemed fairly bright in 1933. Gifford challenged the state's lawmakers, "If the Republican leaders once more betray the welfare of the many for the special interests of the few, voters will rightly demand a complete reorganization of the Republican Party in this State."[45]

The legislature responded by appointing a "sweatshop" commission to investigate labor conditions for women and minors in the state. One of the governor's appointees to the commission was Leila, who provided a personal liaison to the governor and a dynamic presence on the investigatory body. From her long involvement in women's labor problems, Leila was at home on such issues. While serving on the committee, she joined striking workers in picket lines in several places where the sweatshop commission met to dramatize the workers' grievances. An ally was Charlotte E. Carr, Pinchot's deputy secretary of labor and industry, often with Leila at these demonstrations. When the governor increasingly relied on Carr's counsel on labor issues, the alienated secretary of labor resigned in protest in August 1933. Gifford then promoted Carr to his position, and the legislature grudgingly approved her appointment. The governor now had two women cabinet members.[46]

The commission's report exposed the shocking conditions in many sweatshops, with employees sometimes working for fourteen cents a week. Using this information, Governor Pinchot demanded minimum wage legislation for women and the abolition of child labor. The assembly overwhelmingly approved a minimum wage bill for women and children, but the senate defeated it.

In the 1933 session, the legislature again supported old age pensions, but the senate rejected other reform legislation. When Republican chairman Martin exerted pressure on his party's legislators to pursue economy instead of "new fields of governmental activity," Gifford angrily retorted with an international analogy: "The Jews in Germany today are receiving little worse treatment from the infamous Hitler than Jews and Gentiles alike of the working classes have received and are receiving from the Republican Organization of this State." And after the legislature again balked at social legislation later that year, Gifford once more roasted his opponents: "The special session . . . shows that sweatshops and the money lords still control General Martin and that General Martin still controls the Senate."[47]

*   *   *

Gifford Pinchot was for human rights and not just property rights. "It is better to help the small man make a living than to help the rich man make more money," he said. "I fought for him in Pennsylvania. That's why labor is so friendly. I appreciate such friendship." He believed in labor's "Sacred right of protest" and was determined to "safeguard the right of 'collective bargaining,' and advance sound social legislation."[48] "I'm with you 100%," he told an AFL gathering in 1932. Two measures during his administration were promising. One was the passage of an anti-injunction law in 1931, which prohibited judicial restraining orders until an open court hearing and no other law had permitted it. Two years later, he approved a measure outlawing the "yellow-dog" contract, in which a worker agreed not to join a union as a condition of employment.[49]

The hard times had made workers more conscious of their plight, and encouraged by friendly administrations in Harrisburg and Washington, they became more determined in the last half of the Pinchot governorship to improve their working conditions and bargaining rights. The creation of the National Recovery Administration (NRA) in 1933 accepted collective bargaining and labor's right to organize, and many more strikes occurred when workers began asserting their rights.

The greatest difficulty was western Pennsylvania's bituminous coal industry. The UMW aggressively recruited miners and claimed that their union was the sole bargaining agent under the NRA legislation. Besides the resistant coal companies, an obstacle to unionization was the so-called "iron police," a practice in which some county sheriffs appointed deputy sheriffs who the coal companies employed. Company executives had long used these special, private forces to intimidate and even terrorize recalcitrant miners. Having objected to this practice in his first administration, Gifford vowed to change it during his second one. A coal strike in 1931, resulting in some violence and a few deaths, further highlighted the problem. The governor's proposed legislation to put these "industrial police" under the control of the state police failed, but he denied sheriffs' authority to hire such deputies, and the practice gradually subsided. He also tried to make the state police more impartial during labor controversies when intervening in workers' peaceful protests.

The governor's opponents often accused him of inciting radical behavior among workers and abetting communist infiltration of the labor movement. Gifford was no socialist, although he still considered a possible state takeover of the mines if the owners stonewalled improvement in the miners' rights and working conditions. He privately admitted that small groups of communists agitated against their employers, but he deplored opponents who branded all workers as radicals. "A lot of people in this country seem to believe that any time anyone stands up for one's rights that in itself makes him a Communist," he complained.[50]

Despite his outspoken sympathy for workers, Gifford tried to limit labor agitation. In 1933, the UMW began a protracted strike against the H. C. Frick Coke Company, a "captive" coal mine controlled by the United States Steel Corporation.[51] The strike spread, and soon thousands of workers, wielding pool cues, baseball bats, and, in a few cases, guns, were marching in picket lines and setting up road blockades. A county sheriff assembled armed deputies and asked the governor for state police reinforcements, but Gifford demanded the sheriff withdraw his deputies first. When the sheriff declined and banned labor from assembling and picketing, the governor called out about three hundred National Guard troops, insisting that they maintain the same kind of neutrality that he had imposed on the state police.

During the impasse, Gifford asserted that he was committed to collective bargaining and accepted strikes only after direct negotiations had failed. "Not all strikes are wise" or "right," he commented. "Most of them could be avoided entirely by conference and mutual understanding." Peaceful picketing was acceptable, but he also said, "The mine operators have a right to protection of their property."

Union leaders assured him they would give advance notice of their meetings, marches, and picketing activity. The violence declined, but the president of the Frick Company refused to negotiate with his union counterpart. The NRA law complicated the tense situation, which, the UMW insisted, required mining companies to bargain collectively with them. Still, some owners, disagreeing with labor's interpretation of the statute, refused to comply. Governor Pinchot unsuccessfully sought federal mediation, the Frick Company refused to recognize the UMW, and confrontations escalated. To Gifford, the blame lay squarely with U.S. Steel, which, he privately fumed, was willing to countenance settlement of the strike by violence.

In the end, cooler heads prevailed. At a mass meeting of thousands of strikers, Gifford asserted that "90 per cent of the shooting and head-cracking . . . was due to the brutality of company-owned deputy sheriffs," but he warned the strikers, "keep the peace. . . . If you resort to violence then I am against you. . . . Don't put me in a place where I must fight against the men I want to help."[52] He wrote Roosevelt the next day, "You would have been deeply touched to see how these people believe in you. They had a parade four miles long, and it was dotted all over with pictures of you as the miner's friend."[53]

After the parties finally accepted collective bargaining, Gifford expressed his true sentiments to Nettie: "The miners have been simply wonderful," but the "swine of a Steel Trust" acted "like nothing so much as a vicious small child . . . cheating, lying and doing its level best not to prevent trouble but to create trouble."[54]

*   *   *

By 1934, the last of his governor's term, everyone assumed Gifford Pinchot would challenge David A. Reed, the Republican incumbent and bitter opponent of the New Deal, in the upcoming election. Gifford's candidacy would give the party voters a clear-cut choice between an arch-conservative and a reformer. With political change in the offing, the New Deal successes and his gubernatorial achievements could boost his chances. Martin and the Republican Party organization were united behind Senator Reed. They had opposed much of the governor's reform program and were motivated to try to deny legislative achievements that the governor would tout in his senate campaign.

A good example was the highway program. Gifford had worked assiduously to assure the success of his highway building program in rural areas, and he said, "The Highway Department is the greatest relief organization in Pennsylvania."[55] His critics complained that the governor had diverted funds from basic relief needs to road construction.[56] Gifford also used federal RFC money for his road building programs, as was allowed, and resisted efforts to transfer such money from his highway projects to basic relief. Obviously, work relief projects cost much more per worker than the dole, but Gifford argued that most highway funding came from gasoline taxes and motor vehicle registrations and licenses, so those driving on the new roads were paying for them. In addition, he stressed that the highway program had employed more than 80,000 laborers and reduced the burden on the unemployment relief rolls. To its supporters, too, there was the morale factor, whereby those employed valued the worthwhile work they were doing, and more highways were necessary infrastructure for a citizenry that was taking to the automobile as its customary mode of transportation.

In 1933, the senate rejected Gifford's initiative for the state highway department to take over the remaining 53,000 miles of township roads. Perhaps, some thought, the opposition did not want Gifford, who was eyeing the U.S. Senate seat in 1934, to receive additional credit for his road program.[57] As one conservative critic wrote, "Gifford will pave his way to the Senate yet, even if he has to put macadam on every cowpath in the State to do it."[58] In any event, the governor had the last word, as the system of new roads was a physical presence that could not be denied. For generations, Pennsylvania's rural folk would use the term "Pinchot road" to identify with his handiwork.[59]

Over New Year's 1934, Gifford came down with a severe case of shingles, a debilitating illness. Indeed, Leila informed Rosamond, "It's so painful that he has to have [a] wire netting frame to keep the clothes from touching him."[60] During his enforced hospitalization for almost three months, Leila stood in as acting governor, and she would become the unofficial manager of his upcoming senatorial campaign. By the time he recovered, there were only five weeks until the primary election, but Gifford threw himself into the contest, attacking Senator Reed as an "errand-boy of the Mellons."[61] Leila, fully energized, barnstormed around the state, giving speeches, and organized labor was generally behind him.[62]

On election day, Reed received nearly 100,000 votes more than Gifford, who carried Allegheny County, Mellon's power base, but was outpolled in other areas, especially badly in Philadelphia. Had shingles not incapacitated him for a time, Gifford, always an effective vote-getter, would have launched a well-focused, statewide campaign. The result surely would have been closer, but whether he could have won is speculative.

* * *

After the primary, Amos regretted that the defeat of his brother, almost sixty-nine, "makes me pretty sad, because this is probably his last chance for the senatorship."[63] But Gifford and Leila soon sought a cooperative arrangement with the Democrats that might give him another chance for Reed's Senate seat. The Democratic primary victors had been George H. Earle for governor, from an old-line Philadelphia family and most recently the U.S. minister to Austria, and Joseph F. Guffey for senator. The prospects for their success in the general election in a traditionally GOP-dominated state, however, were most uncertain. Some political prognosticators believed that the Democratic nominees would need not just the backing of Pinchot and independent Republicans to prevail but also the substitution of Pinchot for Guffey as their candidate for the U.S. Senate. The scheme presumed that Guffey, despite his long, faithful party service, might be a lackluster candidate and hurt the Democratic ticket.

Gifford turned to Secretary of the Interior Harold Ickes as a liaison to get FDR's intervention for his Senate bid.[64] The scheme started well, and initially, Ickes believed that Gifford, a more able and committed reformer, should be the preferred Democratic senate candidate. More than Gifford, Leila intensively sought Ickes' support, and she spearheaded the effort to get her husband on the Democratic ticket.[65]

She sent Ickes a telegram, talked to him on the phone, met with him in Washington, and followed up with a long letter summarizing her case. Citing primary figures, Leila argued that Guffey "has perhaps a thousand-to-one chance of winning" in November. Moreover, despite their different parties, Mellon, Guffey, and Reed were conspiring with powerful business interests in the state to discredit Gifford and his agenda of liberal reform. Leila further contended

Governor Pinchot breaks ground for a new rural road in York County, Pennsylvania, July 23, 1934, one of several "Pinchot roads," as they were called, that were constructed in the state during the Great Depression. (Pennsylvania State Archives)

that Guffey had promises of patronage from Reed and Mellon, which he would receive regardless of the winner in the election. Gifford soon made much the same plea to Ickes.[66] Ickes relayed the Pinchots' entreaties to the president and told him that he preferred having Guffey withdraw from the race. FDR refused to get involved, however, and Ickes wrote in his diary, "I wish the President had made [Guffey] get off the ticket."[67]

Nevertheless, Gifford continued pursuing the seat. He openly praised FDR and the New Deal and intimated that he would support candidates professing progressive principles, but under no circumstances could he accept Guffey. Two controversial episodes later that summer revealed the tense situation. The first involved Earle and his wife's visit to Grey Towers for lunch. Leila was there, but the governor was away. Leila's and Earle's later accounts of their meeting were totally in conflict, but both parties at Grey Towers were likely interested in bargaining. Earle hoped to get Gifford's endorsement of his gubernatorial candidacy, while Leila's price for such endorsement was the substitution of Gifford for Guffey as the Democratic Senate candidate. The second controversial episode was Leila Pinchot's announcement that she had decided to run as an independent candidate for governor. It was surely a fantasy to think Leila would have any chance in the election, but she might draw some women's and labor votes, which would otherwise go to Earle. Her prospective candidacy could be seen as another ploy to pressure the Democrats to accept her husband as Guffey's replacement. If that happened, then she would quit her race. The Democrats seemed unmoved, however, and six weeks later, Leila withdrew as a candidate.[68]

By September 1934, the Democratic Party leaders that united behind Guffey began their final campaign push for their ticket. James A. Farley, FDR's political adviser and Guffey's friend, came to Pennsylvania and announced that if Governor Pinchot supported anyone for the senate, it would be Guffey. Gifford, not unreasonably, resented the Democratic operative coming into Pennsylvania and telling him, the governor of another party, whom he should support. Then a month before election day, Earle, correctly believing that Gifford would repudiate the Democrats, charged that at their Grey Towers meeting, the Pinchots "had the nerve" to make "the shameful proposition" of dropping Guffey from the ticket and "to take on Gifford Pinchot as the Democratic candidate for Senator." Leila rebutted that it was Earle who had offered Gifford the Senate slot on the ticket in return for the governor's support for his own gubernatorial campaign. Gifford claimed he had two Democratic witnesses to confirm his wife's version of the Grey Towers talk, and he called Earle "a fool and a liar."[69]

Whatever the truth behind these bizarre events, Earle's blast at Gifford freed him from further cooperation with the Democrats. Gifford did an about-face by attacking George Earle and Joe Guffey. His refrain, "I can't stand Guffey," labeled him a Democratic machine politician rather than a reformer and no more preferable than the Republican state bosses he had been fighting. While Gifford did not openly endorse Senator Reed, his attacks on Guffey indicated he preferred the election of a rabid anti-New Deal Republican. A week before the election, Gifford explained to FDR why he could not support the "utterly unfit" Guffey and Earle. Among the complaints, he cited Earle's refusal to join with him and other state party leaders in a September meeting with federal officials to get bipartisan agreement on state funding for relief without having to call an extra legislative session. Squashing that hope, Earle stated, "I refuse to be a party to any sell-out of the taxpayers of Pennsylvania." As Gifford told FDR, "Earle's unprovoked, fantastic, and inexplicable charge that I was selling out Pennsylvania taxpayers . . . set a new mark for cold-blooded attempts to play politics with human misery."[70]

In the end, the Democrats made no changes on their ticket because, as Roosevelt later intimated to Gifford and Leila, "the Pennsylvania Democrats were so certain of victory that they declined to consider any coalition." A common theme in all these political shifts and personal attacks was that Gifford had a consuming desire for the Senate seat, and Leila would run interference for him.[71] Roosevelt accepted Gifford's defense of his break with the Democrats but questioned his implicit support of the anti-New Dealer Reed. And Ickes, who had come to accept Guffey as a loyal Democratic "lamb," concluded that Gifford's fervent chase for the U.S. Senate had distorted his judgment. However, he was willing to give him the benefit of the doubt as he blamed Leila as the more aggressive Pinchot.[72]

It turned out that the Democrats' confidence in their party was well placed, as both Earle and Guffey won their contests, and their party swept the other statewide races. Gifford's late attacks on Earle and Guffey seemed to have had little effect on reform-minded Republicans, many of whom likely voted for them. Earle exulted in the Democrats' victory, commenting, "They say we rode in on Roosevelt's coattails. Hell, he carried us in piggy-back."[73] The 1934 election was indeed historic as the first instance in a midterm election where the president's party had increased its numbers in both houses of Congress.

The lust for power can reveal unlovely aspects of the human personality, and in Gifford's mind, the end goal of a seat in the U.S. Senate seemed to justify his dubious means. If he had succeeded in his quest, he would have become a Democrat closely allied with Franklin Roosevelt and the New Deal. His failure in 1934 squelched that transition and left him in political limbo. He had first entered the political arena as a man without a state and was now in danger of becoming a man without a party. But political careers sometimes take strange turns, and new domestic and foreign challenges would again bring Gifford closer to FDR and the Democrats.

In the longer term, Gifford could be well satisfied with the progressive direction he had given to Pennsylvania politics as, during the Earle administration, much of his unfinished agenda was realized. From 1935 to 1939, the state greatly expanded relief and public works, used federal aid to construct the Pennsylvania Turnpike, passed tax reform measures, and created a more authoritative public utilities commission. Moreover, lawmakers established minimum wage and maximum hours for working women and children and banned discrimination in some industries. Governor Earle also approved laws assuring labor's right to organize, allowed collective bargaining, banned company unions, encouraged reforestation, and approved construction of small dams for flood control and plans to counteract soil erosion.[74]

Collectively, these legislative achievements during the 1930s are referred to as Pennsylvania's Little New Deal. Historians writing about the changes enacted in the Earle administration have acknowledged that Governor Pinchot's contributions in defining and championing the many issues requiring urgent government attention paved the way for the state's later political and social transformation. Gifford Pinchot is a part of that enduring legacy, as subsequent Republican administrations accepted and expanded upon the reforms enacted during his and his successor's governorships.[75]

22.

From New Deal to
Anti-New Deal

By the late 1920s, Alan and Nettie Johnstone were in declining health. After the Great War, Alan retired as a man of leisure. He did not join Crinks on his political campaigns and preferred regular routines, such as enjoying drinks with friends. His health suffered too. In 1928, Nettie turned down Leila and Gifford's invitation to visit them, commenting that "Alan[']s health isn[']t quite up to it and I am afraid of the change for him . . . and I don[']t quite like the risk of cutting off his usual wine" in prohibition America. Alan soon failed precipitously and was committed to a nursing home, where he died in 1932, a month before his seventy-fourth birthday.[1]

Nettie also suffered periodic illnesses and was soon "too weak to see many people without great fatigue." She was too frail to attend Alan's memorial service, but Crinks, who had recently been reelected to the House of Commons, this time from a dockworkers area in Newcastle, represented the family. In her last years, she would appear for company resting on a chaise longue. She died at age sixty-five.[2]

The family deaths did not detract the brothers Pinchot from their political concerns. Amos's sore hip had become arthritic, so by the early 1930s, he walked with a slight limp, sometimes aided by a cane, but that chronic ailment did not limit his output as a writer. Like his brother, the changing political scene seemed to refresh and motivate him. The two men shared similar views on domestic issues, though Amos continued to focus on the economic side, while Gifford's outlook as governor was more political and humanitarian.

Herbert Hoover's distinctive public philosophy fascinated Amos, which he had articulated in a slim volume entitled *American Individualism* (1923).

"Now," Amos cogently observed, "a man's philosophy is perhaps the most important thing about him." Soon after Hoover's electoral triumph in 1928, he published an article in *The Nation*, arguing that Hoover's glowing portrait of the American economic system steadily developing the ideals of progressive individualism was faulty, and the nation's basic industries instead "are dominated by monopoly groups, which have so successfully warred on individualism, equal opportunity, and competition." And Hoover's election would "now guarantee big business and give monopoly and price-fixing a free hand."[3]

Oswald Garrison Villard, *The Nation*'s editor, liked Amos and appreciated his fine writing style. He joshed, "If you weren't so darned lazy, and so comfortably fixed in life, you could make a whopping reputation for yourself!"[4] Needing no prodding, Amos published nine articles over the next four years in *The Nation*, the premier weekly magazine of radical opinion. As he explained to Villard, his purpose "was not just to cuss Hoover, but to show how the great interests build up second rate men whom they control and get the public to vote them into power." His well-researched articles explored the web of utility executives, trade associations, banking interests, and Hoover administration officials in promoting power initiatives that would enrich the utilities.[5]

As the depression deepened, Amos, like Governor Pinchot, attacked what he believed was Hoover's woefully inadequate response to the rapidly growing problem of unemployment relief. He was a member of a citizens' delegation that called on Hoover at the White House in June 1930 to urge him to initiate public works projects. Without hearing them, Hoover brusquely dismissed their concerns and claimed that his consultations with business leaders had already assured him that production would not be cut. "Mr. Hoover," Amos concluded caustically afterward, "had disposed of unemployment. It was a wretched subject, anyhow. . . . We were bundled out of the White House into the sunlight of a world of things which we had just learned did not exist."[6] Another of his articles ridiculed Hoover's emphasis on private relief efforts to reduce citizens' suffering during the depression.[7]

Amos pegged Hoover as representing American producers but ignoring consumers. With the depression, he wrote, Hoover continued to spout the producer-first theory as the engine of prosperity (or what would be called "trickle-down economics") and maintained his ties with big business. The result, Amos argued, was an industry-Republican Party machine alliance and "a large amount of unfair advantage, privilege, and favoritism."[8]

He soon found stark confirmation of Hoover's failings in his insensitive handling of thousands of unemployed military veterans from around the nation, who traveled to Washington, D.C., in the summer of 1932 to demand immediate payment of bonuses for their First World War service. Called the bonus army, the veterans erected makeshift shacks and tents on the Anacostia flats just south of downtown. Congress rejected bonus legislation, and a few protesters were killed in an ensuing riot. General Douglas MacArthur, commanding the army, then exceeded his orders, invaded the bonus marchers' camps, dispersed the remaining settlers with tear gas, and burned down the shanties.

Amos's response was unusual, even for him. He dashed off a short two-act play, dedicated facetiously to "His Excellency" (Hoover). The play was a vicious satire of Hoover and his inner circle. Among the fictitious characters were General Goober (President Hoover), Secretary of State Blimson (Stimson), Secretary of Labor Dope (Doak), and General McJawther (MacArthur). The principals convened at the Blue House (White House), where they plotted the army's invasion of the protesting veterans and their hovels in nearby Anacostia. In the climactic final scene, General Goober directs the attack from the Blue House and watches the routing with glee. "Come on, McJawther!" he extols. "Sail into 'em. . . . Gas 'em, prod 'em, give 'em hell. . . . There come the tanks and the cavalry. . . . How those shacks blaze!"[9]

Amos's screed was his only venture as a playwright. He self-published his thespian contribution a week before the 1932 election and circulated it among friends, but it was likely never performed. His outrage at the president was too extreme—Hoover had actually tried to restrain his military leaders—for public enjoyment in a troubled time.[10]

*   *   *

As the election of 1932 approached, Amos considered the candidacy of Franklin Roosevelt. The fellow New Yorkers from similar social circles knew each other and occasionally corresponded. Amos sent the New York governor his article attacking Hoover's economic policies, which FDR found "delightful," and Amos wholeheartedly supported him for president along with other independent progressives.[11]

Amos joined Roosevelt in a New York hotel on election night. As the returns indicated Hoover's defeat, FDR "sat with the telephone receiver in his right hand," Amos later recounted, and "he was kind enough to put his left arm around me and say: 'Pinchot, we're going to have a truly liberal administration.'"[12] Amos soon argued in a speech, "the liberals are the only natural and sympathetic leaders of that hopeful and important forward movement which . . . is now revived," and "we ought to back Roosevelt up to the nth degree." Following the avalanche of New Deal reform laws in the first hundred days, he gave the president high marks: "Roosevelt is doing a magnificent job and showing wonderful class and courage." In early 1934, Amos was still "pretty hopeful about things in general."[13]

Of course, the first New Deal legislation, emphasizing business-government cooperation and a hodgepodge of relief and public works projects, did not meet Amos's perfectionist standards of the ideal political economy. He thus remarked, "I don't wholly believe in the philosophy behind the new deal," but he allowed that the administration confronted a national "emergency . . . and when we have twelve million people out of work, something must be done, whether it gibes with one's pre-conceptions or not."[14]

During this busy time, Amos wrote a series of bold, risky articles attacking Walter Lippmann, the acknowledged dean of American journalism. He was then writing for the Republican New York *Herald Tribune*, which circulated his syndicated column, "Today and Tomorrow," to more than 125 American newspapers.

Amos had occasionally exchanged ideas with Lippmann on political matters but had become increasingly put off by his ideas and the inflated impact he had on the public. Privately, he labeled him "the great stuffed shirt of American journalism. At once the prophet of Wall Street and the idol of the back country Babbitt, he is a real force for stupidity in American life." A serious correction was needed, Amos believed, and *The Nation* published his four articles about the journalist.[15]

Walter Lippmann's political thought had shifted over time, moving from a free-thinking socialist youth to progressive reformer, then advancing conservative views in the 1920s and, almost belatedly, endorsing the New Deal. Amos provided several examples to show, first, that Lippmann was inconsistent.[16] Another of his criticisms was that Lippmann's slick writing lulled readers into lazy acceptance of his banal pronouncements.[17] Amos Pinchot's larger point was that the journalist "has been fundamentally conservative on major questions for the last twenty years." Amos emphasized that Lippmann had depicted the owners of America's largest corporations as industrial statesmen who had hired far-sighted managers that eschewed the profit motive and were public-spirited. Amos disagreed. In his view, big business was "a cynical money-making machine." Its leaders required no deference, and Lippmann, allied with wealthy captains of industry, was "a salesman of plutocracy."[18]

Amos's hatchet job on Walter Lippmann was devastating—if you were a radical critic of conventional wisdom. Previously, Amos had been mainly the dissenter, opposing imperialism, militarism, war, and monopoly. Now, he was also the great critic, lampooning American elite figures of his era. And regarding American presidents, the consistent thread was that Amos opposed or broke with all of them, going back to the first Roosevelt.

Given such a course, it would not be surprising that FDR would become a target. That would indeed occur, but why the change? One explanation is that Amos was disappointed with the New Deal's constant shifts in policy. His strategy for expressing his mounting opposition to Roosevelt and the New Dealers was to write "open" (public) letters. In one of the first, he provided a fair description of Roosevelt's awkward juggling of the New Deal's dizzying experimentation with an array of different policy initiatives, but Amos, valuing consistency, found them sadly wanting.[19]

Another factor contributing to Amos's break with Roosevelt was that the continuing depression had badly hurt Amos's pocketbook. Increasingly impatient at the puny economic recovery, he had rejected the administration's recovery policies by 1935. He had taken a real hit from the stock market crash and suffered heavy losses in his real estate investments as many tenants in his apartment residences and business offices stopped paying rent. With his income stream drying up, Amos found it difficult to make his mortgage payments. Increasingly, he negotiated second mortgages with banks to reduce interest (and payments) on his loans.[20] To make ends meet, he borrowed from the Pinchot estate fund, diminishing his share of it.[21] His economic troubles continued, however, and Rosamond noted of her father, "He's very worried about finances."[22]

Amos did not specifically link the continued deterioration of his financial situation to his views on the New Deal's economic policies, but an undercurrent of initial hopes turning to mounting distress over his personal situation paralleled his growing disaffection with the New Deal. And during the presidential election of 1936, one of his main arguments against Roosevelt's reelection was that, despite all the New Deal initiatives, the U.S. economy lagged behind the depressed European economies in non-military growth.

Was Amos's family's financial condition really so desperate? Their situation was difficult, and they cut back on their opulent lifestyle and searched for new income sources. Ruth had earned an M.A. in English literature at Columbia, and with Mary and Antoinette (Tony) now in school, she had returned to work in the publishing industry. But though employable there, she did not prosper. She had three jobs, none of which lasted long. When Leila offered to sponsor her for membership in the private Colony Club, Ruth confessed that the cost was too high "[f]or a woman who is earning ten dollars a week at the most and who has no money besides and who is married to a poor man."[23]

Despite the cutbacks, Amos and Ruth managed to maintain the accouterments of an upper-class existence. They held onto their Park Avenue residence and cottage at Grey Towers, and Amos kept his office and secretary downtown. He also could afford occasional trips to California and Florida, and both daughters would be able to enroll at Vassar and graduate without apparent financial aid.[24]

Amos's confusing gyrations were nonetheless mostly consistent with his political philosophy, which was a finely tuned mechanism. Early in the New Deal, he pushed his program for the nationalization of the nation's natural resources and railroads since they were controlled by interlocking directorates of bankers and industrialists. Paul U. Kellogg, a respected social reformer, headed a group of liberals, including Amos, who were preparing a comprehensive reform plan to present to the Roosevelt administration. Amos, an active participant, objected that a draft program stated that the signers supported more planning and referred to the recently enacted Tennessee Valley Authority as "a great laboratory." Such language, Amos complained, would persuade readers of the document that its signers were "not for public ownership."

Kellogg replied, "you're all wet," and anyone would know that the TVA was a stellar example of public ownership. He criticized Amos's "grand house wrecking" position as unhelpful and for lacking a sense of humor and refusing to sign the committee's statement. Even his friend Villard told Amos that Kellogg "gave you just what was coming to you."[25]

In this contretemps, it might seem that Amos was a staunch socialist, but his nationalization proposals were severely limited. As he elaborated to a Roosevelt administration official, "I am one of the old brand of individualists. I don't want to see the railroads taken over as a step to socialism, but as a means of keeping equal opportunity, Billy [William Graham] Sumner's 'social chance', alive." Nationalization, he conceded, involved monopoly and price-fixing, but it was "allegedly in the interests of the public in general" instead of a few private owners.[26]

Here was the nub of Amos Pinchot's political dilemma. On the one hand, he supported a few socialist initiatives but exempted many industries, and he did not push for his earlier program calling for government takeover of mines and other natural resources. On the other hand, as a self-styled Sumner individualist, he expressed a clear bias against socialist programs that protected particular groups in society.[27]

Until late 1934, the dilemma was not obvious because he had joined others on the left, urging the Roosevelt administration to back unions and their bargaining rights. He had opposed the NRA as a step toward "regulation theory," but at the time, he supported workers who were using the labor provisions in the law to demand collective bargaining rights. Likewise, he told Roosevelt and others in his administration that unemployment insurance was "utterly essential" and "simply has to be enacted." His backing of laborers, however, suggested little emotional attachment to their cause, and he mainly hoped that these measures would result in higher wages and more purchasing power to stimulate inflation and lift the nation out of the depression.[28]

Amos wrote President Roosevelt, urging bold inflationary monetary initiatives to get "more new money and a very great deal of it in the public's hands," so that debtors could begin liquidating their fixed obligations. In reply, Roosevelt agreed "in great part about the need of more money in the public's hands, and I think it is on the way, though perhaps too slowly."[29]

Amos also joined a new group, the Sound Money League. The name was a misnomer, for the league leaders wanted an inflationary currency. They proposed taking control of the nation's money supply and credit away from the Federal Reserve Board and giving it to a new kind of nonpartisan central bank, which they called an independent monetary authority.[30] In 1934, Amos wrote long letters to Treasury Secretary Henry Morgenthau and Raymond Moley, one of FDR's economic "brain trust," suggesting schemes that would temporarily expand the supply of paper currency backed by silver, whose price the government would raise by open market purchases of the precious metal. Amos professed no magic solution, but his suggestions were designed to encourage the administration to adopt inflationary measures.[31]

Senior administration officials were then focused on strengthening the federal reserve system with new banking legislation, but an increasingly impatient Amos complained in an open letter that FDR "has not carried through" with his promised reflationary policies. "Every moment of delay on Mr. Roosevelt's part puts off recovery."[32]

At the same time, Amos faced pressure from the left. In the spring of 1934, he became chairman of the People's League for Economic Security, which endorsed heavily graduated income and inheritance taxes and federal ownership of the banking system and natural resources. Although Amos initially praised this "excellent" platform, its distinctly socialist direction soon bothered him. He complained to a professor member, "I have conceived of our league as not standing for socialism but as nevertheless being perfectly willing to receive support from socialists who would work for the part of our program calling for the socialization of certain services. . . . [W]e have got to fish or cut bait. Be for capitalism or against it."

Long opposed to government regulation as a middle ground, Amos, seeing only socialism or capitalism as alternatives, put himself firmly in the capitalist camp. When it became evident that a majority in the league favored the abolition of the profit system, Amos resigned. Individualism, he maintained, "is the main essential of human development; . . . what is needed is not equality but a very great inequality, based, however, not on privilege but on our value to society."[33] Henceforth he would move toward conservative opposition to what he perceived as the government's collectivist policies.

Amos resigned from the league after the Democrats' impressive gains in the mid-term congressional elections in 1934. Amos then wrote his brother, "Obviously, the people wanted to give Roosevelt a good chance to carry out his program. . . . Events are forcing him to the left." During President Roosevelt's second two years, the Second New Deal, as it is sometimes called, did turn to the left.[34]

There was much in that markedly leftward tilt that Amos Pinchot had earlier applauded. The passage of the Social Security Act, which included unemployment insurance provisions that he had endorsed, should have pleased him. And he might well have approved the administration's awkward shift in economic policy to a more active antitrust focus. Trust busting had always been the bedrock of Amos's economic philosophy, and the New Deal leaders hoped that splitting up businesses into smaller units would provide more competition and initiative to stimulate economic growth. Finally, Roosevelt's proposal for enhanced taxation of higher incomes, inheritances, corporate profits, and dividends—what was called a "wealth tax"—was in line with Amos's long-standing interest in addressing the problem of income inequality.

Amos ignored these measures and was sharply critical of the New Deal by 1935. His primary objection to its new direction was the growing powers of the president, which Congress expanded in many pieces of legislation. The additional authority of the presidency has perplexed intellectuals who have correctly pointed to its marked increase under Roosevelt and the New Deal. Of course, a decisive president could exploit the economic crisis and the need for new legislation and use executive orders to enhance presidential power, but it is less clear how inevitable the process was. In any event, Congress could not, or would not, restrict the president's discretionary authority, and the result was a potentially much more powerful chief executive.

Such a trend clashed with Amos's old notions of limited government. Congress would not be blameless in giving enhanced powers to the executive branch, but he mainly criticized Roosevelt, who, in his view, alternately browbeat and sweet-talked Congress to pass legislation giving him more discretionary power. Amos's first target for criticism was the Banking Act of 1935, which broadened the authority of the Federal Reserve Board and gave the president, he protested, "a monstrous prerogative," and he doubted that the people "consciously gave it to Roosevelt." Thereafter, Amos often wrote about the danger of "executive usurpation."[35]

In January 1936, Amos sent out an open letter formally breaking with Roosevelt, and he searched for a Republican candidate to contest the president's reelection. He avoided reactionaries, who "don[']t see the necessity of making the Republican party at least seem progressive and liberal," and he feared that an ultra-conservative Republican nominee would give FDR a smashing victory and might result in a one-party government. Much of the Republican Party establishment also sought a "sane alternative" to the New Deal, and they soon agreed upon Alf M. Landon, the Republican governor of Kansas, who won the party's nomination in June. Amos approved of Landon, a former Bull Moose progressive who had endorsed some New Deal programs and might effectively appeal to voters concerned about the Democratic Party's leftward direction.[36]

Before the election, Amos released another open letter, addressed to Interior Secretary Harold Ickes, explaining why he rejected FDR and supported Landon. Ickes, a fierce Roosevelt loyalist, responded with his own broadside, reminding Amos of his leftwing past: "are you desperately seizing an opportunity to absolve yourself" of your former "extreme radicalism. . . . I have a distinct recollection that Theodore Roosevelt himself included you in his famous 'lunatic fringe.'"[37]

*   *   *

Meanwhile, Gifford's family tried to mend their political fences with the Republican Party in Pennsylvania. The two-time governor still had lingering presidential ambitions but knew he was an extremely long-shot prospect. When no presidential boomlet occurred, he turned his political antenna toward Leila, who wanted to run again for Congress.[38]

Louis McFadden, her Republican adversary in the two previous primaries, had become an extremist—a vociferous critic of the New Deal and an anti-Semite—and discredited by his own party, he lost reelection in 1934 to a

Democrat.[39] McFadden would try to make a comeback in the 1936 primary, but he had no support from the Republican organization. The way was open for Leila to compete for the party's nomination on more favorable terms. Moreover, she had already given speeches castigating Adolf Hitler's persecution of the Jews in Germany, and she might have welcomed the chance to confront McFadden's anti-Semitism.[40]

Leila chose, however, to run in another congressional district covering the northeastern section of Philadelphia, where many textile workers, especially in the hosiery industry, lived and worked. Leila moved in different social circles from these workers, many of whom were socialists, but she had long attacked child labor and sweatshops and picketed with textile laborers in their strikes across the state. She was a modern woman, independent and outspoken, and with her red hair and dressed in bright-colored garments, she made no pretense of being anybody but herself.[41] Many of the workers admired her, and during some strikes in 1933, one lauded her presence, calling her "fiery," "all for the union," and "right out there with us."[42] For her congressional campaign, Leila saw the workers as her political base.

Cornelia (Leila) Pinchot strongly supported organized labor. Appointed to a state committee that investigated sweat shop labor, she (wearing hat) marched here in Mahony City, Pennsylvania, in June 1933, with "sweat shop" strikers whom she exhorted to "fight for a decent wage." She championed labor rights outside Pennsylvania too—for instance, she soon joined African American laundry union workers in Brooklyn, New York, demonstrating for higher wages. (Corbis – Bettmann)

Leila touted her education accomplishments and her long record of support for working families. Her platform stood for old age pensions, unemployment insurance, minimum wage laws, protection against cheap foreign textile imports, higher wages, and opposition to wars that enriched munitions makers, bankers, and profiteers. She received some endorsements from Republican women's clubs and labor leaders in the state. Her opponent was James J. Connolly, a seven-term congressman who had been defeated for reelection two years earlier. Her major thrust against him was to label him "lazy" and "selfish," while she would energetically represent the people in the district.[43]

Connolly had political backing down to the ward level, however, and a consensus among party officials in the district was that she had only modest support and should withdraw. But a determined Leila persevered. Gifford helped, working the phones and consulting with his extensive contacts among Republican operatives in the area. The Connolly forces referred to her as an "interloper," and it was problematic how many of the textile workers were registered Republicans or would change their party affiliation so they could vote for her in the GOP primary. In the last stages, Leila challenged Connolly to a series of debates but received no response.[44]

On primary day, Leila finished a distant second (of four other candidates) behind Connolly, who won close to half the total count. Amos was "terribly sorry" about the result, he wrote Leila, and blamed the Republican Party bosses for her defeat.[45] Leila may also have been a victim of her questionable strategy and, though difficult to measure, a prevailing prejudice against strong, independent-minded women running for political office. Following Gifford's failure to win the U.S. Senate seat two years earlier, for instance, Amos believed that Leila, serving as ad hoc governor during Gifford's shingle's malady and then going overboard in her energetic campaigning for her husband, "gave rather too much the impression that she is a leading power in the administration. No doubt a good many people resented that."[46]

The 1936 contest would be Leila's last, but, only fifty-five and still energetic, she would continue to speak out in support of organized labor and against Hitler's persecution of Jews.

*   *   *

In May 1936, Gifford had a long talk with Landon in Topeka and concluded afterward, "Like Landon decidedly. . . . He said he wanted me to take a 'major part' in the campaign, and asked me to draw planks on labor, about which he knows little, utilities, and conservation." Like his brother, Gifford believed that Landon was the best moderate Republican candidate to have a chance against Roosevelt, and he made speeches and radio talks for him.[47]

Ickes, having already ridiculed Amos's support of Landon, attacked Gifford. In a partisan radio talk in Pennsylvania, he commented that it was "laughable" for Gifford to "pretend" that Landon was a conservationist and that he should be supporting Roosevelt, who "has actually done more for conservation than any one else in our history." But Gifford, he went on, had deserted the president and the New Deal when he failed to replace Joe Guffey as the Democratic nominee for senator two years earlier. In relating this episode publicly for the first time, Ickes emphasized that Gifford was consumed with "political ambition," but when his ploy failed, he had "deserted to the enemy that he had been fighting most of his political life," including reactionaries Reed, Mellon, and Grundy.[48]

FDR won reelection in a landslide. Landon had not used the speeches Gifford prepared for him, but the election results did not disappoint the former Pennsylvania governor. Roosevelt's triumph, Gifford reflected, was "a tremendous defeat for the concentrated wealth and for the States Rights big fellows. It means more and better national security legislation, conservation, labor, and corporation control. . . . It is a smashing defeat of the few for the many."[49]

The Republican debacle was more troublesome for Amos, who was distrustful of the incumbent's purposes but believed that Roosevelt, in his lust for power, would be vulnerable.[50] He was right about FDR's vulnerability; during the campaign, the president allied himself closely with organized labor. In portraying the contest as one between democratic forces fighting against wealthy and selfish "economic royalists," he had deliberately stirred up class antagonism.[51]

Roosevelt would help galvanize his opponents by launching his so-called court-packing plan. In reaction to Supreme Court decisions by aged, life-tenured justices, which had overturned much New Deal legislation, the administration introduced a bill allowing the president to nominate up to six new justices for each still sitting on the court after the age of seventy. The initiative was illegal, but to many lawyers and moderates and conservatives in both parties, the tampering with the traditional appointment process amounted to extra-legal overreach against a sacred institution.

Amos immediately saw that FDR's court reform was open for attack. Always well connected with media elites, Amos worked with Frank Gannett, a Republican who owned many newspapers nationwide, in founding the opposition's principal lobbying group, the National Committee to Uphold

Constitutional Government. Gannett and Amos were among its key leaders, and Amos's old college roommate, Sumner Gerard, served as its treasurer. Amos wanted to make the group "as liberal as we can make it," and the committee tried to recruit Democrats and Republicans who had not been deeply involved in partisan politics.[52]

Emboldened by the new group, Amos charged that the president was "trying to put over a dishonest and devious coup d'état," and fired off a message to members of Congress complaining that the court bill, if passed, would "empower Mr. Roosevelt to . . . control the political and economic life of the country."[53]

He then stepped up his criticism with an open letter, which the Committee to Uphold Constitutional Government circulated widely. Among the numerous favorable reactions, Alf Landon commented that his letter was "one of the most devastating and effective arguments on his administration and the Supreme Court proposal I have seen."[54] The committee flooded newspapers, lawyers, farm organizations, and other groups with literature criticizing the plan, gave radio talks against the bill, and sent urgent last-minute telegrams to opinion elites in states of wavering senators on the bill. Partly because of the widespread public criticism, the Senate, though heavily Democratic, narrowly defeated the measure. It was a stunning defeat for Roosevelt. Giving Amos full credit, Gannett wrote him, "Let me say again that we could not have won the fight if it had not been for you."[55]

FDR was now "on the downgrade," Amos thought, but he worried about the Democrats' patronage machine directed by Postmaster General Farley in Washington, which was "powerful" and "corrupt."[56] Also troublesome to him was the growing influence in the Roosevelt administration of a few hundred dedicated New Dealers, as they were collectively labeled, who drafted new bills that obliging members of Congress dropped in the legislative hopper.[57] They were, Amos thought, anti-business and committed reformers. To Amos, however, their vigorous activity seemed "to show the fascist drift which Mr. Roosevelt is ably leading. . . . They have lots of money and lots of agents and a swell organization to work with. And they know what they're after and they move fast."[58]

Amos also criticized the close relationship between Roosevelt and organized labor. The president, he asserted, was trying to develop "a militant alliance between the staff of the aristocracy of labor and himself." In particular, he distrusted FDR's cooperation with John L. Lewis, the UMW head and also the Congress of Industrial Organizations president, which had recently organized unskilled workers in several major industries across the nation. Amos argued that Roosevelt's embrace of big labor was turning a union movement into a class movement with a socialist agenda. He conceded that FDR might want to preserve capitalism, but "I think he's a collectivist at heart," and his protection of private enterprise will result in "a fascist capitalism."[59]

Amos also resisted two other legislative initiatives. One was an executive re-organization bill, which, Amos charged, gave the president authority to control all agencies in the many executive departments, including the commissions and boards created by Congress to regulate industry and relations between capital and labor. The other was a bill giving a labor board power to fix minimum wages and maximum hours for almost all U.S. industry. If the measures passed, he warned, "they would take vital powers from Congress and the courts" and "set up a kind of one-man government."[60]

These bills stalled in Congress, partly because of mounting concerns among southern and rural conservative members about their sweeping provisions. However, a sharp economic recession later that year also played into the hands of New Deal critics, who pointed to the failure of the administration's recovery efforts. When the recession hit, Amos complained that the introduction of more "radical" legislation "suddenly and quite needlessly knocked [recovery] on the head."[61]

In all these endeavors, Amos Pinchot reiterated the same political philosophy he had espoused twenty-five years earlier in the progressive reform movement. The cornerstone of his faith was still the Jeffersonian free individual. His remedy for America's social ills was grassroots democracy in which moral individuals would empower an aroused Congress to pass legislation undermining entrenched interests in American society. Limited government was preferable to concentrated power, whether in the hands of the president, business monopolies, or labor unions. The economic emergency might require some adjustments to foster recovery, but there were limits beyond which government should not tread. As he told a sympathetic friend, "I happen to believe in democracy," in which the major policy decisions of government were arrived at "not by one man, but by open debate by the representatives of the people. This may be old-fashioned stuff. . . . But it is the theory and the system which, with all its faults, has worked best."[62]

There were nonetheless shifts in his philosophy of government. He no longer advocated the breakup of monopolies, the nationalization of certain public sector entities, and government programs to provide economic security to disadvantaged parts of society. And his conviction that a return to prosperity depended on a revival of economic productivity in the private sector increasingly trumped concerns over labor rights and political reform. Now the federal government should be no more than "a decent, impartial umpire."[63] The New Deal was laying the foundations for what would soon be called the welfare state—that government had an ongoing responsibility for the protection and promotion of the economic and social well-being of its citizens—but that perspective would be alien to his thinking. He did not say so specifically, but his sharp attacks on collectivism and his touting of individualism going back to William Graham Sumner seemed to question much of the progressive legislation enacted into law over the previous forty years.

23.

A Lost Woman

During and after Gifford's second governorship, he and Leila would become more involved with their son, Giff, whose formal schooling would be as erratic as that of his cousins Gifford 2nd and Rosamond. Because of a bad eye problem, which Gifford ruefully reported, "I am afraid he inherited from his Dad," and persistent trouble with his sinuses, he had to withdraw from two boarding schools. He finally enrolled in and graduated from the Thacher School, a boys' boarding school in southern California.[1]

Although Giff was accepted at Yale in the fall of 1933, he flunked out during his freshman year. Returning to the college the following fall with his eyesight restored, he was still plagued by painful sinus infections and thought about dropping out again. It was the youngster's decision, his father had written him, but reflecting on his own positive college years, he hoped Giff would continue at Yale. "You might miss one of the great experiences of your life if you don't," he gently pleaded.[2]

With his health somewhat improved, Giff stayed in college and began seeing a lot of Sarah (Sally) Richards. Her parents lived in New York, where her Yale graduate father was a Wall Street lawyer. (Their home was on Park Avenue, only a block from the Amos Pinchot residence.) Sally was a year older than Gifford and, as a student at Vassar College, was three class years ahead of him. A common interest of the couple was sailing. The adventure to Tahiti had stimulated Giff's interest in the sport, and Sally's father, an avid sailor, had introduced her to the yachting world. Giff and Sally had an on-and-off again courtship, partly because they were so young, but by late 1935, Giff, now twenty, was beginning to assert himself. Regarding his and Sally's future, he told his mother he had been "puzzled" about what he should do about his attraction to his girlfriend but decided to continue seeing Sally regularly. "I'm so damn young I feel I have to scream sometimes to assert my independence because I'm not always sure of it." But of his and Sally's more serious relationship, he was certain. "She loves me stably and deeply I am quite sure," he assured Leila. "Our relation is now happy[,] beautiful[,] deep and completely self[-]respecting."

Already graduated from Vassar, Sally Richards was working in New York. The couple wanted to get married, and by the early spring of 1936, during Leila's congressional primary campaign, Giff pressed their case with his disapproving parents. Having themselves married when much older, they would not easily relate to matrimony to offspring barely twenty. Following an argument with his parents, to whom Giff would apologize for getting "mad" and being "such a fool" with them over their "misunderstandings," his parents agreed to their marriage that summer.[3] Decisive reasons for their relenting attitude were Giff and Sally's long relationship and their determination to be married. Elopement, though perhaps never mentioned directly, was an option. As Sally soon told Leila, "I suppose marriages made in defiance of parents' wishes are very romantic, but I think they must cause a good deal more pain to everyone concerned than could be justified by the momentary thrill of independence."[4]

In June, Sally and Gifford Bryce were married in a Presbyterian service in Wilton, Connecticut, where her parents had a country residence.[5] The groom's dad, outfitted in a new white suit, served as best man. After a sailing honeymoon from Norwalk, Connecticut, to Nantucket and back on a thirty-foot sloop Giff bought with the royalties from his South Seas book, the newlyweds settled in New Haven. In their first summer as a married couple, Giff had to make up a course he had failed "partly as a result of spending more time visiting Sally at Vassar than I did studying at Yale," and Sally also enrolled in a course. Giff's parents grew closer to Sally, and that Thanksgiving, Gifford noted in his diary, "The more I see of that girl the more I think she is a fine person."[6]

As a married man, Gifford Bryce Pinchot lived off campus with Sally and played no part in Yale's social life. The two spent his last college year studying in England. Giff would then enroll in medical school at Columbia University College of Physicians and Surgeons.[7]

* * *

Amos Pinchot tried to keep track of his son and daughter. After their marriage, Gifford 2nd and Janine lived in the United States and had two daughters, Marianne and Diane Rosamond. However, he had difficulty finding employment, and she, having first focused on motherhood, was interested in pursuing a career in the movies. The couple soon separated and were divorced six years after their marriage. Rosamond, now thirty-one and still close to her older brother, worried, "He's still so young that he has to prove his age by swearing, staying up late, and smoking constantly. But he's such a sweet darling boy."[8]

Janine lived in France with the children, and Gifford 2nd set off for southern California, looking for work. He had almost no money, and when a girlfriend in Los Angeles broke up with him, he told his sister, "I want to forget this babe in California" and have you "find me another girl just like you." But Gifford 2nd would never remarry.[9] When he had custody of the children, Gertrude helped with their care and even made the long trip to France to return them to their mother.

By 1936, Gifford 2nd finally found work as an apprentice engineer with the Douglas aircraft company, and he told his father that he had joined the CIO. Despite his anti-union stance, Amos supported his son's decision and added, "I suppose I would join it myself if I were in your place." Even so, it was Gifford 2nd's Aunt Leila who seemed more concerned about the Douglas management "exploiting" the aircraft workers, and she asked him whether she could do anything to spur the union to do more to protect them.[10]

*   *   *

Meanwhile, Rosamond and Bill Gaston experienced a rockier road. The couple had two boys, Billy and Jimmy. But almost from the start, Rosamond and Bill's marriage floundered, and they were soon estranged. Bill had affairs with several women and was a heavy drinker, sometimes not returning home from an evening spent at his speakeasy. When she would say she wanted a divorce, he threatened to take the boys and ruin the Pinchot name. In late May 1932, Rosamond told her husband she was pregnant again, but Bill retorted that she was dull and the "world's worst bitch." In subsequent days, he showed no interest in her pregnancy. "How typical of him!" she wrote in her diary. "Now there's this emptiness. No one in the world to kiss, no one to give all the tenderness I have to give."[11]

Rosamond had an abortion from a doctor whom Leila recommended. During her recovery, she and her boys moved out of the couple's apartment and rented a penthouse apartment on East Seventy-Ninth Street. She intended to go to Nevada for a divorce, but Bill helped deflect that step by sending her flowers during her recovery and offering to visit her. At the time, Rosamond dismissed these gestures, but as she moved out of their apartment, he, weeping, pleaded with her to stay married and help him get an aviation job with the hoped-for Roosevelt administration. Rosamond reflected after their meeting, "I'm afraid that as a husband he'll always be a failure."[12] She nonetheless promised to support him in his job search, and she lacked the willpower to divorce him. Gifford's family was wholly on Rosamond's side and labeled her wayward husband "Beelzebub."

As Rosamond separated from Bill, she befriended Eleanor Roosevelt. Remembering her earlier work with women speakers during the Al Smith campaign, Eleanor recruited Rosamond to help Democratic women speak forcefully in pitching their message in support of FDR's presidential run. On election eve, Rosamond saw Eleanor in Manhattan and, keeping her promise to her husband, asked her if she would say nothing against Bill Gaston if his name came up for an appointment. Eleanor readily assented. Rosamond was still hopeful that keeping her promise might help to reunite him.[13]

Among Rosamond's several glamorous women friends in New York City, her main confidante was Elizabeth (Bessie) Marbury, a veteran theatrical and literary agent. Bessie Marbury was nearly fifty years older than Rosamond, but Rosamond loved her, and they had many conversations on personal and career matters. Bessie may have helped her young friend get an assignment writing a series of articles for *Babies—Just Babies*, a recently launched magazine that Eleanor Roosevelt edited. The publication's mission was to help raise mothers' awareness of childcare issues. Rosamond's piece, "The Most Famous Baby in the World," was about newborn Mary MacArthur, actress Helen Hayes's daughter.[14]

During their intimate talks, Bessie told Rosamond about FDR's earlier affair with his social secretary, Lucy Mercer. Here was another reason Rosamond would identify with the prospective first lady, a kindred spirit suffering from the misconduct of an unfaithful husband. Perhaps, she reflected unrealistically, she and Bill, like Eleanor and FDR, could find a way to coexist as partners, if not intimates. In their first meetings, she confided to Eleanor about her marital problems, and Eleanor had written her cryptically that if she could persevere without bitterness, it would make her "grow and be of more use to all one's friends."[15]

When Marbury died in January 1933, Eleanor Roosevelt invited Rosamond to ride with her to their friend's memorial service at St. Patrick's Cathedral. Before her death, Bessie had also tried to set up an interview with Rosamond to write a regular column for the *New York Journal*, which asked her to prepare a personal reminiscence about her friend. Rosamond complied, and in the *Journal* next to Rosamond's account of Bessie's lifestyle were photographs of the two women friends.[16]

The *Journal*'s editor, perceiving ready name recognition with a Pinchot byline, thought that a regular column by Rosamond would be a hit but emphasized, "You must have definite opinions." The comment was an eye-opener to Rosamond, who reflected, "I having definite opinions! I who never knew what I thought about anything." She soon learned that the *Journal* had rejected her as a prospective columnist.[17]

Shortly afterward, Universal News, a Hearst press service, hired Rosamond to follow the first lady's first days and contribute articles under her byline. The assignment paid only $150 and was only an oral agreement, so perhaps nothing much was expected of her. On the train trip from New York to Washington, D.C., for the inaugural, Eleanor walked through the press car and singled out Rosamond to return to her stateroom, where they had a long talk. During the inauguration parade, Rosamond rode down Pennsylvania Avenue with Governor Pinchot and Cornelia in their new Studebaker, then walked through the White House, including the bedrooms upstairs, until Eleanor appeared again.

Rosamond submitted many articles describing Eleanor Roosevelt's transition to the White House, but only her first piece made it into print. "I guess my stuff duplicated what the other half dozen reporters brought in," she concluded discouragingly.[18] The first lady invited Rosamond to the White House a few more times in these first months, and she also saw the president, who once greeted her, "Hello, Rosamond, how goes the writing?" She also attended a luncheon given by the Roosevelts, and Eleanor gave her more personal time, including another White House tour. When the two parted, Eleanor always kissed her.

The young, beautiful Rosamond contrasted physically with Eleanor's much older and plain appearance, and Rosamond noted the first lady's "awful yellow teeth." Yet she projected an inner beauty Rosamond admired: the soft, pleasant voice, natural warmth, friendly smile, and sweet, intimate personality. After they parted for what would be their last meeting together, Rosamond wrote in her diary, "I felt a real affection in her presence. A great woman."[19]

In the twenty years since her marriage to Gifford, Leila had transformed and reconfigured many rooms in Grey Towers. Her most recent project involved the installation of a large elliptical concrete structure on the patio—what the Pinchots called the Finger Bowl—which was filled with water, and Amos, Gifford, Leila, and their politically savvy dinner guests would sit around the bowl, pass the food on small boat-like trays across the water, and discuss the major topics of the day. Of her attendance at one such dinner, Rosamond felt like "a complete and miserable fool. . . . My interests are vague and uncreative."[20]

She began reading the newspaper and writing copious notes about political developments, but her efforts at self-education competed unsuccessfully with her friends' active social life. She lived in the fast lane and met with many luminaries in Gotham: Elsa Maxwell, Cole Porter, George Gershwin, H. G. Wells, Sinclair Lewis, and Katharine Hepburn, among others. She also attracted several beaus who wanted to go out with her; a favorite was Bennett Cerf, a recent co-founder of Random House. She saw a lot of Cerf, who also visited her a few times at Grey Towers.[21]

One of Rosamond's primary concerns was money. Income from her trust fund was dwindling, and Bill would not help her. She earned some money modeling new fashions in *Vogue* and *Vanity Fair* magazines and promoting Elizabeth Arden's cosmetics and other commercial products, but living in Manhattan and actively socializing with affluent friends was expensive. Prominent among stage directors in the city were George Cukor and David O. Selznick, who helped her relaunch her acting career by getting her parts in summer stock in Sturbridge, Massachusetts, which she liked well enough, if mainly to finance her lifestyle. These "on tops" people, she commented, "have money and are recognized as either smart or clever. They're the people with the power."[22]

One of her New York friends, Zoe Akins, a playwright, poet, and screenwriter, urged Rosamond to travel to Hollywood and stay at a house she owned nearby while trying her luck in the film industry. She emphasized that movies were expanding, and that was where the money was. Rosamond was soon persuaded and, in January 1934, made the first of three trips to Hollywood.

Stage directors Cukor and Selznick, who also spent time in cinematic productions in Hollywood, helped Rosamond get a screen test at Metro Golden Mayer productions, which offered her a movie contract for a year at $300 a month. She had some acting experience in her favor, but at about five feet, ten inches, she knew she was too tall for most roles: "[I'm] a big gangling girl without any real reason (except money) for wanting to go into pictures." She would also face stiff competition from an expanding supply of young lovelies flocking to Hollywood for their chance at fame and fortune. Moreover, now almost thirty and having to exercise regularly and go on starvation diets to stay thin, she faced more competition on the glamour side. She signed the film contract, but with no current roles available, she was told to return in six months.[23]

She made two more trips to Hollywood before learning she would play the part of Queen Anne in an RKO Pictures remake of *The Three Musketeers*. It was a prominent supporting role, but the film, released in late 1935, was a flop. Rosamond later wrote Leila, "I still feel very depressed about myself in the picture." She was taller than the two leading men opposite her, and the cameraman did "absolutely nothing to make any of the women in the picture look presentable."[24]

It is easy to assume that Rosamond had no talent as an actress and that her successful stage debut in *The Miracle* was a fluke.[25] It is true that her early ambivalence about a stage career and her concerns about her failed marriage and child care distracted her from the strong commitment and drive required for theatrical stardom. Still, Rosamond did not question her acting abilities. She also appreciated the creative process of working with directors and other actors and especially liked the intimacy of summer stock productions. She was no brilliant actress, but she was likely correct in believing that her height limited her possible roles in the theater and movies.[26]

On her second foray to Hollywood, Rosamond planned to divorce Bill. He was spreading stories about her loose morals and angrily accusing her of thinking only about her career and neglecting the children. He continued his philandering, and because of his sexual exploits and demeaning comments, Rosamond concluded that Bill Gaston was a "distinctly evil fellow." "Cut him out of your life," she wrote in her diary. "You're really too good for him. . . . He's just attractive. Damn it that's it."[27] But during all her time in California, she never went to Nevada to divorce him. Indeed, Bill had a magnetic pull on her, and other male friends never quite measured up.[28]

The significant development during Rosamond's Hollywood adventure was her budding romantic relationship with Jed Harris, a brilliant but egotistical stage director. Rosamond seemed to be attracted to thespian directors. Earlier it had been Cukor and Selznick, and now Harris. They were enormously talented—Cukor and Selznick would later win Academy Awards for movies they directed. Moreover, these three men had immense casting authority in both the male-dominated theater and in Hollywood. Rosamond, wanting leading parts, felt she had to stay on their good side, and these directors found Rosamond beautiful, desirable, and unattached. She had tolerated Cukor (who was a closet gay) and endured Selznick (who chased her both in Hollywood and New York). Selznick got hopelessly drunk at one New York entertainment with his wife present and insisted on taking Rosamond home. A melee ensued, and he passed out. Eventually, he would proposition her without success. As she commented at the time, "So far I've never had anything with a married man and I'm not going to start with a man whose wife loves him."[29]

Harris was in the same mold but had a somewhat different résumé. As a stage director, he was astonishingly successful. In the late 1920s, when still in his twenties, Harris directed four consecutive Broadway hits in eighteen months, appeared on the cover of *Time* magazine, and playwrights yearned for him to direct their creations. He was handsome, but actors and actresses labeled his personality "diabolical," "consuming," "devouring."[30] When Katharine Hepburn tried to leave one of his less successful plays, which he wanted to take to Chicago, Harris held her to her contract. "My dear," he told her, "the only interest I have in you is the money I can make out of you."[31]

In the early 1930s, Jed Harris met Rosamond during a Hollywood interlude, and he began to see her there and more regularly when they were both in New York. Harris was divorced but was also seeing other women.

As she fell for Jed, her theater acquaintances tried to warn her about him. They bluntly told her that Harris was "a very evil, sinister fellow," "cruel, ruthless and sadistic," in fact, "a monster." Rosamond was aware of Jed's bad reputation but, smitten with him, defended her new lover as extraordinarily talented and dismissed the warnings as coming from jealous colleagues. In any event, her choice of Harris was consistent with her previous mates, and she had noted before her affair with Harris that "People always tell me I have perverted tastes" in men.[32]

When Bill Gaston heard about Rosamond's new romance, he worried she might finally divorce him and marry Harris. Bill had been playing on the Pinchot name and her presumed reluctance to drag it into divorce court, but Harris might change everything. So he developed a plan. Rosamond's mother, Gertrude, suffering from a weak heart and lungs, was in declining health and had recently moved to sunny Tucson, Arizona. Rosamond had moved into her mother's former residence on East Eighty-First Street. In June 1936, when she was away briefly, Bill broke into the apartment and stole her safe box and leather-bound diaries in which she had entered her fulsome reflections. If necessary, he could use her accounts of her romantic liaisons in discrediting her and besmirching the Pinchot name.[33]

Rosamond took no action, and nothing came out publicly about Bill's burglary. Instead, she concentrated on her acting as if nothing had happened. In the summer of 1936, she appeared in stock productions. In January 1937, she was reunited with Max Reinhardt, who directed a five-hour extravaganza entitled *The Eternal Road* in New York.[34] The play, both pageant and opera with a musical score by Kurt Weill, used old Jewish heroic tales of resisting persecution with an implied message of resistance to Hitler's anti-Jewish policies. The production, having a half-year run, was a moderate success. Rosamond played the role of Bathsheba, a small part, for a few months before giving it up.

It would have helped Rosamond to have a strong support network among friends and relatives during her romantic difficulties. But those relationships were changing. The core of her support had been her father, Amos. He had quietly instituted proceedings to ban Bill Gaston from practicing law in New York, and he likely was prepared to support her fully if she decided to divorce her husband. But they apparently never discussed her personal difficulties or a possible strategy for dealing with them. Moreover, Rosamond sensed that Ruth, with her own family a priority, was less welcoming toward her.[35]

Because of these shifts, Rosamond had reservations about visiting her father and Ruth at Grey Towers. She still enjoyed walking in the woods and to Sawkill stream and waterfalls, but she knew she would not eventually inherit Amos's and Ruth's cottage (Mary and Tony would). Besides her father, her other confidant was Leila, and a deeply grateful Rosamond, during one trip to Hollywood, wrote her aunt, "I have never known anyone, in my life, so completely kind and generous as you. You seem to be instinctively generous and I marvel at it."[36]

Gertrude unsuccessfully tried to help her daughter. She cared for Rosamond's children, which gave Rosamond more free time to pursue her social networking and acting engagements but, lonely and in failing health, frequently phoned her daughter. Rosamond knew she could be a comfort to her mother but groused, "my stomach turns over when I think of the cloying affection I'd get in return. How she'd want to hold my hand and kiss me—all the talk of 'spiritual values'—nauseating." While Rosamond embodied the "new," liberated woman, Gertrude still adhered to old-fashioned morality. The two had little in common, and Rosamond would write in her diary, "Poor mother, it's such a shame that I don't like her."[37]

Rosamond had spoken affectionately of her two boys and marveled at their unique, sprouting personalities, and she vowed to spend more time with them. Increasingly, however, they were a drag on her already complicated life. When she first met Harris, she commented about Billy and Jimmy, "I hate them." A surprised Harris replied, "Nobody hates little boys," but she insisted, "Well, I do." When Harris went on to say he could not believe her, Rosamond continued to insist that she hated her boys and didn't know how to be a mother and bring them up.[38] Some women dislike their mothers, as Rosamond disliked Gertrude, and still lead normal lives, but few hate their own children. Perhaps Rosamond expressed her "hate" remarks when she was in one of her depressed moods. In any event, she was emotionally lost and, though entirely speculative, perhaps becoming mentally ill.

If she and Harris decided to marry, an added complication was that he was Jewish (his birth name was Jacob Horowitz). Her previous beaus, Cerf, Cukor, and Selznick, were Jews. Marrying one, however, would likely make her a social outcast among the snobby upper crust in the city. She was willing to defy cultural conventions, but there were limits beyond which might lie real social opprobrium to her and tarnish the Pinchot name.[39] When Rosamond nonetheless told Amos that she wanted to marry Harris, her father complied. It was her life and he wanted to support her. Harris's religion did not seem to bother him.

The question of Rosamond's and Harris's future reached a decision point during Jed's direction of a new play by Thornton Wilder.[40] It was a measure of Harris's Broadway successes that he prevailed upon Wilder to let him direct his new play, *Our Town*. In January 1938, at Princeton, New Jersey, they began rehearsals for the play, which was scheduled to have its world premiere in the college town later that month. Wilder and Harris had a contentious relationship from the start, but after several delays, the play moved toward opening night.[41]

Rosamond had no part in the play but was in Princeton as Harris's special friend. She acted as prop manager and prompter for the rehearsing performers. Wilder later remarked that Harris, while unusually kind to the actors, had been "overtiring" them "with interminable rehearsals, delays and all night work," and "Jed didn't sleep or eat for days."[42] Some cast members, Rosamond, and probably Harris ingested Benzedrine pills, an amphetamine for stimulation, to stay awake and alert. Opening night finally came on the evening of January 22, 1938. Wilder and Harris thought the production before a full house went well, but Wilder, making one criticism about the last act, prompted Harris to explode in a fury.

Several accounts of what happened post-performance backstage sometimes differ in details, but some threads are clear enough.[43] Harris suggested to Rosamond that she should not travel with the troupe to Boston the next day for a two-week warm-up before moving to New York. Perhaps he was trying to distance himself from her, or he may have been genuinely solicitous, thinking of getting her off the Benzedrine and her need to look after her boys. Although Wilder believed that Rosamond, probably through her prompting role, had liked the play, she was dispensable for the production. But Rosamond was fixated on being with Harris, perhaps more so because of the Benzedrine racing through her body. If she did not go to Boston, she wanted to be with him that night. They argued in the presence of the cast right after the show; later the same evening, Harris retreated to a snack shop in town and phoned Rosamond to have a private conversation with her. When Wilder and his sister, famished after nonstop rehearsals and the performance, also stopped at the same shop to get something to eat, they heard Harris in the back talking on the phone. "But Rosamond, no darling," Harris was saying. "Of course I love you but I can't, don't you see, I can't spend the night with you. Yes, I love you, it has nothing to do with not loving you." The Wilders quickly left the shop as they heard Jed, in louder tones, say, "Yes, I love you; of course, I love you." In any event, her entreaties to Harris were woefully timed, as he was utterly exhausted and in no mood for close female companionship.[44]

After the emotional phone conversation, Jed and his sister drove a sullen Rosamond back to Manhattan, where she picked up her car and motored alone to the large house she was renting in the village of Old Brookville, near the north shore of Long Island. She had picked that residence because it was near a prestigious school, which her boys, nine and six, could attend.

Rosamond decided not to make the trek to Boston, and the next evening, cold and snowy, she put her boys to bed in their rented house and, leaving them with their live-in nursemaid, went out for a long drive later that night. When she returned after 3 a.m., she parked the car in the garage, went to her bedroom, and placed two notes on the bed. Returning to the car, Rosamond retrieved a piece of garden hose, sticking one end in the exhaust pipe and the other through a crack in a back window and filling in the rest of the crack with burlap, and got back in the car and started the engine.

At about 6:15 that morning, the cook discovered a lifeless Rosamond in the car and phoned the local police, who shortly confirmed her death by suicide and called Amos Pinchot. The news was a terrible shock to him. An added in-dignity was that he had to drive from Manhattan to Old Brookville to identify his daughter's body, but two of Rosamond's girlfriends agreed to go with him and share the grisly duty. Amos never revealed the contents of Rosamond's two notes, but the police inspector confirmed that they were "confessing her suicidal intentions and distributing her property." The medical examiner's report noted that she had been taking Benzedrine tablets: "Probable motive—committed in fit of reactionary depression from late hours and reaction following wearing off of drug." A blood test confirmed carbon monoxide poisoning, but there was no autopsy, which might have revealed the amount of Benzedrine in her system and other information, such as pregnancy or illness.[45]

Rosamond's death at thirty-three was front page news in the New York newspapers. Since her death, much more is known about suicide (and suicide prevention), but why it happens for individuals in specific situations can still be unfathomable. In Rosamond's case, she felt trapped in a miserable marriage with no escape from her awful predicament, and her tempestuous relationship with Harris may have confirmed her sense of helplessness. In her diary, she had written on occasion, "Sick of the tired life I lead, sick of the untidiness of it and the waste," and "Life seems meaningless." She had contemplated jumping off her apartment balcony in 1934, right after she had invited Bill to her penthouse hoping for lovemaking, only to have him walk out on her. Self-destruction surely existed not far below the surface in her mind, and in the early morning hours of January 24, 1938, even the heartache that she knew her suicide would cause to her loved ones could not stop her from taking the fatal step.[46]

The funeral in Gertrude's New York apartment was private and attended only by Bill Gaston, Jed Harris, Amos and his two daughters, Gifford and Leila, Gifford 2nd, who flew in from California, and a few friends. Gertrude was too ill to make the trip from Tucson. After the service, Rosamond's body was taken to Milford and laid to rest in a small mausoleum in the family cemetery.

*   *   *

In dealing with Rosamond's suicide, the Pinchots, concerned about the reputation of the family name, tried to minimize the downsides of the tragedy. The afternoon newspapers on the day of her death reported that Rosamond was found in the car wearing a white evening gown, silver slippers, and an ermine wrap. That was likely accurate, but foreseeing lurid press speculation over her choice of attire, Amos said she was dressed in sports clothes and a sweater, and the *New York Times* duly used his description in the next day's morning paper.[47]

Rosamond's death also impacted Gifford and Leila's political careers. Gifford had announced in early January that he would run again in 1938 as a candidate for governor of Pennsylvania.[48] Then, right after Rosamond's death, the couple agreed to say as little as possible about it publicly. Ignoring the car asphyxiation and the notes Rosamond left, Leila privately told consoling friends as well as Giff and Sally in England that the cause of Rosamond's death was lack of sleep and an accidental overdose of depressing Benzedrine.[49] These descriptions persuaded Giff, who replied that he was consoled to learn that his cousin had not acted "premeditatively" and that "it seems if just anything had been different it wouldn't have happened."[50]

The family also had to face the question of raising Billy and Jimmy Gaston. In her death notes, Rosamond had apparently expressed her desire to have the two Pinchot families assume this responsibility, and both were sympathetic. Anything would be better than the cursed Beelzebub. But as the surviving parent, Bill was their legal guardian, and a suitable custody arrangement would be required. These negotiations dragged on, and finally, Amos, losing his patience, exploded in anger in a phone conversation with Bill, and the hope for some kind of a shared custodial agreement vanished. And so, nearly eighteen months after Rosamond's death, Leila drove Jimmy and Billy and their belongings from

Grey Towers to New York to return them to their father. Their departure, Gifford commented, "was a horrible wrench but there was no way out. To turn them out to that unspeakable skunk was heartbreaking."[51]

For Gertrude, losing her daughter was devastating and accelerated her declining health. She moved from Tucson to the Los Angeles area to be closer to Gifford 2nd but had lost the will to live. "I can't imagine I can go on living and perhaps I shan't have to," she wrote Leila a month after the suicide. Gertrude died less than a year later.[52]

Meanwhile, Amos was guilt-ridden at not being more involved with Rosamond during her personal troubles and tried to be more of a father to Gifford 2nd. He wrote him more frequently and visited him in Southern California in the winters. Amos's acknowledgments to letters of condolence pouring in after Rosamond's death emphasized his daughter's vitality and many friendships in New York and California. But the pain was deep, and occasionally, he let some of it seep into his replies. He reflected, for example, "I suppose that none of our lives is free from tragedies. But this is the first great one that I have known and it has affected me deeply."[53] The loss of Rosamond came at a time when he was already becoming more pessimistic about his own life. Before her demise, Rosamond herself had noted of her father, then sixty-one, that his life "hasn't been as complete as he might have hoped. . . . His temper[a]ment is unhappy."[54]

In dealing with his sorrow, Amos wrote a sonnet, "To Rosamond," on the second anniversary of her death, which the New York *Herald Tribune* obligingly published:

> Weep not, poor soul. Nor ask to know what sun
> Doth course above that broad and shining land.
> Where she finds rest, and where full rivers run
> In silent splendor to the tidal sand.
> But ride, as she did ride her steed in pride
> Across the hills. And give, as she did give,
> To those whom God, prejudging, has denied
> Compassion and the generous strength to live.
> She was the glow of dawn that leaps afar
> O'er feeble fields to touch the barren height.
> She was the lovely discontented star
> That leans from heaven to give to earth her light.
> And each forsaken creature, man or beast,
> She loved the most as it became the least.[55]

24.

The Human Travails
of War

As Gifford prepared to run for a third gubernatorial term, Leila optimistically wrote Giff that his dad "might have no real opposition," and Gifford noted, "I think we have a better chance than ever before" in the primary.[1] Because of the Republican thrashing in the 1936 election, he was more convinced that the GOP's Old Guard had been repudiated and that only a progressive Republican gubernatorial candidate like himself could succeed in 1938. The growing opposition to the New Deal certainly insinuated a Republican year, and he was the obvious Republican choice on the reform side.

Some party leaders nonetheless approached him with a proposal to put up for governor a ticket of Arthur H. James, a conservative judge strongly opposed to the Democrats' Little New Deal in the state along with Pinchot running for the U.S. Senate. Despite Gifford's long quest for an elusive Senate seat, he now rebutted that he did not want to be in Washington "as just one more in a helpless minority." He also scoffed that "any ticket headed by James could win in the fall, and he gave James's disqualifications "in detail."[2]

But James, with backing from the Republican organization, decided to contest Gifford. Leila still believed that her husband's candidacy was going "unbelievably well" and surmised that Roosevelt and the Democrats were losing support among organized labor, which would help her husband in the upcoming contest.[3] The opposite proved true, however, as labor remained with the Democrats, and Republicans voted in droves for conservatives, including James. Gifford's age (seventy-two years) also may have turned off some voters, and James often mentioned it during the campaign.

These negative forces prevailed on primary day in May when Pennsylvania Republicans gave James more than twice as many votes as Gifford (933,000 to 451,000). Gifford's resounding loss stunned him. Commentators on the election results mostly emphasized that Pinchot's gubernatorial candidacy suffered not just as a reformer but also because of his long association with organized labor in general and John L. Lewis in particular.[4] Now too old to contemplate running for political office again, he could focus on his conservation interests.

* * *

In 1934, Rosamond noted about Amos, "With all his talent he has only written very little." The comment was accurate for his unfinished book projects, but his magazine articles continued nonstop throughout the 1930s. After Rosamond died, Amos published three more open letters attacking Roosevelt and the New Deal. His ten public essays from 1934–1938 totaled nearly two hundred typed pages. Collectively, they may have helped stiffen conservatives' opposition to the New Deal, but their length precluded sympathetic print media from more than referencing them occasionally. And although Amos addressed four of these open letters to Roosevelt, it is questionable whether he read any of them.

In May 1938, Amos charged in another letter that the administration's relief bill would further clothe the president with more executive power and was a boldface White House scheme to buy support in the coming elections.[5] He also criticized pump-priming—that government should spend more on relief and go much more deeply into debt since more people would be employed, generate consumer spending, and set the economy on an upward course. But to Amos's mind, pump-priming had already been tried and left millions still unemployed despite billions in expenditures.[6] Amos advanced no alternative suggestions and did not concede that the New Deal recovery and relief programs, despite their defects, had at least staved off a much deeper depression and possible social revolution. Amos was no libertarian, but he was carrying his anti-government ideas to an extreme.

He soon showed the same attitude in opposing a congressional bill on maximum hours and minimum wages. The pending legislation was an outgrowth of the New Dealers' enthusiasm for curtailing child labor and helping workers at the bottom of the labor market, many of whom were not members of unions. Amos opposed the measure, citing laissez-faire economic theory. Labor was a commodity, he argued, and real high wages could occur only when there was high production of goods and services sold under competitive conditions. All the New Deal laws and promises of Mr. Roosevelt "will not boost real wages—unless the demand for labor is strong."[7]

But among liberals in a mature industrial America, hours limitation and a minimum wage were articles of faith and a necessary, humane restriction of the free market. The New Deal was not quite dead, and Congress passed a somewhat watered-down Fair Labor Standards Act in June 1938, which curtailed child labor and, for many businesses, established a minimum wage and a maximum hours ceiling.[8]

As the mid-term elections approached, Amos issued the last of his open letters on domestic policy, which was a frontal assault on the swelling union movement. He was convinced that it represented the curse of bigness—this time on the labor instead of the capital side.[9] Though overstating the influence of Lewis and his unions, Amos aptly expressed conservatives' fears of the changes the New Deal had wrought and the public unease about persisting union power and influence.[10]

*   *   *

The other major legislative question was executive reorganization. A key piece of the proposed reorganization would transfer conservation activities, including the administration of the forest service and the national forests, from the agriculture to the interior department, which would be renamed the department of conservation.[11] Along with Roosevelt, Ickes and Gifford would be the key players in a disjointed saga. Longtime friends, the three were like-minded partners committed to the cause of conservation. But FDR could never get Gifford to compromise, and he would sometimes vacillate and have sharp confrontations with each of them. On a personal level, Gifford and Ickes, forgetting their friendship, leveled attacks on each other so that the controversy ultimately became a kind of "remarkable psychodrama," with each of the two protagonists determined to prove that the other's arguments were dangerous for the cause of conservation.[12]

Surely personal issues and ideological differences were involved, but at bottom the controversy was mostly bureaucratic, involving markedly divergent ideas about the future oversight of the nation's natural resources. Toward the end of the fight, Gifford would correctly remark that he would have "emphatically opposed" the transfer of forestry from agriculture to the interior even if the positions of Interior Secretary Ickes and Agriculture Secretary Henry A. Wallace had been reversed.[13] Gifford's strong criticisms of Ickes reflected his intense moralistic personality. As early as mid-1935, Gifford had known that Ickes was "red hot to get Dept. Cons. I'm again[st] it strong," and he began working quietly with the new head of the U.S. Forest Service, whom he liked, and other foresters, active and retired, to derail the transfer initiative.[14]

After the president's sweeping reelection victory in 1936, Gifford pessimistically assumed that Congress would rubber stamp the reorganization.[15] He nonetheless decided to oppose it and ripped into the bill during a speaking tour on the West Coast and in articles. He mentioned that forests were a crop and part of agriculture and thus should remain separate from the dissimilar natural resources overseen by the interior. Emphatically, he also pointed out that the plan was more far-reaching than previous reorganization schemes, and he likened Ickes' "personal ambition" to the earlier power grab of the nefarious Secretary of the Interior Fall. Perhaps his most effective argument was that while the interior incumbent was a staunch conservationist, what about his successors? There would be too much pressure from private interests on the new department to keep the conservation features intact. It was infinitely preferable to maintain forestry policy separately in agriculture as a check on these pressures.

Gifford also opposed the dismembering of the conservation work in the agriculture department by giving the new entity authority over questions of soil conservation, grazing, and water and leaving agriculture only with research functions and cooperation with state and local governments on private lands. The separation, he objected, would not be based on use and protection, "which is the only sensible basis, but on the artificial and constantly changing basis of ownership."

More generally, he argued that the reorganization "would hand over to the President the absolute power, without limit in time, to do substantially anything he happened to feel like doing to the whole Government organization of the United States." He could create new departments outside the civil service and effectively "abolish the Congress of the United States" on such matters.[16] Although a Theodore Roosevelt nationalist, Gifford had no problem calling for limitations on executive authority that involved tampering with forest administration. His strong rhetoric was designed to galvanize conservation associations to lobby against the reorganization proposal and reflected his long antipathy toward the interior department dating back to the 1890s.[17]

Gifford never showed much love even for the national park service, which was a part of the interior department. The national parks were a "possible exception" to interior's mismanagement, he allowed, but emphasizing their different missions to the disparagement of the park service, he mused, "The National Forests belong to the people, but the N. Parks belong to the concessionaires."[18]

Ickes responded in kind, and in a radio talk, he "went after Gifford Pinchot pretty savagely."[19] Neither personality was forgiving. Gifford's self-righteous streak surfaced, and Ickes, a self-described "curmudgeon," was equally inflexible. Clare Boothe Luce, Rosamond's socialite friend but later a Republican congresswoman, once said that Ickes had "the soul of a meat axe and the mind of a commissar," and Harold Hopkins would later say of him, "He is stubborn and righteous which is a hard combination."[20]

Amos also weighed in and argued that the plan played into the hands of FDR's grasp for more presidential prerogatives, and he warned that working people, if they valued their freedom, should oppose what would lead to their forced regimentation.[21] Gifford was pleased with his brother's support, saying his "superb" critique "against Franklin, as you put it, is much stronger than even I supposed it could be."[22]

President Roosevelt's firm commitment to the reorganization was critical for its success, but he was smarting from legislative defeats. Moreover, in the first half of 1938, he opposed several uncooperative or conservative Democratic incumbents in the primaries, but his choices would lose in almost every contest. The House of Representatives recommitted the reorganization bill, effectively killing the measure for that year. Ickes was so discouraged that he thought about resigning.[23]

At that point, Secretary of Agriculture Wallace became an active player in the debate. Ickes had thought that the president had forbidden him from speaking on the issue and reminded FDR that the proposed department had been the president's recommendation. His chief failed to reassure him, however. From the start, in fact, Roosevelt had wanted to avoid a major fight on the transfer issue and was unwilling to make it a high-priority goal.[24]

Six months later, the president, still cautious, told Ickes that forests were a crop and might best stay in agriculture. To Ickes, the forests-were-a-crop argument was bunk. "Lumbermen," he asserted, "certainly do not regard themselves as farmers, and lumberjacks join the carpenters' union and not the Grange." But Roosevelt, backing away, suggested that an interdepartmental committee could study the question. If that happened, Ickes complained, there would be no chance of the forestry transfer, and FDR nodded, "maybe not."[25]

Congress soon passed laws reorganizing parts of the executive branch but exempted the forest service. It was a victory for Gifford. In October 1938, he advanced his arguments opposing the forestry transfer in a meeting with Roosevelt and may have influenced the outcome. However, other forces, including Wallace's opposition and a Republican-conservative Democrat coalition in Congress, had effectively stymied almost all New Deal measures, especially those enhancing presidential power.[26]

*   *   *

As 1939 dawned, Gifford noted, "The New Year opens like a set trap. . . . In all my life I have never known a more threatening future."[27] It was indeed a dark and ominous time, with militaristic Germany and Japan on an expansionist warpath. In July 1937, Japan invaded the China mainland, and its troops moved deep into the interior of the country. In Europe, Germany seized the Rhineland, marched into Austria, and, most recently, took over all of Czechoslovakia. Efforts to appease Hitler had obviously failed. The Nazis' pogrom against Jews escalated dramatically, culminating in the violent Kristallnacht, in which scores of Jews were killed and thousands arrested, and Jewish synagogues, homes, and businesses were pillaged and torched.

Gifford wanted the United States to provide economic and military aid to the beleaguered democracies of Europe, but his health, increasingly precarious, prevented his involvement in pro-allied activity.[28] Gifford then lived at his grand house on Rhode Island Avenue in Washington. On January 23, 1939, a taxi he was riding in was smashed by a streetcar. Gifford suffered no broken bones but was badly shaken up. Then a week later, he suffered a heart attack at home, which his physicians believed was triggered by the taxi accident. The attack was serious, and his doctors prescribed several months' rest. Gifford may have become active too soon, for he soon had four more attacks.[29] He was bedridden at home for five months and allowed no visitors except for Leila, his physicians, and a full-time nurse. He gradually recovered but could go full speed only for short periods.

Meanwhile, Gifford and Ickes awkwardly tried to repair their old friendship. Foreign affairs helped bring them together. Just before his accident, Gifford sent the interior secretary a note complimenting him for a recent speech attacking Hitler and the Nazis. Ickes sent a friendly reply, and they began exchanging letters. Ickes was pleased with the reconciliation "because I have always liked Gifford and have approved of most of what he has stood for in public life." (His appreciation of his friend did not extend, however, to his wife, whom Ickes thought had not been "too good for him.") After Gifford's heart setbacks, Ickes sent him some roses and called on him when he was allowed to receive visitors.[30]

Gifford's olive branch to his old friend also had a political purpose. He was distressed that the Republican Party seemed hidebound in its resistance to change. He was still smarting over his primary loss to Arthur James, and after James had won handily in the general election, Gifford concluded that the Republican organization in Pennsylvania was now solidly in the grip of conservatives and that his future influence in the party, even as a senior statesman, would be non-existent. Leila felt even more alienated from the GOP and wrote a journalist friend, "there is no future for the Republican party organized as it is now," and "my continuing to call myself a Republican and to function inside the party amounts to a form of intellectual and political dishonesty."[31]

During an Ickes visit to the Pinchots' Washington home, Gifford and Leila offered to help elect a liberal Democratic presidential candidate in the coming 1940 election and avowed that they wanted nothing in return. They even agreed to support Senator Guffey's reelection—the same person Gifford had earlier said that he "can't stand." Thinking that the Democrats could well use the Pinchots' support in Pennsylvania, Ickes was gratified.[32]

But then, the transfer issue resurfaced. The legislative fight had seemed resolved in 1939, but as the transfer was failing, Roosevelt told Ickes, "I will make a Department of Conservation before I get through with it." Because of his chief's shillyshallying on the question previously, Ickes found the comment unconvincing.[33] But Gifford worriedly wrote letters to faculty members at forestry schools asking them to oppose the transfer and enclosed a draft letter to be sent to Roosevelt—153 of them reached the White House. Gifford's salvo was an overreaction, and Roosevelt, who privately considered his old friend one of the "wild men" on conservation issues, wrote Gifford that he was so angry at Gifford's lobbying that he was now thinking of supporting Ickes on the transfer issue, and he returned all the letters to him. More than that, he lectured his former mentor, comparing Gifford's powerplay with "Coughlin or the United States Chamber of Commerce or the Cattleman's Associations, or, for that matter, horrid things like the K. K. K. itself. . . . And incidentally," he continued, "the days have passed when any human being can say that the Department of Agriculture is wholly pure and honest and the Department of the Interior is utterly black and crooked." Gifford, though admitting that FDR was "Very sore," did not back off and shot back, "To uproot the [Forest] Service from its lifelong surroundings would do great injury." He also sent a letter arguing against the transfer to every member of Congress.[34]

Ultimately, Senator Norris and others, believing the fight over the transfer in an election year might hurt the Democrats in the south and west, persuaded the president to abandon the issue. The U.S. Forest Service remained in the agriculture department, where it still resides today.[35]

Meanwhile, Nazi Germany's invasion of Poland in September 1939 brought on World War II in Europe. Like most Americans at the time, Gifford wanted the United States to stay out of the war if possible but aid the European democracies in their resistance to Hitler. After the German conquest of the low countries and France in May 1940, he joined the newly founded Committee to Defend America by Aiding the Allies. Leila also became more prominent in speaking at rallies, trying to bolster support for persecuted Jews in Europe and more lenient immigration restrictions on Jewish exiles trying to flee the Nazis' grasp.

After Roosevelt decided to run for a third term and the Democrats renominated him and the Republicans chose Wendell Willkie, Gifford fretted over his choice. He liked Willkie's "courage and great drive," and the candidate proved to be the most liberal Republican presidential nominee since the progressive period. His outspoken support for the military draft and aiding Britain in its resistance to Hitler were also encouraging. At the same time, however, there was little chance that Gifford would endorse him. Willkie was a lawyer for private utilities, an industry Gifford had fought most of his political life, and his speeches, Gifford concluded, sounded like "another plutocrat, accepting what progress has been made, but no more." The president then asked to see Gifford, and in late September, he came to their White House meeting in a bargaining mood. What he wanted from FDR in return for his endorsement were three things: no transfer of the forest service, appointment of his choice to fill the forest service chief vacancy, and a good (though unspecified) government job for Leila. But Roosevelt, though friendly, displayed his well-known skills in controlling private conversations. He expressed sympathy for Leila's job search but evaded Gifford's entreaties and talked mostly about the war so that Gifford left the White House meeting "pretty angry." Indeed, he concluded, "so far as bringing up anything, I might just as well not have come."[36]

Gifford and Leila visited Willkie at his home in Indiana, but Gifford then visited FDR again and afterward announced that he was supporting the incumbent, the "man with experience and training" for dealing with the current foreign crisis. "We cannot safely put [a] green hand in charge of ship in this storm," he emphasized.[37]

*   *   *

Meanwhile, Amos Pinchot resurrected his anti-militarist and anti-preparedness arguments, although he accepted more spending on defensive armament. He most strenuously objected to policy initiatives that would endanger strict neutrality and increase the prospect of U.S. military involvement in the European war. His disillusionment with Woodrow Wilson also contributed to his animus against Franklin Roosevelt's alleged lust for power. And already alarmed by FDR's increased authority in the domestic realm, he resisted his assertive foreign policy moves.

Gifford disagreed with Amos's sharp criticisms of Roosevelt's foreign policies, and Leila annotated her brother-in-law's open letters with many question marks. Amos, meanwhile, found another relative who strongly opposed the president—his Uncle Will Eno. Through the years, Will remained connected to the Pinchot family. Although he had been a real estate investor-speculator in New York City, his true passion was traffic management. As far back as the 1880s, he was disturbed by the masses of carts and horses piling into Gotham intersections without rules of the road or traffic signs providing discipline. The advent of the much speedier automobile era greatly increased the need for stop lights, proper signage, and basic driving regulations for traffic safety.

As the youngest Eno sibling, Will was only fifteen years older than Amos. Married but having no children, he had perhaps even more reason to stay connected to his two Pinchot nephews. By 1900, he had begun a career as a traffic consultant, and in 1921, he founded the Eno Center for Highway Traffic Control in Washington, D.C. (The center still exists there today.) He wrote several books on traffic regulation and traveled to Europe to promote his views.[38]

Will Eno was an old-style patrician, usually well dressed in a three-piece tailored suit and sporting a goatee and waxed mustache (sometimes a handlebar one), and generously donated to his alma mater, Yale. Of the two Pinchot nephews, Will was much closer to Amos. Even more than Amos, Will Eno had been an outspoken anti-prohibitionist, believing the noble experiment violated his personal freedom. Arranging for his own supply of alcohol, he had recruited the bartender at a private club in New York, who procured some cases of gin and bottles of vermouth, and Amos had obligingly picked up the booze for both of them.[39] Their second bond was politics. Will, a Republican, had supported Al Smith in the 1928 presidential election on the prohibition issue, as had Amos. He vehemently opposed the New Deal, however, and joined the right-wing American Liberty League.[40] In the late 1930s, Amos became a vice-president of Will's transportation center, which further linked the two men.

Will Eno was also an anti-Semite and an apologist for Hitler's expansionist territorial aims and ruthless anti-Jewish policies. Referring to the British prime minister's appeasement of the German chancellor at the Munich conference, he wrote Amos, "Hurrah for Chamberlain! In my opinion, the greatest man in the

Will Eno, an ultraconservative, nourished his nephew
Amos Pinchot's anti-Semitic and anti-interventionist sen-
timents before World War II. (William Phelps Eno, *The
Story of Highway Traffic Control, 1899-1939*, frontispiece)

world." (By contrast, when appeasement failed, Gifford commented, "Chamberlain, next to Hitler the most dangerous man in the world.")[41] Convinced that
an international Jewish conspiracy existed, Will ranted that American major
media sources "are either owned or controlled by the Jews and they by Russia"
and "most of the business organizations in New York are now in control of the
Jews. . . . Think this over," he warned his nephew, "and you will see why we may
wake up some day and follow Hitler. With 4,500,000 Jews in this country and
750,000 in Germany, there is good reason to begin to think."[42]

Amos found his uncle's anti-Semitic rage rather extreme, as his entire public
life had been filled with friendships with Jews, including Louis Brandeis, Rabbi
Stephen Wise, and Morris Hillquit. Not religious himself, a person's faith had
been unimportant to Amos. If anything, he had indicated some interest in the
plight of persecuted minorities fleeing European repression, Jews among them.

When asked to join an international refugee organization in 1933, he said he would "of course" become a member.[43]

Yet, in the late 1930s, Amos agreed with Will to the extent of arguing that the "American Jews would be wise if they made themselves as inconspicuous as possible for the next few years." When others criticized his position, Amos replied, "the objection to the speaking of Jews as a group seems to me ill-founded. It is one of the things that has been put over on the liberals" by Jewish sympathizers. Jews could be friends, but when they spoke out against religious persecution and public issues, they were lumped together as part of a conspiring Jewish lobby.[44] That perspective was then shared by many anti-interventionists, notably the famed aviator Charles Lindbergh, their most noted spokesman, who, in a speech in September 1941, singled out three groups—the British, the Jews, and the Roosevelt administration—as prominent agitators for U.S. entry into World War II.

In urging American Jews to remain silent, Amos took a position directly at odds with his lifelong commitment to free speech for persecuted individuals and groups going back before World War I, and he had served continuously as an ACLU director and had spoken out in defense of Sacco and Vanzetti. Even in the mid-1930s, he could comment that the ACLU's work "has the distinction of being theoretically sound, and in practice effective."[45] But Amos's obsession with two central questions—resisting Roosevelt's supposed quest for dictatorial powers and keeping the United States out of the approaching European war—trumped the problem of the Jewish plight and their rights.

Amos's Jewish and liberal acquaintances were appalled at his criticism of Jewish activism. Rabbi Stephen Wise commented to a mutual friend, "Jews as a group are not interventionists or isolationists or anything else, but as individuals they have the same right as Amos Pinchot to take a position." He added that they had that right because "We are both American citizens."[46]

Amos claimed that he was "against every form of anti-Semitism" but did not counter anti-Jewish sentiment, which was surging as more Americans turned inward and sought scapegoats for their economic distress. He also encouraged it. Father Coughlin, for example, launched tirades against Jews in his radio broadcasts, which Amos and his Uncle Will listened to with approval. Amos also reveled in isolationist Senator Gerald P. Nye's attack on pro-war propaganda in Hollywood, listing the names of Jewish movie producers. The best that can be said about Amos's thinking about the Jewish predicament is that, because of all the criticism he had received, he acknowledged by the fall of 1941 that it was "a difficult situation," and "it's hard to know what is the best course."[47]

After Germany's takeover of most of Western Europe in mid-1940, Hitler prepared for an all-out assault on Britain. As the Battle of Britain commenced, Roosevelt regularly consulted with Prime Minister Winston Churchill to try to provide all aid short of U.S. military intervention to that island nation.

Much like Amos's active involvement in nongovernmental pressure groups during American neutrality in World War I, in the second, he joined the recently founded America First Committee (AFC). Amos was a member of the organization's national board in Chicago and the New York chapter, and Will joined one in Bridgeport, Connecticut. The AFC had a strong Yale coloration; most of its leadership came from privileged families and Republicans. Still, its detractors included liberal anti-interventionists who decried some AFC members' use of the organization to launch political attacks on the Roosevelt administration.[48] The AFC membership included pacifists, communists, and isolationists but also nationalists and unilateralists, who, downplaying pacifism and supporting rearmament, wanted the United States, unencumbered by foreign commitments, to have the freedom to decide whether and when it might be in the nation's interest to enter the conflict.[49]

Within the America First Committee, Will Eno was a unilateralist. After Germany and Italy attacked France, for example, he was willing for the United States to "strike" militarily against the Axis powers but deplored America's unpreparedness for war, which would make military action against them impossible "perhaps for more than a year." Amos was much closer to the pacifist and isolationist positions, however, and he became a prominent spokesman for the conservative, anti-interventionist viewpoint, which some academic historians, international lawyers, members of Congress, and religious leaders in the America First Committee shared. In trying to avoid war, he nonetheless made some curious rationalizations. Before Germany's onslaught into France and the Low Countries, for example, he was confident that Britain, France, and their allies would prevail against Hitler. He also argued that the Führer was no maniacal monster but a traditional European statesman trying to recover Germany's rightful place as a major player in world politics. After Germany overran much of Western Europe, he wrote, "The collapse of France makes intervention seem to most of us more futile and silly."[50]

In the upcoming presidential election, Amos warmed to Wendell Willkie. He had reservations about Willkie's support of some of FDR's foreign policy moves, but his animus against Roosevelt was so strong that he increasingly praised Willkie's campaign speeches, touting him as the would-be savior of America in a "crusade" against a grasping third-term despot, and predicting his victory at the polls. When he lost to Roosevelt by ten percentage points in the popular vote, Amos admitted that the election results left him "pretty limp and fairly depressed."[51] Gifford, by contrast, campaigned for Roosevelt in some Pennsylvania cities where his choice had comfortably prevailed, and he was well satisfied with the outcome.

A weakness of the isolationist position in 1940–1941 was Americans' deep-seated sympathy for the British people. Linguistic, cultural, and even racial (Anglo-Saxon) affinities and 125 years of peace and common democratic traditions had brought them closer together, and they had fought as allies against Germany in World War I. Many Americans, even those steadfastly against war, were prepared to provide much more economic aid and military supplies short of war to help a nearly bankrupt Great Britain in its deadly struggle against Nazi tyranny. In the summer of 1940, it had been the destroyers-for-bases in which the United States gave Britain fifty older destroyers in return for some of the latter's naval bases in the Caribbean, Bermuda, and Newfoundland. In early 1941, it would be lend-lease.

Some American isolationists argued that the European war was a struggle for hegemony between rival imperialisms, but longtime anti-imperialist Amos Pinchot had a soft spot for the British people. At the outset of the war, he had written, "I can't help feeling a profound admiration for the way the English act in the crisis—the evacuation of the children from London, the calm of the people, and the way the British broadcasters have been talking about the war."[52] This pro-British sentiment, affecting isolationists in varying degrees, worked to the administration's advantage in promoting the lend-lease bill.

Amos labeled lend-lease a "dictatorship bill" since it included enlarged discretionary provisions to the president. He charged that FDR, a devious manipulator, was using his "puppets," Secretary of the Navy Frank Knox and Secretary of War Stimson, to express his viewpoint.[53] Indeed, he proposed that the lend-lease bill should be amended to require the president to appear before Congress to respond to questions about it. And what was worse, Amos thought, it would "make these powers so permanent that he could wreck his country ten times over before Congress could take them from his hands."[54]

Amos's criticisms of growing executive power in the domestic and foreign policy realms were at the forefront of what a later generation of concerned commentators would pejoratively call the "imperial presidency." In any case, such reasoning made no headway in Congress, and public opinion polls showed a decided shift in favor of major military aid to Britain. Amos made no compelling argument against lend-lease to Britain on foreign policy grounds, and indeed he was prepared "to see all aid given to England, to the very limit of what can be given under our laws and the Constitution, without inviting war."[55]

Congress passed lend-lease in early March 1941, and the United States drew closer to Britain. Following incidents involving attacks by German submarines on merchant vessels, Roosevelt asserted "freedom of the seas" and U.S. resistance to Nazi "piracy." Amos complained that the president's direct challenge to German sea power was leading the nation helter-skelter into war, which only Congress could declare as stated in the Constitution. He also quoted from FDR's numerous speeches in the last days before the election in which the president, catering to antiwar sentiment, had asserted, "Your boys are not going to be sent into any foreign wars."[56]

During 1940–1941, Amos and other pacifistic Americans placed their faith in a diplomatic settlement with Germany, but because of the fascists' ruthless conquest of most of Western Europe and all-out air assaults on Britain, it was harder to believe that peace with Hitler was possible. Right after the presidential election, Amos commented, "I am all for a negotiated peace," even though talking with Hitler was "a gamble, perhaps or probably only a truce." But the alternative, he reasoned, would be "a long, horrible war, say four or five years, of mutual extermination," even if Britain should prevail in the end. And a long war would greatly increase the chances of the United States being drawn in— an event, he insisted, that "would be one of the most horrible crimes against humanity." He was right about the prospect of terrible casualties and material devastation in a long war and the increased chances of U.S. military involvement. After the German invasion of the Soviet Union in June 1941, even Amos realized that European peace was remote.[57]

By late summer, Roosevelt and his defense advisers adopted a forward strategy of using U.S. naval ships to convoy merchant ships laden with goods to Britain and the Soviet Union. Shooting incidents with German U-boats on the high seas occurred, and an undeclared war in the Atlantic began. Many prominent Americans, including Amos, joined in a statement charging that Roosevelt's announcement of a shoot-on-sight policy without congressional sanction was "a grave threat to democratic principles of majority rule." In forcing a showdown with Germany, Amos lamented to his Uncle Will, "The administration is no longer in favor of freedom of the seas but for 'control of the seas.'"[58]

Most America Firsters were decidedly Eurocentric, but Amos would also worry about Japan's incursions into China. After FDR called for a "quarantine" of aggressor nations (meaning Japan), Amos criticized the president for arousing war passions in the country. During the presidential campaign, he asserted publicly that Roosevelt and his advisers had convinced themselves that war was "necessary, and if they can't have war with Germany, there is Japan . . . , a policy of war at any price."[59] But only in the fall of 1941 did he again express concerns about the rapidly escalating tensions in U.S-Japan relations, and he wanted an accommodation. Perhaps discussions with Japanese diplomats would succeed. Supporting the leader of a coalition of American pacifist groups, he wrote, "We should keep banging away for peace negotiations and against the crooked attempt of the White House to slip this country into war on rollers greased with falsehood."[60]

After the Japanese air attacks on Pearl Harbor and the Philippines, Amos supported the U.S. decision for belligerency against Japan (and soon also against Germany) and the disbandment of the America First Committee.[61] But with the United States at war, Amos went into an emotional tailspin. Even before that traumatic disaster, Amos had shown signs of depression, as his grief over Rosamond's death was always with him. And he continually worried about his finances. As an escape from his unhappiness, Amos turned to alcohol. He had always loved hard liquor, and during a European trip in the prohibition era, he had bragged, "I frequently had and immensely enjoyed cognac." He later added, "I will not admit I have no other motive in drinking except fear of germs. . . . I like the effect."[62]

Shortly before Mary graduated from Brearley school in 1938, Amos, probably drunk, berated his daughter, who was returning home with her date, for her bad social habits. When Mary tried to defend herself, Amos slapped her across the face. And a month before Pearl Harbor, he told a friend that Ruth's comment about his being "slightly tight" at a recent party the previous evening was "a lenient view" of what was likely his embarrassingly unpleasant behavior at the event.[63]

His disappointments in domestic and foreign policy realms contributed to his emotional distress. He was, it turned out, on the wrong side of history. He had asserted twenty-five years earlier that President Wilson had shown that "narrow nationalism is out of date, that 'America First,' 'America for America Only,' is not only the most contemptible slogan ever invented, but, in the long run, the stupidest and the most dangerous."[64] His disillusionment with Wilson helps explain his rejection of internationalism, but he went to the opposite extreme. It was not just that the world had changed while he had not; it was that he had changed somewhat, with his vision of democracy and freedom shriveled to the point of reflexive and hardened opposition, including his support of anti-Semites, against Roosevelt and his policy agendas.

Even Amos's efforts to draw closer to his children were fraught with tension. In late 1941, Gifford 2nd, now thirty-nine, raised questions about the settlement of Gertrude's modest estate, and Amos thought Janine, his son's former wife, was behind the complaint. Amos admitted "some mistakes" in the settlement and offered to pay his son's expenses to come to New York to talk to him and Gertrude's other executors, but Gifford had not replied. "I am hurt and terribly upset by the way he has acted," Amos wrote his cousin Florence Graves, who lived near his son and was trying to mediate the family impasse. He added, "The break between Gifford and myself and the misunderstandings have been a painful and dreadful experience for both of us, I fear."[65]

It may have seemed to Amos that he was a failure as a property investor, father, and polemicist, and his deteriorating physical and bipolar condition likely accelerated his descent into severe depression. Amos had earlier tried x-ray and sulfapyridine treatments for his arthritic hip, but in 1939, he had complained that he was "no less lame" and still suffered "a little pain at night which breaks my sleep."[66] By the spring of 1942, he came down with a bad case of the grippe and was "overtired" and "out of sorts." Gifford, who saw him then, was "shocked by his appearance," and Amos decided to get rest and treatment in a sanitarium. "My difficulty," he confessed, "has been prolonged insomnia and the attendant exhaustion." Gifford still found Amos "very low in his minds," but when Amos recovered some of his strength, he returned home in early August 1942, where Ruth cared for him with the help of a nurse.[67]

Amos's main social interaction outside his household was with compatriot Will Eno, and he soon visited his uncle at his Saugatuck house. It was a bad decision, as Will, with his extreme political views and own declining health, could not provide Amos with the emotional support he needed.[68] During his stay, Amos closeted himself in a bathroom, locked the door, and, probably with a razor blade, slit veins and arteries in one of his upper forearms. His nurse, with Will's help, finally forced open the door and found Amos bleeding profusely on the floor. They stopped the flow of blood somewhat and called an ambulance, which took him to a nearby hospital. Several blood transfusions saved his life. Gifford's son, now Dr. Gifford Bryce Pinchot, had some of his senior colleagues at Presbyterian Hospital in New York City visit and examined Amos. "His prompt and intelligent action in this whole matter has given me the greatest satisfaction," Gifford (the father) noted of his son. A few weeks later, Dr. Pinchot also helped get Amos transferred to Presbyterian, where he would receive the best treatment and allow him to keep his father informed of his uncle's condition.[69]

Amos regained consciousness and could move around slowly, but he was disoriented and confused and would never consistently interact intelligently with others. Gifford 2nd came from California to see his father, and Gifford visited him many times over the next several months. About half the time, Gifford recorded that he had good conversations with his brother, who was sometimes "cheerful" and "improved," but he also found him "worried at times over the past" and "by hallucinations" and "imaginary incidents."[70] During Amos's convalescence over the next year, he was moved to different hospitals because none was willing to give him the long-term personal care he needed.

Some doctors who examined Amos believed he could slowly recover from his trauma and resume a more normal life. Instead, his condition declined, and he died eighteen months after his attempted suicide.[71] After a funeral service, Amos was buried in the family plot at Milford Cemetery. The gravestone reads simply: "Amos R. E. Pinchot Pvt. N. Y. Cav. Dec. 6, 1873 Feb. 18, 1944." The reference to military service in the Spanish-American War, which was a very unhappy experience for Amos and started him on his lifelong anti-militarist course, is ironic. In his last demented days, Amos probably did not request that epitaph, and it was likely Ruth's decision to honor her husband's patriotism as a former enlisted soldier during the current death struggle against more menacing totalitarian enemies.

*   *   *

Although Amos's passing was not unexpected, the death of Harcourt (Crinks) Johnstone in Britain was unforeseen. In the interwar years, Crinks had loyally tried to revive the fortunes of the ailing Liberal party. A longtime social friend of Winston Churchill, Crinks loved good literature, food, and drink and disliked exercise. Like his mother, Nettie, he appreciated good taste in the arts and having a good time.[72]

When Churchill became prime minister in 1940, he appointed Crinks as minister of overseas trade. The position was not critically important in wartime, but Churchill's action recognized Crinks' steadfast free trade views. A few months later, Crinks was elected to the House of Commons, and in 1943, Churchill made him a part of his privy council, the government's policy group. By all accounts, Crinks was an effective minister during the war, but in March 1945, he suffered a massive stroke and died immediately, two months before his fiftieth birthday. Among the dignitaries attending his funeral were Winston and Clementine Churchill and two future prime ministers, Clement Attlee and

Anthony Eden.[73] A bachelor to the last, Harcourt Johnstone's death marked the end of Nettie's line of the Pinchots.

Meanwhile, in the United States, Gifford was involved in several endeavors. The first was personal—assisting Leila, who was still active in public life, in her quest for a responsible government position. In the fall of 1940, Roosevelt intimated that he intended to offer her something and, according to Gifford, subsequently told his running mate Henry Wallace that "she could be very useful to us."[74] But after his reelection, he had appointed her only as a volunteer in the office of civilian defense. She was pleased to be reconnected with Eleanor Roosevelt, the office's assistant director, whom she lauded for "her passionate integrity," but the office was disbanded after a year. Right after the midterm elections of 1942, the two Pinchots again approached FDR, Gifford imploring him to appoint her as a special assistant to him.[75]

Leila's letter to the president argued that her involvement with women and labor constituencies and her interest in peace plans would be assets to his administration. And trying to discount impressions of her as an independent-minded activist, she asserted that if he made her an assistant, she would not "go haywire on you" and not "make trouble" or "step on anyone's toes."[76] Nothing happened, however, and the Second World War would be another frustrating time for Leila and her search for active public service.

Meanwhile, Gifford contributed to the American war effort. Drawing on his angling expertise, he developed a kit, which included crude fishing gear, for servicemen surviving shipwrecks from enemy attacks. Using the kit, the men could ingest the water from fish they might catch and eat raw to supply their liquid intake and increase their chances of survival until rescued. The U.S. Navy soon adopted his kit, and Gifford briefed Roosevelt on its benefits. It received nationwide publicity when *Reader's Digest* published an article he wrote about it.[77]

Thinking about how to make the postwar world a better place, he also revived and enlarged an initiative dating back to the Theodore Roosevelt presidency.[78] Convinced that a fundamental cause of war was the desire of nations for more territory and additional natural resources, Gifford argued that international cooperation in the conservation and distribution of natural resources would greatly increase the chances for permanent peace in the postwar world.

Wanting the Americas to lead the way in this endeavor, he promoted the idea of an inter-American conference, which would assemble factual data on the forests, waters, lands, minerals, and wildlife existing in each country, and the nations' consumption, imports, and exports. Agreement at the conference would be the basis for inviting nations worldwide to an international conference for further action. Prodded by Gifford Pinchot, an inter-American scientific conference recommended that the American nations should create a commission that would prepare an inventory of the world's natural resources for the convocation of a later international conference on conservation.[79]

Finally, in late June 1944, Gifford, anticipating the victory of the forces of freedom and democracy and caught up in notions of a unified and peaceful postwar world order, again advanced his proposal for an international conservation conference. Wendell Willkie had gone on a worldwide tour and found a widespread consensus for international cooperation and peace, and his book, *One World* (1943), extolling this promise, was the best-selling nonfiction book up to that time. Gifford had not liked Woodrow Wilson, but now in a second, more catastrophic war, some of the former president's universalist ideas appealed to him. The dream of one world seemed both necessary and possible. Following his professional interests, Gifford's vision of peace encompassed conservation as a centerpiece.

Despite their past differences, FDR still considered Gifford "undoubtedly our [nation's] No. 1 conservationist" and, "favorably impressed" with Gifford's idea, asked him to send a memorandum. Submitted in late August 1944, Gifford's proposal called for an international conference in Washington to discuss "the conservation of natural resources, and fair access to them among the Nations, as a vital step toward permanent peace," and it provided suggestions for the U.S. planning of the meeting.[80]

Excited by Gifford's vision of global cooperation, Roosevelt told Gifford that he was pursuing the conference idea, and Gifford accepted his invitation to be a member of the U.S. delegation. FDR doggedly pushed the international conference proposal, urging the state department to consider such an international conference.[81] The department told FDR, however, that such a conference would complicate the work of agencies of the proposed United Nations that were already considering conservation issues in their international dimensions. Department officers warned that a full-scale world meeting on conservation would confuse the issues being discussed in other international forums. The president, who considered the diplomatic corps overly cautious, soon complained that the department had "failed to grasp the real need of finding out more about the world's resources and what we can do to improve them." The department's resistance nonetheless delayed diplomatic movement on the initiative.[82]

FDR informed Gifford in late 1944 that he would discuss the subject with Winston Churchill and Joseph Stalin at the upcoming summit at Yalta. Gifford was thrilled but would again be disappointed. Roosevelt pontificated briefly on the importance of forestry to the two allied leaders at their meeting but more to show his personal interest in the subject than as an issue for discussion.[83] At a press conference on shipboard during his return home, Roosevelt also held forth on the problems of poor countries that had deforested their lands and the need for reforestation and other conservation reforms to assist in their economic development.[84]

The state department continued to drag its feet on the conference initiative, mostly arguing that an international conference should wait until after establishing the United Nations at an upcoming meeting in San Francisco. Roosevelt once again expressed his annoyance but agreed that Gifford Pinchot's plan was "not urgent."[85] Still hoping for a favorable decision, Gifford sent the president a detailed proposal for the anticipated conference, and on April 10, he followed with another letter to him pressing for action.

Roosevelt died two days later. Heartsick at the news, Gifford wrote, "what a loss the world has had! For FDR was certainly the leader of the world toward better things." He persisted with President Truman, who was sympathetic about a conference, but the emerging tensions with the Soviet Union dimmed hopes of major diplomatic initiatives involving progress on worldwide cooperation.[86] The dream of permanent peace was giving way to cold war.

*   *   *

Gifford Pinchot's other project was writing his memoirs. He had earlier begun gathering documents to write a history of the founding and development of the conservation movement in the United States. Gifford had a good sense of history. Always at the center of the movement, he believed that posterity required an authoritative history. He possessed information "which no other man has," and the completed book would be a "public service."

The difficulty was that Gifford had saved everything—reams of diaries, appointment books, family letters, official correspondence, interviews, and speeches. Gifford hired researchers and old forestry compatriots who helped him navigate the collection and transcribe interesting nuggets on the topics he outlined. The expansive project was slow-going.[87]

He was simultaneously struggling with his declining health. He had felt vigorous through most of 1945 and had participated in the fortieth anniversary of the founding of the U.S. Forest Service in November, at which he and Eleanor Roosevelt were the principal speakers. His eightieth birthday the previous month had been a momentous celebration, with a deluge of letters extolling his achievements as forester and politician. His prized gift was two volumes of letters from members of the forest service honoring his leadership. Gifford particularly appreciated the sentiment expressed in the accompanying scroll: "First and foremost American Forester . . . he set in motion those principles which will in no small measure determine the future history of our country. . . . Known affectionately as 'G.P.' by all foresters."[88]

Concerning his history-memoir, a day before the birthday event, he penned in his diary, "FINISHED BOOK!"[89] But it was only a fulsome draft, and while revising it, his health worsened. Suffering from his heart condition and anemia, he required occasional blood transfusions. By the spring of 1946, he was mostly incapacitated and often bedridden. Finally, he came down with pneumonia and died at Grey Towers on October 4, 1946. After his funeral there, he was buried in a Milford cemetery. Governor Edward Martin, Gifford's old foe as Republican Party chairman, issued a proclamation closing all state offices on the day of his service. Gifford's memoir, loyally prepared for publication by Raphael Zon, an old forestry colleague, soon appeared in print posthumously.[90]

Leila continued her support of unions, protective legislation for female workers, and other progressive causes, and she especially touted the memory of her husband's gigantic contributions to the environmental movement. Most memorable, she gave a speech at the dedication of a national forest in Washington State in 1949, renamed for Gifford Pinchot, in which she extolled the importance of her husband's legacy in advancing current and future conservation causes.[91]

25.

Seeking Sisters

Before his last year of college, Leila had written Gifford Bryce, "Remember that by temperament you belong to the type Who DO things in life, not to those who accept life as it comes. . . . You will be happier if you do BIG LEAGUE stuff." Giff did not need to be reminded of the Pinchot values— the impulse to serve the public good—which he had already internalized. Medicine was within that sphere. At the same time, though, he was not an activist for causes like his parents, and Leila's urging to overcome his "inhibitions" and become one could not change him. He had no interest in getting involved in their game of politics, which Leila deeply regretted.[1]

Sally, his loving partner, would support him in college and through the long slog of medical school. The couple had three children, Marianna, Gifford III, and Peter. During World War II, Giff enlisted with the U.S. Navy Medical Corps and served in the Pacific theater. After that conflict, Giff became a medical researcher. He joined the microbiology department at Yale before moving to the biology faculty at Johns Hopkins University in 1958, where he advanced to become a full professor. He published articles on subjects ranging from pathology to bacteriology. Perhaps his most significant scholarly contribution was an article in *Scientific American*, which explained how marine farming had contributed to the food supply and its possibilities for enhancing the future supply. His piece combined his love of science, the sea and marine life, and service to the larger public good—similar priorities of his late father.[2]

Giff mainly absorbed a sense of adventure from his dad and sailing became his passion. Besides extensive cruising, he and Sally engaged in competitive racing, participating in at least eight Bermuda races and a transatlantic one. In 1953, moreover, they sailed their 38-foot yawl from New York to Norway and back, and later made a round-trip sailing adventure trip to Tahiti, recreating part of the voyage that he had experienced with his parents and scientists a generation earlier. A skilled navigator, Sally was arguably the better sailor, but as a measure of women's inferior social standing in that era, the couple always assumed that Giff was the skipper of their boat. They both loved skiing and, taking up flying, became licensed pilots. He found woodworking to his liking too, and after assembling his own shop, he built furniture. In retirement, he constructed small boats culminating in a twenty-five foot steamboat launch in which he and Sally puttered around the Connecticut coast. Reflecting on these multiple interests, Giff once wrote, "It always makes me feel a little guilty to list so many hobbies, but I do feel that we come this way only once and it's silly not to get as much as we can out of the experience."[3]

*   *   *

Amos's daughters, Tony and Mary, had their own sagas. They were bright, precocious, and developed into beautiful young women. Among those who knew them best as they were growing up was their much older half-sister, Rosamond. She was not an admiring relative. To Rosamond, the two were self-absorbed and boy-crazy; their lives seemed to revolve around parties and dances. The older Mary, with blonder hair than her sister, was obsessed with boys. "Being an ardent reader of movie magazines, she's hot for love already at 12," Rosamond observed. She professed to "love little Tony," while "Mary is nice enough when no males are about."[4]

After Rosamond's first return from Hollywood, Tony and Mary had sought her out for stories of her adventures, and she told her sisters what they wanted to hear. The movie magazines that the girls were reading correctly captured the glamour of film stars and their personal lives, she related, and she regaled them with lively tales of seeing Johnny Weissmuller on the *Tarzan* set, meeting Robert Montgomery, or admiring Katharine Hepburn's work ethic, among others.

Amos did not approve of coming out parties for his daughters, but Mary and Tony went to debutante balls of their schoolmates at elite New York hotels. The two girls also thought nothing of attending dances or house parties as far away as Newport, and they also tromped off to boys' prep schools in New England for dance weekends.[5]

Mary and Tony were naturally curious teenagers trying to absorb as much as they could about the outside world. Male companionship was a phase in their lives, and their experiences were not unlike their school friends from similar, affluent backgrounds. Both girls were athletic, and while at Grey Towers, they, like Rosamond earlier, went off on horseback riding jaunts. At Brearley

School, they played competitively on the basketball and tennis teams. As with Rosamond, the two had no exposure to organized religion, but they had a serious side. Aspiring to college, Mary and Tony took a rigorous curriculum and were good students. Smoking was the rage among many school girls then, and Mary indulged in the habit. Her classmates saw her as a social, athletic, and academic standout; in her senior year, they selected her "Miss Brearley," as the girl who best personified the school's ideals.

Rosamond's suicide during Mary's senior year had a distinctly sobering effect. Her half-sister had been Mary's role model, and it was her first experience with family tragedy. One outlet for expressing her sense of loss was to join her father in honoring Rosamond's memory in poetry. In her sophomore year at Vassar, she published a poem about Rosamond, entitled "Requiem," in the *New York Times*.[6] Rosamond's life as a consummate diarist also influenced Mary, who began keeping a journal after her sister's death.

Amos's troubling behavior, including the slap of his daughter for her supposed partying, had not alienated Mary from him, but she worried more about him.[7] While she was at Vassar, Amos had great hopes that she would go on to study medicine. Of her interest, he wrote, "A long hard road to hoe, but she really wants to do it." Mary seriously considered the profession, and a few faculty members at Vassar encouraged her toward that career path.[8]

At Vassar, the parties continued on weekends at men's colleges, with Yale as the females' favored choice. Mary had boyfriends at Brearley, but now older and more self-assured, she was independent and developed her own circle of friends; parties were only part of her stimulating social life. She showed more interest in the domestic political scene and the cataclysmic events abroad. She was not particularly political; however, she joined the left-wing American Labor Party. Despite her father's growing concern over the spread of communistic ideas in the late 1930s, her decision had not bothered him, as he assumed that young people were "naturally radicals and rebels."[9]

Many of Mary's classmates viewed Vassar as preparation for finding a compatible husband and becoming a competent, intelligent housewife; others, including Mary, were preparing for professional careers. Despite her interest in medicine, Mary's real inclinations were more artistic and involved painting and writing, which were much more in line with her parents' avocations. At Vassar she wrote a fictionalized short story and poetry for the college's literary magazine. In any event, because of the interference of the war, everything changed. Mary worked for a woman's magazine the summer after graduation, then became a reporter for United Press, even having her own column. Her half-developed thoughts about a medical career dissolved.

At Brearley and Vassar, Mary's special boyfriend was Bill Attwood, whose family also lived on Park Avenue. He attended Choate and then Princeton. Mary entranced Attwood, but eventually he gave up on her. The blond beauty was too special, he later reflected, and he could never keep up with her wide-ranging interests. Not long after college, Mary found her first long-term live-in boyfriend, Bob Schwartz, a tall, handsome young man of Jewish background from Salem, Ohio. He, too, was a reporter, for the military newspaper *Yank*, and he and other young male employees for the paper lived in a midtown Manhattan hotel.

Already a mature thinker, Mary wanted to make a difference in a chaotic world. Her early passion was peace. Undoubtedly influenced by her father's antiwar views, she saw war and killing as stupid and became an uncompromising pacifist. Although she could not change the world during the current maelstrom, she developed a vision of a more peaceful, humane postwar future and pondered basic questions about the human experience. "There was no crap to her," Schwartz later said of her. "She was concerned with the ethics and aesthetics of life . . . She would say, 'Why are we really here?'"[10] Mary was a seeker, restless about the present and searching for a deeper meaning and purpose in life.

During their love affair, the couple often visited Grey Towers, and they would swim naked in the Sawkill falls and pools on the property. On one occasion at this "romantic palace," as Schwartz remembered the retreat, Mary rebelled from doing the dishes while he sat in the living room reading the newspaper. Schwartz readily agreed with her feminist point and thereafter tried to share household duties with her. They were a young couple in love and seemingly compatible. But after three years together, their relationship ended. More than Mary, it was Bob Schwartz who pulled away. Like Bill Attwood, he could never permanently satisfy Mary's intellectual and aesthetic quests. He also sensed that his lover's mother, Ruth, had a problem with his Jewishness and, though friendly toward him, felt he was socially below the Pinchots, even though Mary, with Tony supporting her, remained committed to him.[11]

It was not long before Mary found another love, Cord Meyer, Jr. He was Mary's age, and his family had amassed a fortune in New York real estate. Cord graduated second in his class from the prestigious St. Paul's School. At Yale, he had played goalie on the hockey team, was a writer and editor for *Yale Literary Magazine*, and was elected to the secret society, Scroll and Key. Academically, he was elected to Phi Beta Kappa and, at graduation, won the prize for the student who had contributed the most intellectually to the college. He was obviously a promising star of the upcoming generation and likely headed for great things.

One of Cord's classmates at St. Paul's and Yale had been his fraternal twin brother, Quentin. The two were close, but the nation went to war as they finished college. Cord and Quentin both enlisted in the Marine Corps. Cord went to officer candidate school and was sent to the South Pacific as a second lieutenant. In July 1944, while leading the first wave of his machine gun platoon ashore on the island of Guam, Cord was critically wounded when a Japanese grenade blew up near his face. The blast blinded him, and he was barely alive when he was finally rescued a day later. During his slow rehabilitation at military medical facilities in Hawaii and New York, he recovered most of his physical strength and the sight in one eye, but his eyesight in the other was permanently impaired. For his wounds, he earned the Purple Heart and Bronze Star.

Like Mary, Cord was a dreamer. He had witnessed the stimulating debate in the Yale community over foreign policy before Pearl Harbor, and after U.S. involvement, he had briefly considered conscientious objection before his enlistment. The shattering war experience made him a committed international reformer, earnestly searching for a new, peaceful world order. In their college years, Mary and Cord had met, but there was no romantic relationship until they began seeing each other in the fall of 1944 during his medical treatments in New York City. Soon they became inseparable. As his health improved, they began going out together. In many ways, they seemed a perfect match. Both were from affluent families, educated at elite colleges, bright and personable, and had broad interests. They shared, moreover, a love of writing. The editor of the *Atlantic* was so impressed with Cord's letters sent home from the Pacific theater (which his father had shown him) that he published them in the magazine.[12] Like Mary, Cord was not religious, but as secular humanists, both were determined to play active roles in pursuing their dream of world peace.

Cord's irenic search would take him to world federalism. During the global conflict, many idealists believed that some kind of supranational government was required to rein in aggressive nation states and prevent major future wars. Their initial hope was the new United Nations, and Cord would have a close-up look at the formative international institution when Harold Stassen, a U.S. delegate to the San Francisco conference launching it, appointed him an assistant for the gathering. While Cord finagled for the job, he and Mary became engaged, and Mary wrote excitedly to her Aunt Leila, "I AM GOING TO BE MARRIED." The nuptials took place on April 19, 1945, in Ruth's Park Avenue apartment before the twenty-four-year-old newlyweds headed off to the West Coast for the conference. After the wedding, Ruth wrote Leila approvingly, "Amos would have felt that Cord was right for Mary, and she for him, I know."[13]

During the U.N. conference proceedings, Cord expressed his reservations about the draft plan for the United Nations. It was "a step in the right direction," he noted, "but there will have to be amendments to make it work." The international organization was essentially a big power alliance, allowing five anti-Axis powers a veto in the Security Council, and people, he emphasized, "should realize the essential condition of international anarchy that will exist as long as the nations are free to make war without regard for any higher law." Nations would have to agree to some limitations on their sovereignty to make the world organization an effective peacemaking institution.[14]

While in San Francisco, Cord received news that Quentin had been killed by a Japanese grenade in Okinawa. Quentin's death hit Cord particularly hard, and he retreated into himself, sometimes shutting himself in a room for hours of lonely contemplation. Mary's efforts to comfort him were unsuccessful. He could well express his complex emotions and sense of vulnerability in his journal, but he was an intensely private individual who rarely expressed his feelings publicly. The bottled-up result would be a somewhat tormented personality.

The San Francisco conference approved the new international organization with the big nations' veto power intact. Though discouraged, Cord remained a committed world federalist. The news of the atomic bombing of two Japanese cities, which ended World War II, convinced him that if mankind would survive the atomic age, the need for world government was even more necessary and urgent. Many internationalists shared his disappointment, including Leila, who was not a world federalist but worked with private associations to promote the new United Nations as an effective instrument for peace. As she wrote Mary in early 1946, "I went with Eleanor [Roosevelt] to one of the sessions. It certainly is not getting off to a good start, is it?"[15]

Cord Meyer, Jr., also had a less attractive side. His intense personality, combined with his obvious intelligence and academic achievements, made him dogmatic, disputing and ridiculing those who disagreed with his opinions. Life to him was not different shades of gray but blacks and whites. The headmaster of St. Paul's School later remembered him: "As a boy he had a fixed habit of going off the deep end; he blew like a gale," and especially on questions of morals and morale, he was sure he was "always right."[16] He usually cooled off quickly after an argument, and Mary, in love and sharing his basic viewpoint, may not have experienced his tempestuous side in San Francisco or immediately afterward when they retreated to a Montana ranch owned by the Meyer family for a month-long, delayed honeymoon. But it erupted on their train trip back to New York when she reviewed an article Cord was writing about the conference for the *Atlantic*. It was about twice as long as assigned, and when Mary, already experienced in magazine writing, suggested extensive cuts, he vehemently disagreed and reinserted the text.[17] Finally, he blew up on his wife and reduced her to tears.

Cord had become well known in the federalist movement as a charismatic speaker and for his book, *Peace or Anarchy* (1947), which lucidly articulated the case for world government. At the founding convention of the United World Federalists, which included idealists, scientists, and intellectuals as members, the delegates elected Cord Meyer, only twenty-six, as their president. It was the main nongovernmental organization dedicated to the pursuit of a supranational government, and with branches in many states and cities, it showed promise to move the dream of global government into the mainstream of political discourse. He was now at the center of a burgeoning movement.

The dream of world government never happened. Emerging tensions with the Soviet Union over communist ideology and its ruthless hegemony over many parts of Eastern Europe doomed the possibility of any realistic diplomatic discussions about a more authoritative international organization. The United Nations became a pawn in the escalating Cold War, and world federalism was a victim of that hardened international climate.

A disillusioned Cord Meyer wrote in early January 1950: "I now doubt the efficacy of any kind of action. Who am I to put myself against the dark and titanic forces that now mass themselves on the horizon of this new half-century?"[18] As he extricated himself from the federalist movement, he hoped to pursue a career as a writer but received no academic offers and was apparently too controversial for a state department job. Finally, Allen Dulles, Deputy Director of Central Intelligence, offered him a place in the agency, joining what would later be called the directorate of plans, the most secret part of the CIA. He was not just abandoning the dream of world peace and becoming a Cold Warrior but would be participating in provocative schemes that made the Cold War hotter.

When the anti-communist paranoia, whipped up by Senator Joseph McCarthy, led to accusations against Cord for his earlier peace and world federalist activities, the agency sent him home until the investigation could clear his name. Cord wrote a long defense of his earlier activism. During his home leave, he interviewed for executive positions with New York publishing companies.

Again, he was passed over, and eventually, the investigation exonerated Cord, allowing him to return to CIA work.[19]

Perhaps sensing his internal conflicts, Allen Dulles promoted Cord to chief of the international organization division in the directorate of plans. The appointment further committed him to the agency; the longer Cord stayed with the CIA, the greater the prospect that he would buy into its hardline, anti-communist culture. Accepting the change was perhaps easier because he had a compulsive work ethic and an inner need for certainty. Among the covert programs he successfully directed were the manipulation of Radio Free Europe and the National Student Association. Another, Operation Mockingbird, involved the secret infiltration of numerous media organizations, with the CIA eventually underwriting the salaries of thousands of journalists who managed to slant news coverage in favor of the CIA's position on specific foreign policy issues. Indicative of the agency's high esteem of Cord's dedication and commitment, he was awarded the CIA's distinguished intelligence medal three times in the coming years—only one officer would ever win as many.

* * *

In her early married years, Mary had given birth to three boys, Quentin (1946), Michael (1947), and Mark (1949), and was a devoted mother. She was attentive to her children's needs, changing diapers and later ferrying them to and from school, and the couple bought a spacious house in McLean, Virginia. But Cord's CIA experience would be disastrous for his marriage. Perhaps in trying to escape his inner turmoil, he became a chain smoker and drank excessively. He also likely engaged in extramarital affairs, sometimes with women Mary knew.

The CIA secrecy annoyed Mary. Agency employees were not allowed to talk about their work with their spouses, which aggravated her. Still, she learned enough about the agency's covert programs that she was more thoroughly disgusted with its missions and operations. As part of the anti-communist witch hunt, Mary too had been labeled a communist dupe for her earlier membership in the American Labor Party, but she was unapologetic about her past activism. Although world peace might now be a chimera, and liberal beliefs in eclipse, she maintained her progressive outlook.

Mary and Cord continued to share their writings, but instead of constructive criticism, they only found faults in the other's creations.[20] Another of the Meyers' disagreements concerned the education of their children. As soon as they were old enough, Mary sent her two oldest boys to the recently founded private Georgetown Day School, which sought to counter the mostly segregated capital city by enrolling many disadvantaged and black children. Making allowances for the students' multicultural backgrounds, the curriculum emphasized social interaction and tolerance as much as scholastic achievement. Cord was angry at Mary for her school choice and wondered how the boys, without rigorous intellectual oversight, would ever qualify for St. Paul's and Yale. But the values of the academic experiment were important to Mary, and the boys stayed in the school. Cord also had poor rapport with his sons. Three boys fairly close in age were naturally rather rambunctious at times as they grew up, but their noise only annoyed him. He was an authoritarian father, and the boys grew to fear his outbursts and criticism.

*　　*　　*

Meanwhile, Antoinette (Tony) Pinchot was coming into her own. At sixteen, she enrolled at Vassar, two years behind Mary. After graduation, as with Mary, her main interest was journalism, and her first job after college was with a woman's magazine. She then became a staff writer for *Vogue*. In 1947, she married Steuart Pittman. Like his new brother-in-law, Cord Meyer, Pittman graduated from St. Paul's School and Yale and had enlisted in the Marine Corps and served in the Pacific during World War II, receiving the Silver Star for his exemplary service. He was a student at Yale Law School when he and Tony married.[21]

Following law school, Pittman joined a Washington law firm, and Tony bore him a boy, Andrew, and three girls, Nancy, Rosamond, and Tamara, in five years. The Pittmans and Meyers saw a lot of each other and maintained contact with Leila, who was now living nearly full time in her Rhode Island Avenue home. In June 1953, Leila hosted a wedding reception at her house for friends of theirs. "The Meyers and Pittmans were there," she wrote Giff and Sally, "and quite added to the beauty and general revelry. Mary looked really beautiful."[22]

Leila may not have known that Mary and Cord's marriage was already in deep trouble, and Tony and Steuart's was becoming stale. Women's employment opportunities were still limited, even for the most privileged among them. The two beautiful women lived in a faster-paced, affluent America where sexual mores, including extramarital sex and divorce, were more tolerated. Without religious grounding as a possible restraint and well connected through their husbands to the elite in the nation's capital, they would inevitably meet and socialize with many successful and powerful men in politics, journalism, and the arts. The temptations of possible new romantic and sexual relationships were ever present for wives and husbands.

Whether Ruth knew of her daughters' marital difficulties, she believed they needed a break from all the child care and other housewife chores. In the summer of 1954, she gave Tony and Mary each a round-trip ticket to Europe and $1,000 in spending money. The European jaunt fueled their sense of independence, and it would become what they would later call "a husband dumping trip."[23] At the end of their travels in Paris, Tony met Ben Bradlee, a married European correspondent for *Newsweek*, and the two fell swiftly in love. As Bradlee later described it, after some socializing with friends and private talking, he and Tony checked into "a small, lovely room [and] spent the next twenty-four hours exploring hungers that weren't there just days ago, and satisfying them with gentle passion, new to me."[24] It would be another year before Tony and Bradlee were married. In between, Tony left Steuart. She consulted a psychiatrist to try to help her understand the reasons for her estrangement from her husband and her new attraction to Bradlee, who was now in Washington as a *Newsweek* reporter. Before their marriage, the lovers divorced their spouses and sorted out the inevitable inter-familial adjustments over the care and upbringing of Tony's four children and Ben's young son. The couple would have two children of their own, Dominic and Marina.

On the European trip with Tony, Mary became intimately involved with a wealthy Italian cruising the Mediterranean in his sloop.[25] The next summer, she and Cord traveled to Europe together and met the Italian who was with an American college co-ed and, without telling her husband about their earlier affair, they again cruised the Mediterranean together. When Cord returned home, Mary stayed on, ostensibly to visit Tony, who was in Paris, but really to see her Italian lover alone and renew their affair. After their second foray together, they believed they were deeply in love. Upon returning home, Mary told Cord about her affair and requested a divorce. Her Italian friend, she explained, would divorce his wife, and the two would marry and live on a ranch in the American West with Cord's boys. He concluded that her decision to abandon virtually everything, take their sons far away from him, and live in unfamiliar surroundings was ridiculous. He reflected in his journal: "My only hope is to allow time to dull her feelings and to permit reality to show through her present intact illusion. One cannot argue with someone who is in love with love."[26]

Only two months later, however, a terrible family tragedy, the death of their middle son, Michael, suddenly interrupted the couple's sorting out of their marriage crisis. Michael, then nine, was killed by an onrushing car on a windy state highway near the front of the Meyers' property. As he and his older brother, Quentin, returned home from a neighbor's house at dusk, Michael crossed the busy road and likely never saw the car that hit him from behind. Mary heard the crash and Quentin's screams and came rushing to the road but could only hold her dead son in her arms and try to console the shocked, grief-stricken driver. Michael would be buried in Milford cemetery next to his grandfather Amos.

The family nightmare might have been a wake-up call for both parents to try to find some basis for saving their marriage, but to Mary, their marriage could not be saved. She soon confronted him again, complaining about his excessive drinking, short temper, resentment toward their children, "cruel and thoughtless in his treatment of her," and "incurably promiscuous" behavior. (Cord later privately regretted "my own tendency to take a perverse pleasure in exercising my power over Mary.") She was waiting for the Italian, but he backed out of their relationship. Mary was profoundly disappointed and felt a real sense of the Italian gigolo's betrayal, but the following summer, she went to Nevada and got a divorce. Cord assented to it, but the divorce was acrimonious.[27]

* * *

Mary's difficulties with her husband seemed to set her on the path of a more daring lifestyle. Michael's death made her more protective of Quentin and Mark, but otherwise, she accelerated her break from the traditional housewife mold. Her Italian lover's desertion made her more cynical about the permanence of male relationships. In an increasingly affluent era, she had no major financial worries after her divorce and easily participated in Washington's social whirl, in which extramarital relationships and divorces were not uncommon.[28] Shortly before her divorce, Mary had moved with her two boys from McLean to a spacious Georgetown apartment, and she found time to satisfy her artistic and sexual longings. Her apartment had a detached garage, which she made into an art studio. She mostly painted there in the colorized modern art tradition popular in Washington then, and she immersed herself as an artist and patron of the rising artistic culture in the city. She took painting lessons from Kenneth Noland, a talented abstract artist in the color school, and they became lovers. Mary stayed with Noland for several years, even though his background—a southerner from a rural background, struggling financially and socially unpretentious—was quite different from Mary's refined world.[29] In 1960, as their romantic involvement was ending, the two, who shared liberal, dovish foreign policy views, apparently cooperated in writing separate letters to the *Washington Post,* complaining about its frivolous coverage of a citizens' disarmament group earnestly promoting an international ban on nuclear testing. The newspaper obligingly published both.[30]

Mary had not offered excuses to Cord for her infidelity but told him that he had not satisfied her sexually and emotionally and "there are so many beautiful men" out there.[31] One of the "beautiful men" she knew was John F. Kennedy. Mary had just turned forty when Kennedy was elected president, but Mary had known him as far back as the winter of 1936 when, only fifteen, she had attended a dance weekend at Choate. Her date for the occasion was Bill Attwood, her favorite beau then, but Kennedy, a freshman at Princeton, had returned to his school alma mater for the dance, and he spent much of the evening cutting in on pretty Mary on the dance floor.

Jack Kennedy likely dated her a few times during her Vassar years. In 1945 while plying his hand at journalism, he and newly married Mary reconnected at least socially when both covered the proceedings of the U.N. conference in San Francisco.[32] In the 1950s, the Meyers' house in McLean was next door to Hickory Hill, the name of Jack and Jacqueline's estate. Jack was now a U.S. Senator, and with busy husbands in government work, Mary and Jackie saw each other frequently. The two couples were part of the same Washington elite. Among other things, Jackie had attended Vassar after Mary, and they both were interested in the arts. In 1956, Jack and Jackie moved to Georgetown, just before Mary's relocation there.

Tony and Ben Bradlee also lived in Georgetown and had grown close to the Kennedys socially. The Bradlees hosted the first of several dinners for the new president. Mary was there and was part of the inner circle of the Kennedys' Georgetown friends.[33] As early as the summer of 1959, Mary may have had a sexual liaison with Kennedy, who was unhappy in his marriage. In any case, after he moved into the White House, Mary became a frequent visitor, not just as a guest to scheduled entertainments but separately and alone. Years later, the public opening of logs of guests entering and leaving the White House documented that, during Kennedy's presidency, Mary Meyer visited seventeen times, and on every occasion but one, First Lady Jackie was away from the city.[34] Mary tried to be discreet and told only a few close friends about her intimate relationship with the president. Though not easy to believe, given the two sisters' closeness, Tony later claimed she did not know about their affair.[35] In any event, Mary began another diary of her activities, which included her visits with Kennedy.

Even before his presidency, Jack Kennedy's compulsive womanizing was well known in the upper social circles of Georgetown. He did not slow down in the White House, and his sexual experiences with office staff and interns as well as visitors from outside, including Mary, have been extensively revealed in the years since his death.

Mary seemed to downplay rumors of Kennedy's sexual exploitation of other women, but she was correct in believing that she was his favorite lover. Sex was the object of his many liaisons, but valuing Mary for her intelligence and ideas, he treated her as a special paramour. She could talk to him about many subjects, ranging from analyzing his womanizing to matters of high domestic and foreign policy, and he would listen and share some of his private thoughts. She had unbelievable access arguably to the most powerful man in the world, but Mary was less interested in power than in her relationship with the president. It was a bonus if she might influence him somewhat in the direction of more peace-oriented and progressive policies. Like several Pinchots before her, she was a risk taker, though in her case, it went to the point of foolhardiness sometimes. Her

Mary Pinchot enjoying herself at President Kennedy's noisy 46th birthday party, on the presidential yacht Sequoia, May 29, 1963. Her sister Tony and husband, Ben Bradlee, also attended the raucous celebration. (John F. Kennedy Library)

sense of high adventure and having fun carried her along, even though her fling with a sitting, married president might not last.

Still a seeker, Mary explored the world of recreational drugs. It is unclear how she got involved in the drug culture, but she knew that the CIA utilized drugs to gain information from informants, and abstract artists with whom she painted and socialized sometimes used drugs as mind-enhancers. Just as she was experimental in her painting, she was becoming an experimentalist in life. In the spring of 1962, she appeared at the office door of Timothy Leary, the LSD guru in Harvard University's psychology department. Mary may have already tried LSD, and after introducing herself, she told him she wanted his help learning how to administer an LSD session for "a very important man."[36] Leary did not pick up that this friend might be the U.S. President, and he did not give Mary special attention. She persisted, however, and consulted with him several times. Mary probably smoked marijuana joints with Kennedy at the White House, but it is less likely that he experimented with LSD.[37]

It seems that Kennedy broke off his trysts with Mary on two occasions in early 1963, but fortunately for the couple, the press never reported on their relationship. By the early summer that year, Mary resumed her visits to the White House.[38] That September, President Kennedy participated in a Pinchot family event—a trip to Milford, Pennsylvania, to accept the gift of Grey Towers from Gifford Bryce Pinchot, Leila and Gifford's son, to the U.S. Forest Service.

Gifford's decision to give up the property evolved from family changes in the previous decade. Leila died in 1960 at the age of seventy-nine. She willed Grey Towers to her son, but as a sailing enthusiast spending his free time with Sally on saltwater far removed from Milford, Gifford Bryce had little desire to live in or maintain the expensive estate. He also understood, however, that Grey Towers was a magnetic lodestar for three generations of Pinchots and that the mansion should be preserved and used to perpetuate his father's conservation legacy and advance future environmental causes. He thus decided to donate the property to the U.S. Forest Service, and after long negotiations involving lawyers, foundations, and Pinchot family members, the transfer arrangements were completed. While the forest service managed the property, a newly created Pinchot Institute for Conservation developed the research and education programs. The institute's initial focus was that Grey Towers would be used as a meeting center for high-level discussions among scientists, environmental activists, government officials, and others on pressing natural resource issues.[39] President Kennedy's visit to Grey Towers was the capstone in this new private-public process.

Presumably, Tony and Mary tried to influence the president's decision to come to Milford, and it certainly helped that the two sisters and Ben Bradlee were his good friends—the two sisters even flew with Kennedy to the Grey Towers event at his request, arriving in the presidential helicopter. Public concerns about the environment were also heating up. For example, Rachel Carson's *Silent Spring*, published a year earlier, was a searing indictment of the obsessive use of DDT and other contaminants in poisoning America's water and food supplies, and had become a best-selling book that stimulated citizens' agitation for conservation. Kennedy's appearance at Grey Towers allowed him to get in front of an emerging domestic political issue, and his public remarks to a crowd of thousands fittingly extolled Gifford Pinchot as a principal founder and leader of the still robust conservation movement. Milford was the president's first stop in a whirlwind tour that would take him to ten western states in five days, where he would make many speeches highlighting conservation themes.[40]

Gifford Bryce's gift did not include the slice of property at Grey Towers that Amos's family had used as their retreat from their New York City residence. In her widowhood, Ruth, now seventy and somewhat reclusive, still lived there part of each year. She was at the dedication, and Kennedy, in fine form throughout his visit, praised Amos in his speech. Afterward, Kennedy took a brief tour of the mansion, then headed with Giff, Mary, and Tony to Ruth's cottage nearby, where her daughters spent much time in their youth, to socialize with their mother and look at family photo albums. Like her late husband, Ruth had gravitated to the political right since the 1930s and become an ardent backer of the ultraconservative Senator Barry Goldwater, who would win the Republican presidential nomination a year later. Despite their political differences, Kennedy and Ruth engaged in pleasant conversation. Giff later recounted that the president had been "very human" toward his aunt and, during the picture taking, had "turned to her with a broad and very friendly grin and said, 'I will send you a copy of this and you can send it on to Barry.'"[41]

*   *   *

On November 19, 1963, eight weeks after the Milford event, an exhibit of Mary Meyer's colorist paintings opened at a Washington gallery, but Kennedy would be assassinated in Dallas, Texas, three days later. Amid her personal trauma over her lover's demise, Mary's show would receive a laudable review, and she continued her serious painting and planned another exhibit. Her rise as a promising artist would be cut short, however, when, on October 12, 1964, she too would be violently killed.[42] Mary's death occurred during a midday

Following his acceptance of Gifford Bryce Pinchot's gift of Grey Towers to the U.S. Forest Service, Milford, Pennsylvania, President Kennedy posed for photographs with (l-r) Gifford Bryce, Antoinette (Tony) Bradlee, Ruth Pinchot, and Mary Pinchot Meyer at Ruth's cottage nearby, September 24, 1963. The photograph may be the only one showing the lovers Kennedy and Mary together. (John F. Kennedy Library)

walk alone on the towpath adjacent to the old C & O Canal that traversed through Georgetown. She often walked along the path as a break from painting in her studio. Someone came up to Mary and accosted her. Mary struggled and screamed, and two men working on the Canal Road below the towpath heard her yells but could not see what was happening. At that point, the assailant pulled a gun and shot her in the head. Though mortally wounded, she managed to get up and tried to get away when the assailant sent a second shot through her back. She died instantly.

Why had she been assaulted and killed? Attempted rape was a possible motive, but it was broad daylight and occurred in a fairly open area. Mary carried no purse or money with her, and there was no good evidence that robbery was the cause. However, the District of Columbia police, finding no more plausible motive, would maintain robbery as the most likely one. Her murder was front page news in the Washington newspapers, which provided their own speculations as to what happened and why.

The police investigation of the tragic event provided no leads about Mary's past activities that might have prompted the attack. However, interviews with witnesses nearby revealed additional information. A white Army lieutenant came forward with his story of seeing an African American man behind her when he jogged on the towpath earlier that evening. The police took into custody Ray Crump, Jr., a twenty-five-year-old indigent black laborer recently released from jail, who gave different explanations for his presence at the canal. He was near her body when the police arrived at the crime scene, and he was charged with the murder. To many, it was an open and shut case—the attacker had been found, and he would be prosecuted and convicted. There were problems with the prosecution, however. The murder weapon was never found, none of Mary's blood or garment fibers turned up on the accused man, and the prosecutor produced no witnesses who saw the actual assault. At the trial, the defense refused to put Crump on the stand where the prosecution's cross-examination could have challenged his credibility. Prosecution witnesses described the black man they saw nearby the murder scene as considerably taller and heavier than the defendant. In this and other ways, the prosecution botched what was already a difficult case. The defendant was ultimately acquitted.

The murder has never been solved, but twelve years after Mary's tragic death, an article in the *National Enquirer* exposed her numerous visits to the White House as President Kennedy's lover and confidant and revealed the possibility that they smoked pot together. Anne Truitt, a close artist friend, and her husband, Jim, were among the few people with whom Mary had confided about her amorous affair. Jim, a journalist who kept meticulous records (and now divorced from Anne), was the principal source for the article.[43] Reviewing the unanswered questions about her murder, the story fueled speculation that more than a single assailant might have been involved. Perhaps, some alleged, the assailant was a hit man working for another person or group. Since her tragic end, several biographies of Mary have been written, which have advanced interpretations of her assassination.[44]

Their stories make for engrossing reading, either inferring or arguing that Mary's assassination and perhaps Kennedy's too were part of an organized conspiracy concocted by the president's haters (the mafia and right-wingers) outside government and in the most secret parts of the Pentagon and CIA. It is not unreasonable to believe Kennedy's assassination was a conspiracy involving more than one disaffected assassin. Further, it is possible that Mary was killed because she supposedly had serious reservations about the conclusions of the recently released Warren Commission, which, in its investigation of Kennedy's death, hurriedly endorsed the single-shooter thesis and knew too much about him and any revelations he may have made to her during their relationship about his suspected enemies. But Mary was a private person, and there seem to be no writings or conversations of what she and her lover communicated to each other or what she may have known about the circumstances leading to Kennedy's death. Much speculation remains. It is also unlikely whether the real killer or possible clandestine operations plotting her death can ever be identified. Now two generations after the events, no one is still alive who might have new details about Mary's murder, and no recordings of people and verifiable written documents with hard evidence, especially intelligence records, have surfaced.

Adding to the mystery surrounding Mary's death was her diary, which was publicly revealed in the *Enquirer* article. On the same day of the murder, Ben Bradlee, Mary's brother-in-law, had the unthankful tasks of phoning Ruth to tell her about her daughter's tragic end and then identifying Mary's body at the morgue. Later accounts of what transpired next differ, sometimes markedly. According to Bradlee's account, published more than thirty years later, on the same evening of Mary's death, Anne Truitt, who was in Tokyo, Japan, with her husband, Jim, then *Newsweek* bureau chief there, had phoned his house and related that Mary had previously instructed Anne, if anything happened to her, to find and give Anne the diary. This was the first Tony and Ben knew of such a diary. When the Bradlees went to Mary's home the next day (or soon thereafter), they discovered James Jesus Angleton, the CIA's director of counterintelligence and a family friend, already inside the house. After returning later the same day to search in the studio, they again found him, this time trying to pick the lock. (Angleton was well known as an expert lock-picker.) In the studio, they found a diary in Mary's handwriting of about ten pages in an artist's sketchbook, mostly filled with some of Mary's color swatches and drawings.

Tony and Ben took the diary home and read it. They were shocked by the first revelations of Mary's long affair with Kennedy. Tony was especially aggrieved. She and Ben had heard many stories of Kennedy's sexual appetite, but they knew nothing about Mary's liaisons with him. Tony felt a sense of betrayal since she was attracted to the president and flattered by his attention, and she believed that Kennedy might have found her more desirable than her sister. While still a senator, he made a pass at Tony, and he even propositioned her during a noisy party in late May 1963, celebrating his forty-sixth birthday on the presidential yacht, *Sequoia*. Tony always turned him down, and after reading Mary's diary, she felt that Kennedy and Mary might have been using her as a decoy to deflect attention from their own affair. The Bradlees then, in a "naive" moment, gave Mary's diary to James Angleton for destruction.[45]

Anne Truitt and Cicely Angleton, the counterintelligence chief's wife, contradicted Bradlee's memoir. They explained in a letter to the *New York Times* that Anne's phone call to the Bradlee house on the evening of the murder was person-to-person to Angleton, who was told about Mary's private diary and her instruction to Anne, in the event of anything happening to her, to find and turn

it over to Angleton for safe-keeping. (They said nothing about Angleton's independent presence at Mary's house and studio after her death or the destruction
of the document.) If the two women's account was accurate, their letter implied
that Bradlee should not have been surprised at Angleton's presence at Mary's
residence nor of the diary ending up in Angleton's hands. Their version might
seem more plausible since Tony gave the diary to Angleton shortly after reading
it.[46] If there were names or descriptions in her diary that might have been closely
scrutinized and provided leads for further investigation into the Kennedy and
Mary murders, the Bradlees never admitted it. To them, the diary was a personal
or family document without policy implications, especially when the president
of the United States was involved.[47] Indeed, though intelligence officials and
family members might have differed about the details of the murders, investigation, trial, and Mary's diary, they were all motivated, at least until the *National
Enquirer* article, to withhold Jack and Mary's love affair and drug activities and
possible misinformation by intelligence operatives from public exposure.

Given Mary's disdain for the CIA, it might seem incongruous that she would
want Angleton, the acknowledged mastermind and overseer of the agency's covert programs, to take possession of her diary. To his critics, he was the supreme
villain of the Cold War. Angleton was a complicated personality, however, as he
was also cultured—well versed in history and foreign affairs, an accomplished
piano player, skilled fisherman, lover of the arts—and a good family man. The
personal connection was important, as he and his wife, Cicely, had been longtime friends with Mary going back to Cord's first days with the CIA. After the
Meyers' divorce, he had been like a second father in raising Mary's two boys.
Mary understood that Angleton, a master of secrets, would protect the diary,
allowing her oldest son, Quentin (Angleton was his godfather), to read it when
he was twenty-one, as she, according to Anne, had also wished, but otherwise
loyally guarding the personal information in it from public disclosure.[48]

After the appearance of the *Enquirer* piece, Tony confronted Angleton, who
admitted that he had not destroyed the diary sketchbook she had turned over
to him. She demanded that he return it to her, which he did. Tony then had the
diary burned in Anne Truitt's presence. Bradlee later wrote that neither he nor
Tony "has any idea what Angleton did with the diary while it was in his possession, nor why he failed to follow Mary and Tony's instructions."[49]

Mary's sudden death was especially upsetting to her two boys (who were
away at college and boarding school) and also Tony. Their intense pain was
more long-lasting because the murder remained unsolved, leaving no closure
for the family. Tony also had to live with the knowledge of her sister's sexual

liaisons with Kennedy and the sense of betrayal in keeping it secret and misleading her. Tony was a seeker in her own way, and she turned to the fine arts and philosophy for peace of mind. She took painting lessons and classes in sculpture at the Corcoran School of Art in Washington and became a proficient sculptor and jeweler. She even had her own exhibition in a small Washington art gallery. She also studied spiritualist philosophy and mysticism and became an ardent disciple of two Russian gurus.[50]

Tony was also backing away from journalism. Bradlee soon became chief editor of the *Washington Post*, gaining accolades for his newspaper's publication of the Pentagon Papers and its investigative reporting of the Watergate burglary, eventually leading to Richard Nixon's resignation from the presidency. But Tony dissociated herself from the profession. Journalism had become shallow to her, so fast-breaking news scoops were trivial compared to her yearning for deeper philosophical insights into life. As Tony and Ben drifted apart, Ben found a new live-in girlfriend, Sally Quinn, a young, attractive *Post* reporter, and after his divorce from Tony, he would marry Sally in 1978. Tony lived her last years in Washington in relative obscurity until her death in 2011.

*   *   *

Beginning with Rosamond's suicide and Amos's downfall and continuing through Mary's several entanglements and finally her murder and Tony's personal travails, that branch of the Pinchots suffered a series of terrible tragedies.[51] But their stories are only part of a larger family epic of the principled, adventuresome, risk-taking Pinchots in a long historical arc of three generations, and their activism resulted in formidable achievements and successes.

By the late 1980s, Amos's and Gifford's sons, Gifford 2nd and Gifford Bryce, had died, and Gifford III and Peter, the sons of Gifford Bryce, were the only ones from that direct line to carry on the Pinchot surname. They both married and had families, and forestry and conservation projects formed an important part of their diverse careers, which also involved organic dairy farming, entrepreneurial and academic innovations, and angel investing.[52] Marianne and Diane Rosamond, the daughters of Gifford 2nd, and Bill and James, Rosamond's sons, also married and had children.[53]

These more recent Pinchot generations have been productive in their own spheres and had their own personal triumphs and disappointments, even if not so dramatic or publicly revealed as the stories of their forebears. As the diaspora continues, the family members have every reason to appreciate the amazing Pinchot legacy.

Abbreviations in the Notes

AJ	Alan Johnstone
AP	Amos Pinchot
APJ	Antoinette Pinchot Johnstone
APP	Amos Pinchot Papers
BTW	Booker T. Washington
CBP	Cornelia Bryce Pinchot
CBPP	Cornelia Bryce Pinchot Papers
FDR	Franklin Delano Roosevelt
GBP	Gifford Bryce Pinchot
GP	Gifford Pinchot
GPP	Gifford Pinchot Papers
HLS	Henry L. Stimson
JRG	James R. Garfield
JWP	James Wallace Pinchot
MEP	Mary Eno Pinchot
NYT	*New York Times*
PMHB	*Pennsylvania Magazine of History and Biography*
PWW	*Papers of Woodrow Wilson*
RPP	Rosamond Pinchot Papers
TR	Theodore Roosevelt
TRP	Theodore Roosevelt Papers
WHT	William Howard Taft
WHTP	William Howard Taft Papers
WP	*Washington Post*
WTS	William Tecumseh Sherman
WW	Woodrow Wilson
WWP	Woodrow Wilson Papers
YDN	*Yale Daily News*
YLM	*Yale Literary Magazine*

Notes on Sources

Writing a credible biography about a past public person requires access to relevant primary materials. Sometimes the sources do not exist or have been lost or destroyed, and the result is that biographers have been constrained in providing full justice to their prominent historical figures. The refrain "no papers" is often enough to discourage historians from trying to tackle the lives of certain historical personages.

Studying the Pinchot family poses the opposite problem of too much documentation. Clio smiled on the Pinchot family. Until at least the advent of the telephone, letter writing was the main mode of personal communication between individuals who were physically separated from one another, and all the Pinchots were not only inveterate travelers but also prolific correspondents. Indeed, one of the requirements that the first-generation Pinchot parents in this book imposed on their children was frequent—at least bi-weekly—letters from them whenever the child or a parent was away from home.

For this book, I mainly perused four collections of Pinchot family papers, all of which are housed in the manuscript division of the Library of Congress. The indispensable resource among these collections is the extensive Gifford Pinchot papers. Consisting of nearly 3,200 archive boxes, his papers comprise the second-largest collection of private papers in the library. Going back three generations before Gifford and his siblings Antoinette and Amos (or when the family emigrated from France to the United States), the Pinchots saved just about everything. The collection thus contains personal (and some business) papers of their father, their mother's diaries, and the correspondence between their immediate and extended family members. More substantively, they include Gifford's diaries, his family letters, much professional and political correspondence, and extensive newspaper clipping files during his career as forester and conservationist and his two stints as governor of Pennsylvania. Several boxes house copies of his speeches and drafts of his many books.

Not surprisingly, the Gifford Pinchot papers are a treasure trove of family history, containing the core of the immediate family's relationships and adventures. I cannot claim to have delved into every box, but I opened the great majority of them and mined the many hundreds that I considered central to the ideas and activities of the entire family. The only published collection from his papers are *The Conservation Diaries of Gifford Pinchot*, edited by Harold K. Steen, a compilation of Gifford's diary entries relating to his forestry and conservation activities. I have cited this published collection where accurate and relevant to assist researchers wanting access to printed sources. But because Gifford wrote in his diaries about a wide range of other subjects, including his personal and family relationships and his extensive political career, the reader will notice many citations herein from his manuscript diaries.

The Amos Pinchot papers comprise 180 boxes further documenting Amos's family ties and involvement in various political and social causes. My research in these boxes revealed crucial information not only about Amos's personal life and the political and social causes in which he participated but also provided important details on the lives of his parents and other family members not duplicated elsewhere.

The third collection, consisting of 570 boxes, is the papers of Gifford's wife, Cornelia (Leila) Bryce Pinchot. She, too, seemed to save all her personal papers—at least from the time of her betrothal to Gifford to her death forty-six years later. Her correspondence with Gifford from their budding romance onward, her activism in feminist causes, and her care for political and social issues at the state, national, and international level are central to her correspondence, but her letters also document the upbringing of their son, Giff, and her involvement with Amos's children.

Leila's close relationship with Amos's oldest daughter, Rosamond, is further documented in the Rosamond Pinchot papers. Comprising six boxes, this fourth Pinchot collection contains many letters between Rosamond and her father and Leila, which along with the young woman's copious private diaries, reveal many details about her schooling, acting career, and troubled marriage during her short life.

Cumulatively, these four Pinchot manuscript collections form arguably the largest collection of family papers in America.

Observant readers will discern that many footnote citations in this book reference direct quotations in the text, and the vast majority of these are from the manuscript papers I consulted. Usually, the fuller context of my analysis comes from other, unquoted (and uncited) letters in the same collection, often the same box.

By contrast, there are relatively few citations of secondary sources, including the extensive and still growing historical literature on family history, forestry, political reform movements, or diplomatic developments, to take some prominent examples. My research strategy included extensive reading in the extant secondary literature, and I am deeply indebted to those who have explored these subjects, often perceptively. Historiography is important, and we historians stand on the shoulders of those in our discipline who have ventured forth before us. For my purposes, the historical literature on the social and cultural life of the patrician class from the mid-nineteenth to mid-twentieth century America was especially helpful. So, too, historical writings about Gifford Pinchot, the best-known family member, including disagreements among them about aspects of his career—for instance, his controversy with John Muir over conservation—have not escaped my attention.

Generally, however, I have not cited in the notes the specific secondary works that I have found most useful. The exceptions are those from which I quote in the text and occasional citations to important but older and sometimes more obscure sources. I have not discussed errors and excesses in other works in my text or footnotes, which are usually more matters of detail rather than fundamental interpretation, but have written my own account from what I have deduced as truthful and reliable.

Moreover, except for Gifford Pinchot and Mary Pinchot Meyer, and to a lesser degree Rosamond, my interpretations of the individuals in this book are unique since very little, if anything, has been written about any of them in any depth. I hope my portraits of all the Pinchots—their personalities and the full range of their travails, illnesses, successes, and failures—will prove helpful and stimulate further explorations of their lives and the events and causes in which they participated.

Endnotes

Chapter 1: Two Rising Entrepreneurs

1. Jackson F. Eno, ed., "The Eno Family From Their Origins in France to the Present, Part I: The Late Middle Ages to the Early 19th Century," *Simsbury Genealogical and Historical Research Library*, 17 (Summer 2010), pp. 1-6; Henry Lane Eno, *The Eno Family: New York Branch* (Princeton, NJ: Princeton University Press, 1920).

2. Amos R. Eno to Lucy Jane Phelps, Feb. 16, 1834, Gifford Pinchot Papers (Manuscript Division, Library of Congress), box 49 (hereafter GPP).

3. Ibid.

4. The Eno and Phelps families intermarried several times by the eighteenth century. Jackson F. Eno, "The Eno Family from Their Origins in France to the Present, Part II: Into the 20th Century," *Simsbury Genealogical and Historical Research Library*, 17 (Fall 2010), pp. 1-7; Oliver S. Phelps, *The Phelps Family of America and Their English Ancestors* (Pittsfield, MA: Eagle Publishing, 1899), pp. 608, 622, passim.

5. Mary Ann (Phelps) Allen to MEP, Jan. 7, 1898, GPP, box 59.

6. Another of Elisha and Lucy's offspring, John Smith Phelps, won election for nine straight terms as a Democratic representative to the U.S. Congress. During the Civil War, John remained loyal to the Union and served as a general in the U.S. Army, and he would become military governor of occupied Missouri. Char Miller, *Gifford Pinchot and the Making of Modern Environmentalism* (Washington, DC: Island Press, 2001), pp. 45-48. (Hereafter, Miller, *Pinchot*.)

7. Ibid.; Mary Pinchot, Recollections, GPP, Box 441. Another of Eno's many speculative ventures was the Flatiron Building (1857).

8. Mary Jane Springman, "The Simsbury Free Library," *Simsbury Genealogical and Historical Research Library*, 14 (Spring, 2007), pp. 1-5.

9. Two siblings younger than Mary died in their infancy. The surviving seven in order of birth were Amos F., Mary Jane (her middle name), John (Jack) Chester, Anna Maria, Antoinette, Henry Clay, and William Phelps.

10. Amos F. Eno to Mary Eno, undated [June 1864], John S. Phelps to Amos R. Eno, Dec. 1, 1861, and Amos F. Eno to Lucy Jane Eno, Feb. 5, 1863, GPP, box 3168.

11. Miller, *Pinchot*, p. 50; MEP, Recollections, GPP, box 441; MEP to GP, June 29 [1896?], ibid., box 72; Amos F. Eno to Sister (Mary), Feb. 10, 1863, ibid., GPP, box 51.

12. James's birth year is usually given as 1831, but notations of family births in James's Bible and other sources listed his birthdate as 1829: M. A. P. Warner to Brother, Aug. 1 [1894], Amos Pinchot Papers (hereafter APP), box 1; P. W. Ells to C. C. D. Pinchot, Nov. 15, 1864, GPP, box 48; census records for 1830 (and later), his passport application in 1864, and Union draft records.

13. Cyrill's middle names were Constantine Désiré. "Cyril" would be the anglicized spelling of the French Cyrille, but he dropped the "e" and not the final "l". Biographical Sketch of James W. Pinchot, July 10, 1936, GPP, box 644, adds details on the French settlers in Milford. Norman B. Lehde, "Origins of the Pinchot Family," *Journal of Forestry*, 63 (Aug. 1965), pp. 582-584, informs James's early years. Additional details on Milford are in Norman Lehde, et al., *Milford, Pennsylvania, 1733-1983: "Heritage 250"* (n.p.: n.p. [1983]).

14. I am grateful to Jean-Charles Cappronnier, President of La Société Historique de Breteuil, for details on the social and economic position of the Pinchot family in Breteuil.

15. Miller, *Pinchot*, pp. 20-21. Passport of Constantine and Marie Pinchot, Aug. 3, 1818, GPP, box 3174. Marie may have had financial resources, which improved the Pinchots' economic position in America.

16. Constantine Pinchot's application for citizenship, Nov. 7, 1818, and Cyrill's certificate of U.S. citizenship, Oct. 11, 1826, are ibid.

17. William Bross to GP, Sept. 9, 1889, ibid., box 77.

18. Charles D. Vail to GP, March 27, 1912, ibid., box 157.

19. Real estate deeds documenting Cyrill's land purchases in Milford are ibid., box 3172. Cyrill's correspondence regarding lumber matters is ibid., box 49.

20. Wallace, James's middle name, came from Cyrill's business associate, and one of Eliza's brothers married a Wallace. Letters from John W. Wallace to C. C. D. Pinchot concerning the lumber trade, are in GPP, box 49. Cyrill C. D. Pinchot's account book for 1863-1871, and his postmaster appointment, March 13, 1865, are ibid., box 76.

21. JWP, "The Yale Summer School of Forestry," *World's Work*, 8 (Oct. 1904), p. 5389.

22. Henry Fitch to JWP, Nov. 9, 1847, Fred R. Bailey to C. C. D. Pinchot, April 15, 1851, and H. S. Mott to C. C. D. Pinchot, March 18, 1852, and April 14, 1852, GPP, box 49; Miller, *Pinchot*, pp. 24-27.

23. Milford in 1860 had 711 residents (U.S. Census, 1860). Edgar had started a wholesale grocery business in the city, but by the 1850s he had become a wholesale druggist.

24. Advertising flyer of Partridge, Pinchot & Warren, July 12, 1858, GPP, box 50. James also speculated a little in an iron mining venture in New Jersey. Correspondence is ibid., box 49.

25. JWP to C. C. D. Pinchot, Dec. 6, 1854, ibid.

26. JWP to Mons. Pinchot & Son, Feb. 22, 1854, ibid., and C. C. D. Pinchot to JWP, May 31, 1854, and July 27, 1854, C. C. D. Pinchot and Sis (Mary A. Pinchot) to Cyrill H. Pinchot, May 6 [1856], ibid., box 70; C. C. D. Pinchot to Cyrill H. Pinchot, Nov. 30, 1856, ibid., box 50.

27. John F. Pinchot to Bub (brother Cyrill), June 1, 1855, ibid., box 49; and John F. Pinchot to Cyrill H. Pinchot, Jan. [1856?], ibid., box 71.

28. JWP to Mons. Pinchot & Son, Aug. 16, 1852, ibid., box 49.

29. JWP to Cyrill H. Pinchot, Aug. 17, 1855, and Dec. 3, 1855, and C. C. D. Pinchot to JWP, March 13, 1855, ibid.

30. J. S. Warren to JWP, Jan. 25, 1874, ibid., box 51. One account asserted that Cyrill joined the Presbyterian church at Milford in 1832, and "for over forty years he continued an active and earnest member, and during that long period was one of its most liberal supporters." Quotation in *Commemorative Biographical Record of Northeastern Pennsylvania*, p. 277.

31. C. C. D. Pinchot to JWP, July 25, 1854, and JWP to C. C. D. Pinchot, Oct. 1, 1852, GPP, box 49.

32. JWP to C. C. D. Pinchot, Nov. 5, 1854, ibid. One listing had James living then at the Mansion Hotel in Brooklyn. *Wilson's Business Directory* (New York: John F. Trow, 1856), p. 307.

33. JWP to Cyrill H. Pinchot, Nov. 16, 1857, and Nov. 5, 1858, GPP, box 50. M. Nelson McGeary, *Gifford Pinchot: Forester-Politician* (Princeton, NJ: Princeton University Press, 1960), p. 3. (Hereafter McGeary, *Pinchot*.) GP, Draft Biographical Sketch of James W. Pinchot, July 10, 1936, GPP, box 644.

34. JWP to Cyrill H. Pinchot, Jan. 1, 1856, Aug. 4, 1856, Oct. 25, 1856, Dec. 11, 1856, Feb. 19, 1857, April 2, 1857, July 21, 1857, April 27, 1858, Sept. 16, 1858, and Nov. 5, 1858, GPP, box 50. Cyrill received outstanding grades in 1857 and 1858. His report cards are in GPP, box 76.

35. JWP to Cyrill H. Pinchot, April 27, 1859, ibid., box 50. Cyrill may have contracted tuberculosis in the winter of 1859 and likely left Union College then, and he did not return there for the 1859–1860 academic year. Student Bill Book for the Class of 1861, Union College, Special Collections.

36. The six, painted between 1861 and 1868, were *Bivouac of Seventh Regiment at Arlington Heights, Virginia*; *Chillon Castle*; *Moonlight*; *Lake Fog*; *Hunter Mountain in the Catskills, After Sunset*; and *Indian Summer*. *Catalogue of Paintings of Sanford Robinson Gifford, N.A.* (New York: Metropolitan Museum of Art, 1881); Waldo S. Pratt to JWP, Dec. 13, 1880, GPP, box 52.

37. Launt Thompson to JWP, Nov. 7, 1861, ibid., box 51; Jervis McEntee Diaries, March 5, 1875 (and many other entries), Jervis McEntee Papers (Archives of American Art); Worthington Whittredge to Joseph Mozier, May 21, 1864, GPP, box 3169; *The Autobiography of Worthington Whittredge, 1820-1910*, ed. John I. H. Bauer (New York: Arno Press, 1969), p. 69. James and Whittredge were still corresponding into the twentieth century.

38. Thompson to JWP, July 23, 1863, GPP, box 51.

39. James then lived near the Fifth Avenue Hotel and could have first met Mary there. McEntee to JWP, Oct. 25, 1863, ibid., box 3169.

40. MEP to GP, Feb. 10 [1894], ibid., box 3170.

41. MEP, Recollections, ibid., box 441; Miller, *Pinchot*, pp. 50-51.

42. The 1862 draft law subjected Northern men between twenty and forty-five to possible military conscription.

43. JWP to C. C. D. Pinchot, April 18, 1861, GPP, box 51. Sanford Gifford would re-enlist two more times.

44. JWP to C. C. D. Pinchot, June 30, 1863, APP, box 1.

45. Launt Thompson to JWP, July 23, 1863, GPP, box 51. Vicksburg fell to Union forces at the same time as Gettysburg.

46. Mary's diary for 1863 contains numerous entries of "Mr. P__" coming to call with violets in hand or staying for dinner. Ibid. box 3170; JWP to Mary Eno, Aug. 29 [1863], ibid., box 51; and U.S. draft notice, Oct. 1, 1863, ibid., box 3174.

47. Neither of James's surviving brothers, Edgar and John, served in the military during the war.

48. On the wedding day, Jervis McEntee was out of town, Launt Thompson got the date wrong, and Eastman Johnson overslept. Eastman Johnson to JWP, May 25, 1864, GPP, box 51; Jervis McEntee to JWP, May 23, 1864, ibid., box 3169.

49. JWP to Mary Eno, Feb. 11 [1864], ibid., box 75.

50. James Warren to JWP, Aug. 12, 1864, ibid., box 3169.

51. C. A. Phelps to Cousin Mollie (Mary), May 10, 1859, ibid., box 50.

52. JWP to MEP, undated, 10:20 p.m., and Aug. 1, 1865, and MEP to JWP, May 21, 1865, ibid., box 51.

53. James had at first expressed, however, "great anxiety over the ugly shape of his head and the absolute hardness of his features." This disquietude soon subsided. MEP, Diary, 1865, Feb. 20, 1868, JWP to MEP, Sept. 10, 1866, ibid., box 3170; and JWP to MEP, Aug. 22, 1865, ibid., box 51.

54. The Phelpses were obviously fixated on the name Lucy, which was the name of Mary's maternal grandmother, mother, and youngest sister, who lived only from 1849–1851.

55. MEP Diary, 1865, Feb. 20, 1868, May 21, 1869, GPP, box 3170; and Lucy Phelps Eno to MEP, June 20, 1869, ibid., box 3168. Lucy Eno had special reasons for sympathy, as Lulie bore her name, and two of her own children, including another Lucy, had died in their infancy.

56. Antoinette was also the name of one of Mary's cousins.

57. MEP Diary, May 6, 1870, GPP, box 3170.

58. JWP to MEP, Feb. 4, 1871, ibid., box 3169; JWP to C.C. D. Pinchot, Oct. 6, 1872, ibid., box 51; Antoinette E. Pinchot, note, Monday, 17th, 1879, APP, box 1.

Chapter 2: The French Connection

1. The sixteen in the household are listed by name in the 1870 U.S. Census.

2. Quotations in Betsy Fahlman, *John Ferguson Weir: The Labor of Art* (Newark: University of Delaware Press, 1997), p. 62.

3. Miller, *Pinchot*, p. 27; John F. Weir to JWP, May 17, 1870, GPP, box 51.

4. "Napoleon; or, The Man of the World," in *The Complete Prose Works of Ralph Waldo Emerson*, ed. G. A. Bettany (New York: Wand, Lock, 1891), pp. 214-223 (quotations on pp. 221-222).

5. Beck and Pinchot in the new partnership named Fr. Beck & Co. agreed to contribute $75,000 in real estate, machinery, inventory, and cash. James contributed $55,000 for a half interest in Beck's store property.-Details are in GPP, box 76.

6. MEP to JWP, Aug. 21 [1878?], ibid., box 54; and JWP to C. C. D. Pinchot, Aug. 12, 1870, ibid., box 51.

7. MEP, Pocket Diary, 1870, ibid., box 3174; and MEP, Outline of Early Life, ibid., box 48.

8. Soon after his return from Europe, Sherman would have two extended torrid extramarital affairs. Fortunately for his Pinchot friendship, his affairs were not revealed until long after all their lifetimes. Michael Fellman, *Citizen Sherman: A Life of William Tecumseh Sherman* (New York: Random House, 1995), pp. 352-370.

9. JWP to C. C. D. Pinchot, July 12, 1872, Aug. 18, 1872, and Sept. 1, 1872, GPP, box 51; and MEP, Outline of Early Life, ibid., box 48.

10. MEP to JWP, Aug. 21 [1878?], ibid., box 54; JWP to MEP, Thursday [1872], ibid., box 3169; and JWP to C. C. D. Pinchot, Feb. 29, 1872, ibid., box 51.

11. JWP to C. C. D. Pinchot, Dec. 9, 1871, and Feb. 29, 1872, ibid.,

12. JWP to MEP, Jan. 30, 1872, ibid., box 3169; MEP to JWP, May 26 [1872], ibid., box 75.

13. GP to JWP, June 2, 1873, and GP to MEP, Aug. 12, 1874, ibid., box 51.

14. JWP to C. C. D. Pinchot, Jan. 24, 1872, ibid. Gifford also saw at close range the German emperor, Wilhelm I, who like the Pinchots summered at Homberg.

15. JWP to C. C. D. Pinchot, Nov. 20, 1869, and WTS to JWP, Feb. 1, 1871, ibid. The amount raised came to £2,000 (about 50,000 francs) as a first installment. Minister E. B. Washburne to Secretary of State Fish, Feb. 8, 1871, RG 59, National Archives.

16. James had come away from his visit to England in 1869 "more than ever impressed with the largeness and wealth as well as the poverty of London." JWP to C. C. D. Pinchot, Dec. 30, 1869, and July 9, 1871, GPP, box 51; JWP to MEP, Sept. 24, 1871, ibid., box 3169.

17. The painting may have been James's idea, but Mary enthusiastically embraced it. Cabanel to JWP, undated, ibid., box 51.

18. McEntee was not told the explicit price but inferred it from his discussion about the portrait with James Pinchot. Jervis McEntee Diaries, May 22, 1873, McEntee Papers.

19. Whittredge to JWP, Feb. 15, 1874, and McEntee to JWP, June 25, 1876, GPP, box 51.

20. Weir to JWP, Oct. 30, 1874, ibid. Whittredge continued to complain of the difficulties facing American artists, though lauding James's "quiet example in loving and encouraging the art of our country." Whittredge to JWP, June 25, 1876, ibid. The Johnson painting James commissioned is entitled *Mrs. Cross*; the bust was completed in 1878. The Eno family was likely involved even earlier, as Henry C. Eno, Mary's immediate younger brother, had etched Whittredge's *The Old Hunting Ground* (1864) in James Pinchot's art collection.

21. JWP to Mother, Aug. 21, 1871, GPP, box 51.

22. JWP to C. C. D. Pinchot, Sept. 24, 1871, ibid. The ex-emperor's sudden death in January 1873 ended James's library initiative. The Metropolitan Museum later returned the Napoleon statue long term to Grey Towers, the Pinchot's Milford home, where it is still positioned today.

23. With money in short supply, James reflected, "If I had been in New York[,] I could have made some money doubtless, but it is sad to think how much that opportunity has cost to so many." JWP to C. C. D. Pinchot, Oct. 4 [1873], GPP, box 71.

24. JWP to C. C. D. Pinchot, Dec. 6, 1873, and Dec. 20, 1873, ibid., box 51.

25. JWP to C. C. D. Pinchot, Dec. 20, 1873, JWP to Mother, Jan. 3, 1874, and JWP to Brother, Feb. 4, 1874, ibid.

26. MEP, Diary, Sept. 1-Oct. 20, 1874, ibid., box 3170.

27. MEP to JWP, Aug. 21, ibid., box 54. The year 1888 has been written on this letter, but internal evidence suggested it was written much earlier, probably in 1878.

28. MEP to JWP, Aug. 21 [1878?], ibid.

29. An aunt of Mary Pinchot and her family lived in Saybrook. For the first summer there, the Pinchots gave up their New York rental house and rented another nearby in the fall.

30. MEP to GP, Sept. 16 [1889], GPP, box 54. Gifford admitted that Bar Harbor was the "Most beautiful place in itself I know of anywhere." GP, Diary, Aug. 8, 1891, ibid., box 1.

31. MEP to GP, Sept. 16 [1889], ibid., box 54.

32. JWP to C. C. D. Pinchot, Oct. 13, 1872, and Feb. 23, 1872, ibid., box 51.

33. MEP, Outline of Early Life, ibid., box 48.

34. In a June 10, 1875, agreement, James Pinchot and Frederick Beck entered into co-partnership with three others, with Beck and Pinchot, being "special partners," each contributing $25,000, and the others lesser amounts of cash, goods, or machinery for five years. Pinchot was to receive ten percent of the profits.

35. MEP to JWP, Aug. 21 [1878?], GPP, box 54. Later, she again asked him to forgive her for her criticisms. MEP to JWP, Dec. 28 [1885], ibid., box 53.

36. Minutes of the Advisory Committee, Jan. 21, 1878, box 3168. In early 1877, James gave $1,000 to the Metropolitan Museum of Art. Gifford later believed his father gave $2,500 or $3,500 to the museum. GP, Draft Biographical Sketch of James W. Pinchot, July 10, 1936, ibid., box 644.

37. Ibid.

38. JWP to GP, Sept. 28, 1892, ibid., box 55.

39. MEP to JWP, March 11 [1883], ibid., box 75. She also wrote him: "It is only because you do not do yourself justice that I complain of you. When you are at your best I am always satisfied with and proud of you." MEP to JWP, Dec. 28 [1885], ibid.

40. MEP to JWP, March 11 [1883], ibid., box 53.

41. GP, Draft Biographical Sketch of James W. Pinchot, July 10, 1936, ibid., box 644. James's letters to Richard Butler, the chair of the American committee, are in American Committee of the Statue of Liberty Correspondence (Manuscripts and Archives, New York Public Library), box 1. Launt Thompson to JWP, Aug. 21, 1884, APP, box 1.

42. JWP to MEP, Feb. 21, 1886, GPP, box 52. One estimate of a total cost (unfurnished) of $19,000 is surely too low, even allowing for a twenty-plus price inflation for our own time. Rebecca Philpot to author, e-mail, March 4, 2016.

43. MEP to JWP, Feb. 7 [1886], GPP, box 53.

44. The painting and statue are currently in a front room of Grey Towers, and the bust of Lafayette is located in a niche on the second floor.

45. JWP to MEP, June 5, 1890, GPP, box 54.

46. MEP to JWP, March 11 [1883]. ibid., box 75.

47. JWP to MEP, March 14 [1886], ibid., box 54 and MEP to GP, March 11 [1890], ibid., box 72.

Chapter 3: The Education of Christian Patricians

1. A German governess and a tutor of the children were still in friendly contact with family members thirty-five years later. Eugenie Rausch to MEP, Sept. 20, 1909, GPP, box 3169; Augusta T. Daniel to GP, June 4 [1915?], ibid., box 75.

2. JWP to MEP, Dec. 13, 1885, ibid., box 52.

3. 1880 U.S. Census.

4. McCadden sometimes failed to awaken Gifford for church because she believed he needed the extra sleep.

5. At its founding in 1877, Mary served as chairman of the society's committee on paintings and later chaired the needlework department. James and his older brother Edgar signed on as lifetime members and were also involved. Mary also served as the society's president for a time later in the 1890s.

6. MEP to JWP, Aug. 21 [1878], GPP, box 54.

7. MEP to JWP [Jan. 1, 1886], ibid., box 53.

8. MEP to JWP, Dec. 24, 1885, ibid. Nettie may have borrowed the name "Mousatilla" from a character in some children's books published mid-century.

9. MEP to GP, Nov. 13, 1887, ibid., box 3170; MEP to GP, March 14 [1890], ibid., box 72.

10. MEP to GP, Jan. 14 [1882] ibid., box 73. Even later, she told him that his birth had been "the happiest day of my life" and "how thankful I am that God gave you to me." MEP to GP, Aug. 11 [1913], ibid., box 3170.

11. MEP to GP, Wednesday [1884?], ibid., box 72.

12. MEP, Diary, July 7, 1876, ibid., box 3170; GP to My Dear Teacher, Oct. 19, 1877, ibid., box 52.

13. Gifford believed that his father never knew he had heard his praise of him, but Gifford's biographer has perceptively suggested that James did indeed intend Gifford to hear him. Miller, *Pinchot*, pp. 19-20. GP to John MacMullen, Nov. 6, 1879, GPP, box 52. Gifford Pinchot, *Just Fishing Talk* (New York: Telegraph Press, 1936), pp. 71-75 (quotations on p. 75).

14. Quotations ibid., pp. 73, 74.

15. Quotation in GP, *Breaking New Ground* (New York: Harcourt, Brace, 1947), p. 2.

16. In 1869, James's artist friend John Weir began a forty-four-year tenure as founding dean of the Yale School of Fine Arts. Mary's distinguished maternal grandfather was a Yale alumnus, and Henry, John (Jack), and William Eno were Yale graduates.

17. James was particularly interested in Winchester, Eton, and Rugby.

18. MEP to JWP, undated [1888], GPP, box 75; MEP, Journal [1877], ibid., box 39.

19. MEP to GP, Nov. 26 [1880], ibid., box 52. Gifford's separation at Canterbury was acceptable because he lived in a minister's home where they said their prayers at night.

20. She also wrote him, "The closer you can get in knowledge of [Paul] and in following him, the nobler and broader your life will be. There is no human character in secular or sacred history [who] is so much held up as a model for boys. To imitate him in all things possible, my son, is the best counsel I can give you. Try every day to read a few words of his and hold them close to your heart." MEP to GP, Oct. 17, [1880] and Oct. 10 [1880], and other complimentary references to Paul are ibid.

21. JWP to GP, Sept. 30 [1880], and Oct. 14-15, 1880, and MEP to GP, Oct. 14, 1880, ibid.

22. JWP to GP, Oct. 14, 1880, Nov. 22, 1882, and Feb. 17, 1882, ibid. Even Mary thought that Gifford's modest spending on candy was "very extravagant." MEP to GP, Jan. 27, 1882, ibid.

23. JWP to GP, Dec. 5, 1881, Nov. 25, 1881, and Jan. 10, 1883, ibid.

24. MEP to GP, Oct. 22 [1880], and JWP to GP, Nov. 3, 1880, ibid.

25. GP to MEP, Nov. 1 [1880], ibid. After Gifford's housemother at Exeter met James, she said to Gifford, "Well, you've a father to be proud of," to which Gifford replied, "I know I have." GP to MEP, Dec. 4, 1881, ibid.

26. GP to MEP, Feb. 21, 1882, ibid.

27. MEP to GP, May 1 [1882], ibid., box 72.

28. GP to MEP, May 8, 1882, Oct. 18, 1880, and Oct. 20 [1880], ibid., box 52. About one-third of the Exeter students attended the Episcopal church. GP to Parents, undated fragment [Fall 1883?], ibid., box 75.

29. Ibid. Records of his expenses are in GP, Pocket Diary, 1880, ibid., box 39, and GP, Diary, ibid., box 1.

30. GP to MEP, Feb. 2, 1882, Feb. 8, 1882, and Feb. 14, 1882, ibid., box 52; MEP to GP, Feb. 27 [1882], ibid., box 72; GP to MEP, March 1, 1882, ibid., box 52.

31. JWP to GP, Feb. 17, 1882, and June 23, 1883, ibid.

32. JWP to GP, undated, ibid., box 75.

33. Nearly eighty years later, the Republican Party chairman in Pennsylvania, ruefully reflecting on the many difficulties Gifford had caused him, commented that his father should have taken his son to the woodshed a few more times. Edward Martin, Oct. 21, 1961, cited in James A. Kehl and Samuel J. Astorino, "A Bull Moose Responds to the New Deal: Pennsylvania's Gifford Pinchot," *PMHB*, 88 (Jan. 1964), p. 43.

34. AP to GP, April 11 [1894], GPP, box 71.

35. GP to MEP, Feb. 11 [1914], ibid., box 68. *The Conservation Diaries of Gifford Pinchot*, ed. Harold K. Steen (Washington, DC.: Island Press, 2001), July 27, 1891, p. 13; GP, Diary, Jan. 12, 1897, GPP, Box 2, and Jan. 29, 1911, ibid., box 5.

36. GP to MEP, Feb. 8, 1882, ibid., box 52; GP to MEP, Feb. 21, 1882, ibid., box 10.

37. JWP to GP, May 30, 1882, ibid., box 52.

38. GP to JWP, May 18, 1882, ibid. Much later, Gifford related that he and his companion had taken the two surviving owls back to school and tamed them. GP to Gifford Pinchot 2nd, Dec. 21, 1921, ibid., box 244.

39. JWP to GP, May 18, 1882, and MEP to GP, May 18, 1882, ibid., box 52; MEP to GP, May 12 and May 13 [1882], ibid., box 72; MEP to GP, May 13 [1882], ibid., box 72.

40. W. Nutting to JWP, undated, ibid., box 71. *Yale Class Book, 1889*, ed. William Whitney Ames (New Haven, CT: Price, Lee, and Adkins, 1889), p. 64.

41. GP to MEP, Nov. 2, 1883, and MEP and JWP to GP, Nov. 5 [1883], GPP, box 72.

42. GP to Parents, Nov. 6, 1883, ibid., box 52.

43. MEP to GP, Nov. 11 [1883], ibid., box 73.

44. JWP to Cyrill H. Pinchot, Oct. 25, 1856, ibid., box 50; JWP to GP, Dec. 4, 1882, ibid., box 52.

45. Among works exploring Christian manliness (sometimes called muscular Christianity), see Norman Vance's, *The Sinews of the Spirit: The Ideal of Christian Manliness in Victorian Literature and Religious Thought* (Cambridge: Cambridge University Press, 1985).

46. Antoinette E. Pinchot to GP, Oct. 14, 1883, and GP to MEP, Oct. 28, 1883, GPP, box 52.

47. At Exeter, a classmate had a pistol, and Gifford had bought the bullets. James put a stop to their target practice, then bought his son a shotgun for his Adirondack sojourn. GP to JWP, Feb. 29 [1884], ibid., box 71, and GP to Parents, Jan. 18, 1884, ibid., box 10.

48. GP to JWP, Feb. 29 [1884], ibid., box 71, and MEP to GP, March 2 [1884], ibid., box 72.

49. In preparing for the examinations, Gifford noted, "I believe I shall have a condition in arithmetic, and probably one or two others." But later, he thought: "(I actually had five.)" GP to Parents, June 29, 1885, ibid., box 10.

50. The bankruptcy or suspended operations of a few New York financial institutions had already intensified speculation of another impending failure. Geoffrey C. Ward, *A Disposition to Be Rich: How a Small-Town Pastor's Son Ruined an American President, Brought on a Wall Street Crash, and Made Himself the Best-Hated Man in the United States* (New York: Alfred A. Knopf, 2012).

51. The bank had to cover a good part of the deposits totaling about $4.5 million. The bank directors paid $345,000, William Walter Phelps $90,000, shareholders pledged additional amounts, and Amos R. Eno the rest. They also had to cover another shortfall of $95,000, which John had withdrawn as a bank loan to himself. Eno's statement and interview regarding Phelps's involvement is in the *Commercial Advertiser*, Jan. 6, 1888, p. 1. Also, Hugh M. Herrick, comp., *William Walter Phelps: His Life and Public Services* (New York: Knickerbocker Press, 1904), pp. 141-146.

52. The extradition treaty was with Britain, which still controlled Canada's foreign relations. Details about cross-border enforcement are in Katherine Unterman, "Boodle Over the Border: Embezzlement and the Crisis of International Mobility, 1880-1900," *Journal of the Gilded Age and Progressive Era*, 11 (April 2012), pp. 151-189. John left with his family for Canada when law enforcement officials began to close in on him. Authorities had also watched his house in Manhattan, but he managed to elude them.

53. John Eno to MEP, Feb. 1, 1883, GPP, box 3169. Other statements through April 1884 are ibid.

54. MEP to JWP, Dec. 4 [1885], ibid., box 70; MEP to JWP [Jan. 1, 1886], and JWP to MEP, Jan. 15, 1886, ibid., box 53. Mary's $50,000 of bond money had been the second of such gifts from her father, and the one James had turned over to Mary at her request more than a decade earlier.

55. MEP, Diary, May 12-June 1, 1884, GPP, box 39.

56. Widely touted as the Republican presidential nominee in the upcoming election, Sherman had squashed speculation, saying "I will not accept if nominated, and will not serve if elected."

57. Sherman also provided an over-simplified Civil War analogy: "I remember during the war of having caught my soldiers in the very act of pillage which was death by martial law, but I said[,] 'Boys[,] this is wrong, I will shut my eyes for half an hour by which time you must be in your camps.' They lived to do heroic work afterward." WTS to Chester A. Arthur, June 16, 1884, Chester A. Arthur Papers (Manuscript Division, Library of Congress), reel 3.

58. WTS to MEP, June 23, 1884, GPP, box 53. In 1872, John had obtained a U.S. passport.

59. F. J. Phillips to WTS, June 21, 1884, William T. Sherman Papers (Manuscript Division, Library of Congress), reel 20.

60. Under British law, the definition of forgery was narrow, and a person could be extradited only if the offense was clearly in violation of the treaty provisions.

61. Sherman also advised Mary that her father's and brother's financial burdens shrank in comparison to the plight of his former comrade in arms, Ulysses S. Grant, who had pitifully small financial resources to pay his multi-millions in debts. WTS to MEP, June 2, 1884, Sept. 25, 1884, and May 24, 1884, GPP, box 53.

62. Mary, for her part, was annoyed at certain friends of William Walter Phelps (though not Phelps himself) for taking credit for the bank's rescue, since it was her father's money that had really saved it. Hard feelings also developed between her and her father, with Mary believing that he had failed to oversee John and had then practically disowned him.

63. JWP to MEP, Feb. 21, 1886, GPP, box 53.

64. JWP to MEP, March 14, 1886, March 15, 1886, and April 27, 1886, ibid.

65. Mary was already working with Secretary of State James G. Blaine. WTS to MEP, Jan. 4, 1891, GPP, box 55; *NYT*, March 10, 1891, p. 2; GP, Diary, March 10, 1891, GPP, box 1.

66. In 1890, Canada would finally succeed in having a new extradition treaty negotiated with the United States, which covered fraud and embezzlement, among other offenses.

67. Quotation in Unterman, "Boodle over the Border," p. 172. Mary Pinchot Eno, John's second oldest child, said she was giving a dance for seventy people. Mary P. Eno to MEP, April 19, 1892, GPP, box 55.

68. GP to Pats of D '87, Feb. 23, 1893, ibid., box 3175. John's reappearance angered Nettie, who said he was an "impenitent thief," "beast," and "ought to be poisoned." APJ to GP, Dec. 30 [1894], ibid., box 3168, and Jan. 3 [1895], ibid., box 70.

69. MEP to GP, Nov. 13 [1893], ibid., box 72.

70. Frances Cleveland to MEP, Dec. 31, 1893, ibid., box 56.-

71. GP to MEP, Feb. 17, 1885, ibid., box 53.-

72. MEP, Diary, March 19, 1885, ibid., box 39. Later dates for this year in Mary's diary have been torn out and lost, and no correspondence between Gifford and Kitty during their "romance" has been found.

73. Catharine Howland Hunt to GP, Nov. 20 [1886?], ibid., box 70; Catharine Howland Hunt to GP, Dec. 31, 1888, ibid., box 54.

74. Catharine Howland Hunt to JWP, Easter Sunday [April 5] 1885, and Antoinette E. Pinchot to JWP, Easter Sunday 1885, ibid., box 53. The biography of Richard Morris Hunt by Kitty's mother does not

mention the episode. Catherine Clinton Howland Hunt, Biography of Richard Morris Hunt (unpublished manuscript, Library of Congress), Vol. III.

75. GP to JWP, Sept. 27, 1885, GPP, box 53.

Chapter 4: A New Profession

1. Quotations in *Breaking New Ground*, p. 1. GP to JWP, July 16, 1905, GPP, box 63.

2. As a tangible link, James soon made a "generous" gift (but less than $10,000) in Gifford's name to the American Museum of Natural History in New York. Albert S. Bickmore to JWP, Sept. 16, 1879, APP, box 1; *Building the American Museum, 1869-1927* (New York: American Museum of Natural History, 1928), pp. viii-ix.

3. George Perkins Marsh, *Man and Nature; Or, Physical Geography as Modified by Human Action* (New York: Charles Scribner, 1864), pp. 301, 328, 236, passim. Appreciative reviews of the book were published in *NYT*, July 25, 1864, and *North American Review*, 99 (July 1864), pp. 318-320. In the 1890s his book was reissued with a revised title, *Earth as Modified by Human Action*.

4. Mark Stoll, "'Sagacious' Bernard Palissy: Pinchot, Marsh, and the Connecticut Origins of American Conservation," *Environmental History*, 16 (January 2011), pp. 5-15. Both Marsh and James Pinchot owned a complete edition of Palissy's works (p. 12).

5. JWP, "Yale Summer School of Forestry," p. 5389.

6. This view of James is sympathetically developed in Nancy P. Pittman, "James Wallace Pinchot (1831–1909): One Man's Evolution toward Conservation in the Nineteenth Century," *Yale Forestry and Environmental Science Centennial News* (Fall 1999), pp. 1-7.

7. GP to MEP, March 21, 1886, GPP, box 53. James delayed introducing Gifford to Marsh's book, as he did not want to distract his son from his studies. While at Exeter, he sent Gifford a book of Emerson's essays but told him not to read them until through college. JWP to GP, Nov. 5, 1882, ibid., box 52. And James told Gifford during his freshman year at Yale that he should focus on his courses and could later explore his interests in forestry. JWP to GP, Jan. 19, 1886, ibid., box 53. In sum, James consistently took the long view.

8. Gifford may have benefitted somewhat from changes that were gradually transforming Yale from a small college to a modern university. It began calling itself a university in 1887, and a new president, Timothy Dwight, began expanding the graduate school and professional training. George Wilson Pierson, *Yale College: An Educational History, 1871-1921* (New Haven: Yale University Press, 1952), pp. 95-106. Some of Gifford's science courses came from the Sheff side, others from the academic. There were 134 entering freshman on the academic side in Gifford's class.

9. GP to JWP, Dec. 11, 1885, GPP, box 53.

10. *Breaking New Ground*, p. 4. Pierson, *Yale College*, p. 300. Brewer had already published a map of the forests of the United States along with accompanying commentary. Gifford took his course in meteorology. GP to MEP, Dec. 19 [1886], GPP, box 71.

11. Yale then had a complicated system and arcane names for honors. George Wilson Pierson, *A Yale Book of Numbers. Historical Statistics of the College and University, 1701-1976* (Yale University, 1983). Gifford's grade point averages (with 4.0 perfection, 3.0 honor grade, and 2.75 quality grade) for the four years were 3.12, 2.86, 2.70, and 2.88. Yale College Student Grade Books, vol. 7 (Manuscripts and Archives, Yale University Library).

12. Gifford later quoted approvingly a line in the Yale song recounting college days, "We had a good time and studied – some." Quotation in *Breaking New Ground*, p. 4.

13. GP to JWP, Sept. 27, 1885, GPP, box 53.

14. GP to MEP, Nov. 3, 1885, and Helen C. Parsons to GP, Jan. 6, 1886, ibid.

15. Gifford also was taken into the back room of a saloon and forced to play some silly games for the sophomores' entertainment. GP to JWP, Sept. 27, 1885, ibid.; GP to MEP, Oct. 11 [1885], ibid., box 71; and GP to MEP, Nov. 3, 1885, ibid., box 53.

16. JWP to AP, Nov. 15, 1885, ibid.

17. *Breaking New Ground*, pp. 3-5.

18. Gifford managed to stay on the team for one game, in which he scored a touchdown and "excelled" as a running back during the thrashing of a high school team. MEP to GP, Nov. 5 [1883], GPP, box 72; JWP to GP, Sept. 30, 1885, and GP to MEP, Nov. 8, 1885, ibid., box 53; *YDN*, Nov. 16, 1885, p. 1.

19. He also had tried crew in the winter, but his poor eyes forced him to give it up.

20. GP to MEP, May 21, 1886, and JWP to GP, Monday night [May 24, 1886], GPP, box 53.

21. GP to MEP, June 11, 1886, ibid.

22. The celebratory aspect was muted out of respect for James's mother, Eliza, whose health was failing, and she would die in her native Milford a month later.

23. Another attraction was the editors' modest remuneration. GP to MEP, Nov. 6, 1887, GPP, box 53. GP, "Izaak Walton's Will," *YLM*, 52 (May 1887), pp. 326-327. Earlier at Exeter, Gifford had obtained a copy of Walton's masterpiece, and for the Lit had used Walton's *Angler* as a point of departure for short book reviews. GP, "Portfolio," *YLM*, 52 (April 1887), pp. 287-288.

24. Frank I. Paradise to GP, Jan. 24, 1888, GPP, box 54. Gifford sensed that a partying and less religious faction in the class together with the backers of other failed candidates for the board had caused his defeat. GP to MEP, Sunday [late Jan. 1888], ibid., box 71.

25. MEP to GP, Wednesday, Jan. 24 [1888], Friday [April 1888], and Sunday [May 27, 1888], ibid., box 3170. Gifford had been uncommunicative, because he was sick in bed with the measles and thus probably escaped the initiation shenanigans.

26. GP, Journal, Dec. 19, 1890, ibid., box 33.

27. GP to JWP, Sunday [Oct. 14, 1888], and GP to MEP, Monday [Oct. 15, 1888], ibid., box 54.

28. JWP to GP, Monday [Oct. 1888], ibid., box 71; GP to MEP, Oct. 21, 1888, ibid., box 54.

29. The program of the 25th anniversary dinner, Nov. 12, 1913, is ibid., box 3179.

30. MEP to GP, March 5 [1882], ibid.

31. William Walter Phelps to JWP, April 10, 1883, ibid., box 52. A stimulating overview of Amos's life is Nancy Pittman Pinchot, "Amos Pinchot: Rebel Prince," *Pennsylvania History*, 66 (Spring 1999), pp. 166-198.

32. AP to MEP, Thursday, July 31 [1884], GPP, box 73.

33. AP to GP, Sunday [c. 1900], ibid., box 54; McCadden to GP, April 27, 1890 [1891], and Maria Furman to GP, Sunday, March 6, 1890 [1892], ibid., box 77; McEntee to JWP, May 20, 1886, ibid., box 53.

34. AP to MEP, Jan. 1, 1886, ibid.; GP to JWP, Jan. 27, 1889, ibid., box 54.-

35. AP to GP, undated [October 1887], ibid., box 73; GP to JWP, Jan. 27, 1889, ibid., box 54.

36. Gifford also won the DeForest Medal for oratory, which was a briefer version of the Townsend study. His DeForest-prize oration was published as "The Quakers of the Seventeenth Century," *YLM*, 55 (Oct. 1889), pp. 26-30 (quotation on p. 30). The typescript of his Townsend essay (forty pages) is in GPP, box 3179.

37. Antoinette E. Pinchot to GP, undated [June 1889], ibid., box 54.-

38. GP to JWP, Oct. 14, 1888, ibid. A small notebook, dated Oct. 1888, with four pages of Gifford's notes on New Haven trees is ibid., box 31.

39. *Breaking New Ground*, p. 5; *Conservation Diaries*, Jan. 15, 1889, p. 63.

40. GP to MEP, Feb. 16, 1889, GPP, box 54.

41. JWP to GP, Jan. 6, 1888, ibid.

42. GP to MEP, Feb. 16, 1889, and Reynolds to GP, March 23, 1889, ibid.

43. GP to MEP, Oct. 9, 1888, ibid.

44. Quotation in Miller, *Pinchot*, p. 72; *Breaking New Ground*, pp. 3, 5.

45. One of his Lit essays was a fictional discussion between a devotee of Bishop Berkeley, the idealistic philosopher, who had argued, in Gifford's words, that "all things exist only in the presentation of our senses," and a businessman, who in his anguish over a financial reversal was visited during a trance by a menacing apparition holding a crucifix. Horrified, the businessman shook off the ghost by throwing a metal vase at him. When the man awoke, an indentation of the crucifix on the vase remained. Gifford expressed no opinion about the incident but clearly believed that ideas were real or could be perceived as such. "A Modern Victim of the Inquisition," *YLM*, 53 (April 1888), pp. 312-314.

46. GP to Charles O. Gill, Aug. 30, 1902, GPP, box 85.

47. GP to MEP. undated [Feb. 1889], ibid., box 10. The printed course syllabus and Gifford's lecture notes are ibid., box 31. Herbert Spencer, the British philosopher who popularized the optimistic view of evolution as a theory of inevitable progress in lectures in the United States, was a personal friend of James and Mary Pinchot, and James in particular respected Spencer's views.

48. GP to MEP, Tuesday [Autumn 1888], ibid., box 31. Because his father had recently sold a tract of land in Manhattan, which he had earlier put in Gifford's name, for $10,000 (but kept the five per cent mortgage), Gifford would also receive the monthly interest income.

49. MEP to GP, Wed., Jan. 12 [1887], Nov. 3 [1888], and Dec. 2 [1888?], GPP, box 3170.
50. MEP to GP, April 8, 1889, and April 15, 1889, ibid.
51. GP to JWP, March 10, 1889, ibid., box 54.
52. *Breaking New Ground*, p. 6.
53. GP, Diary, June 15, 1891, GPP, box 1.
54. Quotation in Char Miller, *Seeking the Greatest Good: The Conservation Legacy of Gifford Pinchot* (Pittsburgh: University of Pittsburgh Press, 2013), p. 30.

Chapter 5: Practical Forestry

1. *Breaking New Ground*, p. 6. His father gave him his watch and $5,000 to finance the trip. GP, Journal, Oct. 5, 1889, GPP, box 31.
2. GP, Journal, Oct. 17, 1889, ibid.
3. *Breaking New Ground*, p. 9.
4. *Conservation Diaries*, Oct. 22, 1889, p. 32.
5. GP, Journal, Nov. 9, 1889, GPP, box 33. During her earlier European travels, Gifford's mother had sent him brochures about the Nancy program. MEP to GP, Jan. 12 [1886], ibid., box 3170.
6. First quotation in *Breaking New Ground*, p. 8; GP, Journal, Oct. 22, 1889, GPP, box 31.
7. GP to MEP, Jan. 22, 1890, ibid., box 54.
8. Schlich soon confirmed Gifford's low opinion of the Nancy forestry school. GP, Diary notes, c. Jan. 1890, ibid., box 972; *Conservation Diaries*, May 15, 1890, and Supplemental Diary, 1890, pp. 38, 34; GP to JWP, May 11, 190, GPP, box 54.
9. JWP to MEP, Feb. 8, 1892, ibid., box 3169; GP to MEP, Jan. 18, 1889, ibid., box 10; GP to JWP, Jan. 27, 1889, ibid., box 54; penultimate quotation in McGeary, *Pinchot*, p. 22. GP to MEP, Feb. 26, 1890, and GP to Antoinette E. Pinchot, Nov. 4, 1889, GPP, box 54.
10. First quotation in McGeary, *Pinchot*, p. 22; JWP to GP, GPP, box 3169.
11. *Conservation Diaries*, March 24, 1890, p. 35, and July 12, 1890, p. 39.
12. GP to MEP, Oct. 20, 1890, GPP, box 54; *Conservation Diaries*, Nov. 3, 1890, p. 41. For their part, the European students disliked Gifford's competitive edge and work ethic. GP to MEP, March 6, 1890, GPP, box 54.
13. GP to JWP, April 28, 1890, and GP to MEP, Aug. 31, 1890, ibid.
14. GP to JWP, May 11, 1890, ibid. Extracts from the *Garden and Forest* articles are in *Gifford Pinchot: Selected Writings*, ed. Char Miller (University Park: Pennsylvania State University Press, 2016), pp. 23-28. (Hereafter, GP, *Selected Writings*.)
15. *Conservation Diaries*, July 19, 1890, p. 39, July 28, 1890, p. 40, Nov. 21, 1890, p. 41. Brandis even made Gifford his German translator during their excursion with the British students. Having studied the language since childhood, Gifford picked it up again quickly and did passably well in his added role.
16. *Conservation Diaries*, March 24, 1890, p. 35; GP to JWP, Aug. 14, 1890, GPP, box 54.
17. Quotations in McGeary, *Pinchot*, p. 23.
18. JWP to GP, Jan. 20, 1889, GPP, box 3169.
19. JWP to GP, Jan. 20, 1890, and undated [Oct. 31, 1890], ibid.
20. *Breaking New Ground*, p. 4.
21. GP to JWP, June 9, 1890, GPP, box 54.
22. MEP to GP, Sunday, Oct. 26 [1889], ibid., box 3170, and MEP to GP, Aug. 27 [1890], ibid., box 54.
23. GP to JWP, Jan. 7, 1890, ibid.
24. GP to JWP, Aug. 14, 1890, ibid.
25. GP to JWP, May 6, 1890 and May 11, 1890, and GP to MEP, Oct. 5, 1890, ibid.
26. Quotation from a Fernow letter are in GP to JWP, Aug. 3, 1890, ibid.
27. Ibid. Predictably, Brandis preferred that Gifford find better prospects in managing a private forestry reserve than government forestry.
28. Sargent to GP, Aug. 2, 1890, and MEP to JWP, Aug. 10 [1890], ibid.
29. Quotation in Miller, *Pinchot*, p. 91.
30. *Conservation Diaries*, Oct. 10, 21, 1890, p. 64.
31. GP to JWP, Oct. 20, 1890, GPP, box 54; quotation in McGeary, *Pinchot*, p. 23.

32. *Breaking New Ground*, p. 21.

33. "Government Forestry Abroad," *Publications of the American Economic Association*, 6 (May 1891), pp. 5-54 (quotations on pp. 30, 54).

34. Quotations in Miller, *Pinchot*, p. 92. Moreover, Fernow's paper at the same conference, which stressed the "difficulties" and "negative elements" of forest administration, was discomfiting. B. E. Fernow, "Practicality of an American Forest Administration," *Publications of the American Economic Association*, pp. 77-91 (quotations on pp. 77, 80).

35. JWP to GP, May 13 [1892], GPP, box 55.

36. GP, *Breaking New Ground*, p. 46.

37. *Conservation Diaries*, Dec. 31, 1890, p. 64, Feb. 3, 1891, p. 65, and March 14, 1891, p. 66.

38. James, perhaps from conversations with his friend Richard Morris Hunt, whom Vanderbilt had hired to design his elaborate chateau, had learned about the estate and its forested lands. JWP to GP, Feb. 2, 1891, GPP, box 55; GP, Diary, Feb. 20, 1891, ibid., box 1.

39. The mammoth estate also included a terrace the size of a football field, a nine-hundred-foot-long esplanade, a large walled garden, a forty-acre nursery, and an arboretum.

40. Thorstein Veblen's *The Theory of the Leisure Class* (1899), for example, incisively satirized what he termed the economically useless and wasteful activities of "conspicuous consumption" practiced by the dominant social elite in America.

41. Quotation in Justin Martin, *Genius of Place: The Life of Frederick Law Olmsted* (New York: Da Capo Press, 2011), p. 267.

42. Quotation ibid., p. 362.

43. *Breaking New Ground*, p. 49. James and Olmsted were both long-time members of the Century Association. Frederick Law Olmsted to James Gall, Jr., May 4, 1891, *The Papers of Frederick Law Olmsted: The Last Great Projects, 1890-1895*, eds. Charles E. Beveridge, et al. (Baltimore: Johns Hopkins Press, 2015), 9, p. 341. Moreover, Olmsted had grown up in Hartford, Connecticut, and Amos Eno's job sixty years earlier was in the Hartford dry goods store of Olmsted's father. Olmsted knew about the prominence of the Enos and James's connection with that family. MEP, biography of her father, undated, GPP, box 48. James occasionally asked Olmsted to visit Grey Towers, but he was always too busy to make the trip. *Papers of Frederick Law Olmsted*, 9, pp. 790, 792n13.

44. GP to JWP, March 16, 1893, GPP, box 56. Olmsted offered tips to Gifford on salary, Vanderbilt accepted Gifford's request for $2,500 for up to five years, and his employment also included subsistence, a horse, travel expenses, and a small house as living quarters.

45. *Conservation Diaries*, Oct. 18, 1891 and Dec. 31, 1891, p. 52.

46. GP to Fernow, Jan. 18, 1892, GPP, box 961; GP, Notes, Sept. 19, 1892, ibid., box 972; and Fernow to GP, Sept. 19, 1892, ibid., box 961.

47. Gifford Pinchot, *Biltmore Forest: The Property of Mr. George W. Vanderbilt* (Chicago: R. R. Donnelley, 1893), p. 14; GP to JWP, March 13, 1892, GPP, box 55.

48. Gifford thought he had the support of the North Carolina commissioners but soon learned that the promised funds were spent on other projects. Gifford then advanced his own funds for the project, which consisted mainly of photographs of the practice of forestry at Biltmore, until the state reimbursed him.

49. GP, *Biltmore Forest*, pp. 18, 25, 37-40, passim.

50. Fernow to GP, July 9, 1894, GPP, box 961; *Breaking New Ground*, p. 54; Robert E. Wolf, "National Forest Timber Sites and the Legacy of Gifford Pinchot: Managing a Forest and Making It Pay," *American Forests: Nature, Culture, and Politics*, ed. Char Miller (Lawrence: University Press of Kansas, 1997), pp. 89-92; Brian Balogh, "Scientific Forestry and the Roots of the Modern American State: Gifford Pinchot's Path to Progressive Reform," *Environmental History*, 7 (April 2002), pp. 211-215.

51. GP, *Breaking New Ground*, p. 69; GP to JWP, May 26, 1892, GPP, box 55.

52. Word of Vanderbilt's interest in these properties might raise the prices inordinately, so Gifford became "Mr. Gifford," or someone whose connection to Biltmore was presumably less obvious.

53. Quotations in Miller, *Pinchot*, pp. 113-114.

54. GP to Parents, Nov. 12, 1894, GPP, box 57. Gifford's salary was reduced to perhaps $500 a year.

55. Quotation in Carl A. Schenck, *Biltmore Story: Recollections of the Beginnings of Forestry in the United States*, ed. Ovid Butler (St. Paul: Minnesota Historical Society, 1955), p. 20.

56. George W. Vanderbilt to GP, Aug. 15, 1895, GPP, box 962; *Conservation Diaries*, March 9, 1896, p. 61, and Sept. 17, 1895, p. 60.

57. Vanderbilt to GP, Jan. 15, 1896, GPP, box 963. Gifford (and Vanderbilt too) perceived the many Appalachian mountaineers as fiercely independent American citizens. To Schenck, however, they were lowly, thieving peasants poaching on someone else's property. Schenck, *Biltmore Story*, pp. 44, 30.

58. Schenck later wrote that Gifford promised Vanderbilt a four percent profit from Big Creek.

59. Quotations in Schenck, *Biltmore Story*, pp. 50, 37.

60. *Conservation Diaries*, March 9, 1896, p. 61.

61. GP to JWP, Dec. 2, 1897, GPP, box 964; Schenck, *Biltmore Story*, p. 49.

62. Ibid., p. 50; GP to Brandis, June 26, 1905, GPP, box 95; *Conservation Diaries*, Feb. 19, 1897, p. 61.

63. In 1914, Overton Price surmised that a new crop of trees would be ready for commercial lumbering by 1930. Harold T. Pinkett, *Gifford Pinchot: Private and Public Forester* (Urbana: University of Illinois Press, 1970), pp. 27-30; *Breaking New Ground*, pp. 66, 69; McGeary, *Pinchot*, p. 30.

Chapter 6: Affairs of the Heart and Mind

1. MEP to JWP, Jan. 1 [1886], GPP, box 53.

2. Antoinette E. Pinchot, Diary, Jan. 1, 3, 1889, ibid., box 47.

3. Antoinette E. Pinchot, Diary, Jan. 9, 13, 14, 1889, ibid. She referred to Barclay as "sweet" five times in these entries.

4. McCadden to GP, April 27, 1890 [1891], ibid., box 77; AJ to MEP, Tuesday [Jan. 1892?], ibid., box 70.

5. Antoinette E. Pinchot to MEP, Sunday [Sept. 1891], ibid., box 55; MEP to GP, Jan. 3 [1892], ibid., box 72.

6. GP, Diary, July 27-28, 1891, Oct. 4, 1891, ibid., box 1.

7. AJ to MEP, Tuesday [Jan. 1892?], ibid., box 70.

8. Alan's and Nettie's romance was part of a growing transatlantic pattern of male members of the British aristocracy marrying women from wealthy American families. Social and intellectual factors fostering this development are explored in Dana Cooper, *Informal Ambassadors: American Women, Transatlantic Marriages, and Anglo-American Relations, 1865-1945* (Kent, Ohio: Kent State University Press, 2014).

9. Antoinette E. Pinchot to GP, Wednesday [Oct. 1891], GPP, box 55.

10. GP, Diary, July 7, 1891, ibid., box 1. Grandfather Amos likewise opposed the marriage and considered cutting Nettie out of his will, although Mary believed that "would make no difference in N's or Johnstone's determination." MEP to JWP, June 13 [1892], ibid., box 73.

11. GP, Diary, Dec. 25, 1891, ibid., box 1; AJ to MEP, Jan. 22, 1891 [1892], ibid., box 55.

12. Antoinette E. Pinchot to GP, Monday [winter 1891-1892], ibid., box 71.

13. MEP, draft response on Alan Johnston to MEP, March 12, 1892, ibid., box 55. A girlfriend of Gifford labeled the no-contact order "hateful." Maria Furman to GP, Sunday, March 6, 1891 [1892], ibid., box 77.

14. AJ to MEP, April 8, 1892, and Lord Derwent to JWP, March 26, 1891, ibid., box 55.

15. Antoinette E. Pinchot to GP, Wednesday [Oct. 1891], ibid., box 70.

16. MEP to JWP, May 26, 1892, ibid., box 55. Nettie had a relapse after hearing that her best friend, Kitty Hunt, was engaged, but she soon recovered. MEP to JWP, June 13 [1892], ibid., box 73.

17. Mary's contribution, increasing the couple's allowance, came from another monetary gift that her father had given her. MEP to GP, April 14 [1890], ibid., box 72; AJ to MEP, Tuesday [June 1893?], ibid., box 56.

18. MEP to GP, Aug. 9 [1894?], ibid., box 72.

19. *Yale Class Book, 1889*, p. 87; Fisher to GP, July 18, 1893, and Donnelley to GP, May 9, 1893, GPP, box 78..

20. GP, Diary, Oct. 24, 1889, ibid., box 31. The last quotation is in McGeary, *Pinchot*, p. 22.

21. GP to MEP, Jan. 18 (?), 1889, GPP, box 10; Furman to GP, Nov. 2, 1889, April 19, 1891, Dec. 16, 1889, Jan. 19, 1890, May 3, 1890, Sept. 28, 1890, ibid., box 77.

22. *Conservation Diaries*, Aug. 12, 13, 1891, Oct. 2, 1891, Dec. 2, 3, 1891, pp. 13-14.

23. Gifford consulted his old girlfriend Maria for a woman's perspective on how to deal with Trix. Maria suggested that he long delay his replies to Trix's letters. Sam Fisher to GP, Dec. 5 and 11, 1891, GPP, box 77. Soon learning that Trix was "very bitter" at Gifford for his inattention, Maria "had a beautiful smile all

to myself." Maria Furman to GP, Sunday, March 6, 1891 [1892], ibid., box 77. Beatrix Jones to GP, Sept. 6 [1892], and Tuesday [April] 5, 1892, ibid. Beatrix would later become a pre-eminent landscape gardener, and Gifford would recommend her for landscape gardening jobs. GP to William A. Boring, Jan. 8, 1900, and Henry Y. Satterlee to GP, Aug. 23, 1900, ibid., box 83.

24. Maria Furman to GP, Sept. 1, 1891, ibid., box 77; GP, Diary, Sept. 11, 14, 1891, ibid., box 1.

25. GP to Pats of D '87, Feb. 23, 1893, ibid., box 3175.

26. Maria Furman to GP, Sept. 26, 1891, and Monday, Sept. 28, 1890 [1891], ibid., box 77; GP, Diary, Nov. 24, 1891, ibid., box 1; and GP to Pats of D '87, Feb. 23, 1893, ibid., box 3175. Gifford suffered from the "bad blues" in trying to get over Maria. GP, Diary, Dec. 12, 1891, ibid., box 1.

27. GP, Diary, Jan. 23, 1892, ibid., box 1. Bond's full name was William Key Bond Emerson.

28. GP to JWP, Jan. 27, 1889, ibid., box 54; GP to Parents, June 5, 1887, ibid., box 53.

29. He occasionally expressed interest in her during his college years. GP, Journal, Dec. 21, 1890, and GP to Pats of D '87, Feb. 23, 1893, GPP, box 3175..

30. Sam Fisher to GP, Jan. 2, 1891 [1892], ibid., box 77.

31. Natalie's later letters to Gifford are ibid., box 78. Natalie would marry John Nicholas Brown, from one of the oldest Rhode Island families, in 1897. Her younger sister, Edith Stuyvesant Dresser, would marry Gifford's former boss, George W. Vanderbilt, in 1898.

32. GP to MEP, Saturday [April 1892], ibid., box 55; GP to Pats of D '87, Feb. 23, 1893, ibid., box 3175.

33. Ibid.

34. Florence Adele Sloane, *Maverick in Mauve: The Diary of a Romantic Age* (Garden City, N.Y.: Doubleday, 1983), pp. 74-82 (first and last quotations on pp. 74, 82); Sloane to GP, May 29 [1893], GPP, box 80.

35. Furman to GP, Jan. 19, 1890, ibid., box 77.

36. GP, Diary, Sept. 25, 1891, ibid., box 1; JWP to MEP, May 24, 1892, ibid., box 55. Catharine (Kitty) Howland Hunt married Livingston Hunt in July 1892.

37. JWP to GP, March 23, 1893, ibid., box 56.

38. MEP to GP, Aug. 27 [1890], ibid., box 54; MEP to GP, Nov. 10 [1889], ibid., box 3170; MEP to GP, 7th [1893?], ibid., box 72.

39. Three months after Gifford and Maria parted in Roslyn, Mamee was still "much concerned" about their relationship, and he assured her that there was "no cause for the least alarm." GP, Diary, Jan. 10, 1892, ibid., box 1.

40. He had earlier hoped to go abroad for six months for further study of the European forests but used the shorter time at Aix-les-Bains to make side trips to discuss diverse forestry matters with his mentors.

41. Quotation in Sloane, *Maverick in Mauve*, pp. 16-17.

42. Laura likely suffered from pulmonary consumption. It was not until the early twentieth century that laboratory tests first began to identify the tubercle bacilli. Moreover, X-ray technology did not yet exist. The word "tuberculosis" did not even come into common usage until the twentieth century. Gifford Pinchot later destroyed all his correspondence with Laura in which there may have been references to consumption, and there is no mention of it in surviving letters of his family or classmates. It seems that even the word consumption was unmentionable among people of high social position.

43. The two were Tom Buchanan and Horace (Hod) Walker. The records of the Woodmere Cemetery, Detroit, Michigan, indicate that Walker died of phthisis, or tuberculosis of the lungs. I am grateful to Gail Hershenzon at the cemetery for this information. Hod's illness is documented in GP, Diary, GPP, box 1.

44. Quotation in James G. Bradley, "The Mystery of Gifford Pinchot and Laura Houghteling," *Pennsylvania History*, 66 (Spring 1999), p. 202. Laura and Gifford's love affair is chronicled in Paula Ivaska Robbins, *On Strawberry Hill: The Transcendent Love of Gifford Pinchot and Laura Houghteling* (Tuscaloosa: University of Alabama Press, 2017).

45. Of Richet, Gifford commented, "He is unwilling to reverse all his [scientific] beliefs bec[ause] of a thing which cannot be repeated at will." GP, Diary, July 8, 1890, GPP, box 33. Richet would eventually develop the notion of a "sixth sense," which is the ability to perceive hypothetical vibrations of unknown origin without contradicting anything in the science of physiology.

46. *Conservation Diaries*, p. 9; and GP, Diary, Feb. 2, 1891, GPP, box 1. The book, by Henry Drummond, was *Natural Law in the Natural World* (1884), which claimed that until conversion, man lives in an inorganic world spiritually but, after being converted and born again, enters the organic world

spiritually. Gifford, still conflicted by the challenges of evolution to religion, bought the argument. Drummond's critics, including some scientists and clerics, rejoined that inorganic man before his rebirth could not be responsible for his behavior—"a stone cannot sin," as W. S. Rainsford, the rector of the Episcopal Church near Gramercy Park that the Pinchots sometimes attended, later expressed it. W. S. Rainsford, *The Story of a Varied Life: An Autobiography* (Garden City, NY: Doubleday, Page, 1922), p. 390.

47. Bradley, "Mystery of Gifford Pinchot and Laura Houghteling," p. 210, gives a list of books the two read together. Doris Stillman, "Spirit: Notes on references to spiritualism in books in Grey Towers Library" (Grey Towers, National Historic Landmark) surveys the Pinchot collection of books on spiritualism.

48. Helen Sootin Smith, Introduction to *The Gates Ajar* (Cambridge, MA: Belknap Press, 1964), and Emily Midorikawa, *Out the Shadows: Six Visionary Victorian Women in Search of a Public Voice* (New York: Counterpoint, 2021), are two among many analyses of spiritualism in that era.

49. Fisher to GP, July 17, 1893, and Sept. 25, 1893, and Horace Walker to GP, July 19, 1893, GPP, box 78.

50. Donnelley to GP, Nov. 16, 1893, and Pat Clark to GP, Sept. 7, 1893, ibid., box 78.

51. GP to MEP, March 30, 1893, ibid., box 56; GP to MEP, April 8, 1893, ibid., box 961.

52. Julia McNamee to GP, June 30, 1893, ibid., box 78.

53. GP to JWP and MEP, undated [Fall 1893], ibid., box 962.

54. APJ to MEP, Friday [Nov.? 1893], and Tuesday [Nov.? 1893], ibid., box 56.

55. APJ to GP, undated, and Sunday [Nov.? 1893?], ibid., box 70.

56. Donnelley to GP, Nov. 30, 1893, ibid., box 78; GP to MEP, Dec. 1, 1893, ibid., box 56.

57. Quotations in Bradley, "Mystery of Gifford Pinchot and Laura Houghteling," pp. 205-206. No death record for Laura Houghteling has been found in the records of the District of Columbia.

58. APJ to MEP, Thursday [Feb. 8, 1894], GPP, box 56.

59. JWP to GP, May 3, 1894, ibid., box 3169.

60. APJ to MEP, Oct. 20 [1894]. Oct. 23 [1894], Oct. 29 [1894], Nov. 16 [1894], and AJ to MEP, Nov. 20, 1894, ibid., box 57.

61. GP, Diary, April 13, 1894, and April 22, 1894, ibid., box 1; GP to MEP, Oct. 5, 1894, ibid., box 57; GP, Diary, Jan. 12, 1897, ibid., box 2; Jan. 24, 1911, ibid., box 5.

62. Maria F. Emerson to GP, Sept. 8, 1894, ibid., box 78, and Maria F. Emerson to GP July 23, 1895, and Aug. 21, 1895, ibid., box 79.

Chapter 7: Forestry Stirrings

1. Henry S. Graves, "Early Days with Gifford Pinchot," *Journal of Forestry*, 63 (August 1965), pp. 585-586. GP to Graves, March 8, 1893, and April 10, 1893, GPP, box 410.

2. JWP to GP, Sept. 9, 1892, ibid., box 55; JWP to GP, April 10, 1896, ibid., box 57; and AP to GP, Aug. 30, 1896, ibid., box 58.

3. Reynolds to GP, undated [mid-1897], ibid., box 79.

4. Quotation in *Breaking New Ground*, pp. 84-85.

5. Ibid., p. 85.

6. Gifford Pinchot credited Sargent's journal with distributing "more information about American forests and forest trees than all other periodicals combined." *Breaking New Ground*, p. 91. A complimentary essay is Char Miller, "A High-Grade Paper: *Garden and Forest* and Nineteenth-Century American Forestry," *Arnoldia*, 60, no. 2 (2000), pp. 19-38.

7. Gibbs appointed two additional men who decided not to participate.

8. *Breaking New Ground*, pp. 89-94.

9. Ibid., pp. 94-95.

10. S. B. Sutton, *Charles Sprague Sargent and the Arnold Arboretum* (Cambridge, MA: Harvard University Press, 1970), p. 156; GP to JWP and MEP, July 20, 1896, GPP, Box 58; GP to MEP, Oct. 5, 1892, ibid., Box 56.

11. At his father's urging, Gifford may have diluted his critical submission of Sargent's outline before publication. GP to JWP and MEP, Nov. 12, 1894, and JWP to GP, Nov. 14, 1894, ibid., box 57. His published remarks also accepted military training until a government school of forestry could be created. "A Plan to Save the Forests," *Century Magazine*, 49 (Feb. 1895), p. 630. Gifford later noted the common bias then "in favor of Army–officer control," and "I fell for it to some extent myself." *Breaking New Ground*, pp. 95, 87.

12. Ibid., p. 101; *Conservation Diaries*, May 16, 1896, p. 72.

13. GP to MEP and JWP, July 20, 1896, GPP, box 58; John Muir to GP, Oct. 28, 1896, Dec. 17, 1896, ibid., box 963; *Breaking New Ground*, p. 103.

14. JWP to GP, July 23, 1896, Aug. 9, 1896, Sept. 1, 16, 1896, GPP, box 58. James continued to admonish his son. JWP to GP, March 1, 1897, and April 6, 1897, ibid.

15. Quotation in McGeary, *Pinchot*, p. 39; GP to JWP and MEP, July 20, 1896, GPP, box 58; *Conservation Diaries*, Aug. 26, 1896, p. 74.

16. Quotation in Sutton, *Charles Sprague Sargent*, p. 165.

17. The bill passed by Congress gave the interior secretary broad powers to permit sales of timber on the reserves but also authorized the president to keep or cancel all or any part of any reserve. Cleveland vetoed it.

18. *Report of the Committee Appointed by the National Academy of Sciences upon the Inauguration of a Forest Policy for the Forested Lands of the United States to the Secretary of the Interior, May 1, 1897* (Washington, DC: Government Printing Office, 1897).

19. To gain better insight into lawmakers' views, he sometimes took home issues of the *Congressional Record* as nighttime reading.

20. Quotations in *Breaking New Ground*, p. 112.

Chapter 8: Brotherly Love in Peace and War

1. McCadden to GP, April 27, 1890 [1891], and Sept. 14, 1890, and Maria Furman to GP, May 3, 1890, GPP, box 77; GP, Diary, Dec. 21, 1890, ibid., box 33. *The Yale Class Book '97*, eds., George L. Parker and Edward P. Newton (New Haven, CT: O. A. Dorman, 1897), pp. 200, 201. As he matured, Amos announced that he preferred his middle Eno name to Toots, and after his grandfather Amos died, he was called Amos.

2. AP to MEP, Oct. 9, 1889, AP to MEP, Nov. 16, 1889, GPP, box 54; MEP to GP, Nov. 3 [1889], ibid., box 3170.

3. Cushing to JWP, Dec. 10, 1889, APP, box 1.

4. MEP, Diary, June 18, 1885, GPP, box 39; MEP to JWP, June 6 [1890], ibid., box 54; MEP to AP, Aug. 3 [1890], ibid., box 75; AP to GP, Aug. 31 [1892?], ibid., box 71.

5. MEP to GP, Dec. 22 [1889], ibid., box 3170. Report cards for Amos at Westminster are ibid., boxes 54 and 56.

6. AP to MEP, Sunday, Dec. 8 [1891], ibid., box 72.

7. AP to MEP, undated [1893], and AP to MEP, May 10 [1893], ibid., box 73.

8. GP to MEP, Oct. 5, 1893, ibid., box 56; AP to JWP, Sunday, Sept. 30 [Oct. 1] [1893], APP, box 3.

9. Gifford sent Amos an account of his love affair with his lost Laura, and after Nettie's baby died in Washington, Gifford took the baby's coffin, accompanied by Uncle Mo and young Amos, to Simsbury for burial. AP to GP, Saturday, Feb. 10, 1894, GPP, box 56; GP, Diary, March 4, 1894, ibid., box 1.

10. MEP, Diary, Feb. 13, 1888, ibid., box 3174; MEP to GP, Sunday, Nov. 27 [1881], ibid., box 72; Reynolds to GP, Oct. 4, 1893, ibid., box 78.

11. AP to GP, April 16, 1892, ibid., box 55; AP to GP, Monday, April 30 [1894], ibid., box 71. Amos's grade point averages (with 4.0 being perfection and 2.0 passing) during his four years were 2.59, 2.59, 2.48, and 2.56. Yale College Student Grade Books, vol. 9. (Manuscripts and Archives, Yale University Library)

12. AP to GP, April 30 [1894], GPP, box 71; AP to GP, Sept. 26 [1895], ibid., box 57; AP to MEP, May 20 [1894], AP to MEP, Monday, March 5 [1894], AP to MEP, Sunday [Fall 1895?], ibid., box 73; AP to MEP, Thursday, June 27 [1895], ibid., box 72; AP to GP, Aug. 30, 1896, ibid., box 58. Amos also tied for fourth place among classmates voting for "the greatest social light." *Yale Class Book '97*, pp. 180, 158.

13. AP to GP, undated [c. Oct. 1896], GPP, box 71; GP to JWP, Sept. 15, 1895, ibid., box 57; AP, "A Mountain Ride," *YLM*, 60 (Jan. 1895), pp. 185-186. Amos's article was based on his visit to Gifford at Biltmore the previous summer. AP to GP, Oct. 23 [1895] and Dec. 7 [1895], GPP, box 71; GP, Diary, Nov. 23, 1895, ibid., box 2.

14. GP, Diary, April 10, 21, 27, 1897, ibid. In their correspondence, the brothers did not mention the subject of Amos's essay.

15. *Yale Class Book '97*, pp. 124-128.

16. JWP to GP, Dec. 12, 1889, GPP, Box 3169; MEP to GP, Nov. 17 [1889], ibid., box 3170; MEP to JWP, April 20 [1892?], ibid., box 75; MEP to JWP, Aug. 15, 1891, ibid., box 57; MEP to JWP, June

17 [1895], June 21 [1895], and July 26 [1895], ibid.; APJ to JWP, June 18 [1895], MEP to JWP, July 19 [1895], ibid., box 73; JWP to MEP, Aug. 23, 1895, ibid., box 57.

17. AP to GP, Oct. 3, 1892, ibid., box 55; MEP to JWP, Aug. 26 [1895], ibid., box 57.

18. GP to MEP, June 20, 1897, and Binger Hermann to GP, June 25, 1897, ibid., box 964.

19. AP to MEP, July 25, 1897, and AP to JWP, July 28, 1897, ibid., box 58.

20. AP to MEP, Aug. 15, 1897, ibid.; *Conservation Diaries*, Sept. 5, 1897, p. 83.

21. GP, Diary, Nov. 7, 1897, GPP, box 2.

22. Abbot agreed that Pinchot's service on the forest commission had been "a great mistake" and that his acceptance of the position of forest agent showed "the lack of appreciation of proprieties usual among gentlemen." Quotations in Sutton, *Charles Sprague Sargent*, p. 168, and Brandis to GP, Aug. 9, 1897, GPP, box 964.

23. JWP to GP, undated, ibid., box 3169.

24. Arnold Hague to GP, Feb. 11, 1898, GP to Sargent, April 16, 1898, and Sargent to GP, April 20, 1898, ibid., box 964.

25. GP to JWP, Dec. 5, 1897, ibid., box 58.

26. *Conservation Diaries*, April 5, 1897, p. 77.

27. GP to JWP, Dec. 5, 1897, GPP, box 58. The scheme involved Mark Hanna, the president's campaign manager and then a U.S. senator; Republican Party power brokers Whitelaw Reid and Levi P. Morton; Grant La Farge, a friend of Gifford; and John A. Porter, McKinley's private secretary. La Farge to H. M. Hanna, March 16, 1897, ibid., box 964. Whitelaw Reid to John Addison Porter, Dec. 13, 1897, ibid., box 80. *Conservation Diaries*, Dec. 18, 1897, and Jan. 5, 1898, pp. 86, 92.

28. Gifford Pinchot's study was published in *Report on Examination of the Forest Reserves*, 55th Congress, 2nd session, Senate Doc. No. 189 (Washington, DC: Government Printing Office, 1898), pp. 35-118.

29. Quotation in Pinkett, *Pinchot*, p. 35.

30. Gifford wrote another book, *The Adirondack Spruce: A Study of the Forest in Ne-Ha-Sa-Ne Park* (New York: The Critic, 1898). The goal as always was sustained yield—"the great object of foresters the world over," Gifford later put it.

31. *Conservation Diaries*, May 11, 1898, p. 93. Amos also encouraged Gifford to accept the position. Remarkably, Gifford apparently did not discuss the offer with his parents, perhaps suggesting that they now acquiesced in Gifford's considered judgment on forestry matters.

32. A few years later, the forestry division moved to offices in the Atlantic Building on F Street, closer to downtown Washington. Gifford's formal title was forester, but the head was commonly called chief forester and, much later, the chief. In 1907, the forester's salary was increased to $5,000.

33. A week before the *Maine* explosion, the publication of a stolen letter written by the Spanish minister in Washington disparaging President McKinley had inflamed American opinion. The latest scholarship on the *Maine* explosion supports the internal detonation interpretation, but key U.S. naval and political figures covered up the true cause. Kenneth C. Wenzer, "The USB *Maine* Conspiracy," *Federal History Journal*, 12 (2020), pp. 75-98.

34. Before Spain, the United States had volatile diplomatic crises with Italy (1891), Chile (1891), and Great Britain (1895); the last is noted below in the text.

35. Alan wrote Mary Pinchot during the crisis, "Nettie and I don't discuss the Venezuelan question. Whatever happens (and God grant a peaceful solution may be come to) our love will remain the same and my affection for you all will be undiminished." AJ to MEP, Dec. 23, 1895, GPP, box 57.

36. AP to GP, Sunday, Feb. 2 [1890], and Antoinette E. Pinchot to GP, Nov. 6 [c. 1887], ibid., box 71; GP to MEP, March 26, 1894, ibid., box 962.

37. AP to GP, Oct. 29 [1897], ibid., box 71.

38. AP to MEP, Friday [March 1898], ibid., box 59.

39. APJ to MEP, June 4 [1898], ibid.

40. AP to Parents, May 3, 11, 23, 1898, and AP to MEP, undated [May 1898], ibid. William C. Cammann, et al., *The History of Troop "A", New York Cavalry U.S.V. from May 2 to November 28, 1898 in the Spanish-American War* (New York: R. H. Russell, 1899). James also investigated getting Amos a commission as an officer, but Amos liked his unit and the prospect of a short war finally ended these family discussions.

41. Marcia Houghteling to GP, April 22 [1898], GPP, box 3168; MEP to GP, June [July] 5 [1898], ibid., box 59.

42. AP to GP, June 23, 1898, ibid.

43. MEP to GP, June [July] 5 [1898], MEP to GP, Aug. 2 [1898], ibid.; GP, Diary, July 27, 1898, ibid., box 2.

44. *History of Troop "A"*, pp. 139-145, 171-183, passim. Only one other troop member was discharged for reasons other than sickness or reassignment to other units.

45. Ibid., pp. 54, 343-348. His only malady Amos mentioned during training was "a slight attack of the trots and a pain in my tum, from which I am now recovering." GP to MEP, July 5, 17, 1898, and APJ to MEP, July 25 [1898], GPP, box 59.

46. GP to MEP, April 8, 1892, ibid., box 55; AP to MEP, July 25, 1897, ibid., box 58; GP, Diary, July 15, 1897, ibid., box 2; JWP to GP, Sunday [?], ibid., box 71. James also complained occasionally of mild neuralgia. Amos had seen a doctor on his western trip, and by the end of his summer adventure he had seemed perfectly well.

47. *History of Troop "A"*, pp. 144-145, 174, 183 (quotations on pp. 144, 145).

48. The parents contacted Mary's brother Will in Saugatuck regarding the possibility of chartering a yacht to rescue Amos, but the *Relief* seemed a better and quicker way to retrieve him. MEP, Diary, Aug. 22, 1898, GPP, box 41; GP to JWP and MEP, undated [late Aug. 1898], William P. Eno to MEP, Aug. 24, 1898, and JWP to GP, Aug. 26, 1898, ibid., box 59.

49. Ibid.; MEP, Diary, Aug. 25, 1898, ibid., box 41. Margaret Livingston Chanler was the third youngest of ten children whose father had married into the wealthy Astor family. Both parents died in the mid-1870s, and the young children became well-off orphans. For her good work during the war, Margaret was sometimes referred to as "Sister Margaret" or the "Angel of Puerto Rico." She was also involved in women's causes.

50. AP to GP, Jan. 29, 1899, GPP, box 59; MEP, Diary, Dec. 27, 1898, April 21, 1899, ibid., box 41. Amos was appreciative of his good treatment there. He would give Dr. Criel a box of cigars for "his having undoubtedly saved my life by getting me out of Utuado," and he and James would socialize with Chanler as a way of thanking her personally. Gifford spelled the doctor's name "Kriel," but neither name was further identified.

51. GP, Diary, Aug. 29, Sept. 20, 29, Oct. 6, 1898, GPP, box 2; McCadden to GP, Oct. 10, 1898, ibid., box 59.

52. JWP to GP, Sat., Aug. 26 [1898], ibid. For a college reunion, Amos wrote that he had contracted typhoid during the war. *Sexennial Record of the Class of Yale Ninety-Seven*, ed. Graham Sumner (New York: Robert Grier Cooke, 1905), p. 87. Amos may have mentioned typhoid disingenuously, since full recovery was more likely than from malaria.

53. Once, Gifford complained that he was "touched" by malaria. GP to MEP, April 8, 1892, GPP, box 55.

54. AP to GP, Jan. 29, 1899, ibid., box 59. In that era, going out west for hunting or other adventures was a common prescription for depressed or nervous men from wealthy families.

55. AP to JWP and MEP, March 22, 1899, AP to MEP, March 3, 1899, and March 23, 1899, GP to JWP, April 30, 1899, and GP to MEP, June 23, 1899, ibid.; AP to GP, undated [March 1899], ibid., box 71; AP to JWP, March 2, 1899, APP, box 1.

Chapter 9: Family Matters

1. JWP to GP, March 14, 1896, GPP, box 56; JWP to GP, Sept. 16, 1896, APJ to MEP, Friday [Oct. or Nov. 1896], ibid., box 58; George W. Tyler to MEP, Feb. 21, 1898, ibid., box 59; MEP, Diary, Feb. 21, 1898, ibid., box 41.

2. Amos R. Eno's will, Feb. 21, 1895, and two codicils dated that year and 1896, are ibid., box 3171.

3. AP to GP, Oct. 29 [1897], ibid., box 71; JWP to GP, Jan. 19, 1898, ibid., box 59.

4. New York *Sun*, Nov. 24, 1897, p. 1.

5. Most of the later changes provided for additional compensation to the siblings without children. William P. Eno to JWP, May 14, 1899, GPP, box 3169.

6. JWP to GP, July 9, 1898, ibid., box 59.

7. There were twelve shares in the residuary estate: Amo held two (which he gave up); Antoinette Wood and John Eno and his children, one each; and the remaining seven were divided equally (2-1/3 each) to siblings Mary, Henry, and Will. Even John and his children got a small portion of this residual estate.

8. William P. Eno to GP, Sept. 29, 1898, GPP, box 3168; William P. Eno to MEP, Jan. 2, 1899, and William P. Eno to JWP, May 14, 1899, ibid., box 3169. Three years after her grandfather's death, Nettie whined that "somebody in the U.S.A. . . . owes me a hell of a lot of money. . . . I don't want to be a nuisance, but it's setting pretty d___ inconvenient." APJ to GP, Feb. 22 [1901], ibid., box 70.

9. JWP to AJ, Dec. 18, 1901, APP, box 1; JWP to GP, April 28, 1900, GPP, box 60; *NYT*, May 15, 1901, p. 1, and June 29, 1907, p. 2. Will promptly "flipped" the Flatiron Building for a handsome profit. Will and his two brothers bought the Fifth Avenue Hotel for $4.25 million. Will (and perhaps Amo too) shortly disposed of his interest in the land company.

10. MEP to GP, June 24 [1899], GPP, box 72; APJ to MEP, Aug. 2 [1899], ibid., box 59.

11. AP to MEP, Monday, March 5 [1900], and AP to GP, Feb. 21 [1900], ibid., box 73.

12. MEP, Diary, May 17, 1900, ibid., box 42; APJ to MEP, May 31 [1900], and AP to GP, May 22, 1900, ibid., box 60.

13. MEP to AP, Aug. 12 [1901], ibid., box 72; HL to GP, Feb. 27, 1900, GP to HLS, Feb. 28, 1900, ibid., box 967; GP to Amos Gaunce, Dec. 6, 1899, Gaunce to GP, Nov. 4, 1900, ibid., box 81; HLS to GP, Oct. 24, 1900, ibid., box 83.

14. AP to GP, Nov. 18, 1900, ibid., box 60.

15. AP to MEP, Friday, April 19 [1901], ibid.

16. Gertrude M. Pinchot to GP, May 22, 1901, ibid.

17. AP to GP, May 31, 1901, ibid.

18. APJ to MEP, June 15 [1899], ibid., box 59. Earlier, Alan declined two offers from Liberal Party whips to stand for seats in the House of Commons, partly because he saw small chance of success in the elections.

19. APJ to MEP, March 17 [1898] and March 5 [1898], ibid.

20. APJ to MEP, June 4 [1898], ibid.

21. APJ to MEP, Oct. 6 [1898], ibid. Mary Pinchot's 1902 portfolio showed she had $9,000 in outstanding loans to Nettie. Financial statement attached to Edward A. Mead to GP, June 20, 1902, GPP, box 3171.

22. APJ to MEP, March 19 [1898], and Monday [Nov.?] 11 [1898], ibid., box 59.

23. APJ to MEP, Wednesday [August 1901], ibid., box 61.

24. The racing results of Alan's horses are derived from the London *Times* from 1901-1910. A friend later confirmed that his horses ran "not without some degree of success." London *Times*, Aug. 4, 1932, p. 12.

25. APJ to MEP, Wednesday [Aug. 1901], Tuesday [Aug. 1901, Wednesday [Aug.] 28 [1901], Aug. 30 [1901], GPP, box 61; *WP*, Aug. 18, 1908, p. 7.

26. Mary had increasingly found the expenses and affectations of her daughter's social world harmful. MEP to JWP, July 23 [1895?], GPP, box 73.

27. AP to GP, June 23, 1901, ibid., box 60.

28. MEP to GP, July 2, 1901, and June 27 [1901], ibid., box 72.

29. Ibid.; APJ to Catharine Hunt, Dec. 17 [1901], ibid., box 70. Nettie suffered from a bad heart, swollen throat, congestion of the bowels and uterus, and a floating kidney. She also complained of neuralgia, rheumatism, and depression. APJ to MEP, Nov. 14 [1901], Nov. 20 [1901], Dec. 10 [1901], Dec. 28 [1901], and AJ to MEP, Feb. 3, 1902, ibid., box 61.

30. AP to GP, June 23 [1901], ibid., box 60.

31. APJ to Catharine Hunt, Dec. 17 [1901], APJ to MEP, Nov. 14 [1901], ibid., box 61; AP to GP, ibid., box 71; APJ to MEP, Thursday [July 3, 1902?], and July 14, 1902, ibid., box 61.

32. Nettie had the chinchillas made into a big, soft muff and long stole. APJ to MEP, Sunday [Aug.] 26 [1901], Nov. 20 [1901], and Jan. 3, 5 [1902], ibid.

33. MEP to JWP, Oct. 3 [1902], ibid., box 62.

34. JWP to GP, March 17, 23, 1899, ibid., box 59. The Gramercy Park house was sold for $76,500. JWP to GP, Saturday [1906?], ibid., box 64.

35. GP to JWP, April 29, 1902, ibid., box 62. Architectural drawings for alterations to the house (1921) are in Prints & Photographs Division, Library of Congress. *Breaking New Ground*, pp. 150-151, 241, 317-318. A later description of the Pinchot mansion said it had fifty-four rooms. Washington *Evening Star*, April 3, 1955, p. D-2.

36. *Washington Wife: Journal of Ellen Maury Slayden from 1897–1919* (New York: Harper and Row, 1962), Jan. 11, 1905, pp. 64–65.

37. APJ to MEP, Aug. 21 [1899], GPP, box 59.

38. APJ to MEP, Jan. 2 [1907], ibid., box 65. Second quotation in Slayden, *Washington Wife*, Jan. 11, 1905, p. 64.

39. Unsigned card to MEP, Feb. 6 [?], and APJ to MEP, undated fragment, GPP, box 75.

40. Later, La Farge informed Gifford that the cost of the house was $75,994.15 ($2.65 million today) and the addition $32,522.76. C. G. La Farge to GP, June 19, 1912, ibid., box 157.

41. Quotation in Pinkett, *Pinchot*, p. 48.

42. One of Gifford's first acts as forester was the issuance of a directive, Circular 21, October 15, 1898, which offered his division's help to owners of private wood lots and forest lands in developing plans for practical lumbering.

43. GP to MEP, Aug. 22, 1899, GPP, box 59.

44. In his first three years as forester, the appropriations for his division increased more than six times and the number of employees sixteen times. A successful innovation was his hiring of summer interns at an economical rate, so that of the 123 people in the division in 1900, sixty-one were students.

45. GP to Redfield Proctor (R-VT), Sept. 4, 1902, GPP, box 85. Proctor was chairman of the Senate Agriculture and Forestry Committee.

46. *Breaking New Ground*, p. 152.

47. GP to JWP, March 27, 1893, GPP, box 961. Gifford's thinking may have been guided by Brandis, who had preached that successful management of forest tracts in America should precede any forestry school.

48. JWP to GP, Oct. 24, 1894, and GP to JWP, Nov. 12, 1894, ibid., box 57.

49. *Conservation Diaries*, May 2, 1898, p. 92. Fernow's career is explored in Andrew Denny Rogers, III, *Bernard Eduard Fernow: A Story of North American Forestry* (Princeton, NJ: Princeton University Press, 1951).

50. Gifford may have first met Hadley in October 1899 when he accompanied his Uncle Will to a meeting with the new president to discuss Will's gift of $3,000 to the university to upgrade the campus grounds. GP, Diary, Oct. 14, 1899, GPP, box 2; *YDN*, Feb. 2, 1900, p. 2.

51. Arthur T. Hadley to GP, Dec. 8, 1899, GPP, box 966.

52. GP to Hadley, Dec. 15, 1899, ibid.; AP to GP, Sunday [Dec. 17, 1899], ibid., box 54; GP, Diary, Jan. 27, 29, 1900, ibid., box 3.

53. Gifford and Mamee soon added another $90,000 to the endowment, with the university pledging to raise another $50,000 to assure its longer-term financial health.

54. GP to JWP, Aug. 25, 1903, GPP, box 62; Harry S. Graves to GP, Sept. 1 [1900]. ibid., box 969. *Conservation Diaries*, March 14, 1903, p. 114. In its first years, the forest school had only two faculty members plus temporary appointments, and the forestry students also took science-oriented courses in the Yale Sheffield School offered by Brewer and other professors.

55. *Conservation Diaries*, Jan. 27, 29, 1900, July 25, 1903, pp. 114, 115; Q. R. Craft, "Camp Life at the Yale Summer School of Forestry," *Forestry and Irrigation*, 10 (Sept. 1904), pp. 427–431. The summer school lasted until 1929.

56. S. S. Minturn to GP, March 12 [1902], GPP, box 70; AP to GP, Oct. 15 [1902], ibid., box 71.

57. JWP to GP, Dec. 22, 1902, ibid., box 62; Gertrude M. Pinchot to GP, tel., Feb. 13, 1903, ibid.; Gertrude M. Pinchot to GP, undated [mid-Feb. 1903], ibid., box 68.

58. AP to GP, May 28, 1903, June 10, 1903, ibid., box 62; and Gertrude M. Pinchot to GP, April 5 [1903], ibid., box 71.

59. AP to GP, June 10, 1903, and GP to AP, July 21, 1903, ibid., box 62.

60. W. W. Rockhill to GP, Jan. 26 [1904], GPP, box 409a; GP, Diary, Jan. 28, 1904, ibid., box 4; AP to GP, June 4, 1904, ibid., box 63; AP, Note on Chapter on Roosevelt [1927?], APP, box 122; *Conservation Diaries*, Oct. 19, 1904, p. 137.

61. GP to AP, April 17, 1903, and July 21, 1903, GPP, box 71; *WP*, Nov. 11, 1910, p. 4, and Nov. 1, 1912, p. 7.

62. Alan was awarded Knight Commander of the Royal Victorian Order. He had hoped to get Knight Commander of the Order of St. Michael and St. George. AJ to JWP, Dec. 15, 1905, GPP, box 64. Instead, he was subsequently awarded Knight Grand Cross of the Royal Victorian Order.

63. Gertrude M. Pinchot to GP, Sept. 16 [1904], and Oct. 21 [1904], ibid., box 63.

Chapter 10: Political Awakenings

1. MEP, to GP, Monday [1892?], GPP, box 3170.
2. MEP to GP, Oct. 28 [1894], ibid., box 72.
3. JWP to GP, Nov. 10, 1894, ibid., box 3169.
4. MEP to GP, March 11, 1883, ibid., box 52. Regarding Stowe's book, Mary thought "that every American youth ought to read the book." MEP to GP, June 29 [1896], ibid., box 72.
5. MEP to GP, Oct. 28 [1894], ibid.
6. Mary did not seem to object to the male-only memberships in private clubs. After the Century Association, in 1897 Gifford joined the Cosmos Club in Washington, D.C., an elitist society composed mainly of scientists. MEP to GP, Jan. 22 [1898], ibid., box 59.
7. MEP to GP, Aug. 4, 1896, ibid., box 72; JWP to GP, Oct. 2, 1896, ibid., box 3169.
8. Reynolds to GP, Jan. 12, 1894, ibid., box 70; Reynolds to GP, Feb. 10, 1896, ibid., box 80.
9. Reynolds to GP, Dec. 14, 1898, ibid.; *Breaking New Ground*, p. 71.
10. Reynolds to GP, Aug. 19, 1895, GPP, box 79; GP, Diary, Nov. 2, 1895, ibid., box 2.
11. APJ to MEP, Saturday [early March 1894], ibid., box 56. In London, the Johnstones lived a stone's throw from Anna Roosevelt, Theodore's older sister, and Anna "cheered" Nettie during her pregnancy with Crinks and "is a very great support." AJ to MEP, Jan. 17, 1895, ibid., box 57. Correspondence between Mary Pinchot and various Roosevelts is ibid., box 72.
12. GP, Diary, May 21, 1894, ibid., box 1; quotation in Douglas Brinkley, *The Wilderness Warrior: Theodore Roosevelt and the Crusade for America* (New York: HarperCollins, 2009), p. 341.
13. La Farge and Roosevelt had probably nominated Gifford for membership in the Boone and Crockett Club in 1897, and Governor Roosevelt had appointed La Farge's professional partner to the position of state architect.
14. TR to GP, Feb. 18, 1899, GPP, box 81.
15. Gifford recalled that the temperature on the mountain read -23° some 3,000 feet below the summit. GP to A. Lawrence Rotch, Jan. 28, 1900, ibid., box 576.
16. C. Grant La Farge, "A Winter Ascent of Tahawus," *Outing*, 36 (April 1900), pp. 1-7 (La Farge quotation on p. 7); GP, Diary, Feb. 10, 1899, GPP, box 2.
17. In a terse diary reference, Gifford noted, "Boxed and wrestled w. T.R. before dinner," which he slightly expanded in his memoirs: "Roosevelt bested me in wrestling, but I had the honor of knocking the future President of the United States off his very solid pins." GP, Diary, Nov. 27, 1899, ibid., Box 3; *Breaking New Ground*, p. 145.
18. GP to MEP, Tuesday [Jan. 1882?], GPP, box 52; MEP to GP, March 12 [1884], ibid., box 72.
19. GP to MEP, Oct. 6, 1901, ibid., box 968; *The Works of Theodore Roosevelt* (New York: Charles Scribner's Sons, 1926), 15, pp. 103-104.
20. His limited knowledge came mainly from Dietrich Brandis and his forestry work much earlier in Burma and British India.
21. At Yale Law School, Ahern wrote a thesis on the necessity of forest legislation (his wife was an art student affiliated with Yale class of 1895). In one letter about management of the Philippine forests, Ahern asked Gifford nine meaty questions. Ahern to GP, Feb. 11, 1898, GPP, box 965; *Conservation Diaries*, July 22, 1896, and July 23, 1898, pp. 73, 18; *Directory of the Living Non-Graduates of Yale University: Issue of 1914* (New Haven: Yale, 1914), p. 222. After Yale, Ahern taught forestry at a state college in Montana. His courses might have been the first formal forestry instruction in America, antedating even the curriculums at Biltmore and Cornell. Lawrence Rakestraw, "Forest Missionary: George Patrick Ahern, 1894-1899," *Montana, The Magazine of Western History*, 9 (Oct. 1959), pp. 36-44; *Breaking New Ground*, pp. 93, 100.
22. First quotation in Pinkett, *Pinchot*, p. 52; GP to WHT, April 6, 1901, GPP, box 640; Ahern to GP, Feb. 18, 1902, ibid. Last quotation in Lawrence Rakestraw, "George Patrick Ahern and the Philippine Bureau of Forestry, 1900-1914," *Pacific Northwest Quarterly*, 58 (July 1967), pp. 144-145.
23. GP to James Wilson, Oct. 17, 1902, GPP, box 86.
24. GP to Gertrude M. Pinchot, Nov. 8, 1902, ibid,. box 62; GP to JWP, Nov. 6, 1902, ibid., box 640. Gifford's summary of his Philippine travels is in GP, *Selected Writings*, pp. 34-38.

25. *Conservation Diaries*, Nov. 27, 1902, p. 126. Gifford's (and Ahern's) recommendations were printed in *Report of the Forestry Bureau of the Philippine Islands for the Year Ended September 1, 1903* (Bureau of Insular Affairs, War Department), pp. 315-325.

26. GP to G. P. Gilder, March 22, 1900, GPP, box 81.

27. The U.S. military's behavior in the Philippines resulted in major excesses, though the number and specifics are in dispute.

28. GP to TR, Nov. 22, 1902, GPP, box 640; *Washington Star*, Jan. 6, 1903, p. 8; *Conservation Diaries*, Jan. 9, 1903, p. 135.

29. GP to Anson Phelps Stokes, March 27, 1902, and GP to Edward W. Reed, June 16, 1902, GPP, box 86; *Breaking New Ground*, p. 233.

30. *Conservation Diaries*, Jan. 18, 1891, p. 11; GP to MEP, April 8, 1892, GPP, box 55.

31. GP, Lecture on Forests and Forest Work in the Philippines, March 16, 1903, ibid., box 640; GP to BTW, Nov. 10, 1900, ibid., box 83; and GP to BTW, March 1, 1906, ibid., box 104. Ahern had much more democratic views: the Filipinos "hate the Americans and their customs even more heartily than they ever hated the [Spanish] friar. We have, in the public schools, abused their customs and religion and now we are reaping the harvest." Ahern to GP, June 25, 1902, GPP, box 640. And while in charge of the Philippine forests from 1900 to 1914, Ahern's purpose was to help the Filipino people prosper from their forests, and he stressed the need for more scientific research to evaluate the utility of the Philippine woods for various commercial purposes.

32. Carlos Sulit, "Yale in Philippine Forestry," *Yale Forest School News*, 38 (July 1950), pp. 50-51; GP to Hadley, Nov. 9, 1900, GPP, box 83; GP to Graves, Jan. 16, 1902, ibid., box 84. By 1910, only two Filipino students had graduated from the Yale Forest School. In 1910, a forestry school in the Philippines opened. Rakestraw, "George Patrick Ahern and the Philippine Bureau of Forestry," pp. 145ff.; Greg Bankoff, "Breaking New Ground? Gifford Pinchot and the Birth of 'Empire Forestry' in the Philippines, 1900-1905," *Environment and History*, 15 (2009), pp. 369-393; and Bankoff, "First Impressions: Diarists, Scientists, Imperialists and the Management of the Environment in the American Pacific, 1899-1902," *Journal of Pacific History*, 44 (Dec. 2009), pp. 261-280.

33. A variation on this theme for another part of Asia is Jerry Israel, "'For God, for China and for Yale' – The Open Door at Work," *American Historical Review*, 75 (Feb. 1970), pp. 796-807.

34. GP to Albert J. Beveridge, July 16, 1903, GPP, box 86.

35. When James R. Garfield became secretary of the interior in 1907, he would draft executive orders that withdrew oil and phosphate lands from private interests until Congress passed laws disposing of them. Resistance in Congress had caused the government efficiency committee's report to be shelved without publication.

36. *Conservation Diaries*, June 7, 1903, and Oct. 21, 1903, p. 135; GP to TR, March 30, 1903, Theodore Roosevelt Papers (Manuscript Division, Library of Congress), reel 3 (hereafter TRP).

Chapter 11: Empire Builder and Anti-Preservationist

1. GP, *Selected Writings*, pp. 39-42 (quotations on pp. 41, 42).

2. Wanting to build on this momentum, Gifford persuaded the association to hire the seasoned forestry professional, Edward A. Bowers, to launch an aggressive membership drive. Bowers' best efforts brought meager results, however, and, in his view, served only to deplete the association's treasury.

3. By July 1905, twenty-four of the fifty-five new foresters had received master's degrees from the new Yale Forest School.

4. GP to George W. Woodruff, Feb. 2, 1903, ibid., box 89.

5. GP to Herbert A. Smith, Sept. 26, 1904, GP to TR, Sept. 22, 1904, ibid., box 94; GP to Andrew Carnegie, March 1904, ibid., box 90.

6. Reynolds to GP, Dec. 21, 1903, and GP to Reynolds, Dec. 28, 1903, ibid., box 88. Quotation in Theodore Roosevelt, *An Autobiography* (New York: Macmillan, 1913), p. 313. After Upton Sinclair's *The Jungle* exposed the unsanitary conditions in the meat-packing facilities in Chicago, Roosevelt sent Reynolds and another government official to make surprise visits to the Chicago plants. Horrified by the conditions, Reynolds jokingly wrote Gifford that "my own personal investigations have led me to become a vegetarian." Reynolds to GP, April 15, 1905, GPP, box 103.

7. GP to TR, Sept. 22, 1905, ibid, box 98.

8. GP, extract from *Report of the Forester*, 1909, p. 13. (GPP, box 974.)

9. First quotation in Pinkett, *Pinchot*, p. 71. William B. Greeley, *Forests and Men* (New York: Doubleday, 1951), p. 66.

10. Any letter not answered within thirty-six hours, he wrote, should result in "a special inquiry." *Recommendation on Policy, Organization, and Procedure for the Bureau of Forestry in the Philippine Islands*, p. 321.

11. Quotation in *Breaking New Ground*, p. 265. The full title was *The Use of National Forest Reserves*. By the 1980s, the slender manual, still in use, expanded to twenty-seven volumes and about 20,000 pages. Michael Frome, *The Forest Service* (Boulder, Col.: Westview Press, 2nd ed., 1984), p. 52.

12. Quotation in Pinkett, *Pinchot*, p. 73.

13. *Washington Star*, March 23, 1906, p. 1; MEP to JWP, March 24, 1906, GPP, box 64. The efficiency committee was called the Keep Committee, named after its chairman, Assistant Treasury Secretary Charles H. Keep.

14. TR to GP, July 27, 1901, ibid., box 968.

15. Garfield, the French Ambassador Jules Jusserand, and Lawrence Murray, an assistant secretary of commerce, were other regular participants.

16. A legendary walk with Jusserand and several other men to the Virginia side of the Potomac River, for example, is detailed in TR, *Autobiography*, p. 52; and *The Reminiscences of Hans J. Jusserand* (Freeport, N.Y.: Books for Libraries Press, 1972 edition), pp. 335-336.

17. GP, Diary, Oct. 11, 1905, GPP, box 3.

18. GP to JWP, Thanksgiving Day, 1905, ibid., box 64. When Gifford's father died a few years later, this letter was found on his desk, suggesting, perhaps, its emotive resonance on James, who had so often preached such values to his children.

19. Rainsford to GP, undated [c. 1899], and GP to Rainsford, Nov. 3, 1899, ibid., box 81. Rainsford was also a good friend of Theodore Roosevelt.

20. GP to Rainsford, Nov. 16, 1899, ibid. He also socialized with a friend of his parents, Henry Y. Satterlee, who was the first Episcopal bishop of Washington and initiated the purchase of land upon which the Washington Cathedral would be built. Because of his strong Episcopalian focus, Gifford would henceforth affiliate with the Anglican church.

21. Beveridge also endeared himself to Gifford's parents, becoming a regular visitor to Grey Towers (he affectionately called his hosts his "Majesty" and "Lady Mother"). Albert J. Beveridge to GP, May 21, 1903, June 17, 1903, June 23, 1903, and Oct. 14, 1903, GPP, box 86.

22. Beveridge to GP, Oct. 14, 1903, ibid.; Beveridge to GP Nov. 15, 1906, GP to Beveridge, Nov. 22, 1906, Beveridge to GP, July 30, 1907, ibid., box 100; Beveridge to JWP, Sept. 14, 1905, ibid., box 64.

23. Before the 1916 law, Congress created a Children's Bureau to investigate and report on all matters relating to the welfare of children. Thereafter, Congress would not enact restrictions on child labor until the later years of the New Deal. Gifford early served on the national board and local D.C. chapter of the Boy Scouts. Documentation is in GPP, box 142.

24. MEP, June 21, 1903, ibid., box 968.

25. For the government, competitive bidding would raise more revenue to pay for efficient management of the forests.

26. GP, *The Fight for Conservation* (New York: Nabu Press, 1910), p. 4.

27. Fred E. Weyerhaeuser to GP, Oct. 27, 1898, GPP, box 965. As early as 1898, Weyerhaeuser responded to the forestry division's Circular 21.

28. Weyerhaeuser may have sensed that because only the large and established lumber companies could meet the detailed prescribed federal government's cutting requirements. It was prudent to show interest in its goal of long-term forest sustainability. Quotations in McGeary, *Pinchot*, p. 85.

29. GP to TR, Sept. 23, 1905, TRP, reel 59.

30. Gifford's defense of the administration's forest policy is summarized in his forty-two-page pamphlet, *The Use of the National Forests, 1907* (U.S. Department of Agriculture, 1907). The lumbermen's apparent acceptance of Pinchot's message on national forestry is presented in Robert F. Ficken, "Gifford Pinchot Men: Pacific Northwest Lumbermen and the Conservation Movement, 1902-1910," *Western Historical Quarterly*, 13 (April 1962), pp. 165-178. Gifford's disarming of critics in one state is told in G. Michael McCarthy, "The Pharisee Spirit: Gifford Pinchot in Colorado," *PMHB*, 97 (July 1973), pp. 362-378.

31. *Congressional Record*, Feb. 18, 1907; GP to JWP, Sept. 8, 1905, GPP, box 64; GP to WHT, Oct. 29, 1906, ibid., box 975.

32. TR was willing to use "the bully pulpit" of the presidency to achieve his reform agenda. When Congress refused to give him specific authority of law, he issued executive orders. He published more such orders than any of his predecessors. Unless the Constitution or Congress specifically prohibited him from protecting the nation's national resources, he felt a responsibility to act for the general welfare, and government lawyers provided examples of court decisions upholding the supervisory power of the executive.

33. Quotation in McGeary, *Pinchot*, p. 89; McCarthy, "Pharisee Spirit," pp. 376-378.

34. *Breaking New Ground*, p. 337. *The Letters of Theodore Roosevelt*, eds. Elting E. Morison, et al. (Cambridge, Mass.: Harvard University Press, 1952), 6, pp. 975n-976n.

35. *Breaking New Ground*, pp. 321-329 (quotations on pp. 323, 322).

36. Ibid., pp. 325-326. The concept was an adaptation of British theorist Jeremy Bentham's utilitarian doctrine.

37. Arizona and New Mexico would soon become states to make forty-eight. The White House also invited all members of Congress, the Supreme Court, the cabinet, several lay leaders, and the Inland Waterways Commission.

38. Since no money had been appropriated for the expenses of the conference, Gifford and Mary presumably absorbed the entire cost.

39. *Proceedings of a Conference of Governors in the White House, Washington, DC, May 13-15, 1908* (Washington, DC: Government Printing Office, 1909), p. 193; quotation in McGeary, *Pinchot*, p. 99.

40. *Report of the National Conservation Commission*, 60th Cong., 2nd Sess., S. Doc. 676 (3 vols., Washington, DC: Government Printing Office, February 1909), passim. On the state level, "Pinchotism" became a pejorative word associated with meddling government rangers, inspectors, and bureaucrats who, it was alleged, treated the local residents as dishonest citizens and imposed "carpet-bag rule" on them. Democrats in Colorado won the election in 1908, in part, by successfully making discontent with the forest service a lively campaign issue.

41. Quotation in Frome, *Forest Service*, p. 45; McGeary, *Pinchot*, p. 89.

42. Quotation ibid., p. 88; *Congressional Record*, 60th Cong., 1st Sess., pp. 5,370, 4,137, and 4,140.

43. He nowhere seemed to reflect, for example, that TR's announcement that he would not run for re-election shortly after his election victory in 1904 might have accounted somewhat for his declining leverage over Congress toward the end of his administration.

44. James Wilson to GP, Feb. 28, 1907, GPP, box 974. Similarly, his friend Senator Proctor of Vermont noted that the "quite hostile" senators from the forest reserve states were "scolding very badly about the additional reserves." Redfield Proctor to GP, March 12, 1907, ibid.

45. GP to Proctor, March 14, 1907, ibid.

46. George Bird Grinnell, ed., *American Big Game in the Haunts: The Book of the Boone and Crockett Club* (New York: Forest and Stream, 1904), pp. 485-489, passim.

47. GP to AP, May 21, 1903, GPP, box 62. As a sportsman, he once roasted a buck deer's horns in the campfire coals and, after chewing on them, pronounced that "they were not at all bad." GP to Family, July 24, 1897, ibid., box 964.

48. During the Roosevelt presidency, Gifford twice went salmon fishing in New Brunswick, Canada. (On the second one, he sent the biggest, a 25 pounder, to Roosevelt's home in Oyster Bay.) GP to MEP, June 22, 1904, ibid., box 63; GP to Redfield Proctor, April 17, 1905, ibid., box 97; GP to Charles F. Holder, April 3, 1906, ibid., box 102.

49. Charles Frederick Holder, *Recreations of a Sportsman on the Pacific Coast*. (New York: G. P. Putnam, 1910), pp. 305-317. This book also relates other salt water fishing exploits by Gifford.

50. Muir to GP, Dec. 16, 1897, GPP, box 964.

51. *Survey of Forest Reserves*, pp. 38-39, 48, 52, 56, 58, 65, 71-72, 80, 83, 86, 90, 101, 107-108, 110, 117.

52. GP to JWP, Sept. 9 and 19, 1906, GPP, box 64.

53. Robert U. Johnson to GP, Sept. 4, 1908, GP to Johnson, Sept. 15, 1908, and Johnson to GP, Sept. 17, 1908, GPP, box 576. Sargent, Fernow, and Muir and his people, among others, were not invited, even though TR claimed that the governor's conference was the greatest conservation gathering ever.

54. Earlier, Interior Secretary Hitchcock twice rejected the city's request for a dam at Hetch Hetchy, and its prospects then languished.

55. To be sure, the Hetch Hetchy dam would provide for the good of Bay area people for the indefinite future, but preservationists believed that despoliation of a natural wonder was not just for the longest time—but probably forever.

56. *Breaking New Ground*, p. 103.

57. GP, *Selected Writings*, pp. 187-190. A documentary record of the dispute is Char Miller, ed., *Hetch Hetchy: A History in Documents* (Peterborough: Broadview Press, 2020).

58. Plunkett had been involved in cattle raising in Wyoming in the 1880s, about the same time that Roosevelt was trying his hand at ranching in the Dakotas.

59. *Letters of Theodore Roosevelt*, 6, p. 1241.

60. *Breaking New Ground*, p. 340. Gifford was just beginning to show an interest in women's issues. GP to JWP, Aug. 19, 1904, and GP to MEP, Aug. 11, 1904, GPP, box 63. Some of Mary's anti-urban biases may have rubbed off on her son. MEP to JWP, undated [1888], GPP, box 75; MEP, Journal, [1877], ibid., box 39; MEP to JWP, Aug. 21 [1902], ibid., box 73.

61. Quotation in McGeary, *Pinchot*, p. 101.

62. Gifford would come to know well Henry, a commission member, as well as his son Henry C. and grandson Henry A., both of whom would subsequently serve as secretaries of agriculture. His greater understanding and appreciation of rural life would serve as the basis of much of his public support in his later political career.

63. Gill had captained the Yale football team while attending the Yale Divinity School and was selected to the first All-American football team.

64. *The Country Church: The Decline of Its Influence and the Remedy* (1913); and *Six Thousand Country Churches* (1919). Correspondence regarding the first book is in GPP, boxes 132, 143, and 156.

65. GP, *Selected Writings*, pp. 83-89.

66. Archibald Butt to Mother, Oct. 21 [1908], *The Letters of Archie Butt*, ed. Lawrence F. Abbott (New York: Doubleday, Page, 1924), p. 147.

67. *Conservation Diaries*, Jan. 28, 1907 and Nov. 9, 1907, p. 140; TR to GP, March 2, 1909, *Letters of Theodore Roosevelt*, ed. Morison, 6, p. 1,541; *Proceedings of a Conference of Governors*, p. 10. A recent summation of the Roosevelt-Pinchot collaboration is Char Miller, "Play, Work, and Politics: The Remarkable Partnership of Theodore Roosevelt and Gifford Pinchot," in Char Miller and Clay S. Jenkinson, eds., *Theodore Roosevelt: Naturalist in the Arena* (Lincoln: University of Nebraska Press, 2020), pp. 101-110.

Chapter 12: Family Turmoil

1. GP to JWP, Thanksgiving Day, 1905, GPP, box 64; GP to JWP, Aug. 30, 1902, and AJ to JWP, Jan. 5, 1904, ibid., box 62.

2. AP to GP, Feb. 7, 1905, and GP to MEP, May 28, 1905, ibid., box 63; AP to GP, Sept. 24, 1905, and Jan. 24, 1906, ibid., box 64.

3. AP to GP, April 18, 1907, ibid., box 65.

4. James's brothers Edgar and John had both died in 1900. JWP to GP, June 6 [1905], GPP, box 63.

5. Quotation in Char Miller, "Keeper of His Conscience? Pinchot, Roosevelt, and the Politics of Conservation," in *Theodore Roosevelt: Many-Sided American*, eds. Natalie A. Naylor, Douglas Brinkley, and John Allen Gable (Interlaken, NY: Heart of the Lakes, 1992), pp. 241-242.

6. MEP to JWP, 18th [1906], GPP, box 70.

7. MEP to GP, July 24 [1907], GP to AP, Dec. 5, 1907, ibid., box 65.

8. APJ to MEP, Jan. 7 [1908], ibid., box 65; MEP to Miss Sheffield, April 3 [1908], ibid., box 73. Alan's stay was short, as on orders of the king he had to return to England before James's death.

9. AP to MEP, Nov. 16, 1908, ibid., box 66.

10. AP to GP, March 28, 1907, JWP to GP, March 26, 1907, ibid., box 65; JWP to GP, Friday, June 13[14] [1907], ibid., box 71. Even after Gifford's financial rescue, Amos was still in debt, so Gifford soon loaned him another $33,000.

11. AP to MEP, July 8, 1908, and Nov. 12, 1908, and GP to MEP, July 11, 1909, ibid., box 66.

12. Gertrude M. Pinchot to GP, April 1, 1908, ibid., box 65; typewritten statement, undated [1908], APP, box 2.

13. MEP to GP, Sept. 1 [1908], GPP, box 66; MEP, Diary, Oct. 11, 1908, ibid., box 43.

14. U.S. Census (1910).

15. AP to MEP, Nov. 16, 1908, AP to GP, Jan. 28, 1909, GPP, box 66; AP to GP, Feb. 1 [1909], ibid., box 71.

16. AP to MEP, April 22, 1909, ibid.

17. MEP to GP, Sept. 1 [1908] and May 27 [1909], ibid.; AP to GP, Monday, June 7 [1909], ibid., box 71. The introverted Gertrude wrote that Amos and she "are asked out a great deal, but I arrange to have 2 or 3 home evenings as it is awful never to be alone." Gertrude M. Pinchot to GP, Sunday [1909], ibid., box 72.

18. Gertrude M. Pinchot to GP, Thursday [c. June 10, 1909], ibid., box 66.

19. GP to MEP, Sept. 28, 1907, ibid., box 65; GP to MEP, Aug. 20, 1908, ibid., box 121.

20. MEP to GP, Aug. 19 [1904], ibid., box 72.

21. APJ to AP, Sunday [Jan.?] 19 [1913?], APP, box 4.

22. MEP, Diary, June 30, 1909, GPP, box 42; AP to MEP, Monday, Aug. 16, 1909, GP to MEP, Aug. 5, 1909, and Gertrude M. Pinchot to GP, Aug. 16-17 [1909], ibid., box 66. In her last letter, Gertrude related that she had found a paper Amos had written explaining the depth of "'atrophied will' (his own expression) . . . and pessimism, and utter hopelessness, and the comradeship of the lost[,] who need not hope that life holds any beauty or balm because their own nature destroys Everything." (She did not share the paper with Gifford, however.)

23. Quotation in Nancy Pittman Pinchot, "Amos Pinchot," p. 181.

24. Gertrude M. Pinchot to GP, Oct. 22 [1909], GPP, box 3168; GP to MEP, Oct. 24, 1909, ibid., box 66.

25. Gifford had seen a lot of James and Helen Garfield during Roosevelt's presidency, and James and Gifford were then writing a book on the Roosevelt policies, which was never finished because of an escalating political controversy around them. Helen N. Garfield to GP, Oct. 22, 1909, ibid., box 121.

26. GP to AP, undated [c. Nov. 1907], APP, box 4.

27. Amos told his brother that he sought an unsalaried appointment to a commission revising the city charter, which, "will be exceedingly interesting and exactly in the line I care most about," but he did not get the appointment. AP to GP, April 5, 1908, GPP, box 65.

28. Gertrude M. Pinchot to GP, Aug. 16-17 [1909], ibid., box 66.

29. Gertrude M. Pinchot to GP, Thursday [c. June 10, 1909], ibid.

Chapter 13: Political Rebellion

1. GP, Diary, Nov. 24, 1907, GPP, box 2.

2. As governor-general of the Philippines, Taft supported Gifford's forestry recommendations, and in 1906, Gifford decided not to running against Taft for election as a Yale trustee. GP to Z. Bennett Phelps, May 18, 1906, ibid., box 103.

3. *Papers Relating to the Foreign Relations of the United States*, 1909 (Washington: Government Printing Office, 1914), p. 3.

4. Quotation in Henry F. Pringle, *The Life and Times of William Howard Taft: A Biography* (New York: Farrar and Rinehart, 1939), 1, p. 479. Ballinger also unsuccessfully opposed the creation of a national forest in Alaska.

5. He even opposed them inside the forests where they might conflict with mining entries that Congress had authorized.

6. GP to JRG, May 3 and 22, 1909, GPP, box 121; GP to MEP, June 10, 1909, ibid., box 66.

7. Quotation in McGeary, *Pinchot*, pp. 123-124; Newell to GP, undated [Dec. 1909], GPP, box 124.

8. Ballinger canceled an agreement of dubious legality between the forest service and the Indian office of the interior department, in which the former managed the Native American timber lands. GP to MEP, July 4, 11, 1909, ibid., box 66.

9. One paper headlined, "Pinchot in Danger of Losing His Place." *NYT*, Aug. 12, 1909, p. 2.

10. GP to MEP, Aug. 16, 1909, Aug. 29, 1906, and Sept. 6, 1909, GPP, box 66.⁻

11. Quotation in McGeary, *Pinchot*, p. 128.

12. GP to WHT, Aug. 10, 1909, *Investigation of the Department of the Interior and of the Bureau of Forestry*, 61st Congress, 3rd Sess., Doc. No. 719 (Washington, DC: Government Printing Office, 1911), 4, pp. 1218-1219 (quotation on p. 1218). (Hereafter, *Investigation*.)

13. Ibid., pp. 1187-1191.

14. Quotation in Pringle, *Taft*, 1, p. 494.

15. Ibid., pp. 479-481.

16. GP, speech to National Irrigation Congress, Spokane, Aug. 10, 1909. GPP, box 974.

17. Notes of Conversation between President Taft and GP, Sept. 24, 1909, ibid., box 13.

18. GP to MEP, Sept. 27, 1909, and GP to MEP, Aug. 31, 1909, ibid. Quotation in McGeary, *Pinchot*, p. 150.

19. Quotations in Pringle, *Taft*, 1, pp. 480, 492.

20. GP to MEP, Oct. 30, 1909, GPP, box 66; GP to Lew Welsh, Oct. 6, 1909, ibid., box 127; GP, *The Fight for Conservation* (New York: Nabu Press, 1910), ch. 7, passim.

21. "Are the Guggenheims in Charge of the Department of the Interior?" *Collier's Weekly*, 44 (Nov. 13, 1909), pp. 15-17.

22. *Investigation*, 7, pp. 3,755 and 3,756; quotation in McGeary, *Pinchot*, p. 156.

23. Overton W. Price and A. C. Shaw to GP, Jan. 5, 1910, *Investigation*, 4, pp. 1275-1279.

24. HLS to GP, Jan. 5, 1910, Henry L. Stimson Papers (Manuscripts and Archives, Yale University Library), reel 5.

25. Gifford likely acted hastily to get his case to the public before the president's imminent release of his report to Congress on the Glavis case. Gifford may have shown Secretary Wilson the letter without elaboration, and the latter may have approved it without a careful reading. In any event, the explosive reaction in Congress was highly embarrassing to Wilson, who, thinking he had been misled, was understandably angry with Gifford.

26. *Investigation*, 4, pp. 1283-1285 (quotations on p. 1284).

27. Taft also fired Price and Shaw. Ibid., pp. 1289-1290 (quotation on p. 1290); MEP, Diary, Jan. 7, 1910, GPP, box 43.

28. This was advice given to Gifford during his earlier conflict with Professor Sargent.

29. Gifford's lawyer friend George Woodruff also urged him to temper his view of the law. But Gifford at best revised his views on the law in a nuanced fashion. McGeary, *Pinchot*, p. 130.

30. AP to GP, Sept. 5, 1909, and Nov. 11, 1909, GPP, box 66.

31. GP to MEP, Aug. 31, 1909, ibid.

32. Mary Pinchot pronounced that Glavis's testimony was "admirably given" and he had withstood the cross-examination "wonderfully well." MEP, Diary, Jan. 31, 1910, and Feb. 14, 1910, ibid., box 43. Also, Melvin Urofsky, *Louis D. Brandeis: A Life* (New York: Pantheon Books, 2009), pp. 259-260.

33. Gifford also had to admit that he was not always accurate with the facts. *Investigation*, 4, p. 1219.

34. GP to George W. Pepper, Feb. 5, 1910, GPP, box 67.

35. Quotation in Urofsky, *Brandeis*, p. 258.

36. Because of executive privilege, Brandeis could not access White House documents. The reasoning behind executive privilege is that the president, if he is to be effective, requires full and frank advice from his subordinates, but he will get it from them only when they are assured that their communications will be protected from public disclosure.

37. *Investigation*, 7, pp. 3978, 4090.

38. The stenographer was twenty-four-year-old Frederick M. Kerby. He had earlier held back his information for fear of losing his job. Ibid., 8, p. 4397.

39. *NYT*, May 15, 1910, p. 1; MEP, Diary, May 14, 1910, GPP, box 43. Last quotation in Norman Hapgood, *The Changing Years* (New York: Farrar and Rinehart, 1930), p. 190.

40. There had been no scandal since the Grant administration, and Grant himself was never suspected of dishonesty. In his farewell remarks to his forest service compatriots, Gifford said, "You are servants of the people of the United States. Keep that in mind with the utmost clearness." GP, Talk to Meeting of all the members of the Forest Service, Jan. 8, 1910, George Dudley Seymour Papers (Manuscripts and Archives, Yale University Library), Series I, box 24.

41. *Investigation*, 9, pp. 4936-4937, and 4953; *NYT*, May 15, 1910, p. 1.

42. GP to Brandeis, June 14, 1910, GPP, box 129. Ballinger fired Frederick Kerby, but a newspaper syndicate promised him another job. Gifford complimented Kerby for coming forth to testify. McGeary, *Pinchot*, p. 189.

43. Gifford enthused that Graves was "the best man in this country for the work." Quotation ibid., p. 186.

44. A tragic sequel involved Gifford's associate forester, Overton Price, a tense personality, who, tormented by his behavior that led to the firing of his boss, became deeply depressed. Despite Gifford's best efforts in trying to help Price get another government job and neurasthenic treatments, he took his own life in June 1914. Documentation is in the Woodrow Wilson Papers (Manuscript Division, Library of Congress), reel 289, and GPP boxes 6, 47, 149, 166, 3170.

45. Janes Penick, Jr., *Progressive Politics and Conservation: The Ballinger-Pinchot Affair* (Chicago: University of Chicago Press, 1968), pp. ch. 8, passim.

46. *Conservation Diaries*, April 11, 1910, p. 145. Roosevelt's honors included his belated acceptance of the Nobel Peace Prize for his successful presidential mediation of the Russo-Japanese War.

47. AP, "Two Revolts Against Oligarchy: The Insurgent Movements of the Fifties and of To-day," *McClure's Magazine*, 35 (Sept. 1910), pp. 581-590; Gertrude M. Pinchot to AP, Sunday [Aug.? 1910], APP, box 2; Helen Garfield to GP, Aug. 16, 1910, GPP, box 132; GP to MEP, Sept. 6, 1910, ibid., box 10.

48. Text in *Works of Theodore Roosevelt*, 17, pp. 5-22.

49. GP to JRG, Aug. 16, 1910, GPP, box 132. The drafting of Roosevelt's Osawatomie speech has been variously credited to Herbert Croly, with Gifford Pinchot composing the final text, Gifford's draft, Aug. 31, 1910, is in the Cornelia Bryce Pinchot Papers (Manuscript Division, Library of Congress), II:59. (Hereafter CBPP)

50. GP to MEP, Sept. 6, 1910, GPP, box 10.

51. The reformers made few gains in the Eastern states, and in Indiana, the legislature denied the re-election bid of Albert Beveridge, a strong reformer. The Republican progressives' most notable triumph was their election of Hiram Johnson as governor of California. In many states, reformers had successfully championed legislative and constitutional reforms—for example, the primary, allowing voters to choose their nominees directly; the initiative and referendum, whereby citizens could enact measures in the absence of legislative action; and the recall of judges or their decisions when they flouted the popular will.

52. *Investigation*, 1, pp. 91-92; GP to AP, Feb. 3, 1911, GPP, box 149; GP to Brandeis, June 27, 1911, ibid., box 143.

53. *Conservation Diaries*, June 26, 1911, p. 146; and TR to GP, June 28, 1911, TRP, reel 367.

54. GP to Henry Wallace, May 27, 1911, GPP, box 152. The president's appointments of Fisher as interior secretary and Stimson as his secretary of war, both friends of Gifford, were indicative of Taft's moderate direction.

55. A spurious magazine article in mid-1911, for instance, alleged another possible scandal involving the withdrawal of Alaskan public lands from a national forest around Controller Bay in Alaska, but the journalist's allegations were in fact soon discredited.

56. Moreover, when Secretary Fisher, who had visited the same area a few weeks earlier, arrived in Seward, a banner displayed the message, "Conservation Prices . . . coal, $17 per ton . . . Wood, $7 a cord . . . . But you must not mine your own coal, nor cut your own wood . . . All reserved for future generations . . . Signed . . . G. Pinchot . . . 'Pinhead.'" McGeary, *Pinchot*, pp. 208-209 (quotation on p. 209).

57. GP to APJ, May 7, 1923, GPP, box 252. At one point during his tense visit, a Gifford supporter came down to the dock at one town wearing a gun as a warning to demonstrators who wanted to prevent him and his party from disembarking from their steamer.

58. Quotation in McGeary, *Pinchot*, p. 209.

59. Daniel Guggenheim to GP, Jan. 10, 1917, and GP to Guggenheim, Feb. 9, 1917, GPP, box 204.

60. GP, "A Look Ahead in Politics," *Saturday Evening Post*, 184 (Oct. 7, 1911), pp. 3-4, 61-62.

61. GP to MEP, Oct. 23, 1910, GPP, box 10; TR to HLS, Nov. 16, 1910, Morison, 7, p. 165.

62. MEP to GP, Aug. 4 [1910], Jan. 5 [1911], and Aug. 31 [1910], GPP, box 3170.

63. Slayden, *Washington Wife*, Nov. 20, 1911, pp. 163-164.

64. MEP to GP, Sept. 11 [1910?], GPP, box 3170.

65. By mid-1911, Gifford was "almost certain" that TR would avoid coming out for Taft. GP to AP, May 26, 1911, ibid., box 149

66. AP to GP, Sept. 7, 1911, ibid., box 152; AP to GP, Sept. 29, 1911, ibid., box 149.

67. GP, Diary, July 21, 1911, ibid., box 5; William Kent to TR, Sept. 13, 1911, TR to Kent, Sept. 19, 1911, and TR to Theodore Roosevelt, Jr., Aug. 22, 1911, Morison, 7, pp. 343-344 and note 1, p. 338, and p. 336. TR to Arthur Hamilton Lee, Aug. 22, 1911, ibid., p. 338.

68. GP to Henry Wallace, June 28, 1911, GPP, box 152.

69. John H. Hannan to AP, July 15, 1911, and GP to AP, Aug. 24, 1911, APP, box 5; GP, Diary, Aug. 28, 1911, GPP, box 5; AP to Walter L. Houser, Nov. 2, 1911, APP, box 6.

70. AP to JRG, Oct. 8, 1911, ibid. *La Follette's Autobiography*, p. 596; GP, Diary, Dec. 25 and 28, 1911, GPP, box 5.

71. AP to Medill McCormick, Sept. 22, 1911, APP, box 5; AP to Walter L. Houser, Oct. 30, Nov. 2 and 3, 1911, and McCormick to GP, Nov. 13, 1911, ibid., box 6; AP to GP, Feb. 16, 1912, GPP, box 159. Part of the senator's weakness as a candidate was his decision to spend many weeks writing his autobiography instead of stumping the country and getting himself and his reform message better known nationally.

72. GP, Diary, Nov. 12, 1911, ibid., box 5; JRG to GP, Nov. 28, 1911, and Dec. 2, 1911, ibid., box 145.

73. For example, at a convention of Ohio progressives, Gifford, Garfield, and others blocked an endorsement of the Wisconsin candidate and instead approved a resolution supporting any "Progressive Republican." To La Follette, the vote was a betrayal. *La Follette's Autobiography*, p. 575.

74. GP, Diary, Jan. 22, 1912, GPP, box 5. GP to Charles R. Crane, March 5, 1911, ibid, box 144. La Follette was also deeply concerned about the health of his teenage daughter who required an operation.

75. GP, Diary, Feb. 15 and 18, 1912, ibid., box 5.

76. GP, Diary, Feb. 5, 15 and 18, 1912, ibid., box 5; GP to La Follette, Feb. 17, 1912, ibid., box 158; Washington *Evening Star*, Oct. 2, 1912, p. 2, and Dec. 8, 1912, p. 8.

77. GP to AP, Feb. 28, 1912, GPP, box 159; MEP to GP, undated [May 1912], ibid., box 3170.

78. AP to TR, Feb. 14, 1912, TRP, reel 129; GP, Diary, Feb. 9, 1912, GPP, box 5; GP to AP, Feb. 15, 1912, ibid., box 159. Roosevelt also let Amos know that he might have to avoid some politically hazardous issues. TR to AP, Feb. 15, 1912, Morison, 7, p. 505-506. MEP to GP, [June] 15 [1912], GPP, box 72.

79. *NYT*, March 11, 1912, p. 4; AP to TR, March 11, 1912, TRP, reel 133. Subsequently, Amos urged Roosevelt to enunciate more clearly that the central message of his campaign was his fight for the "people" against "privilege." AP to TR, March 26, 1912, tel., ibid., reel 135.

80. AP to Joseph M. Dixon, March 21, 1912, and AP to Gaylord U. Smith, April 1, 1912, tel., APP, box 6. A copy of the pamphlet is in GPP, box 1071.

81. After reading an earlier draft, La Follette remarked, "It is the best thing that has been done along that line." La Follette to AP, Nov. 14, 1911, APP, box 6. *Pearson's* required the author to include a prefatory statement explaining the objections of other magazines.

82. AP, "President Taft – Candidate for Re-election," *Pearson's Magazine*, 27 (May 1912), pp. 533-544 (quotation on p. 533). Another article by Amos dealt with a reciprocity treaty with Canada. The Taft forces successfully won Senate approval, but Amos called it "a special interest scheme designed to win over the manufacturing interests in eastern and contested Midwestern states for Taft's renomination at the expense of farmers and consumers." AP, "The Reciprocity Illusion," *Success Magazine*, 14 (Oct. 1911), pp. 30, 42-44.

83. AP to TR, May 9, 1912, TRP, reel 140; TR to AP, May 11, 1912, ibid., reel 376; *Letters of Theodore Roosevelt*, 7, p. 541n.; Morris, *Colonel Roosevelt*, pp. 185, 187.

84. Ibid., pp. 188, 636-637, 638-639.

85. *Works of Theodore Roosevelt*, 17, p. 231.

86. Doris Kearns Goodwin, *The Bully Pulpit: Theodore Roosevelt, William Howard Taft, and the Golden Age of Journalism* (New York: Simon and Schuster, 2013), p. 702.

87. *NYT*, June 30, 1912, p. 6; GP, Diary, Aug. 3-5, 1912, GPP, box 5; GP to MEP, Aug. 6, 1910, ibid., box 10. Amos apparently wrote one plank linking the high cost of living to business, which TR rejected as "utter folly." Morris, *Colonel Roosevelt*, p. 649n.

88. Eugene Debs, the American Socialist Party's presidential nominee, would garner more than 900,000 votes (six percent) in the election.

89. P. S. Stahlnecker to BTW, Dec. 28, 1910, GPP, box 140; GP to H. A. Slattery, July 25, 1912, ibid., box 161; Amos R. E. Pinchot, *History of the Progressive Party, 1912-1916* (New York: New York University Press, 1958), p. 162.

90. The Progressive Party platform advocated direct primaries, the direct election of senators, woman suffrage, and the initiative, referendum, and limited recall of judicial decisions. It championed a national health system and graduated federal income and inheritance taxes, a more flexible currency system, a downward revised tariff, and nonpartisan commissions to regulate big business combinations. It also called for a universal minimum wage, an eight-hour maximum work day for women and juveniles, plus welfare

benefits, broader workers compensation laws, limitation of injunctions in labor disputes, farm relief, and rules facilitating the organization of labor unions.

91. Among other possible influences on Gertrude was The Triangle Shirtwaist Factory fire in lower Manhattan (March 1911), in which 145 garment workers (123 of whom were women) perished; it dramatized the plight of poor workers. After the fire, an investigation found that the exits and fire escapes had been regularly locked to prevent employees from taking breaks from their work under trying conditions.

92. GP to Gertrude M. Pinchot, Feb. 29, 1912, GPP, box 159.

93. New York *Sun*, March 17, 1912, p. 13; GP to Gertrude M. Pinchot, April 22, 1912, GPP, box 159.

94. MEP to GP, Sept. 25 [1912], and GP to Gertrude M. Pinchot, Oct. 24, 1912, ibid.

95. The title was an obvious takeoff of Republican journalist William Allen White's biting editorial in 1896, "What's the Matter with Kansas," which had attacked the upstart Populist Party.

96. For his essay, Amos solicited material from New York urban social reformers but apparently did not consult other reformers' writings, including those by Albert F. Bentley, Herbert Croly, and Walter E. Weyl.

97. *What's the Matter with America: The Meaning of the Progressive Movement and the Rise of the New Party* (n.p.: n.p., 1912), passim.

98. Edwin B. H. Tower to AP, Oct. 2, 1912, APP, box 7; typewritten statement [1908], ibid., box 2. Amos declined an earlier invitation to run for Congress. MEP to GP, Sept. 5 [1912], GPP, box 71. On the eve of Progressive Party nomination convention, Amos and other insurgents appealed successfully to Roosevelt to force the withdrawal of the head of New York's delegation to the convention—"a conspicuous exponent of corrupt minority rule," Amos called him. Gifford then wrote their mother, "I was very proud in the fight Amos made." GP, Diary, Aug. 1, 1912, ibid., box 5; AP, et al., to TR, Aug. 4, 1912, APP, box 7; GP to MEP, Aug. 6, 1912, GPP, box 10.

99. Bates, also a Yale graduate, had defeated Amos as the Republican candidate for assemblyman four years earlier, but the two reformers were friends and agreed on the issues.

100. AP to Hiram Johnson, Oct. 5, 1912, and AP to MEP, Oct. 19, 1912, APP, box 7.

101. AP to Hiram Johnson, Oct. 5, 1912, ibid. The boundaries of this congressional district had been redrawn after the 1910 census, introducing another uncertain element in the election.

102. AP to Mark Sullivan, Oct. 5, 1912, and AP to Thomas G. Patten, Oct. 30, 1912, APP, box 7.

103. AP, campaign leaflet, copy in GPP, box 3174.

104. AP to Henry Moskowitz, Oct. 18, 1912, AP to Jacob H. Schiff, Oct. 25, 1912, Robert G. Barkley to AP, Oct. 30, 1912, and AP to Sir, Nov. 2, 1912, APP, box 7. Mamee also contributed generously to local Progressive Party coffers and to individual progressive candidate races in New York and Pennsylvania.

105. Gifford had been campaigning in the Midwest, Pennsylvania, and New England. Representative of his diary entries are Aug. 4, 5, Sept. 30, Oct. 1, 1912, ibid., box 5.

106. GP to AP, Oct. 31, 1912, and Charles F. Darby to AP, Oct. 16, 1912, APP, box 7.

107. AP to Beveridge, Oct. 8, 1912, AP to Brandeis, Oct. 8, 1912, and AP to McCormick, Oct. 8, 1912, APP box 7; GP, Diary, Oct. 15, 1912, GPP, box 5.

108. AP to Brandeis, Oct. 8, 1912, APP, box 7.

109. To qualify as a voter in Pennsylvania, one-year residency was required. George R. Bull to GP, Oct. 28, 1911, GPP, box 143.

110. Hapgood to AP [Nov.] 7 [1912], APP, box 7. Patten received 13,704 votes; Pinchot, 6,644; and the Republican, Socialist, and independent candidates garnered 4,942, 2,085, and 21 votes respectively. Helene Maxwell Hooker, introduction to AP, *History of the Progressive Party*, pp. 44, 271. Bates also failed in his congressional bid.

Chapter 14: New Directions

1. MEP to GP, Nov. 11, 1912, GPP, box 3170; MEP, Diary, Nov. 10, 1912, ibid., box 44; TR to GP, Nov. 11, 1912, Morison, 7, p. 637.

2. APJ to AP, Sept. 24 [1912], APP, box 3; GP, Diary, Nov. 11-20, 1912, GPP, box 5.

3. GP to AP, Dec. 1, 1912, ibid., box 159.

4. AP to TR, Dec. 23, 1912, and GP to TR, Dec. 17, 1912, APP, box 8. Some radical reformers charged that ten percent of Americans owned ninety percent of the wealth. Gifford wanted good evidence but learned that government agencies had no statistics on income distribution and few on wages.

5. TR to GP, Nov. 11, 1912, Morison, 7, pp. 637-638; GP to Hiram Johnson, Dec. 28, 1912, GPP, box 157.

6. GP, Diary, Dec. 8, 10, 1912, ibid., box 5

7. TR to AP, Dec. 5, 1912, Morison, 7, pp. 661-670; TR to GP, Jan. 3, 1913, GPP, box 170. Ironically, the leading owners of U.S. Steel, unhappy with Perkins's political activities, tried to force him to give up his directorship, but a determined Perkins successfully resisted these efforts. John A. Garraty, *Right-hand Man: The Life of George W. Perkins* (New York: Harper, 1960), pp. 290-295.

8. GP to TR, Dec. 17, 1912, Morison, 7, p. 677n1; GP to AP, Dec. 21, 1912, GPP, box 159.

9. GP, Diary, Feb. 4, 1913, ibid., box 5.

10. Quotation in Morris, *Colonel Roosevelt*, p. 186.

11. William Allen White to GP, April 20, 1914, GPP, box 186.

12. *Conservation Diaries*, June 13, 1913, p. 141.

13. GP, Diary, June 13, 1913, GPP, box 5; MEP to TR, June 13 [1913], TRP, reel 176.

14. *Conservation Diaries*, June 24 and July 12, 1913, p. 141; TR to MEP, June 20, 1913, TRP, reel 356. TR, *Autobiography*, p. 409. MEP to TR, Nov. 29 [1913], and GP to TR, Dec. 10, 1913, TRP, reel 181.

15. GP, Diary, April 3, 14, 16, 1911, GPP, box 5; MEP, Diary, June 21, 1911, ibid., box 44.

16. Cornelia's parents listed eight household servants (the Pinchots had nine) in the 1910 census. Edward Cooper had even been elected mayor of New York for a term.

17. Cornelia Bryce Pinchot, "In Search of Adventure," *These Modern Women: Autobiographical Essays from the Twenties*, ed. Elaine Showalter (Old Westbury, NY: Feminist Press, 1978), pp. 121-126 (quotations on pp. 123, 124).

18. Ibid., p. 124; *NYT*, June 13, 1913, p. 7, March 11, 1914, p. 11, and July 7, 1914, p. 9. Many earlier *NYT* stories referred to her life as a sportswoman and socialite. She was also a prime leader of a group called the Conference on Unemployment Among Women.

19. GP, Diary, March 15, 1913, and April 4, 8, 1913, GPP, box 5; GP to Frances A. Kellor, April 15, 1913, ibid., box 167. Leila joined the Progressive Service, headed by Frances Kellor, who served as an officer of Leila's women's unemployment group. *NYT*, May 3, 1914, p. 12; Kellor to GP, undated [Nov. 2, 1914], GPP, box 179.

20. GP, Diary, June 22, 1913, ibid., box 5. Leila caught no fish and Gifford only one small one.

21. MEP, Diary, Oct. 21, 1911, Nov. 1, 1912, March 15, 1913, ibid., box 44. Leila's visit to Grey Towers in 1911 came when Gifford was away on his Alaska trip.

22. Bradley, "Mystery of Gifford Pinchot and Laura Houghteling," pp. 211-213, claims that Mary arranged for the coming together of the couple. Miller, *Pinchot*, pp. 177-181, 204-205, 411, argues, however, that Gifford and Cornelia as "commanding personalities" (p. 411) began seeing each other without Mary's prodding. The narrative here agrees more with the latter interpretation and tries to provide additional perspective.

23. Moreover, in late 1913, Mary and Nettie visited Edith and Lloyd Bryce, who had recently completed his diplomatic assignment, in Roslyn. Mary's cultivation of Dutch contacts included dinner and tea invitations to the Netherlands Minister to the United States and his wife, and Mary twice had dinner at the Dutch Legation. MEP, Diary, Sept. 6, 1911, Dec. 6, 1911, and May 10, 1913, GPP, box 44; Slayden, *Washington Wife* (Nov. 20, 1911), p. 163. Ship passenger lists document Leila's three arrivals in New York from Liverpool during her father's tenure as minister.

24. GP to AP, Oct. 7, 1913, GPP, box 169; MEP, Diary, Nov. 30, 1913, Dec. 2, 1913, and March 7, 1914, ibid., box 44. In the latter visit, Gifford went to Asheville to attend the funeral of George Vanderbilt.

25. Quotation in CBP, "In Search of Adventure," p. 126.

26. *NYT*, Oct. 4, 1913, p. 1.

27. Gifford lectured on the Chautauqua circuit during the summer of 1913 and followed with a long fishing trip in Florida.

28. GP, Diary, March 16, 1914 and April 8, 1914, GPP, box 5.

29. GP, Diary, June 14, 1914, ibid.; Gertrude M. Pinchot to AP, Tuesday, July 21 [1914], APP, box 4.

30. MEP, Diary, May 7, 1914, GPP, box 44.

31. Frances A. Kellor to MEP, July 31 [1914], ibid., box 68.

32. In early July, Alan Johnstone traveled to America to pay his respects to Mrs. Pinchot, but he embarked from New York on August 7 to return to his post as British Minister in the Netherlands, as the military conflict and the precarious position of that nation required his immediate presence at The Hague.

33. Cornelia E. Bryce to GP [July 29, 1914] and undated, attached to this letter, CBPP, box III 1.

34. Cornelia E. Bryce to GP [Aug. 6, 1914], ibid.; GP, Diary, Aug. 8, 1914, GPP, box 5.

35. *NYT*, Aug. 16, 1914, p. 15.

36. GP to TR, Dec. 10, 1913, TRP, reel 181. Palmer would later serve as President Wilson's attorney general and become infamous for his so-called "Palmer raids" against radicals after the First World War. Gifford never liked Palmer, early labeling him "a scamp." GP, Diary, May 18, 1913, GPP, box 5.

37. Walter Davenport, *Power and Glory: The Life of Boies Penrose* (New York: Putnam, 1931), pp. 206, 208-209.

38. GP to Medill McCormick, Jan. 31, 1914, GPP, box 180; GP to JRG, Jan. 21, 1914, ibid., box 177.

39. Amos argued that monopolies felt responsibility only to their shareholders, used their enormous power to bankrupt smaller competitors, and were not just anti-union but failed to pay their workers a living wage and used espionage to keep them in line. AP, "The Cost of Private Monopoly to Public and Wage-Earner," *Annals of the American Academy of Political and Social Science*, 48 (July 1913), pp. 164-188 (quotations on pp. 184, 185). He elaborated his complaint about collusion between big trusts, their control of common carriers, and their subversion of rate regulation in the public interest in AP, "The Biggest Thing Between You and Prosperity," *Pearson's Magazine*, 34 (Sept. 1915), pp. 225-240.

40. Amos came to accept Louis Brandeis's arguments in favor of breaking up the trusts and began forcefully attacking the Perkins view. Brandeis thanked him for exposing "the futility of monopoly, of banker management, and of the so-called 'regulation' of monopoly." AP to Louis D. Brandeis, Oct. 8, 1912, APP, box 7; Brandeis to AP, July 18, 1913, ibid., box 9.

41. GP to H. D. W. English, Jan. 21, 1914, GPP, box 176.

42. GP to Gilson Gardner, Jan. 23, 1913, ibid., box 165; GP to AP, Jan. 25, 1913, ibid., box 169; GP to AP, Feb. 2, 1914, ibid., box 182; AP to GP, Oct. 14, 1914, APP, box 12; AP to GP, Jan. 23, 1913, ibid., box 8.

43. AP to GP, Jan. 23, 1913, ibid., box 8; AP to Daniel Kiefer, June 17, 1915, ibid., box 15. To Amos, large landholdings were another kind of monopoly. Prodded by George Record, an independent reformer and friend, he read Henry George's writings on imposing a single tax on unimproved land to bring about more equitable land distribution. AP to George L. Nelson, Aug. 31, 1914, APP, box 11.

44. AP to GP, April 20, 1914, A. Nevin Detrich to AP, April 20, 1914, and GP to AP, April 20, 21, 1914, ibid.; AP to GP, April 23, 1914, GPP, box 182.

45. MEP to AP, April 22, 1914, APP, box 10; AP to MEP, April 24, 1914, GPP, box 68.

46. GP, Diary, March 20, 1914, ibid., box 5. Amos's letter was soon leaked to newspapers and printed in garbled form. Trying to set the record straight, Amos then released the full text. New York *Evening World*, June 10, 1914, p. 1.

47. Beveridge to GP, Sat. night [June 20, 1914], GPP, box 174; Medill McCormick to GP, June 22, 1914, ibid., box 180; JRG to GP, June 24, 1914, ibid., box 177.

48. GP to AP, Sept. 13, 1914, APP, box 11. Because this was the first election in which U.S. senators were elected by popular ballot, Penrose might have felt he had to get out on the hustings, but Gifford's energetic speaking schedule further motivated him.

49. GP to AP, March 13, 1914, GPP, box 182; GP to AP, Sept. 13, 1914, Stahlnecker to AP, Sept. 14, 1914, and GP to AP, Sept. 18, 1914, APP, box 11.

50. GP to BTW, March 27, 1914, BTW to GP, April 3, 1914, GP to BTW, April 7 and 22, 1914, GPP, box 185; Turner Speller to GP, March 28, 1914, ibid., box 184; GP to W. Bishop Johnson, July 21, 1914, ibid., box 179; Stahlnecker to Speller, Sept. 14, 1914, and Oct. 9, 1914, ibid., box 184.

51. Irving Fisher, a year ahead of Gifford at Yale and also a bonesman, corresponded with Gifford on a wide range of public issues.‑

52. In seeking black support and distancing himself from the Democrats, Gifford could have lambasted the Wilson administration's recent segregation of government departments in Washington and criticized the many disenfranchisement and segregation laws and lynchings throughout the southern states. But, in a speech to a black church in the city on April 14, 1914, he did not mention these issues, and instead, simply lauded African Americans for their economic and educational progress and predicted a bright future for the race. Washington *Evening Star*, April 17, 1914, p. 11; the speech is in GPP, box 774.

53. GP to Charles Nordhoff, Feb. 17 and 24, 1942, ibid., box 322.

54. A copy is ibid., box 1078.

55. GP, Diary, May 20, 1914, ibid., box 5.

56. GP to TR, Oct. 17, 1914, tel., TRP, reel 192; and TR to GP, Oct. 18, 1914, tel., Morison, 8, p. 825.

57. A discouraged Dean Lewis withdrew as the party's gubernatorial nominee two months before the election. Lewis had thrown his support to the Democratic nominee, but the Republican candidate won handily anyway. GP to APJ, Nov. 9, 1914, GPP, box 179.

58. In California. Hiram Johnson was reelected governor, and Francis J. Heney finished second for the U.S. Senate seat but badly trailed the victor in votes.

59. APJ to AP, April 30 [1911?], APP, box 3.

60. MEP to GP, [Aug.] 22 [1913], GPP, box 3170.

61. A classic account is Henry F. May, *The End of American Innocence: A Study of the First Years of Our Own Time, 1912-1917* (New York: Alfred A. Knopf, 1959).

62. AP to Patrick Quinlan, May 26, 1913, APP, box 9.

63. In this letter of protest, Amos said he belonged to no church and had never met the incarcerated preacher, although he had found that one of his books had "a more helpful and deeply religious conception of real Christianity than most of the ministers of the Gospel." AP to John Purroy Mitchel, May 15, 1914, ibid., box 11.

64. For example, *The Masses*, 4 (July 1913), p. 2.

65. Quotations in Max Eastman, *Enjoyment of Living* (New York: Harper, 1948), p. 455. *The Masses* required regular infusions of money.

66. *NYT*, March 6, 1914, p. 20.

67. The Paterson strike failed. Quinlan's first trial ended in a hung jury, but he was quickly tried again and convicted; he served two years in prison. The New York pastor did not get out of jail until the end of his six-month sentence. The Associated Press eventually dropped the lawsuit against *The Masses*.

68. AP to APJ, Dec. 21, 1914, APP, box 12. Helpful in unraveling Amos's evolving political thought is Rex Oliver Mooney, Amos Pinchot and Atomistic Capitalism: A Study in Reform Ideas (Ph.D. dissertation, Louisiana State University, 1973).

69. AP to C. H. Myers, Nov. 7, 1914, and AP to Hugh O'Neill, Dec. 4, 1914, APP, box 12.

70. The limitation of Amos's appeal was revealed when he severely criticized the *New Republic*, the most articulate periodical championing progressivism, for its focus on "symptoms and incidentals" and its failure to "follow through" on its "illusory" reform proposals. The editors replied that Amos overlooked the practical complexities that reformers faced, failed to discuss the necessary means to the desired end, and countered his reform ideas about railroads. "A Communication," *New Republic*, 3 (May 29, 1915), pp. 95-98.

71. AP, "The Failure of the Progressive Party," *The Masses*, 6 (Dec. 1914), pp, 9-10.

72. AP to G. B. Shaw, Oct. 29, 1914, APP, box 12.

73. In particular, Floyd Dell, one of the young *Masses* editors, wrote then and later about the changing roles of women.

74. Draft public letter, undated [late March 1915], APP, box 13. Gertrude's ongoing support of the Sangers is recorded in Ellen Chesler, *Woman of Valor: Margaret Sanger and the Birth Control Movement in America* (New York: Simon & Schuster, 1992), pp. 132, 154, 156, 167, 275.

75. *New York Tribune*, Jan. 5, 1917, p. 5.

76. *NYT*, Feb. 19, 1917, p. 11. Amos drafted the statement that Gertrude made to the governor.

Chapter 15: A Military Hospital

1. Mary gave the house, which cost $34,037.50, to her daughter as a gift. Mrs. Mead to APJ, April 22, 1915, APP, box 13.

2. *WP*, September 4, 1914, p. 7; Gertrude M. Pinchot to AP, Saturday [1912], ibid., box 3.

3. APJ to GP, Oct. 15 [1914], GPP, box 71; APJ to AP, April 29, 1915, APP, box 13; APJ to GP, [June] 28 [1915?], GPP, box 3168; APJ to AP, Dec. 31 [1917], APP, box 3.

4. APJ to GP, Oct. 15 [1914], GPP, box 71; APJ to GP, [June] 28 [1915?], ibid., box 3168.

5. Slayden, *Washington Wife* (Nov. 20, 1911), p. 163.

6. A newspaper account of Nettie, "handsomely gowned" and wearing "almost priceless" jewelry (*WP*, June 16, 1907, p. 11) is only one of several featuring her stylish appearances at entertainments.

7. Earlier, Nettie reportedly was "highly indignant" of New York City clergy for failing to open their churches during extreme hot weather to the poor. *Washington Times*, July 11, 1911, p. 6. She also fired off a letter to *The Masses*, rebutting an article critical of the British Army and the Allied cause in the Great War. "An Englishwoman Protests," *The Masses*, 6 (May 1915), p. 20.

8. Washington *Herald*, Nov. 16, 1913, p. 2.

9. APJ to GP, Jan. 18 [1919], GPP, box 222. After a lunch with Nettie a day earlier, Colonel Edward M. House, Wilson's aide and an Anglophile, concluded, "She is an intelligent and charming woman." Edward M. House, Diary, Nov. 12, 1913, Edward M. House Papers (Manuscripts and Archives, Yale University Library), Series II, Vol. 1.

10. APJ to GP, Oct. 15 [1914], GPP, box 71; *WP*, Sept. 4, 1914, p. 7.

11. AP to APJ, Nov. 17, 1914, APP, box 12; AP to APJ, April 23, 1915, ibid., box 13.

12. GP to Charles F. Holder, Dec. 8, 1914, GPP, box 178.

13. APJ to GP, Oct. 15 [1914], ibid., box 71; AP to APJ, Nov. 17, 1914, and Dec. 21, 1914, APP, box 12; APJ to GP, Dec. 14, [1914], GPP, box 71; GP to APJ, Dec. 11, 19, 1914, ibid., box 179.

14. APJ to GP, Dec. 14 [1914], ibid., box 71.

15. GP, Diary, Jan. 31, 1915, ibid., box 5.

16. GP to A. K. Fisher, May 5, 1915, and GP to Henry Wallace, May 5, 1915, ibid., box 188.

17. GP, Diary, Feb. 15, 1915, ibid., box 5.

18. GP to Henry Wallace, Jan. 26, 1916, ibid., box 201.

19. APJ to AP, Jan. 3, 1915, cablegram, ibid., box 189; APJ to GP, April 29, 1915, APP, box 12.

20. GP to Mabel Boardman, April 27, 1915, GPP, box 187.

21. Harold James Reckitt, *V.R. 76: A French Military Hospital* (London: William Heinemann, 1921), pp. 6-16, 32, 38, 51, 270-271, 279, 289, passim (quotation on p. 9). The official name was Hôpital Militaire V.R. 76, but those serving there usually called it the Johnstone-Reckitt Hospital or the Ris (or Ris-Orangis) Hospital. After the United States entered the war, the letterhead of the facility used the title Hospital Under Three Flags, with the foundation name below it.

22. Quotations in Reckitt, *V.R. 76*, pp. 38, 39.

23. APJ to AP, Oct. 27 [1916], APP, box 3.

24. Dr. A. Aribert de Jax, quotation in Reckitt, *V.R. 76*, p. 253.

25. APJ to GP, March 1 [1916] and April 1 [1916], and APJ to Reckitt, March 1, 1916, GPP, box 197; APJ to Gertrude M. Pinchot, Dec. 15, 1916, cable, ibid., box 199. Later the expenses soon went up to about $12,000 a month. Reckitt, *V.R. 76*, p. 290.

26. APJ to CBP, March 22 [1916] and March 30 [1916], GPP, box 68.

27. APJ to CBP, March 22 [1916], ibid.

28. AP to GP, March 12 [1915], ibid., box 191.

29. APJ to AP, Oct. 29 [1915], APP, box 3.

30. If they lost, each of the eight would receive $200,000 (or $50,000 less than the six Pinchot and Eno beneficiaries in Amo's last will would have received). A former judge and a law partner of Sumner Gerard handled the testimony for the Pinchots' side.

31. At the second trial, Amos Pinchot again representing the plaintiffs, the family prevailed, but the judge set aside the verdict and urged the parties to settle out of court, which they did. Each of the eight plaintiffs received on paper about $250,000, but given the attorneys' costs (only Amos received none except for expenses), they received probably one-half that amount. It had been a miserable grind for Amos, but it would help Nettie with her postwar financial difficulties.

32. APJ to GP, July 27 [1918], GPP, box 213. A list of donors to the hospital and financial statements are in Reckitt, *V.R. 76*, pp. 284-287, 289-292.

33. APJ to GP, Oct. 11[1916], GPP, box 70. Regarding Ford and women pacifists' efforts, see David S. Patterson, *The Search for Negotiated Peace: Women's Activism and Citizen Diplomacy in World War I* (New York: Routledge, 2008), pp. 148ff.-

34. AP to Harcourt Johnstone, Jan. 30, 1917, APP, box 19; Gertrude M. Pinchot to GP, Saturday [Jan. 27, 1917], and GP to Gertrude M. Pinchot, Jan. 30, 31, 1917, GPP, box 207.

35. APJ, to GP, April 13 [1917], ibid., box 213; APJ to GP, April 24, 1917, ibid., box 207. Nettie's comments to Reckitt, quotation in Reckitt, *V.R. 76*, p. 7.

Chapter 16: War and Dissent

1. GP, Our Interest in the World War, Open Forum, Bronx, N.Y., March 12, 1916; and Patriotism, Milford, Pa., July 5, 1915, GPP, box 774.
2. AP to GP, June 4 [1907], ibid., box 71; AP to MEP, April 24, 1914, ibid., box 68.
3. AP, "Conscription," *Harper's Weekly*, 59 (Nov. 14, 1914), p. 463. Among those perishing on the *Lusitania* was Amos's political ally, Lindon Bates, Jr., who was traveling to help with the Belgian relief effort. A day before the ship's departure from New York, Amos had declined Bates's invitation to join him for the voyage. AP to Lindon Bates, May 11, 1915, APP, box 13.
4. Patterson, *Search for Negotiated Peace*, pp. 189-191 (quotations on pp. 189, 191).
5. Ibid., pp. 187-199 (quotations on p. 190). The AUAM also formed branches in several states.
6. AP to WW, Jan. 27, 1916, *The Papers of Woodrow Wilson* (Princeton, NJ: Princeton University Press, 1981), 36, p. 22 (hereafter *PWW*). AP to Robert M. Thompson, May 9, 1916, APP, box 1; *NYT*, March 30, 1916, p. 4.
7. *PWW*, 36, p. 120. Amos was one of only two who made the entire tour. Two outspoken western opponents of preparedness were William Jennings Bryan—who resigned as secretary of state in protest of Wilson's firm dealings with Germany after the *Lusitania* sinking—and Henry Ford.
8. AP to WW, Jan. 27, 1916, and AP to Norman Hapgood, Jan. 29, 1916, *PWW*, 36, p. 22.
9. Ibid., p. 86; Brandeis to AP, Feb. 10, 1916, APP, box 15.
10. The full text of this letter is in Urofsky, *Brandeis*, p. 459.
11. AP to George F. Porter, May 9, 1916, APP, box 16.
12. New York *Sun*, May 14, 1916, p. 3, and May 16, 1916, p. 3. An undated copy of her protest (in the WPP's behalf) to Governor Whitman is in APP, box 26.
13. The other three were A. A. Berle, Wise, and John A. McSparran, master of the Pennsylvania State Grange.
14. *PWW*, 36, p. 645.
15. Quotation in Patterson, *Search for Negotiated Peace*, p. 197; AP to George F. Porter, May 9, 1916, APP, box 16.
16. On his western trip, Wilson called for expanding the navy to become the undisputed biggest in the world. He did not repudiate the remark but substituted "most adequate" navy for "greatest" in the official text. He was likely sensitive to affronting Britain, which claimed to have the largest navy. Patterson, *Search for Negotiated Peace*, p. 385n25.
17. *NYT*, June 24, 1916, p. 4; AP to WW, tel., June 28, 1916, *PWW*, 37 (1981), p. 321.
18. Harry Overstreet, Irving Fisher, and Gertrude Pinchot to WW, June 27, 1916, ibid., pp. 308-309; *NYT*, June 30, 1916, p. 3.
19. Ibid., p. 7. The headline of Amos Pinchot's newspaper article was, "We Can Have Peace If We Want It: An Open Letter About Mexico." He also printed his piece as a pamphlet, which Crystal Eastman circulated to the WPP mailing list. Crystal Eastman to AP, Aug. 5, 1916, APP, box 16.
20. WW to AP and Gertrude M. Pinchot, July 3, 1916, *PWW*, 37, p. 348. Wilson had already thanked Amos for his earlier (June 28) telegram and for Gertrude's visit. WW to AP, June 30, 1916, ibid., p. 336.
21. Pershing's forces pursued Villa for another six months while the commission conducted difficult talks for a peaceful settlement. The slow progress in the negotiations prompted the New York branch of the WPP to urge completion of the agreement. Gertrude M. Pinchot (for WPP, N.Y. branch) to WW, tel., Jan. 5, 1917, ibid., 40 (1982), p. 418.
22. GP to TR, June 4, 1916, GPP, box 199.
23. Quotation in McGeary, *Pinchot*, p. 256.
24. Quotations ibid.
25. President Wilson had signed into law a measure giving the government control over railroad lands in Alaska and had vetoed a bill giving away land in national forests. GP to Henry L. Eno, March 13, 1913, GPP, box 165; GP, Diary, March 5, 10, 18, 1913, ibid., box 5.
26. GP to APJ, Feb. 1, 1916, GPP, box 197. Gifford convinced himself that "the Democratic Senators are trying hard to give away the public resources right and left, and the White House does nothing to stop them." Gifford also accused the administration of "taking large numbers of [government] jobs out from under the merit system and making spoils of them" and of "squeezing out" his friend Frederick Newell as head of the Reclamation Service.

THE PINCHOTS

27. GP to WW, January 29, 1916, *PWW*, 36, p. 48-51; WW to Franklin K. Lane, March 9, 1916, ibid., p. 277. William Kent to AP, July 26, 1916, APP, box 16. Other Wilson supporters debunked conservationists' concerns about Wilson. GP to H. G. Palmer, Sept. 20, 1916, and Norman Hapgood to the Editor, Sept. 30 [1916], [New York?] *Herald*, newspaper clipping, ibid., box 17. A recent history of the election does not mention conservation as an issue. Lewis L. Gould, *The First Modern Clash over Federal Power: Wilson versus Hughes in the Election of 1916* (Lawrence: University Press of Kansas, 2016).

28. GP to APJ, May 24, 1915, and Sept. 9, 1915, GPP, box 189; GP to APJ, Feb. 1, 1916, ibid., box 197.

29. AP to Edward C. Stucke, Dec. 4, 1914, APP, box 12.

30. AP to Norman Hapgood, March 13, 1916, ibid., box 15.

31. GP to AP, Sept. 4, 1916, ibid; AP to GP, Sept. 21, 1916, GPP, box 199.

32. *NYT*, Oct. 17, 1916, p. 3.⁻

33. *Grand Rapids* (Mich.) *News*, Nov. 2, 1916, APP, box 17; TR to AP, Nov. 3, 1916, Morison, 8, p. 1122.

34. CBP to AP, Monday [Nov. 1916], APP, box 3.

35. AP, "What the Election Means," *The Masses*, 9 (Jan. 1917), pp. 18-20. AP to S. S. Wise, Jan. 2, 1917, APP, box 18.

36. AJ to AP, Nov. 8, 1914, ibid., box 3.

37. Quotations in AP, *War and the King Trust: An Address to the Anglo-German Club* (n.p.: n.p. [late January 1917], passim. Also, AP, "The Courage of the Cripple," *The Masses*, 9 (March 1917), pp. 19-21.

38. *New York Tribune*, Dec. 24, 1916, p. 2; GP to APJ, Jan. 25, 1917, GPP, box 205. As Wilson's peace initiative percolated through European capitals, Alan Johnstone was replaced as the British Minister to the Netherlands. The recall apparently came at the behest of a new coalition British government.

39. AP to A. W. Ricker, Dec. 26, 1916, APP, box 18.

40. Amos's historical argument is in *New Republic*, 10 (March 10, 1917), pp. 163-164. Thinking in time, the AUAM leadership emphasized the parallels between U.S armed neutrality in its "quasi-war" against France (1798–1800) and the current crisis over German submarines. In the former, the two nations fought naval battles but avoided formal declarations of war until they could resolve the contentious issues peacefully. The AUAM embraced a paper written by Carleton J. H. Hayes, a history professor at Columbia University. Hayes' paper was published in *The Survey*, 37 (Feb. 10, 1917), pp. 535-538. Wald to WW, Feb. 8, 1917, *PWW*, 41 (1983), pp. 168-169.

41. The AUAM presentation to Wilson is ibid., pp. 305-308.

42. AP to Robert La Follette, March 5, 1917, APP, box 19.

43. AP, "Keep Out of War," *The Public*, 20 (March 16, 1917), p. 251; AP to Emily Greene Balch, April 6, 1917, APP, box 20. Amos founded a new group, the Committee for Democratic Control, which allied with the EPF's referendum proposal. One purpose was to give voice to citizens' resistance to involvement in the war by publicizing the district results, which ranged from four-to-one to eleven-to-one against war and for the referendum. Committee's advertisement, *New Republic*, 10 (March 3, 1917), p. 145. A war referendum was of dubious legality, however—the U.S. Constitution explicitly gives Congress the power to declare war.

44. In early March, New York antiwar reformers asked Amos to run as an independent candidate in a special election for a congressional seat in Manhattan. Amos declined the invitation. It would be the last time he would consider running for political office.

45. APJ to GP, April 24, 1917, GPP, box 199; AP to Norman Hapgood, May 17, 1917, APP, box 22.

46. A discussion of Amos Pinchot and the ACWF is John W. Hillje, "New York Progressives and the War Revenue Act of 1917," *New York History*, 53 (Oct. 1972), pp. 437-459.

47. AP to Daniel Kiefer, Feb. 14, 1918, APP, box 27; AP to Warren J. Stone, tel., April 12, 1917, ibid., box 20.

48. Amos's statement before the Senate Finance Committee, May 15, 1917, APP, box 74; ACWF advertisement, *Washington Times*, April 1, 1917, p. 16. AP, et al., to Editor, April 10, 1917, APP, box 20; AP to William J. Stone, tel., March 30, 1917, ibid., box 18. Amos wanted to conscript all incomes above $100,000 but said ACWF members were willing to negotiate a lower figure. AP to Henry Wharton, April 20, 1917, APP, box 20. Other features included an excess profits tax on businesses, the sale of all war supplies and services like transportation to be limited to a reasonable profit, and false income tax returns would be a felony.

49. AP to E. D. O'Dea, April 26, 1917, ibid., box 19.

50. GP to Rainsford, March 22, 1917, GPP, box 207; GP to APJ, May 31, 1917, ibid., box 205.

51. For example, the newspaper publisher E. W. Scripps to AP, tel., April 10, 1917, APP, box 20.

52. The ACWF early spent $20,000 on publicity, about half of which Amos paid for. AP to Chester B. Goodrick, June 19, 1918, ibid.

53. AP to Claude Kitchin, Aug. 10, 1918, ibid.

54. AP to Goodrick, June 19, 1918, and AP to J. Milbourne Shortliffe, Oct. 12, 1918, ibid. Although the excess profits tax was repealed and tax rates were reduced in the more conservative 1920s, the principle of progressive income taxation remained intact and became a permanent part of the U.S. tax structure.

55. *NYT*, March 13, 1917, p. 4. AP, "The Commercial Policy of Conscription," *The Masses*, 9 (May 1917), pp. 6, 8.

56. WW, War Message to the Congress, April 2, 1917, *PWW*, 41, p. 526. Amos hosted a small dinner party for House at his apartment. The guests, an amused House wrote in his diary, were composed "of long haired men and short haired women." House, Diary, April 13, 1917, House Papers, Series 2, Vol. 5.

57. Quotation in David M. Kennedy, *Over Here: The First World War and American Society* (Oxford: Oxford University Press, 1980), p. 26. The AUAM would soon be defunct.

58. *PWW*, 42 (1983), June 14, 1917, p. 104; AP to Crystal Eastman, June 15, 1917, APP, box 23.

59. AP, Max Eastman, and John Reed to WW, July 12, 1917, and WW to AP, July 13, 1917, *PWW*, 43, pp. 165, 164. AP to James McK. Cattell, July 26, 1917, APP, box 23. Wilson's secretary also wrote Amos, saying the president "is making a very thorough investigation and will go to the bottom of the matter in any case." Joseph P. Tumulty to AP, July 16, 1917, ibid.

60. AP to Albert S. Burleson, July 13, 1917, Burleson to WW, July 16, 1917, and WW to AP, July 17, 1917, *PWW*, 43 pp. 164, 187-188, and 193.

61. Hand, quotation ibid., p. 166.

62. AP to Louis Wiley, July 26, 1917, APP, box 23.

63. AP (and five others) to WW, Sept. 26, 1917, *PWW*, 44 (1983), pp. 266-267 (quotations on p. 266).

64. Quotations ibid, 45 (1984), Nov. 12, 1917, p. 14, and Dec. 4, 1917, p. 105.

65. House, Diary, Feb. 11, 1918, House Papers, Series II, Vol. 6.

66. The Tammany candidate for mayor won in a landslide.

67. AP to Roger Baldwin, Oct. 6, 1917, APP, box 24; AP to John Hays Hammond, Dec. 11, 1917, ibid., box 26.

68. GP, Diary, April 26, 1917, GPP, box 5; GP to AP, May 22, 1917, ibid., box 207; GP to A. W. Dimock, ibid., box 203; GP to TR, June 21, 1917, ibid., box 208; GP to James A. McSparran, Aug. 19, 1917, ibid., box 206; GP to AP, Aug. 31, 1917, APP, box 24.

69. GP to Henry C. Wallace, Oct. 26, 1917, GPP, box 210. Hogs were the most important livestock sector, and the interests of farmers, meat packers (or middlemen), consumers, and the provisioning of allied troops in Europe were all involved.

70. House, Diary, Oct. 7 and 16, 1917, House Papers, Series 2, Vol. 5; GP to House, Oct. 20, 1917, GP to Hoover, Oct. 25, 1917, and Hoover to GP, Oct. 27, 1917, GPP, box 205.

71. Actually, the food administration soon adopted some of Gifford's proposals for guaranteed price supports, and Gifford reflected, "my resignation may have had some share in bringing it about." GP to House, Nov. 29, 1917, ibid.; Hoover to WW, Nov. 19, 1917, *PWW*, 45, p. 85. Hoover's challenges as food administrator are recounted in George H. Nash, *The Life of Herbert Hoover: Master of Emergencies, 1917-1918* (New York: W. W. Norton, 1996), p. 165ff.

72. Alvey A. Adee to GP, Oct. 10, 1918, and GP to Robert Lansing. Oct. 15, 1918, GPP, box 216; APJ to GP, Nov. 28, 1918, ibid., box 213. The state department soon informed Gifford that he could apply again, but that application too was denied.

73. TR to P. C. March, Sept. 1, 1918, ibid., box 214; M. Churchill to GP, Oct. 19, 1918, ibid., box 212.

74. GP to Will H. Hays, Nov. 8, 1918, ibid., box 213; GP to TR, Nov. 18, ibid., box 215.

75. AP to Gertrude M. Pinchot, March 4, 1918, APP, box 27; AP to Frank Harris, Jan. 31, 1918, ibid., box 26.-

76. AP to Gilson Gardner, April 13, 1918, ibid., box 27.

77. AP to WW, May 24, 1918, *PWW*, 48 (1985), pp. 146-147.

78. WW to Thomas W. Gregory, June 1, 1918, ibid., p. 220; AP to Owen R. Lovejoy, June 19, 1918, APP, box 27.

79. AP, *Peace or Armed Peace: An Open Letter from Amos Pinchot to the American Representatives of the coming International Peace Conference*, Nov. 11, 1918, passim (quotations on p. 15), copy in APP, box 134. Despite the administration's deplorable record on civil liberties, Amos was somewhat hopeful of its Committee on Public Information that was issuing propaganda to boost the war and Wilson's peace aims. AP to George Creel, Nov. 14, 1917, ibid., box 26.

80. *New York Tribune*, Nov. 1, 1918, p. 14.

81. AP to W. Forbes Morgan, Jan. 16, 1919, APP, box 29.

82. AP, *Protecting the Old Order* (New York: n.p., March 12, 1919), passim (quotations on p. 3), copy in GPP, box 3045. In 1918, the Supreme Court had overturned a federal law regulating goods made by child labor that were sold in interstate commerce but had upheld, in a tie vote, a state law regulating women's wages.

83. AP, *Protecting the Old Order*, p. 2.

84. *NYT*, May 26, 1919, p. 17. Amos's retrospective view of the entire Wilson presidency is his article, "Eight Years of Woodrow Wilson," *Reconstruction*, 3 (March 1921), pp. 103-107.

85. AP to GP, April 7, 1919, and GP to AP, April 12, 1919, GPP, box 224.

86. AP to William E. Borah, Aug. 20, 1919, and AP to Hiram Johnson, Aug. 28, 1919, APP, box 30. Even some strongly opposed to the peace settlement like Johnson allowed that Wilson may not have deliberately lied about the secret treaties but had had a lapse of memory.

87. Nettie agreed with Gifford's distrust of the president. Concerning the U.S. government's refusal to issue Gifford a passport to visit Europe, she wrote, "I don't see how anything could be much stupider. . . . I simply boil when I think of it. . . . It shows how personal and vindictive people can be." APJ to GP, Nov. 28 [1918], GPP, box 213.

88. After the conference, Wilson would tour devastated places in Belgium.

89. Wilson probably knew about the rejection but may not have been consulted about it.

90. APJ to GP, Jan. 18, 1919, GPP, box 222.

91. APJ to CBP, June 28 [1919], CBPP, box I:7.

Chapter 17: From the Depths

1. In 1900, the school had moved from Dobbs Ferry, New York, to Simsbury, Connecticut, after a generous donation of land from a wealthy alumnus.

2. AP to Arthur Nock, June 14, 1918, and AP to Cushing, March 5, 1918, APP, box 27; AP to Cushing, Nov. 7, 1918, APP, box 28. The school continued awarding the cup, perhaps without Amos's financing, and Cushing wrote him, "The remembrance of you is thus perpetuated in our grateful hearts." Cushing to AP, June 2, 1920, ibid., box 32.

3. AP to John M. Hopkins, Nov. 7, 1918, ibid., box 29. The students spent the fall and spring terms in Lake Placid, New York, and the winter term in Coconut Grove, Florida.

4. AP to CBP, July 22, 1916, CBPP, box I:5. If anything, Gertrude seemed more willing to live apart, and during the late summer of 1917, she did not return from Quebec to join Amos and the Gerards for a two-week vacation at Fire Island near New York City.

5. Anonymous [Ruth Pinchot], "A Deflated Rebel," *The Nation*, 124 (Jan. 5, 1927), pp. 11-12 (quotation on p. 12). Her article was later reproduced under her own name in *These Modern Women: Autobiographical Essays from the Twenties*, ed. Elaine Showalter (Old Westbury, NY: Feminist Press, 1978), pp. 58-62.

6. Max Eastman, *Enjoyment of Living* (New York: Harper, 1948), pp. 294-295, 309, 311, 335-338 (quotation on p. 337).

7. "Blackberry Branch," a short poem by Ruth Pickering, is in *Pearson's Magazine*, 38 (Sept. 1917), p. 104. Her articles were a fictionalized story of the frustrations of an ambitious woman stenographer working for an insensitive male employer ("Up a Blind Alley," ibid., p. 115), and a profile of a female playwright and song writer, "Clare Kummer: The Year's New Playwright," ibid., (Jan. 1918), pp. 316-317.

8. AP to Mrs. James W. Warbasse, Oct. 6, 1917, APP, box 24. One thought was that Amos would become the chief editor, but that did not happen.

9. Quotation in Nancy Pittman Pinchot, "Amos Pinchot: Rebel Prince," p. 188.

10. Ruth Pickering to AP, Feb. 14, 1918, APP, box 27.

11. She wrote that if the andirons had been given to John Keats, "he never would have written 'Small, busy flames play through the fresh laid coals,' but [if] he could have made a grand flight into all the forests of the world, he might have written very much earlier in his life 'in darkly clustered trees that fledge the wild-ridged mountains steep by steep.'" The poetic quotations are from John Keats, "To My Brother" (1819) and "Ode to Psyche" (1818). Ruth Pickering to AP, undated, APP, box 24; AP to Horace B. Liveright, July 5, 1918, APP, box 28.

12. Gertrude M. Pinchot to AP, Sept. 4 [1918], ibid., box 3.

13. Helen Gerard to AP, Sept. 15, 1918, Ruth Pickering to AP, undated, ibid.

14. Gertrude M. Pinchot to CBP, Oct. 10 [1918], CBPP, box I:7; Helen Gerard to AP, Oct. 2, 1918, APP, box 29. Amos's Uncle Will and Aunt Nettie also supported him and his new love. William P. Eno to AP, Nov. 28, 1918, ibid., box 28.

15. CBP to AP, undated [April 1917], ibid., box 3; Jerin Haron to GP, Sept. 7, 1922, GPP, box 3178. Gertrude also supported Leila during her recovery from a planned appendectomy. Gertrude M. Pinchot to CBP, Monday [early March 1919], CBPP, box I:7. Leila would seek several physicians' advice for getting pregnant into the 1920s, but she never conceived again.

16. AP to CBP, Feb. 26, 1919, ibid.; Virginia T. Hyde to AP, Feb. 9 [1919], GPP, box 73.

17. As part of the settlement, Amos paid her $1,500 a month, which seemed to satisfy Gertrude. Sumner Gerard, who handled the details of the divorce settlement, calculated that Amos' annual income after taxes was about $50,000, and he suggested the $1,500 figure to Amos. Sumner Gerard to AP, Feb. 19, 1919, APP, box 29.

18. Gertrude M. Pinchot to CBP, Monday [March 1919], CBPP, box I:7.

19. AP to CBP, Oct. 4, 1919, ibid., box I:35.

20. Gifford and Leila, Aunt Nettie Wood, the Gerards, and Ruth's parents and two sisters were among those attending the wedding. *New York Tribune*, Aug. 10, 1919, p. 8.

21. AP to George Foster Peabody, Dec. 19, 1918, and AP to Herbert S. Bigelow, Dec. 20, 1918, APP, box 28.

22. AP, "The Case for a Third Party: II," *The Freeman*, I (July 7, 1920), p. 394.

23. Glenn E. Plumb, a veteran lawyer representing railway unions, devised the Plumb plan in 1918. President Wilson, in his distracted and weakened state, failed to act, thereby missing an opportunity to regain his faltering labor support.

24. AP to Frederic C. Howe, Oct. 21, 1919, APP, box 30; AP to W. J. MacDonald, Feb. 5, 1920, ibid., box 31.-

25. AP, "Government by Evasion," *The Freeman*, I (Aug. 18, 1920), p. 539; AP, "The Case for a Third Party: II," p. 396.

26. Hopkins had been an early Progressive Party activist in New Jersey in 1912. Committee of 48 Platform (revised), undated, copy in APP, box 87; AP, *Facts*, 1 (Dec. 11, 1919), p. 1.

27. Ibid.

28. There was violent racial strife in East St. Louis; Washington, D.C.; Chicago; and several other cities in 1919 and 1920.

29. AP to Charles T. Hallinan, May 1, 1920, APP, box 31.

30. The Chicago Federation of Labor, in its disagreement with the conservative direction of the American Federation of Labor, had founded the party.

31. AP to E. W. Scripps, Feb. 17, 1920, and AP to G. F. Stevens, Feb. 25, 1920, APP, box 31.

32. Quotations in Eugene M. Tobin, *Organize or Perish: America's Independent Progressives, 1913-1933* (New York: Greenwood Press, 1986), p. 116. Elizabeth McKielen, *Chicago Labor and the Quest for a Democratic Diplomacy, 1914-1924* (Ithaca, NY: Cornell University Press, 1995), pp. 146-155.

33. Quotations in AP, "Government by Evasion," p. 540.

34. Alan Benson, the Socialist candidate for president in 1916, was even more critical of the liberal elites comprising the Committee of 48. "The best thing that can be said of some," he wrote, "is that they are politicians; the best that can be said of others is that they are well-meaning gentlemen whose wealth has prevented them from having the slightest knowledge of life – and the best that can be said of others is that, believing themselves to be democrats, they are, in fact hopeless snobs." Quotations in Tobin, *Organize or Perish*, p. 117.

35. Quotation ibid.

36. AP to Robert M. La Follette, June 25, 1920, APP, box 31. The Wisconsin senator was strongly supported by antiwar, discontented progressives and organized labor but hated by many prowar liberals.

37. The Labor leaders' confident behavior actually belied a weakened movement. Besides the growing conservative mood nationally, the socialists were disunited. The beleaguered Socialist Party fielded Eugene Debs as its presidential candidate in 1920, and he garnered more than 900,000 votes, more than three times the number of the Farmer-Labor candidate, even though Debs was still in jail. And the AFL, which endorsed no candidate, nonetheless put forward planks that weaned away less extreme socialists from the new party. J. A. H. Hopkins, "Facts About the Chicago Convention," summarized the Committee of 48's differences with the Farmer-Labor group; copy in APP, box 88.

38. AP to Z. B. Cutler, July 21, 1920, AP to Lincoln Steffens, Oct. 6, 1920, and Gilson Gardner to R. P. Scripps, July 19, 1920, ibid., box 32.

39. Congress had meanwhile passed the Esch-Cummins (or Transportation) Act of 1920, which restored the railroads to private ownership with compensation. The new railroad labor board, which the owners dominated, would prove hostile to railroad workmen in the 1920s.

40. AP to J. A. H. Hopkins, Nov. 26, 1920, APP, box 32.

41. AP, "'Oh! Say, Can You See?'" *The Freeman*, 2 (Oct. 20, 1920), pp. 129-130 (quotations on p. 130).

42. The Bryce parents had died, and Leila, her sister, and her brother inherited their assets. Leila was very well off; one indication was her gift of $100,000 (about $1.3 million today) to a newly established Mary Eno Pinchot Fund at the Yale Forest School. Gifford had set up the fund in 1918.

43. CBP to GP, undated, GPP, box 73; GP to CBP, July 21 [1916], Aug. 24, 1917, and May 20, 1923, ibid., box 3169.

44. GP, Diary, Jan. 8, 1918, GPP, box 6, GP to Denny O'Neil, Jan. 12, 1918, ibid., box 215; GP to APJ, Jan. 24, 1918, ibid., box 213.-

45. Agreement between GP, CBP, and George Woodruff, April 18, 1918, ibid., box 3179.

46. GP to Denny O'Neil, Feb. 28, 1918, and O'Neil to GP, June 4, 1918, ibid., box 215; quotation in McGeary, *Pinchot*, p. 273.

47. Quotations ibid. Gifford followed up with an open letter repeating his criticisms of Penrose. GP to Republican Senators, Feb. 7, 1919, GPP, box 458.

48. APJ to CBP, April 9 [1920], CBPP, box I:12.

49. CBP to Herbert Croly, April 5, 1920, and CBP to Carrie Chapman Catt, Aug. 26, 1920, ibid., box I:10.

50. CBP to APJ, Jan. 20, 1920, ibid., box I:12.

51. GP, press release, April 16, 1919, GPP, box 3179. Gifford early dismissed the Committee of 48 as a third-party option, saying that he would rely on rank-and-file Republicans to check the Old Guard leaders. GP to J. A. H. Hopkins, Feb. 7, 1919, ibid., box 221.

52. GP to AP, Jan. 15, 1920, and GP to APJ, Jan. 23, 1920, ibid., box 232.

53. GP to James R. Reynolds, June 15, 1920, and July 27, 1920, ibid., box 235.

54. *NYT*, Aug. 31, 1920, p. 3.

55. Gifford, who had gotten to know Wallace intimately during their service together on the U.S. Food Administration, had strongly encouraged his friend to accept the cabinet post. GP to Henry C. Wallace, Nov. 9, 1924, GPP, box 257.

56. Quotation in McGeary, *Pinchot*, p. 272.

57. GP to Warren G. Harding, Nov. 15, 1922, and Harding to GP, Nov. 18, 1922, GPP, box 1084.

58. GP to John C. Shaffer, Dec. 29, 1921, ibid., box 3175. At the same time, Gifford wanted Harding to succeed, and he helped administration officials devise new language for the reorganization package that would paper over the abandoned transfer issue. GP to Henry C. Wallace, Dec. 16, 1922, ibid., box 1088.

59. Drafts of Gifford's and the NCA's statements and press releases on the issue are ibid., box 495.

60. *Gifford Pinchot: Selected Writings*, pp. 191-193. For his criticism of the Ford proposal, Gifford also gathered information from old-time conservationists in Washington. Additional documentation is in GPP, box 674.

61. CBP to Harry Slattery, April 8, 1921, CBPP, box I:16. J. Stanley Lemons, "The Sheppard-Towner Act: Progressivism in the 1920s," *Journal of American History*, 55 (March 1969), pp. 776-786. Because of increasing conservative political dominance and declining feminist focus, the law was not renewed in the late 1920s and allowed to lapse.

62. The census bureau defines "rural" as any population, housing, or territory with less than 2,500 residents. The 1920 census was the first where a majority of the U.S. population was urban.
63. CBP to APJ, Jan. 20, 1920, CBPP, box I:12.
64. AP to CBP, Jan, 3, 1920, and Jan. 8, 1920, APP, box 2; CBP to APJ, Jan. 20, 1920, CBPP, box I:12.
65. "Report of Committee of Grange," *Forest Leaves*, 17 (Feb. 1919), pp. 4-6.
66. GP to William C. Sproul, July 3, 1919, GPP, box 226; McGeary, *Pinchot*, pp. 273-274. For the lion analogy expressed by Gifford's maternal great-grandmother, see above, p. .
67. GP, et al., to Sproul, Oct. 21, 1919, GPP, box 226.
68. GP to James B. Reynolds, March 20, 1920, ibid., box 235.
69. A 1920 article Gifford published, which argued for reclaiming the state's wasted lands, is in GP, *Selected Writings*, pp. 121-123.
70. The chairman's salary went from $5,000 to $8,000. An anonymous, handwritten note on a printed flyer, "That $3,000 Grab," undated [1922], noted that it was "being put under every door in Harrisburg." Copy in GPP, box 1098.

Chapter 18: The Limits of Power

1. A. Nevin Detrich, Gifford's campaign chairman in his Senate run in 1914, become secretary of Gifford's gubernatorial campaign. Detrich to GP, Jan. 27, 1922, GPP, box 1081; GP to Lawrence O. Murray, Feb. 1, 1922, ibid., box 1122; GP to APJ, March 6, 1922, ibid., box 1121.
2. GP to AP, March 9, 1922, APP, box 34. Gifford contributed $82,257.97 ($29,500 of which was Leila's) of the $118,033.27 expended on the campaign. The expenditures of his opponent would be fifteen percent higher. Joseph Albert Falco, Political Background and First Gubernatorial Administration of Gifford Pinchot, 1923-1927 (Ph.D. dissertation, University of Pittsburgh, 1956) (hereafter Falco, Pinchot), pp. 142-143. This dissertation and William B. Hingston, Gifford Pinchot, 1922-1927 (University of Pennsylvania, 1962) (hereafter Hingston, Pinchot), provide invaluable details on Gifford's first governorship.
3. Falco, Pinchot, pp. 114-118, 123-124, 135-136, 141. Indicative of Grundy's importance, four medium-sized counties that he controlled would vote decisively for Pinchot in the primary.
4. Quotation in McGeary, *Pinchot*, p. 280.
5. Hingston, Pinchot, pp. 76-77; GP to George E. Alter, April 20, 1922, GPP, box 1090.
6. The report of the commission was published as *Reorganization of the State Government of Pennsylvania* (April 1922), copy in CBPP, box I:24. In 1922, the voters disapproved of the proposed changes in the state constitution, so the state government would have to find extra-constitutional measures to bring about administrative reform.
7. Falco, Pinchot, pp. 205-207.
8. The agreement provided that if the district chairman were a man, the vice chair would be a woman, and the chairmen were obliged to consult with their vice chairs on issues coming before the committee. From 1922 to 1930, all twelve women elected to the Pennsylvania legislature (some for more than one term) were Republicans. Jeanne H. Schmedlen, *History of Women in the Pennsylvania House of Representatives, 1923-2005* (Harrisburg: Pennsylvania House of Representatives, 2005), pp. 200-201.
9. Falco, Pinchot, pp. 119, 136. A Warburton statement, undated, is in CBPP, box I:27; CBP to APJ, April 8, 1922, ibid., box I:23.
10. Esther P. Lape to CBP, undated [May 16, 1922], ibid., box I:22. Lape was an activist for women's rights, health care, peace, and other liberal causes and also a friend of Eleanor Roosevelt.
11. GP, "The Influence of Women in Politics," *Ladies Home Journal*, 39 (Sept. 1922), pp. 12, 116. In 1922, fifty women ran for state offices in Pennsylvania, and eight of the thirty-eight women candidates for the state house of representatives were elected.
12. An Appeal to Colored Voters of Pennsylvania, undated [May 1922], CBPP, box I:27; Charles Fred White to CBP, May 8, 1922, and clipping from Philadelphia *Advocate*, May 6, 1922, GPP, box 1098. The Pinchot campaign sent out 3,000 copies of this newspaper story for distribution to black voters in the Pittsburgh area. D. Edward Long to John N. English, May 11, 1922, ibid., box 1092. By the early 1920s, the black population made up about 3.5 percent of Pennsylvania residents; by 1930, rising black migration from the South would increase it to 4.5 percent.

13. He later referred to Alter as "quiet, kindly, likeable, indolent – a respectable lawyer with no stomach for a fight." Quotation in Hingston, Pinchot, p. 78.

14. Edward W. Biddle to CBP, May 11, 1922, CBPP, box I:21. Gifford Pinchot for Governor, campaign leaflet, undated [early May 1922], GPP, box 1098; second quotation in Pinchot campaign leaflet, undated [c. April 1922], GPP, box 1127. NYT, May 7, 1922, p. 31.

15. Rosamond Pinchot to AP, Jan. 24 [1923], APP, box 2.

16. GP to AP, April 27, 1922, GPP, box 1125.

17. If the Vares had withheld more early results, Gifford thought, the Vares' dishonest "gang" could have manufactured sufficient votes to bring about Alter's triumph. McGeary, Pinchot, p. 284.

18. Esther P. Lape to CBP, undated [May 16-17, 1922], CBPP, box I:22; GP to William Kent, July 1, 1922, GPP, box 1121.

19. Hingston, Pinchot, pp. 94-100, 104-105.

20. McSparran had been one of the delegates, who had earlier carried the anti-preparedness message to President Wilson.

21. Philadelphia Evening Ledger, Nov. 6, 1922, p. 18, also included an article by Leila appealing for women's votes. Friendly newspapers presented Gifford as the moderate reformer, genial family man, and outdoor enthusiast. In the election, Gifford did less well in places where McSparran had strong connections with the Grange. P. S. Stahlnecker to CBP, Sept. 5, 1923, GPP, box 257.

22. APJ to CBP, undated [May 1922], CBPP, box I:32.

23. APJ to GP, Feb. 15 [1920], GPP, box 231.

24. APJ to CBP, [Nov.] 16th [1922], CBPP, box I:23. A summary of Crinks's political career is set forth in Jaime Reynolds and Ian Hunter, "'Crinks' Johnstone," Journal of Liberal History, 26 (Spring 2000), pp. 14-18.

25. Leila was also annoyed with Amos over family financial matters. CBP to AP, Dec. 13, 1921, and AP to CBP, Dec. 19, 1921, CBPP, I-16.

26. Slattery to CBP, Aug. 21, 1919, GPP, box 495.

27. CBP to Harry A. Slattery, Nov. 29, 1922, Harry A. Slattery Papers (David M. Rubenstein Rare Book and Manuscript Library, Duke University), box 1.

28. Quotation in John W. Furlow, "Cornelia Bryce Pinchot: Feminism in the Post-Suffrage Era," Pennsylvania History, 43 (Oct. 1976), p. 332; CBP to AP, undated [1917], APP, box 3.

29. During the 1916 campaign, Amos declined an invitation to speak at a Democratic rally in Hartford because his Aunt Nettie Wood, a prominent Republican woman in Connecticut, had objected, "and I do not want to hurt her feelings." AP to W. L. Cushing, Nov. 1 and 2, Dec. 1, 1916, APP, box 17.

30. Slattery was then helping Amos with a book project. Amos wrote an intemperate press statement attacking many former Republican progressives for supporting Coolidge instead of La Follette in the 1924 presidential campaign, which prompted the referenced long editorial in a Philadelphia newspaper extolling the "eminent" and "esteemed" Governor Gifford, while castigating Amos as "a pronounced pacifist" and "radical agitator," who believes that "marriage is a capitalist trick to enslave the masses." Philadelphia North American, Oct. 10, 1924, and Ruth Pinchot to CBP, Wednesday [Oct. 22 or 29, 1924?], CBPP, box I:49.

31. McGeary, Pinchot, p. 290.

32. The mansion was inadequate for official functions. Gifford would recommend the construction of a new executive mansion on a site Leila picked out, but it would be another forty years before a new governor's house was built. Mamie McCadden, the Pinchots' trusted servant, dating back to Gifford's birth, also moved to Harrisburg, but she soon suffered from dementia and died two years later at age eighty.

33. "Quotation in Paul B. Beers, Pennsylvania Politics Today and Yesterday: The Tolerable Accommodation (University Park: Pennsylvania State University Press, 1980), pp. 87-88. Gifford would tell his brother, "I think, and always have thought, that you overestimate the number of people who vote intelligently on any but the very simplest and clearest of issues." GP to AP, Dec. 2, 1924, GPP, box 255.

34. GP, Selected Writings, pp. 130-134 (quotations on pp. 133, 134).

35. Gifford would later comment that the able speaker, C. Jay Goodnough, without ties to any political faction, was "one of the luckiest things I ever did" as governor. Quotation in Hingston, Pinchot, p. 124.

36. Clyde L. King to AP, June 19, 1923, APP, box 3.

37. Falco, Pinchot, pp. 163-175; Hingston, Pinchot, pp. 148-154.

38. GP to Robert Y. Stuart, Dec. 20, 1922, GPP, box 1086; GP to AP, Jan. 8, 1923, ibid., box 255; Clyde L. King to GP, Jan. 14, 1927, ibid., box 277. King's estimated savings were based on a hypothetical projection of what the Sproul government would have spent if it had stayed in office another four years.

39. GP to APJ, Jan. 28, 1923, ibid., box 252.

40. CBP to Mrs. H. H. Durchschlag, Feb. 27, 1923, and CBP to Elizabeth R. Cosgrove, March 1, 1923, CBPP, box I:35; CBP to R. A. Haynes, Feb. 24, 1923, ibid., box III:6.

41. CBP to Harry A. Slattery, Nov. 29, 1922, Slattery Papers, box 1; CBP to Sarah J. Sparks, March 1, 1923, CBPP, box I:35.

42. The vote was 107 to 100 in the house, but passage required a majority (or 105) of its 208 members. That all members voted (one had died) in the chamber revealed the significance of the measure. The many Democrat votes from rural areas contributed to the passage of the bill. Falco, Pinchot, pp. 210ff. The measure excluded private residences making their own alcoholic beverages. Hingston, Pinchot, p. 140.

43. After the First World War, Gifford showed less interest in organized religion, which Leila eschewed altogether, but his religious-moralistic perspective endured. Falco, Pinchot, pp. 225-228. Documentation on Gifford's oversight of moving pictures is in GPP, boxes 1404 and 1528.

44. In 1921, for example, the Boone and Crockett Club had asked for his resignation, presumably for his criticisms of TR and the war. Amos threatened to sue if his membership was not restored, and Gifford fully supported his brother. The club backed off and Amos resumed his membership. Correspondence is in APP, boxes 33 and 34.

45. GP to CBP, June 6, 1923, CBPP, box I:35. Moreover, the recent repeal of prohibition enforcement in neighboring New York State was an early sign of eroding support for prohibition. Other states then were also moderating their enforcement laws.

46. GP to APJ, May 29, 1923, GPP, box 252.

47. There were more than 4,000 breweries and distilleries in Pennsylvania that held federal permits allowing the production of alcohol for medicinal and industrial purposes. When the treasury assistant secretary intimated that the federal permits allowing the state police to inspect permit-holding breweries and distilleries were valid only for "normal business hours," Gifford mocked the limitation, saying, "Criminals work mainly at night" and the string attached to the supposed federal-state cooperation would "hobble the officers of the law." Quotations in *NYT*, Dec. 17, 1923, p. 7.

48. GP to F. E. Olmsted, Oct. 31, 1923, GPP, box 253; *NYT*, May 12, 1924, p. 4.

49. Even after leaving the governorship, he would comment privately, "I have a good many sins on my conscience, but one of them is not sitting still, and letting [Mellon] get away with the dry business, so far as I was able to prevent it." GP to APJ, May 20, 1927, GPP, box 277.

50. Falco, Pinchot, pp. 217-218; Thomas R. Pegram, "Brewing Trouble: Federal, State, and Private Authority in Pennsylvania Prohibition Enforcement under Gifford Pinchot, 1923-27," *PMHB*, 138 (April 2014), pp. 169ff.

51. GP, address to WCTU convention, Erie, Pennsylvania, Oct. 6, 1923, GPP, box 776.

52. Quotation in McGeary, *Pinchot*, p. 307; *NYT*, Sept. 27, 1925, p. 16.

53. APJ to GP, July 16 [1923], and GP to APJ, Aug. 3, 1923, GPP, box 277; APJ to GP, Aug. 13 [1923], ibid., box 252.

54. GP to Calvin Coolidge, Sept. 10, 1923, Calvin Coolidge Papers (Manuscript Division, Library of Congress), reel 55.

55. GP to Coolidge, tel., Dec. 8, 1924, and Coolidge to GP, Dec. 12, 1924, GPP, box 1370. Quotation in McGeary, *Pinchot*, p. 307. Gifford's statement, Oct. 25, 1925, is in GPP, box 780.

56. A precedent in Gifford's mind was President Roosevelt's intervention in the anthracite coal strike in 1902. In 1919, Coolidge, as governor of Massachusetts, had intervened to end a strike of Boston policemen, so it was not unreasonable to believe he would play an active role in arbitrating the current impasse.

57. Hingston, Pinchot., pp. 174-177; Coolidge to GP, Sept. 7, 1923, Coolidge Papers, reel 115.

58. GP to AP, Nov. 18, 1923, APP, box 36. GP, "Wages, Margins and Anthracite Prices," *Annals of the American Academy of Political and Social Science*," 111 (Jan. 1924), pp. 61-81.

59. *NYT*, Aug. 9, 1915, p. 7; GP to AP, Aug. 8, 1915, APP, box 2; AP to GP, Aug. 12, 1915, GPP, box 191.

60. AP, "Railroads and the Mechanics of Social Power," *The Nation*, 117 (Oct. 17, 1923), pp. 429-431, (Oct. 24, 1923), pp. 458-460, and (Oct. 31, 1923), pp. 488-490. He soon issued the three articles as a pamphlet.

61. AP to GP, Aug. 29, 1923, APP, box 35.

62. Among the questions: Did the governor have the authority for such drastic actions? Would other Pennsylvania politicians support him? Would not such a course alienate him from the Republican Party

mainstream, which already viewed him as somewhat radical, at a time when he had national ambitions? Would the owners not challenge the governor's orders in the courts?

63. Amos's compatriot George Record weighed in with his own analysis, but he and Amos found the governor's response "most discouraging" and "a mistake." GP to AP, Nov. 18, 1923, GP to George L. Record, Oct. 23, 1923, APP, box 36; AP to Antoinette Wood, Nov. 12, 1923, ibid., box 2.

64. Among key reasons for the failure, the two Republican senators from Pennsylvania did not endorse it. Hingston, Pinchot, pp. 178-180.

65. William Vare's brother, Edwin, died a few weeks before the 1922 general election, but William was annoyed at Gifford's attacks on wets like himself and Mellon.

66. Ralph B. Strassburger, the victor, was married to the heiress of the Singer Sewing Machine Company.

67. NYT, April 24, 1924, p. 3.

68. CBP to Mrs. Frank T. Griswold, April 25, 1924, APP, box 3. As a last-ditch appeal before the election, Leila arranged to send out 1,800 letters to women supporters and telephoned others. The disappointing result prompted Minnie Washburton to resign from her position on the Republican state committee.

69. GP to APJ. Jan. 25, 1924, and March 31, 1924, GPP, box 252.

70. Quotation in McGeary, Pinchot, p. 315.

71. GP to APJ, Feb. 28, 1925, and April 1, 1925, GPP, box 261.

72. Quotation in McGeary, Pinchot, p. 311.

73. Falco, Pinchot, pp. 228-232.

74. Quotation in Jean Christie, Morris Llewellyn Cooke: Progressive Engineer (New York: Garland, 1983), p. 70.

75. Report of the Giant Power Survey Board to the General Assembly of the Commonwealth of Pennsylvania (Harrisburg: Telegraphy Printing [1925]).

76. Quotations in Christie, Morris Llewellyn Cooke, pp. 77, 79.

77. GP to Morris L. Cooke, Feb. 18, 1925, GPP, box 1435. The two fired commissioners refused to leave their positions, and a state court ruled in their favor. Pinchot's four appointees still held a majority, but they often did not vote as a bloc, and the senate rejected two other nominees.

78. GP to Coolidge, Nov. 27, 1925, Coolidge Papers, reel 115.

79. GP to AP, Nov. 14, 1927, APP, box 40.

80. Quotations in report of fact-finding committee of the Committee of 76, undated [Nov. 1925], GPP, box 781.

81. For example, the legislature rejected ten election reform bills, passed another in such diluted form that Gifford vetoed it, and approved a constitutional amendment, which went nowhere.

82. GP to Henry S. Drinker, Feb. 11, 1926, GPP, box 260; NYT, Feb. 20, 1926, p. 2. A summary of the issues is GP, The Extra Session: A Report to the People, Harrisburg, March 1, 1926.

83. Quotations in McGeary, Pinchot, p. 317.

84. Hingston, Pinchot, pp. 306-317. A Johnstown newspaper, May 12, 1926, p. 1 (clipping in GPP, box 267), features Lewis and Murray endorsing Gifford Pinchot at two mass meetings.

85. Church leaders and reformers tried to persuade either Pepper or Pinchot to withdraw from the race. Both refused, however, and the UMW declared that the coal miners were "thoroughly determined . . . to elect Governor Pinchot, in whom they have great confidence" and to defeat the anti-union Pepper. Quotations in Falco, Pinchot, p. 304. GP to AP, March 16, 1926, GPP, box 266; GP to George W. Norris, April 9, 1926, ibid., box 263.

86. In addition, Pepper's use of post office patronage and his organization in black areas likely eroded Gifford's appeal among African Americans. CBP to AP, undated [April 1926]. APP, box 3; J. E. Philpot to P. S. Stahlnecker, March 27, 1926, GPP, box 1131.

87. Hingston, Pinchot, pp. 317-328.

88. NYT, Sept. 14, 1926, p. 1. Gifford's campaign funding was a family affair. Of the $187,000 spent, he contributed $44,000, Leila $40,000, his Aunt Nettie Wood $50,000, and Amos $10,000. His campaign expenses (without being paired with any candidate for governor) paled in contrast to those of his two competitors. Pepper and his allied candidate for governor spent a whopping $1.8 million during the 1926 primary contest. Vare (paired with a gubernatorial candidate) spent $796,000, but the chicanery of his electioneering led to his undoing. Hingston, Pinchot. p. 329.

89. GP to president of the U.S. Senate, Jan. 8, 1927, GPP, box 781. The U.S. Senate is the judge of its elections but, except in very close ones, has only rarely refused to seat the apparent victor because of voting irregularities, including excessive campaign expenditures. I am grateful to Mary Baumann, Senate Historical Office, for this information.

90. Regarding patronage, for example, all the governor's appointments before the election were delayed until Stahlnecker approved them, but the Pinchot forces attacked Pepper officials when they supposedly pressured municipal workers to vote for Pepper. Hingston, Pinchot, pp. 305, 315.

91. GP to APJ, Sept. 28, 1926, ibid., box 261; NYT, Dec. 4, 1926, p. 36. Text of the speech is in GPP, box 781. Gifford also attacked "the worst elements in public life" for trying to subvert the direct primary, which stood for transparency in politics, and bring about a return to a boss-run convention system. Text in Selected Writings, pp. 150-153.

92. Message by Governor Gifford Pinchot to the General Assembly of Pennsylvania (n.p: n.p., Jan. 4, 1927), copy in GPP, box 781; NYT, Jan. 5, 1927, p. 9.

93. GP to APJ, Feb. 5, 1927, GPP, box 277; NYT, Jan. 17, 1927, p. 22.

Chapter 19: Women's Aspirations

1. Amos made one trip to southern France to see Nettie and Alan and a home they built. Amos and Ruth had bought a house on East Thirty-Eighth Street in New York, but in late 1926, they would sell the house and move back to 1125 Park Avenue.

2. MEP to AP, Monday [Summer 1912?], APP, box 3.

3. RP to AP, Oct. 16 [1922], ibid., box 2.

4. Rosamond Pinchot to AP, undated [1923?], ibid.

5. Rosamond Pinchot to AP, Jan. 17 [1923], undated [March 25, 1922], and M[ay?] 23 [1923], undated [Sept. 1922?], ibid. At the end of the winter term, her grades were in the low 70s (passing was 60), and the comment was, "Academic work fair and could be much better." Report card for period ending March 22, 1922, ibid.

6. Rosamond Pinchot to AP, undated [1922?] and undated [Summer 1923], ibid.

7. The Miracle, by Karl Vollmöller, had been first produced in London in 1911 and had also been made into a silent film.

8. Rosamond's acting experience consisted of her participation with her brother in a patriotic play during the First World War, written by a young Milford local, in which Gifford 2nd also participated. Gifford Pinchot 2nd to AP, undated [Sept. 1918], APP, box 28. She was also in the cast of a play at Ethel Walker, an experience she enjoyed.

9. Rosamond Pinchot, undated manuscript, Rosamond Pinchot Papers (Manuscript Division, Library of Congress), box OV2 (hereafter RPP).

10. One article publicizing the upcoming production included interviews with Reinhardt, Gest, and Rosamond. NYT, Nov. 26, 1923, p. 15.

11. AP to APJ, Dec. 14, 1923, and AP to Rosamond Pinchot, Dec. 14, 1923, APP, box 2.

12. Quotation in Bibi Gaston, The Loveliest Woman in America (New York: William Morrow, 2008), p. 16.

13. AP to APJ, Jan. 17, 1924, APP, box 2. Opening night reviews in NYT, Jan. 16, 1924, and in New York World, Jan. 16, 1924, are in RPP, box 2.

14. CBP to AP, Jan. 18, 1924, APP, box 3. Gifford was too busy to make opening night, but he would later see Rosamond in performance.

15. Quotation in Gaston, Loveliest Woman, pp. 35-36.

16. Quotations ibid., pp. 36, 37.

17. AP to APJ, Oct. 14, 1926, APP, box 3.

18. Quotations in NYT, April 15, 1927, p. 27, and Aug. 8, 1927, p. 6; Rosamond Pinchot to AP, Sept. 10 [1927], APP, box 40. It may have been during this European tour that Iris Tree, a bohemian British poet and actress, called Rosamond "the loveliest woman in America," and newspaper articles thereafter sometimes used the phrase when writing about Rosamond.

19. Quotations in Gaston, Loveliest Woman, pp. 42, 43.

20. CBP to AP, Jan. 30, 1928, APP, box 3. Some newspaper accounts reported that Gertrude also was present at the wedding, but she was away from her New York residence that winter.

21. Rosamond Pinchot to AP, July 3 [1928], July 9 [1928], and July 15 [1928], APP, box 41.

22. Anonymous [Ruth Pinchot], "A Deflated Rebel," *The Nation*, 124 (Jan. 5, 1927), pp. 11-12 (quotation on p. 12).

23. Ruth asked Leila not to show her piece to Gifford, who "would think it so vulgar to be without reserve." Ruth Pinchot to CBP, Wednesday [Jan. 15, 1927?], CBP to Ruth Pinchot, Jan. 10, 1927, and CBP to Ruth Pinchot, Jan. 25, 1927, CBPP, box I:105.

24. Anonymous [CBP], "In Search of Adventure," *The Nation*, 124 (June 8, 1927), pp. 630-632 (quotation on p. 632).

25. Slattery resigned from the National Conservation Association in 1923 (which soon closed down entirely) to serve as counsel representing various clients suing government officials involved in the Harding scandals. Slattery may have written his letter to Amos at his own behest, but Gifford surely knew about it.

26. AP to GP, March 31, 1927, and Harry A. Slattery to AP, April 11, 1927, APP, box 40.

27. AP to Slattery, April 19, 1927, and Ruth Pinchot to CBP, Monday [April 18, 1927?], ibid.

28. AP, "The Flag and the Dollar," *The Forum*, 78 (Sept. 1927), pp. 435-442; *NYT*, May 12, 1931, p. 3.

29. Legal scholars and many luminary literati, believing the evidence against the accused men was unconvincing, demanded a new trial. A committee's review of the case confirmed the jury's guilty verdict, however, and the governor of Massachusetts refused to commute the sentence.

30. *NYT*, Aug. 13, 1927, p. 5, and Aug. 16, 1927, p. 12.

31. Ibid., Sept. 23, 1928, II, p. 4, and Nov. 11, 1928, II, p. 4. Amos had probably met Janine earlier that summer when he traveled to the mineral baths at Carlsbad, Germany, to get the health "cure," including treatment of his chronically sore hip, and to see his son. Janine's mother subsequently kept him informed of her daughter's amorous relationship with Gifford 2nd. Lola Jahiel Voisin to AP, June 7, 1928, Sept. 3, 1928, and Nov. 11, 1928, APP, box 41.

32. Gabriel Voisin's memoir, *Men, Women and 10,000 Kites* (London: Putnam, 1963), pp. 177, 179, 188, 205, has some references to the early life of his daughter Janine (though not named).

33. Quotation in McGeary, *Pinchot*, p. 327. The working title was So This Is Politics, draft in GPP, box 1038.

34. For example, during the 1920s, no woman had yet been elected to the U.S. Senate.

35. CBP to Ruth Pinchot, April 26, 1924, APP, box 2.

36. CBP to APJ, March 24, 1928, CBPP, box I:136.

37. CBP to Hiram Johnson, Oct. 10, 1920, ibid., box I:12; CBP to AP, Dec. 1, 1923, APP, box 2.

38. Roosevelt may have made these remarks at Gifford and Leila's wedding; in any event, Gifford later said that he was present when TR said it.

39. Campaign materials, including newspaper clippings and endorsements, are in CBPP, box I:128. The Grange refused to back either candidate.

40. Philadelphia *Inquirer*, April 26, 1928, p. 3; GP to APJ, May 2, 1928, GPP, box 291.

41. Rosamond Pinchot to AP, Aug. 6 [1928], and clipping from New York *Evening Journal*, Sept. 22, 1928, APP, box 41.

42. AP to John J. Raskob, Oct. 4, 1928, ibid. Amos gave $1,000 to the Democratic National Committee to circulate his letter. Henry Moskowitz to AP, Oct. 5, 1928, ibid.-

43. Raskob also headed the Democratic National Committee during the campaign.

44. George W. Norris to GP, July 14, 1928, and Aug. 2, 1928, and GP to Norris, July 23, 1928, GPP, box 24.

45. GP's 1920 statement, reproduced ibid., Box 295; GP to APJ, Oct. 28, 1928, and Sept. 26, 1928, ibid., box 291.

Chapter 20: The Widening Horizons of Conservation

1. GP, *Selected Writings*, pp. 135-142 (quotation on p. 135). His slightly more optimistic appraisal of forestry in Pennsylvania is GP, "Outlook for Forestry in Pennsylvania," *American Forestry*, 29 (Jan. 1923), p. 19.

2. Miller, *Pinchot*, pp. 286-289 (quotation on p. 287).

3. Ibid.

4. GP, "The Blazed Trail of Forest Depletion," *American Forestry*, 29 (June 1923), pp. 323-328, 373- 374.

5. GP to Robert Y. Stuart, Nov. 15, 1928, and Stuart to GP, Nov. 21, 1928, GPP, box 296.

6. GP, *Selected Writings*, pp. 67-70 (quotation of p. 69).

7. Ibid., pp. 104-108. Quotations in GP, "Blazed Trail of Forest Depletion," p. 374.

8. George P. Ahern, *Deforested America* (privately printed, 1928), quotations on pp. 71, 70. Elsewhere, Ahern disparagingly defined Greeleyism as "the lumbermen leading the Forest Service by the hand." Quotation in Frome, *Forest Service*, p. 26.

9. George P. Ahern, *Deforested America: Statement of the Forest Situation in the United States*, 70th Congress, 2nd Session, Sen. Doc. 216 (Washington, Government Printing Office, 1929).

10. GP to Raphael Zon, Dec. 26, 1928, GPP, box 289; McGeary, *Pinchot*, p. 334.

11. Quotation ibid, p. 335.

12. GP to APJ, Sept. 26, 1928, GPP, box 291; CBP to APJ, March 24, 1928, CBPP, box I:136.

13. GP to Lewis Stimson, Sept. 9, 1910, GPP, box 138; GP to Louis D. Brandeis, Dec. 8, 1914, ibid., box 174.

14. GP to APJ, Oct. 27, 1928, ibid., box 291. Woodruff backed out when Gifford moved forward with his plans. *Fortieth Reunion of '89*, p. 48. The schooner had been a two-masted ship, but the main boom of 72 feet was unwieldly, so the previous owner had added a mizzen mast. GP to George C. Pardee, Jan. 2, 1929, GPP, box 314.

15. GP, *To the South Seas* (Philadelphia: John C. Winston, 1930), pp. 2-12, 15, 16, 22 (quotations on pp. 8, 6); GP to APJ, Oct. 27, 1928, GPP, box 291.

16. First quotations in GP, *To the South Seas*, p. 55.

17. His diary of the entire voyage is in GPP, box 16.

18. Completing her negative portrait, Leila bewailed that Giff was miserable in the hot weather and suffering from a fever and big boils on his buttocks, so "he also hates it – has not smiled in weeks." CBP to AP, undated [May 1929], CBP to AP, undated [May 10, 1929], and CBP to AP, Sunday, May 19 [1929], CBPP, box III:1.

19. CBP to AP, undated [May 1929], and undated, ibid.

20. CBP to Ruth Pinchot, undated, ibid.

21. CBP to AP, Sunday, May 19 [1929], ibid.; GP to AP, July 16, 1929, APP, box 41.

22. In his book about the voyage, Gifford never gives the first captain's name and mentions in only a few sentences the smashed crankcase that led to the firing of the captain. GP to AP, May 8, 1929, GPP, box 3169; GP, *To the South Seas*, p. 22; CBP, diary, April 15, 1929, CBPP, box III:2; GP to AP, Aug. 9, 1929, APP, box 41; Morris Gregg, quotation in Miller, *Pinchot*, p. 301. GP, Diary, May 8, 1929, GPP, box 3169. Gifford even advanced the departing captain an extra month's salary, paid for his travel home, and gave him a letter of recommendation, though "with a strained conscience." GP, Diary, May 5-16, 1929, ibid., box 6.

23. *NYT*, Oct. 27, 1929, 8, p. 2, and June 1, 1930, 8, p. 5; George C. Pardee, to GP, April 23, 1931, and GP to Pardee, May 7, 1931, GPP, box 314.

24. Gifford mailed several hundred copies of his book to friends and political contacts. A few details about the voyage here are taken from Gifford Bryce Pinchot, *Giff and Stiff in the South Seas* (Philadelphia: John C. Winston, 1933).

25. GP, *To the South Seas*, p. 490. The captain and crew sailed the schooner, loaded with wildlife and specimens, back to its winter quarters in Savannah, Georgia.

26. GP to Henry S. Graves, Dec. 9, 1929, GPP, box 308; GP to George W. Woodruff, Jan. 4, 1930, ibid., box 320. The minority report is in GP, *Selected Writings*, pp. 67-70.

27. For example, Gifford would subsequently stay at Graves's house during his visits to New Haven.

28. Industry-forestry collaboration was tried at the federal level during Franklin D. Roosevelt's New Deal, with the enactment of the National Industrial Recovery Act, but the established lumber code in this program was barely in place when the Supreme Court declared the law unconstitutional.

29. GP to Morris L. Cooke, Feb. 20, 1925, and April 14, 1925, GPP, box 1435.

30. GP, press release, May 11, 1928, APP, box 41. He cited the electric power companies' invasion of educational institutions, including the distribution of free pamphlets to high school students and the writing of economics textbooks favorable to the utility viewpoint.

31. GP, *The Power Monopoly; Its Make-up and Menace* (1928). Four companies, he claimed, owned over ninety percent of the power, including the Morgan-Mellon concerns which controlled more than fifty percent. He also publicized these views in GP, "The Gigantic Strides of the Power Monopoly in the United States," *Current History*, 30 (April 1929), pp. 40-42. Quotation in McGeary, *Pinchot*, p. 341.

32. Quotations ibid., p. 346.

Chapter 21: Toward a New Deal

1. Grundy, the senate incumbent, was contesting in his own primary but seemed mostly interested in defeating Vare's man in the governor race. Details are in McGeary, *Pinchot;* Richard C. Keller, *Pennsylvania's Little New Deal* (New York: Garland, 1982); and John W. Furlow, Jr., An Urban State Under Siege: Pennsylvania and the Second Gubernatorial Administration of Gifford Pinchot, 1931-1935 (Ph.D. dissertation, University of North Carolina, 1973). Quotation in McGeary, *Pinchot,* p. 349.

2. GP to AP, March 26, 1930 and April 14, 1930, GPP, box 314. John L. Lewis, UMW president, supported Brown, but the rank-and-file miners stood solidly behind Gifford's candidacy.

3. The vote totals: 633,000 for Pinchot, 613,000 for Brown, and 281,000 for Phillips.

4. Keller, *Pennsylvania's Little New Deal,* pp. 21-24. The Democratic winner in the gubernatorial primary, John M. Hemphill, received only 121,000 votes compared with more than two million for the three main Republican aspirants.

5. Because many registered Republicans would be voting for a Democrat, the anti-Pinchot Republicans also ran Hemphill as a gubernatorial nominee of a new Liberal Party. McGeary, *Pinchot,* p. 352.

6. Quotation in Keller, *Pennsylvania's Little New Deal,* p. 23.

7. Leila Pinchot profusely thanked McSparran for his endorsement. CBP to McSparran, Oct. 23, 1930, CBPP, box I:118.

8. Quotation in McGeary, *Pinchot,* p. 353. Grundy's complicated relationship with Gifford Pinchot is presented in Ann Hawkes Hutton, *The Pennsylvanian: Joseph R. Grundy* (Philadelphia: Dorrance, 1962), pp. 204-207, passim.

9. The Pennsylvania constitution prohibited governors from serving consecutive terms from 1878 to 1968. One governor had won two nonconsecutive terms in the nineteenth century.

10. First quotation in McGeary, *Pinchot,* p. 358; *Christian Century,* 47 (Nov. 19, 1930), pp. 1408-1410.

11. Keller, *Pennsylvania's Little New Deal,* p. 23.

12. GP, *Selected Writings,* pp. 154-157 (quotations on pp. 155, 156).

13. McGeary, *Pinchot,* p. 365.

14. Quotations in Keller, *Pennsylvania's Little New Deal,* p. 39.

15. McGeary, *Pinchot,* pp. 366-367.

16. For example, Gifford attacked King's "deplorable change of front" and King charged that the PSC acronym stood for "Pinchot Service Commission." Quotations ibid., p. 369.

17. McGeary calculated that, up until these late confirmations, the governor had appointed seventeen commissioners during his two governorships. (They could serve until rejected.) The senate rejected only two but failed to confirm any of them. Ibid.

18. Furlow, Urban State, pp. 260-261; GP to APJ, Oct. 24, 1931, GPP, box 310. For the key position of committee secretary, Gifford appointed economist Paul H. Douglas, who would later become a U.S. Senator from Illinois.

19. Furlow, Urban State, pp. 245-246. Quotations in Keller, *Pennsylvania's Little New Deal,* p. 71. There was no precise data on falling economic output and mounting unemployment. Various estimates for Pennsylvania during the early 1930s are given in Joseph M. Speakman, *At Work in Penn's Woods: The Civilian Conservation Corps in Pennsylvania* (University Park: Penn State University Press, 2006), pp. 14-19.

20. The $1 million limitation had become part of the state constitution in 1873 when the annual state budget was only $7 million. By 1935, the budget amounted to more than $200 million. Furlow, Urban State, p. 250.

21. Furlow, Urban State, pp. 256-257; quotation in Keller, *Pennsylvania's Little New Deal,* pp. 71-72.

22. GP to AP, Dec. 4, 1931, GPP, box 314; GP to AP, Dec. 16, 1931, ibid., box 1722.

23. Quotations in Keller, *Pennsylvania's Little New Deal,* pp. 75, 76.

24. Quotations in McGeary, *Pinchot,* pp. 374, 375.

25. Furlow, Urban State, pp. 287-289; McGeary, *Pinchot,* p. 376. New York Governor Franklin Roosevelt was then developing a similar program for his state. The subsequent federal CCC programs in Pennsylvania are documented in Speakman, *At Work in Penn's Woods,* passim.

26. *NYT,* Aug. 14, 1931, p. 9. The governor reiterated his social justice perspective in testimony before a U.S. Senate committee and the case for federal assistance in a magazine article, "The Case for Federal Relief," *Survey,* 67 (Jan. 1, 1932), pp. 347-349.

27. Furlow, *Urban State*, p. 246; Keller, *Pennsylvania's Little New Deal*, pp. 77, 88. Unemployment in the Commonwealth would grow nine months later to thirty-seven percent, or nearly 1.5 million people.

28. In 1934, Gifford thwarted the legislators' move to reduce the salaries of all government employees, including their own, although he voluntarily took a ten-percent cut in his own pay.

29. Quotation in Keller, *Pennsylvania's Little New Deal*, p. 83.

30. The complicated amendment process meant that an income tax, even if approved, could not take effect before 1933. Woodruff to GP, Sept. 3, 1930, GPP, box 320. The state constitution permitted flat taxes, so for the special legislative session Governor Pinchot announced a modest one-percent income tax, but the Republican-controlled legislature defeated the proposal.

31. A new state distribution board followed these guidelines. Furlow, *Urban State*, pp. 250-255, 275, 279.

32. Quotation ibid., p. 274.

33. GP, Statement, June 13, 1932, GPP, box 3179; quotation in *NYT*, June 3, 1931, p. 1. Gifford received assurances at least from Senator Hiram Johnson of California that he would not be a candidate.

34. Quotation ibid., Aug. 14, 1931, p. 9.

35. Stephen Stahlnecker to Harold L. Ickes, April 1932, GPP, box 2003. After their participation together in TR's "bull moose" campaign of 1912, Gifford and Ickes corresponded intermittently about political issues, and Leila and Ickes exchanged thoughts on their mutual gardening interests.

36. Replies are ibid, boxes 2004 and 2007. Quotation in Kehl and Astorino, "A Bull Moose Responds to the New Deal," p. 42.

37. Quotation in McGeary, *Pinchot*, p. 392. For example, Governor Pinchot, seeing that he had no chance as a favorite son at the GOP convention, stayed home in Harrisburg.

38. GP Diary, Feb. 19, 1912, GPP, box 1; FDR's speech, Sept. 14, 1935, *Franklin D. Roosevelt and Conservation, 1911-1945*, ed. Edgar B. Nixon (Hyde Park, NY: Franklin D. Roosevelt Library, 1957), 1, pp. 429-431.

39. Additionally, for his South Seas adventure, Gifford asked Franklin to support his nomination for membership in the New York Yacht Club. The two also explored possibilities of interstate cooperation on the utility issue, though little was accomplished in that area. FDR to GP, Dec. 3, 1930, GP to FDR, Jan. 21, 1931, FDR to GP, April 2, 1931, FDR to GP, June 11, 1931, GP to FDR, June 11, 1931, FDR to GP, June 15, 1931, GP to FDR, June 18, 1931, GPP, box 1732; *NYT*, June 16, 1931, p. 33, and Jan. 17, 1932, p. 26.

40. GP to FDR, Dec. 1, 1932, GPP, box 1862; last quotation in McGeary, *Pinchot*, pp. 393-394. Leila, Gifford, and niece Rosamond attended the inauguration ball.

41. Furlow, *Urban State*, pp. 284-285.

42. Ibid., pp. 285-287.

43. Governor Pinchot pardoned a leftwing activist who had been convicted for violating an anti-sedition law. In defense of his action, Gifford wrote unapologetically, "To imprison a man for publicly expressing his views on a political subject does not repress communism. It encourages opposition to the government, breeds hatred and disloyalty, and is thoroughly un-American." He also criticized the University of Pittsburgh, which had fired a professor for his activist liberal views, and he reacted negatively to an initiative to dismiss a University of Pennsylvania professor as an alleged Nazi propagandist. He announced; "if academic freedom has been destroyed in Germany[,] it is not for us to destroy it here." Gifford made academic freedom a necessary condition for state aid to Pennsylvania's public universities. Quotations in McGeary, *Pinchot*, pp. 384-385.

44. Gifford especially lauded the "personal help" of three of its leaders in winning "several hot fights" in the house. Quotation in McGeary, Pinchot, p. 395; FDR to Joseph F. Guffey, May 19, 1933, reproduced in Joseph F. Guffey, *Seventy Years on the Red-Fire Wagon: From Tilden to Truman Through New Freedom and New Deal* (privately printed, 1952), p. 78.

45. Quotation in Keller, *Pennsylvania's Little New Deal*, pp. 59-60.

46. Carr would antagonize, among others, Joseph Grundy, who had already broken with Gifford over the governor's reform agenda, for her activism and her publicizing of allegations of his company's discriminatory policies against labor and working women.

47. Quotations in McGeary, *Pinchot*, p. 377.

48. Quotations in Furlow, *Urban State*, pp. 321, 335, and 321.

49. Quotation ibid., p. 322; McGeary, *Pinchot*, pp. 376-377.

50. Quotation ibid., p. 385.

51. The financially strapped coal companies paid their already low wage workers even less, especially those who lived in company-owned towns and bought their goods on credit in company-owned stores. Publicizing this paternalistic practice, Gifford presented an example of a miner who ended up with no cash in his pay envelope after the company had tallied all his debts and expenses to the owners. A UMW priority was to sign up such miners and undermine the company unions.

52. Quotations in Furlow, Urban State, p. 335, and McGeary, Pinchot, p. 381. Muriel Earley Sheppard, Cloud by Day: The Story of Coal and Coke and People (Chapel Hill: University of North Carolina Press, 1947), pp. 119-149, passim, captures the complexities and uncertainties of the labor strife in western Pennsylvania in the early 1930s.

53. Quotation in McGeary, Pinchot, p. 381.

54. GP to APJ, Oct. 5, 1933, GPP, box 326.

55. Quotation in Furlow, Urban State, p. 287.

56. Keller, Pennsylvania's Little New Deal, p. 84.

57. Ibid.; Furlow, Urban State, pp. 287-290; McGeary, Pinchot, p. 376.

58. Isidor Feinstein, "A Gentleman in Politics," American Mercury, 28 (May 1933), pp. 83-84 (quotation on p. 84).

59. Keller, Pennsylvania's Little New Deal, p. 84.

60. Rosamond Pinchot, Diary, March 31, 1934, RPP, box 1.

61. McGeary, Pinchot, pp. 396-397; quotation in Keller, Pennsylvania's Little New Deal, p. 134.

62. However, John L. Lewis, withheld his endorsement, arguing that he was supporting his longtime associate, UMW secretary-treasurer Thomas Kennedy, who was running as Democratic candidate for lieutenant governor, and that it would be "improper" to take sides in other contests. John L. Lewis to CBP, April 25, 1934, and CBP to Lewis, April 26, 1934, CBPP, box I:295.

63. AP to William P. Eno, May 16, 1934, APP, box 3.

64. Gifford, at Ickes's behest, had sent a letter to newly elected President Roosevelt, endorsing his friend for the position of interior secretary. McGeary, Pinchot, p. 409. Moreover, Gifford persuaded Secretary Ickes to hire Slattery as a personal assistant. Correspondence is in GPP, boxes 328 and 2072 and Ickes Papers, box 162. Ickes had been raised in Pennsylvania and, after moving away, retained interest in the politics of the Keystone State.

65. Roosevelt objected to cabinet secretaries taking sides in primary contests (unless in their home state), even Republican ones. CBP to Harold Ickes, tel., April 12, 1934, GP to Ickes, April 14, 1934, Ickes to GP, April 17 and 24, 1934, ibid.

66. CBP to Harold Ickes, July 19, 1934, ibid. Leila also revived charges that Guffey had been involved in the embezzlement of alien property money and had been in cahoots with Andrew Mellon. The episode was old news, however, and would have little impact on his electability. Guffey's defense is given in his Seventy Years on the Red-Fire Wagon, pp. 58-60.

67. The Secret Diary of Harold L. Ickes (New York: Simon and Schuster, 1953), 1, p. 208. Gifford wrote Roosevelt that the president had "suggested that I should run for the Senate with Democratic support." GP to FDR, Oct. 29, 1934, Ickes Papers, box 162. If Roosevelt had said that to him, he backed off after the primary.

68. NYT, Sept. 8, 1934, p. 1, and Sept. 18, 1934, p. 4.

69. Earle is quoted in GP to FDR, Oct. 29, 1934, GPP, box 2104; last quotation in Keller, Pennsylvania's Little New Deal, p. 140.

70. GP to FDR, Oct. 29, 1934, GPP, box 2104. In this letter, Gifford also cited Guffey's allegedly shady past and Earle's "lie" about his and Leila's earlier meeting at Grey Towers.

71. Because of Gifford's senatorial ambitions, William A. Schnader, the Republican nominee for governor, felt compelled to issue a statement denying that he had made any deal with Pinchot to unseat Reed for excessive campaign expenditures, if he was elected governor.

72. GP to FDR, Oct. 29, 1934, GPP, box 2104; Keller, Pennsylvania's Little New Deal, p. 141; Ickes, Secret Diary, 1, p. 207 (Oct. 20, 1934).

73. Quotation in Furlow, Urban State, p. 494. In the election to the Pennsylvania General Assembly, the Republicans still dominated the senate, but the Democrats took control of the house for the first time since 1877. Keller, Pennsylvania's Little New Deal, pp. 150-151. The Democrats would control both houses of the Pennsylvania legislature after 1936, and Guffey would be reelected to the U.S. Senate in 1940.

74. These last two measures were sometimes called the Little Wagner Act and Little AAA (Agricultural Adjustment Act), named after the New Deal legislation that had initiated similar changes on the federal level.

75. Keller, *Pennsylvania's Little New Deal*, passim; Randall M. Miller and Willam Pencak, eds., *Pennsylvania: A History of the Commonwealth* (University Park: Pennsylvania State University Press, 2002), pp. 296ff.

Chapter 22: From New Deal to Anti-New Deal

1. APJ to CBP, Aug. 23 [1928], CBPP, box I:118; APJ to GP, Nov. 23 [1928], GPP, box 291; London *Times*, Aug. 2, 1932, p. 12, and Aug. 4, 1932, pp. 12, 13.

2. APJ to CBP, Nov. 13 [1927], CBPP, box I:118; London *Times*, July 4, 1934, p. 17, and July 5, 1934, p. 9.

3. AP, "Hoover and the Big Lift," *The Nation*, 127 (Dec. 26, 1928), pp. 706-708 (quotations on pp. 706 and 707).

4. Oswald Garrison Villard to AP, Dec. 14, 1928, APP, box 41.

5. AP, "VII. Hoover and Power, *The Nation*, 133(Aug. 5, 1931), pp. 125-128, and "VIII. Hoover and Power" (Aug. 12, 1931), pp. 151-153. Amos said his pieces had involved "an enormous amount of research . . . because I don't want to have any comeback." AP to Villard, July 9, 1931, APP, box 43.

6. AP, "We Met Mr. Hoover," *The Nation*, 132 (Jan. 14, 1931), pp. 43-44 (quotation on p. 44). Privately, Amos complained that Hoover "has refuted all affirmative action, until he has been literally kicked into doing something" about unemployment relief. AP to Russell Doubleday, Jan. 9, 1931, APP, box 42.

7. AP, "Relief: 1931 Style," *The Nation*, 133 (Dec. 16, 1931), pp. 660-662.

8. AP, "IV. Captain Hoover: Afloat in a Sieve," *The Nation*, 134 (March 23, 1932), pp. 336-338.

9. AP, *General Goober at the Battle of Anacostia* (privately printed, 1932), unpaginated, copy in APP, box 134.

10. Copies could be obtained for ten cents from bookstores or by mail. Harry Slattery asked for fifty copies, but the number of requests for the play was likely small.

11. AP to FDR, March 17, 1932, and FDR to AP, March 21, 1932, APP, box 43; AP to FDR, Aug. 11, 1932, and Nov. 5, 1932, ibid., box 44; *NYT*, Sept. 26, 1932, p. 1, and Oct. 30, 1931, p. 22.

12. AP to Hiram Johnson, Oct. 2, 1940, APP, box 60.

13. AP, *The American Liberal and the Liberal Program*, speech to Community Forum, Nov. 13, 1932, copy ibid., box 133; AP to Saul Haas, Dec. 18, 1932, AP to Francis J. Heney, Aug. 4, 1933, and AP to Gilson Gardner, Jan. 31, 1934, ibid., box 45.

14. AP to Mitchell Kennerly, Aug. 31, 1933, ibid.

15. AP to H. W. L. Dana, June 30, 1933, and AP to Francis Hackett, Aug. 17, 1933, ibid. Amos focused on Lippmann's books, *Drift and Mastery* (1914), *A Preface to Morals* (1929), and the *A Preface of Politics* (1913).

16. Amos also faulted Lippmann for criticizing Roosevelt as an aspiring presidential candidate but then endorsing him just before the election.

17. An example was Lippmann's treatment of the Sacco and Vanzetti case, in which he posed as a fair and impartial observer. His columns after their execution, Amos charged, tried to allay conservatives' fears. Lippmann's biographer concedes Amos Pinchot's and other critics' point. Ronald Steel, *Walter Lippmann and the American Century* (New York: Vintage Books, 1980), pp. 231-232.

18. AP, "Walter Lippmann, I. 'The Great Elucidator,'" *The Nation*, 137 (July 5, 1933), pp. 7-10; "Walter Lippmann, II. 'The New Tammany,'" ibid. (July 12, 1933), pp. 36-38; "Walter Lippmann, III. Obfuscator de Luxe," ibid. (July 19, 1933), pp. 67-70; and "Walter Lippmann, IV. On Democracy," ibid. (August 2, 1933), pp. 126-130.

19. AP to Felix Frankfurter, July 15, 1935, CBPP, box I:328.

20. Amos mostly did not evict his tenants but hoped that better economic times would allow them to begin paying rent again.

21. AP to Lewis E. Meyers, Jan. 21, 1932, and AP to Ben B. Lindsey, Jan. 8, 1932, APP, box 43; AP to William P. Eno, March 18, 1933, and April 18, 1933, ibid., box 3; AP to GP, April 5, 1933, GPP, box 327. Amos (and Gifford and Nettie) also received $100,000 (about $1.5 million today) from the

will of Aunt Antoinette Eno Wood, who had died in 1930. She also left $100,000 to her only surviving sibling, Will Eno, and lesser amounts to her grandnieces and grandnephews. In memory of her parents, she gave $350,000 (plus a maintenance fund) for construction of a new town hall in her native Simsbury, Connecticut.

22. Rosamond Pinchot, Diary, Nov. 16, 1933, RPP, box 1. Before long, Amos was saying that "[i]f it wasn't for the family estate[,] I'd be out of a job myself no doubt and on the beach," and he worried that Mary, then at Vassar, might have to withdraw and that he could not afford to enroll Tony there. AP to Bill and Florence Graves, Oct. 19, 1938, APP, box 57; AP to Gifford Pinchot 2nd, May 1, 1940, ibid., box 3.

23. Ruth Pinchot to CBP, Dec. 10, 1935, CBPP, box I:323; Ruth Pinchot to GP, Tuesday [1938], GPP, box 369. Ruth first worked as a managing editor of a new, glossy art publication, which soon folded, then as a researcher for $25 a week for a writer of historical novels, and finally as an editor for *North American Review*, which also shut its doors. Ruth's professional résumé (c. 1932) is in APP, box 65.

24. During the 1930s, Amos and Ruth reduced their live-in servants from four to two, and they rented the empty rooms to college students who had summer jobs in the city. U.S. Census, 1930 and 1940.

25. AP to Paul U. Kellogg, May 4, 1934, Kellogg to AP, May 7, 1934, AP to Kellogg, May 11, 1934, Kellogg to AP, May 14, 1934, and Oswald G. Villard to AP, May 9, 1934, APP, box 46. Others in the group supported public ownership in principle but accepted a more generic statement that would better appeal to the president. Correspondence is ibid.

26. AP to Joseph B. Eastman, April 11, 1934, ibid.

27. Amos exempted the automobile industry, airlines, and department stores, for example, because he believed they were competitive industries.

28. AP to George L. Record, July 7, 1933, APP, box 45; AP to FDR, April 26, 1934, and Aug. 10, 1934, and AP to Edwin E. Witte, Sept. 13, 1934, ibid., box 46.

29. AP to FDR, June 28, 1934, and FDR to AP, June 30, 1934, ibid. Amos also sent him a new book, *Monetary Statesmanship* (1934) by Norman Lombard, which was a relatively short survey and did not strongly enunciate a particular viewpoint.

30. *NYT*, Oct. 1, 1934, p. 6.

31. AP to Henry L. Morgenthau, Aug. 28, 1934, and AP to Raymond Moley, Aug. 17, 1934, APP, box 46. Although Amos gave a radio talk touting reflation and sounded out high-profile Americans, neither the Sound Money League nor his own proposals gained traction.

32. AP, letter to 200 Editors, Aug. 8, 1934, GPP, box 327.

33. AP to Henry Pratt Fairchild, April 7, 1934, April 9, 1934, Sept. 20, 1934, and Nov. 10, 1934, APP, box 46. Amos's problem with socialists in the 1930s was reminiscent of his earlier unhappy experience with labor radicals and socialists in trying to form a third party in 1920.

34. AP to GP, Nov. 12, 1934, GPP, box 327.

35. AP to Members of Congress, Jan. 24, 1936, APP, box 66; AP to William P. Eno, May 29, 1935, ibid., box 3. Amos wrote an earlier public letter warning about the "disturbing" discretionary powers given to the president. AP to GP, April 16, 1935, GPP, box 337.

36. AP to Members of Congress, Jan. 24, 1936, APP, box 65; AP to William P. Eno, June 5, 1936, and AP to CBP, April 29, 1936, ibid., box 3. He also asked Landon not to demand a return to the full gold standard, which some archconservatives favored.

37. AP to Harold L. Ickes, Oct. 14, 1936, ibid., box 50. Amos claimed that the committee wanted to publish ten million copies of his open letter, but internal bickering in the Republican national committee apparently prevented it. *Conservation Diaries*, Nov. 4, 1936, p. 169. Amos's choice of Ickes as recipient is curious, as he had earlier called him "an old and dear friend," and the interior secretary had obligingly served as the conduit for the book on monetary policy that Amos intended for the president's reading. AP to William P. Eno, March 18, 1933, APP, box 3; Ickes to AP, Oct. 19, 1936, ibid., box 50.

38. Trying to validate his Republican credentials, Gifford publicly released his letter to President Roosevelt, charging that Democratic appointees overseeing Works Progress Administration projects in Pennsylvania had unfairly favored Democrats and politicized the recovery effort there. The letter annoyed

Roosevelt, who rejoined that Gifford's barb lacked specifics and was obviously politically motivated, and he replied only because he considered Gifford a personal friend. Gifford followed with another open letter containing quotations from aggrieved citizens. McGeary, *Pinchot*, pp. 413-414.

39. In late 1932, McFadden turned against President Hoover for accepting a reduction in European war debts to U.S. banks and twice introduced resolutions for his impeachment (the second also blamed Roosevelt for the bonus army fiasco), but the House overwhelmingly voted to table both resolutions. McFadden was becoming a political pariah in his own party.

40. GP to GBP, May 14, 1933, GPP, box 327.

41. *WP*, July 7, 1933, p. 16, and Aug. 3, 1933, p. 1.

42. Sharon McConnell-Sidorick, *Silk Stockings and Socialism: Philadelphia's Radical Hosiery Workers from the Jazz Age to the New Deal* (Chapel Hill: University of North Carolina Press, 2017), pp. 115, 119, 187, 209, 260n22 (quotations on p. 209).

43. *NYT*, February 4, 1936, p. 11, and March 5, 1936, p. 7. CBP's campaign literature is in CBPP, boxes I:349-352.

44. Morris Gregg, Diary, ibid., box I:350; *NYT*, March 10, 1936, p. 11, April 1, 1936, p. 14, and April 5, 1936, IV, p. 11; Philadelphia *Evening Bulletin*, April 29, 1936, p. 20; CBP to James J. Connolly, April 7 and 11, 1936, CBPP, box I:346.

45. Leila received 12,302 votes, 6,268 behind Connolly. *Philadelphia Inquirer*, April 30, 1936, p. 4; AP to CBP, April 29, 1936, APP, box 3. Connolly would be defeated in the general election in November.

46. AP to William P. Eno, May 16, 1934, APP, box 3.

47. Gifford entertained vague hopes that he might become Landon's running mate on the Republican ticket, but his name was early dropped from consideration. *NYT*, May 29, 1936, p. 13; *Conservation Diaries*, May 28, 1936, June 2 and 12, 1936, p. 168; GP to AP, Oct. 20, 1936, APP, box 50.

48. Ickes did not mention Leila by name but as Gifford's "trusted emissary" in trying to get his support for replacing Guffey with her husband in 1934. Ickes, radio address, Altoona, Oct. 19 [1936], Ickes Papers, box 162.

49. Gifford's one concern was that the election would bring too much power to Democratic city bosses. *Conservation Diaries*, Nov. 5, 1936, p. 169.

50. AP to Walter Jeffrey, Nov. 12, 1936, APP, box 50.

51. FDR's anti-business rhetoric rivaled that of Andrew Jackson (to whom he compared himself), and about his opponents shouted, "I welcome their hatred." David M. Kennedy, *Freedom from Fear: The American People in Depression and War, 1929-1945* (New York: Oxford University Press, 1999), pp. 278-286 (quotation on p. 282).

52. After the election, Amos convened a small group of FDR opponents to fashion an anti-administration strategy, but their first meeting had been "a flop." AP to Earl Harding, Jan. 29, 1937, APP, box 51. Richard Polenberg, *Reorganizing Roosevelt's Government: The Controversy Over Executive Reorganization* (Cambridge, Mass.: Harvard University Press, 1966), pp. 55-63 (quotation on p. 56).

53. AP to Members of Congress, Feb. 13, 1937, and AP to Albert G. Rutherford, Feb. 17, 1937, APP, box 51.

54. AP to FDR, April 26, 1937, and Alf M. Landon to AP, May 6, 1937, ibid., box 52. Amenable to some limitation on the court's powers by constitutional amendment, Amos thought that at least a six-to-three majority might be required to overturn legislation. AP to Albert G. Rutherford, Feb. 17, 1937, ibid., box 51.

55. Quotation in Polenberg, *Reorganizing Roosevelt's Government*, p. 63.

56. AP to W. C. Dennis, April 7, 1937, and AP to Florence J. Harriman, March 2, 1937, APP, box 51.

57. These New Dealers were mostly young lawyers and economists and formed "a faction within the administration." Quotation in Kennedy, *Freedom from Fear*, p. 353.

58. AP to Roy Howard, July 22, 1937, APP, box 53.

59. AP to Irving Fisher, Jan. 6, 1937, AP to Frederick A. Delano, Jan. 12, 1937, and AP to Max Eastman, June 15, 1937, ibid., box 52.

60. AP to FDR, July 26, 1937, ibid., box 53.

61. AP to CBP, July 11, 1938, CBPP, box I:374.

62. AP to Florence J. Harriman, March 2, 1937, APP, box 51.

63. Quotation in Polenberg, *Reorganizing Roosevelt's Government*, p. 60.

Chapter 23: A Lost Woman

1. GP to APJ, Feb. 10, 1931, GPP, box 310. Horace D. Taft to GP, Nov. 10, 1930, GP to Taft, Jan. 15, 1931, Jan. 21, 1931, tel., Jan. 30, 1931, and Feb. 14, 1931, GPP, box 318. When Nettie learned of Giff's eye problem, she reminded her brother of the miserable time when Gifford had had to leave Exeter because of his failing eyesight, only to have their parents send the two of them to suffer a bitter cold winter together in a cabin in the Adirondacks. By contrast, a special reason for Thacher was the warm climate. APJ to GP, March 8, 1931, ibid.

2. GP to GBP, Oct. 23, 1934, ibid., box 327.

3. GBP to CBP, undated [Fall 1935], undated [Winter 1936], and undated [March 1936], CBPP, box I:342.

4. Sarah Richards to CBP, April 15 [1936], ibid.

5. In his freshman year, Giff first met Sally at a dance in Wilton. There were few Presbyterian churches in Connecticut, but the Richards' Presbyterian pastor in New York City performed the ceremony in an Episcopal Church in Wilton.

6. First quotation in Gifford B. Pinchot, *Loki and Loon: A Lifetime Affair with the Sea* (New York: Dodd, Mead, 1985), p. 13. This book provides details of the married couple's many sailing and racing adventures over the next forty-five years. *NYT*, April 16, 1936, p. 22, and June 14, 1936, II, p. 3; GP, Diary, Nov. 25, 1936, GPP, box 7.

7. Giff's name is entirely absent from the Yale class yearbook of 1938, the year of his graduation.

8. Rosamond Pinchot, Diary, July 3, 1933, RPP, box 1. Gifford 2nd confided to Rosamond that he had to pay Janine 9,000 francs for an operation that Rosamond assumed was for an abortion. Because Gifford 2nd had been in the United States, Janine's new boyfriend was likely responsible. Ibid., Nov. 25, 1933.

9. Ibid., July 25, 1933 and Aug. 1, 1933. Gifford 2nd was also involved with a young movie actress, but she eventually ended the relationship and married someone else. William Graves to AP, July 17, 1938, and AP to Belle Gurnee, July 21, 1938, APP, box 56.

10. AP to William P. Eno, May 29, 1935 and Aug. 3, 1936, and AP to Gifford Pinchot 2nd, Jan. 20, 1937, ibid., box 3; CBP to Gifford Pinchot 2nd, March 23, 1939, GPP, box 369.

11. Quotations in Gaston, *Loveliest Woman*, p. 110.

12. Quotation ibid., p. 111. The two took turns taking care of their boys, and Bill's mother in Maine and Gertrude and Leila helped too. All the while, Rosamond hoped that her husband might swear off other women and be reconciled to her.

13. Bill then phoned her. "We talked and I'm still so fond of him," she confessed in her diary. On New Year's Eve she added, "Have a longing for him tonight. . . . Bill, you have been very false, and still, I know that you in your own way you love me. Human love what a farce it can be!" Quotations ibid., pp. 120, 121.

14. Ibid., pp. 128-130; *Eleanor Roosevelt Encyclopedia*, eds. Maurine H. Beasley, Holly C. Shulman, Henry R. Beasley (Westport, CT: Greenwood, 2001), pp. 44-45. Rosamond's article would be the only one for the publication, which soon folded.

15. Eleanor Roosevelt to Rosamond Gaston, Nov. 25, 1932, reproduced in Gaston, *Loveliest Woman*, p. 121.

16. Ibid., pp. 127-129; *New York Journal*, Jan. 23, 1933, p. 3.

17. Gaston, *Loveliest Woman*, pp. 122-130 (quotations on p. 130); Rosamond Pinchot, Diary, Feb. 18, 1933, RPP, box 1.

18. Ibid., March 4, 5, and 7, 1933. Rosamond's article for this press service was not found, and it may have been used without her byline.

19. Rosamond's only reservation about the first lady was that she lacked fashion sense, mixing up colors in her outfits confusedly and choosing dreadful accessories. Gaston, *Loveliest Woman*, pp. 117-122, 128, 132-137 (quotations on pp. 122, 137). A year later, Rosamond saw her at a formal dinner and remarked, "Mrs. Roosevelt, all teeth, kissed me." Quotation ibid., p. 213.

20. Ibid., pp. 130, 132-134 (quotation on p. 130).

21. Ibid., pp. 138-141, 213-214, 218, 238-239. When Cerf was not romancing her, he would talk to Gifford about book publishing, or Leila about politics or children's books, or bat the tennis ball with a half-lame Amos.

22. Ibid., p. 138; Rosamond Pinchot, Diary, July 30, 1933, Nov. 5 and 16, 1933, RPP, box 1. Bill Gaston then had a job with Lehman Brothers, but he would soon lose it.

Endnotes

23. Gaston, *Loveliest Woman*, pp. 141-147, 203-206 (quotation on p, 203).
24. Quotation ibid., p. 227.
25. One harsh judgment of Rosamond's acting ability is Martin Gottfried, *Jed Harris: The Curse of Genius* (Boston: Little, Brown, 1984), pp. 158ff.
26. Despite her realistic assessment of the Hollywood scene, she still harbored vague dreams of becoming a star there and make her enough money to buy a beach house in Southern California, divorce Bill, and begin a new life with her boys. Her father was still her hero, and she further reflected that he could visit her frequently in the sunny climes to alleviate his arthritic discomfort. She waited a while for another assignment, but nothing happened. Gaston, *Loveliest Woman*, p. 208.
27. Quotations ibid., pp. 218, 207.
28. Ibid., pp. 211-212. Bennett Cerf was, for instance, "a darling little fellow, . . . but not enough man for me." Rosamond Pinchot, Diary, July 12, 1933, RPP, box 1.
29. Gaston, *Loveliest Woman*, pp. 141, 144-145, 203, 219, 220, 223-224; Rosamond Pinchot, Diary, Nov. 7, 1934, RPP.
30. Quotations in Gaston, *Loveliest Woman*, p. 226.
31. Katharine Hepburn, *Me: Stories of My Life* (New York: Random House, 1991), pp. 169-170 (quotation on p. 170).
32. Another theater director commented that Rosamond had a masochistic streak about her most intimate male friends. Gaston, *Loveliest Woman*, pp. 210, 227, 233, 239 (quotations on pp. 233 and 210).
33. The diaries covering the period from mid-1934 to mid-1936 were never recovered.
34. Rosamond had earlier been reunited in Hollywood with Reinhardt, who with his wife had fled the rising anti-Semitic atmosphere in his native Austria. Rosamond deeply admired Reinhardt. Gaston, *Loveliest Woman*, pp. 220-222, 232-234.
35. After one mix-up with Ruth, for example, Rosamond despite Ruth's assurances thought she was resentful. Rosamond Pinchot, Diary, Oct. 29, 1933, RPP, box 1.
36. RP to CBP, March [1935], CBPP, box I:323. Toward Jed, however, Leila was more standoffish. Gaston, *Loveliest Woman*, pp. 227-229, 233.
37. Rosamond Pinchot, Diary, Oct. 1, 16, 1933, RPP, box 1.
38. Ibid., April 24, 1933; Gaston, *Loveliest Woman*, p. 226. The boys had accompanied Rosamond on her second trip to Hollywood; her mother and other relatives cared for them on her other visits there.
39. The New York *Social Register*, a listing of the city's establishment families, had already dropped Rosamond's name for becoming an actress, considered a low-grade career for a privileged woman. She had brushed off that slight.
40. Wilder had already won a Pulitzer Prize for his novel, *The Bridge of San Luis Rey* (1927).
41. The Harris versus Wilder theme is explored in Tappan Wilder's "Afterward" to *Our Town: A Play in Three Acts* (New York: HarperCollins, 2003), pp. 158-160; also *The Selected Letters of Thornton Wilder*, eds. Robert G. Wilder and Jackson R. Bryer (New York: HarperCollins, 2008), pp. 335-337.
42. Quotations ibid., p. 336.
43. Gottfried, *Jed Harris*, pp. 168-169.
44. Quotations in Gaston, *Loveliest Woman*, pp. 242-243.
45. Ibid., pp. 244-245 (quotations ibid., p. 245).
46. Deciding against suicide in 1934, she judged that it would have made her father's life "intolerable" and "would kill him too." Quotations ibid., pp. 209, 210, and 213.
47. Cf. New York *Journal-American*, Jan. 24, 1938, p. 1, *New York Post*, Jan. 24, 1938, p. 1, and *NYT*, Jan. 25, 1938, p. 1. The morning *New York Herald Tribune*, Jan. 25, 1938, p. 1, also reported that she was dressed in an evening gown, slippers, and ermine coat. In the final act of *Our Town*, Emily, the main character, has died in childbirth but reappears in a white dress to talk to the other revived dead in the graveyard. Rosamond's clothing may have been her way of linking her own demise with Jed Harris and the play.
48. GP, Diary, Jan. 10, 1938, GPP, box 7.
49. GP to GBP, Jan. 29, 1938, ibid., box 364; CBP to Mrs. George H. Richards, Feb. 7, 1938, CBPP, box I:374.
50. GBP to CBP, undated [Feb. 1938], ibid. Only two days after the funeral, Gifford wrote his brother saying not a word about the recent tragic events surrounding Rosamond's death. GP to AP, Jan. 29, 1938, APP, box 54.

51. GP, Diary, July 5, 1939, GPP, box 7. Gifford's son overheard Amos's angry phone conversation with Bill but apparently provided no details. Gaston, *Loveliest Woman*, p. 252.

52. Gertrude Pinchot to CBP, Feb. 23 [1938], CBPP, box I:379; William Graves to AP, July 17, 1938, APP, box 56.

53. AP to Alice Severance, July 13, 1938, and AP to Belle Gurnee, July 31, 1938, ibid.

54. Rosamond Pinchot, Diary, May 1, 1934, RPP, box 1.

55. New York *Herald Tribune*, Jan. 25, 1940, p. 22. This was Amos's only foray into the poetic realm.

Chapter 24: The Human Travails of War

1. CBP to GBP, Nov. 1, 1937, CBPP, box I:364; GP, Diary, Jan. 18, 1938, GPP, box 7.

2. Ibid.

3. CBP to GBP, March 25, 1938, CBPP: box I:374; CBP to GBP, Nov. 1, 1937, ibid., box I:364.

4. CBP to GBP, March 25, 1938, ibid., box I:374; *NYT*, Oct. 16, 1938, p. 4.

5. Roosevelt "took special exception to assertions that he wished to be dictator – an American Hitler, Mussolini, or Stalin." Robert Dallek, *Franklin D. Roosevelt: A Political Life* (New York: Viking, 2017), p. x.

6. Amos's letter also dismissed in a few paragraphs the ideas of John Maynard Keynes, the noted British economist and principal architect of the theory, who had influenced Roosevelt's economic advisers to expand pump-priming. AP to FDR, May 17, 1938, CBPP, box I:374.

7. AP to Roy Howard, Aug. 19, 1937, APP, box 53.

8. The minimum wage was forty cents an hour and maximum weekly hours were forty.

9. He argued that higher taxes, labor demands, and an administration that was less concerned with reducing unemployment than with sustaining relief programs were hurting business efforts toward recovery. AP to John L. Lewis, Sept. 3, 1938, CBPP, box I:374.

10. Labor unions were politically vulnerable, and the Taft-Hartley Act, which invalidated the closed shop and placed restrictions on other union activities, would become law nine years later in a Republican-controlled Congress.

11. The department of conservation was as much Roosevelt's idea as Ickes', but the latter enthusiastically promoted the proposed consolidation, arguing that it "will prevent overlapping and clashing and jealousies in the future." Ickes, *Secret Diaries*, 2, p. 22.

12. Quotation in Miller, *Gifford Pinchot*, p. 435.

13. Quotation in Nixon, *Roosevelt and Conservation*, 2, p. 415.

14. GP, Diary, June 14, 1935, GPP, box 7; McGeary. *Pinchot*, p. 410.

15. *Conservation Diaries*, Jan. 12, 1937, p. 187.

16. GP, Diary, Feb. 26, 1937, GPP, box 7. Text of GP's speeches are in *Gifford Pinchot: Selected Writings*, pp. 71-75, and in APP, box 52.

17. Gifford often pointed out that, in 1905, the forest reserves had been transferred from interior to the new forest service in the agriculture department precisely because of interior's regular mishandling of them. Subsequently, the Ballinger affair and the Harding scandals confirmed his low opinion of the department.

18. Quotations in GP, "Old Evils in New Clothes," *Journal of Forestry*, 35 (May 1937), p. 435; and GP, Diary, Aug. 19, 1937, GPP, box 7. Congress had created the National Park Service in 1916.

19. Ickes, *Secret Diary*, 2, pp. 131-132 (May 2, 1937), and quotation on p. 238 (Nov. 4, 1937).

20. Harold L. Ickes, *The Autobiography of a Curmudgeon* (New York: Reynal and Hitchcock, 1943). Quotations in Douglas Brinkley, *Rightful Heritage: Franklin D. Roosevelt and the Land of America* (New York: HarperCollins, 2016), p. 488.

21. AP to FDR, Jan. 29, 1938, CBPP, box I:374.

22. GP to AP, Jan. 29, 1938, APP, box 55. Although Gifford was not known for seeking conservative support, his arguments against reorganization as executive overreach found allies among conservatives in Congress who hammered away in opposition to the initiative as a dangerous expansion of presidential power.

23. Ickes, *Secret Diary*, 1, pp. 601-602 (May 22, 1936).

24. GP, Diary, Feb. 28, 1937, GPP, box 7. Ickes cogently argued that Congress regarded the issue as an interdepartmental fight, and he objected to getting between the departments "unless the President really wanted the bill." Ickes, *Secret Diary*, 2, pp. 292-293. (Jan. 18, 1938) (quotation on p. 292).

25. Ibid., p. 488 (Oct. 16, 1938) and pp. 624-625 (April 29, 1939) (quotations on p. 624). The most FDR offered Ickes at the time was the transfer of a few parts of agriculture (but not forestry) to interior.

26. Opponents of reorganization also benefitted from the lack of strong public pressure for administrative change. Although Gifford could rely on foresters and other conservationists to speak up against transfer, other pressure groups—labor unions, farm organizations, and even lumbermen's groups— did not get excited about the question.

27. *Conservation Diaries*, Jan. 1, 1939, p. 176.

28. CBP to GBP, June 10, 1938, CBPP, box I:374. During his recent gubernatorial primary campaign, he had often felt out of breath and tired. Afterward, he was still unable to generate much sustained energy. His doctors prescribed a long period of rest, and he did not conduct any speaking tours against the executive reorganization plan in 1938.

29. Two of the attacks were relatively mild, and Gifford preferred to think they were only digestive upsets.

30. Quotations in Ickes, *Secret Diary*, 2, p. 565 (Jan. 29, 1939); also, ibid., p. 635 (April 29, 1939).

31. The party's high command informed Gifford, for example, that he could not campaign in Nebraska for George W. Norris, Gifford's main ally in the U.S. Senate, since Norris had broken with the party and was running for reelection as an independent. GP, Diary, Oct. 5, 1936, GPP, Box 7; CBP to William Hard, July 7, 1938, CBPP, box I:374.

32. Ickes, *Secret Diary*, 2, p. 488 (Oct. 16, 1938), and pp. 624-626 (April 29, 1939).

33. Ickes, *Secret Diary*, 3, pp. 106, 108 (Jan. 21, 1940).

34. Nixon, *Roosevelt and Conservation*, 2, pp. 176, 413-415 (quotations on pp. 176, 413, 415); penultimate quotation in McGeary, *Pinchot*, p. 411.

35. Ickes, furious at his defeat, submitted his resignation, but Roosevelt persuaded him to stay on. Gifford and Ickes continued to attack each other personally, and Gifford at one point privately called the interior secretary an "American Hitler." Quotation ibid., p. 422.

36. GP, Diary, Sept. 28, 30, 1940, GPP, box 7.

37. Ibid., Aug. 13, 1940, June 26, 1940, and Oct. 9, 1940.

38. During Theodore Roosevelt's presidency, Will prevailed upon Gifford to obtain TR's letters of introduction to carry his ideas on traffic management to European cities. During Gifford's first governorship, when the Pennsylvania capital city had hired him for advice on its traffic problems, he stayed in the governor's mansion during his consultancy. He soon repaid this hospitality by lending Governor Pinchot his horse for Coolidge's inaugural parade in Washington. William Phelps Eno, *The Story of Highway Traffic Control, 1899-1939* (Eno Foundation for Highway Traffic Control, 1939), pp. 161-163, passim; CBP to William P. Eno, Feb. 12, 1923, CBPP, box I:31.

39. Eno to AP, May 19, 1928, and AP to Eno, May 24, 1928, APP, box 3.

40. Amos sometimes gently disagreed with his uncle's extreme views, such as his outrage at the administration's decision to go off the full gold standard. Eno to AP, June 1, 1936, and June 4, 1936, and AP to Eno, June 5, 1936, ibid.

41. Eno to AP, Sept. 30, 1938, ibid.; GP to Samuel Fisher, May 9, 1940, Samuel H. Fisher Papers (Manuscripts and Archives, Yale University Library), box 26.

42. Eno to AP, Dec. 10, 1938, APP, box 3. Eno also believed that the only major non-Jewish department store was Wanamaker's.

43. AP to Jay Lovestone, May 13, 1933, ibid., box 45.

44. AP to Eno, Dec. 12, 1938, ibid., box 3; Philip C. Jessup to AP, Oct. 10, 1941, AP to Jessup, Oct. 15, 1941, and AP to John Haynes Holmes, Oct. 29, 1941, ibid., box 63.

45. AP to Roger N. Baldwin, July 16, 1936, ibid., box 50. The ACLU recognized some limits to freedom of speech, and in 1940, its leadership (including Amos Pinchot) voted to ban directors who were Communists, because the party advocated the overthrow of the U.S. government, but they still supported Communists' right to free speech.

46. Quotation in Miller, *Pinchot*, p. 322. Wise had already criticized Amos for abandoning the New Deal.

47. AP to Eno, Dec. 12, 1940, and Aug. 4, 1941, APP, box 3; AP to John Haynes Holmes, Oct. 29, 1941, ibid., box 63.

48. The Yale connection is told in Marc Wortman, "The Forgotten Antiwar Movement," *Yale Alumni Magazine*, 79 (July-Aug. 2016), pp. 34-42. Neither Amos Pinchot nor Will Eno is mentioned in the article.

49. *NYT*, April 2, 1940, p. 12, Feb. 10, 1941, p. 10, and March 24, 1941, p. 16.

50. AP to Eno, April 12, 1940, and June 18, 1940, APP, box 3.

51. AP to Eno, Sept. 27, 1940, AP to Hiram Johnson, Oct. 2, 1940, AP, handwritten comment on Wendell Willkie to AP, Sept. 9, 1940, AP to Willkie, Oct. 11, 1940, ibid., box 60; AP to Douglas Johnson, Nov. 7, 1940, ibid., box 61; AP to Gifford Pinchot, 2nd, Nov. 11, 1940, ibid., box 3.

52. AP to Gifford Pinchot, 2nd, Sept. 28, 1939, ibid.

53. AP to CBP, Jan. 29, 1941, ibid.; *NYT*, May 10, 1941, p. 9. Roosevelt had appointed Knox, Landon's running mate in 1936, and Stimson before the election to give his foreign policies a more nonpartisan thrust. Under lend-lease, the president's discretionary provisions included decisions on which country would receive U.S. aid and how much.

54. AP to FDR, Feb. 9, 1941, APP, box 61; AP to FDR, July 11, 1941, ibid., box 62; *NYT*, Feb. 10, 1941, p. 10.

55. The "all aid" comment was in a footnote, however, perhaps suggesting Amos's lingering resistance to lend lease. AP to FDR, Feb. 9, 1941, APP, box 61.

56. Quotations (along with other FDR antiwar remarks) in AP to FDR, July 11, 1941, ibid., box 62.

57. AP to Edgar J. Cook, Nov. 28, 1940, and AP to Roy Howard, Nov. 19, 1940, ibid., box 61. Lend-lease aid was soon extended to the Soviet Union.

58. *NYT*, Sept. 15, 1941, p. 2; AP to Eno, Oct. 2, 1941, APP, box 3.

59. AP, interview, Sept. 10, 1940, ibid., box 60.

60. AP to FDR, Jan. 29, 1938, CBPP, box I:374; AP to Frederick J. Libby, Nov. 3, 1941, APP, box 64.

61. Unlike some other Roosevelt haters, he did not countenance a conspiracy among the president and his close military and security aides for deliberately antagonizing the Japanese militarists to launch the surprise attack, thereby getting the United States into the European war through the "back door."-

62. AP to William P. Eno, April 10, 1923, APP, box 2; AP to CBP, Dec. 4, 1931, ibid., box 3.

63. Nina Burleigh, *A Very Private Woman: The Life and Unsolved Murder of Presidential Mistress Mary Meyer* (New York: Bantam, 1998), p. 61; AP to Mrs. Clyde, Nov. 5, 1941, APP, box 64.

64. AP, "What the Election Means," *The Masses*, 9 (Jan. 1917), p. 18.

65. AP to Florence Graves, Feb. 9, 1942, and Feb. 17, 1942, APP, box 64.

66. AP to Gifford Pinchot, 2nd, May 17, 1939, June 17, 1940, and Sept. 28, 1939, ibid., box 3. He considered surgery but apparently was told that an operation could not help him. Hip replacement surgery did not yet exist as an option.

67. AP to Lewis Glavis, April 8, 1942, ibid., box 64; GP, Diary, July 13, 20, Aug. 3, 4, 1942, GPP, box 8; AP to E. S. Webster, Jr., June 24, 1942, APP, box 64.

68. John A. Montgomery, *Eno: The Man and the Foundation: A Chronicle of Transportation* (Westport, CT: Eno Foundation for Transportation, 1988), pp. 129-130.

69. *NYT*, Aug. 7, 1942, p. 1; GP, Diary, Aug. 6, 21, 24, 31, 1942, GPP, box 8.

70. GP, Diary, Aug. 16, 27, 31, Sept. 8, 14, 20, 29, Dec. 12, 1942, ibid.

71. In Amos's final days, the family had to decide whether they wanted him to have a lobotomy, a controversial procedure today. However, it was then considered a promising operation for disturbed patients, making them more pleasant and easier to care for. Ruth, Mary, and Tony decided against it. Oska Diethelm to GP, Jan. 29, 1944, and Ruth Pinchot to GP, Feb. 7, 1944, GPP, box 397.

72. Crinks came to know Churchill mainly through an elite political dining group called the Other Club, which Churchill had co-founded before the Great War and for which Crinks later served as secretary. Reynolds and Hunter, "'Crinks' Johnstone," pp. 14-18.

73. Under the terms of a wartime electoral truce, Crinks had been unopposed in his election to Commons.

74. GP to FDR, Nov. 18, 1942, GPP, box 392.

75. CBP, quotation in Blanche Wiesen Cook, *Eleanor Roosevelt: The War Years and After, 1939-1962* (New York: Viking, 2016), 3, p. 408; GP to FDR, Nov. 18, 1942, GPP, box 392.

76. Ibid.

77. GP to FDR, May 12, 1942, GPP, box 388. Gifford's article was rewritten and published in the April 1943 issue.

78. Regarding TR's initiative, see above, pp. - .

79. *Gifford Pinchot, Selected Writings*, pp. 109-114; *NYT*, May 12, 1940, p. 15.

80. Nixon, *Roosevelt and Conservation*, 2, pp. 415, 591-594 (quotations on pp. 415, 592 and 593). Gifford's meeting with Roosevelt also had a political purpose. Disturbed by the Republican Party's conservative establishment, Wendell Willkie visited Gifford to complain that progressive Republicans had nowhere to turn and also argued that liberal Democrats felt saddled by conservatives in their own party. He suggested that they found a third-party movement uniting reform elements. Gifford was enthusiastic and floated the suggestion to the president at their June meeting. Roosevelt, in turn, dispatched his close adviser, Samuel Rosenman, to talk to Willkie. The initiative died aborning with Willkie's death that October and FDR's six months later. Samuel I. Rosenman, *Working with Roosevelt* (New York: Da Capo Press, 1972), pp. 463-470.

81. Roosevelt twice asserted that "Conservation is the basis of permanent peace." Quotations in Nixon, *Roosevelt and Conservation*, 2, pp. 599-600.

82. Ibid., pp. 606-608, 612-613, 615-616 (quotation on p. 612). U.N. agencies, the Economic and Social Council and the Food and Agricultural Organization, were considering conservation along with many other international issues.

83. Ibid., pp. 627-628, passim. At Yalta, FDR mentioned the subject of forestry "jokingly" and expounded on the economic problems of deforested nations before returning to the discussion of more immediately important topics. *Foreign Relations, Conferences at Malta and Yalta*, 1945, pp. 715-716.

84. Nixon, *Roosevelt and Conservation*, 2, pp. 632-633.

85. Roosevelt conceded that the conference idea was "not urgent." Ibid., pp. 634-643 (quotation on p. 636). The department also argued again that international agencies were already considering conservation issues.

86. GP, Diary, March 28, 1945, and April 12, 1945, GPP, box 8; Nixon, *Roosevelt and Conservation*, 2, pp. 644-648.

87. Quotations in McGeary, *Pinchot*, p. 427. Gifford had already donated all his papers to the Library of Congress. Until his death in 1944, Herbert (Dol) Smith in particular worked closely with him on the memoir.

88. Quotations ibid., p. 425.

89. GP, Diary, Aug. 10, 1945, GPP, box 8.

90. Not surprisingly, Ickes wrote a mostly negative review of the memoir, claiming that Gifford's bitter and unnecessary attacks in it about the interior department badly hurt the conservation cause. *NYT*, Nov. 23, 1947, VII, p. 6. An evaluation of the memoir, and its limitations as authoritative history, are in Miller, *Pinchot*, pp. 361-368.

91. Drafts of Leila's speech at the dedication of the Gifford Pinchot National Forest, Oct. 15, 1949, are in CBPP, box II:62.

Chapter 25: Seeking Sisters

1. CBP to GBP, Aug. 1, 1937, CBPP, box I:364; GBP, *Loki and Loon*, p. 128.

2. Gifford B. Pinchot, "Marine Farming," *Scientific American*, 233 (Dec. 1970), pp. 14-21.

3. Quotation ibid., p. 10. GBP, *Loki and Loon*, pp. 5, 137-138, 207, passim; *NYT*, Dec. 1, 1985, p. 27

4. Rosamond Pinchot, Diary, Aug. 1, 1933, and Oct. 9, 1933, RPP, box 1.

5. Rosamond Pinchot, Diary, Aug. 1, 1933, ibid. The girls also went to parties at other faraway sites like the Hamptons (Long Island) and Black Point (near New London). Gaston, *Loveliest Woman*, pp. 138, 205-206.

6. Her poem, published at the same time her father published his in the *Herald Tribune*, read:
"I saw her lying there so calm and still,
With one camellia placed beside her head.
She looked the same, and yet, her soul and will
Being gone, she did seem dead.

"I thought, if one so loved and beautiful
Should wish to leave, perhaps there was a voice
That called her back – and she was dutiful.
Somewhere the gods rejoice.

"In some far place, where all the lovely things
Of earth are born, the gods no longer weep.
She was returned to them. And what she brings
We lose, but always keep."
NYT, Jan. 25, 1940, p. 20.

7. Mary had stayed at home in the summer of 1940 to help her father and went to California with him on a vacation.

8. AP to Gifford Pinchot, 2nd, Sept. 30, 1941, APP, box 3.

9. AP to Gifford Pinchot, 2nd, Dec. 5, 1939, ibid.

10. Quotations in Burleigh, *Very Private Woman*, pp. 75, 76. Because Schwartz, a fervent anti-Nazi, disagreed with her about the war, the two rarely discussed it.

11. Peter Janney, *Mary's Mosaic: The CIA Conspiracy to Murder John F. Kennedy, Mary Pinchot Meyer, and Their Vision for World Peace* (New York: Skyhorse, 2015), pp. 161-164.

12. Cord Meyer, Jr., "On the Beaches," *Atlantic*, 174 (Oct. 1944), pp. 42-46.

13. Mary Pinchot to CBP, Jan. 11 [1945], and Ruth Pinchot to CBP, May 2, 1945, CBPP, box I:410. During their courtship, Cord took courses at Yale Law School but gave it up when his eyes still bothered him.

14. *NYT*, May 3, 1945, p. 16.

15. CBP to Cord Meyer, Jr., Nov. 20, 1945, and CBP to Mary Pinchot Meyer, Jan. 29, 1946, CBPP, box I:410. President Truman appointed Mrs. Roosevelt as a member of the U.S. delegation at the United Nations.

16. Quotation in Burleigh, *Very Private Woman*, p. 86.

17. The published article is Cord Meyer, Jr., "A Serviceman Looks at Peace," *Atlantic*, 176 (Sept. 1945), pp. 1-6.

18. Cord Meyer, Journal, Jan. 3, 1950, Cord Meyer, Jr. Papers (Manuscript Division, Library of Congress), box 5.

19. Correspondence relating to Cord's job search is ibid. Still hoping for an academic or diplomatic appointment, he withheld acceptance of the agency's offer until September 1951. In his first few years with the CIA, he continued to look for alternative employment outside of government. Lester Markel to Meyer, March 31, 1954, ibid.

20. Cord Meyer, Journal, March 18, 1950, May 24, 1951, and June 8, 1951, Meyer Papers, box 5.

21. The Pinchots had a strong attraction to Yale, as beginning with Gifford and Amos (and three of their mother's brothers), their two boys also went to Yale (and Giff married the daughter of a Yale alumnus), and two of Amos's three daughters married Eli men.

22. CBP to GBP and Sally Pinchot [July 5, 1953], CBPP, box 1:60.

23. Quotation in Janney, *Mary's Mosaic*, p. 187.

24. Ben Bradlee, *A Good Life: Newspapering and Other Adventures* (New York: Simon & Schuster, 1995), p. 159.

25. Mary wrote a short story of a woman's brief extramarital affair. Cord dismissed the story, he later recalled, as "sophomoric in emotion and badly written" but, suspecting that it was autobiographical, roughly criticized it "with so little respect for her feelings." Cord Meyer, Journal, Oct. 18, 1955, Meyer Papers, box 5.

26. Ibid., Pittman provided Cord with a copy of his earlier separation agreement with Tony to use as a guide for his brother-in-law's separation from Mary. Pittman to Cord Meyer, April 11, 1957, ibid.

27. Janney, *Mary's Mosaic*, pp. 190-191 (first quotations on p. 191); Cord Meyer, Journal, Sept. 3, 1958 (last quotation). Mary gained alimony and custody of the two boys, but Cord was given control over their education. He withdrew the boys from Georgetown Day and enrolled them in St. Albans, a traditional Episcopal school in Washington, DC, and later they would be sent to boarding schools in New England.

28. As financial backup, Mary also inherited a family trust fund of unknown amount, from which she could get income at age twenty-one. At Vassar she was withdrawing "only" $500 for clothes and other necessities. AP to Gifford Pinchot, 2nd, Sept. 3, 1941, APP, box 3.

29. Married with children, Noland was going through a drawn-out divorce. He would soon pursue artistic success in New York.

30. *WP*, Oct. 12, 1960, p. A16.

31. Quotation in Janney, *Mary's Mosaic*, p. 191.

32. Kennedy and Cord Meyer did not get along well at the conference, either because Cord's foreign policy views were more radical than Kennedy's or because he was jealous of the attention JFK was giving Mary, or both. Much later, Cord supported Kennedy (after Humphrey) for the presidency in 1960 and hoped to get a political appointment in the new administration. He was told by a mutual friend that because of "some incident" at the 1945 conference that was now an "impossibility." Cord Meyer, Journal, March 21, 1963, Meyer Papers, box 5.

33. Walter Lippmann, oral history interview, c. 1964, p. 13 (John F. Kennedy Library).

34. Burleigh, *Very Private Woman*, pp. 180, 187ff., 326n17, and 328n52-330. There may have been many more White House visits, as individuals escorted into the building by Kennedy aides were often not identified by name. Mary and Jack also talked sometimes on the phone.

35. Now divorced, Cord Meyer also seemed unaware of Mary's liaisons with Kennedy and reflected quizzically about JFK in his journal: "To his strange competitiveness, he adds a curiosity and interest in my private life and that I find unexplainable, even to the point of asking about a bathing suit that was sent anonymously by someone and that I returned to Mary thinking it was hers." Cord Meyer, Journal, March 21, 1963, Meyer Papers, box 5.

36. Quotation in Burleigh, *Very Private Woman*, p. 170.

37. Robert Greenfield, *Timothy Leary: A Biography* (New York: Harcourt Books, 2006), pp. 186, 549. Leary would be fired from Harvard the next year for his drug experiments.

38. The press silence on Kennedy's sexual indiscretions during his lifetime allowed the American public to assume that he and Jackie were a glamorous and happily married couple who were devoted to their small children. The silence seems inexplicable today, but informal constraints then existed—Kennedy's friendly behavior toward White House reporters, their culpability in many cases with extramarital affairs of their own, and, most of all, the unwritten rule that the private lives of the first family were off limits to investigative journalism.

39. Miller, *Seeking the Greatest Good*, pp. 2-3, 13.

40. Edward P. Cliff, head of the U.S. Forest Service, oral history interview, July 2, 1964 (Kennedy Library); *Public Papers of the Presidents of the United States: John F. Kennedy, 1963* (Washington, DC: Government Printing Office, 1964), pp. 704-719.

41. Quotation in Norman B. Lehde, *When President Kennedy Visited Pike County* (Milford, PA: Pike County Chamber of Commerce, 1964), p. 38. The U.S. Senate's approval of the limited nuclear test ban treaty with the Soviet Union that same morning, signaling a reduction in Cold War tensions, likely contributed to Kennedy's buoyant mood at the Milford event. He would spend time discussing disarmament during his western trip.

42. A review of her exhibit noted that the results of Mary's hard work were "gratifying indeed," and several of the paintings "seem particularly rewarding." *WP*, Nov. 24, 1963, p. G10. An appreciation of her colorist paintings, "lyrical and emotional rather than coolly calculated," is ibid., Oct. 25, 1964, p. G10. In March 1966, the Washington Gallery of Modern Art also had an exhibition of Mary's paintings.

43. An Anne Truitt abstract sculpture painted yellow and white, *Mary's Light* (1962), honors Mary Pinchot Meyer.

44. The interpretations are Burleigh, *Very Private Woman*, and Janney, *Mary's Mosaic*. Janney was a childhood friend of Michael Meyer, who was killed in the earlier automobile accident. A third book, Michael Pinchot, *Mary & JFK: Presidential Mistress Mary Pinchot-Meyer* (self-published, 2013), traces Mary's life up to just before Kennedy's assassination, then becomes a fictionalized account of Kennedy surviving the assassination attempt and his marriage to Mary and their subsequent short life together, finally reverting back to the real-life events of Kennedy's and Mary's actual deaths and subsequent speculation about them. Michael Pinchot says he is no relation to the Pinchots in this book but is distantly related to JFK. Michael Pinchot to author, e-mail, Jan. 22, 2016. There have also been at least two novels and a play based on the Mary-Kennedy connection.

45. Bradlee, *Good Life*, pp. 266-270 (quotation on p. 270); Burleigh, *Very Private Woman*, pp. 167-170; Sally Bedell Smith, *Grace and Power: The Private World of the Kennedy White House* (New York: Random House, 2004), pp. 410-411; Janney, *Mary's Mosaic*, pp. 228-229, 366.

46. *NYT*, Nov. 5, 1995, book review section, p. 5. Angleton's children later repeated the Anne Truitt-Cicely Angleton version. *WP*, Dec. 3, 2011, p. A13.

47. Bradlee, *Good Life*, pp. 269-270. In addition, Peter Janney developed a conspiracy theory, which centered on Angleton, "a consummate, pathological liar and a master of duplicity." He also proffered that

Mary's diary-sketchbook was not the "real" diary, which Angleton (and perhaps Bradlee) had seized and concealed in a visit to Mary's house after her murder. Further, he thinks that the white witness identifying Crump at the latter's trial, while likely not Mary's assassin, may have been involved in her murder. Janney, *Mary's Mosaic*, pp. 72-87, 321-412, passim (quotations on pp. 78, 80).

48. Jefferson Morley, *The Ghost: The Secret Life of CIA Spymaster James Jesus Angleton* (New York: St. Martin's Press, 2017), pp. 78-82, 164; Janney, *Mary's Mosaic*, p. 83.

49. Quotation in Bradlee, *Good Life*, p. 271. Angleton was noted for having an archivist mentality and saving everything, so he likely had already made copies of it.

50. Janney, *Mary's Mosaic*, p. 366.

51. One consequence perhaps was that Mary and Cord's two sons, Quentin and Mark, never married and lived reclusive lives.

52. Contributions to conservation by Gifford's direct descendants and other professional environmentalists are recorded in Miller, *Seeking the Greatest Good*, passim.

53. Bibi Gaston, *Loveliest Woman*, in alternate chapters traces her own journey of learning about her grandmother Rosamond and more about the lives of her father, Bill, and his brother, James (her uncle).

Index

Pennsylvania Woman Suffrage Association, 261
Pennsylvania Railroad, 268, 317
Penrose, Boies, 206, 208–10, 262, 268
Pentagon Papers, 405
People's League for Economic Security, 343
Pepper, George Wharton, 181, 268, 287–88, 319
Perkins, George W., 196–97, 199–201, 207–208, 235–36, 300
Pershing, John J., 144, 233–34
Phelps, Elisha, 2
Phelps, John, 4
Phelps, John Jay, 2
Phelps, Lucy. *See* Lucy Phelps Eno
Phelps, Lucy Smith, 2
Phelps, William Walter, 55
Philadelphia Centennial Exposition, 27
Philippines, 114, 142–45, 308, 379
Phillips, Thomas W., Jr., 317–18
Phillips Exeter Academy, 37–40, 55–56
Pickering, Ruth. *See* Ruth Pickering Pinchot
Pinchot, Amos Richards Eno, American War Finance Committee, 240–42; anti-interventionist and antimilitarist activism, 229–32, 376–79; antisemitism, 375, 379; childhood and education, 103–107; civil liberties and dissent, 242–45, 248; Committee of 48, 256–60; cultural rebellion, 211–16; fishing and hunting exploits, 108, 119, 122–23, 133–34, 198, 299; health issues, 116–19, 133–34, 174–76, 255–56; marital problems and divorce, 172–74, 193, 252–56; marriage to Gertrude Minturn, 122–23; marriage to Ruth Pickering, 253; opposition to U.S. military intervention in Mexico, 233–36; peace ideas and activism, **231**; political philosophy, 207, 213–15, 256, 342–45, 350–51; Progressive Party, 192–97, 199–201, 206–208; prohibition and alcohol, 106, 266, 299–300, 373, 379; relations with his children, 133, 252–53, 255, 291–92, 294–95, 364, 380–81; relations with his siblings, 113–14, 116–17, 118, 122, 126, **199**, 299–300; Sacco and Vanzetti trial, 300, 375; service in Spanish-American War, 113–18; suicide attempt and death, 380–81; support for

and opposition to New Deal, 339–41, 341–45, 348–51; U.S. Congress candidacy, 195–97; writings, 176, 185, 191, 194–95, 253, 260, 281, 338–39, 364
Pinchot, Antoinette (2nd generation). *See* Antoinette (Nettie) Pinchot Johnstone
Pinchot, Antoinette (3rd generation). *See* Antoinette (Tony) Bradlee
Pinchot, Constantine, 5–6
Pinchot, Cornelia (Leila) Bryce, attitudes toward prohibition, 263, 266, 276; candidacies for U.S. Congress, 301–303, 324, 346–47; commitment to women's issues, 261, 263, 328, 385; courtship of and marriage to Gifford Pinchot, 203–205, 220, 261–62; death of, 398; Grey Towers, **302**; opposition to child labor and sweatshops, 328, **346**–47; relations with Amos and family, 255–56, 266, 273–74, 303, 341–42, 373; relations with Eleanor Roosevelt and the Roosevelt administration, 325–26, 372, 382, 392; relations with Rosamond and her sons, 295, 298, 354, 360, 363–64; relations with son Gifford Bryce, 221, 310, 352–53, 386; South Seas voyage, 310–14; support for free speech, 313, 327; support for Gifford's political career and legacy, 206, 268–69, 271, 277, 288, 317, 332–35, 365, 371–72, 385; support for Jewish people, 372
Pinchot, Cyrill Constantine Désiré, 5–6, 8–9, 18
Pinchot, Cyrill H., 9–10, 33, 40
Pinchot, Diane Rosamond, 354, 405
Pinchot, Edgar, 7–9
Pinchot, Eliza, 6, 23
Pinchot, Gertrude Minturn, **174**, 205; cultural and reform interests, 193–94, 211–12, 215–16, 227–28, 232, 234; death of, 364; health issues, 123, 168, 172–73; marital troubles and divorce, 252–56, 294; marriage to Amos Pinchot, 122–23, 185; relations with Rosamond, 292, 295, 298, 360; spiritualism, 174–75; views of Amos's health problems, 123, 133–34, 135, 172–73, 176
Pinchot, Gifford, Biltmore social life, 84, **85**, 86; courtship of and marriage to Cornelia Bryce, 203–205, 220, 261–62;

About the Author

David S. Patterson is the author of two books: *Toward a Warless World: The Travail of the American Peace Movement* and *The Search for Negotiated Peace: Women's Activism and Citizen Diplomacy in World War I.*

Patterson's career as an academic and government historian includes teaching diplomatic history, peace history, and women's history at major universities and his service for several years as chief editor of U.S. Department of State's *Foreign Relations of the United States*, a long-standing, multi-volume documentary series.

His work on the Pinchot family is an outgrowth of his growing concerns about the global environmental challenges, which Gifford Pinchot first confronted more than a century ago, and his ongoing research into Amos Pinchot's commitment to civil liberties and antiwar movements.

Among his awards, Patterson was the recipient of a Mershon Social Science Fellowship and a National Endowment for the Humanities travel grant. While teaching in China, he was named the Sir Run Run Shaw Professor of American History at the Johns Hopkins University-Nanjing University Center for Chinese and American Studies. More recently, he served as a visiting fellow at the Rothermere American Institute at the University of Oxford. He has a Ph.D. in history from the University of California, Berkeley.

Besides history, his other passions include choral singing, golf, and, like the Pinchots, the central importance of family. Patterson and his wife live in Maryland, within commuting distance of their son and wife and grandchildren.